Betty Larson

232-6896

Large Quantity Recipes

Large Quantity Recipes

Fourth Edition

MARGARET E. TERRELL, D.Sc.
Professor Emeritus, University of Washington

DOROTHEA B. HEADLUND
Foodservice consultant

VNR VAN NOSTRAND REINHOLD
New York

Copyright © 1989 by Van Nostrand Reinhold
Library of Congress Catalog Card Number 88-10805
ISBN 0-442-20486-8

Printed in the United States of America
Designed by Kathryn Parise

Van Nostrand Reinhold
115 Fifth Avenue
New York, New York 10003

Van Nostrand Reinhold International Company Limited
11 New Fetter Lane
London EC4P 4EE, England

Van Nostrand Reinhold
480 La Trobe Street
Melbourne, Victoria 3000, Australia

Macmillan of Canada
Division of Canada Publishing Corporation
164 Commander Boulevard
Agincourt, Ontario M1S 3C7, Canada

16 15 14 13 12 11 10 9 8 7 6 5 4 3 2 1

Library of Congress Cataloging-in-Publication Data
Terrell, Margaret E.
  Large quantity recipes.

  Includes index.
  1. Quantity cookery. I. Headlund, Dorothea B.
II. Title.
TX820.T415 1989   641.5′7   88-10805
ISBN 0-442-20486-8

CONTENTS

2 BEVERAGES AND COCKTAILS **41**

3 SOUPS **61**

9 SAUCES, RELISHES, AND STUFFINGS **229**

PREFACE

Success in large quantity foodservice depends largely upon the quality of the food served. Meals of dependable goodness and appeal will cause diners to "walk the extra mile" to enjoy them. A reputation for consistently providing dependable goodness in food is not achieved by chance. Successful managers rely upon a file of recipes that have been standardized to meet the needs, tastes, and buying power of a specific clientele. Such a file is a highly significant management tool. Alert operators know that in addition to solving problems and meeting the costs of operation, competing for and satisfying clientele is vital and should not be risked through guesswork.

The recipes in this book have been professionally tested in large, successful, public foodservice kitchens. Each recipe has been carefully chosen, based on popularity when served in both large and small food operations, such as a commercial restaurant, university and school foodservice, hospital and nursing home service, industrial plants, and church kitchens. Consideration was given in recipe selection and methods of preparation to the following points:

1. A sufficient number of recipes within each menu classification to provide variety and interest in menus.
2. Recipes of demonstrated popularity.
3. Recipes, when prepared according to directions, will provide food of good quality.
4. Directions for preparation stated clearly and simply in logical order of procedure.
5. Preparation methods that utilize equipment commonly found in large kitchens.

6. Foods with sufficient range in variety and cost to permit ready adaptation to specific needs.

Ingredient measurements in the recipes are stated in both metric and U.S. customary weight and volume. Persons preparing the recipes may use the measurements with which they are most familiar, thus lessening the chances of making errors. The use of both weight and volume facilitates converting market supplies into recipe quantities, or recipe quantities into market orders. Weight is recognized as the quickest, easiest, and most accurate means of measurement for most products. This fact emphasizes the importance of having conveniently placed scales of dependable accuracy for use when preparing food.

Tables to aid in recipe calculation and preparation have been included in an Appendix, with additional tables included within chapters as they pertain to specific preparation. Table A-1, in the Appendix, gives the approximate equivalents in metric and U.S. customary measures of weight; the abbreviations used in the recipes are given in Table A-4. It is sometimes necessary to substitute another item for the one stated in the recipe. Table A-5 lists ingredients that permit such substitutions.

There is considerable variation in the sizes of containers used in food departments. The serving pans referred to in these recipes measure approximately 12 × 20 × 2 inches, half pans 10 × 12 × 2 inches, loaf pans 9 × 5 × 3 inches, and baking sheets 18 × 26 × 1 inches. Although fractional variations may be common, these measurements should guide any calculations required for adjustment in particular cases.

Control of food costs calls for control of portions, as well as control of ingredient amounts in recipes. Table A-6 lists food portioning aids. Table A-7 states cooking temperatures for different products.

The recipe quantities in most instances are based on amounts sufficient for fifty adult portions. This amount has proven to be convenient for increasing for larger groups or for dividing by 4, 6, or 8 to adjust for home quantities. In each instance, adjustment by weight is the most reliable, as it allows less variation due to handling technique, or equipment. Table A-3 provides the comparative approximate weight and volume of foods, and gives equivalent measurements of ingredients to aid in such calculations.

The purpose of this book is to provide foodservice managers with a reliable source of dependable recipes to aid them in developing a useful "working file" adapted to meet the needs of their establishments. It has been the conscious goal in the development of these recipes to promote the improvement of the quality of foods served to the dining public.

CHAPTER 1 _____Breads

Bread is a favorite food throughout the world, and one that lends itself to many interesting variations. The leavening used in bread determines its classification as a "quick" bread or a "yeast" bread. Quick action is obtained through rapid release of the carbon dioxide leavening formed by the chemical reaction of an alkali, such as soda, and an acid, such as cream of tartar, buttermilk, molasses, or vinegar. Yeast requires time for fermentation in a warm (82°F/28°C), moist, draft-free atmosphere. Low temperature retards yeast growth and high temperature kills the yeast plants. Salt, fat, and sugar retard the growth of yeast plants. An increase in the amount of these ingredients, as required in sweet breads, calls for an increased amount of yeast.

Quick Breads

When making quick breads, mix the liquid ingredients into the dry ingredients only enough to moisten the dry ingredients. Stirring the batter tends to develop gluten strands in the flour and spoils both the tenderness and texture of the muffins or other quick breads. Avoid overmixing, unless the batter contains sufficient fat and sugar, as in a cake batter, to counteract the toughening of the gluten. A rich batter, such as a cake batter, requires extra mixing to develop volume. A properly mixed quick bread batter is likely to appear lumpy and undermixed when put into the pan. Use double-action baking powder for batters that are to be held for a time before baking. This type of baking powder, containing such acids as sodium aluminum sulfate and calcium acid phosphate, releases most of the carbon dioxide at baking temperatures.

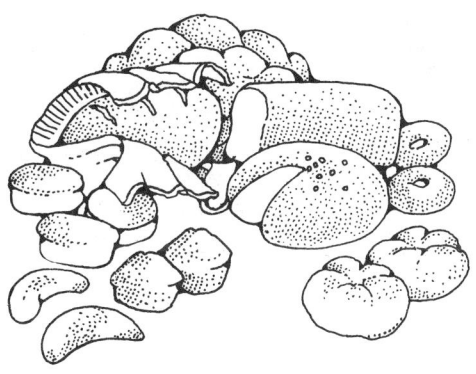

Baking Powder Biscuits
50 Biscuits (2-in diameter)
Bake, 450°F/232°C, 12–15 min

| Metric | | Ingredients | U.S. | |
Weight	Volume		Weight	Volume
1.14 kg	2.37 l	Flour, all-purpose	2 lb, 8 oz	2½ qt
57 g	60 ml	Sugar	2 oz	4 tbsp
57 g	79 ml	Baking Powder	2 oz	⅓ cup
14 g	15 ml	Salt	½ oz	1 tbsp
454 g	474 ml	Shortening	1 lb	2 cups
681 g	711 ml	Milk	1 lb, 8 oz	3 cups

Procedure

1. Sift together flour, sugar, baking powder, and salt. Blend in mixer using flat paddle at low speed.
2. Cut fat into 4 oz/114 g pieces and drop into dry ingredients. Mix at low speed for 1 minute. Scrape beater and bowl. Continue mixing until mixture resembles rice or coarse meal.
3. Add ¾ of the milk and mix slightly. Add last quarter of milk cautiously, using only enough to make a soft dough that can be kneaded.
4. Knead dough on lightly floured board about 15 times. Divide in half. Roll to ½-inch thickness. Cut with 2-inch cutter or into 2-inch squares with a knife. Place on ungreased baking sheet. Brush tops with milk just before baking.
5. Bake at 450°F/232°C for 12 to 15 minutes. (Biscuits may be cut and held in the refrigerator for as long as an hour before baking, if desired.

Variations

Cheese Biscuits Add 12 oz/340 g grated cheddar cheese to dry ingredients.

Marmalade Pinwheels Divide dough in half. Roll each lot ¼-inch thick. Spread 1 cup/237 ml marmalade on each half. Roll as for jelly roll. Cut each roll into 25 1-inch slices. Place cut side down on greased baking sheet.

Cheese Rolls Roll dough ¼-inch thick. Sprinkle with 1 lb/454 g grated cheddar cheese and roll as for jelly roll. Slice roll 1-inch thick and place cut side up on baking sheet.

Drop Biscuits Add ¾ cup/178 ml milk. Drop from tablespoon onto greased baking sheet.

Shortcake Biscuits
50 Biscuits (2-in diameter)
Bake, 425°F/218°C, 15 min

Metric		Ingredients	U.S.	
Weight	Volume		Weight	Volume
1.14 kg	2.37 l	Flour, all-purpose	2 lb, 8 oz	2 ½ qt
227 g	237 ml	Sugar	8 oz	1 cup
57 g	79 ml	Baking Powder	2 oz	⅓ cup
14 g	15 ml	Salt	½ oz	1 tbsp
454 g	474 ml	Shortening	1 lb	2 cups
567 g	592 ml	Milk	1 lb, 4 oz	2 ½ cups
114 g	118 ml	Eggs, beaten (2 lge)	4 oz	½ cup

Procedure

1. Blend dry ingredients. Cut shortening into dry ingredients.
2. Combine milk and beaten eggs and stir into dry ingredients to form a soft dough (as soft as can be easily handled).
3. Turn dough onto lightly floured board and knead 10 to 12 times. Roll to ¾-inch thickness. Cut with a 2-inch cutter and place on ungreased baking sheet. Let stand 10 minutes before baking.
4. Bake at 425°F/218°C for 15 minutes.

Butterscotch Biscuits
50 Biscuits
Bake, 375°F/190°C, 15 min

Metric		Ingredients	U.S.	
Weight	Volume		Weight	Volume
1.02 kg	2.13 l	Flour, pastry	2 lb, 4 oz	2 ¼ qt
14 g	15 ml	Salt	½ oz	1 tbsp
36 g	53 ml	Baking Powder	1 ¼ oz	3 ½ tbsp
454 g	474 ml	Shortening	1 lb	2 cups
681 g	711 ml	Milk	1 lb, 8 oz	3 cups
227 g	237 ml	Butter or Margarine	8 oz	1 cup
510 g	711 ml	Brown Sugar	1 lb, 2 oz	3 cups

Procedure

1. Blend flour, salt, and baking powder. Cut in shortening. Add milk to make a soft dough. Turn onto floured board and knead lightly. Divide dough into 2 portions. Roll each portion to oblong shape approximately 25 inches long, ¼ inch thick.
2. Cook butter or margarine and brown sugar to creamy stage. Cool. Spread each half of dough with half of this mixture. Roll like jelly roll and cut each half into 25 1-inch slices.
3. Place slices cut side up on greased baking sheets. Bake at 375°F/190°C for 15 minutes.

Variation

4 oz/114 g chopped nuts or 6 oz/170 g raisins may be sprinkled on top of sugar-butter mixture before rolling.

Cinnamon Buns
50 Buns
Bake, 425°F/218°C, 20 min

Metric		Ingredients	U.S.		
Weight	Volume		Weight		Volume
1.02 kg	2.13 l	Flour, pastry	2 lb,	4 oz	2 ¼ qt
43 g	60 ml	Baking Powder		1 ½ oz	4 tbsp
114 g	118 ml	Sugar		4 oz	½ cup
14 g	15 ml	Salt		½ oz	1 tbsp
227 g	237 ml	Shortening		8 oz	1 cup
227 g	237 ml	Eggs, beaten (4 lge)		8 oz	1 cup
454 g	474 ml	Milk (approx.)	l lb		2 cups
		Filling			
170 g	178 ml	Butter or Margarine, softened		6 oz	¾ cup
454 g	632 ml	Brown Sugar	1 lb		2 ⅔ cups
7 g	15 ml	Cinnamon		¼ oz	1 tbsp
227 g	355 ml	Raisins, seeded		8 oz	1 ½ cups

Procedure

1. Blend flour, baking powder, sugar, and salt. Add shortening and blend until mixture resembles rice or coarse meal.
2. Combine eggs and 1 cup/237 ml of milk. Stir into dry ingredients. Add enough additional milk to make a soft dough, as soft as can be handled easily.
3. Divide dough in half. Roll ¼-inch thick and about 25 inches long. Spread each half of the dough with half of the softened butter or margarine. Blend brown sugar and cinnamon and sprinkle half over each half of the dough. Sprinkle with raisins. Press raisins into dough.
4. Roll as for jelly roll and cut ¾-inch slices. Place slices in greased muffin pans or on a greased baking sheet, cut side up.
5. Bake at 425°F/218°C for 20 minutes.

Dumplings
50 Dumplings

Metric		Ingredients	U.S.		
Weight	Volume		Weight		Volume
1.70 kg	2.84 l	Biscuit Mix (see p.2)	3 lb,	12 oz	3 qt
57 g	355 ml	Parsley, chopped		2 oz	1 ½ cups
71 g	237 ml	Chives, chopped		2 ½ oz	1 cup
	10 ml	Poultry Seasoning			2 tsp
907 g	947 ml	Milk	2 lb		1 qt

Procedure

1. Blend parsley, chives, and poultry seasoning into biscuit mix. Add milk and stir just enough to moisten dry ingredients.
2. Drop with a No. 20 scoop on top of stew arranged in serving pans. Cover tightly and steam in steam cooker or in 400°F/205°C oven for 15 or 20 minutes.

Cheese Wafers or Sticks
About 100 Sticks or Wafers
Bake, 400°F/205°C, 10 min

Metric		Ingredients	U.S.	
Weight	Volume		Weight	Volume
454 g	947 ml	Cheddar Cheese, grated	1 lb	1 qt
454 g	474 ml	Butter or Margarine	1 lb	2 cups
	⅝ ml	Pepper		⅛ tsp
	1 ¼ ml	Cayenne Pepper		¼ tsp
	10 ml	Salt		2 tsp
454 g	947 ml	Flour, pastry	1 lb	1 qt
57 g	59 ml	Egg, beaten (1 lge)	2 oz	¼ cup

Procedure

1. Cheese may be grated or, if soft enough, may be put through a wire sieve. Blend cheese, butter or margarine, and seasonings.
2. Blend cheese mixture with flour until well mixed.
3. Roll dough between layers of waxed paper to ¼-inch thickness.
4. Cut into wafers with a small cookie cutter, or cut into sticks ¼ to ½ inch wide. Carefully place on cookie sheet to avoid breaking. Brush tops with beaten egg.
5. Bake at 400°F/205°C for 10 minutes.

Scotch Scones
48 Scones
Bake, 400°F/205°C, 20 min

Metric		Ingredients	U.S.	
Weight	Volume		Weight	Volume
681 g	1.42 l	Flour, pastry	1 lb, 8 oz	1 ½ qt
227 g	237 ml	Sugar	8 oz	1 cup
28 g	40 ml	Baking Powder	1 oz	2 ⅔ tbsp
14 g	15 ml	Salt	½ oz	1 tbsp
227 g	237 ml	Shortening	8 oz	1 cup
170 g	178 ml	Eggs, beaten (3 lge)	6 oz	¾ cup
170 g	178 ml	Milk	6 oz	¾ cup
	5 ml	Vanilla		1 tsp

Procedure

1. Blend dry ingredients. Cut in shortening to meal-like fineness.
2. Blend eggs, milk, and vanilla. Stir into dry ingredients to form soft dough. Turn onto lightly floured board and knead 10 to 12 times.
3. Divide dough in half for easy handling. Roll each into rectangle 24 inches long and 6 inches wide. Cut through center lengthwise and divide into 6 pieces crosswise. Cut each rectangle diagonally to make 24 triangles.
4. Place triangles on greased baking sheet. Bake at 400°F/205°C for 20 minutes.

Variations

1. Add 8 oz/227 g seedless raisins or currants to dough.
2. Add 1 tbsp/15 ml grated orange rind and 1 tbsp/15 ml grated lemon rind (or 2 tbsp/30 ml of either) to the dough.

Whole Wheat Biscuits
48 Biscuits (2½-in diameter)
Bake, 425°F/218°C, 12 min

Metric		Ingredients	U.S.		
Weight	Volume		Weight		Volume
681 g	1.42 l	Flour, all-purpose	1 lb,	8 oz	1½ qt
43 g	60 ml	Baking Powder		1½ oz	4 tbsp
21 g	22 ml	Salt		¾ oz	1½ tbsp
681 g	1.42 l	Flour, whole wheat	1 lb,	8 oz	1½ qt
340 g	355 ml	Shortening		12 oz	1½ cups
1.02 kg	1.07 l	Milk (approx.)	2 lb,	4 oz	4½ cups

Procedure

1. Sift together all-purpose flour, baking powder, and salt. Stir in whole wheat flour.
2. Cut shortening into dry ingredients until mixture resembles corn meal. Add milk to make a soft dough that leaves sides of bowl.
3. Turn onto lightly floured board and knead lightly (about 15 turns).
4. Roll to ½-inch thickness. Cut with 2½-inch cutter and place on baking sheet. Bake at 425°F/218°C 10 or 12 minutes.

MUFFINS

Plain Muffins
48 Muffins (No. 20 Scoop)
Bake, 400°F/205°C, 20–25 min

Metric		Ingredients	U.S.		
Weight	Volume		Weight		Volume
1.14 kg	2.37 l	Flour, all-purpose	2 lb,	8 oz	2½ qt
227 g	237 ml	Sugar		8 oz	1 cup
57 g	79 ml	Baking Powder		2 oz	⅓ cup
14 g	15 ml	Salt		½ oz	1 tbsp
454 g	504 ml	Oil or Shortening, melted	1 lb		2⅛ cups
227 g	237 ml	Eggs, beaten (4 lge)		8 oz	1 cup
907 g	947 ml	Milk	2 lb		1 qt

Procedure

1. Combine dry ingredients. Blend liquid ingredients and add to dry ingredients. Stir just enough to moisten dry ingredients.
2. Using a No. 20 scoop, fill well-greased muffin pans to ⅔ full.
3. Bake at 400°F/205°C for 20 to 25 minutes.

Applesauce Puffs

48 Muffins (No. 20 Scoop)
Bake, 400°F/205°C, 25 min

Metric		Ingredients	U.S.	
Weight	Volume		Weight	Volume
1.28 kg	2.60 l	Biscuit Mix	2 lb, 13 oz	2 ¾ qt
255 g	266 ml	Sugar	9 oz	1 ⅛ cups
11 g	23 ml	Cinnamon		1 ½ tbsp
510 g	533 ml	Applesauce	1 lb, 2 oz	2 ¼ cups
255 g	266 ml	Milk	9 oz	1 ⅛ cups
255 g	266 ml	Eggs, beaten (5 med)	9 oz	1 ⅛ cups
114 g	118 ml	Margarine, melted	4 oz	½ cup
		Topping		
114 g	118 ml	Margarine, melted	4 oz	½ cup
255 g	266 ml	Sugar	9 oz	1 ⅛ cups
	5 ⅝ ml	Cinnamon		1 ⅛ tsp

Procedure

1. Combine biscuit mix with sugar and cinnamon.
2. Mix applesauce, milk, eggs, and margarine. Add to dry ingredients and mix just enough to moisten dry ingredients.
3. Using a No. 20 scoop, fill greased muffin pans to ⅔ full.
4. Bake at 400°F/205°C for 12 minutes.
5. Cool slightly. Dip tops of puffs in melted margarine, and then in mixture of sugar and cinnamon.

Blueberry Muffins

48 Muffins (No. 20 Scoop)
Bake, 400°F/205°C, 25 min

Metric		Ingredients	U.S.	
Weight	Volume		Weight	Volume
907 g	1.89 l	Flour, pastry	2 lb	2 qt
35 g	53 ml	Baking Powder	1 ¼ oz	3 ½ tbsp
14 g	15 ml	Salt	½ oz	1 tbsp
227 g	237 ml	Sugar	8 oz	1 cup
454 g	829 ml	Blueberries, fresh	l lb	3 ½ cups
312 g	316 ml	Oil or Butter, melted	11 oz	1 ⅓ cups
227 g	237 ml	Eggs, beaten (4 lge)	8 oz	1 cup
605 g	632 ml	Milk	1 lb, 5 ⅓ oz	2 ⅔ cups

Procedure

1. Blend sugar, flour, baking powder, and salt. Mix oil, eggs, and milk. Combine all ingredients, including blueberries, and mix just enough to moisten dry ingredients.
2. Using a No. 20 scoop, fill greased muffin pans to ⅔ full.
3. Bake at 400°F/205°C for 25 minutes.

Note: Fresh whole cranberries may be substituted for blueberries.

Blueberry Corn Muffins

48 Muffins (No. 20 Scoop)
Bake, 400°F/205°C, 25 min

Metric		Ingredients	U.S.		
Weight	Volume		Weight		Volume
567 g	869 ml	Corn Meal	1 lb,	4 oz	3 ⅔ cups
425 g	889 ml	Flour, all-purpose		15 oz	3 ¾ cups
283 g	296 ml	Sugar		10 oz	1 ¼ cups
32 g	45 ml	Baking Powder		1 ⅛ oz	3 tbsp
	5 ml	Salt			1 tsp
23 g	38 ml	Lemon Rind, grated			2 ½ tbsp
595 g	1.07 l	Blueberries	1 lb,	5 oz	4 ½ cups
227 g	237 ml	Eggs, slightly beaten (4 lge)		8 oz	1 cup
850 g	889 ml	Milk	1 lb,	14 oz	3 ¾ cups
312 g	326 ml	Butter or Margarine, melted		11 oz	1 ⅜ cups

Procedure

1. Combine corn meal, flour, sugar, baking powder, salt, and grated lemon rind. Mix well.
2. Gently mix blueberries into dry ingredients. Stir only enough to coat the berries.
3. Combine eggs, milk, and melted butter or margarine.
4. Make a well in the center of the blueberry mixture. Pour liquid ingredients into well and stir just enough to moisten dry ingredients.
5. Using a No. 20 scoop, fill greased muffin pans to ⅔ full.
6. Bake at 400°F/205°C for 25 minutes.

Bran Muffins

56 Muffins (No. 20 Scoop)
Bake, 375°F/190°C, 15 min

Metric		Ingredients	U.S.		
Weight	Volume		Weight		Volume
255 g	1.07 l	All-Bran		9 oz	4 ½ cups
227 g	237 ml	Water, boiling		8 oz	1 cup
227 g	237 ml	Eggs, slightly beaten (4 lge)		8 oz	1 cup
425 g	592 ml	Brown Sugar		15 oz	2 ½ cups
907 g	947 ml	Buttermilk	2 lb		1 qt
227 g	237 ml	Butter or Margarine, melted		8 oz	1 cup
454 g	947 ml	Flour, all-purpose	1 lb		1 qt
20 g	25 ml	Soda			1 ⅔ tbsp
	5 ml	Salt			1 tsp
142 g	889 ml	40% Bran Flakes		5 oz	3 ¾ cups

Procedure

1. Mix All-Bran cereal with boiling water and let stand for 20 minutes.
2. Add beaten eggs, brown sugar, buttermilk, and melted butter or margarine.
3. Sift flour, soda, and salt together. Add to mixture.
4. Add 40% Bran Flakes.
5. Using a No. 20 scoop, fill greased muffin pans to ⅔ full.
6. Bake at 375°F/190°C for 15 minutes or until nicely browned.

Bran-Honey Nut Muffins

4 ½ doz Muffins (No. 20 Scoop)
Bake, 400°F/205°C, 20 min

Metric		Ingredients	U.S.	
Weight	Volume		Weight	Volume
907 g	1.89 l	Flour, pastry	2 lb	2 qt
43 g	60 ml	Baking Powder	1 ½ oz	4 tbsp
28 g	30 ml	Salt	1 oz	2 tbsp
454 g	474 ml	Sugar	1 lb	2 cups
57 g	237 ml	All-Bran	2 oz	1 cup
114 g	237 ml	Nuts, chopped	4 oz	1 cup
454 g	474 ml	Eggs, beaten (8 lge)	1 lb	2 cups
681 g	711 ml	Milk	1 lb, 8 oz	3 cups
340 g	237 ml	Honey	12 oz	1 cup
199 g	237 ml	Shortening, melted	7 oz	1 cup

Procedure

1. Blend flour, baking powder, salt, and sugar. Mix in All-Bran and nuts.
2. Combine eggs, milk, honey, and melted shortening. Add to dry ingredients, stirring just enough to moisten them.
3. Using a No. 20 scoop, fill greased muffin pans to ⅔ full.
4. Bake at 400°F/205°C for 20 minutes.

Corn Muffins

48 Muffins (No. 20 Scoop)
Bake, 400°F/205°C, 20–25 min

Metric		Ingredients	U.S.	
Weight	Volume		Weight	Volume
709 g	1.07 l	Corn Meal	1 lb, 9 oz	4 ½ cups
596 g	1.18 l	Flour, pastry	1 lb, 5 oz	5 cups
170 g	178 ml	Sugar	6 oz	¾ cup
49 g	70 ml	Baking Powder	1 ¾ oz	4 ⅔ tbsp
21 g	22 ml	Salt	¾ oz	1 ½ tbsp
227 g	237 ml	Eggs, well-beaten (4 lge)	8 oz	1 cup
605 g	632 ml	Milk	1 lb, 5 ⅓ oz	2 ⅔ cups
283 g	316 ml	Shortening, melted	10 oz	1 ⅓ cups

Procedure

1. Blend well corn meal, flour, sugar, baking powder, and salt.
2. Combine eggs, milk, and melted shortening. Stir into dry ingredients just enough to dampen them. Using a No. 20 scoop, fill greased muffin pans to ⅔ full.
3. Bake at 400°F/205°C for 20 to 25 minutes.

Cranberry Muffins
48 Muffins (No. 20 Scoop)
Bake, 400°F/205°C, 25 min

Metric		Ingredients	U.S.		
Weight	Volume		Weight		Volume
1.05 kg	2.13 l	Flour, cake or pastry	2 lb,	5 oz	2 ¼ qt
57 g	80 ml	Baking Powder		2 oz	5 ½ tbsp
283 g	316 ml	Sugar		10 oz	1 ⅓ cups
14 g	15 ml	Salt		½ oz	1 tbsp
283 g	296 ml	Eggs, beaten (5 lge)		10 oz	1 ¼ cups
511 g	533 ml	Milk	1 lb,	2 oz	2 ¼ cups
283 g	355 ml	Shortening, melted		10 oz	1 ½ cups
397 g	829 ml	Cranberries, whole fresh		14 oz	3 ½ cups

Procedure

1. Blend dry ingredients. Combine eggs, milk, and shortening. Mix with cranberries into dry ingredients, stirring only enough to moisten. Batter will be lumpy.

2. Using a No. 20 scoop, fill greased muffin pans to ⅔ full.

3. Bake at 400°F/205°C for 25 minutes.

Creole Muffins
54 Muffins (No. 20 Scoop)
Bake, 400°F/205°C, 20 min

Metric		Ingredients	U.S.		
Weight	Volume		Weight		Volume
681 g	1.42 l	Flour, pastry	1 lb,	8 oz	1 ½ qt
43 g	60 ml	Baking Powder		1 ½ oz	4 tbsp
28 g	30 ml	Salt		1 oz	2 tbsp
170 g	178 ml	Sugar		6 oz	¾ cup
397 g	592 ml	Corn Meal		14 oz	2 ½ cups
227 g	237 ml	Eggs, beaten (4 lge)		8 oz	1 cup
907 g	947 ml	Milk	2 lb		1 qt
227 g	266 ml	Shortening, melted		8 oz	1 ⅛ cups
114 g	158 ml	Green Pepper, chopped		4 oz	⅔ cup
28 g	30 ml	Onion, grated		1 oz	2 tbsp
114 g	158 ml	Pimiento, chopped		4 oz	⅔ cup
170 g	355 ml	Cheddar Cheese, grated		6 oz	1 ½ cups

Procedure

1. Blend flour, baking powder, salt, sugar, and corn meal.
2. Combine eggs, milk, and shortening. Combine all ingredients and stir only until dry ingredients are moistened.
3. Using a No. 20 scoop, fill greased muffin pans to ⅔ full.
4. Bake at 400°F/205°C for 20 minutes.

Oat-Bran Muffins

48 Muffins (No. 20 Scoop)
Bake, 400°F/205°C, 25–30 min

Metric		Ingredients	U.S.	
Weight	Volume		Weight	Volume
907 g	947 ml	Water, boiling	2 lb	1 qt
114 g	474 ml	All-Bran	4 oz	2 cups
227 g	474 ml	Oats, rolled	8 oz	2 cups
312 g	474 ml	Raisins	11 oz	2 cups
170 g	237 ml	Brown Sugar	6 oz	1 cup
198 g	237 ml	Vegetable Oil	7 oz	1 cup
227 g	237 ml	Eggs, beaten (4 lge)	8 oz	1 cup
567 g	1.18 l	Flour, pastry	1 lb, 4 oz	5 cups
43 g	60 ml	Baking Powder	1 ½ oz	4 tbsp
57 g	237 ml	Milk Solids, nonfat	2 oz	1 cup
14 g	15 ml	Salt	½ oz	1 tbsp

Procedure

1. Pour boiling water over All-Bran, oatmeal, and raisins. Stir in brown sugar and let mixture cool. Stir in oil and eggs.
2. Blend flour, baking powder, milk solids, and salt. Add all at once to cereal mixture. Stir only until dry ingredients are moistened.
3. Using a No. 20 scoop, fill greased muffin pans to ⅔ full.
4. Bake at 400°F/205°C for 25 to 30 minutes.

Sour Cream Whole Wheat Muffins

48 Muffins (No. 20 Scoop)
Bake, 375°F/190°C, 20 min

Metric		Ingredients	U.S.	
Weight	Volume		Weight	Volume
227 g	237 ml	Margarine	8 oz	1 cup
510 g	711 ml	Brown Sugar	1 lb, 2 oz	3 cups
510 g	533 ml	Eggs, beaten (9 lge)	1 lb, 2 oz	2 ¼ cups
681 g	1.42 l	Flour, whole wheat	1 lb, 8 oz	1 ½ qt
	5 ml	Salt		1 tsp
	10 ml	Baking Soda		2 tsp
681 g	711 ml	Sour Cream	1 lb, 8 oz	3 cups
	10 ml	Vanilla		2 tsp
114 g	237 ml	Nuts, chopped	4 oz	1 cup

Procedure

1. Cream margarine and sugar 5 minutes at low speed on mixer.
2. Scrape down sides of mixing bowl. Add eggs to creamed mixture. Mix at medium speed.
3. Stir dry ingredients together. Add dry ingredients to creamed mixture, alternating with sour cream.
4. Add vanilla and fold in nuts.
5. Using a No. 20 scoop, fill well-greased muffin pans to ⅔ full.
6. Bake at 375°/190°C for 20 minutes.

GRIDDLE CAKES

Plain Griddle Cakes

50 Cakes (No. 20 Scoop)

Metric		Ingredients	U.S.		
Weight	Volume		Weight		Volume
1.14 kg	2.37 l	Flour, all-purpose	2 lb,	8 oz	2 ½ qt
114 g	118 ml	Sugar		4 oz	½ cup
57 g	79 ml	Baking Powder		2 oz	⅓ cup
14 g	15 ml	Salt		½ oz	1 tbsp
454 g	474 ml	Shortening, melted	1 lb		2 cups
340 g	355 ml	Eggs, beaten (6 lge)		12 oz	1 ½ cups
1.82 kg	1.89 l	Milk	4 lb		2 qt

Procedure

1. Mix dry ingredients thoroughly.
2. Combine melted shortening, eggs, and milk.
3. Stir liquids into dry ingredients only enough to moisten the dry ingredients. The batter will be lumpy.

4. Using a No. 20 scoop, dip the batter onto a hot griddle.

Bread Crumb Griddle Cakes

50 Cakes (No. 20 Scoop)

Metric		Ingredients	U.S.		
Weight	Volume		Weight		Volume
624 g	1.54 l	Bread Crumbs, dry	1 lb,	6 oz	6 ½ cups
1.93 kg	2.01 l	Milk	4 lb,	4 oz	8 ½ cups
156 g	158 ml	Butter or Margarine		5 ½ oz	⅔ cup
454 g	474 ml	Eggs, well-beaten (8 lge)	1 lb		2 cups
340 g	711 ml	Flour, all-purpose		12 oz	3 cups
14 g	15 ml	Salt		½ oz	1 tbsp
43 g	55 ml	Baking Powder		1 ½ oz	3 ⅔ tbsp

Procedure

1. Pour milk over crumbs. Melt butter and add to mixture. Add well-beaten eggs to crumb mixture. Blend flour, salt, and baking powder. Stir into crumb mixture until moistened. Batter will be lumpy.

2. Using a No. 20 scoop, measure onto hot griddle.

Buckwheat Griddle Cakes

50 Cakes (No. 20 Scoop)

| Metric | | Ingredients | U.S. | |
Weight	Volume		Weight	Volume
733 g	1.24 l	Flour, buckwheat	1 lb, 10 oz	5 ¼ cups
18 g	25 ml	Baking Powder		1 ⅔ tbsp
	¾ tsp	Soda		¾ tsp
21 g	22 ml	Salt	¾ oz	1 ½ tbsp
85 g	90 ml	Sugar	3 oz	6 tbsp
227 g	237 ml	Eggs, well-beaten (4 lge)	8 oz	1 cup
1.70 kg	1.78 l	Buttermilk	3 lb, 12 oz	7 ½ cups
71 g	79 ml	Butter or Margarine, melted	2 ½ oz	⅓ cup

Procedure

1. Blend dry ingredients. Combine eggs, buttermilk, and shortening. Stir into flour mixture until it is moistened.

2. Using a No. 20 scoop, measure onto hot griddle.

Buttermilk Griddle Cakes

50 Cakes (No. 20 Scoop)

| Metric | | Ingredients | U.S. | |
Weight	Volume		Weight	Volume
907 g	1.89 l	Flour, pastry	2 lb	2 qt
14 g	15 ml	Salt	½ oz	1 tbsp
12 g	15 ml	Soda		1 tbsp
11 g	15 ml	Baking Powder		1 tbsp
57 g	60 ml	Sugar	2 oz	4 tbsp
170 g	178 ml	Eggs, beaten (3 lge)	6 oz	¾ cup
2.04 kg	2.13 l	Buttermilk or Sour Milk	4 lb, 8 oz	2 ¼ qt
85 g	90 ml	Shortening, melted	3 oz	6 tbsp

Procedure

1. Blend dry ingredients. Combine eggs, buttermilk, and butter or margarine, and stir into flour mixture.

2. Using a No. 20 scoop, measure onto hot griddle.

Corn Meal Griddle Cakes
50 Cakes (No. 20 Scoop)

Metric		Ingredients	U.S.	
Weight	Volume		Weight	Volume
511 g	770 ml	Corn Meal	1 lb, 2 oz	3 ¼ cups
1.13 kg	1.18 l	Water, boiling	2 lb, 8 oz	5 cups
57 g	50 ml	Shortening, melted	2 oz	3 ⅓ tbsp
567 g	592 ml	Milk	1 lb, 4 oz	2 ½ cups
94 g	50 ml	Molasses	3 ⅓ oz	3 ⅓ tbsp
283 g	296 ml	Eggs, beaten (5 lge)	10 oz	1 ¼ cups
255 g	533 ml	Flour, bread	9 oz	2 ¼ cups
43 g	50 ml	Baking Powder	1 ½ oz	3 ⅓ tbsp
14 g	15 ml	Salt	½ oz	1 tbsp

Procedure

1. Add corn meal slowly to boiling water and stir until smooth.
2. Add shortening, milk, molasses, and eggs to corn meal. Mix thoroughly.
3. Blend dry ingredients and add to corn meal mixture. Mix until well blended. Batter will be lumpy.
4. Using a No. 20 scoop, measure onto hot griddle.

WAFFLES

Corn Meal Waffles
50 Waffles

Metric		Ingredients	U.S.	
Weight	Volume		Weight	Volume
1.59 kg	3.31 l	Flour, all-purpose	3 lb, 8 oz	3 ½ qt
1.22 kg	1.89 l	Corn Meal	2 lb, 11 oz	2 qt
85 g	118 ml	Baking Powder	3 oz	½ cup
16 g	20 ml	Soda		4 tsp
37 g	40 ml	Salt	1 ⅓ oz	2 ⅔ tbsp
170 g	178 ml	Sugar	6 oz	¾ cup
510 g	474 ml	Egg Yolks (24 med)	1 lb, 2 oz	2 cups
4.54 kg	4.74 l	Buttermilk	10 lb	5 qt
454 g	533 ml	Shortening, melted	1 lb	2 ¼ cup
681 g	711 ml	Egg Whites (24 med)	1 lb, 8 oz	3 cups
170 g	178 ml	Sugar	6 oz	¾ cup

Procedure

1. Blend dry ingredients. Beat egg yolks and mix with buttermilk and melted shortening. Combine mixtures.
2. Beat egg whites until stiff but moist. Gradually add sugar and beat until whites will stand in peaks. Fold into batter lightly.
3. Measure ½ cup (118 ml) or No. 8 scoop onto hot waffle iron.

Plain Waffles
50 Waffles

Metric		Ingredients	U.S.	
Weight	**Volume**		**Weight**	**Volume**
1.82 kg	3.78 l	Flour, all-purpose	4 lb	4 qt
114 g	158 ml	Baking Powder	4 oz	⅔ cup
37 g	40 ml	Salt	1⅓ oz	2⅔ tbsp
510 g	474 ml	Egg Yolks (24 med)	1 lb, 2 oz	2 cups
2.27 kg	2.37 l	Milk	5 lb	2½ qt
454 g	533 ml	Shortening, melted	1 lb	2¼ cups
681 g	711 ml	Egg Whites (24 med)	1 lb, 8 oz	3 cups

Procedure

1. Blend flour, baking powder, and salt.
2. Beat egg yolks and combine with milk and melted shortening. Stir into flour mixture.
3. Beat whites until stiff but moist. Fold into batter.

4. Measure ½ cup (118 ml) or No. 8 scoop onto hot waffle iron.

Note: Keep reserve supply refrigerated.

Variations

Add one of the following to the batter or sprinkle a proportionate amount on the batter before closing the iron:

1. 2 cups/474 ml chopped cooked bacon
2. 1 qt/947 ml pecans
3. 2 cups/474 ml finely diced cooked ham
4. 2 qt/1.89 l shredded coconut

Graham Waffles
50 Waffles

Metric		Ingredients	U.S.	
Weight	**Volume**		**Weight**	**Volume**
1.36 kg	2.84 l	Flour, graham	3 lb	3 qt
1.36 kg	2.84 l	Flour, all-purpose	3 lb	3 qt
49 g	60 ml	Soda	1¾ oz	4 tbsp
28 g	30 ml	Salt	1 oz	2 tbsp
170 g	237 ml	Brown Sugar	6 oz	1 cup
1.36 kg	1.42 l	Eggs, beaten (24 med)	3 lb	1½ qt
5.44 kg	5.68 l	Buttermilk	12 lb	6 qt
596 g	711 ml	Butter, melted	1 lb, 5 oz	3 cups

Procedure

1. Blend dry ingredients. Combine eggs, buttermilk, and butter. Stir into dry ingredients until moistened.

2. Measure ½ cup (118 ml) or No. 8 scoop onto hot waffle iron.

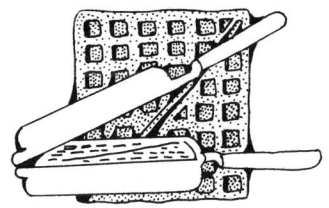

Sour Cream Waffles
50 Waffles

Metric		Ingredients	U.S.	
Weight	**Volume**		**Weight**	**Volume**
1.82 kg	3.79 l	Flour, all-purpose	4 lb	4 qt
14 g	20 ml	Soda		4 tsp
19 g	20 ml	Salt		4 tsp
114 g	118 ml	Sugar	4 oz	½ cup
907 g	947 ml	Eggs, separated (16 lge)	2 lb	1 qt
3.63 kg	3.79 l	Sour Cream, thick	8 lb	1 gal

Procedure

1. Blend dry ingredients. Beat yolks and combine with sour cream. Mix with dry ingredients.
2. Beat whites until stiff but not dry. Fold into batter.
3. Measure ½ cup (118 ml) or No. 8 scoop onto hot waffle iron.

Note: Keep reserve batter refrigerated.

PAN BREADS

Almond Coffee Cake
48 Servings (3 × 3 in.)
Bake, 350°F/177°C, 40 min

Metric		Ingredients	U.S.	
Weight	**Volume**		**Weight**	**Volume**
255 g	266 ml	Butter or Margarine	9 oz	1 ⅛ cups
623 g	652 ml	Sugar	1 lb, 6 oz	2 ¾ cups
283 g	296 ml	Eggs (5 lge)	10 oz	1 ¼ cups
964 g	1.07 l	Flour, cake	2 lb, 2 oz	4 ½ cups
43 g	59 ml	Baking Powder	1 ½ oz	¼ cup
	5 ml	Salt		1 tsp
114 g	237 ml	Milk Solids	4 oz	1 cup
681 g	711 ml	Water	1 lb, 8 oz	3 cups
		Topping		
57 g	59 ml	Margarine	2 oz	¼ cup
227 g	237 ml	Almond Paste	8 oz	1 cup
510 g	711 ml	Brown Sugar	1 lb, 2 oz	3 cups
114 g	237 ml	Cornflakes	4 oz	1 cup

Procedure

1. Cream shortening on mixer at medium speed for 10 minutes. Add sugar gradually and cream until light and fluffy.
2. Beat eggs until light and add to creamed mixture. Continue beating for 2 minutes at medium speed.
3. Sift dry ingredients together. Combine all of the ingredients and mix at low speed for 1½ minutes. Scrape sides and bottom of bowl and mix at medium speed for 10 seconds.
4. Pour mixture into greased baking sheet (18 × 26 × 1 in.).
5. Blend topping ingredients and sprinkle on top of batter.
6. Bake at 350°F/177°C for 40 minutes.

Blueberry Coffee Cake

48 Servings (3 × 3 in)
Bake, 400°F/205°C, 30 min

| Metric | | Ingredients | U.S. | | |
Weight	Volume		Weight		Volume
1.70 kg	2.84 l	Biscuit Mix	3 lb,	12 oz	3 qt
340 g	355 ml	Sugar		12 oz	1 ½ cups
340 g	355 ml	Eggs, beaten (6 lge)		12 oz	1 ½ cups
198 g	237 ml	Salad Oil		7 oz	1 cup
907 g	947 ml	Milk	2 lb		1 qt
		Topping			
454 g	829 ml	Blueberries	1 lb		3 ½ cups
255 g	355 ml	Brown Sugar		9 oz	1 ½ cups
114 g	178 ml	Biscuit Mix		4 oz	¾ cup
	5 ml	Cinnamon			1 tsp
71 g	79 ml	Butter, melted		2 ⅔ oz	⅓ cup

Procedure

1. Stir sugar into biscuit mix. Combine beaten eggs, oil, and milk. Mix into dry ingredients until dry ingredients are just moistened.
2. Spread batter into a greased baking sheet (18 × 26 × 1 in). Sprinkle blueberries over batter. Combine remaining ingredients and sprinkle on top of blueberries.
3. Bake at 400°F/205°C for 30 minutes or until nicely browned.

Variations

Other fresh fruits may be used in place of the blueberries, such as 1 qt/947 ml sliced apples, sliced peaches, apricot halves, or prune plums with halves cut side up on the batter.

Cornbread

48 Servings (3 × 3 in)
Bake, 425°F/218°C, 30 min

| Metric | | Ingredients | U.S. | | |
Weight	Volume		Weight		Volume
793 g	1.24 l	Corn Meal	1 lb,	12 oz	5 ¼ cups
681 g	1.42 l	Flour, pastry	1 lb,	8 oz	1 ½ qt
43 g	60 ml	Baking Powder		1 ½ oz	¼ cup
170 g	178 ml	Sugar		6 oz	¾ cup
28 g	30 ml	Salt		1 oz	2 tbsp
454 g	474 ml	Eggs, beaten (8 lge)	1 lb		2 cups
1.02 kg	1.07 l	Milk	2 lb,	4 oz	4 ½ cups
199 g	237 ml	Shortening, melted		7 oz	1 cup

Procedure

1. Blend dry ingredients. Combine eggs, milk, and melted shortening. Stir into dry ingredients just enough to dampen them.
2. Spread into greased baking sheet (18 × 26 × 1 in).
3. Bake at 425°F/218°C for 30 minutes or until done.

Cranberry Coffee Cake
50 Servings
Bake, 325°F/163°C, 30 min

Metric		Ingredients	U.S.		
Weight	Volume		Weight		Volume
935 g	1.89 l	Flour, all-purpose	2 lb,	1 oz	2 qt + ¼ cup
38 g	55 ml	Baking Powder		1 ⅓ oz	3 ⅔ tbsp
28 g	30 ml	Salt		1 oz	2 tbsp
	15 ml	Soda			1 tbsp
623 g	652 ml	Sugar	1 lb,	6 oz	2 ¾ cups
312 g	652 ml	Nuts, chopped		11 oz	2 ¾ cups
737 g	770 ml	Banana, mashed	1 lb,	10 oz	3 ¼ cups
623 g	652 ml	Milk	1 lb,	6 oz	2 ¾ cups
340 g	355 ml	Eggs, beaten (6 lge)		12 oz	1 ½ cups
312 g	316 ml	Margarine, melted		11 oz	1 ⅓ cups
1.25 kg	1.30 l	Cranberry sauce	2 lb,	12 oz	5 ½ cups
312 g	316 ml	Sugar, granulated		11 oz	1 ⅓ cups

Procedure

1. Blend dry ingredients. Stir in nuts.
2. Combine banana, milk, eggs, and margarine. Add to flour, stirring just enough to blend.
3. Pour into a greased baking sheet (18 × 26 × 1 in).
4. Spread cranberry sauce over top of cake and sprinkle with sugar.
5. Bake at 400°F/205°C for 25 to 30 minutes.

Snickerdoodle Coffee Cake
48 Servings (3 × 3 in)
Bake, 375°F/190°C, 30 min

Metric		Ingredients	U.S.		
Weight	Volume		Weight		Volume
1.36 kg	2.84 l	Flour, cake	3 lb		3 qt
64 g	90 ml	Baking Powder		2 ¼ oz	6 tbsp
23 g	22 ml	Salt			4 ½ tsp
1.02 kg	1.07 l	Sugar	2 lb,	4 oz	4 ½ cups
340 g	533 ml	Raisins		12 oz	2 ¼ cups
255 g	266 ml	Eggs, well-beaten (5 med)		9 oz	1 ⅛ cups
1.25 kg	1.24 l	Milk	2 lb,	12 oz	5 ¼ cups
510 g	533 ml	Margarine, melted	1 lb,	2 oz	2 ¼ cups
		Topping			
283 g	296 ml	Sugar		10 oz	1 ¼ cups
5 g	15 ml	Cinnamon			1 tbsp

Procedure

1. Blend dry ingredients. Mix in raisins.
2. Combine eggs, milk, and margarine. Stir into dry ingredients just until dry ingredients are moistened.
3. Spread batter onto greased baking sheet (18 × 26 × 1 in). Sprinkle top with mixture of cinnamon and sugar.
4. Bake at 375°F/190°C for 30 minutes.

Streusel Coffee Cake

48 Servings (3 × 3 in)
Bake, 350°F/177°C, 45 min

Metric		Ingredients	U.S.		
Weight	Volume		Weight		Volume
9 g	10 ml	Salt		⅓ oz	2 tsp
1.59 kg	3.31 l	Flour, all-purpose	3 lb,	8 oz	3½ qt
1.39 kg	1.45 l	Sugar	3 lb,	1 oz	6⅛ cups
793 g	829 ml	Butter or Margarine	1 lb,	12 oz	3½ cups
28 g	35 ml	Soda		1 oz	2⅓ tbsp
16 g	35 ml	Cinnamon		½ oz	2⅓ tbsp
	18 ml	Cloves, ground			3½ tsp
212 g	474 ml	Walnuts, chopped		7½ oz	2 cups
1.59 kg	1.66 l	Buttermilk	3 lb,	8 oz	1¾ qt

Procedure

1. Mix salt, flour, and sugar. Add butter or margarine and blend until mixture is fine grained.
2. Reserve 1 lb, 8 oz/681 g of this mixture for topping.
3. To the remaining mixture, add soda, cinnamon, cloves, and chopped nuts. Blend well.
4. Add buttermilk and stir just enough to moisten dry ingredients.
5. Spread onto greased baking sheet (18 × 26 × 1 in). Sprinkle reserved topping over batter. Bake at 350°F/177°C for 45 minutes or until done.
6. Cut cake into 48 portions (6 × 8).

Southern Spoon Bread

48 Servings (3 × 3⅓ in)
Bake, 300°F/149°C, 60–70 min

Metric		Ingredients	U.S.		
Weight	Volume		Weight		Volume
5.44 kg	5.68 l	Milk	12 lb		6 qt
907 g	1.42 l	Corn Meal, yellow	2 lb		1½ qt
43 g	45 ml	Salt		1½ oz	3 tbsp
681 g	711 ml	Water	1 lb,	8 oz	3 cups
511 g	474 ml	Egg Yolks, beaten (24 med)	1 lb,	2 oz	2 cups
681 g	711 ml	Egg Whites (24 med)	1 lb,	8 oz	3 cups
	2½ ml	Cream of Tartar			½ tsp

Procedure

1. Scald milk, Mix corn meal and salt with water and stir into milk. Cook until thickened. Remove from heat.
2. Add a small amount of hot corn meal to egg yolks, then stir yolks into hot corn meal.
3. Add cream of tartar to egg whites. Whip whites until stiff but moist. Fold whites into corn meal. Divide batter into two greased serving pans (12 × 20 × 2 in).
4. Bake at 300°F/149°C for 1 hour or until nicely browned and knife inserted in center comes out clean.

LOAF BREADS

Applesauce Raisin Bread

3 Loaves (2 lb/907 g)
Bake, 350°F/177°C, 60 min

| Metric | | Ingredients | U.S. | |
Weight	Volume		Weight	Volume
170 g	178 ml	Eggs, beaten (3 lge)	6 oz	¾ cup
681 g	711 ml	Applesauce	1 lb, 8 oz	3 cups
170 g	178 ml	Oil or Shortening, melted	6 oz	¾ cup
340 g	355 ml	Sugar, granulated	12 oz	1 ½ cups
128 g	178 ml	Brown Sugar	4 ½ oz	¾ cup
227 g	355 ml	Raisins, seedless	8 oz	1 ½ cups
681 g	1.42 l	Flour, all-purpose	1 lb, 8 oz	1 ½ qt
20 g	30 ml	Baking Powder		2 tbsp
	7 ½ ml	Soda		1 ½ tsp
	10 ml	Salt		2 tsp
	10 ml	Cinnamon		2 tsp
	15 ml	Nutmeg		1 tbsp
277 g	474 ml	Walnuts, chopped	8 oz	2 cups

Procedure

1. Combine eggs, applesauce, oil, and sugars. Add raisins.
2. Blend well flour, baking powder, soda, salt, and spices. Stir into sugar mixture. Add nuts. Mix well and divide into 3 greased loaf pans (9 × 5 × 3 in).
3. Bake at 350°F/177°C for 1 hour or until it tests done.

Banana Bread

3 Loaves (2 lb/907 g)
Bake, 350°F/177°C, 1 hr

| Metric | | Ingredients | U.S. | |
Weight	Volume		Weight	Volume
283 g	296 ml	Shortening	10 oz	1 ¼ cups
567 g	592 ml	Sugar	1 lb, 4 oz	2 ½ cups
283 g	296 ml	Eggs, well-beaten (5 lge)	10 oz	1 ¼ cups
596 g	1.24 l	Flour, all-purpose	1 lb, 5 oz	5 ¼ cups
28 g	40 ml	Baking Powder	1 oz	2 ⅔ tbsp
	3 ¾ ml	Soda		¾ tsp
	10 ml	Salt		2 tsp
766 g	829 ml	Bananas, ripe, mashed	1 lb, 11 oz	3 ½ cups
227 g	474 ml	Nuts, chopped	8 oz	2 cups

Procedure

1. Cream shortening and sugar until well blended. Beat in eggs.
2. Blend flour, baking powder, soda, and salt. Add to creamed mixture alternately with bananas, blending well after each addition. Stir in nuts.
3. Pour 2 lbs/907 g into each of 3 greased loaf pans (9 × 5 × 3 in).
4. Bake at 350°F/177°C for 1 hour.

Apricot-Orange Bread

3 Loaves (2 lb/907 g)

Bake, 350°F/177°C, 50 min

Metric		Ingredients	U.S.		
Weight	Volume		Weight		Volume
170 g	355 ml	Apricots, dried		6 oz	1 ½ cups
681 g	3 lge	Oranges	1 lb,	8 oz	3 lge
		Water, boiling			
170 g	296 ml	Raisins, seedless		6 oz	1 ¼ cups
681 g	711 ml	Sugar	1 lb,	8 oz	3 cups
85 g	90 ml	Shortening, melted		3 oz	6 tbsp
14 g	15 ml	Vanilla		½ oz	1 tbsp
150 g	158 ml	Eggs, beaten (3 med)		5 ¼ oz	⅔ cup
681 g	1.42 l	Flour, pastry	1 lb,	8 oz	1 ½ qt
	5 ml	Salt			1 tsp
	15 ml	Soda			1 tbsp
	30 ml	Baking Powder			2 tbsp
170 g	355 ml	Nuts, chopped		6 oz	1 ½ cups

Procedure

1. Soak apricots 30 minutes. Drain. Squeeze juice from oranges. Add boiling water to make 2 cups.
2. Grind rinds, apricots, and raisins. Add to juice.
3. Stir sugar, shortening, and vanilla into fruit. Add beaten eggs. Blend dry ingredients and stir into fruit mixture. Add nuts.
4. Pour into 3 greased loaf pans (9 × 5 × 3 in). Bake at 350°F/177°C for 50 minutes or until done. Turn out on rack and let cool.

Boston Brown Bread

3 Loaves (2 ¾ lb/1.25 kg)

Steam for 2 hr

Metric		Ingredients	U.S.		
Weight	Volume		Weight		Volume
624 g	1.07 l	Corn Meal	1 lb,	6 oz	4 ½ cups
227 g	474 ml	Flour, rye		8 oz	2 cups
340 g	711 ml	Flour, whole wheat		12 oz	3 cups
15 g	21 ml	Soda		½ oz	1 ½ tbsp
15 g	15 ml	Salt		½ oz	1 tbsp
681 g	474 ml	Molasses	1 lb,	8 oz	2 cups
1.36 kg	1.42 l	Sour Milk	3 lb		1 ½ qt
340 g	533 ml	Raisins		12 oz	2 ¼ cups

Procedure

1. Thoroughly blend dry ingredients. Stir in molasses, sour milk, and raisins until well blended.
2. Pour into 3 greased loaf pans (9 × 5 × 3 in). Cover well with brown paper, then with lid or larger pan. Steam for 2 hours.

Cranberry-Nut Bread

3 Loaves (2⅛ lb/967 g)
Bake, 350°F/177°C, 1 hr

| Metric | | Ingredients | U.S. | |
Weight	Volume		Weight	Volume
681 g	1.42 l	Cranberries, fresh, whole	1 lb, 8 oz	1½ qt
340 g	355 ml	Orange Juice	12 oz	1½ cups
	1½ tsp	Orange Rind, grated		1½ tsp
227 g	237 ml	Butter or Margarine	8 oz	1 cup
170 g	178 ml	Eggs, beaten (3 lge)	6 oz	¾ cup
681 g	1.42 l	Flour, all-purpose	1 lb, 8 oz	1½ qt
681 g	711 ml	Sugar, granulated	1 lb, 8 oz	3 cups
21 g	30 ml	Baking Powder	¾ oz	2 tbsp
	7½ ml	Soda		1½ tsp
14 g	15 ml	Salt	½ oz	1 tbsp
170 g	355 ml	Pecans, coarsely chopped	6 oz	1½ cups

Procedure

1. Cook cranberries, orange juice, and rind over medium heat for 5 minutes. Remove from heat, add margarine, and stir until melted. Cool.
2. Add beaten eggs and blend.
3. Blend dry ingredients and nuts. Combine mixtures and stir until well mixed. Pour 2⅛ lb/967 g into each of 3 greased loaf pans (9 × 5 × 3 in).
4. Bake at 350°F/177°C for 1 hour or until it tests done. Remove from pans immediately and cool on rack.

Peanut Butter Bread

3 Loaves (2⅛ lb/964 g)
Bake, 350°F/177°C, 1 hr

| Metric | | Ingredients | U.S. | |
Weight	Volume		Weight	Volume
340 g	355 ml	Peanut Butter	12 oz	1½ cups
170 g	178 ml	Butter or Margarine	6 oz	¾ cup
14 g	45 ml	Orange Rind, grated	½ oz	3 tbsp
510 g	533 ml	Sugar	1 lb, 2 oz	2¼ cups
170 g	178 ml	Eggs (3 lge)	6 oz	¾ cup
340 g	355 ml	Applesauce	12 oz	1½ cups
766 g	1.50 l	Flour, all-purpose	1 lb, 11 oz	6¾ cups
	2½ ml	Soda		½ tsp
	30 ml	Baking Powder		2 tbsp
14 g	15 ml	Salt	½ oz	1 tbsp
510 g	533 ml	Milk	1 lb, 2 oz	2¼ cups
85 g	178 ml	Peanuts, coarsely chopped	3 oz	¾ cups

Procedure

1. Cream together peanut butter, butter or margarine, orange rind, and sugar. Beat in eggs. Add applesauce and mix well.
2. Sift dry ingredients together and add to peanut butter mixture alternately with milk. Add peanuts.
3. Divide into 3 greased loaf pans (9 × 5 × 3 in). Bake at 350°F/177°C for 1 hour.

Carrot Bread

3 Loaves (2 ½ lb/1.14 kg)
Bake, 350°F/177°C, 1 hr

Metric		Ingredients	U.S.	
Weight	Volume		Weight	Volume
907 g	947 ml	Sugar	2 lb	1 qt
454 g	474 ml	Salad Oil	1 lb	2 cups
340 g	355 ml	Eggs, beaten (6 lge)	12 oz	1 ½ cups
681 g	1.42 l	Flour, pastry	1 lb, 8 oz	1 ½ qt
21 g	30 ml	Baking Powder	¾ oz	2 tbsp
	15 ml	Soda		1 tbsp
	20 ml	Cinnamon		4 tsp
	2 ½ ml	Salt		½ tsp
227 g	474 ml	Nuts, chopped	8 oz	2 cups
793 g	1.42 l	Carrots, raw, grated	1 lb, 12 oz	1 ½ qt

Procedure

1. Combine sugar, oil, and eggs.
2. Blend flour, baking powder, soda, cinnamon, salt, and nuts. Add to sugar mixture. Stir in carrots and mix well.
3. Pour 2 ½ lb/1.14 kg into each of 3 greased loaf pans (9 × 5 × 3 in). Bake at 350°F/177°C for 1 hour or until it tests done.

Raisin-Orange Bread

3 Loaves (2 ¼ lb/1.02 kg)
Bake, 350°F/177°C, 1 hr

Metric		Ingredients	U.S.	
Weight	Volume		Weight	Volume
907 g	1.89 l	Flour, pastry	2 lb	2 qt
21 g	30 ml	Baking Powder		2 tbsp
	10 ml	Soda		2 tsp
14 g	15 ml	Salt	½ oz	1 tbsp
567 g	632 ml	Sugar	1 lb, 4 oz	2 ⅔ cups
114 g	237 ml	Nut Meats, chopped	4 oz	1 cup
283 g	415 ml	Raisins	10 oz	1 ¾ cups
85 g	237 ml	Orange Rind, grated	3 oz	1 cup
170 g	178 ml	Eggs, well-beaten (3 lge)	6 oz	¾ cup
368 g	395 ml	Milk	13 oz	1 ⅔ cups
368 g	395 ml	Orange juice	13 oz	1 ⅔ cups
100 g	118 ml	Shortening, melted	3 ½ oz	½ cup

Procedure

1. Blend flour, baking powder, soda, salt, and sugar. Add nuts, raisins, and grated orange rind.
2. Combine eggs, milk, orange juice, and melted shortening. Add to dry ingredients, stirring until they are moistened.
3. Scale 2 ¼ lb/1.02 kg batter into each of 3 greased loaf pans (9 × 5 × 3 in).
4. Bake at 350°F/177°C, for 1 hour or until they test done.

Date-Nut Bread

3 Loaves (2 ½ lb/1.14 kg)
Bake, 300°F/149°C, 1 ¼ hrs

Metric			U.S.	
Weight	Volume	Ingredients	Weight	Volume
681 g	1.07 l	Dates, chopped	1 lb, 8 oz	4 ½ cups
14 g	20 ml	Soda		1 ½ tbsp
737 g	769 ml	Water, boiling	1 lb, 10 oz	3 ¼ cups
85 g	90 ml	Butter or Margarine	3 oz	6 tbsp
790 g	829 ml	Sugar	1 lb, 12 oz	3 ½ cups
227 g	237 ml	Eggs, well-beaten (4 lge)	8 oz	1 cup
21 g	22 ml	Vanilla	¾ oz	1 ½ tbsp
	7 ½ ml	Salt		1 ½ tsp
907 g	1.89 l	Flour, all-purpose	2 lb	2 qt
227 g	474 ml	Pecans, chopped	8 oz	2 cups

Procedure

1. Mix dates, soda, and water; and let stand 20 minutes.
2. Thoroughly cream butter or margarine and sugar. Beat in eggs and vanilla.
3. Blend salt, flour, and nuts. Add alternately to creamed mixture with dates and water.
4. Divide batter into 3 greased loaf pans (9 × 5 × 3 in). Bake at 300°F/149°C for 1 ¼ hours or until it tests done.

Prune Bread

3 Loaves (2 ½ lb/1.14 kg)
Bake, 325°F/163°C, 1 hr

Metric			U.S.	
Weight	Volume	Ingredients	Weight	Volume
907 g	947 ml	Prunes, coarsely chopped	2 lb	1 qt
907 g	947 ml	Water, boiling	2 lb	1 qt
14 g	20 ml	Soda		4 tsp
57 g	59 ml	Butter or Margarine	2 oz	¼ cup
539 g	553 ml	Sugar	1 lb, 3 oz	2 ⅓ cups
114 g	118 ml	Eggs (2 lge)	4 oz	½ cup
10 g	10 ml	Vanilla	⅓ oz	2 tsp
15 g	30 ml	Orange Rind, grated		2 tbsp
907 g	1.89 l	Flour, all-purpose	2 lb	2 qt
14 g	20 ml	Baking Powder		4 tsp
	10 ml	Salt		2 tsp
227 g	474 ml	Walnuts, chopped	8 oz	2 cups

Procedure

1. Pit and coarsely chop uncooked prunes. Pour boiling water over prunes. Stir in soda and let stand to cool.
2. Cream butter or margarine and sugar. Add eggs, vanilla, and orange rind.
3. Blend flour, baking powder, and salt. Add to sugar mixture alternately with prunes. Add nut meats.
4. Pour 2 ½ lb/1.14 kg batter into each of 3 greased loaf pans (9 × 5 × 3 in)
5. Bake at 325°F/163°C, 1 hour or until they test done.

Nut Bread

3 Loaves (2 ½ lb/1.14 kg)
Bake, 350°F/177°C, 1 hr

Metric		Ingredients	U.S.	
Weight	Volume		Weight	Volume
1.02 kg	2.16 l	Flour, all-purpose	2 lb, 4 oz	2 ¼ qt
454 g	474 ml	Sugar	1 lb	2 cups
28 g	40 ml	Baking Powder	1 oz	2 ⅔ tbsp
14 g	15 ml	Salt	½ oz	1 tbsp
170 g	178 ml	Shortening, melted	6 oz	¾ cup
454 g	474 ml	Eggs, beaten (8 lge)	1 lb	2 cups
907 g	947 ml	Milk	2 lb	1 qt
340 g	711 ml	Walnuts, chopped	12 oz	3 cups

Procedure

1. Blend dry ingredients. Combine shortening, eggs, and milk. Add to dry ingredients with chopped nuts. Stir just enough to dampen dry ingredients.
2. Divide into 3 greased loaf pans (9 × 5 × 3 in).
3. Bake at 350°F/177°C for 1 hour or until it tests done.

Praline Coffee Cake

3 Loaves (3 lb/1.36 kg)
Bake, 350°F/177°C, 40–50 min

Metric		Ingredients	U.S.	
Weight	Volume		Weight	Volume
227 g	237 ml	Butter or Margarine	8 oz	1 cup
454 g	632 ml	Brown Sugar	1 lb	2 ⅔ cups
10 g	60 ml	Cinnamon, ground		2 tbsp
227 g	474 ml	Pecans, coarsely chopped	8 oz	2 cups
340 g	355 ml	Shortening	12 oz	1 ½ cups
340 g	355 ml	Sugar	12 oz	1 ½ cups
15 g	15 ml	Vanilla	½ oz	1 tbsp
454 g	474 ml	Eggs, beaten (8 lge)	1 lb	2 cups
681 g	1.07 l	Raisins, chopped	1 lb, 8 oz	4 ½ cups
681 g	1.42 l	Flour, all-purpose	1 lb, 8 oz	1 ½ qt
10 g	15 ml	Baking Powder		1 tbsp
10 g	15 ml	Soda		1 tbsp
14 g	15 ml	Salt	½ oz	1 tbsp
681 g	711 ml	Sour Cream	1 lb, 8 oz	3 cups

Procedure

1. Blend butter or margarine, brown sugar, and cinnamon. Add chopped pecans. Reserve for filling and topping on coffee cake.
2. Cream shortening, sugar, and vanilla until light and fluffy. Add eggs gradually. When well blended, stir in chopped raisins.
3. Sift together dry ingredients and add alternately with sour cream to raisin mixture.
4. Pour 1 ½ lb/681 g of batter into each of 3 greased loaf pans (9 × 5 × 3 in). Sprinkle 4 oz/113 g brown sugar–pecan mixture over batter in each pan. Divide remaining batter on top of pecan mixture and sprinkle remainder of pecan mixture on top.
5. Bake at 350°F/177°C for 40 to 50 minutes or until cakes test done. Let stand 10 minutes in pans, then turn out on racks to cool.

Note: Loaves may be baked in 2 tube pans (10 in), if desired.

Poppy Seed–Lemon Loaf
3 Loaves (2 lb/907 g)
Bake, 350°F/177°C, 45–50 min

Metric			U.S.		
Weight	Volume	Ingredients	Weight		Volume
42 g	79 ml	Poppy Seed		1 ½ oz	⅓ cup
397 g	415 ml	Milk		14 oz	1 ¾ cups
793 g	1.66 l	Flour, all-purpose	1 lb,	12 oz	1 ¾ qt
31 g	45 ml	Baking Powder			3 tbsp
14 g	15 ml	Salt		½ oz	1 tbsp
596 g	711 ml	Shortening, melted	1 lb,	5 oz	3 cups
567 g	711 ml	Sugar	1 lb,	4 oz	3 cups
397 g	415 ml	Eggs (7 lge)		14 oz	1 ¾ cups
28 g	45 ml	Lemon Rind, grated		1 oz	3 tbsp

Procedure

1. Add poppy seed to milk and let stand.
2. Blend flour, baking powder, and salt. Cream shortening and sugar. Add eggs gradually, beating well after each addition. Add lemon rind.
3. Add flour mixture and milk alternately to creamed mixture, beating after each addition. Divide batter evenly into 3 greased loaf pans (9 × 5 × 3 in).
4. Bake at 350°F/177°C for 45 to 50 minutes or until it tests done.

Yeast Breads

Compressed yeast and active dry yeast are the two types of yeast commonly used in large kitchens and bake shops. They differ in the amount of moisture contained (compressed has approximately 70% and active dry approximately 8%) and in the amount required for comparable leavening. Recipes may be adjusted according to the following ratios:

Compressed		Active Dry		Compressed		Active Dry	
grams	ounces	grams	ounces	grams	pounds	grams	ounces
28	1	14	½	681	1 ½	276	9 ¾
57	2	21	¾	907	2	361	12 ¾
114	4	43	1 ½	1.135	2 ½	454	16
227	8	92	3 ¼	1.36	3	546	19 ¼
340	12	135	4 ¾	1.82	4	723	25 ½
454	16	184	6 ½	2.27	5	907	32

Temperature is an important factor in the fermentation of yeast to leaven yeast breads. Compressed yeast should be softened in warm water (82°F/27.7°C to 85°F/29.4°C), and active dry yeast at 100°F/37.7°C to 110°F/43.3°C. Crumble or sprinkle the yeast on top of the water and let it stand 5 minutes, then stir and dissolve. Processing may be simplified with active dry yeast by stirring it into the beginning mixture of flour, sugar, and salt. In this method, blend a third of the flour required in the recipe with the active dry yeast, sugar, salt, and dry milk solids (if used). In the mixer, blend melted shortening or oil, beaten egg, and 120°F/49°C water. Add dry ingredients at low speed, then increase to high speed, and beat for 2 or 3 minutes. Add enough flour to form a satisfactory dough.

White Bread or Rolls
6 Loaves (1 ½ lb/681 g) or 100 Rolls (1 ½ oz/43 g)
Bake, 350°F/177°C, 20–25 min

Metric		Ingredients	U.S.		
Weight	Volume		Weight		Volume
170 g	178 ml	Eggs, beaten (3 lge)		6 oz	¾ cup
170 g	178 ml	Oil or Margarine, melted		6 oz	¾ cup
1.13 kg	1.42 l	Water, warm (120°F/49°C)	2 lb,	8 oz	1 ½ qt
1.14 kg	2.37 l	Flour, bread	2 lb,	8 oz	2 ½ qt
170 g	178 ml	Sugar		6 oz	¾ cup
170 g	355 ml	Milk Solids		6 oz	1 ½ cups
	20 ml	Salt			4 tsp
43 g	90 ml	Yeast, active dry		1 ½ oz	6 tbsp
1.14–1.36 kg	2.37–2.84 l	Flour, bread	2 ½–3 lb		2 ½–3 qt

Procedure

1. Put eggs, oil or margarine, and water in mixer bowl.
2. Combine flour, sugar, milk solids, salt, and yeast and add to the liquids. Mix at medium speed for 3 minutes.
3. Gradually add sufficient flour to form a soft dough (just enough flour for the dough to clear the mixer bowl). Mix at medium speed for 10 minutes.
4. Place dough in a greased bowl in a warm place to rise until doubled in bulk. Knead down and let rest for 10 minutes. Shape into loaves and place in greased pans (9 × 5 × 3 in). Let rise until double in size.
5. Bake at 350°F/177°C for 20 to 25 minutes or until nicely browned.

Cheese Bread
6 Loaves (1½ lb/681 g)
Bake, 350°F/177°C, 25–30 min

Metric		Ingredients	U.S.		
Weight	Volume		Weight		Volume
1.25 kg	2.60 l	Flour, bread	2 lb,	12 oz	2 ¾ qt
170 g	178 ml	Sugar		6 oz	¾ cup
15 g	30 ml	Salt		½ oz	2 tbsp
	3 ¾ ml	Mustard, dry			¾ tsp
43 g	90 ml	Yeast, active dry		1 ½ oz	6 tbsp
1.36 kg	2.84 l	Sharp Cheddar Cheese, shredded	3 lb		3 qt
1.36 kg	1.42 l	Water, warm	3 lb		1 ½ qt
1.14–1.36 kg	2.37–2.84 l	Flour, bread	2 ½–3 lb		2 ½–3 qt

Procedure

1. Blend the dry ingredients and cheese. Add water and mix at medium speed for 3 minutes.
2. Add enough flour to form a soft dough. Knead at medium speed for 10 minutes. The dough should clear the sides of the bowl when enough flour has been added.
3. Put in a greased container in a warm place to rise until doubled in bulk.
4. Knead down and let rest for 10 minutes.
5. Form into loaves and place in greased pans (9 × 5 × 3 in). Let rise until double in size.
6. Bake at 350°F/177°C for 25 to 30 minutes or until nicely browned.

Cranberry Anadama Bread

4 Loaves (2 lb/907 g)
Bake, 350°F/177°C, 25–40 min

Metric		Ingredients	U.S.	
Weight	Volume		Weight	Volume
227 g	237 ml	Water, warm	8 oz	1 cup
57 g	4 cakes	Yeast, compressed	2 oz	4 cakes
340 g	711 ml	Cranberries, fresh	12 oz	3 cups
21 g	30 ml	Orange Rind, grated	¾ oz	2 tbsp
114 g	118 ml	Sugar	4 oz	½ cup
213 g	316 ml	Corn Meal, yellow	7 ½ oz	1 ⅓ cups
227 g	237 ml	Water, cold	8 oz	1 cup
907 g	947 ml	Water, boiling	2 lb	1 qt
28 g	30 ml	Salt	1 oz	2 tbsp
85 g	90 ml	Shortening	3 oz	6 tbsp
312 g	237 ml	Molasses	11 oz	1 cup
1.70 kg	3.31 l	Flour, bread	3 lb, 12 oz	3 ½ qt
28 g	30 ml	Milk	1 oz	2 tbsp

Procedure

1. Grind cranberries, using coarse blade. Add orange rind and sugar.
2. Soften yeast in warm water and let stand.
3. Mix corn meal in cold water and add to boiling water. Cook for 3 minutes, stirring until thickened. Remove from heat. Add salt, shortening, and molasses. Mix well. Cool to lukewarm.
4. Stir in yeast and cranberries. Add 2 ½ qt/2.37 l flour and mix well. Knead in remaining flour until smooth and satiny.
5. Let rise until double in size. Punch down and let rest for 10 minutes. Form 4 loaves and place in greased pans (9 × 5 × 3 in). Let rise until double in bulk (about 45 min).
6. Brush tops with milk. Bake at 350°F/177°C, 25 to 40 minutes.

Orange Bread

6 Loaves (1½ lb/681 g)
Bake, 350°F/177°C, 25–30 min

Metric		Ingredients	U.S.	
Weight	Volume		Weight	Volume
340 g	355 ml	Eggs, beaten (6 lge)	12 oz	1 ½ cups
1.36 kg	1.42 l	Water, warm	3 lb	1 ½ qt
151 g	158 ml	Oil or Shortening, melted	5 ⅓ oz	⅔ cup
255 g	711 ml	Orange Rind, grated	9 oz	3 cups
1.14 kg	2.37 l	Flour, bread, white	2 lb, 8 oz	2 ½ qt
170 g	178 ml	Sugar	6 oz	¾ cup
21 g	22 ml	Salt	¾ oz	1 ½ tbsp
85 g	237 ml	Milk Solids	3 oz	1 cup
43 g	90 ml	Yeast, active dry	1 ½ oz	6 tbsp
1.14–1.36 kg	2.37–2.84 l	Flour, bread	2 ½–3 lb	2 ½–3 qt

1. Put egg, warm water (120°F/49°C), orange rind, and melted shortening in mixer bowl.
2. Combine flour, sugar, salt, milk solids, and yeast. Add to liquids in mixer. Mix at medium speed for 3 minutes.
3. Gradually add flour to form a soft dough. (The dough will clear the sides of the bowl when enough flour has been added.)
4. Knead at low speed for 10 minutes. Place in a greased container and let rise in a warm place until doubled in bulk (about 1½ hrs).
5. Knead down. Let rest for 10 minutes.
6. Shape loaves and place in greased loaf pans. Let rise until doubled in size.
7. Bake at 350°F/177°C for 25 to 30 minutes or until nicely browned.

Fruit Bread

4 Loaves (1½ lb/681 g)
Bake, 350°F/177°C, 25–40min

Metric		Ingredients	U.S.	
Weight	Volume		Weight	Volume
340 g	711 ml	Flour, bread	12 oz	3 cups
227 g	237 ml	Sugar	8 oz	1 cup
14 g	15 ml	Salt	½ oz	1 tbsp
43 g	6 pkgs	Yeast, active dry	1½ oz	6 pkgs
5 g	15 ml	Lemon Rind, grated		1 tbsp
227 g	237 ml	Milk	8 oz	1 cup
114 g	118 ml	Shortening	4 oz	½ cup
340 g	355 ml	Water	12 oz	1½ cups
227 g	237 ml	Eggs, beaten (4 lge)	8 oz	1 cup
170 g	355 ml	Flour, bread	6 oz	1½ cups
454–681 g	947 ml–1.18 l	Flour, bread	1–1½ lb	4–5 cups
454 g	592 ml	Raisins, seedless, white	1 lb	2½ cups
114 g	178 ml	Mixed Candied Fruit	4 oz	¾ cup

Procedure

1. Blend 3 cups/711 ml of flour, sugar, salt, yeast, and lemon peel.
2. Scald milk and water. Add shortening. Remove from heat and stir until shortening has almost melted. When temperature has cooled to 110°F/43°C, stir in flour-yeast mixture. Beat at medium speed for 2 minutes. Scrape mixer bowl as needed.
3. Add eggs and another 1½ cups/355 ml flour. Beat at high speed for 2 minutes. Stir in enough additional flour to make a moderately stiff dough. Knead until smooth and elastic.
4. Place in a greased bowl and let rise until double (about 40 min). Punch down. Let rest 10 minutes.
5. Knead in raisins and candied fruit.
6. Shape into 4 loaves. Place in greased loaf pans (9 × 5 × 3 in) and let rise until double in size (about 45 min).
7. Bake at 350°F/177°C for 25 to 45 minutes or until bread tests done.

Note: A delicious dough for Hot Cross Buns.

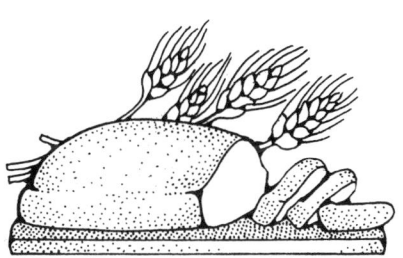

Orange Rye Bread

6 Loaves (1½ lb/681 g)
Bake, 350°F/177°C, 30–35 min

Metric		Ingredients	U.S.	
Weight	Volume		Weight	Volume
85 g	178 ml	Flour, bread	3 oz	¾ cup
43 g	90 ml	Yeast, active dry	1½ oz	6 tbsp
340 g	355 ml	Water, 115°F/46°C	12 oz	1½ cups
	15 ml	Sugar, granulated		1 tbsp
312 g	237 ml	Molasses	11 oz	1 cup
170 g	178 ml	Oil	6 oz	¾ cup
21 g	23 ml	Salt	¾ oz	1½ tbsp
128 g	355 ml	Orange Rind, grated	4½ oz	1½ cups
568 g	1.18 l	Flour, rye	1 lb, 4 oz	1¼ qt
1.14 kg	1.18 l	Water, boiling	2 lb, 8 oz	1¼ qt
454 g	947 ml	Flour, bread	1 lb	1 qt
681–907 g	1.42–1.89 l	Flour, bread	1½–2 lb	1½–2 qt

Procedure

1. Mix bread flour, yeast, water, and sugar together well, and let stand for 15 minutes (until very foamy).
2. Mix molasses, oil, salt, orange rind, rye flour, and boiling water. Let cool to 115°F/46°C.
3. Add yeast mixture and 1 quart of bread flour. Mix at medium speed for 3 minutes.
4. Add enough bread flour to form a soft dough. Knead at low speed for 10 minutes.
5. Put dough in a greased bowl and let it rise in a warm place until it has doubled in bulk. Knead down and let it rest for 10 minutes.
6. Shape into loaves and place in greased pans (9 × 5 × 3 in). Let rise until double in bulk.
7. Bake at 350°F/177°C for 30 to 35 minutes or until done.

Dark Rye Bread

6 Loaves (1½ lb/681 g)
Bake, 350°F/177°C, 30–35 min

Metric		Ingredients	U.S.	
Weight	Volume		Weight	Volume
85 g	178 ml	Flour, bread	3 oz	¾ cup
	15 ml	Granulated Sugar		1 tbsp
43 g	90 ml	Yeast, active dry	1½ oz	6 tbsp
340 g	355 ml	Water (115°F/46°C)	12 oz	1½ cups
681 g	355 ml	Molasses, black strap	1 lb, ½ oz	1½ cups
170 g	178 ml	Oil	6 oz	¾ cup
21 g	23 ml	Salt	¾ oz	1½ tbsp
681 g	1.42 l	Flour, rye, dark	1 lb, 8 oz	1½ qt
1.02 kg	1.07 l	Water, boiling	2 lb, 4 oz	4½ cups
681 g	1.42 l	Flour, bread	1 lb, 8 oz	1½ qt
454–907 g	947 ml–1.89 l	Flour, bread	1–2 lb	1–2 qt

1. Combine flour, sugar, yeast, and warm water. Mix well and let stand for 15 minutes (until foamy).
2. Mix molasses, oil, salt, rye flour, and boiling water. Let cool to 115°F/46°C. Add bread flour and yeast mixture. Beat at medium speed for 3 minutes.
3. Add enough flour to form a soft dough. Knead at medium speed for 8 to 10 minutes, until smooth and elastic.
4. Put dough in a greased bowl in a warm place to rise until doubled in bulk.
5. Knead down. Let rest for 10 minutes. Form into loaves and place in greased loaf pans (9 × 5 × 3 in).
6. Let rise until double in size (about 45 min).
7. Bake at 350°F/177°C for 30 to 35 minutes.

Potato Raisin Bread

6 Loaves (1½ lb/681 g)
Bake, 350°F/177°C, 30 min

Metric			U.S.		
Weight	Volume	Ingredients	Weight		Volume
1.36 kg	1.42 l	Potato Water, warm	3 lb		1½ qt
283 g	355 ml	Potatoes, cooked, mashed		10 oz	1½ cups
57 g	59 ml	Sugar		2 oz	¼ cup
368 g	711 ml	Flour, bread		13 oz	3 cups
43 g	90 ml	Yeast, active dry		1½ oz	6 tbsp
170 g	178 ml	Eggs, beaten (3 lge)		6 oz	¾ cup
227 g	237 ml	Oil or fat, melted		8 oz	1 cup
15 g	15 ml	Salt		½ oz	1 tbsp
170 g	178 ml	Sugar		6 oz	¾ cup
10 g	30 ml	Cinnamon			2 tbsp
681 g	1.42 l	Flour, bread	1 lb,	8 oz	1½ qt
454 g	711 ml	Raisins	1 lb		3 cups
.907–1.14 kg	1.89–2.37 l	Flour, bread	2–2½ lb		2–2½ qt

Procedure

1. Put warm potato water (120°F/49°C) and mashed potatoes in mixer bowl. Mix sugar, flour, and yeast together and stir into the potato water until smooth. Cover the bowl and let stand until the mixture is bubbly (about 20 min).
2. Add the eggs, melted fat or oil, salt, sugar, cinnamon, and 1½ lbs/681 g of flour. Mix at medium speed for 3 minutes.
3. Add enough flour gradually to form a soft dough. The mixture will clear the bowl when sufficient flour has been added. Continue mixing at slow speed for about 8 minutes. (The dough should be smooth and elastic.) Add raisins and mix for 2 minutes.
4. Let the dough rise until it is double in bulk (about 1½ hrs).
5. Punch the dough down. Cover and let it rest for 10 minutes. Divide into 6 loaves and place in greased loaf pans (9 × 5 × 3 in) and let rise until double in size.
6. Bake at 350°F/177°C for 30 minutes.

Herb Bread

6 Loaves (1½ lb/681 g)
Bake, 350°F/177°C, 30 min

Metric		Ingredients	U.S.	
Weight	Volume		Weight	Volume
340 g	355 ml	Eggs, beaten (6 lge)	12 oz	1 ½ cups
170 g	178 ml	Oil or Margarine, melted	6 oz	¾ cup
1.36 kg	1.42 l	Water, warm (120°F/49°C)	3 lb	1 ½ qt
1.14 kg	2.37 l	Flour, bread	2 lb, 8 oz	2 ¼ qt
170 g	178 ml	Sugar	6 oz	¾ cup
170 g	652 ml	Milk Solids, instant	6 oz	2 ¾ cups
21 g	23 ml	Salt	¾ oz	1 ½ tbsp
	15 ml	Sage, powdered		1 tbsp
	15 ml	Thyme, ground		1 tbsp
	15 ml	Marjoram		1 tbsp
	30 ml	Caraway Seed		2 tbsp
43 g	90 ml	Yeast, active dry	1 ½ oz	6 tbsp
1.14–1.36 kg	2.37–2.84 l	Flour, bread, white	2 ½–3 lb	2 ½–3 qt

Procedure

1. Combine beaten eggs, oil, and water in mixer bowl.
2. Stir together flour, sugar, milk solids, salt, herbs, and yeast in a separate bowl and add to liquids in the mixer bowl.
3. Beat at medium speed until smooth and elastic (about 3 min).
4. Add enough flour to form a soft dough. Knead until smooth (about 10 min).
5. Put in a greased bowl and let rise in a warm place until doubled in size (about 1½ hrs).
6. Knead down. Let rest about 10 minutes. Shape loaves and place in greased loaf pans (9 × 5 × 3 in).
7. Let rise until double in size (about 45 min).
8. Bake at 350°F/177°C for 30 minutes.

Four Grain Bread

6 Loaves (1½ lb/681 g)
Bake, 350°F/177°C, 30–45 min

Metric		Ingredients	U.S.	
Weight	Volume		Weight	Volume
170 g	355 ml	Oatmeal, quick-cooking	6 oz	1 ½ cups
681 g	711 ml	Water, boiling	1 lb, 8 oz	3 cups
170 g	178 ml	Butter or Margarine	6 oz	¾ cup
241 g	178 ml	Molasses, medium dark	8 ½ oz	¾ cup
28 g	30 ml	Salt	1 oz	2 tbsp
681 g	711 ml	Water, cool	1 lb, 8 oz	3 cups
255 g	355 ml	Flour, whole wheat	9 oz	1 ½ cups
128 g	355 ml	All-Bran cereal	4 ½ oz	1 ½ cups
191 g	355 ml	Flour, rye	6 ¾ oz	1 ½ cups
156 g	237 ml	Corn Meal	5 ½ oz	1 cup
681 g	1.42 l	Flour, bread, white	1 lb, 8 oz	1 ½ qt
43 g	90 ml	Yeast, active dry	1 ½ oz	6 tbsp
1.36–1.59 kg	2.84–3.31 l	Flour, bread, white	3–3 ½ lb	3–3 ½ qt

1. Stir oatmeal into boiling water and bring to boiling. Remove from heat. Add butter, molasses, and salt. Stir in cool water to bring temperature of the mixture to 120°F/49°C.
2. Blend flours, cereal, and yeast in mixer bowl. Add liquid mixture and beat to mix well (about 3 min).
3. Gradually add enough white flour to form a soft dough. Knead until smooth and elastic.

4. Place dough in a greased bowl in a warm place and let rise until double in bulk. Knead down and let rest for 10 minutes.
5. Shape into loaves and place in greased loaf pans (9 × 5 × 3 in). Let rise until double in size.
6. Bake at 350°F/177°C for 30 to 40 minutes.

Whole Wheat Bread or Rolls

6 Loaves (1½ lbs/681 g) or 100 Rolls (1½ oz/43 g)
Bake, 350°F/177°C, 30 min

Metric		Ingredients	U.S.		
Weight	Volume		Weight		Volume
170 g	178 ml	Eggs, beaten (3 lge)		6 oz	¾ cup
170 g	178 ml	Oil or Shortening, melted		6 oz	¾ cup
242 g	178 ml	Molasses		8½ oz	¾ cup
1.36 kg	1.42 l	Water, warm	3 lb		1½ qt
1.14 kg	2.37 l	Flour, white	2 lb,	8 oz	2½ qt
28 g	30 ml	Sugar		1 oz	2 tbsp
20 g	20 ml	Salt			5 tsp
43 g	90 ml	Yeast, active dry		1½ oz	6 tbsp
170 g	355 ml	Milk Solids		6 oz	1½ cups
1.14–1.36 kg	2.37–2.84 l	Flour, whole wheat	2½–3 lb		2½–3 qt

Procedure

1. Put beaten eggs, oil or melted shortening, molasses, and warm water (120°F/49°C) in mixer bowl.
2. Combine white flour, sugar, salt, yeast, and milk solids and add to the liquid mixture. Mix at medium speed for 3 minutes.
3. Gradually add whole wheat flour to form a soft dough (just enough flour until dough clears the bowl). Mix at low speed for 10 minutes.

4. Place in a greased bowl to rise until double in bulk.
5. Knead down. Let rest for 10 minutes.
6. Shape in loaves, place in greased loaf pans (9 × 5 × 3 in). Let rise until double in size (about 45 min).
7. Bake at 350°F/177°C for 25 minutes or until nicely browned.

Variations

1. Add chopped walnuts (12 oz/340 g or 3 cups/711 ml) before adding the whole wheat flour.
2. Add raisins (1 lb/454 g or 3 cups/711 ml) and 2 tbsp/

30 ml of cinnamon just before adding the whole wheat flour.

Roll Varieties

Bowknots Roll dough ³⁄₈ inch thick. Brush with melted butter or margarine. Cut strips ½ inch by 9 inches, and twist them by placing a hand on each end of strip and twisting or rolling dough on board, in opposite directions. Loop the twist into a single knot with one end coming up through the center of the loop.

Buns Form 1½ to 2½ oz/43 to 72 g balls of dough by rotating the dough lightly against the board while held lightly in the palm of the hand.

Cloverleaf Rolls Form ½ oz/14 g balls of dough (as described under buns). Place 3 small balls together in a muffin cup.

Crescent Rolls Roll dough to ⅛-inch thickness in a circle (as for pie crust). Brush with melted butter or margarine. Cut circle into 12 triangles (or pie-shaped wedges). Beginning with the wide outside edge, roll up triangle toward its tip. Place rolls 2 inches apart on greased baking sheet with tip underneath roll and ends curved to form a crescent.

Fan Tan or Butterflake Rolls Roll dough into a very thin rectangle. Brush with melted butter or margarine. Cut into 1¼-inch-wide strips. Place 5 or 6 flat strips evenly, one on top of the other. Slice through the layers into 1½-inch slices. Place in greased muffin pans with cut end down.

Parkerhouse Rolls Roll dough to ³⁄₈-inch thickness. Cut with 1½- to 2½-inch biscuit cutter, according to size desired. Let dough rest a few minutes after cutting. Brush biscuits with melted butter or margarine. Crease them across the center with the back of a table knife and fold them over.

Poppy Seed or Sesame Rolls Shape dough as desired. Brush with mixture of 1 egg white (beaten until foamy) and 2 tbsp/30 ml of water. Sprinkle top of rolls generously with seeds.

Brioche
48 Rolls (2 oz/57 g)
Bake, 375°F/190°C, 15–25 min

Metric		Ingredients	U.S.	
Weight	Volume		Weight	Volume
454 g	947 ml	Flour, bread	1 lb	1 qt
28 g	4 pkgs	Yeast, active dry	1 oz	4 pkgs
57 g	118 ml	Milk, nonfat dry	2 oz	½ cup
227 g	237 ml	Sugar	8 oz	1 cup
14 g	15 ml	Salt	½ oz	1 tbsp
6 g	10 ml	Lemon Rind, grated		2 tsp
340 g	355 ml	Eggs, well-beaten (6 lge)	12 oz	1 ½ cups
85 g	79 ml	Egg Yolks, beaten (4 lge)	3 oz	⅓ cup
199 g	237 ml	Butter or Margarine, melted	7 oz	1 cup
681–907 g	1.42–1.89 l	Flour, bread	1 ½–2 lb	1 ½–2 qt
454 g	474 ml	Water (120°F/49°C)	1 lb	2 cups

Procedure

1. Blend well 1 lb/454 g flour, yeast, dry milk, sugar, and salt.
2. Combine grated lemon rind, beaten eggs and yolks, melted butter or margarine, and water. Mix well at low speed and add blended dry ingredients. Beat rapidly for 2 or 3 minutes.
3. Add enough flour at slow speed to form a soft dough. Knead for 10 minutes. Place in a greased bowl and let rise until double in bulk. Knead down and refrigerate 6 hours or overnight.
4. Divide a fourth of the dough (24 oz/681 g) and set aside. Shape the remainder into 48 balls (1½ oz/43 g) and place in muffin or brioche pans. Make an indentation on top of each ball. Shape the remainder of the dough into 48 small balls. Brush small balls and those in pans with mixture of 1 egg white, beaten until foamy, and 2 tbsp water. Press a small ball in indentation in top of large ball in pan.
5. Let rise until double in size (about ½ hr). Bake at 375°F/190°C for 15 to 25 minutes or until nicely browned.

Potato Rolls

100 Rolls (1 oz/28 g)
Bake, 375°F/190°C, 15–25 min

Metric		Ingredients	U.S.	
Weight	Volume		Weight	Volume
28 g	2 cakes	Yeast, compressed	1 oz	2 cakes
114 g	118 ml	Water, lukewarm	4 oz	½ cup
567 g	711 ml	Potatoes, mashed	1 lb, 4 oz	3 cups
454 g	474 ml	Milk	1 lb	2 cups
170 g	178 ml	Eggs, beaten (3 lge)	6 oz	¾ cup
76 g	79 ml	Sugar	2 ⅔ oz	⅓ cup
21 g	22 ml	Salt	¾ oz	1 ½ tbsp
227 g	266 ml	Butter or Margarine, melted	8 oz	1 ⅛ cups
1.36 kg	2.84 l	Flour, bread	3 lb	3 qt

Procedure

1. Dissolve yeast in lukewarm water (85°F/29.4°C).
2. Slowly add milk to mashed potatoes, mixing until smooth. Stir in beaten eggs, sugar, salt, yeast, and butter or margarine.
3. Stir in flour to make a soft dough, as soft as can be kneaded. Knead thoroughly.
4. Put in greased bowl. Brush top with melted shortening. Let rise in warm place until double in size (about 2 hrs). Punch down. Let rest 10 minutes.
5. Shape into rolls. Brush tops with melted butter or margarine. Let rise until double in size.
6. Bake at 375°F/190°C for 20 minutes. Brush tops with butter or margarine and let cool on rack.

Bran Rolls

100 Rolls (1 oz/28 g)
Bake, 375°F/190°C, 15–25 min

Metric		Ingredients	U.S.	
Weight	Volume		Weight	Volume
114 g	474 ml	All-Bran	4 oz	2 cups
454 g	474 ml	Water, boiling	1 lb	2 cups
340 g	355 ml	Shortening	12 oz	1 ½ cups
283 g	296 ml	Sugar	10 oz	1 ¼ cups
7 g	10 ml	Salt		2 tsp
57 g	4 cakes	Yeast, compressed	2 oz	4 cakes
454 g	474 ml	Water, lukewarm	1 lb	2 cups
227 g	237 ml	Eggs, beaten (4 lge)	8 oz	1 cup
1.13–1.36 kg	2.36–2.84 l	Flour, bread	2 ½–3 lb	2 ½–3 qt

Procedure

1. Pour boiling water over All-Bran. Stir in shortening until melted. Add sugar and salt. Cool to lukewarm.
2. Crumble yeast on warm water and let stand to soften. Stir into cooled All-Bran mixture. Add eggs.
3. Mix in enough flour to make a soft dough. Knead in more flour as needed until dough is smooth and elastic. Place in greased bowl. Grease top of dough. Let rise until double in bulk (about 2 hrs). Punch down. Dough may be refrigerated for later use or shaped at this point.
4. Shape rolls and let rise until double in size.
5. Bake at 375°F/190°C, 15 to 25 minutes. Brush tops with melted butter or margarine and let cool on rack.

Basic Sweet Rolls
50 Rolls (1½ oz/43 g)
Bake, 375°F/190°C, 15–25 min

Metric		Ingredients	U.S.	
Weight	Volume		Weight	Volume
454 g	947 ml	Flour, bread	1 lb	1 qt
28 g	4 pkgs	Yeast, active dry	1 oz	4 pkgs
57 g	118 ml	Milk, nonfat dry	2 oz	½ cup
170 g	178 ml	Sugar	6 oz	¾ cup
21 g	22 ml	Salt	¾ oz	1 ½ tbsp
227 g	237 ml	Eggs, well-beaten (4 lge)	8 oz	1 cup
150 g	178 ml	Butter or Margarine, melted	5 ¼ oz	¾ cup
567 g	592 ml	Water, warm	1 lb, 4 oz	2 ½ cups
907 g–1.13 kg	1.89–2.36 l	Flour, bread	2–2 ½ lb	2–2 ½ qt

Procedure

1. Blend well 1 lb/454 g flour, yeast, dry milk, sugar, and salt.
2. Combine beaten eggs, melted butter or margarine, and warm water. Mix well at low speed. Add blended dry ingredients. Beat at high speed for 3 minutes. Scrape bowl as needed.
3. Add enough flour to form a soft dough. Beat at low speed or knead in additional flour as needed. The rich dough tends to be sticky. Avoid mixing in too much flour. Use just enough for the dough to be rea-sonably easy to handle. Knead dough until it is smooth and satiny.
4. Place in greased bowl. Brush top with melted fat. Let rise in a warm, draft-free place until double in bulk (about 1½ hrs). Punch down. Let rest 10 minutes. Shape. Let rise until double in size (about 45 min).
5. Bake at 375°F/190°C, 15 to 25 minutes. Brush tops with butter. Remove from pans and cool on rack.

Sweet Roll Varieties

Cinnamon Rolls Roll Sweet Roll dough into a rectangle ⅜ inch thick. Spread with ¼ cup/59 ml softened butter or margarine. Sprinkle with mixture of 2 cups/474 ml sugar, 2 tbsp/30 ml cinnamon, and 8 oz/227 g raisins. Roll as for jelly roll. Cut in 1-inch slices and place cut side down ½ inch apart on greased baking sheet (18 × 26 × 1 in). Let rise until double in size (about 45 min).

Kolache Shape Sweet Roll dough into 1½ oz/ 43 g balls and place 1 inch apart on greased baking sheet (18 × 26 × 1 in). Brush rolls with melted butter or mar-garine. Press a cavity with the thumb or finger in the center of each roll. Fill cavity with rounded tea-spoonful of filling. Filling: Mix well 1½ lb/681 g chopped cooked prunes, 8 oz/227 g chopped orange marmalade, 4 oz/114 g chopped walnuts, 1 tsp/5 ml cinnamon, and ⅛ tsp ground cloves. Let rise until double in size. Bake at 375°F/190°C for 20 to 25 min-utes.

Marmalade Rolls Roll Sweet Roll dough into a rectan-gle ⅜ inch thick. Spread with 12 oz/340 g thick or-ange marmalade. Roll as for jelly roll. Make 1-inch slices and place cut side down 1 inch apart on greased baking sheet (18 × 26 × 1 in). Let rise. Bake at 375°F/190°C, 20 to 25 minutes. Brush with butter or glaze with syrup from the marmalade after bak-ing.

Orange Rolls Roll Sweet Roll dough into a rectangle ⅜ inch thick. Spread with ¼ cup/59 ml of softened butter or margarine. Sprinkle with blended mixture of 1½ oz/43 g orange rind, grated, and 6 oz/170 g sugar. Roll as for jelly roll. Make 1-inch slices and place cut side down ½ inch apart on greased baking sheet or in greased muffin pans. After baking, while the rolls are still hot, glaze them with blended mix-ture of 3 oz/85 g corn syrup, 2 tbsp/10 g grated or-ange rind, 6 oz/170 g sugar, and ¼ cup/59 ml hot water.

Pecan Rolls Roll Sweet Roll dough into a rectangle ⅜ inch thick. Spread with ¼ cup/59 ml creamed but-ter or margarine. Sprinkle with 1 cup/237 ml brown sugar. Roll as for jelly roll. Make 1-inch slices. Blend 6 oz/170 g brown sugar, 4 oz/114 g softened butter or margarine, and 3 oz/85 g water. Put 1 tsp/5 ml of mixture in bottom of greased muffin pans and add 4 or 5 pecan halves to each cup. Place slice of dough on top. Let rise until double in size. Bake at 375°F/ 190°C, 20 to 25 minutes or until nicely browned. In-vert on rack and cool. Brush tops with butter.

Hot Cross Buns

50 Rolls (1½ oz/43 g)

Bake, 375°F/190°C, 20–25 min

Metric		Ingredients	U.S.	
Weight	Volume		Weight	Volume
454 g	947 ml	Flour, bread	1 lb	1 qt
28 g	4 pkgs	Yeast, active dry	1 oz	4 pkgs
57 g	118 ml	Milk, nonfat dry	2 oz	½ cup
170 g	178 ml	Sugar	6 oz	¾ cup
9 g	10 ml	Salt		2 tsp
5 g	15 ml	Cinnamon		1 tbsp
	⅝ ml	Cloves		⅛ tsp
	5 ml	Nutmeg		1 tsp
170 g	178 ml	Eggs, well-beaten (3 lge)	6 oz	¾ cup
170 g	178 ml	Butter or Margarine, melted	6 oz	¾ cup
454 g	474 ml	Water, warm	1 lb	2 cups
681–907 g	1.42–1.89 l	Flour, bread	1½–2 lb	1½–2 qt
150 g	237 ml	Raisins, seedless	5⅓ oz	1 cup
114 g	118 ml	Mixed Candied Fruit, chopped	4 oz	½ cup
		Frosting		
142 g	237 ml	Confectioner's Sugar	5 oz	1 cup
43 g	45 ml	Milk	1½ oz	3 tbsp
14 g	15 ml	Butter or Margarine	½ oz	1 tbsp
5 g	5 ml	Orange Juice Concentrate		1 tsp

Procedure

1. Blend 1 lb/454 g flour, yeast, dry milk, sugar, salt, and spices.
2. Mix beaten eggs, butter or margarine, and warm water in mixer at low speed. Add blended dry ingredients. Beat at high speed for 2 or 3 minutes. Scrape bowl as needed.
3. Add enough flour to form a soft dough. Knead in raisins and fruit. Add as much flour as needed. Rich dough tends to be sticky; avoid adding excess flour. Add just enough for dough to be reasonably easy to handle. Knead for 10 minutes or until dough is smooth and elastic.
4. Place dough in greased bowl in a warm, draft-free place. Let rise until double in size (about 2 hrs). Knead down. Let rest 10 minutes. Shape into 1½ oz/43 g balls and place in greased pans barely touching. Brush with melted butter or margarine. A cross may be slashed with knife on top of each roll, if desired. Let rise until double in size (about 1 hr).
5. Bake at 375°F/190°C for 20 to 25 minutes. Brush with melted butter or margarine. Blend frosting ingredients. Apply with a pastry tube to form a cross on top of rolls.

Prune Nut Rolls

60 Rolls (2 ½ oz/71 g)

Bake, 375°F/190°C, 20–25 min

Metric		Ingredients	U.S.	
Weight	Volume		Weight	Volume
454 g	474 ml	Water, warm	1 lb	2 cups
227 g	237 ml	Eggs, beaten (4 lge)	8 oz	1 cup
199 g	237 ml	Butter or Margarine, melted	7 oz	1 cup
227 g	237 ml	Sugar	8 oz	1 cup
9 g	10 ml	Salt		2 tsp
227 g	474 ml	Flour, Bread	8 oz	2 cups
28 g	4 pkgs	Yeast, active dry	1 oz	4 pkgs
57 g	118 ml	Milk, nonfat dry	2 oz	½ cup
283–340 g	592–711 ml	Flour, bread	10–12 oz	2 ½–3 cups
		Filling		
1.36 kg	1.42 l	Prunes, soaked, chopped	3 lb	1 ½ qt
227 g	237 ml	Sugar	8 oz	1 cup
	2 ½ ml	Salt		½ tsp
4 g	10 ml	Cinnamon		2 tsp
	5 ml	Nutmeg		1 tsp
12 g	20 ml	Lemon Rind, grated		4 tsp
227 g	474 ml	Walnuts, chopped	8 oz	2 cups
		Glaze		
170 g	178 ml	Lemon Juice	6 oz	¾ cup
510 g	947 ml	Powdered Sugar	1 lb, 2 oz	1 qt

Procedure

1. Combine water, eggs, butter or margarine, sugar, and salt in mixer. Beat at low speed for ½ minute.
2. Blend 2 cups/474 ml flour, dry yeast, and dry milk, and add to liquids. Beat rapidly for 3 minutes.
3. At slow speed add enough flour to make a soft dough. Knead until smooth and satiny. Place in greased bowl in warm, draft-free place and let rise until double in bulk (about 2 hrs).
4. Knead down. Let rest 10 minutes. Roll out on a lightly floured board, in a rectangle ⅜ inch thick. Spread with prune filling. Roll as for jelly roll. Make 1-inch slices and place cut side down on greased baking sheet (18 × 26 × 1 in) about 1 inch apart. Brush tops with melted butter or margarine.
5. Let rise until double in size. Bake at 375°F/190°C, 20 to 25 minutes. Brush with lemon glaze while hot.

Danish Pastry

48 Rolls (1¾ oz/50 g)
Bake, 375°F/190°C, 15–25 min

Metric		Ingredients	U.S.	
Weight	Volume		Weight	Volume
454 g	947 ml	Flour, bread	1 lb	1 qt
28 g	4 pkgs	Yeast, active dry	1 oz	4 pkgs
57 g	118 ml	Milk, nonfat dry	2 oz	½ cup
170 g	178 ml	Sugar	6 oz	¾ cup
10 g	10 ml	Salt		2 tsp
454 g	474 ml	Eggs, well-beaten (8 lge)	1 lb	2 cups
100 g	118 ml	Butter or Margarine, melted	3½ oz	½ cup
340 g	355 ml	Water, warm	12 oz	1½ cups
681–907 g	1.42–1.89 l	Flour, bread	1½–2 lb	1½–2 qt
199 g	237 ml	Butter or Margarine, softened	7 oz	1 cup

Procedure

1. Blend well 1 lb/454 g flour, yeast, dry milk, sugar, and salt.
2. Combine eggs, butter or margarine, and warm water. Mix well at low speed. Add blended dry ingredients. Beat at high speed for 2 or 3 minutes. Scrape bowl as needed.
3. Add enough flour to form a soft dough. Knead for 10 minutes or until dough is smooth and satiny.
4. Roll dough into a rectangle ⅜ inch thick. Spread with ⅔ softened butter or margarine. Fold dough in half crosswise. Spread with remaining butter or margarine. Fold lengthwise. Stretch or roll lightly. Fold into a rectangle and place in a greased pan. Cover and place in refrigerator overnight.
5. Roll dough into a rectangle. Let rest on bench for 10 minutes. Shape as desired. Brush with melted butter or margarine, or an egg mixture made with 1 egg white beaten until foamy and 2 tbsp/30 ml water.
6. Let rise until double in size (about 30 min). Bake at 375°F/190°C for 15 to 25 minutes or until nicely browned.

Variation

Butter Horns or Snail Shape   Roll the dough to ⅜-inch thickness. Cut strips 2 × 9 inches. Twist strips by moving the ends in opposite directions against the board. Swirl the strips loosely to form snail shape. Arrange 1 inch apart on a greased baking sheet (18 × 26 × 1 in). Bake at 375°F/190°C, 15 to 25 minutes.

CHAPTER 2

Beverages and Cocktails

Beverages

Beverages are enjoyed for stimulation and refreshment, whether alone or as a part of a meal. Rich, appealing flavor, sparkling color, and temperature add important values for enjoyment. The temperature should be icy cold or piping hot. This fact makes equipment valuable that helps to maintain the desired temperature. The substance of a beverage should be clear on the tongue and not leave a cloying sensation in the mouth.

HOT BEVERAGES

Coffee
50–60 Cups (6 oz/170 g)

Metric		Ingredients	U.S.	
Weight	Volume		Weight	Volume
454 g	1.18 l	Coffee, ground	1 lb	5 cups
9.1–10.9 kg	9.5–11.4 l	Water	20–24 lb	2½–3 gal

Procedure

1. Heat water to boiling.
2. Measure coffee accurately into container for brewing.
3. Permit measured amount of water to pour over the ground coffee.
4. Remove coffee grounds as soon as coffee has filtered through.
5. Permit brew to stand a few minutes (about 10) to ripen before serving.
6. Maintain 185°–200°F/85°–95°C temperature during service.

Variations

For Cafe au Lait, brew coffee double strength and heat an equal quantity of milk to scalding temperature. Serve equal amounts of hot milk and coffee per portion.

HOW TO CONTROL COFFEE QUALITY

1. Suitable equipment Choose a coffee maker that will (a) yield an excellent brew; (b) maintain palatable temperature; (c) provide quantity needed at suitable speed; and (d) will require a minimum of labor to operate and maintain. The equipment needs to be thoroughly and easily cleanable. One type of coffee maker is not likely to be best for all situations. Eight- or twelve-cup decanter models may serve well in service dining rooms, for example, but may not be fast enough for serving a fast-moving cafeteria line.

2. Good coffee Choose a coffee blend and a degree of roast that will be popular with the specific clientele. Select a grind suitable for the equipment to be used (fine, regular, or coarse). When testing blends, note comparative color, flavor, aroma, body, and holding quality. Some of the best coffees become bitter in a comparatively short time. Coffee is best in quality when freshly roasted, ground, and brewed.

3. Correct proportions Determine proportions of water to coffee according to the strength of brew favored by the clientele.

4. Fresh water Be sure that the water is fresh and freshly brought to boiling temperature. Avoid stale, brackish, alkaline, or strongly chlorinated water. Water filters are available and advisable in localities where the nature of the water injures the coffee quality.

5. Proper temperature The temperature of the water is significant in drawing flavorful oils from the coffee. The water poured over ground coffee should be between 204°F/96°C and 212°F/100°C. After brewing, a temperature of 185°F/85°C should be maintained.

Chocolate
50 Servings (6 oz/170 g)

| Metric | | Ingredients | U.S. | |
Weight	Volume		Weight	Volume
340 g	355 ml	Sugar	12 oz	1 ½ cups
5 g	5 ml	Salt		1 tsp
	10 ml	Cinnamon (optional)		2 tsp
1.82 kg	1.89 l	Water, hot	4 lb	2 qt
681 g	1.42 l	Chocolate, unsweetened, shaved	1 lb, 8 oz	1 ½ qt
7.26 kg	7.57 l	Milk, hot	16 lb	2 gal
15 g	15 ml	Vanilla	½ oz	1 tbsp

Procedure

1. Mix dry ingredients in hot water and simmer until sugar is completely dissolved (about 3 min).
2. Reduce heat, add shaved chocolate, and stir constantly until chocolate is melted and smooth.
3. Add milk and heat to scalding temperature.
4. Add vanilla and beat until frothy.

Note: 2 tsp/10 ml of instant coffee may be substituted for cinnamon.

Cocoa
50 Servings (6 oz/170 g)

| Metric | | Ingredients | U.S. | |
Weight	Volume		Weight	Volume
283 g	592 ml	Cocoa, unsweetened	10 oz	2 ½ cups
681 g	711 ml	Sugar	1 lb, 8 oz	3 cups
21 g	20 ml	Salt	¾ oz	1 ½ tbsp
907 g	947 ml	Water, cold	2 lb	1 qt
9.07 kg	9.46 l	Milk, hot	20 lb	2 ½ gal

Procedure

1. Thoroughly mix cocoa, sugar, and salt. Add the water and mix until smooth. Heat to boiling and simmer slowly for 5 minutes.

2. Add cocoa mixture to hot milk. Stir until well-blended and heat to scalding. Beat until frothy with a whip to prevent scum forming on surface.

Variations

Flavor with one of the following: 1 tbsp/15 ml vanilla, 2 tbsp/30 ml instant coffee, or 2 tsp/10 ml cinnamon.

Each cup may be decorated with a large marshmallow or whipped cream.

Tea
50 Servings (6 oz/170 g)

Metric			U.S.	
Weight	Volume	Ingredients	Weight	Volume
57 g	175 ml	Tea	2 oz	¾ cup
9.07 kg	9.46 l	Water, boiling	20 lb	2½ gal

Procedure

1. Put tea in cheesecloth bag, and place in glass, chinaware, or stainless steel container.
2. Pour freshly boiling water over tea. Let stand 1 to 5 minutes. Remove tea bag. Hold brew at 190°F/88°C.

Note: For individual bags, use heated container and boiling water.

Hot Spiced Tea
50 Servings (7 oz/198 g)

Metric			U.S.	
Weight	Volume	Ingredients	Weight	Volume
45 g	10 2-in	Cinnamon Sticks	1½ oz	10 2-in
	10 ml	Cloves		2 tsp
114 g	2 rinds	Orange Rind	4 oz	2 rinds
57 g	1 rind	Lemon Rind	2 oz	1 rind
1.82 kg	1.89 l	Water, hot	4 lb	2 qt
907 g	947 ml	Sugar	2 lb	1 qt
907 g	947 ml	Orange Juice	2 lb	1 qt
454 g	474 ml	Lemon Juice	1 lb	2 cups
57 g	175 ml	Tea	2 oz	¾ cup
7.26 kg	7.57 l	Water, boiling	16 lb	2 gal

Procedure

1. Tie spices and rinds loosely in cheesecloth bag. Simmer in 2 qt/1.89 l of water for 20 minutes. Remove bag from liquid.
2. Add sugar and stir until dissolved. Add fruit juices.

3. Brew tea in 2 gal/7.57 l boiling water. Combine with spice mixture. Heat to simmering temperature before serving.

Hot Spiced Cider
50 Servings (5 oz/140 g)

| Metric | | Ingredients | U.S. | |
Weight	Volume		Weight	Volume
65 g	15 2-in	Cinnamon Sticks	2 ¼ oz	15 2-in
12 g	30 ml	Cloves, whole		2 tbsp
10 g	30 ml	Allspice, whole		2 tbsp
	5 ml	Mace		1 tsp
	5 ml	Salt		1 tsp
	few grains	Cayenne Pepper		few grains
1.25 kg	1.66 l	Brown Sugar	2 lb, 12 oz	1 ¾ qt
7.26 kg	7.57 l	Cider	16 lb	2 gal

Procedure

1. Tie spices loosely in cheesecloth bag. Add spices and brown sugar to cider.
2. Heat cider slowly to boiling point. Lower heat to simmer 15 minutes. Remove spice bag. Serve piping hot.

Mulled Apricot Nectar
50 Servings (6 oz/170 g)

| Metric | | Ingredients | U.S. | |
Weight	Volume		Weight	Volume
7.26 kg	7.57 l	Apricot Juice	16 lb	2 gal
1.82 kg	1.89 l	Orange Juice	4 lb	2 qt
340 g	237 ml	Honey	12 oz	1 cup
340 g	3 med	Lemons, sliced	12 oz	3 med
45 g	10 2-in	Cinnamon Sticks	1 ½ oz	10 2-in
	10 ml	Cloves, whole		2 tsp
	10 ml	Allspice, whole		2 tsp

Procedure

1. Tie spices and lemon slices loosely in cheesecloth. Add to juices and honey. Heat slowly to simmering. Simmer 10 minutes.
2. Let stand 30 minutes. Remove spice bag. Reheat for service.

Wassail

50 Servings (6 oz/170 g)

Metric		Ingredients	U.S.	
Weight	Volume		Weight	Volume
8.17 kg	8.51 l	Apple Juice or Cider	18 lb	2 ¼ gal
45 g	10 2-in	Cinnamon Sticks	1 ½ oz	10 2-in
28 g	1 rind	Lemon Rind, cut in strips	1 oz	1 rind
	5 ml	Nutmeg, grated		1 tsp
3 g	10 ml	Allspice, whole		2 tsp
237 g	247 ml	Lemon Juice	8 oz	1 cup
907 g	947 ml	Pineapple Juice	2 lb	1 qt
340 g	237 ml	Honey	12 oz	1 cup

Procedure

1. Tie spices and lemon rind loosely in cheesecloth bag. Add to cider and simmer for 10 minutes. Let stand 30 minutes.

2. Remove spice bag. Add remaining ingredients. Heat to simmering and serve immediately.

COLD BEVERAGES

Apricot Punch

50 Servings (5 oz/140 g)

Metric		Ingredients	U.S.	
Weight	Volume		Weight	Volume
3.63 kg	3.79 l	Apricot Juice	8 lb	1 gal
907 g	947 ml	Orange Juice	2 lb	1 qt
227 g	237 ml	Pineapple Juice	8 oz	1 cup
114 g	120 ml	Lemon Juice	4 oz	½ cup
2.27 kg	2.37 l	Ginger ale, chilled	5 lb	2 ½ qt

Procedure

1. Blend fruit juices and chill.

2. Add chilled ginger ale immediately before serving.

Cranberry Juice Cocktail
50 Servings (5 oz/140 g)

Metric		Ingredients	U.S.	
Weight	**Volume**		**Weight**	**Volume**
4.54 kg	4.74 l	Cranberry Juice	10 lb	5 qt
227 g	237 ml	Lemon Juice	8 oz	1 cup
	⅝ ml	Bitters		⅛ tsp
2.27 kg	2.37 l	Ginger ale, chilled	5 lb	2½ qt

Procedure

1. Blend juices and bitters. Chill.

2. Add chilled ginger ale immediately before serving.

Cranberry Apple Punch
50 Servings (5 oz/140 g)

Metric		Ingredients	U.S.	
Weight	**Volume**		**Weight**	**Volume**
170 g	237 ml	Cinnamon Candies	6 oz	1 cup
454 g	474 ml	Water, boiling	1 lb	2 cups
3.63 kg	3.79 l	Cranberry Juice	8 lb	1 gal
1.82 kg	1.89 l	Apple Juice	4 lb	2 qt
115 g	118 ml	Lemon Juice	4 oz	½ cup
1.60 kg	1.66 l	Ginger ale, chilled	3 lb, 8 oz	1¾ qt

Procedure

1. Dissolve cinnamon candies in boiling water. Cool. Add fruit juices and chill thoroughly.

2. Blend in chilled ginger ale just before serving.

Lemon Orange Punch
50 Servings (5 oz/140 g)

Metric		Ingredients	U.S.	
Weight	**Volume**		**Weight**	**Volume**
511 g	533 ml	Lemonade Concentrate	1 lb, 2 oz	2¼ cups
511 g	533 ml	Orange Concentrate	1 lb, 2 oz	2¼ cups
3.63 kg	3.79 l	Water	8 lb	1 gal
454 g	474 ml	Grenadine Syrup	1 lb	2 cups
2.27 kg	2.37 l	Ginger ale	5 lb	2½ qt

Procedure

1. Refrigerate liquids until well-chilled.

2. Blend well shortly before serving.

Citrated Orange Punch

50 Servings (5 oz/140 g)

Metric		Ingredients	U.S.	
Weight	**Volume**		**Weight**	**Volume**
567 g	592 ml	Orange Juice	1 lb, 4 oz	2 ½ cups
170 g	178 ml	Lemon Juice	6 oz	¾ cup
35 g	40 ml	Citric Acid	1 ¼ oz	2 ½ tbsp
1.13 kg	1.18 l	Water, boiling	2 lb, 8 oz	1 ¼ qt
793 g	829 ml	Sugar	1 lb, 12 oz	3 ½ cups
4.54 kg	4.74 l	Water, cold	10 lb	5 qt

Procedure

1. Squeeze oranges and lemons. Chop rinds and add to juice.
2. Dissolve citric acid powder in boiling water. Stir in sugar until dissolved. Add fruit and chill overnight. Strain.
3. Add cold water before serving.

Note: Appetizing and inexpensive. Decorate with fresh fruit or balls of fruit sherbet.

Lemon Lime Punch

(Emerald)
50 Servings (5 oz/140 g)

Metric		Ingredients	U.S.	
Weight	**Volume**		**Weight**	**Volume**
681 g	711 ml	Sugar	1 lb, 8 oz	3 cups
907 g	947 ml	Water, boiling	2 lb	1 qt
1.02 kg	1.07 l	Lemonade Concentrate	2 lb, 4 oz	4 ½ cups
340 g	355 ml	Lime Juice	12 oz	1 ½ cups
1.36 kg	1.42 l	Pineapple Juice	3 lb	1 ½ qt
2.72 kg	2.84 l	Water, cold	6 lb	3 qt
	⅝ ml	Bitters		⅛ tsp
	1 ¼ ml	Green Coloring		¼ tsp
1.60 kg	1.66 l	Ginger ale, chilled	3 lb, 8 oz	1 ¾ qt

Procedure

1. Dissolve sugar in boiling water. Cool. Blend all ingredients except ginger ale and chill.
2. Add chilled ginger ale shortly before serving.

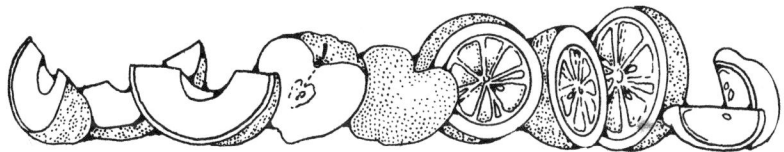

Fruit Punch
50 Servings (5 oz/140 g)

| Metric | | Ingredients | U.S. | |
Weight	Volume		Weight	Volume
567 g	592 ml	Water, boiling	1 lb, 4 oz	2 ½ cups
1.36 kg	1.42 l	Pineapple, crushed	3 lb	1 ½ qt
567 g	592 ml	Sugar	1 lb, 4 oz	2 ½ cups
28 g	60 ml	Orange Rind, grated	1 oz	4 tbsp
681 g	711 ml	Tea, strong, hot	1 lb, 8 oz	3 cups
567 g	592 ml	Lemon Juice	1 lb, 4 oz	2 ½ cups
907 g	947 ml	Orange Juice	2 lb	1 qt
681 g	711 ml	Maraschino Cherries and Juice	1 lb, 8 oz	3 cups
2.27 kg	2.37 l	Ginger ale, chilled	5 lb	2 ½ qt

Procedure

1. Combine boiling water, crushed pineapple, sugar, and grated orange rind. Simmer 10 minutes. Remove from heat. Add tea. Cool.

2. Add juices and cherries. Chill. Add ginger ale just before serving.

Tomato Juice Cocktail
50 Servings (5 oz/140 g)

| Metric | | Ingredients | U.S. | |
Weight	Volume		Weight	Volume
7.25 kg	7.60 l	Tomato Juice	16 lb	5 ½ cans (46 oz)
227 g	237 ml	Sugar	8 oz	1 cup
15 g	15 ml	Salt	½ oz	1 tbsp
227 g	237 ml	Lemon Juice	8 oz	1 cup
	2 ½ ml	Hot Pepper Sauce		½ tsp
45 g	45 ml	Celery Salt	1 ½ oz	3 tbsp

Procedure

1. Combine all ingredients, except lemon juice. Cook 30 minutes. Strain and add lemon juice.

2. Chill well before serving.

Rhubarb Punch

50 Servings (5 oz/140 g)

| Metric | | Ingredients | U.S. | |
Weight	Volume		Weight	Volume
4.55 kg	9.47 l	Rhubarb, diced	10 lb	2 ½ gal
3.65 kg	3.79 l	Water	8 lb	1 gal
1.35 kg	1.45 l	Sugar	3 lb	1 ½ qt
681 g	711 ml	Water, chilled	1 lb, 8 oz	3 cups
340 g	355 ml	Lime Juice, chilled (6 limes)	12 oz	1 ½ cups
1.60 kg	1.66 l	Ginger ale, chilled	3 lb, 8 oz	1 ¾ qt
		Red Coloring		

Procedure

1. Cook fresh or frozen rhubarb in water until tender. Strain out juice through cheesecloth.
2. Heat juice with sugar, stirring until sugar is dissolved. Chill.
3. Add lime juice, cold water, and ginger ale. Color with red coloring to a very light pink.

Loganberry Punch

50 Servings (5 oz/140 g)

| Metric | | Ingredients | U.S. | |
Weight	Volume		Weight	Volume
907 g	947 ml	Sugar	2 lb	1 qt
907 g	947 ml	Water, boiling	2 lb	1 qt
681 g	711 ml	Lemon Juice	1 lb, 8 oz	3 cups
1.82 kg	1.89 l	Loganberry Juice	4 lb	2 qt
907 g	947 ml	Orange Juice	2 lb	1 qt
1.82 kg	1.89 l	Water, cold	4 lb	2 qt
	1 ⅔ ml	Mint Flavoring		⅓ tsp
793 g	829 ml	Ginger ale, chilled	1 lb, 12 oz	3 ½ cups

Procedure

1. Dissolve sugar in boiling water. Cool. Blend all ingredients except ginger ale and refrigerate until well chilled.
2. Add chilled ginger ale shortly before serving.

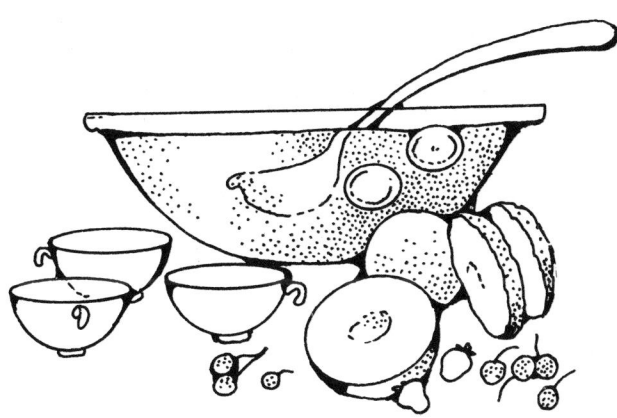

Raspberry Mint Crush
50 Servings (5 oz/140 g)

Metric		Ingredients	U.S.	
Weight	Volume		Weight	Volume
1.47 kg	1.54 l	Sugar	3 lb, 4 oz	6 ½ cups
1.59 kg	1.66 l	Water, boiling	3 lb, 8 oz	1 ¾ qt
567 g	947 ml	Raspberries, fresh	1 lb, 4 oz	1 qt
7 g		Mint Leaves and Stems	¼ oz	
1.36 kg	1.42 l	Lime Juice	3 lb	1 ½ qt
1.36 kg	1.42 l	Water, cold	3 lb	1 ½ qt
1.60 kg	1.66 l	Ginger Ale, chilled	3 lb, 8 oz	1 ¾ qt
	50 sprigs	Mint Leaves		50 sprigs

Procedure

1. Dissolve sugar in boiling water. Cool.
2. Crush raspberries with mint leaves and stems.
3. Combine with lime juice, sugar solution, and cold water.
4. Let stand in refrigerator for at least 2 hours. Strain.

Add chilled ginger ale and serve with finely chopped ice and sprig of mint in glass.

Note: Sparkling water may be used in place of one quart of cold water.

Ice Ring for Fruit Punch

Fill a large ring mold one third full of water and freeze. Select attractive fruit and mint leaves and arrange them on the ice. Add just enough water to cover and freeze decoration into position. Fill ring mold with water and freeze again. The ring mold selected should be large enough to permit the serving ladle to pass through the center easily during service.

Items from which decoration may be selected include:

Cherries, fresh or maraschino

Berries, such as blueberries, raspberries, strawberries

Kumquat slices and leaves

Slices of small lemons or limes

Mint sprigs

Quarter-slices of orange, rind on

Mandarin oranges segments

MILK AND SHERBET DRINKS

Apricot-Orange Float
50 Servings (6 oz/170 g)

Metric		Ingredients	U.S.	
Weight	Volume		Weight	Volume
2.75 kg	2.85 l	Apricot Nectar	6 lb	3 qt
454 g	474 ml	Lemon Juice	1 lb	2 cups
2.05 kg	2.15 l	Milk	4 lb, 8 oz	2 ¼ qt
681 g	474 ml	Honey	1 lb, 8 oz	2 cups
2.72 kg	3.79 l	Orange Sherbet	6 lb	1 gal

Procedure

1. Combine juices, milk, honey, and half the sherbet. Blend at high speed until smooth (about 1 min).

2. Pour into chilled glasses. Add No. 30 scoop sherbet to each serving.

Sherbet Punch
50 Servings (5 oz/140 g)

Metric		Ingredients	U.S.	
Weight	Volume		Weight	Volume
454 g	474 ml	Sugar	1 lb	2 cups
907 g	947 ml	Water, boiling	2 lb	1 qt
227 g	237 ml	Lemon Juice	8 oz	1 cup
1.36 kg	1.42 l	Pineapple Juice	3 lb	1 ½ qt
2.27 kg	2.37 l	Ginger ale, chilled	5 lb	2 ½ qt
1.36 kg	1.89 l	Sherbet	3 lb	2 qt

Procedure

1. Dissolve sugar in boiling water. Cool. Blend with juices and chill.
2. Add chilled ginger ale and sherbet just before serving.

Note: If sherbet is served in the individual portions, it is advisable to shape the balls with a No. 70 scoop and freeze them ready for service. A colorful sherbet, such as cranberry, raspberry, orange, or lime may be used.

Eggnog
50 Servings (5 ½ oz/160 g)

Metric		Ingredients	U.S.	
Weight	Volume		Weight	Volume
340 g	316 ml	Egg Yolks (16 lge)	12 oz	1 ⅓ cups
567 g	592 ml	Sugar	1 lb, 4 oz	2 ½ cups
	10 ml	Salt		2 tsp
5.44 kg	5.68 l	Milk	12 lb	1 ½ gal
567 g	592 ml	Egg Whites (16 lge)	1 lb, 4 oz	2 ½ cups
340 g	355 ml	Sugar	12 oz	1 ½ cups
28 g	30 ml	Vanilla	1 oz	2 tbsp
454 g	474 ml	Brandy (optional)	1 lb	2 cups
227 g	237 ml	Rum (or flavoring to taste)	8 oz	1 cup
454 g	947 ml	Whipped Cream	1 lb	1 qt
15 g	30 ml	Nutmeg	½ oz	2 tbsp

Procedure

1. Blend egg yolks with sugar and salt. Beat in milk and cook into a soft custard over medium heat, stirring constantly. When mixture will coat spoon, remove from heat. Cool.

2. Beat egg whites, gradually adding sugar after egg whites become frothy. Continue beating until whites form soft peaks.

3. Fold custard into whites and stir in flavoring until well-blended. Chill for several hours or overnight.

4. Serve garnished with whipped cream and sprinkle with nutmeg.

Place quantity of flavoring and syrup indicated in glass, add milk sufficient for an 8 oz/227 g serving and blend well. A simple syrup may be made by boiling 1 lb/454 g sugar, 1 lb/454 g water, and 1 tbsp/15 ml corn syrup (to retard crystallization) until the sugar is dissolved.

Banana   2 oz/57 g mashed banana and 1 tbsp/15 ml simple syrup. (For 50 servings use 6 lb/2.72 kg bananas, 3¼ lb/1.47 kg simple syrup, and 3 gal/11.36 l milk.)

Caramel   1½ tbsp/22½ ml fountain syrup or syrup made as follows: Melt 3 lb/1.36 kg brown sugar in heavy pan over low heat, stirring constantly. Remove from heat and gradually add 1½ qt/1.42 l hot water. Heat and stir until sugar is fully dissolved. Cool. Add 1 tsp/5 ml salt and 2 tbsp/30 ml vanilla.

Chocolate   2 tbsp/30 ml fountain syrup or cocoa mixture (see recipe, Hot Beverages).

Coffee   2 tsp/10 ml instant coffee and 2 tbsp/30 ml simple syrup.

Maple   2 tbsp/30 ml maple syrup.

Orange   3 oz/85 g orange juice and 1 tbsp/15 ml simple syrup. (For 50, use 4¾ qt/4.5 l orange juice and 2 gal/757 l milk.)

Raspberry or Strawberry   2 tsp/10 ml berry topping or 1 tbsp/15 ml crushed berries, and 1 tbsp/15 ml simple syrup.

Fruit Cocktails

Melon Ball and Raspberry Cocktail
50 Servings (3½ oz/95 g)

Metric		Ingredients	U.S.	
Weight	Volume		Weight	Volume
2.27 kg	3.80 l	Melon Balls	5 lb	1 gal
1.36 kg	2.13 l	Raspberries, fresh	3 lb	2¼ qt
340 g	711 ml	Pineapple Juice	12 oz	3 cups
14 g	15 ml	Lemon Juice	½ oz	1 tbsp
800 g	829 ml	Ginger ale, chilled	1 lb, 12 oz	3½ cups

Procedure

1. Make balls of canteloupe, casaba, and honeydew with ball cutter. Chill.
2. Heap melon and raspberries in cocktail glasses.
3. Blend fruit juices and chilled ginger ale. Pour over fruit.

Broiled Grapefruit
50 Servings (½ Grapefruit)

Metric		Ingredients	U.S.	
Weight	Volume		Weight	Volume
	25 fruit	Grapefruit, size 80		25 fruit
151 g	158 ml	Butter	5⅓ oz	⅔ cup
227 g	237 ml	Sugar	8 oz	1 cup
227 g	50 items	Cherries or Butter Mints	8 oz	50 items

Procedure

1. Cut fruit in half. Cut segments from membrane. With scissors clip out center and membrane, leaving segments in place.
2. Sprinkle each half with teaspoonful sugar and ½ tsp butter.
3. Broil for about 15 minutes or until fruit is well-heated and edge of skin is lightly browned.
4. Garnish center with cherry or mint. Serve immediately.

Note: A tablespoonful of Sherry, Orange Curaçao, or Framboise may be added to each portion just before serving.

Grapefruit-Tarragon Cocktail
50 Servings (5 oz/142 g)

Metric			U.S.	
Weight	Volume	Ingredients	Weight	Volume
907 g	1.18 ml	Avocado, peeled, diced	2 lb	1 ¼ qt
57 g	59 ml	Lemon Juice	2 oz	¼ cup
3.63 kg	4.74 l	Grapefruit Sections	8 lb	5 qt
793 g	1.42 l	Cucumbers, peeled, diced	1 lb, 12 oz	1 ½ qt
681 g	1.07 l	Pineapple, fresh, diced	1 lb, 8 oz	4 ½ cups
681 g	1.07 l	Tarragon Jelly Cubes	1 lb, 8 oz	4 ½ cups
1.14 kg	1.18 l	Pineapple and Green Pepper Cocktail Sauce (see SAUCES)	2 lb, 8 oz	5 cups

Procedure

1. Marinate avocado in lemon juice to prevent browning.
2. Thoroughly chill ingredients. Arrange fruit and cucumbers in cocktail glasses. Top with tarragon jelly cubes and cocktail sauce. Garnish with parsley or watercress.

Tarragon Jelly Cubes
3 cups/711 ml

Metric			U.S.	
Weight	Volume	Ingredients	Weight	Volume
22 g	45 ml	Granulated Gelatin	¾ oz	3 tbsp
170 g	178 ml	Water, cold	6 oz	¾ cup
75 g	90 ml	Tarragon Vinegar	2 ⅔ oz	6 tbsp
	11 ¼ ml	Salt		2 ¼ tsp
35 g	50 ml	Sugar	1 ½ oz	3 ⅓ tbsp
397 g	415 ml	Water, boiling	14 oz	1 ¾ cups

Procedure

1. Dissolve gelatin in cold water.
2. Add vinegar, salt, and sugar.
3. Pour boiling water over mixture. Stir until well-dissolved.
4. Pour gelatin into shallow pan (11 ½ × 7 × 2 in), so as not to exceed depth of of ½ inch. Chill.
5. When set, cut into ½ inch squares. Serve 6 cubes per cocktail.

Avocado and Celery Rings
50 Servings (4 oz/114 g)

Metric		Ingredients	U.S.	
Weight	Volume		Weight	Volume
3.63 kg	3.78 l	Avocado, diced	8 lb	4 qt
114 g	118 ml	Lemon Juice	4 oz	½ cup
907 g	1.89 l	Celery Rings	2 lb	2 qt
227 g	237 ml	Cream Cheese	8 oz	1 cup
170 g	178 ml	Chili Sauce	6 oz	¾ cup
170 g	178 ml	Catsup	6 oz	¾ cup
340 g	355 ml	Mayonnaise	12 oz	1 ½ cups
	5 ml	Salt		1 tsp

Procedure

1. Marinate avocado in lemon juice. Arrange avocado and celery rings in cocktail glasses.
2. Blend cream cheese, chili sauce, catsup, mayonnaise, and salt. Spoon mixture over avocado and celery rings.
3. Chill and serve with lemon or parsley garnish.

Canteloupe and Pineapple
50 Servings (3 ½ oz/100 g)

Metric		Ingredients	U.S.	
Weight	Volume		Weight	Volume
2.27 kg	3.79 l	Canteloupe Balls	5 lb	4 qt
1.82 kg	1.89 l	Pineapple Tidbits	4 lb	2 qt
907 g	947 ml	Pineapple Juice	2 lb	1 qt
28 g	30 ml	Lemon Juice	1 oz	2 tbsp
	1 ¼ ml	Mint Flavoring		¼ tsp
	2 drops	Green Coloring		2 drops
	50 sprigs	Mint		50 sprigs

Procedure

1. Combine melon and pineapple. Arrange in cocktail glasses.
2. Blend juices, mint flavoring, and green coloring. Pour over fruit.
3. Chill well and garnish with mint sprigs before serving.

Sherry Fruit Cup
50 Servings (5 oz/142 g)

| Metric | | Ingredients | U.S. | |
Weight	Volume		Weight	Volume
1.82 kg	1.89 l	Peaches, drained, diced	4 lb	2 qt
1.15 kg	1.20 l	Pineapple, drained, diced	2 lb, 8 oz	5 cups
681 g	711 ml	Apricots, drained, quartered	1 lb, 8 oz	3 cups
1.36 kg	1.42 l	Pears, drained, diced	3 lb	1 ½ qt
454 g	711 ml	Seedless Grapes	1 lb	3 cups
1.15 kg	1.20 l	Apricot Juice	2 lb, 8 oz	5 cups
340 g	355 ml	Sherry	12 oz	1 ½ cups
227 g	50	Maraschino Cherries	8 oz	50

Procedure

1. Combine all fruit except cherries. Add apricot juice and chill thoroughly.

2. Shortly before serving, add sherry. Arrange fruit in glasses and garnish with maraschino cherry.

Orange Fruit Cup
50 Servings (5 oz/142 g)

| Metric | | Ingredients | U.S. | |
Weight	Volume		Weight	Volume
1.60 kg	2.15 l	Oranges, drained, diced	3 lb, 8 oz	2 ¼ qt
1.36 kg	1.42 l	Pineapple, drained, diced	3 lb	1 ½ qt
1.36 kg	1.42 l	Seedless Grapes	3 lb	1 ½ qt
397 g	474 ml	Pears, drained, diced	14 oz	2 cups
907 g	1.42 l	Bananas, diced	2 lb	1 ½ qt
681 g	1.07 l	Strawberries, quartered	1 lb, 8 oz	4 ½ cups
681 g	711 ml	Orange Juice	1 lb, 8 oz	3 cups
114 g	118 ml	Lemon Juice	4 oz	½ cup
227 g	237 ml	Pineapple Juice	8 oz	1 cup
227 g	50	Maraschino Cherries	8 oz	50

Procedure

1. Combine all fruit except cherries. Add combined fruit juices and chill well.

2. Arrange in glasses and garnish with a maraschino cherry.

Seafood Cocktails

Avocado and Crab Cocktail
30 Servings (5 oz/142 g)

Metric		Ingredients	U.S.	
Weight	**Volume**		**Weight**	**Volume**
1.80 kg	2.85 l	Avocado, diced	4 lb	3 qt
60 g	60 ml	Lemon Juice	2 oz	¼ cup
1.36 kg	2.85 l	Celery Rings	3 lb	3 qt
1.36 kg	1.42 l	Cream Cheese	3 lb	1 ½ qt
340 g	355 ml	Mayonnaise	12 oz	1 ½ cups
340 g	355 ml	Chili Sauce	12 oz	1 ½ cups
60 g	60 ml	Lemon Juice	2 oz	¼ cup
	2 drops	Hot Pepper Sauce		2 drops
1.36 kg	2.37 l	Crabmeat or Shrimp	3 lb	2 ½ qt
397 g	50 slices	Lemon Slices	14 oz	50 slices
57 g	50 sprigs	Parsley	2 oz	50 sprigs

Procedure

1. Marinate avocado in lemon juice. Arrange with celery rings in cocktail glasses.
2. Blend cream cheese, mayonnaise, chili sauce, lemon juice, and hot pepper sauce.
3. Remove shell or hard particles from crabmeat. Set aside legs or attractive pieces for garnish. Fold remainder into sauce.
4. Place spoonful of crab mixture on top of celery and avocado. Garnish with crab, lemon slice, and parsley.

Salmon and Cucumber Cocktail
50 Servings (3 ½ oz/100 g)

Metric		Ingredients	U.S.	
Weight	**Volume**		**Weight**	**Volume**
2.72 kg	4.26 l	Salmon, steamed, flaked	6 lb	4 ½ qt
1.36 kg	2.37 l	Cucumbers, peeled, diced	3 lb	2 ½ qt
454 g	947 ml	Celery, minced	1 lb	1 qt
75 g	237 ml	Chives, chopped	2 ½ oz	1 cup
227 g	237 ml	Sour Cream, thick	8 oz	1 cup
28 g	30 ml	Lemon Juice	1 oz	2 tbsp
14 g	15 ml	Tarragon Vinegar	½ oz	1 tbsp
227 g	237 ml	Mayonnaise	8 oz	1 cup

Procedure

1. Remove bones from salmon carefully to avoid breaking fish.
2. Set aside 50 attractive pieces for garnish. Arrange remaining flaked salmon with cucumber in cocktail glasses. Chill.
3. Blend celery, chives, sour cream, lemon juice, vinegar, and mayonnaise. Chill.
4. Spoon sauce over cocktails and garnish with salmon flakes and parsley sprigs.

Crab Cocktail
50 Servings (3 ½ oz/100 g)

Metric		Ingredients	U.S.	
Weight	Volume		Weight	Volume
3.63 kg	5.70 l	Crabmeat	8 lb	6 qt
907 g	1.90 l	Celery, chopped	2 lb	2 qt
227 g	237 ml	Catsup	8 oz	1 cup
227 g	237 ml	Mayonnaise	8 oz	1 cup
114 g	118 ml	Lemon Juice	4 oz	½ cup
	2 ½ ml	Salt		½ tsp
	50 slices	Lemon Slices		50 slices

Procedure

1. Select 50 attractive pieces of crabmeat and set aside. (There are approximately 18 legs in 1 lb crabmeat.)
2. Flake remaining crabmeat, careful to remove shell particles.
3. Blend celery, catsup, mayonnaise, lemon juice, and salt. Mix with crabmeat. Fork lightly into glasses. Garnish with attractive piece of crabmeat and lemon slice.

Note: If catsup used is quite tart, reduce amount of lemon juice.

Halibut and Shrimp Cocktail
50 Servings (4 oz/114 g)

Metric		Ingredients	U.S.	
Weight	Volume		Weight	Volume
2.72 kg	4.26 l	Halibut, cooked, flaked	6 lb	4 ½ qt
60 g	60 ml	Lemon Juice	2 oz	¼ cup
	2 ½ ml	Salt		½ tsp
907 g	1.89 l	Celery Rings	2 lb	2 qt
454 g	474 ml	Sweet Pickles, minced	1 lb	2 cups
227 g	237 ml	Chili Sauce	8 oz	1 cup
454 g	474 ml	Mayonnaise	1 lb	2 cups
907 g	1.54 l	Shrimp, small Alaska	2 lb	6 ½ cups

Procedure

1. Remove halibut bones. Mix halibut with lemon juice and salt. Arrange flakes in glasses alternately with celery rings.
2. Blend pickles, chili sauce, and mayonnaise. Ladle over halibut and celery. Garnish with small shrimp and parsley.

Clam and Tomato Juice
50 Servings (5 oz/142 g)

Metric		Ingredients	U.S.	
Weight	Volume		Weight	Volume
3.63 kg	3.79 l	Clam Broth	8 lb	1 gal
3.18 kg	3.31 l	Tomato Juice	7 lb	3 ½ qt
454 g	474 ml	Lemon Juice	1 lb	2 cups
	5 ml	Worcestershire Sauce		1 tsp
14 g	15 ml	Salt	½ oz	1 tbsp
397 g	50 slices	Lemon Slices, thin	14 oz	50 slices

Procedure

1. Blend ingredients thoroughly. Serve hot or chilled.   2. Garnish with very thin slice of lemon floated on top.

Oyster Cocktail
50 Servings (3 ½ oz/100 g)

Metric		Ingredients	U.S.	
Weight	Volume		Weight	Volume
4.77 kg	6.63 l	Oysters	10 lb, 8 oz	1 ¾ gal
1.02 kg	1.07 l	Catsup	2 lb, 4 oz	4 ½ cups
170 g	178 ml	Lemon Juice	6 oz	¾ cup
85 g	90 ml	Worcestershire Sauce	3 oz	6 tbsp
	5 ml	Salt		1 tsp
	2 ½ ml	Cayenne Pepper		½ tsp
85 g	178 ml	Horseradish, grated	3 oz	½ cup

Procedure

1. Set aside 50 oysters for garnish.
2. Combine remaining ingredients. Mix carefully with remaining oysters. Chill.

3. Arrange in cocktail glasses with an oyster on top.

Shrimp Cocktail
50 Servings (3 ¼ oz/92 g)

Metric		Ingredients	U.S.	
Weight	Volume		Weight	Volume
2.27 kg	3.79 l	Shrimp	5 lb	1 gal
1.59 kg	3.31 l	Celery, diced	3 lb, 8 oz	3 ½ qt
227 g	237 ml	Cream Cheese	8 oz	1 cup
454 g	474 ml	Catsup	1 lb	2 cups
227 g	237 ml	Lemon Juice	8 oz	1 cup
10 g	10 ml	Hot Pepper Sauce		2 tsp
21 g	22 ml	Salt	¾ oz	1 ½ tbsp
	50 sprigs	Parsley		50 sprigs

1. Reserve 50 of the largest shrimp for garnish.
2. Mix remaining shrimp and celery and arrange in glasses. Chill.
3. Combine cream cheese, catsup, lemon juice, hot pepper sauce, and salt. Chill.

4. Spoon sauce over cocktails and garnish each with one of the reserved shrimp and a sprig of parsley.

Hors D'Oeuvres

Tasty tidbits of food that stimulate the appetite are used for hors d'oeuvres, either hot or cold. The items may be simple or elaborate in preparation, as well as in serving arrangement. Nippy cheeses, piquant salads, pickles, cold meats, crisp and refreshing vegetables, and similar foods form a large selection from which to choose these appetizers. Stimulation of the appetite calls for creating an appearance of delectable goodness, adequate supply, and glistening freshness. It is best to avoid skimpy and heterogeneous small items scattered over a large tray. The foods that dry quickly, discolor, or appear to be "leftover" detract from an appealing effect.

Hors d'oeuvres may be served with liquid refreshments before a meal, in an individual assortment as the first course of a meal, or as an accompaniment to the salad course. Assorted hors d'oeuvres, canapés, and small salads may be used as a first course of a meal with omission of the regular salad course. When selecting items for such an appetizer plate, choose those that provide variety in color, form, texture, flavor, and size on the plate. Listed below are foods that may be used as hors d'oeuvres.

HORS D'OEUVRES SUGGESTIONS

Cheese

1. Cubes of brick, Cheddar, Edam, Swiss, Blue, and smoked cheeses.
2. Tiny Cheddar apples made of softened cheese with a blush of paprika and a whole clove stem and blossom end.
3. Cherry tomato, hollowed, filled with spicy cheese with watercress stem and leaf.
4. Pecan, walnut, or candied grapefruit peel sandwiched together with Sherry-flavored Cheddar or cream cheese.
5. Celery hearts filled with pimiento cheese, softened Cheddar, or mixture of Blue and cream cheese.
6. Fresh apple wedge with Cheddar or apricot with cream cheese.

Eggs, Hard-Cooked

1. Halves of small or peewee size eggs garnished with mayonnaise and anchovy fillet, caviar, and onion, or stuffed-olive slice.
2. Quartered with dressing garnish and pimiento.
3. Stuffed eggs—small size cut across and tips trimmed so as to set level, garnished with anchovy, caper, pimiento, or paprika.

Fish

1. Anchovies skewered with pearl onion, cucumber, or stuffed olive.
2. Crab legs—half frosted with cocktail sauce.
3. Smoked clams or oysters.
4. Pickled herring.
5. Salmon, smoked or kippered.
6. Shrimp, plain or marinated in garlic French dressing.
7. Sardines.

Fruit

1. Spiced apricots, crabapples, apple rings, white grapes, prunes, melon rind.
2. Filled apples—Core firm, flavorful apples, making hole 1 ¼ inch in diameter. Fill center with softened Cheddar. Chill. Cut into sections, let apple fall open, forming a rosette.
3. Dates filled with nuts and cream cheese.
4. Stuffed prunes. Remove pit, stuff with apple or plum butter and top with walnut, or fill with nuts and cream cheese.
5. Fresh strawberries, husk on and tip dipped into powdered sugar.
6. Wedges or balls of fresh melon, watermelon, canteloupe, honeydew.

Meat

1. Ham Rolls. Slice cooked ham very thin, spread with chive cheese and roll tightly. Chill. Cut into 2-inch lengths. Diameter of rolls should be about ¾ inch.
2. Chipped Beef Rolls. Fill thin slices with Cheddar and minced green pepper, or Blue and cream cheese. Roll as ham rolls.
3. Dices of ham, summer sausage, smoked turkey or chicken. Skewer on picks with other foods such as pickled pearl onion, celery, olive, or green pepper.
4. Frankfurter or pepperoni rings skewered with celery or pickle.
5. Small slices of salami or Thuringer cut in half and rolled in cornucopia and filled with Blue and cream cheese mixture.
6. Sautéed chicken liver wrapped with crisp bacon.
7. Broiled bacon wrapped around olive, pickled onion, or tomato.
8. Surprise Balls. Soften smoked liver sausage, form ball around ½ stuffed olive and roll in finely chopped parsley.
9. Stack alternate slices ⅛ inch thick, 3 salami and 2 club-Swiss cheese. Cut stack to form cubes and skewer with pick.

Pickles

1. Olives—ripe, green, and stuffed.
2. Cucumber pickles—sweet, mustard, mixed, and dill.
3. Beets—whole, sliced, and quartered.
4. Pickled Italian sweet peppers.
5. Pickled pearl onions.
6. Pickled mushrooms.
7. Spiced nuts.
8. Pickled fruits—peach, apricot, crabapple, prune, grape.
9. Stuffed dills. Hollow large straight pickles lengthwise with apple corer. Fill with softened Cheddar and pimiento. Slice across pickles into ⅜-inch-thick slices.

Vegetables

1. Sticks—carrot, green pepper, turnip, celery, cucumber, zucchini.
2. Celery—curls, hearts, and stuffed.
3. Tomato—wedges or small whole.
4. Marinated—cauliflower or zucchini raw or lightly cooked, marinated in French dressing.
5. Peppers—sweet or hot, red or green, whole, sticks, or rings.
6. Onion—rings or sweet onion or fresh tender young onions.
7. Radishes—whole with one tiny leaf, roses, or accordion cut.

CHAPTER 3 _____ *Soups*

Production of appetizing soups calls for the use of well-chosen materials used in sufficient quantity to yield rich flavor and substance. A miserly use of materials or improper preparation of stock will result in an insipid, watery product that has little nourishment or enjoyment value. The choice of soup for a menu should be done with thought for other dishes to be served in the meal, in terms of richness, flavor, color, texture, and consistency. Care is needed to avoid repeating the chief flavoring food in subsequent courses.

Soup Stock

Stock imparts rich, appetizing flavor to soups and is the single most important ingredient in most soups. It merits careful attention for this reason. Brown stock, made with partially browned beef bones and meat, and white stock, made with chicken and/or veal, are the varieties used in largest quantity. Ham, lamb, and fish stocks may be required in specific recipes.

The cooking of the meat and bones for stock should begin in cold water. As the liquid comes slowly to a simmer, a foamy material, commonly referred to as scum, will rise to the surface. The scum should be skimmed off as it accumulates. If this is not removed, or if the broth boils, the scum will break down and scatter grey wisps through the stock. Lukewarm water is better than cold or boiling water for dissolving flavorful extractives. If the water is allowed to boil, the bones and vegetables will release substances that will make the broth cloudy. The meat and bones should be allowed to simmer slowly—beef for 6 to 8 hours, chicken or veal for 4 to 5 hours, and fish for 1 ½ hours.

Strain the broth, cooling it as rapidly as possible, and refrigerate overnight. When cooling, the lid of the soup container should be left ajar. If covered, the steam will not escape, and the broth will remain at lukewarm temperature. It is important to remember that holding meats or broth for very long at lukewarm temperature is hazardous to sanitation. This liquid, before clarification, is known as broth, and after clarification, is called stock.

The fat that rises to the top of the broth helps to protect it from contamination. It is advisable to let it remain until stock is clarified for use. When removing the fat, take care to avoid roiling the sediment that has settled to the bottom of the kettle. After removing the fat, decant the gelatinous stock from the top. This can be done best when the gelatin has a syrupy consistency. Further clarification can be accomplished by stirring ground meat and egg white into the cool broth, and slowly heating it to boiling. The coagulated mixture will rise to the top and can be skimmed off or removed by straining the stock through cheesecloth.

Stock is highly perishable and should be kept carefully refrigerated until used. If it is necessary to keep stock for later use, or if the flavor is not as strong as desired, reduce it in volume. This can be done by boiling it down to half measure (demiglace) or one fourth (glace) to evaporate some of its water content and to concentrate its strength. In the reduced state, it will be thick, rubbery, and strong-flavored. It should be frozen for holding. It can be brought back to its former state by dissolving in boiling water.

Commercial soup bases are widely used due to lower cost and greater convenience, but rarely compare in quality with a good stock, freshly made. The soup base should be chosen carefully to insure desired quality. Some are available that enhance rich flavor and others that spoil the flavor of any dish in which they are used.

The amount of meat substance contained in commercial soup base varies considerably. It is wise to obtain samples of bases available and test them in an identical manner, and at the same time to make comparisons of quality. The meat essence is the most important and the most expensive element. (Satisfactory strength of sampling can be obtained by dissolving ½ oz/15 g of base in 2 cups/474 ml boiling water.) Do not be misled by the flavor of vegetable salts. Be alert to the degree of rich, sweet, meaty flavor, as well as to the strength and agreeableness of taste and aroma.

White Stock (Consommé)
3 gal/11.36 l

| Metric | | | U.S. | |
Weight	Volume	Ingredients	Weight	Volume
9.98 kg		Chicken and/or Veal	22 lb	
16.34 kg	17.04 l	Water	36 lb	4½ gal
227 g	474 ml	Celery, chopped	8 oz	2 cups
454 g	711 ml	Onions, chopped	1 lb	3 cups
297 g	474 ml	Carrots, chopped	10½ oz	2 cups
	7½ ml	Peppercorns, crushed		1½ tsp
114 g	118 ml	Salt	4 oz	½ cup
	2 leaves	Bay Leaves		2 leaves
227 g	237 ml	Egg Whites, beaten (8 lge)	8 oz	1 cup
	8 shells	Egg Shells, crushed		8 shells
28 g	8 sprigs	Parsley	1 oz	8 sprigs
7 g	15 ml	Thyme Leaves		1 tbsp
	10 ml	Marjoram		2 tsp

Procedure

1. Cut up chicken or veal knuckles. Add cold water to cover and slowly heat to simmering. Simmer for 3 to 4 hours. Remove scum as it forms. Add vegetables and seasonings. Cook until tender.
2. Strain. Cool kettle of broth in cold, running water. Refrigerate overnight.
3. Remove fat from broth. Add egg whites and shells. Heat broth to boiling. Simmer 15 minutes. Let stand until sediment settles. Strain through cheesecloth or fine strainer.

Brown Stock (Bouillon)
3 gal/11.36 l

Metric		Ingredients	U.S.	
Weight	Volume		Weight	Volume
13.60 kg		Beef Neck and Shanks	30 lb	
18.14 kg	18.92 l	Water, cold	40 lb	5 gal
454 g	947 ml	Celery, diced	1 lb	1 qt
907 g	1.89 l	Onions, quartered	2 lb	1 ½ qt
340 g	711 ml	Carrots, diced	12 oz	3 cups
156 g	237 ml	Turnips, diced	5 ½ oz	1 cup
	7 ½ ml	Peppercorns, crushed		1 ½ tsp
	3 leaves	Bay Leaves		3 leaves
	5 ml	Cloves, whole		1 tsp
28 g	8 sprigs	Parsley	1 oz	8 sprigs
	15 ml	Basil Leaves		1 tbsp
	15 ml	Thyme Leaves		1 tbsp
	10 ml	Marjoram Leaves		2 tsp
114 g	118 ml	Salt	4 oz	½ cup

Procedure

1. Saw bones to expose marrow, and cut up meat.
2. Brown meat and bones to desired degree. (The amount of browning will determine the color and flavor of the stock.)
3. Place meat and bones in the stock kettle and cover with cold water. Let stand about 30 minutes. Bring slowly to simmering temperature, and let simmer for 4 to 6 hours.
4. Remove scum by skimming as it forms on top of broth. Add vegetables and seasonings. Cook until vegetables are tender.
5. Strain. Cool by setting kettle in cold, running water in sink. Refrigerate overnight. Remove fat congealed on top. Decant stock, being careful not to roil sediment.

Stock Made with Instant Base
1 gal/3.79 l

Metric		Ingredients	U.S.	
Weight	Volume		Weight	Volume
3.63 kg	3.79 l	Water, boiling	8 lb	1 gal
114 g	118 ml	Soup Base	4 oz	½ cup

Procedure

1. Dissolve soup base by stirring boiling water into it gradually until it is completely dissolved.
2. Use in recipes in same manner as other stocks. (Bases vary in amount of salt contained and herbs. Note whether adjustment needs to be made in recipes to allow for the seasoning contained in the soup base.)

Stock Soups

English Garden Soup
3 gal/11.36 l

Metric		Ingredients	U.S.	
Weight	Volume		Weight	Volume
227 g	237 ml	Margarine, melted	8 oz	1 cup
681 g	829 ml	Onions, finely chopped	1 lb, 8 oz	3 ½ cups
681 g	947 ml	Leeks, finely chopped	1 lb, 8 oz	1 qt
9.07 kg	9.46 l	Beef Stock	20 lb	2 ½ gal
227 g	474 ml	Celery, finely chopped	8 oz	2 cups
1.36 kg	2.13 l	Carrots, finely chopped	3 lb	2 ½ qt
681 g	1.07 l	White Turnips, chopped	1 lb, 8 oz	4 ½ cups
227 g	237 ml	Barley	8 oz	1 cup
	7 ½ ml	Pepper		1 ½ tsp
42 g	45 ml	Salt	1 ½ oz	3 tbsp
14 g	15 ml	Worcestershire Sauce	½ oz	1 tbsp

Procedure

1. Sauté onions and leeks in melted margarine.
2. Combine all ingredients, except Worcestershire sauce, and simmer until vegetables are tender.
3. Add Worcestershire sauce just before serving.

Borsch
3 gal/11.36 l

Metric		Ingredients	U.S.	
Weight	Volume		Weight	Volume
454 g	711 ml	Onions, chopped	1 lb	3 cups
283 g	296 ml	Margarine	10 oz	1 ¼ cups
454 g	947 ml	Cabbage, chopped	1 lb	1 qt
454 g	711 ml	Carrots, chopped	1 lb	3 cups
454 g	947 ml	Celery, chopped	1 lb	1 qt
681 g	789 ml	Potatoes, diced	1 lb, 8 oz	3 ⅓ cups
9.07 kg	9.46 l	Beef Stock	20 lb	2 ½ gal
1.36 kg	1.42 l	Tomatoes, canned	3 lb	1 ½ qt
1.36 kg	1.66 l	Beets, canned, diced	3 lb	1 ¾ qt
1.13 kg	1.18 l	Beet Juice	2 lb, 8 oz	1 ¼ qt
76 g	79 ml	Lemon Juice	2 ⅔ oz	⅓ cup
28 g	30 ml	Salt	1 oz	2 tbsp
	2 ½ ml	Pepper		½ tsp
850 g	889 ml	Sour Cream	1 lb, 14 oz	3 ¾ cups

Procedure

1. Sauté onions in margarine until lightly browned. Add with cabbage, carrots, celery, and potatoes to beef stock. Simmer until vegetables are tender.
2. Sieve tomatoes. Add tomatoes, beets, juices, and seasonings to soup. Continue cooking until thoroughly heated.
3. Serve each portion topped with tablespoon of sour cream.

Chicken Rice Soup
3 gal/11.36 l

Metric		Ingredients	U.S.	
Weight	Volume		Weight	Volume
10.89 kg	11.36 l	Chicken Stock	24 lb	3 gal
604 g	947 ml	Onions, chopped	1 lb, 5 ⅓ oz	1 qt
454 g	947 ml	Celery, diced	1 lb	1 qt
454 g	474 ml	Rice, uncooked	1 lb	2 cups
340 g	415 ml	Chicken Fat, melted	12 oz	1 ¾ cups
227 g	474 ml	Flour, all-purpose	8 oz	2 cups
14 g	15 ml	Salt	½ oz	1 tbsp
567 g	889 ml	Chicken Meat, diced, cooked	1 lb, 4 oz	3 ¾ cups

Procedure

1. Cook onions, celery, and rice in stock until tender.
2. Add flour and seasonings to melted fat and blend to make a roux. Stir the roux into the soup and cook until slightly thickened.
3. Simmer chicken meat in soup for 5 minutes before serving.

Minestrone Soup
3 gal/11.36 l

Metric		Ingredients	U.S.	
Weight	Volume		Weight	Volume
795 g	1.04 l	Beans, dried navy	1 lb, 12 oz	4 ⅜ cups
9.07 kg	9.46 l	Water	20 lb	2 ½ gal
227 g	237 ml	Salad Oil	8 oz	1 cup
907 g	1.42 l	Onions, chopped	2 lb	1 ½ qt
14 g	4 cloves	Garlic, minced	½ oz	4 cloves
454 g	947 ml	Celery, diced	1 lb	1 qt
454 g	711 ml	Carrots, chopped	1 lb	3 cups
1.36 kg	1.42 l	Tomatoes, canned	3 lb	1 ½ qt
298 g	237 ml	Ham Soup Base	10 ½ oz	1 cup
14 g	15 ml	Salt	½ oz	1 tbsp
	2 ½ ml	Pepper		½ tsp
	10 ml	Basil		2 tsp
227 g	474 ml	Macaroni, A.P.	8 oz	2 cups
454 g	592 ml	Potatoes, diced	1 lb	2 ½ cups
454 g	829 ml	Green Beans, canned, drained	1 lb	3 ½ cups

Procedure

1. Wash and sort dry beans. Cook beans in water until tender.
2. Sauté onions, garlic, and celery in oil. Add to beans.
3. Add carrots to soup and cook until tender.
4. Add tomatoes, ham soup base, and seasonings. Simmer.
5. Add macaroni and cook until almost tender.
6. Add potatoes and cook until tender.
7. Add green beans and heat through.

Creole Soup
3 gal/11.36 l

Metric		Ingredients	U.S.	
Weight	Volume		Weight	Volume
170 g	296 ml	Onions, finely chopped	6 oz	1 ¼ cups
170 g	266 ml	Green Pepper, chopped	6 oz	1 ⅛ cups
340 g	355 ml	Butter or Margarine	12 oz	1 ½ cups
283 g	596 ml	Flour, all-purpose	10 oz	2 ½ cups
8.17 kg	8.51 l	Beef Stock	18 lb	2 ¼ gal
3.63 kg	3.79 l	Tomato Puree	8 lb	1 gal
43 g	45 ml	Salt	1 ½ oz	3 tbsp
	10 ml	Pepper		2 tsp
	2 ½ ml	Cayenne Pepper		½ tsp
114 g	237 ml	Macaroni Rings	4 oz	1 cup
1.81 kg	1.89 l	Water, boiling	4 lb	2 qt
28 g	30 ml	Salt	1 oz	2 tbsp
57 g	118 ml	Horseradish, prepared	2 oz	½ cup
14 g	15 ml	Vinegar	½ oz	1 tbsp

Procedure

1. Sauté onions and green pepper in butter or margarine for 5 minutes. Add flour and blend. Add stock, stirring until mixture thickens.
2. Add tomato puree. Simmer for 30 minutes. Add salt, pepper, and cayenne pepper.
3. Drop macaroni in vigorously boiling, salted water. Cook until tender. Rinse.
4. Just before serving, add horseradish, vinegar, and macaroni.

Vegetable Soup
3 gal/11.36 l

Metric		Ingredients	U.S.	
Weight	Volume		Weight	Volume
4.54 kg		Beef Bones (or Beef Base 12 oz/340 g)	10 lb	
10.89 kg	11.36 l	Water	24 lb	3 gal
567 g	869 ml	Carrots, chopped	1 lb, 4 oz	3 ⅔ cups
340 g	711 ml	Celery, chopped	12 oz	3 cups
227 g	355 ml	Onions, chopped	8 oz	1 ½ cups
283 g	592 ml	Cabbage, chopped	10 oz	2 ½ cups
2.04 kg	2.13 l	Tomatoes, fresh, cubed	4 lb, 8 oz	2 ¼ qt
681 g	1.00 l	Potatoes, diced	1 lb, 8 oz	4 ½ cups
57 g	60 ml	Salt	2 oz	4 tbsp
	5 ml	Pepper		1 tsp
14 g	79 ml	Parsley, chopped	½ oz	⅓ cup

Procedure

1. Combine bones and water and simmer 4 hours. Strain.
2. Add remaining ingredients, except parsley, to the broth. Cook until vegetables are tender (about 1 hr).
3. Add parsley just before serving.
4. Yield: 50 servings, 1 cup/237 ml.

Oxtail Soup
3 gal/11.36 l

Metric		Ingredients	U.S.	
Weight	Volume		Weight	Volume
227 g	237 ml	Shortening	8 oz	1 cup
681 g	829 ml	Onions, diced	1 lb, 8 oz	3 ½ cups
114 g	178 ml	Leeks, diced	4 oz	¾ cup
227 g	474 ml	Celery, diced	8 oz	2 cups
3.18 kg	3 tails	Oxtails, cut up (approx.)	7 lb	3 tails
7.26 kg	7.57 l	Beef Stock	16 lb	2 gal
	2 leaves	Bay leaves		2 leaves
	1 ¼ ml	Thyme		¼ tsp
	5 ml	Pepper		1 tsp
57 g	60 ml	Salt	2 oz	4 tbsp
766 g	947 ml	Tomato Puree	1 lb, 11 oz	1 qt
907 g	1.42 l	Carrots, finely diced	2 lb	1 ½ qt
681 g	947 ml	Turnips, finely diced	l lb, 8 oz	1 qt
2.72 kg	2.84 l	Water	6 lb	3 qt
227 g	237 ml	Barley	8 oz	1 cup
57 g	59 ml	Worcestershire Sauce	2 oz	¼ cup
114 g	118 ml	Sherry (optional)	4 oz	½ cup

Procedure

1. Sauté onions, leeks, and celery in shortening. Combine with oxtails, 1 gallon beef stock, seasonings, and tomato puree. Simmer until tender (about 2 hrs).
2. Cook carrots and turnips in water until tender. Add with barley and remainder of beef stock to soup. Cook 30 minutes.
3. Just before serving add Worcestershire sauce and Sherry.

Ruby Consommé
3 gal/11.36 l

Metric		Ingredients	U.S.	
Weight	Volume		Weight	Volume
7.26 kg	7.57 l	Tomato Juice	16 lb	2 gal
3.63 kg	3.79 l	Chicken Stock	8 lb	1 gal
42 g	90 ml	Onions, minced	1 ½ oz	6 tbsp
454 g	947 ml	Celery, chopped	1 lb	1 qt
	2 cloves	Garlic, minced		2 cloves
42 g	45 ml	Sugar	1 ½ oz	3 tbsp
14 g	15 ml	Salt	½ oz	1 tbsp
	2 ½ ml	Cloves, whole		½ tsp
114 g	118 ml	Lemon Juice	4 oz	½ cup
19 g	20 ml	Worcestershire Sauce	⅔ oz	4 tsp

Procedure

1. Simmer tomato juice, stock, onions, celery, garlic, and seasonings for 45 minutes.
2. Add lemon juice and Worcestershire sauce. Stir well and strain. Serve immediately.

Navy Bean Soup
3 gal/11.36 l

Metric		Ingredients	U.S.	
Weight	Volume		Weight	Volume
1.36 kg	1.66 l	Navy Beans	3 lb	7 cups
10.9 kg	11.36 l	Water	24 lb	3 gal
340 g	474 ml	Onions, chopped	12 oz	2 cups
340 g	711 ml	Celery, chopped	12 oz	3 cups
85 g	89 ml	Bacon Fat or Margarine	3 oz	6 tbsp
142 g	118 ml	Ham Soup Base	5 oz	½ cup
21 g	23 ml	Salt	¾ oz	1 ½ tbsp
284 g	592 ml	Flour, all-purpose	10 oz	2 ½ cups
	10 ml	Pepper		2 tsp
283 g	296 ml	Margarine, melted	10 oz	1 ¼ cups
	30 ml	Parsley, chopped		2 tbsp

Procedure

1. Sort and wash navy beans.
2. Cook navy beans in water until beans are about half-cooked.
3. Sauté onions and celery in bacon fat or margarine. Add to the beans and water.
4. Add ham soup base and salt. Simmer until beans are tender.
5. Add flour and pepper to melted margarine to make a roux. Add water to roux to make a runny mixture. Stir into soup and cook until thickened.
6. Sprinkle with chopped parsley and serve.

French Onion Soup
3 gal/11.36 l

Metric		Ingredients	U.S.		
Weight	Volume		Weight		Volume
2.95 kg	6.16 l	Onions, thinly sliced	6 lb,	8 oz	6 ½ qt
198 g	207 ml	Margarine, melted		7 oz	⅞ cup
7.72 kg	8.05 l	Water	17 lb		8 ½ qt
298 g	237 ml	Beef Soup Base		10 ½ oz	1 cup
14 g	15 ml	Garlic Salt		½ oz	1 tbsp
28 g	30 ml	Salt		1 oz	2 tbsp
	2 leaves	Bay Leaves			2 leaves
71 g	148 ml	Flour, all-purpose		2 ½ oz	10 tbsp
	6 ¼ ml	Pepper			1 ¼ tsp
85 g	89 ml	Margarine, melted		3 oz	6 tbsp

Procedure

1. Sauté onions in margarine until lightly browned. Add water, beef base, garlic salt, salt, and bay leaves. Simmer.
2. Add flour and pepper to melted margarine to make a roux. Add warm water to make a runny mixture.
3. Bring soup to boiling. Add roux to soup, stirring vigorously. Cook until raw starch flavor has disappeared.

Note: This soup may be made hearty enough for a main dish by topping with a thick slice of French bread, generously spread with Cheddar cheese. Place on soup and melt for an instant under broiler.

Greek Chicken-Lemon Soup
3 gal/11.36 l

| Metric | | Ingredients | U.S. | |
Weight	Volume		Weight	Volume
10.89 kg	11.36 l	Chicken Broth	24 lb	3 gal
793 g	947 ml	Rice, long-grain	1 lb, 12 oz	1 qt
681 g	711 ml	Lemon Juice	1 lb, 8 oz	3 cups
1.36 kg	1.42 l	Eggs, well-beaten (24 lge)	3 lb	1½ qt

Procedure

1. Simmer rice in chicken broth for 25 minutes.
2. Add lemon juice slowly, stirring constantly.
3. Stir 2 cups of broth into well-beaten eggs, then combine eggs with hot mixture, stirring constantly. Heat just below simmering until eggs are cooked (about 2 minutes).

Note: This soup may be served either hot or chilled.

Potage Printanier
3 gal/11.36 l

| Metric | | Ingredients | U.S. | |
Weight	Volume		Weight	Volume
7.26 kg	7.57 l	Water	16 lb	2 gal
114 g	178 ml	Carrots, julienne	4 oz	¾ cup
227 g	474 ml	Onions, shredded	8 oz	2 cups
340 g	711 ml	Cabbage, shredded	12 oz	3 cups
114 g	237 ml	Turnips, julienne	4 oz	1 cup
114 g	237 ml	Celery, julienne	4 oz	1 cup
567 g	592 ml	Tomatoes, canned, chopped	1 lb, 4 oz	2½ cups
227 g	474 ml	Potatoes, raw, julienne	8 oz	2 cups
227 g	415 ml	Green Beans, cut	8 oz	1¾ cups
298 g	237 ml	Beef Soup Base	10½ oz	1 cup
43 g	45 ml	Salt	1½ oz	3 tbsp
227 g	237 ml	Margarine	8 oz	1 cup
198 g	415 ml	Flour, all-purpose	7 oz	1¾ cups
	7½ ml	Pepper		1½ tsp
1.81 kg	3.79 l	Water	4 lb	2 qt

Procedure

1. Combine carrots, onions, cabbage, turnips, celery, and tomatoes with water in soup kettle. Simmer until vegetables are tender.
2. Add potatoes and cook until they are tender. Add green beans.
3. Add beef base and salt to soup.
4. Melt margarine. Add flour and pepper to margarine to make a roux. Combine with water to make a runny mixture. Add to soup, stirring vigorously. Cook until soup is thickened and raw starch flavor has disappeared.

Lentil Soup
3 gal/11.36 l

Metric		Ingredients	U.S.		
Weight	Volume		Weight		Volume
9.55 kg	9.94 l	Water	21 lb		10½ qt
1.59 kg	1.89 l	Lentils	3 lb,	8 oz	2 qt
114 g	158 ml	Bacon Fat		4 oz	⅔ cup
397 g	592 ml	Onions, finely chopped		14 oz	2½ cups
397 g	829 ml	Celery, finely chopped		14 oz	3½ cups
397 g	592 ml	Carrots, finely chopped		14 oz	2½ cups
198 g	158 ml	Beef Base		7 oz	⅔ cup
14 g	15 ml	Salt		½ oz	1 tbsp
14 g	15 ml	Sugar		½ oz	1 tbsp
85 g	89 ml	Margarine, melted		3 oz	6 tbsp
43 g	89 ml	Flour, all-purpose		1½ oz	6 tbsp
	6⅔ ml	Pepper			1⅓ tsp

Procedure

1. Add water to lentils in soup kettle and cook until tender. Check water level and bring to original amount as needed.
2. Sauté onions and celery in bacon fat.
3. Add vegetables, beef base, salt, and sugar to soup. Cook until carrots are tender.
4. Add flour and pepper to melted margarine to make a roux. Add warm water to make a runny mixture.
5. Add mixture to soup and cook until soup has thickened and raw starch flavor has disappeared.

Bisques, Chowders, Gumbos, and Stews

Fish Chowder, New England
3 gal/11.36 l

Metric		Ingredients	U.S.		
Weight	Volume		Weight		Volume
567 g	711 ml	Salt Pork or Bacon, diced	1 lb,	4 oz	3 cups
454 g	711 ml	Onions, chopped	1 lb		3 cups
1.71 kg	1.89 l	Potatoes, finely diced	3 lb,	12 oz	2 qt
3.63 kg	3.79 l	Water, boiling	8 lb		1 gal
57 g	60 ml	Salt		2 oz	¼ cup
	7½ ml	Pepper, white			1½ tsp
2.72 kg	4.26 l	Cod Fillet, 1-in cubes	6 lb		4½ qt
3.63 kg	3.79 l	Milk, scalded	8 lb		1 gal

Procedure

1. Fry salt pork or bacon. Remove it from fat and sauté onions.
2. Combine meat, onions, potatoes, and boiling water. Cook until potatoes are almost tender (about 20 min).
3. Add seasonings, fish, and milk. Simmer for 10 minutes or until fish and potatoes are entirely cooked.

Note: If fresh cod, red snapper, or other light fish is used, fillet the fish and proceed as above.

Clam Chowder, New England
3 gal/11.36 l

Metric		Ingredients	U.S.	
Weight	Volume		Weight	Volume
454 g	592 ml	Salt Pork or Bacon	1 lb	2 ½ cups
907 g	1.42 l	Onions, chopped	2 lb	1 ½ qt
4.08 kg	4.26 l	Water and Clam Liquor	9 lb	4 ½ qt
1.82 kg	2.84 l	Potatoes, finely chopped	4 lb	3 qt
227 g	237 ml	Butter or Margarine	8 oz	1 cup
114 g	237 ml	Flour, bread	4 oz	1 cup
1.82 kg	1.89 l	Light Cream, scalded	4 lb	2 qt
907 g	947 ml	Milk, scalded	2 lb	1 qt
71 g	75 ml	Salt	2 ½ oz	5 tbsp
	5 ml	Pepper		1 tsp
1.36 kg	3.79 l	Clams, chopped meat	3 lb	2 ¼ qt

Procedure

1. Dice salt pork or bacon and fry until lightly browned. Add onions and sauté slowly until tender, covering pot to retain moisture.
2. Combine liquor from clams and water. Add onions, bacon, and potatoes. Cook until potatoes are tender.
3. Melt butter or margarine, add flour, and blend. Slowly add cream and milk. Stir until thickened and smooth. Season with salt and pepper. Add sauce to soup. Add clams and simmer for 20 minutes or until tender.

Clam Chowder, Manhattan
3 gal/11.36 l

Metric		Ingredients	U.S.	
Weight	Volume		Weight	Volume
454 g	592 ml	Salt Pork or Bacon	1 lb	2 ½ cups
454 g	711 ml	Onions, chopped	1 lb	3 cups
454 g	947 ml	Celery, chopped	1 lb	1 qt
	5 ml	Thyme		1 tsp
1.82 kg	2.84 l	Potatoes, finely chopped	4 lb	3 qt
1.82 kg	1.89 l	Water	4 lb	2 qt
28 g	30 ml	Salt	1 oz	2 tbsp
2.95 kg	3.31 l	Tomatoes, canned, strained	6 lb, 8 oz	3 ½ qt
2.89 kg	3.31 l	Clams, chopped and liquor	6 lb, 6 oz	3 ½ qt
	10 ml	Pepper, white		2 tsp
227 g	237 ml	Margarine or Butter	8 oz	1 cup
28 g	178 ml	Parsley, finely chopped	1 oz	¾ cup

Procedure

1. Dice salt pork or bacon and fry until lightly browned. Add onions and celery and cook until tender. Add thyme.
2. Cook potatoes in salted water for 10 minutes. Add bacon, onions, celery, tomatoes, clams, and pepper and continue simmering for 30 minutes.
3. Add margarine just before serving and simmer for 5 minutes.
4. Stir in parsley and serve.

Salmon Chowder
3 gal/11.36 l

Metric		Ingredients	U.S.		
Weight	Volume		Weight		Volume
454 g	947 ml	Celery, finely chopped	1 lb		1 qt
170 g	355 ml	Carrots, shredded		6 oz	1 ½ cups
170 g	295 ml	Onions, finely chopped		6 oz	1 ¼ cups
907 g	947 ml	Water	2 lb		1 qt
2.27 kg	2.36 l	Salmon, boned, flaked	5 lb		2 ½ qt
3.41 kg	3.56 l	Evaporated Milk	7 lb,	8 oz	3 ¾ qt
3.41 kg	3.56 l	Water	7 lb,	8 oz	3 ¾ qt
	7 ½ ml	Soda			1 ½ tsp
37 g	40 ml	Salt		1 ⅓ oz	2 ⅔ tbsp
	10 ml	Pepper			2 tsp
227 g	237 ml	Shortening		8 oz	1 cup
283 g	592 ml	Flour, bread		10 oz	2 ½ cups
28 g	178 ml	Parsley, chopped		1 oz	¾ cup

Procedure

1. Combine vegetables and water and cook until tender.
2. Stir in milk, water, soda, salt, and pepper. Add salmon.
3. Melt shortening and blend in flour. Add some of the hot mixture to the roux and stir until thick and smooth. Stir into soup. Simmer for 30 minutes, stirring frequently. Add parsley and serve.

Tuna Chowder
3 gal/11.36 l

Metric		Ingredients	U.S.		
Weight	Volume		Weight		Volume
1.36 kg	2.13 l	Potatoes, diced	3 lb		2 ¼ qt
454 g	947 ml	Celery, diced	1 lb		1 qt
907 g	1.42 l	Onions, diced	2 lb		1 ½ qt
1.82 kg	1.89 l	Tomato Juice	4 lb		2 qt
1.82 kg	1.89 l	Water, boiling	4 lb		2 qt
1.47 kg	4 cans	Tuna Fish	3 lb,	4 oz	4 cans (13 oz)
340 g	355 ml	Butter or Margarine		12 oz	1 ½ cups
170 g	355 ml	Flour, bread		6 oz	1 ½ cups
28 g	30 ml	Salt		1 oz	2 tbsp
	5 ml	Pepper			1 tsp
227 g	237 ml	Ham Soup Base		8 oz	1 cup
5.45 kg	5.68 l	Milk	12 lb		6 qt
28 g	178 ml	Parsley, chopped		1 oz	¾ cup

Procedure

1. Combine vegetables and water. Cook until vegetables are tender.
2. Drain tuna, break into large flakes, and combine with vegetables.
3. Melt butter or margarine. Blend in flour, soup base, and seasonings. Gradually stir in milk. Cook until thickened. Combine all ingredients and heat to serving temperature.

Salmon and Potato Chowder

3 gal/11.36 l

Metric		Ingredients	U.S.	
Weight	**Volume**		**Weight**	**Volume**
1.36 kg	1.66 l	Salt Pork or Bacon	3 lb	1 ¾ qt
340 g	533 ml	Onions, chopped	12 oz	2 ¼ cups
3.63 kg	5.68 l	Potatoes, finely diced	8 lb	6 qt
2.04 kg	2.13 l	Water	4 lb, 8 oz	2 ¼ qt
41 g	79 ml	Flour, bread	1 ½ oz	⅓ cup
4.54 kg	4.73 l	Milk, scalded	10 lb	5 qt
1.36 kg	1.42 l	Salmon, boned, flaked	3 lb	1 ½ qt
43 g	45 ml	Salt	1 ½ oz	3 tbsp
	5 ml	Pepper		1 tsp
85 g	90 ml	Butter or Margarine	3 oz	6 tbsp

Procedure

1. Fry pork slowly until light brown and crisp. Add onions and cook slowly for 5 minutes. Drain, saving melted fat.
2. Combine potatoes, pork, onions, and water. Cook until tender.
3. Blend flour with fat. Stir in milk until well-blended. Cook for several minutes. Add all ingredients and simmer for 20 minutes.

Washington Chowder

3 gal/11.36 l

Metric		Ingredients	U.S.	
Weight	**Volume**		**Weight**	**Volume**
454 g	592 ml	Bacon, diced	1 lb	2 ½ cups
85 g	118 ml	Bacon Fat	3 oz	½ cup
454 g	947 ml	Onions, minced	1 lb	1 qt
5.00 kg	5.21 l	Water	11 lb	5 ½ qt
2.95 kg	3.31 l	Tomatoes, canned, chopped	6 lb, 8 oz	1 No. 10 can
2.72 kg	3.79 l	Potatoes, finely diced	6 lb	1 gal
57 g	59 ml	Salt	2 oz	¼ cup
2.95 kg	3.31 l	Corn, canned, and liquor	6 lb, 8 oz	1 No. 10 can
113 g	158 ml	Bacon Fat	4 oz	⅔ cup
57 g	118 ml	Flour, bread	2 oz	½ cup
	15 ml	Pepper		1 tbsp
227 g	474 ml	Milk Solids, nonfat	8 oz	2 cups

Procedure

1. Fry diced bacon. Remove bacon from drippings.
2. Add chopped onions to bacon fat and sauté until lightly browned.
3. To soup kettle, add water, tomatoes, onions, and bacon. Simmer.
4. Add potatoes and salt and cook until potatoes are almost tender.
5. Add corn and cook 15 minutes.
6. Melt bacon fat and add flour and pepper to make a roux. Mix milk solids with water and add to roux. Mixture should be runny.
7. Add milk mixture to soup, stirring vigorously. Cook until raw starch flavor disappears.

Corn Chowder
3 gal/11.36 l

Metric		Ingredients	U.S.		
Weight	Volume		Weight		Volume
454 g	474 ml	Bacon, diced	1 lb		2 cups
85 g	118 ml	Bacon Fat		3 oz	½ cup
681 g	711 ml	Onions, finely chopped	1 lb,	8 oz	3 cups
6.35 kg	6.63 l	Water	14 lb		7 qt
114 g	237 ml	Celery, finely chopped		4 oz	1 cup
454 g	829 ml	Green Pepper, chopped	1 lb		3 ½ cups
567 g	947 ml	Potatoes, diced small	1 lb,	4 oz	1 qt
3.00 kg	3.31 l	Corn, cream-style	6 lb,	10 oz	1 No. 10 can
43 g	38 ml	Ham Soup Base		1 ½ oz	2 ½ tbsp
114 g	237 ml	Flour, all-purpose		4 oz	1 cup
170 g	237 ml	Bacon Fat		6 oz	1 cup
43 g	45 ml	Salt		1 ½ oz	3 tbsp
	5 ml	White Pepper			1 tsp
6.81 g	1.42 l	Milk Solids, nonfat	1 lb,	8 oz	1 ½ qt
114 g	711 ml	Parsley, chopped		4 oz	3 cups

Procedure

1. Fry diced bacon. Remove bacon and sauté onions in drippings.
2. Combine water, onions, celery, and green pepper, and cook until vegetables are tender.
3. Add potatoes and cook until almost tender.
4. Add bacon and corn. Dissolve ham soup base in soup. Bring soup to boiling.
5. Combine flour, bacon fat, and seasonings to make a roux. Combine milk solids with water and add to roux. Mixture should be runny.
6. Add roux and milk solid mixture to soup, stirring vigorously. Cook until raw starch flavor disappears.
7. Add parsley and serve.

Oyster Stew
3 gal/11.36 l

Metric		Ingredients	U.S.		
Weight	Volume		Weight		Volume
3.63 kg	4.26 l	Oysters, with liquor	8 lb		4 ½ qt
255 g	266 ml	Butter or Margarine		9 oz	1 ⅛ cups
7.26 kg	7.57 l	Milk	16 lb		2 gal
255 g	266 ml	Butter or Margarine		9 oz	1 ⅛ cups
42 g	45 ml	Salt		1 ½ oz	3 tbsp
	5 ml	Pepper, white			1 tsp
1.02 kg	1.07 l	Milk, cold	2 lb,	4 oz	4 ½ cups
85 g	178 ml	Flour, all-purpose		3 oz	¾ cup

Procedure

1. Heat oysters with butter or margarine.
2. Scald milk with butter or margarine and seasonings. Mix cold milk with flour and stir into scalded milk. Cook, stirring until thickened. Combine with oysters and heat over hot water for 15 minutes. Serve immediately.

Oyster Bisque
3 gal/11.36 l

Metric		Ingredients	U.S.	
Weight	**Volume**		**Weight**	**Volume**
3.18 kg	3.31 l	Oysters	7 lb	3 ½ qt
142 g	158 ml	Butter or Margarine	5 oz	⅔ cup
71 g	158 ml	Flour, bread	2 ½ oz	⅔ cup
6.35 kg	6.63 l	Milk, hot	14 lb	7 qt
15 g	17 ml	Celery Salt	½ oz	3 ½ tsp
	17 ½ ml	Paprika		3 ½ tsp
454 g	474 ml	Eggs, beaten (8 lge)	1 lb	2 cups
66 g	415 ml	Parsley, chopped	2 ⅓ oz	1 ¾ cups

Procedure

1. Heat oysters, drain, and save liquor. Grind oysters fine.
2. Melt butter or margarine; add flour and blend. Add hot milk slowly, stirring until thick and smooth. Add liquor, celery salt, and paprika.
3. Add eggs by first adding some of hot mixture to them. Then stir egg mixture into hot mixture. Stir and cook for 3 minutes.
4. Add oysters and mix well.
5. Sprinkle with parsley and serve.

Note: Clams, lobster, or shrimp may be used in place of oysters.

Salmon Bisque
3 gal/11.36 l

Metric		Ingredients	U.S.	
Weight	**Volume**		**Weight**	**Volume**
2.72 kg	3.56 l	Salmon, boned, flaked	6 lb	3 ¾ qt
1.36 kg	1.42 l	Tomatoes or juice	3 lb	1 ½ qt
57 g	1 bunch	Parsley, chopped	2 oz	1 bunch
227 g	355 ml	Onions, chopped	8 oz	1 ½ cups
57 g	118 ml	Celery Leaves, chopped	2 oz	½ cup
2.72 kg	2.84 l	Water	6 lb	3 qt
340 g	355 ml	Butter or Margarine	12 oz	1 ½ cups
340 g	711 ml	Flour, bread	12 oz	3 cups
4.08 kg	4.26 l	Milk	9 lb	4 ½ qt
57 g	60 ml	Salt	2 oz	4 tbsp
	15 ml	Paprika		1 tbsp

Procedure

1. Simmer salmon, tomatoes, parsley, onions, and celery leaves in water for 20 minutes.
2. Make white sauce with remaining ingredients. Stir in salmon mixture slowly. Do not boil mixture.

Note: Other fish may be used in place of the salmon.

Chicken Bisque
3 gal/11.36 l

| Metric | | Ingredients | U.S. | |
Weight	Volume		Weight	Volume
9.07 kg	9.46 l	Water, boiling	20 lb	2 ½ gal
378 g	296 ml	Chicken Soup Base	13 ⅓ oz	1 ¼ cups
605 g	632 ml	Margarine	1 lb, 5 ⅓ oz	2 ⅔ cups
605 g	1.97 l	Flour, all-purpose	1 lb, 5 ⅓ oz	5 ⅓ cups
382 g	553 ml	Pimiento, chopped	13 ½ oz	2 ⅓ cups
340 g	592 ml	Green Pepper, chopped	12 oz	2 ½ cups
340 g	592 ml	Chicken, diced	12 oz	2 ½ cups
	6 ⅔ ml	Pepper, white		1 ⅓ tsp
	10 ml	Salt		2 tsp

Procedure

1. Dissolve chicken base in boiling water.
2. Melt margarine and add flour to make a roux.
3. Stir a small amount of broth into the roux, then combine it with the broth and cook until slightly thickened.
4. Add chicken, pimiento, green pepper, and seasonings. Continue cooking until thoroughly heated and flour has lost its raw taste.

Gumbo Creole
3 gal/11.36 l

| Metric | | Ingredients | U.S. | |
Weight	Volume		Weight	Volume
283 g	296 ml	Onions, chopped	10 oz	1 ¼ cups
	1 clove	Garlic, minced		1 clove
149 g	178 ml	Salad Oil	5 ¼ oz	¾ cup
170 g	345 ml	Flour, bread	6 oz	1 ½ cups
1.82 kg	1.89 l	Tomatoes, canned, chopped	4 lb	2 qt
9.07 kg	9.46 l	Chicken or Beef Broth	20 lb	2 ½ gal
57 g	118 ml	Celery, finely chopped	2 oz	½ cup
	2 ½ ml	Paprika		½ tsp
28 g	30 ml	Salt	1 oz	2 tbsp
9 g	59 ml	Parsley, chopped	⅓ oz	¼ cup
	2 cloves	Cloves, whole		2 cloves
	2 leaves	Bay Leaves		2 leaves
	⅝ ml	Thyme, crushed		⅛ tsp
	5 ml	Pepper		1 tsp
340 g	474 ml	Okra, canned or fresh, sliced	12 oz	2 cups
340 g	595 ml	Shrimp, raw, cleaned, E.P.	12 oz	2 ½ cups
681 g	1.89 l	Crabmeat, fresh, E.P.	1 lb, 8 oz	2 qt

Procedure

1. Sauté onion and garlic in oil. Add flour and mix until smooth. Put in large pot or steam kettle and add tomatoes. Stir until mixture thickens. Add broth, celery, and seasonings, and simmer for 2 hours.
2. Ten minutes before serving, add okra, shrimp, and crabmeat.

Bouillabaisse

4 gal/15.15 l

| Metric | | Ingredients | U.S. | |
Weight	Volume		Weight	Volume
3.63 kg	3.79 l	Water, boiling	8 lb	1 gal
4.54 kg	8 doz	Clams in Shell	10 lb	8 doz
1.14 kg	1.89 l	Shrimp, fresh or canned	2 lb, 8 oz	2 qt
1.36 kg	1.89 l	Lobster	3 lb	2 qt
1.36 kg	2.21 l	Crabmeat	3 lb	2 ⅓ qt
3.63 kg	5.68 l	Haddock, Cod, or Sole	8 lb	1 ½ gal
71 g	118 ml	Onions, chopped	2 ½ oz	½ cup
57 g	118 ml	Celery, chopped	2 oz	½ cup
28 g	8 cloves	Garlic, minced	1 oz	8 cloves
454 g	474 ml	Salad Oil	1 lb	2 cups
2.95 kg	3.31 l	Tomatoes, chopped	6 lb, 8 oz	1 No. 10 can
	6 leaves	Bay Leaves		6 leaves
	10 ml	Thyme Leaves		2 tsp
	15 ml	Saffron		1 tbsp
85 g	90 ml	Salt	3 oz	6 tbsp
	5 ml	Black Pepper		1 tsp
	45 ml	Orange Peel, chopped		3 tbsp
9 g	59 ml	Parsley, chopped	⅓ oz	¼ cup
907 g	947 ml	Sherry	2 lb	1 qt

Procedure

1. Steam clams in boiling water. Save liquor. Remove meat from shells.
2. Clean shrimp and lobster. Cut lobster into chunks. Flake crab meat.
3. Remove bones and skin from fish and cut into 2-inch chunks.
4. Sauté onions, celery, and garlic in oil until tender.
5. Combine liquor, onions, celery, garlic, oil, tomatoes, seasonings, orange peel, and parsley. Simmer until flavors are mingled.
6. Add fish and continue cooking for 10 minutes. Add Sherry.
7. Garnish top of stew with toasted French bread sprinkled with saffron.

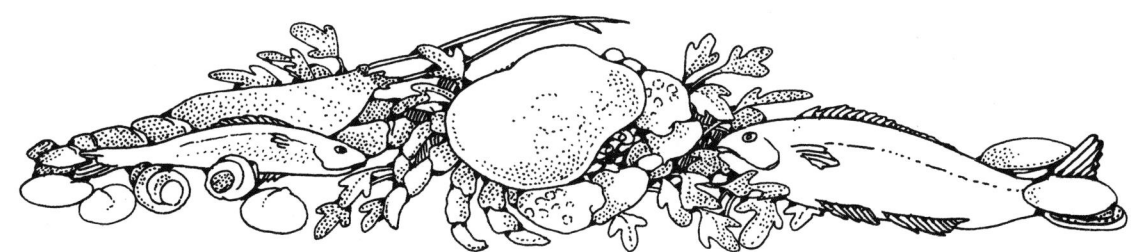

Cream Soups

Cream of Asparagus Soup
3 gal/11.36 l

Metric		Ingredients	U.S.	
Weight	Volume		Weight	Volume
340 g	355 ml	Butter or Margarine	12 oz	1 ½ cups
170 g	355 ml	Flour, bread	6 oz	1 ½ cups
8.17 kg	8.51 l	Milk, hot	18 lb	9 qt
57 g	60 ml	Salt	2 oz	¼ cup
	2 ½ ml	Pepper, white		½ tsp
2.95 kg	2.84 l	Asparagus, cooked, finely ground	6 lb, 8 oz	3 qt

Procedure

1. Melt butter or margarine, add flour, and blend. Add milk slowly, stirring constantly until sauce is smooth and thickened. Add salt and pepper.

2. Stir in ground asparagus and heat thoroughly.

Cream of Broccoli Soup
3 gal/11.36 l

Metric		Ingredients	U.S.	
Weight	Volume		Weight	Volume
4.54 kg	5.92 l	Broccoli, cooked, sieved	10 lb	6 ¼ qt
4.54 kg	4.74 l	Béchamel Sauce	10 lb	5 qt
907 g	947 ml	Milk, hot	2 lb	1 qt

Procedure

1. Blend sieved broccoli with Béchamel sauce, add hot milk, and either heat or chill thoroughly according to the temperature desired for service.
2. Garnish with a sprinkling of paprika.

Note: Creamed soups may be made by combining other sieved vegetables with Béchamel sauce, such as Cream of Asparagus, Carrot, Cauliflower, Celery, Green Pea, or Spinach.

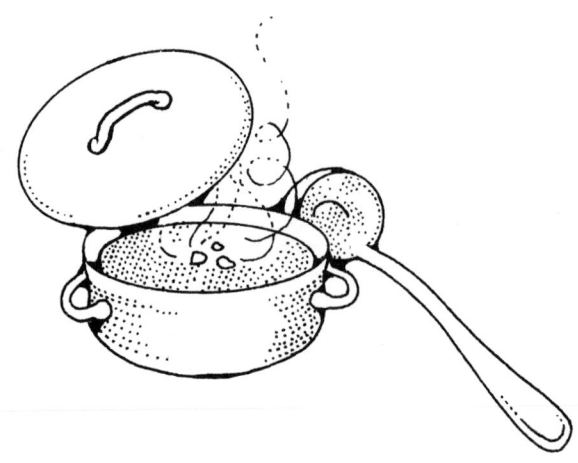

Cream of Cauliflower Soup

3 gal/11.36 l

Metric		Ingredients	U.S.		
Weight	Volume		Weight		Volume
57 g	59 ml	Margarine		2 oz	¼ cup
227 g	355 ml	Onions, finely chopped		8 oz	1 ½ cups
227 g	474 ml	Celery, finely chopped		8 oz	2 cups
8.17 kg	8.51 l	Water	18 lb		2 ¼ gal
298 g	237 ml	Chicken Soup Base		10 ½ oz	1 cup
28 g	30 ml	Salt		1 oz	2 tbsp
850 g	1.42 l	Cauliflower, chopped	1 lb,	14 oz	1 ½ qt
483 g	504 ml	Margarine	1 lb,	1 oz	2 ⅛ cups
425 g	889 ml	Flour, all-purpose		15 oz	3 ¾ cups
	5 ml	Pepper, white			1 tsp
681 g	711 ml	Cream, half and half, hot	1 lb,	8 oz	3 cups

Procedure

1. Melt margarine and sauté onions and celery in margarine until golden.
2. Add onions and celery to water in soup kettle and simmer.
3. Add chicken base and salt to soup. Add cauliflower and cook until almost tender.
4. Melt margarine and add flour and pepper to make a roux. Add warm water to make a runny mixture. Add to soup, stirring vigorously. Cook until raw starch flavor has disappeared.
5. Add hot cream and serve.

Cream of Celery Soup

3 gal/11.36 l

Metric		Ingredients	U.S.		
Weight	Volume		Weight		Volume
1.02 kg	2.13 l	Celery, stalks and leaves	2 lb,	4 oz	2 ¼ qt
340 g	533 ml	Carrots, chopped		12 oz	2 ¼ cups
302 g	474 ml	Onions, chopped		10 ⅔ oz	2 cups
3.63 kg	3.79 l	Water	8 lb		1 gal
	1 ⅔ ml	Celery Seed			⅓ tsp
57 g	59 ml	Salt		2 oz	¼ cup
	7 ½ ml	Celery Salt			1 ½ tsp
99 g	80 ml	Chicken Soup Base		3 ½ oz	5 ⅓ tbsp
283 g	296 ml	Margarine		10 oz	1 ¼ cups
283 g	592 ml	Flour, bread		10 oz	2 ½ cups
	3 ¾ ml	Pepper, white			¾ tsp
	3 ¾ ml	Paprika			¾ tsp
567 g	1.18 l	Milk Solids, nonfat	1 lb,	4 oz	1 ¼ qt

Procedure

1. Chop celery stalks and leaves. Add celery, carrots, and onions to water with celery seed and cook until tender.
2. Add salt, celery salt, and chicken soup base.
3. Melt margarine and add flour, pepper, and paprika to make a roux. Mix milk solids with water and add to roux. Mixture should be runny.
4. Add mixture to soup, stirring vigorously. Cook until raw starch flavor disappears.

Cream of Corn Soup
3 gal/11.36 l

| Metric | | Ingredients | U.S. | |
Weight	Volume		Weight	Volume
9.07 kg	9.46 l	Water, hot	20 lb	2 ½ gal
114 g	237 ml	Onions, chopped	4 oz	¾ cup
4.00 kg	3.79 l	Corn, cream-style	8 lb, 13 oz	1 gal
227 g	178 ml	Chicken Soup Base	8 oz	¾ cup
227 g	237 ml	Butter or Margarine	8 oz	1 cup
198 g	415 ml	Flour, all-purpose	7 oz	1 ¾ cups
454 g	947 ml	Milk Solids, nonfat	1 lb	1 qt
28 g	30 ml	Salt	1 oz	2 tbsp
	10 ml	Pepper, white		2 tsp
	5 ml	Celery Salt		1 tsp
57 g	355 ml	Parsley, chopped	2 oz	1 ½ cups

Procedure

1. Add onions to hot water and cook until tender.
2. Add corn and bring to a boil. Add chicken soup base.
3. Make a roux of margarine and flour. Mix the powdered milk with warm water. Combine the roux and powdered milk mixture. Mixture should be runny.
4. Add roux and milk mixture to soup, stirring vigorously.
5. Add seasonings and continue cooking until raw starch flavor has disappeared.
6. Add parsley and serve.

Cream of Mushroom Soup
3 gal/11.36 l

| Metric | | Ingredients | U.S. | |
Weight	Volume		Weight	Volume
907 g	3.31 l	Mushrooms	2 lb	3 ½ qt
170 g	178 ml	Butter or Margarine	6 oz	¾ cup
340 g	533 ml	Onions, chopped	12 oz	2 ¼ cups
340 g	711 ml	Celery, chopped	12 oz	3 cups
113 g	119 ml	Butter or Margarine	4 oz	½ cup
9.07 kg	9.46 l	Water	20 lb	2 ½ gal
142 g	119 ml	Chicken Soup Base	5 oz	½ cup
28 g	30 ml	Salt	1 oz	2 tbsp
425 g	889 ml	Flour, bread	15 oz	3 ¾ cups
	5 ml	Pepper, white		1 tsp
454 g	474 ml	Butter or Margarine	1 lb	2 cups
908 g	947 ml	Milk	2 lb	1 qt

Procedure

1. Wash mushrooms in salted water. Drain and slice.
2. Sauté mushrooms lightly in margarine. Reserve.
3. Sauté onions and celery in margarine.
4. Add chicken soup base and salt to water in soup kettle. Add onions and celery and simmer.
5. Melt butter or margarine and add flour and pepper to make a roux. Stir milk into roux to make a white sauce.
6. Add white sauce to soup, stirring vigorously. Cook until mixture is thickened. Add sautéed mushrooms to soup.

Green Pea and Bacon Soup
3 gal/11.36 l

| Metric | | Ingredients | U.S. | |
Weight	Volume		Weight	Volume
2.72 kg	4.26 l	Green Peas	6 lb	4½ qt
454 g	711 ml	Onions, chopped	1 lb	3 cups
227 g	474 ml	Celery, chopped	8 oz	2 cups
	10 ml	Thyme		2 tsp
28 g	30 ml	Salt	1 oz	2 tbsp
170 g	178 ml	Butter or Margarine	6 oz	¾ cup
85 g	178 ml	Flour, all-purpose	3 oz	¾ cup
7.26 kg	7.57 l	Milk	16 lb	2 gal
57 g	60 ml	Salt	2 oz	4 tbsp
	5 ml	Pepper		1 tsp
454 g	711 ml	Bacon, cooked, diced	1 lb	3 cups

Procedure

1. Cook peas, onions, celery, thyme, and salt in water to cover, until vegetables are tender. Drain and purée vegetables.
2. Melt butter or margarine. Blend in flour. Gradually stir in milk and seasonings. Cook until smooth and thickened.
3. Combine white sauce and pureed vegetables. Add chopped, crisp bacon and heat to serving temperature (190°F/88°C).

Split Pea Soup
3 gal/11.36 l

| Metric | | Ingredients | U.S. | |
Weight	Volume		Weight	Volume
454 g	711 ml	Onions, chopped	1 lb	3 cups
85 g	89 ml	Butter or Margarine	3 oz	6 tbsp
1.59 kg	1.89 l	Split Peas, dried	3 lb, 8 oz	2 qt
9.07 kg	9.46 l	Water	20 lb	2½ gal
227 g	474 ml	Celery and Leaves, chopped	8 oz	2 cups
21 g	79 ml	Parsley, chopped	¾ oz	⅓ cup
227 g	178 ml	Ham Soup Base	8 oz	¾ cup
14 g	15 ml	Salt	½ oz	1 tbsp
170 g	355 ml	Flour, all-purpose	6 oz	1½ cups
	5 ml	Pepper		1 tsp
198 g	207 ml	Butter or Margarine, melted	7 oz	⅞ cup
57 g	118 ml	Milk Solids, nonfat	2 oz	½ cup

Procedure

1. Sauté onions in butter or margarine until tender.
2. Sort and wash peas. Combine peas, water, sautéed onions, celery, celery leaves, and parsley. Cook slowly 3 to 4 hours until peas are very soft.
3. Add ham soup base and salt.
4. Add flour and pepper to melted margarine to make a roux. Mix milk solids with water and add to roux. Mixture must be runny.
5. Add roux to soup, stirring constantly. Cook until soup is thickened and raw starch flavor has disappeared.

Turkey Almond Soup
3 gal/11.36 l

Metric		Ingredients	U.S.		
Weight	Volume		Weight		Volume
7.26 kg	7.57 l	Turkey Stock	16 lb		2 gal
	4 sprigs	Parsley, chopped			4 sprigs
	5 ml	Sage Leaves, ground			1 tsp
	5 ml	Rosemary Leaves			1 tsp
	2½ ml	Thyme Leaves, ground			½ tsp
2.38 kg	3.79 l	Potatoes, diced	5 lb,	4 oz	1 gal
454 g	711 ml	Onions, chopped	1 lb		3 cups
227 g	474 ml	Celery, chopped		8 oz	2 cups
227 g	355 ml	Carrots, chopped		8 oz	1 ½ cups
1.82 kg	1.89 l	White Sauce, medium	4 lb		2 qt
14 g	15 ml	Salt		½ oz	1 tbsp
454 g	711 ml	Turkey Meat, diced	1 lb		3 cups
227 g	474 ml	Almonds, chopped		8 oz	2 cups

Procedure

1. Turkey stock may be from bones and trim from roast turkey or freshly boiled stock. Tie herbs loosely in cheesecloth. Add them and vegetables to boiling stock. Allow them to cook until vegetables are very tender. Remove herbs and puree vegetables.

2. Blend vegetable puree, stock, white sauce, and salt. Heat to simmering. Add turkey meat and almonds and serve.

Peanut Butter Soup
3 gal/11.36 l

Metric		Ingredients	U.S.		
Weight	Volume		Weight		Volume
227 g	237 ml	Butter or Margarine		8 oz	1 cup
907 g	1.42 l	Onions, finely chopped	2 lb		1 ½ qt
454 g	947 ml	Celery, finely chopped	1 lb		1 qt
114 g	237 ml	Flour, all-purpose		4 oz	1 cup
14 g	15 ml	Salt		½ oz	1 tbsp
	10 ml	Pepper			2 tsp
	10 ml	Thyme			2 tsp
7.26 kg	7.57 l	Chicken Broth	16 lb		2 gal
681 g	632 ml	Peanut Butter, chunky	1 lb,	8 oz	2 ⅔ cups
907 g	947 ml	Cream, half and half	2 lb		1 qt
170 g	178 ml	Lemon Juice		6 oz	¾ cup

Procedure

1. Melt butter or margarine. Sauté onions and celery until tender. Add flour, salt, pepper, and thyme. Gradually add hot chicken broth, stirring until smooth and thickened.

2. Blend in peanut butter and cream. Heat to simmering but do not allow to boil. Remove from heat. Stir in lemon juice and serve at once.

Cheese Soup (Duchess)
3 gal/11.36 l

Metric		Ingredients	U.S.	
Weight	Volume		Weight	Volume
9.07 kg	9.46 l	Chicken Stock	20 lb	2 ½ gal
454 g	711 ml	Carrots, finely diced	1 lb	3 cups
454 g	711 ml	Onions, finely chopped	1 lb	3 cups
681 g	711 ml	Butter or Margarine	1 lb, 8 oz	3 cups
454 g	947 ml	Flour, bread	1 lb	1 qt
28 g	30 ml	Salt	1 oz	2 tbsp
	5 ml	Pepper, white		1 tsp
2.72 kg	2.84 l	Milk	6 lb	3 qt
454 g	947 ml	Cheddar Cheese, ground	1 lb	1 qt

Procedure

1. Cook carrots and onions in chicken stock until tender.
2. Make white sauce with butter or margarine, flour, seasonings, and milk. Combine with soup, stirring vigorously. Cook until raw starch flavor has disappeared and soup has thickened.
3. Remove soup from heat and add cheese, stirring until cheese has melted and mixture is well-blended.

Cream of Tomato Soup
3 gal/11.36 l

Metric		Ingredients	U.S.	
Weight	Volume		Weight	Volume
1.82 kg	1.89 l	Tomato Juice	4 lb	2 qt
1.82 kg	1.89 l	Tomato Puree	4 lb	2 qt
	3 leaves	Bay Leaves		3 leaves
227 g	355 ml	Onions, sliced	8 oz	1 ½ cups
57 g	60 ml	Sugar	2 oz	4 tbsp
	10 ml	Soda		2 tsp
		White Sauce		
340 g	355 ml	Butter or Margarine	12 oz	1 ½ cups
170 g	355 ml	Flour, bread	6 oz	1 ½ cups
7.26 kg	7.57 l	Milk, hot	16 lb	2 gal
57 g	60 ml	Salt	2 oz	4 tbsp
14 g	30 ml	Pepper	½ oz	2 tbsp

Procedure

1. Heat tomato juice, puree, bay leaves, onions, and sugar for 1 hour. Strain. Stir in soda.
2. Melt butter or margarine. Blend in flour. Gradually stir in milk and seasonings. Cook until smooth and thickened.
3. Stir tomato mixture slowly into white sauce shortly before service. Heat, but do not boil.

Mulligatawny Soup
3 gal/11.36 l

Metric		Ingredients	U.S.	
Weight	Volume		Weight	Volume
85 g	89 ml	Butter or Margarine	3 oz	6 tbsp
454 g	711 ml	Onions, chopped	1 lb	3 cups
9.07 kg	9.46 l	Chicken Stock, rich	20 lb	2 ½ gal
1.14 kg	1.18 l	Apples, tart, peeled and diced	2 lb, 8 oz	5 cups
198 g	237 ml	Rice	7 oz	1 cup
28 g	30 ml	Salt	1 oz	2 tbsp
170 g	178 ml	Butter or Margarine, melted	6 oz	¾ cup
142 g	296 ml	Flour, all-purpose	5 oz	1 ¼ cups
	10 ml	Pepper, white		2 tsp
10 g	25 ml	Curry Powder		5 tsp
283 g	296 ml	Cream, 20%, hot	10 oz	1 ¼ cups
907 g	1.89 l	Chicken, cooked and diced	2 lb	2 qt

Procedure

1. Sauté onions in butter or margarine for 5 minutes. Add to chicken stock in soup kettle.
2. Add apples and cook until almost tender.
3. Add rice and salt. Boil gently for 20 minutes, or until rice is cooked.
4. Add flour, white pepper, and curry powder to melted butter or margarine to make a roux. Add roux to soup, stirring vigorously, and cook until raw starch flavor has disappeared.
5. Add cream and diced chicken.

Pepper Pot Soup
3 gal/11.36 l

Metric		Ingredients	U.S.	
Weight	Volume		Weight	Volume
57 g	60 ml	Butter or Margarine	2 oz	¼ cup
57 g	118 ml	Onions, finely chopped	2 oz	½ cup
227 g	474 ml	Green Pepper, chopped	8 oz	2 cups
227 g	474 ml	Celery, chopped	8 oz	2 cups
1.36 kg	1.66 l	Potatoes, diced	3 lb	1 ¾ qt
7.26 kg	7.57 l	Stock, beef, hot	16 lb	2 gal
28 g	30 ml	Salt	1 oz	2 tbsp
142 g	296 ml	Flour, all-purpose	5 oz	1 ¼ cups
	5 ml	Pepper, white		1 tsp
340 g	355 ml	Butter or Margarine, melted	12 oz	1 ½ cups
681 g	711 ml	Milk, hot	1 lb, 8 oz	3 cups
14 g	30 ml	Red Pepper, chopped	½ oz	2 tbsp

Procedure

1. Melt butter or margarine and sauté onions, green pepper, and celery.
2. Add sautéed vegetables, potatoes, and salt to stock and cook until potatoes are tender.
3. Add flour and pepper to melted margarine and stir to make a roux. Add hot milk. Stir until smooth and thickened.
4. Add milk mixture to soup, stirring vigorously. Cook until raw starch flavor has disappeared. Garnish with chopped red pepper and serve.

Chicken Soup
4 ½ gal/16.11 l

Metric		Ingredients	U.S.	
Weight	**Volume**		**Weight**	**Volume**
9.07 kg	9.46 l	Chicken Stock	20 lb	2 ½ gal
681 g	1.42 l	Onions, chopped	1 lb, 8 oz	1 ½ qt
227 g	474 ml	Celery, chopped	8 oz	2 cups
227 g	296 ml	Rice	8 oz	1 ¼ cups
142 g	158 ml	Chicken Fat	5 oz	⅔ cup
142 g	296 ml	Flour, bread	5 oz	1 ¼ cups
2.27 kg	2.37 l	Milk, hot	5 lb	2 ½ qt
567 g	592 ml	Cream, hot, 20%	1 lb, 4 oz	2 ½ cups
57 g	60 ml	Salt	2 oz	4 tbsp
	5 ml	Pepper		1 tsp
681 g	1.42 l	Chicken, cooked, diced	1 lb, 8 oz	1 ½ qt

Procedure

1. Simmer onions and celery in stock for 1 hour. Add rice and cook until tender.
2. Make roux with chicken fat and flour. Stir in cream and milk. Cook until smooth and thickened. Add to stock.
3. Add seasonings and chicken meat. Serve immediately.

Cream of Potato Soup
3 gal/11.36 l

Metric		Ingredients	U.S.	
Weight	**Volume**		**Weight**	**Volume**
3.63 kg	32 med	Potatoes, chopped	8 lb	32 med
312 g	474 ml	Onions, chopped	11 oz	2 cups
3.63 kg	3.79 l	Water	8 lb	1 gal
227 g	237 ml	Butter or Margarine	8 oz	1 cup
57 g	118 ml	Flour, all-purpose	2 oz	½ cup
5.44 kg	5.68 l	Milk, hot	12 lb	6 qt
	7 ½ ml	Pepper		1 ½ tsp
85 g	90 ml	Salt	3 oz	6 tbsp
	10 ml	Celery Salt		2 tsp
57 g	1 bunch	Parsley, chopped	2 oz	1 bunch

Procedure

1. Cook potatoes and onions in water until soft. Puree or mash without draining.
2. Melt butter or margarine, add flour and blend. Add hot milk and seasonings. Stir until smooth and thickened.
3. Add potato mixture to sauce. Heat thoroughly. Garnish with chopped parsley.

Chilled Soups

Avocado Soup
2 gal/7.57 l

Metric		Ingredients	U.S.	
Weight	Volume		Weight	Volume
2.72 kg	2.84 l	Ripe Avocados, mashed	6 lb	3 qt
114 g	118 ml	Lemon Juice	4 oz	½ cup
2.27 kg	2.37 l	Chicken Broth	5 lb	2 ½ qt
85 g	118 ml	Onions, grated	3 oz	½ cup
28 g	79 ml	Hot Pepper, minced	1 oz	⅓ cup
1.36 kg	1.42 l	White Sauce, medium	3 lb	1 ½ qt
21 g	22 ml	Salt	¾ oz	1 ½ tbsp
	2 ½ ml	Pepper		½ tsp
907 g	947 ml	Sour Cream	2 lb	1 qt
	1 drop	Green Coloring (if needed)		1 drop

Procedure

1. Stir lemon juice into avocado as soon as mashed to prevent discoloration.
2. Heat chicken broth, onions, and hot pepper. Blend in white sauce, salt, and pepper. Cool.
3. Blend avocado and sour cream into cold broth mixture. Add coloring, if needed, to make soup a delicate green.
4. Chill and serve.

Vichyssoise (Potato-Onion Soup)
3 gal/11.36 l

Metric		Ingredients	U.S.	
Weight	Volume		Weight	Volume
1.36 kg	2.37 l	Onions, chopped	3 lb	2 ½ qt
	1 leaf	Bay Leaf		1 leaf
	2 ½ ml	Peppercorns, crushed		½ tsp
3.63 kg	3.79 l	Chicken Stock, rich	8 lb	1 gal
454 g	1.89 l	Potato, dehydrated	1 lb	2 qt
	10 ml	Celery Salt		2 tsp
3.63 kg	3.79 l	Cream, half and half	8 lb	1 gal
28 g	30 ml	Salt	1 oz	2 tbsp
14 g	79 ml	Chives, Parsley or Watercress, chopped	½ oz	⅓ cup

Procedure

1. Combine onions, bay leaf, peppercorns, and stock. Cook covered until onions are very tender. Remove bay leaf and strain onions through a sieve or china cap strainer.
2. While hot, stir in dehydrated potato. Add celery salt, cream, and salt.
3. Chill thoroughly. Serve, garnished with chopped chive, parsley or watercress.

Note: If fresh potatoes are used, dice and cook them with onions using 6 lb/2.72 kg. The chicken stock may be 1 gal/3.79 l water and 6 oz/170 g chicken soup base.

Gazpacho
2 ½ gal/9.47 l

Metric		Ingredients	U.S.	
Weight	**Volume**		**Weight**	**Volume**
1.82 kg	1.89 l	Beef Stock	4 lb	2 qt
3.63 kg	3.79 l	Tomato Juice	8 lb	1 gal
283 g	296 ml	Lemon Juice	10 oz	1 ¼ cups
454 g	711 ml	Onions, minced	1 lb	3 cups
20 g	20 ml	Garlic, minced	¾ oz	6 cloves
454 g	947 ml	Celery, minced	1 lb	1 qt
454 g	829 ml	Cucumber, finely chopped	1 lb	3 ½ cups
454 g	947 ml	Green Pepper, minced	1 lb	1 qt
907 g	1.66 l	Tomatoes, finely chopped	2 lb	1 ¾ qt
28 g	30 ml	Salt	1 oz	2 tbsp
15 g	15 ml	Tabasco Sauce	½ oz	1 tbsp
15 g	15 ml	Worcestershire Sauce	½ oz	1 tbsp
681 g	711 ml	Tarragon Wine Vinegar	1 lb, 8 oz	3 cups
28 g	30 ml	Sugar	1 oz	2 tbsp

Procedure

1. Blend ingredients well. Chill thoroughly.
2. Distribute vegetables carefully when serving. A thin slice of cucumber, seasoned with vinegar and salt, is an appetizing garnish.

Fruit Soup
3 gal/11.36 l

Metric		Ingredients	U.S.	
Weight	**Volume**		**Weight**	**Volume**
1.82 kg	2.84 l	Prunes, pitted, chopped	4 lb	3 qt
567 g	947 ml	Raisins, seedless	1 lb, 4 oz	1 qt
454 g	3 whole	Lemons, chopped	1 lb	3 whole
227 g	1 ½ whole	Oranges, chopped	8 oz	1 ½ whole
1.82 kg	1.89 l	Applesauce	4 lb	2 qt
	5 3-in	Cinnamon Sticks		5 3-in
454 g	474 ml	Sugar	1 lb	2 cups
	5 ml	Salt		1 tsp
7.26 kg	7.57 l	Juice, pineapple or apple	16 lb	2 gal
71 g	118 ml	Cornstarch	2 ½ oz	½ cup
454 g	474 ml	Water, cold	1 lb	2 cups
114 g	118 ml	Butter or Margarine	4 oz	½ cup

Procedure

1. Combine all ingredients except cornstarch, cold water, and butter. Simmer until fruit is tender (about 45 min).
2. Mix cornstarch with cold water. Stir into hot fruit mixture. Continue cooking and stirring until thickened and the cornstarch is clear.
3. Remove from heat. Stir in butter or magarine until melted. Chill well before serving.

CHAPTER 4 _Cheese, Egg, Cereal, and Vegetable Entrées_

It is necessary to carefully control temperatures when cooking cheese and egg dishes. High temperature and prolonged cooking time toughens the protein and, in cheese, will cause fat to separate and drain from the cheese. Soufflés cooked at a high temperature will sag quickly when taken from the oven, and custards will become watery and spongy, rather than smooth and tender. Timbales are custards used as nutritious extenders for other foods.

Certain procedures will insure good results when cooking eggs. Eggs taken from refrigeration for immediate cooking need to be warmed gradually to prevent the shells from breaking. Start cooking the eggs in cold water or let them stand for a few minutes in warm water. Eggs cooked at 212°F/100°C will be hard in 10 to 12 minutes, soft-cooked in 3 minutes, and medium-cooked in 4 minutes. Plunge them immediately into cold, running water to halt cooking. This will prevent over-cooking and the development of a ferrous-sulfide (greenish) ring around the yolk.

When used as a main dish, cereals and vegetables need protein foods, fats, and nuts added to achieve richness. Cooking them in well-flavored meat broth, or in water to which a good commercial soup base has been added, helps add flavor. A definite form adds appetite appeal. Avoid mushy, ''hashed-up'' mixtures and flat, insipid, or thin flavors. Palatability can often be heightened through the use of a flavorful sauce.

Table 1
Cooking of Pastas, Dried Beans, and Cereals

Metric		Ingredients	U.S.		
Weight	Volume		Weight		Volume
3.41 kg	4.50 l	Beans, kidney or lima	7 lb,	8 oz	4 ¾ qt
10.89 kg	11.37 l	Water, boiling	24 lb		3 gal
85 g	90 ml	Salt		3 oz	6 tbsp
		OR			
3.18 kg	4.10 l	Beans, navy or pea	7 lb		4 ⅓ qt
9.07 kg	9.46 l	Water, boiling	20 lb		2 ½ gal
71 g	75 ml	Salt		2 ½ oz	5 tbsp

Wash beans. Cover with boiling water and let stand 2 hours or longer. Simmer until tender (about 2 ½ hrs). Approximate yield—15 lb/681 kg.

Table 1
Cooking of Pastas, Dried Beans, and Cereals (*cont.*)

Metric		Ingredients	U.S.	
Weight	Volume		Weight	Volume
1.36 kg	2.37 l	Corn meal or Farina	3 lb	2 ½ qt
21 g	22 ml	Salt	¾ oz	1 ½ tbsp
1.82 kg	1.89 l	Water, cold	4 lb	2 qt
7.26 kg	7.57 l	Water, boiling	16 lb	2 gal

Mix salt and corn meal or farina with cold water. Stir into boiling water. Cook 15 minutes, stirring frequently. Yield—50 Servings (6¾ oz/190 g).

Metric		Ingredients	U.S.	
1.36 kg	1.89 l	Hominy Grits	3 lb	2 qt
21 g	22 ml	Salt	¾ oz	1 ½ tbsp
10.89 kg	11.37 l	Water, boiling	24 lb	3 gal

Add salt to boiling water. Add grits gradually, stirring vigorously. Cover and cook at low heat for 25–30 minutes, stirring occasionally. Approximate yield—50 Servings (5 oz/142 g).

Metric		Ingredients	U.S.	
1.82 kg		Macaroni, Noodles, or Spaghetti	4 lb	
114 g	118 ml	Salt	4 oz	½ cup
10.89 kg	11.37 l	Water, boiling	24 lb	3 gal
57 g	59 ml	Salad Oil	2 oz	¼ cup

Break into desired lengths. Add salt and oil to boiling water. Boil macaroni 5–7 minutes, noodles 4–5 minutes, and spaghetti 6–8 minutes or until tender. Drain; rinse with cold water. Drain well. Approximate yield—12 lb/5.45 kg.

Metric		Ingredients	U.S.	
1.36 kg	4.26 l	Oatmeal, quick	3 lb	4 ½ qt
21 g	22 ml	Salt	¾ oz	1 ½ tbsp
7.72 kg	8.53 l	Water, boiling	17 lb	2 ¼ gal

Add salt to boiling water. Stir in oatmeal. Reduce heat. Simmer 3 minutes. Turn off heat, cover, and let stand 5 minutes. Approximate yield—50 Servings (5 oz/142 g).

Metric		Ingredients	U.S.		
1.59 kg	1.89 l	Rice	3 lb,	8 oz	2 qt
28 g	30 ml	Salt		1 oz	2 tbsp
3.63 kg	3.79 l	Water, boiling	8 lb		1 gal
57 g	59 ml	Salad Oil		2 oz	¼ cup

Add salt and oil to boiling water. Stir in rice. Reduce heat. Cover tightly and continue cooking—in moderate oven for 25 minutes, in steam cooker for 25–30 minutes, or on range top for 20–25 minutes—until water is absorbed and rice is tender. Approximate yield—7 qt/6.63 l.

Cheese Dishes

Mexican Cheese Scramble
48 Servings (½ cup/118 ml)

Metric		Ingredients	U.S.	
Weight	Volume		Weight	Volume
1.70 kg	3.56 l	Cheddar Cheese, grated	3 lb, 12 oz	3 ¾ qt
227 g	237 ml	Butter or Margarine	8 oz	1 cup
2.04 kg	2.15 l	Corn, cream-style	4 lb, 8 oz	2 ¼ qt
454 g	947 ml	Green Pepper, chopped	1 lb	1 qt
151 g	237 ml	Onions, finely chopped	5 ⅓ oz	1 cup
340 g	355 ml	Eggs, slightly beaten (6 lge)	12 oz	1 ½ cups
43 g	45 ml	Salt	1 ½ oz	3 tbsp
7 g	15 ml	Paprika	¼ oz	1 tbsp
907 g	947 ml	Tomato Puree	2 lb	1 qt
1.82 kg	48 slices	Toast	4 lb	48 slices

Procedure

1. Melt cheese and butter or margarine in double boiler. Add corn, green pepper, and onions. Cook until green pepper is almost tender.
2. Add eggs to hot mixture by first adding small amount of hot mixture to eggs and then stirring into hot mixture until well-blended.
3. Add salt, paprika, and puree. Heat thoroughly.
4. Serve on toast. Garnish with crisp bacon or browned link sausage.

Cheese and Corn Pudding
50 Servings (6 oz/170 g)
Bake, 325°F/163°C, 1 hr

Metric		Ingredients	U.S.	
Weight	Volume		Weight	Volume
227 g	237 ml	Shortening	8 oz	1 cup
454 g	947 ml	Green Pepper, chopped	1 lb	1 qt
1.47 kg	1.54 l	Corn, whole kernel	3 lb, 4 oz	6 ½ cups
397 g	355 ml	Egg Yolks, beaten (18 med)	14 oz	1 ½ cups
3.63 kg	3.79 l	Milk, scalded	8 lbs	1 gal
907 g	1.89 l	Bread Crumbs	2 lbs	2 qt
907 g	1.89 l	Cheese, ground	2 lbs	2 qt
57 g	60 ml	Salt	2 oz	4 tbsp
	2 ½ ml	Pepper		½ tsp
	2 ½ ml	Paprika		½ tsp
7 g	15 ml	Mustard, dry	¼ oz	1 tbsp
511 g	533 ml	Egg Whites, stiffly beaten (18 med)	1 lb, 2 oz	2 ¼ cups

Procedure

1. Sauté green pepper in shortening. Drain corn. Mix all ingredients, except egg whites. Fold in whites.
2. Divide mixture into 2 greased pans (12×20×2 in).
3. Bake at 325°F/163°C, 1 hour, or until inserted knife blade comes out clean.

Cheese Fondue

50 Servings (5 ½ oz/156 g)
Bake, 350°F/177°C, 30–40 min

Metric		Ingredients	U.S.		
Weight	Volume		Weight		Volume
227 g	355 ml	Onions, chopped	8 oz		1 ½ cups
227 g	474 ml	Green Pepper, chopped	8 oz		2 cups
227 g	316 ml	Pimiento, chopped	8 oz		1 ⅓ cups
227 g	237 ml	Shortening, melted	8 oz		1 cup
43 g	45 ml	Salt	1 ½ oz		3 tbsp
	5 ml	Paprika			1 tsp
7 g	15 ml	Mustard, dry	¼ oz		1 tbsp
21 g	20 ml	Worcestershire Sauce	¾ oz		4 tsp
1.36 kg	2.84 l	Cheddar Cheese, ground	3 lb		3 qt
2.72 kg	2.84 l	Milk, scalded	6 lb		3 qt
907 g	2.13 l	Bread, soft, diced	2 lb		2 ¼ qt
681 g	632 ml	Eggs Yolks, beaten (32 med)	1 lb,	8 oz	2 ⅔ cups
907 g	947 ml	Egg Whites, beaten (32 med)	2 lb		1 qt

Procedure

1. Sauté onions, green pepper, and pimiento in shortening. Add salt, paprika, mustard, and Worcestershire sauce.
2. Stir vegetable mixture and cheese into hot milk, stirring until cheese is melted. Pour over bread. Cool slightly. Add beaten egg yolks, tossing mixture lightly to mix.
3. Fold in beaten egg whites. Divide mixture into 2 greased serving pans (12×20×2 in).
4. Bake at 350°F/177°F for 30 or 40 minutes, or until inserted knife blade comes out clean. Serve with parsley, tomato, or green pea sauce.

Tomato Rarebit (Ringtum Diddy)

48 Servings (½ cup/118 g)

Metric		Ingredients	U.S.		
Weight	Volume		Weight		Volume
170 g	178 ml	Butter or Margarine	6 oz		¾ cup
283 g	592 ml	Flour, bread	10 oz		2 ½ cups
3.18 kg	3.31 l	Milk	7 lb		3 ½ qt
1.82 kg	3.79 l	Cheddar Cheese, grated	4 lb		4 qt
907 g	947 ml	Tomato Puree	2 lb		1 qt
	5 ml	Soda			1 tsp
	15 ml	Mustard, dry			1 tbsp
	⅝ ml	Cayenne Pepper			⅛ tsp
114 g	118 ml	Worcestershire Sauce	4 oz		½ cup
114 g	118 ml	Sugar	4 oz		½ cup
43 g	45 ml	Salt	1 ½ oz		3 tbsp
	5 ml	Onion Salt			1 tsp

Procedure

1. Melt butter or margarine, add flour, and blend. Cook 3 minutes. Add milk slowly, stirring to prevent lumping. Cook until thickened.
2. Add remaining ingredients. Stir until smooth.
3. Serve on crackers, toast, or rice.

Cheese Soufflé

48 Servings (5 oz/142 g)
Bake, 300°F/149°C, 1–1 ½ hrs

| Metric | | Ingredients | U.S. | |
Weight	Volume		Weight	Volume
255 g	533 ml	Flour, all-purpose	9 oz	2 ¼ cups
510 g	533 ml	Margarine, melted	1 lb, 2 oz	2 ¼ cups
2.72 kg	2.84 l	Milk, hot	6 lb	3 qt
28 g	30 ml	Salt	1 oz	2 tbsp
	⅝ ml	Cayenne Pepper		⅛ tsp
28 g	30 ml	Prepared Mustard	1 oz	2 tbsp
	2 ½ ml	Worcestershire Sauce		½ tsp
907 g	1.89 l	Cheddar Cheese	2 lb	2 qt
1.02 kg	947 ml	Eggs Yolks, beaten (48 med)	2 lb, 4 oz	1 qt
1.36 kg	1.42 l	Egg Whites, stiffly beaten (48 med)	3 lb	1 ½ qt

Procedure

1. Add flour to melted margarine and stir until smooth. Add seasonings to roux and blend.
2. Add roux to hot milk, stirring constantly. Cook to a thick, smooth sauce.
3. Remove from heat. Add grated cheese and stir until well-blended.
4. Add small amount of hot cheese sauce to slightly beaten egg yolks. Then stir egg yolk mixture into cheese sauce.
5. Fold cheese mixture into stiffly beaten egg whites. (The egg whites should be stiff but not dry.)
6. Pour 5 ½ qts/5.21 l cheese soufflé mixture into 2 serving pans (12 × 20 × 2), greased in the bottom only.
7. Bake pans of soufflé in pans of hot water at 300°F/149°C for 1 to 1 ½ hours, or until a knife blade inserted in the center of the soufflé comes out clean. Serve immediately.

Welsh Rarebit

50 Servings (½ cup/118 ml)

| Metric | | Ingredients | U.S. | |
Weight	Volume		Weight	Volume
255 g	266 ml	Butter or Margarine	9 oz	1 ⅛ cups
255 g	533 ml	Flour, bread	9 oz	2 ¼ cups
28 g	30 ml	Salt	1 oz	2 tbsp
	3 ¾ ml	Pepper, white		¾ tsp
24 g	25 ml	Worcestershire Sauce		1 ⅔ tbsp
	7 ½ ml	Mustard, dry		1 ½ tsp
3.41 kg	3.56 l	Milk	7 lb, 8 oz	3 ¾ qt
2.04 kg	4.26 l	Cheddar Cheese, grated	4 lb, 8 oz	4 ½ qt

Procedure

1. Melt butter or margarine. Add flour and seasonings. Blend. Cook over low heat 3 to 5 minutes. Stir while cooking.
2. Add milk slowly, stirring until mixture is thick and flour loses its raw taste. Add cheese and blend.
3. Serve on toasted buns.

Cheese and Vegetable Shortcake
50 Servings (½ cup)

Metric		Ingredients	U.S.	
Weight	Volume		Weight	Volume
227 g	237 ml	Margarine	8 oz	1 cup
227 g	355 ml	Onions, chopped	8 oz	1 ½ cups
454 g	947 ml	Celery, chopped	1 lb	1 qt
170 g	355 ml	Flour, bread	6 oz	1 ½ cups
2.95 kg	1 No. 10 can	Tomatoes, canned	6 lb, 8 oz	1 No. 10 can
567 g	1.03 l	Green Beans, cooked, drained	1 lb, 4 oz	4 ⅓ cups
340 g	533 ml	Carrots, chopped, cooked, drained	12 oz	2 ¼ cups
28 g	30 ml	Salt	1 oz	2 tbsp
28 g	30 ml	Sugar	1 oz	2 tbsp
	1 ¼ ml	Pepper		¼ tsp
1.36 kg	2.84 l	Cheese, sharp Cheddar, ground	3 lb	3 qt
	50	Biscuits		50

Procedure

1. Sauté onions and celery in margarine slowly until tender. Add flour and stir until smooth.
2. Add tomatoes and cheese, stirring constantly until sauce is thickened and the cheese has melted. Add green beans and carrots.
3. Serve the sauce over hot biscuits.

Fluffy Cheese-Rice Omelet
50 Servings (4½ oz/121 g)
Bake, 325°F/163°C, 45–60 min

Metric		Ingredients	U.S.	
Weight	Volume		Weight	Volume
681 g	829 ml	Rice, uncooked	1 lb, 8 oz	3 ½ cups
15 g	15 ml	Salt	½ oz	1 tbsp
2.27 kg	2.37 l	Water, boiling	5 lb	2 ½ qt
793 g	741 ml	Egg Yolks (36 med)	1 lb, 12 oz	3 ⅛ cups
149 g	178 ml	Butter or Margarine, melted	5 ¼ oz	¾ cup
43 g	45 ml	Salt	1 ½ oz	3 tbsp
	2 ½ ml	Pepper		½ tsp
681 g	1.42 l	Cheddar Cheese, grated	1 lb, 8 oz	1 ½ qt
2.72 kg	2.84 l	Milk, warm	6 lb	3 qt
1.02 kg	1.07 l	Egg Whites (36 med)	2 lb, 4 oz	4 ½ cups
28 g	30 ml	Worcestershire Sauce	1 oz	2 tbsp

Procedure

1. Add rice and salt to boiling water. Stir and cover tightly. Cook on low heat for about 15 minutes. Remove from heat and let stand covered for 10 minutes.
2. Beat egg yolks well. Add butter or margarine, salt, and pepper.
3. Combine cheese with warm milk and stir until melted. Add egg yolk mixture slowly, stirring constantly. Add to rice.
4. Beat egg whites until stiff but not dry. Fold egg whites and Worcestershire sauce into rice mixture. Divide into 2 greased pans (12 × 20 × 2 in).
5. Bake at 325°F/163°C for 45 to 60 minutes or until a knife blade inserted comes out clean.

Note: This has a custard-like consistency. It is very nice served with Pea and Pimiento Sauce or Asparagus Sauce.

Egg Dishes

Egg Cutlets
50 Servings (6.6 oz/179 g)
Deep Fry, 350°F/177°C

Metric		Ingredients	U.S.	
Weight	**Volume**		**Weight**	**Volume**
5.22 kg		Eggs, hard-cooked, cubed (8 ½ doz)	11 lb, 8 oz	5 ¾ qt
454 g	474 ml	Butter or Margarine	1 lb	2 cups
340 g	711 ml	Flour, bread	12 oz	3 cups
1.82 kg	1.89 l	Milk	4 lb	2 qt
43 g	45 ml	Salt	1 ½ oz	3 tbsp
	5 ml	Worcestershire Sauce		1 tsp
	5 ml	Paprika		1 tsp
28 g	30 ml	Onion Juice	1 oz	2 tbsp
	2 ½ ml	Pepper, white		½ tsp
454 g	474 ml	Milk	1 lb	2 cups
1.06 kg	2.37 l	Bread Crumbs	2 lb, 5 ⅓ oz	2 ½ qt

Procedure

1. Melt butter or margarine, add flour, and blend. Cook 3 minutes. Add milk slowly, stirring to prevent lumping. Cook until thickened and flour loses its raw flavor. Add seasonings.
2. Fold eggs into sauce and cool mixture.
3. Measuring with a No. 10 dipper, shape into cutlets, about ½ inch thick.
4. Dip cutlets in milk, and then in bread crumbs. Refrigerate for 2 hours or longer. If refrigerated overnight, remove from refrigerator an hour before cooking.
5. Fry in deep fat at 350°F/177°C until golden brown. Serve with strips of bacon, creamed ham, peas, or shrimp.

Egg Timbales
50 Servings (5.3 oz/150 g)
Bake, 275°F/135°C, 1 hr

Metric		Ingredients	U.S.	
Weight	**Volume**		**Weight**	**Volume**
340 g	355 ml	Butter or Margarine	12 oz	1 ½ cups
170 g	355 ml	Flour, bread	6 oz	1 ½ cups
4.08 kg	4.26 l	Milk	9 lb	4 ½ qt
	1 ¼ ml	Celery Salt		¼ tsp
35 g	37 ml	Salt	1 ¼ oz	2 ½ tbsp
	1 ¼ ml	Pepper, white		¼ tsp
2.95 kg	3.08 l	Eggs, slightly beaten (52 lge)	6 lb, 8 oz	3 ¼ qts

Procedure

1. Make white sauce with butter or margarine, flour, and milk. Add seasonings. Pour over slightly beaten eggs.
2. Divide into 2 greased serving pans (12 × 20 × 2 in).
3. Bake at 275°F/135°C for 1 hour or until inserted knife blade comes out clean.

Note: 1 lb/454 g seafood, chopped, cooked ham, or poultry may be added.

Mushroom Omelet

48 Servings (4.4 oz/124 g)
Bake, 275 °F/135°C, 30 min

Metric		Ingredients	U.S.	
Weight	Volume		Weight	Volume
454 g	474 ml	Butter or Margarine	1 lb	2 cups
227 g	474 ml	Flour, bread	8 oz	2 cups
2.72 kg	2.84 l	Milk, hot	6 lb	3 qt
28 g	30 ml	Salt	1 oz	2 tbsp
	2 ½ ml	Pepper		½ tsp
1.22 kg	1.27 l	Eggs, separated (24 med)	2 lb, 11 oz	5 ⅜ cups
1.36 kg	4.26 l	Mushrooms, diced	3 lb	4 ½ qt
227 g	237 ml	Butter or Margarine	8 oz	1 cup

Procedure

1. Make white sauce with butter or margarine, flour, milk, and seasonings.
2. Beat egg yolks. Add to hot sauce by first adding a little hot sauce to yolks and then stirring them into sauce. Stir constantly.
3. Sauté mushrooms in butter or margarine and add to mixture.
4. Beat whites until stiff but not dry. Fold into mixture.
5. Grease 2 pans (12 × 20 × 2 in) on bottom only. Divide mixture into pans.
6. Bake at 275°F/135°C for 30 minutes or until an inserted knife blade comes out clean.

Plain Soufflé

50 Servings (4 ½ oz/128 g)
Bake, 275°F/135°C, 1 hr

Metric		Ingredients	U.S.	
Weight	Volume		Weight	Volume
454 g	474 ml	Butter or Margarine	1 lb	2 cups
454 g	947 ml	Flour, bread	1 lb	1 qt
3.63 kg	3.79 l	Milk	8 lb	4 qt
28 g	30 ml	Salt	1 oz	2 tbsp
	1 ¼ ml	Pepper, white		¼ tsp
	2 ½ ml	Worcestershire Sauce		½ tsp
2.04 kg	2.13 l	Eggs, separated (41 med)	4 lb, 8 oz	2 ¼ qt

Procedure

1. Make white sauce with butter or margarine, flour, milk, and seasonings. Cool to 120°F/49°C.
2. Beat egg yolks slightly. Stir into white sauce.
3. Beat whites until stiff but not dry. Pour sauce slowly over whites while operating mixer at low speed.
4. Grease 2 serving pans (12 × 20 × 2 in) on bottom only, and divide soufflé into pans, using care to distribute egg white evenly.
5. Bake at 275°F/135°C for an hour or until inserted knife blade comes out clean.

Note: 1 lb/454 g of shrimp, crabmeat, chicken, or vegetable may be added to the soufflé if desired, by folding into the sauce before adding whites. Serve soufflé with a modification of white or Béchamel sauce.

Egg Foo Yung
50 Servings (4 oz/114 g)
Pan Fry

Metric		Ingredients	U.S.			
Weight	Volume		Weight		Volume	
227 g	237 ml	Butter or Margarine		8 oz	1 cup	
681 g	947 ml	Meat, cold, chopped, or Small Shrimp	1 lb,	8 oz	1 qt	
681 g	947 ml	Celery, diced	1 lb,	8 oz	1 qt	
793 g	1.81 l	Onions, chopped	1 lb,	12 oz	1 ¼ qt	
907 g	2 No. 2 ½ cans	Bean Sprouts, drained	2 lb		2 No. 2 ½ cans	
2.38 kg	2.48 l	Eggs, well-beaten (48 med)	5 lb,	4 oz	2 ⅝ qt	
43 g	45 ml	Salt		1 ½ oz	3 tbsp	
	5 ml	Pepper			1 tsp	
57 g	60 ml	Soy Sauce		2 oz	4 tbsp	

Procedure

1. Brown meat lightly in butter or margarine. Remove from fat. Add celery and onions and cook until partly tender and brown.
2. Combine all ingredients.
3. Cook portions separately on griddle or in individual fry pans, lightly greased. Use a No.12 scoop for dipping.

Macaroni, Noodle, and Spaghetti Dishes

Macaroni Milanese
50 Servings (4.6 oz/132 g)
Bake, 425°F/218°C, 30 min

Metric		Ingredients	U.S.		
Weight	Volume		Weight		Volume
1.02 kg	1.89 l	Macaroni, uncooked, 1-in	2 lb,	4 oz	2 qt
1.82 kg	1.89 l	Tomato Puree	4 lb		2 qt
	5 ml	Peppercorns			1 tsp
	1 leaf	Bay Leaf			1 leaf
28 g	30 ml	Sugar		1 oz	2 tbsp
227 g	316 ml	Onions, finely chopped		8 oz	1 ⅓ cups
340 g	355 ml	Butter or Margarine		12 oz	1 ½ cups
170 g	355 ml	Flour, bread		6 oz	1 ½ cups
1.82 kg	1.89 l	Brown Stock, hot	4 lb		2 qt
1.14 kg	2.37 l	Ham, chopped	2 lb,	8 oz	2 ½ qt

Procedure

1. Cook macaroni in boiling, salted water until tender. Drain, rinse, and drain thoroughly.
2. Simmer together puree, peppercorns, bay leaf, and sugar for 20 minutes. Strain.
3. Sauté onions in margarine, add flour, and blend. Slowly add browned stock, stirring until smooth.
Add strained tomato mixture and simmer for 15 minutes.
4. Arrange alternate layers of macaroni and ham in 2 greased serving pans (12 × 20 × 2 in). Pour tomato mixture over top.
5. Bake at 425°F/218°C for 30 minutes.

Italian Macaroni

50 Servings (5 oz/142 g)

Bake, 350°F/177°C, 30 min

Metric		Ingredients	U.S.	
Weight	Volume		Weight	Volume
907 g	1.66 l	Macaroni, uncooked	2 lb	1¾ qt
340 g	355 ml	Butter or Margarine	12 oz	1½ cups
283 g	474 ml	Onions, chopped	10 oz	2 cups
340 g	711 ml	Green Pepper, chopped	12 oz	3 cups
170 g	355 ml	Flour, bread	6 oz	1½ cups
2.95 kg	1 No. 10 can	Tomato Puree, hot	6 lb, 8 oz	1 No. 10 can
28 g	30 ml	Salt	1 oz	2 tbsp
14 g	15 ml	Worcestershire Sauce	½ oz	1 tbsp
	5 ml	Basil, dry, crushed		1 tsp
454 g	947 ml	Cheddar Cheese, grated	1 lb	1 qt

Procedure

1. Cook macaroni in boiling, salted water until tender. Drain, rinse in cold water, and drain thoroughly.
2. Sauté onions and green pepper in butter or margarine until tender, but do not brown. Add flour, stirring until smooth. Add tomato puree, and seasonings. Stir until thickened. Add macaroni and mix well.
3. Divide mixture into 2 greased pans (12 × 20 × 2 in). Sprinkle with cheese and bake at 350°F/177°C until browned (about 30 min).

Macaroni and Cheese

50 Servings (6.5 oz/184 g)

Bake, 350°F/177°C, 30 min

Metric		Ingredients	U.S.	
Weight	Volume		Weight	Volume
1.36 kg	2.52 l	Macaroni, uncooked	3 lb	2⅔ qt
681 g	711 ml	Butter or Margarine	1 lb, 8 oz	3 cups
340 g	711 ml	Flour, pastry	12 oz	3 cups
43 g	45 ml	Salt	1½ oz	3 tbsp
	⅝ ml	Curry Powder		⅛ tsp
	1¼ ml	Mustard, dry		½ tsp
	10 ml	Pepper		2 tsp
5.44 kg	5.68 l	Milk	12 lb	1½ gal
28 g	30 ml	Worcestershire Sauce	1 oz	2 tbsp
1.36 kg	2.84 l	Cheddar Cheese, grated	3 lb	3 qt

Procedure

1. Cook macaroni in 2 gal/7.57 l of water with 6 tbsp/90 ml salt and ¼ cup/59 ml of oil until tender. Drain, rinse, and drain thoroughly.
2. Make white sauce with butter or margarine, flour, seasonings, and milk. Stir in Worcestershire sauce and 2½ lb /1.14 kg cheese. Stir well until cheese is melted and sauce is smooth.
3. Mix sauce with macaroni. Divide mixture into 2 well-greased serving pans (12 × 20 × 2 in). Sprinkle 4 oz/114 g cheese on top of each pan of macaroni and garnish with paprika.
4. Bake at 350°F/177°C until thoroughly heated (about 30 min).

Note: Mixture appears moist, but upon baking has firm consistency.

Macaroni, Broccoli, and Cheese

50 Servings (5.8 oz/165 g)
Bake, 350° F/177°C, 30 min

Metric		Ingredients	U.S.	
Weight	Volume		Weight	Volume
1.36 kg	2.53 l	Macaroni, uncooked	3 lb	2 ⅔ qt
227 g	237 ml	Butter or Margarine	8 oz	1 cup
170 g	355 ml	Flour, all-purpose	6 oz	1 ½ cups
28 g	30 ml	Salt	1 oz	2 tbsp
	5 ml	Pepper		1 tsp
2.72 kg	2.84 l	Milk	6 lb	3 qt
907 g	948 ml	Salad Dressing	2 lb	1 qt
1.36 kg	2.84 l	Cheddar Cheese, grated	3 lb	3 qt
1.36 kg	2.84 l	Broccoli, chopped	3 lb	3 qt
198 g	947 ml	Bread crumbs, buttered	7 oz	2 cups

Procedure

1. Cook macaroni in salted water until tender. Drain and rinse with cold water.
2. Make white sauce with butter or margarine, flour, seasonings, and milk.
3. Blend white sauce and salad dressing (cooked or mayonnaise type). Mix in half of cheese and the macaroni. Divide into 2 greased serving pans (12 × 20 × 2 in). Distribute chopped broccoli over the top and sprinkle with the other half of the cheese and the bread crumbs.
4. Bake at 350°F/177°C until brown and the broccoli is tender (about 30 min).

Macaroni and Mushroom Casserole

50 Servings (6.4 oz/180 g)
Bake, 375°F/190°C, 40 min

Metric		Ingredients	U.S.	
Weight	Volume		Weight	Volume
907 g	1.66 l	Macaroni, uncooked	2 lb	1 ¾ qt
227 g	237 ml	Butter or Margarine	8 oz	1 cup
907 g	3.31 l	Mushrooms, sliced	2 lb	3 ½ qt
170 g	237 ml	Onions, chopped	6 oz	1 cup
227 g	474 ml	Flour, bread	8 oz	2 cups
3.63 kg	3.79 l	Milk	8 lb	1 gal
907 g	1.89 l	Cheddar Cheese, grated	2 lb	2 qt
43 g	45 ml	Salt	1 ½ oz	3 tbsp
	7 ½ ml	Pepper		1 ½ tsp
198 g	474 ml	Bread Crumbs	7 oz	2 cups
114 g	118 ml	Butter or Margarine	4 oz	½ cup

Procedure

1. Cook macaroni in boiling, salted water until tender. Drain and rinse.
2. Sauté onions and mushrooms in butter or margarine, browning slightly. Add flour, stirring until smooth.
3. Add milk, stirring until mixture is thick and flour is cooked. Stir in cheese, salt, and pepper, stirring until cheese is melted.
4. Arrange macaroni and sauce in alternate layers in 2 greased serving pans (12 × 20 × 2 in). Sprinkle with buttered crumbs.
5. Bake at 375°F/190°C for 40 minutes.

Macaroni with Vegetables
50 Servings (7 ½ oz/212 g)
Bake, 350°F/177°C, 30 min

| Metric | | Ingredients | U.S. | |
Weight	Volume		Weight	Volume
681 g	1.26 l	Macaroni, uncooked	1 lb, 8 oz	1 ⅓ qt
1.59 kg	2.37 l	Carrots, diced	3 lb, 8 oz	2 ½ qt
1.36 kg	1.26 l	Peas	3 lb	1 ⅓ qt
907 g	1.66 l	Turnips, diced	2 lb	1 ¾ cups
227 g	355 ml	Onions, diced	8 oz	1 ½ cups
681 g	1.42 l	Celery, diced	1 lb, 8 oz	1 ½ qt
283 g	296 ml	Butter or Margarine	10 oz	1 ¼ cups
340 g	711 ml	Flour, all-purpose	12 oz	3 cups
2.72 kg	2.84 l	Milk, hot	6 lb	3 qt
	5 ml	Pepper		1 tsp
43 g	45 ml	Salt	1 ½ oz	3 tbsp
907 g	1.89 l	Cheddar Cheese, grated	2 lb	2 qt

Procedure

1. Cook macaroni in boiling, salted water. Drain and rinse.
2. Steam carrots, turnips, onions, and celery until partly cooked.
3. Make white sauce with shortening, flour, and milk. Add seasonings and cheese and stir until smooth and cheese is melted. Combine all ingredients.
4. Divide into 2 greased pans (12 × 20 × 2 in). Top with buttered crumbs.
5. Bake at 350°F/177°C until brown (about 30 min).
Note: Serve with strips of crisp bacon.

Sausage Casserole
60 Servings (7.4 oz/205 g)
Bake, 350°F/177°C, 45–60 min

| Metric | | Ingredients | U.S. | |
Weight	Volume		Weight	Volume
1.02 kg	2.84 l	Noodles, uncooked	2 lb, 4 oz	3 qt
1.36 kg	2.84 l	Bread Crumbs, dry	3 lb	3 qt
1.82 kg	1.89 l	Country Sausage	4 lb	2 qt
340 g	355 ml	Ground Beef	12 oz	1 ½ cups
2.95 kg	1 No. 10 can	Tomatoes, canned, chopped	6 lb, 8 oz	1 No. 10 can
681 g	711 ml	Catsup	1 lb, 8 oz	3 cups
28 g	30 ml	Salt	1 oz	2 tbsp
454 g	947 ml	Sharp Cheese, grated	1 lb	1 qt
227 g	355 ml	Onion, chopped	8 oz	1 ½ cups
1.82 kg	1.89 l	Water	4 lb	2 qt

Procedure

1. Cook noodles in boiling, salted water until tender. Wash and drain.
2. Combine bread crumbs, sausage, and beef. Mix well. Distribute meat through noodles. Divide mixture into 2 greased pans (12 × 20 × 2 in).
3. Combine remaining ingredients and spread over top of casseroles.
4. Bake at 350°F/177°C until meat is cooked, about 45 to 60 minutes.

Lasagna

60 Servings (7.4 oz/205 g)
Bake, 350°F/177°C, 1 ½ hrs

Metric		Ingredients	U.S.	
Weight	Volume		Weight	Volume
1.36 kg		Lasagna Noodles, uncooked	3 lb	
8.17 kg	8.53 l	Water, boiling	18 lb	2 ¼ gal
57 g	59 ml	Salt	2 oz	¼ cup
57 g	59 ml	Salad Oil	2 oz	¼ cup
283 g	296 ml	Eggs, beaten (5 lge)	10 oz	1 ¼ cups
681 g	1.07 l	Onions, finely chopped	1 lb, 8 oz	4 ½ cups
14 g	4 cloves	Garlic, minced	½ oz	4 cloves
85 g	79 ml	Oil, for meat sauce	3 oz	⅓ cup
1.59 kg	1.66 l	Ground Beef, lean	3 lb, 8 oz	1 ¾ qt
454 g	474 ml	Mushrooms, canned, chopped	1 lb	2 cups
21 g	22 ml	Salt	¾ oz	1 ½ tbsp
681 g	711 ml	Tomato Paste	1 lb, 8 oz	3 cups
907 g	947 ml	Tomato Sauce	2 lb	1 qt
	15 ml	Oregano, dry, crushed		1 tbsp
	5 ml	Basil, dry, crushed		1 tsp
1.36 kg	1.42 l	Spinach, frozen, chopped	3 lb	1 ½ qt
21 g	22 ml	Salt	¾ oz	1 ½ tbsp
907 g	947 ml	Cottage Cheese	2 lb	1 qt
283 g	296 ml	Eggs, beaten (5 lge)	10 oz	1 ¼ cups
227 g	474 ml	Parmesan Cheese, grated	8 oz	2 cups
1.02 kg	2.13 l	Cheddar Cheese, grated	2 lb, 4 oz	2 ¼ qt

Procedure

1. Cook noodles in boiling water with salt and salad oil, until tender. Rinse with cold water and drain thoroughly. Toss lightly with beaten eggs, using care not to break noodles.
2. Sauté onions and garlic in 3 oz/85 g oil. Add meat, brown, and separate. Drain off excess fat. Add mushrooms and liquid, salt, tomato paste, sauce, oregano, and basil. Mix well. Simmer, adding water if needed.
3. Blend spinach, salt, cottage cheese, beaten eggs, and parmesan cheese.
4. Layer half of each mixture into 2 greased serving pans (12 × 20 × 2 in), beginning with meat sauce. Cover with noodles, add spinach, cover with noodles, and top with meat sauce.
5. Bake at 350°F/177°C for 1 hour. Spread grated cheddar cheese evenly over top and bake for another 20 minutes.

Baked Chicken and Noodles
50 Servings (6.7 oz/190 g)
Bake, 400°F/205°C, 30 min

| Metric | | Ingredients | U.S. | |
Weight	Volume		Weight	Volume
907 g	2.52 l	Noodles, uncooked	2 lb	2 ⅔ qt
7.26 kg	7.58 l	Water, boiling	16 lb	2 gal
57 g	60 ml	Salt	2 oz	4 tbsp
114 g	118 ml	Butter or Margarine	4 oz	½ cup
454 g	474 ml	Milk, hot	1 lb	2 cups
283 g	296 ml	Butter or Margarine	10 oz	1 ¼ cups
170 g	355 ml	Flour, all-purpose	6 oz	1 ½ cups
2.50 kg	2.60 l	Milk, hot	5 lb, 8 oz	2 ¾ qt
57 g	60 ml	Salt	2 oz	4 tbsp
	10 ml	Pepper		2 tsp
2.50 kg	2.60 l	Chicken Gravy	5 lb, 8 oz	2 ¾ qt
2.27 kg	4.74 l	Chicken, cooked, minced	5 lb	5 qt
227 g	474 ml	Cheddar Cheese, grated	8 oz	2 cups
114 g	355 ml	Bread Crumbs	4 oz	1 ½ cups

Procedure

1. Cook noodles in boiling water with 4 tbsp/60 ml salt. Rinse and drain. Reheat and add 4 oz/114 g butter or margarine and let it be absorbed. Add 2 cups hot milk and let it be absorbed by noodles.
2. Make white sauce with butter or margarine, flour, milk, and seasonings. Mix with chicken gravy.
3. Mix half the sauce with noodles and divide into 2 greased pans (12 × 20 × 2 in). Combine remaining sauce with chicken and spread over noodles. Combine cheese and crumbs and sprinkle over top. Bake at 400°F/205°C until brown.

Italian Delight
50 Servings (7 oz/198 g)
Bake, 350°F/177°C, 30 min

| Metric | | Ingredients | U.S. | |
Weight	Volume		Weight	Volume
907 g	2.53 l	Noodles, uncooked	2 lb	2 ⅔ qt
5.44 kg	5.68 l	Water, boiling	12 lb	1 ½ gal
28 kg	30 ml	Salt	1 oz	2 tbsp
1.36 kg	1.78 l	Beef, cubed	3 lb	7 ½ cups
454 g	947 ml	Green Pepper, chopped	1 lb	1 qt
1.14 kg	1.78 l	Onions, finely chopped	2 lb, 8 oz	7 ½ cups
681 g	2.13 l	Mushrooms, sliced	1 lb, 8 oz	2 ¼ qt
170 g	178 ml	Butter or Margarine	6 oz	¾ cup
1.14 kg	1.18 l	Corn, whole, drained	2 lb, 8 oz	5 cups
2.04 kg	2.13 l	Tomato Soup	4 lb, 8 oz	2 ¼ qt
57 g	355 ml	Parsley, finely chopped	2 oz	1 ½ cup
	7 ½ ml	Worcestershire Sauce		1 ½ tsp
57 g	59 ml	Salt	2 oz	¼ cup
454 g	947 ml	Cheddar Cheese, grated	1 lb	1 qt

1. Cook noodles in boiling salted water until tender. Rinse with cold water and drain thoroughly.
2. Brown cubed beef.
3. Sauté green pepper, onions, and mushrooms (if fresh) in butter or margarine.

4. Combine all ingredients and mix.
5. Divide mixture into 2 serving pans (12 × 20 × 2 in) and bake at 350°F/177°C for 30 minutes or until browned.

Note: If canned mushrooms are used, drain before adding.

Tuna Noodle Casserole

64 Servings
Bake, 350°F/177°C, 30 min

| Metric | | | U.S. | |
Weight	Volume	Ingredients	Weight	Volume
1.36 kg	3.79 l	Noodles	3 lb	4 qt
8.17 kg	8.51 l	Water	18 lb	2 ¼ gal
57 g	59 ml	Salt	2 oz	¼ cup
9 g	10 ml	Celery Salt	⅓ oz	2 tsp
142 g	237 ml	Onion, finely chopped	5 oz	1 cup
907 g	1.89 l	Celery, diced ⅓ inch	2 lb	2 qt
907 g	3.31 l	Mushrooms, sliced	2 lb	3 ½ qt
227 g	237 ml	Butter or Margarine	8 oz	1 cup
2.21 kg	2.60 l	Tuna Fish, undrained	4 lb, 14 oz	2 ¾ qt
340 g	474 ml	Pimientos	12 oz	2 cups
454 g	474 ml	Butter or Margarine	1 lb	2 cups
227 g	474 ml	Flour, all-purpose	8 oz	2 cups
49 g	53 ml	Salt	1 ¾ oz	3 ½ tsp
7 g	15 ml	Pepper, white	¼ oz	1 tbsp
3.63 kg	3.79 l	Milk	8 lb	1 gal
681 g	1.42 l	Cheddar Cheese, grated	1 lb, 8 oz	1 ½ qt
397 g	947 ml	Bread Crumbs	14 oz	1 qt
114 g	118 ml	Butter or Margarine	4 oz	½ cup

Procedure

1. Cook noodles in boiling water to which salt and celery salt have been added. When tender, drain and rinse in cold water. Drain well.
2. Sauté finely chopped onions, celery, and mushrooms until tender in butter or margarine.
3. Flake tuna fish and chop pimientos.
4. Melt butter or margarine, add flour and seasonings, and blend. Slowly add milk. Stir until thickened and smooth. Add cheese and stir until it is well blended.

5. Combine noodles, tuna, vegetables, and cheese sauce.
6. Pour into greased servings pans (12 × 20 × 2 in). Mix bread crumbs with melted butter or margarine and sprinkle on top.
7. Bake at 350°F/177°C for 30 minutes.

Halibut Noodle Casserole

60 Servings (6.6 oz/188 g)
Bake, 325°F/163°C, 1 hr

Metric		Ingredients	U.S.		
Weight	Volume		Weight		Volume
3.63 kg		Halibut, raw	8 lb		
454 g	189 ml	Noodles, fine, uncooked	1 lb		2 qt
340 g	355 ml	Butter or Margarine		12 oz	1 ½ cups
170 g	355 ml	Flour, all-purpose		6 oz	1 ½ cups
21 g	22 ml	Salt		¾ oz	1 ½ tbsp
	2 ½ ml	Pepper			½ tsp
	5 ml	Paprika			1 tsp
3.63 kg	3.79 l	Milk, hot	8 lb		1 gal
681 g	1.42 l	Cheddar Cheese, grated	1 lb,	8 oz	1 ½ qt
28 g	23 ml	Worcestershire Sauce		1 oz	1 ½ tbsp
227 g	237 ml	Lemon Juice		8 oz	1 cup
227 g	474 ml	Cheddar Cheese, grated		8 oz	2 cups

Procedure

1. Measure the fish at its thickest point to determine cooking time. Allow 10 minutes per inch. Steam halibut. Drain; remove skin and bones. Flake.
2. Cook noodles in boiling, salted water until tender. Drain and rinse.
3. Melt butter or margarine. Add flour and stir until smooth. Add seasonings. Add roux to hot milk, stirring constantly. Cook until sauce is thick and there is no starchy flavor. Stir in 1 lb, 8 oz/681 g of cheese until melted. Add Worcestershire sauce and lemon juice. Remove from heat.
4. Mix fish, noodles, and sauce together lightly. Divide into 2 greased serving pans (12 × 20 × 2 in). Sprinkle 4 oz/114 g cheese on top of each casserole.
5. Bake at 325°F/163°C for about 1 hour.

Note: 3 lb/1.36 kg of shrimp and 5 lb/2.27 kg of red snapper may be substituted for the halibut.

Spaghetti Milanese

60 Servings (6.4 oz/181 g)
Bake, 350°F/177°C, 30 min

Metric		Ingredients	U.S.		
Weight	Volume		Weight		Volume
907 g	1.42 l	Onion, chopped	2 lb		1 ½ qt
681 g	1.42 l	Celery, chopped	1 lb,	8 oz	1 ½ qt
340 g	355 ml	Butter or Margarine		12 oz	1 ½ cups
170 g	355 ml	Flour, bread		6 oz	1 ½ cups
4.54 kg	1 ½ No. 10 cans	Tomato Puree	10 lb		1 ½ No. 10 cans
	7 ½ ml	Basil, ground			1 ½ tsp
	2 leaves	Bay Leaves			2 leaves
	⅝ ml	Thyme			⅛ tsp
57 g	60 ml	Salt		2 oz	4 tbsp
114 g	118 ml	Sugar		4 oz	½ cup
	7 ½ ml	Pepper			1 ½ tsp
1.82 kg	3.79 l	Spaghetti, uncooked	4 lb		4 qt
681 g	1.42 l	Sharp Cheddar Cheese, grated	1 lb,	8 oz	1 ½ qt

1. Brown onions and celery in butter or margarine. Add flour and mix until smooth.
2. Add tomato puree and blend. Add spices. Simmer for 2 hours.
3. Cook spaghetti in 3 gal/11.37 l water with ½ cup/118 ml salt. When tender, rinse in cold water and drain well.
4. Combine spaghetti and sauce. Arrange in serving pans, sprinkle with cheese, and bake at 350°F/177°C for 30 minutes.

Italian Spaghetti

60 Servings (9.9 oz/281 g)

Bake, 375°F/190°C, 30 min

Metric		Ingredients	U.S.	
Weight	Volume		Weight	Volume
1.82 kg	1.89 l	Ground Beef	4 lb	2 qt
454 g	711 ml	Onions, chopped	1 lb	3 cups
227 g	474 ml	Green Pepper, chopped	8 oz	2 cups
	1 clove	Garlic, minced		1 clove
5.90 kg	6.15 l	Tomatoes, canned	13 lb	6 ½ qt
	15 ml	Chili Powder		1 tbsp
	5 ml	Paprika		1 tsp
7 g	15 ml	Pepper	¼ oz	1 tbsp
114 g	118 ml	Salt	4 oz	½ cup
57 g	59 ml	Sugar	2 oz	¼ cup
	⅝ ml	Cayenne Pepper		⅛ tsp
28 g	30 ml	Worcestershire Sauce	1 oz	2 tbsp
	5 ml	Oregano		1 tsp
1.82 kg	3.79 l	Spaghetti, uncooked	4 lb	4 qt
227 g	474 ml	Cheddar Cheese, grated	8 oz	2 cups

Procedure

1. Brown meat. Add onions, green pepper, and garlic. Sauté until tender.
2. Add remaining ingredients, except for spaghetti and cheese. Simmer for about 3 hours. Yield: 7 qt /6.63 l sauce.
3. Cook spaghetti in salted water until tender. Drain and rinse. Mix with sauce.
4. Divide into 2 greased serving pans (12 × 20 × 2 in). Sprinkle with cheese using 4 oz/114 g for each pan.
5. Bake at 375°F/190°C for 30 minutes or until thoroughly heated.

Spaghetti Cheese Casserole
50 Servings (7 ½ oz/212 g)
Bake, 350°F/177°C, 30 min

Metric		Ingredients	U.S.	
Weight	Volume		Weight	Volume
1.82 kg	3.79 l	Spaghetti, uncooked	4 lb	4 qt
340 g	355 ml	Butter or Margarine	12 oz	1 ½ cups
170 g	355 ml	Flour, all-purpose	6 oz	1 ½ cups
43 g	45 ml	Salt	1 ½ oz	3 tbsp
	5 ml	Pepper		1 tsp
2.72 kg	2.84 l	Milk	6 lb	3 qt
1.36 kg	2.84 l	Cheddar Cheese, grated	3 lb	3 qt
907 g	1.89 l	Green Pepper, chopped	2 lb	2 qt
	10 ml	Paprika		2 tsp
14 g	15 ml	Worcestershire Sauce	½ oz	1 tbsp

Procedure

1. Break spaghetti into desired lengths and cook in boiling, salted water. Rinse and drain.
2. Make white sauce with butter or margarine, flour, salt, pepper, and milk. Add grated cheese, green pepper, paprika, and Worcestershire sauce. Mix sauce with spaghetti.
3. Divide mixture into 2 greased pans (12 × 20 × 2 in). Sprinkle with paprika.
4. Bake at 350°F/177°C for 30 minutes.

Note: Serve with mushroom sauce. (See modified Béchamel in Sauce Section.)

Rice and Other Cereal Casseroles

Browned Rice
50 Servings (5 oz/142 g)

Metric		Ingredients	U.S.	
Weight	Volume		Weight	Volume
511 g	533 ml	Butter or Margarine	1 lb, 2 oz	2 ¼ cups
1.36 kg	1.66 l	Rice	3 lb	1 ¾ qt
1.82 kg	2.84 l	Onions, finely chopped	4 lb	3 qt
21 g	6 cloves	Garlic, minced	¾ oz	6 cloves
43 g	45 ml	Salt	1 ½ oz	3 tbsp
	2 ½ ml	Pepper		½ tsp
2.72 kg	2.84 l	Bouillon or Consommé	6 lb	3 qt
2.72 kg	2.84 l	Water	6 lb	3 qt

Procedure

1. Melt shortening in frying pan and add rice. Add chopped onions and garlic. Fry until golden brown.
2. Add seasonings to bouillon or consommé and water and heat. Add fried rice to liquid and let simmer in open kettle until rice is cooked and has absorbed the liquid. Cover to retain heat.
3. Yield: 16 pounds or 50 servings (5 oz/142 g).

Note: This is very good served with meat dishes.

Almonds, Cheese, and Rice

50 Servings (6.8 oz/193 g)

Bake, 375°F/190°C, 45–60 min

Metric		Ingredients	U.S.	
Weight	Volume		Weight	Volume
454 g	474 ml	Mushrooms, fresh, sliced	1 lb	2 cups
114 g	158 ml	Onions, chopped	4 oz	2/3 cup
283 g	474 ml	Almonds, chopped	10 oz	2 cups
170 g	178 ml	Butter or Margarine	6 oz	3/4 cup
1.13 kg	1.18 l	Rice, uncooked	2 lb, 8 oz	1 1/4 qt
567 g	1.34 l	Cheddar Cheese, grated	1 lb, 4 oz	5 2/3 cups
340 g	474 ml	Stuffed Olives, sliced	12 oz	2 cups
28 g	178 ml	Parsley, chopped	1 oz	3/4 cup
43 g	45 ml	Salt	1 1/2 oz	3 tbsp
	2 1/2 ml	Pepper		1/2 tsp
6.35 kg	6.63 l	Chick Stock	14 lb	1 3/4 gal

Procedure

1. Sauté mushrooms, onions, and almonds in butter or margarine until lightly browned.
2. Combine with rice, cheese, olives, and parsley. Divide into 2 greased serving pans (12 × 20 × 2 in).
3. Add salt and pepper to chicken stock. Pour stock over mixture in serving pans. Cover and bake for 45 minutes at 375°F/190°C, or until rice is tender.

Almonds, Chicken, and Rice Casserole

50 Servings (7 oz/198 g)

Bake, 350°F/177°C, 1 hr

Metric		Ingredients	U.S.	
Weight	Volume		Weight	Volume
1.02 kg	1.18 l	Rice, converted, raw	2 lb, 4 oz	1 1/4 qt
3.18 kg	3.31 l	Water, boiling	7 lb	3 1/2 qt
454 g	711 ml	Onions, chopped	1 lb	3 cups
340 g	355 ml	Butter or Margarine	12 oz	1 1/2 cups
227 g	474 ml	Flour, bread	8 oz	2 cups
28 g	30 ml	Salt	1 oz	2 tbsp
	5 ml	Pepper		1 tsp
	10 ml	Thyme		2 tsp
1.36 kg	1.42 l	Chicken Broth	3 lb	1 1/2 qt
1.36 kg	1.42 l	Cream, half and half	3 lb	1 1/2 qt
340 g	474 ml	Pimiento, chopped	12 oz	2 cups
85 g	533 ml	Parsley, chopped	3 oz	2 1/4 cups
2.72 kg	3.79 l	Chicken, cooked, cubed	6 lb	1 gal
312 g	474 ml	Almonds, blanched, slivered	11 oz	2 cups

Procedure

1. Stir rice into boiling water. Cover tightly, reduce heat to low, and cook for 20 minutes.
2. Sauté onions in butter and margarine. Add flour and seasonings. Stir until well-mixed. Gradually add chicken broth and cream. Stir and cook until thickened and smooth.
3. Combine all ingredients and mix well. Pour mixture into 2 greased serving pans (12× 20 × 2 in). Bake at 350°F/177°C until lightly browned (about 1 hr).

Beef and Almond Rice

50 Servings (8 oz/227 g)
Bake, 375°F/190°C, 1 hr

| Metric | | Ingredients | U.S. | |
Weight	Volume		Weight	Volume
1.36 kg	1.42 l	Ground Beef	3 lb	1 ½ qt
1.02 kg	3.31 l	Mushrooms, fresh, sliced	2 lb, 4 oz	3 ½ qt
1.56 g	237 ml	Onions, minced	5 ½ oz	1 cup
255 g	355 ml	Almonds, chopped	9 oz	1 ½ cups
1.36 kg	1.66 l	Rice, converted, raw	3 lb	1 ¾ qt
28 g	178 ml	Parsley, chopped	1 oz	¾ cup
170 g	237 ml	Pimiento, chopped	6 oz	1 cup
907 g	1.89 l	Cheddar Cheese, grated	1 lb	2 qt
170 g	178 ml	Beef Soup Base	6 oz	¾ cup
114 g	118 ml	Soy Sauce	4 oz	½ cup
28 g	30 ml	Salt	1 oz	2 tbsp
	5 ml	Pepper		1 tsp
	10 ml	Basil, dry, crushed		2 tsp
5.44 kg	5.68 l	Water, boiling	12 lb	6 qt
454 g	947 ml	Cheddar Cheese, grated	1 lb	1 qt

Procedure

1. Brown beef until pink disappears. Add onions and mushrooms and lightly brown. Add almonds, rice, parsley, pimiento, and cheese.
2. Stir soup base and seasonings into boiling water.
3. Divide meat mixture into 2 greased serving pans (12 × 20 × 2 in) and pour liquid mixture over it. Cover and bake at 375°F/190°C for 1 hour or until liquid has been absorbed.
4. Sprinkle remaining cheese over hot casserole.

Singapore Ham and Rice

50 Servings (5.8 oz/164 g)
Bake, 350°F/177°C, 30 min

| Metric | | Ingredients | U.S. | |
Weight	Volume		Weight	Volume
283 g	296 ml	Butter or Margarine	10 oz	1 ¼ cups
340 g	711 ml	Green Pepper, chopped	12 oz	3 cups
454 g	711 ml	Onions, chopped	1 lb	3 cups
3.41 kg	5.68 l	Ham, cooked, diced	7 lb, 8 oz	6 qt
255 g	355 ml	Brown Sugar	9 oz	1 ½ cups
	15 ml	Curry Powder		1 tbsp
907 g	947 ml	Orange Juice	2 lb	1 qt
21 g	59 ml	Orange Peel, grated	¾ oz	¼ cup
5.44 kg	5.68 l	Rice, cooked	12 lb	6 qt
14 g	15 ml	Salt	½ oz	1 tbsp

Procedure

1. Sauté onions and green pepper in butter or margarine. Add remaining ingredients and mix thoroughly.
2. Divide into 2 serving pans (12 × 20 × 2 in). Cover and bake at 350°F/177°C until liquid is absorbed (about 30 min).

Diced Ham with Rice and Peas

50 Servings (6.6 oz/187 g)

Steam, 20–30 min

| Metric | | Ingredients | U.S. | |
Weight	Volume		Weight	Volume
1.36 kg	1.66 l	Rice, converted, uncooked	3 lb	1 ¾ qt
454 g	711 ml	Onions, chopped	1 lb	3 cups
340 g	355 ml	Shortening or Bacon Fat	12 oz	1 ½ cups
14 g	15 ml	Salt	½ oz	1 tbsp
	2 ½ ml	Pepper		½ tsp
	10 ml	Thyme		2 tsp
170 g	178 ml	Chicken Soup Base	6 oz	¾ cup
4.08 kg	4.26 l	Water, hot	9 lb	1 ⅛ gal
1.36 kg	1.42 l	Ham, cooked, diced	3 lb	1 ½ qt
1.36 kg	2.13 l	Peas, frozen	3 lb	2 ¼ qt
227 g	237 ml	Pimiento, chopped	8 oz	1 cup

Procedure

1. Sauté rice and onions until lightly browned in fat. Add seasonings and soup base dissolved in hot water. Cover tightly and steam at low temperature for 20 minutes, or until rice is tender.

2. Stir diced ham, peas, and pimiento into rice. Simmer for 10 or 15 minutes, or until thoroughly heated.

Cottage Cheese, Rice, and Nut Loaf

50 Servings (7.6 oz/215 g)

Bake, 350°F/177°C, 1 hr

| Metric | | Ingredients | U.S. | |
Weight	Volume		Weight	Volume
793 g	1.89 l	Bread Crumbs	1 lb, 12 oz	2 qt
2.72 kg	2.84 l	Milk	6 lb	3 qt
212 g	207 ml	Egg Yolks, beaten (10 med)	7 ½ oz	⅞ cup
2.38 kg	2.84 l	Rice, cooked	5 lb, 4 oz	3 qt
3.63 kg	3.79 l	Cottage Cheese, ground	8 lb	1 gal
793 g	1.66 l	Walnuts, chopped	1 lb, 12 oz	1 ¾ qt
28 g	178 ml	Parsley, chopped	1 oz	¾ cup
57 g	60 ml	Salt	2 oz	4 tbsp
	5 ml	Pepper		1 tsp
	2 ½ ml	Sage or Poultry Seasoning		½ tsp
283 g	296 ml	Egg Whites, beaten (10 med)	10 oz	1 ¼ cup

Procedure

1. Soak bread crumbs in milk, until soft. Add remaining ingredients except egg whites and mix well.
2. Fold in stiffly beaten egg whites.
3. Divide into 2 greased pans (12 × 20 × 2 in).
4. Bake at 350°F/177°C for 1 hour, or until inserted knife comes out clean.
5. Serve with tomato sauce.

Note: More sage may be used if desired.

Pork and Rice Casserole

48 Servings (5.8 oz/164 g)
Bake, 375°F/190°C, 30 min

| Metric | | | U.S. | |
Weight	Volume	Ingredients	Weight	Volume
681 g	1.42 l	Cheddar Cheese, grated	1 lb, 8 oz	1 ½ qt
1.82 kg	2.37 l	Rice, cooked	4 lb	2 ½ qt
454 g	711 ml	Onions, chopped	1 lb	3 cups
681 g	1.42 l	Celery, chopped	1 lb, 8 oz	1 ½ qt
227 g	474 ml	Green Pepper, chopped	8 oz	2 cups
2.27 kg	2.37 l	Pork, cooked, diced	5 lb	2 ½ qt
454 g	711 ml	Raisins, chopped	1 lb	3 cups
766 g	711 ml	Pineapple, crushed	1 lb, 11 oz	3 cups
28 g	30 ml	Salt	1 oz	2 tbsp
	2 ½ ml	Pepper		½ tsp
	10 ml	Poultry Seasoning		2 tsp
454 g	474 ml	Milk	1 lb	2 cups
114 g	118 ml	Lemon Juice	4 oz	½ cup

Procedure

1. Set aside half of the cheese for topping. Combine all of the other ingredients, including half of the cheese. Spread mixture into 2 serving pans (12 × 20 × 2 in) and sprinkle the cheese over top.

2. Bake at 375°F/190°C until thoroughly heated (about 30 min).

Hamburger, Rice, and Tomato Casserole

48 Servings (6 oz/170 g)
Bake, 350°F/177°C, 1 hr

| Metric | | | U.S. | |
Weight	Volume	Ingredients	Weight	Volume
1.14 kg	1.36 l	Rice, uncooked	2 lb, 8 oz	5 ¾ cups
340 g	533 ml	Onions, finely chopped	12 oz	2 ¼ cups
57 g	59 ml	Shortening	2 oz	¼ cup
1.82 kg	1.89 l	Hamburger	4 lb	2 qt
2.95 kg	3.31 l	Tomatoes	6 lb, 8 oz	1 No. 10 can
	2 ½ ml	Pepper		½ tsp
78 g	82 ml	Salt	2 ¾ oz	5 ½ tbsp
1.36 kg	1.42 l	Water	3 lb	1 ½ qt
57 g	60 ml	Sugar	2 oz	4 tbsp
	10 ml	Chili Powder		2 tsp

Procedure

1. Cook rice until tender in 8 qt/7.57 l boiling water with 4 tbsp salt. Wash and drain. Place 5 pounds/2.27 kg each in 2 greased pans (12 × 20 × 2 in).
2. Sauté onions in shortening. Add hamburger and cook for 10 minutes, stirring frequently.
3. Combine remaining ingredients. Add meat mixture and heat.
4. Scale 6 ¼ lbs/2.84 kg into pans containing rice. Mix thoroughly.
5. Bake at 350°F/177°C for 1 hour. Mark each pan into portions, making six cuts across and four lengthwise, for serving.

Chicken Risotto

75 Servings (8 oz/227 g)
Bake, 425°F/218°C, 25–30 min

Metric		Ingredients	U.S.	
Weight	Volume		Weight	Volume
1.82 kg	2.13 l	Rice, converted, raw	4 lb	2 ¼ qt
454 g	474 ml	Butter or Margarine	1 lb	2 cups
454 g	711 ml	Onions, chopped	1 lb	3 cups
227 g	474 ml	Green Pepper, chopped	8 oz	2 cups
340 g	474 ml	Mushrooms, sliced	12 oz	2 cups
3.63 kg	3.79 l	Chicken Stock	8 lb	1 gal
2.08 kg	1.89 l	Evaporated Milk	4 lb, 9 oz	2 qt
	10 ml	Thyme		2 tsp
	10 ml	Salt		2 tsp
	5 ml	Pepper		1 tsp
75 g	79 ml	Lemon Juice	2 ⅔ oz	⅓ cup
3.41 kg	5.33 l	Chicken, cooked, diced	7 lb, 8 oz	5 ⅝ qt
567 g	947 ml	Peas, frozen	1 lb, 4 oz	1 qt
340 g	711 ml	Cheddar Cheese, grated	12 oz	3 cups

Procedure

1. Brown rice lightly in butter or margarine. Add onions, green pepper, and mushrooms. Cook until onions are transparent. Stir in stock, evaporated milk, seasonings, lemon juice, and diced chicken.
2. Divide mixture into 2 servings pans (12 × 20 × 2 in). Cover and bake at 425°F/218°C for 20 minutes.
3. Stir peas into mixture and sprinkle cheese over the top. Bake, uncovered, 5 or 10 minutes longer until cheese has melted.
4. Serve with cream sauce or chicken gravy.

Broccoli Rice Casserole

48 Servings
Bake, 325°F/163°C, 1 ¼ hrs

Metric		Ingredients	U.S.	
Weight	Volume		Weight	Volume
1.70 kg	2.37 l	Broccoli, chopped	3 lb, 12 oz	2 ½ qt
170 g	178 ml	Butter or Margarine	6 oz	¾ cup
454 g	711 ml	Onions, chopped	1 lb	3 cups
28 g	30 ml	Salt	1 oz	2 tbsp
	5 ml	Pepper		1 tsp
	2 ½ ml	Nutmeg		½ tsp
681 g	711 ml	Eggs, slightly-beaten (12 lge)	1 lb, 8 oz	3 cups
2.72 kg	2.84 l	Milk	6 lb	3 qt
2.07 kg	2.84 l	Rice, long-grained, cooked	4 lb, 9 oz	3 qt
454 g	1.89 l	Sharp Cheese, grated	1 lb	2 qt

Procedure

1. Cook broccoli. Drain well.
2. Sauté onion in butter or margarine. Add seasonings.
3. Combine all of the ingredients and pour into 2 greased serving pans (12 × 20 × 2 in).
4. Bake at 325°F/163°C for 1 ¼ hours or until inserted silver knife comes out clean.
5. Cut each pan 4 × 6.

Fricandellos

50 Servings (8 oz/227 g)

Bake, 350°F/177°C, 1 hr

Metric		Ingredients	U.S.	
Weight	Volume		Weight	Volume
5.44 kg	5.68 l	Ground Beef or Ham, raw	12 lb	1 ½ gal
1.36 kg	1.66 l	Rice, uncooked	3 lb	1 ¾ qt
454 g	474 ml	Eggs, beaten (8 lge)	1 lb	2 cups
907 g	1.42 l	Onions, ground	2 lb	1 ½ qt
43 g	45 ml	Salt	1 ½ oz	3 tbsp
	10 ml	Pepper		2 tsp
368 g	355 ml	Evaporated Milk	13 oz	1 ½ cups
1.82 kg	1.89 l	Tomato Puree	4 lb	2 qt
1.82 kg	1.89 l	Water	4 lb	2 qt
454 g	947 ml	Celery, chopped	1 lb	1 qt
	1 leaf	Bay Leaf		1 leaf
	10 ml	Salt		2 tsp

Procedure

1. Combine ground beef or ham, uncooked rice, eggs, onions, salt, pepper, and evaporated milk. Mold into 100 balls, using a No. 20 scoop. Arrange in serving pans (12 × 20 × 2 in).

2. Cook tomato puree, water, celery, bay leaf, and salt.
3. Pour tomato mixture over balls, cover, and bake at 350°F/177°C for 1 hour or until rice is tender.

Chicken and Wild Rice Croquettes

50 Servings (4.6 oz/131 g)

Fry, 360°F/182°C

Metric		Ingredients	U.S.		
Weight	Volume		Weight		Volume
681 g	947 ml	Wild Rice, raw	1 lb,	8 oz	1 qt
1.81 kg	1.89 l	Water, boiling	4 lb		2 qt
170 g	178 ml	Chicken Fat or Butter or Margarine		6 oz	¾ cup
85 g	178 ml	Flour, bread		3 oz	¾ cup
907 g	947 ml	Chicken Stock	2 lb		1 qt
43 g	45 ml	Salt		1 ½ oz	3 tbsp
	15 ml	Pepper, white			1 tbsp
43 g	45 ml	Onion Juice		1 ½ oz	3 tbsp
43 g	45 ml	Lemon Juice		1 ½ oz	3 tbsp
4.08 kg	8.51 l	Chicken Meat, finely diced	9 lb		9 qt
227 g	237 ml	Eggs, whole (4 lge)		8 oz	1 cup
		Cracker Crumbs			

Procedure

1. Wash wild rice thoroughly in cold running water. Drain well.
2. Add rice to boiling water. Cover tightly and steam over low heat approximately 45 minutes or until water is absorbed.
3. Melt fat, add flour, and blend. Add chicken stock slowly, stirring to make smooth, heavy gravy. Add salt, pepper, and juices. Mix well. Add chicken meat and wild rice. Mix well.
4. Shape 100 croquettes, measuring with a No. 16 scoop. Chill for 2 hours.
5. Beat eggs slightly. Dip chilled croquettes in egg and roll in finely ground crumbs. Fry in deep fat at 360°F/182°C until brown.

CHEESE, EGG, CEREAL, AND VEGETABLE ENTRÉES

Cheese Rice Croquettes
50 Servings (5.2 oz/128 g)
Fry, 350°F/177°C

Metric		Ingredients	U.S.		
Weight	Volume		Weight		Volume
3.63 kg	4.74 l	Rice, cooked	8 lb		5 qt
1.70 kg	3.56 l	Cheese, grated	3 lb,	12 oz	3 ¾ qt
142 g	474 ml	Cracker Crumbs		5 oz	2 cups
511 g	533 ml	Eggs, beaten (10 med)	1 lb,	2 oz	2 ¼ cups
28 g	30 ml	Salt		1 oz	2 tbsp
	3 ¼ ml	Pepper			¾ tsp
21 g	20 ml	Worcestershire Sauce		¾ oz	1 ½ tbsp
	7 ½ ml	Mustard, dry			1 ½ tsp
	3 ¾ ml	Curry Powder			¾ tsp
454 g	474 ml	Milk	1 lb		2 cups
99 g	118 ml	Eggs, beaten (2 med)		3 ½ oz	½ cup
793 g	1.89 l	Bread Crumbs	1 lb,	12 oz	2 qt

Procedure

1. Stir 2 ½ lbs/1.14 kg raw rice into vigorously boiling water. Cover tightly. Reduce heat to low and cook for 20 minutes or until tender.
2. Combine rice with cheese, cracker crumbs, eggs, and seasonings.
3. Shape into croquettes, measuring with a No. 20 scoop. Make 100 croquettes.
4. Combine milk and 2 beaten eggs. Dip croquettes in egg mixture and then in crumbs. Refrigerate overnight, or at least 2 hours. If refrigerated overnight, remove from refrigerator about 1 hour before cooking.
5. Cook in deep fat at 350°F/177°C.

Note: Very good served with Hawaiian fruit sauce, or creamed ham or chicken.

Jambalaya
50 Servings (7.6 oz/215 g)

Metric		Ingredients	U.S.		
Weight	Volume		Weight		Volume
681 g	1.07 l	Onions, chopped	1 lb,	8 oz	4 ½ cups
681 g	1.42 l	Celery, diced	1 lb,	8 oz	1 ½ qt
340 g	355 ml	Bacon or Ham Fat		12 oz	1 ½ cups
3.63 kg	3.79 l	Spiced Ham, cubed	8 lb		1 gal
1.36 kg	1.66 l	Rice, uncooked	3 lb		1 ¾ qt
681 g	711 ml	Tomatoes	1 lb,	8 oz	3 cups
340 g	355 ml	Ham Stock		12 oz	1 ½ cups
227 g	237 ml	Catsup		8 oz	1 cup
28 g	30 ml	Salt		1 oz	2 tbsp
106 g	79 ml	Worcestershire Sauce		3 ¾ oz	⅓ cup

Procedure

1. Sauté onions and celery in fat until lightly browned.
2. Add remaining ingredients and heat to boiling temperature. Let simmer, stirring frequently until rice is tender and mixture is thick.

Note: Diced ham, chicken, or shrimp may be substituted for the spiced ham.

Turkey and Rice Balls

50 Servings (6 oz/170 g)
Bake, 350°F/177°C, 45–50 min

Metric		Ingredients	U.S.		
Weight	Volume		Weight		Volume
907 g	1.18 l	Rice, converted, raw	2 lb		5 cups
28 g	30 ml	Salt		1 oz	2 tbsp
2.27 kg	2.37 l	Water, boiling	5 lb		2½ qt
227 g	237 ml	Butter or Margarine		8 oz	1 cup
170 g	355 ml	Flour, all-purpose		6 oz	1½ cups
14 g	15 ml	Salt		½ oz	1 tbsp
	5 ml	Pepper			1 tsp
	5 ml	Poultry Seasoning			1 tsp
1.82 kg	1.89 l	Milk	4 lb		2 qt
454 g	947 ml	Celery, chopped	1 lb		1 qt
312 g	474 ml	Onions, chopped		11 oz	2 cups
114 g	118 ml	Pimiento, chopped		4 oz	½ cup
28 g	178 ml	Parsley, minced		1 oz	¾ cup
212 g	474 ml	Walnuts, chopped		7½ oz	2 cups
1.82 kg	2.84 l	Turkey, cooked, diced	4 lb		3 qt
681 g	1.42 l	Cornflake Crumbs	1 lb,	8 oz	1½ qt

Procedure

1. Cook rice in boiling, salted water, tightly covered for 20 minutes.
2. Melt butter or margarine, add flour and seasonings, and stir until blended. Add milk gradually and cook until sauce is thickened.
3. Combine all of the ingredients except cornflake crumbs. Chill for 3 or 4 hours or overnight.
4. Shape into balls using a No. 8 scoop. Roll in cornflake crumbs and arrange in greased serving pans (12 × 20 × 2 in). Bake at 350°F/177°C for 50 minutes.
5. Serve with turkey gravy or condensed mushroom soup.

Note: Ground turkey (6 lb/2.72 l) may be cooked and used in place of diced turkey.

Frankfurters and Rice

50 Servings (10 oz/283 g)
Bake, 350°F/177°C, 30 min

Metric		Ingredients	U.S.		
Weight	Volume		Weight		Volume
681 g	1.42 l	Celery, diced	1 lb,	8 oz	1½ qt
454 g	632 ml	Onions, chopped	1 lb		3 cups
57 g	59 ml	Oil or Shortening, melted		2 oz	¼ cup
2.95 kg	1 No. 10 can	Tomatoes, canned	6 lb,	8 oz	1 No. 10 can
28 g	59 ml	Chili Powder		1 oz	¼ cup
43 g	45 ml	Salt		1½ oz	3 tbsp
2.27 kg	2.37 l	Water and Olive liquor	5 lb		2½ qt
1.45 kg	1.66 l	Rice, uncooked	3 lb,	3 oz	1¾ qt
1.19 kg	1.66 l	Ripe Olives, sliced	2 lb,	10 oz	1¾ qt
4.54 kg	100	Frankfurters	10 lb		100
567 g	1.18 l	Cheddar Cheese, grated	1 lb,	4 oz	1¼ qt

1. Sauté celery and onions lightly in oil, and add tomatoes, chili powder, salt, and liquid. Heat to boiling.
2. Divide rice and olives into 2 serving pans (12 × 20 × 2 in) and pour half of the vegetable mixture over each. Mix well.
3. Cover tightly and bake at 350°F/177°C for 20 or 30 minutes, or until rice is tender.

4. Arrange frankfurters on top of the rice. Sprinkle cheese evenly over each pan and bake until cheese is melted (about 10 min).

Note: Cut the frankfurters on the diagonal part way through to enhance appearance of casserole.

Spanish Rice
50 Servings (6.8 oz/192 g)
Bake, 350°F/177°C, 30 min

Metric		Ingredients	U.S.	
Weight	Volume		Weight	Volume
2.15 kg	2.60 l	Rice, uncooked	4 lb, 12 oz	2¾ qt
6.35 kg	5.21 l	Water, boiling	14 lb	1⅜ gal
38 g	40 ml	Salt	1⅓ oz	2⅔ tbsp
454 g	711 ml	Onions, chopped	1 lb	3 cups
454 g	947 ml	Green Pepper, chopped	1 lb	1 qt
227 g	237 ml	Bacon Fat or Bacon, chopped	8 oz	1 cup
2.72 kg	2.84 l	Tomatoes	6 lb	3 qt
2.72 kg	2.84 l	Tomato Puree	6 lb	3 qt
114 g	118 ml	Salt	4 oz	½ cup
	10 ml	Pepper		2 tsp
	10 ml	Chili Powder		2 tsp
43 g	45 ml	Sugar	1½ oz	3 tbsp
	2½ ml	Mustard, dry		½ tsp
	5/16 ml	Cayenne Pepper		1/16 tsp
28 g	30 ml	Worcestershire Sauce	1 oz	2 tbsp

Procedure

1. Add rice to boiling salted water. Stir and cover tightly. Cook over low heat 20 minutes until water is absorbed and rice is tender. Remove from heat and let stand covered 10 minutes.
2. Sauté onions and green pepper in bacon fat until tender.

3. Heat tomatoes and tomato puree. Add other ingredients and bring to boiling. Mix well with rice.
4. Divide into 2 greased serving pans (12 × 20 × 2 in).
5. Bake at 350°F/177°C for about 30 minutes.

Vegetable Entrées

Baked Bean Delight
50 Servings (7.3 oz/206 g)
Bake, 250°F/121°C, 2 hrs

| Metric | | | U.S. | |
Weight	Volume	Ingredients	Weight	Volume
9.07 kg	9.73 l	Baked Beans, canned	20 lb	3 No. 10 cans
340 g	553 ml	Onions, grated	12 oz	2 ⅓ cups
340 g	711 ml	Green Pepper, chopped	12 oz	3 cups
14 g	15 ml	Salt	½ oz	1 tbsp
454 g	947 ml	Cheddar Cheese, grated	1 lb	1 qt
199 g	237 ml	Butter or Margarine, melted	7 oz	1 cup

Procedure

1. Mix together baked beans, onions, green pepper, and salt.
2. Pour into serving pans to bake. Sprinkle grated cheese evenly over top of beans, and pour melted margarine over grated cheese.
3. Bake at 250°F/121°C for 2 hours.

Baked Beans, Boston
50 Servings (8 ½ ozs/241 g)
Bake, 350°F/177°C, 3 ½ hrs

| Metric | | | U.S. | |
Weight	Volume	Ingredients	Weight	Volume
3.18 kg	4.11 l	White or Pea Beans, small	7 lb	4 ⅓ qt
907 g	947 ml	Ham or Salt Pork, cubed	2 lb	1 qt
57 g	60 ml	Salt	2 oz	¼ cup
340 g	474 ml	Brown Sugar	12 oz	2 cups
57 g	118 ml	Mustard, dry	2 oz	½ cup
57 g	45 ml	Vinegar	2 oz	3 tbsp
312 g	237 ml	Molasses, dark	11 oz	1 cup
1.82 kg	1.89 l	Water, hot, and bean liquid	4 lb	2 qt

Procedure

1. Wash beans. Cover with boiling water and soak overnight. Simmer slowly until tender (about 1 ½ hrs). Drain and save liquid.
2. Put beans in serving pans for baking. Distribute cubed ham or salt pork among beans.
3. Mix remaining ingredients and pour over beans. Add additional boiling water if needed to cover beans. Cover and bake at 350°F/177°C for 3 ½ hours. Cover may be removed for the last ½ hour to allow beans to brown.

Note: If light molasses is used, use 1 ½ cups and reduce hot water to 5 ½ cups. Omit ham or pork for meatless entrée.

Weights During Preparation

Beans, dry   7 lb   Beans, cooked   14 lb   Beans, baked   26 ½ lb

Baked Lima Beans

50 Servings (8.6 oz/245 g)

Bake, 350°F/177°C, 2 hrs

Metric		Ingredients	U.S.		
Weight	Volume		Weight		Volume
3.41 kg	4.50 l	Lima Beans, dry (or cooked—16 ½ lbs)	7 lb,	8 oz	4 ¾ qt
2.04 kg	2.01 l	Stock (from ham and beans)	4 lb,	4 oz	8 ½ cups
907 g	947 ml	Ham, chopped	2 lb		1 qt
57 g	59 ml	Salt		2 oz	¼ cup
1.36 kg	1.42 l	Tomato Puree	3 lb		1 ½ qt
227 g	316 ml	Brown Sugar		8 oz	1 ⅓ cups
227 g	355 ml	Onions, grated		8 oz	1 ½ cups
7 g	15 ml	Mustard, dry		¼ oz	1 tbsp
28 g	37 ml	Vinegar		1 oz	2 ½ tbsp
	5 ml	Pepper			1 tsp

Procedure

1. Wash beans. Cover with boiling water and soak overnight.
2. Cook beans in ham broth until skins crack. Drain and save liquid.
3. Mix chopped ham with beans and place in serving pans. Blend liquid with remaining ingredients and pour over ham and beans. Bake at 350°F/177°C for 2 hours.

Note: Omit ham for meatless entrée.

Lima Beans with Green Pepper and Pimiento

50 Servings (8.3 oz/236 g)

Bake, 350°F/177°C, 2 hrs

Metric		Ingredients	U.S.		
Weight	Volume		Weight		Volume
3.41 kg	4.50 l	Lima Beans, dry (or cooked—16 ½ lb)	7 ½ lb		4 ¾ qt
10.89 kg	11.36 l	Water, boiling	24 lb		3 gal
85 g	90 ml	Salt		3 oz	6 tbsp
227 g	316 ml	Pimiento, chopped		8 oz	1 ⅓ cups
227 g	267 ml	Margarine or Bacon Fat, melted		8 oz	1 ½ cups
454 g	711 ml	Onions, chopped	1 lb		3 cups
227 g	474 ml	Green Pepper, chopped		8 oz	2 cups
7 g	15 ml	Paprika		¼ oz	1 tbsp
114 g	79 ml	Molasses, dark		4 oz	⅓ cup
283 g	237 ml	Corn syrup, dark		10 oz	1 cup
2.72 kg	2.84 l	Bean Liquid	6 lb		3 qt
14 g	15 ml	Salt		½ oz	1 tbsp

Procedure

1. Wash beans. Cover with boiling water and soak overnight. Add salt and cook until tender. Drain and save liquid.
2. Mix remaining ingredients with liquid and add beans.
3. Pour into greased pans and bake at 350°F/177°C for 2 hours.

Note: Add more liquid if needed.

Swedish Brown Beans
50 Servings (10 oz/283 g)
Bake, 350°F/177°C, 1½–2 hrs

| Metric | | | U.S. | |
Weight	Volume	Ingredients	Weight	Volume
8.17 kg	8.51 l	Water, hot	18 lb	2 ¼ gal
2.72 kg	3.56 l	Pinto beans	6 lb	3 ¾ qt
43 g	45 ml	Salt	1 ½ oz	3 tbsp
114 g	118 ml	Oil	4 oz	½ cup
99 g	178 ml	Cornstarch	3 ½ oz	¾ cup
170 g	178 ml	Water, cold	6 oz	¾ cup
511 g	533 ml	Bacon, diced	1 lb, 2 oz	2 ¼ cups
255 g	355 ml	Onions, diced	9 oz	1 ½ cups
	3 cloves	Garlic		3 cloves
3.41 kg	3.56 l	Catsup	7 lb, 8 oz	3 ¾ qt
	2 ½ ml	Hot Pepper Sauce		½ tsp
	7 ½ ml	Worcestershire Sauce		1 ½ tsp
234 g	178 ml	Molasses, light	8 ¼ oz	¾ cup
766 g	1.07 l	Brown Sugar	1 lb, 11 oz	4 ½ cups
	5 ml	Pepper		1 tsp
227 g	237 ml	Vinegar	8 oz	1 cup
	5 ml	Mustard, dry		1 tsp

Procedure

1. Pour hot water over beans and soak overnight.
2. Add salt and oil. Heat to boiling and simmer until tender (about 1 to 1½ hrs). Drain.
3. Combine cornstarch with cold water and add to remaining ingredients. Combine with beans carefully to prevent mashing.

4. Pour into serving pans (12 × 20 × 2 in) and bake at 350°F/177°C for 1½ to 2 hours.

Note: Very nice served with ham or roast pork.

Mushroom Patties
50 Servings (3.9 oz/110 g)
Fry on hot griddle

| Metric | | | U.S. | |
Weight	Volume	Ingredients	Weight	Volume
567 g	829 ml	Onions, finely chopped	1 lb, 4 oz	3 ½ cups
114 g	118 ml	Margarine or Vegetable Oil	4 oz	½ cup
1.25 kg	1.30 l	Eggs, beaten (22 lge)	2 lb, 12 oz	5 ½ cups
1.82 kg	6.63 l	Mushrooms, fresh, chopped	4 lb	1 ¾ gal
114 g	158 ml	Pimiento, chopped	4 oz	⅔ cup
	2 ½ ml	Sage, powdered		½ tsp
43 g	45 ml	Salt	1 ½ oz	3 tbsp
454 g	1.07 l	Bread Crumbs	1 lb	4 ½ cups
57 g	60 ml	Celery Salt	2 oz	4 tbsp
114 g	118 ml	Water	4 oz	½ cup
681 g	711 ml	Tomatoes	1 lb, 8 oz	3 cups
454 g	947 ml	Bread, soft, diced	1 lb	1 qt

1. Sáute onions in margarine or vegetable oil.
2. Combine onions with remaining ingredients in order given.

3. Dip patties with a No. 20 scoop and fry on a hot griddle until brown, turning once.

Note: Serve with Béchamel Sauce.

Celery and Pecan Loaf

50 Servings (4.6 oz/131 g)

Bake, 350°F/177°C, 40–45 min

Metric		Ingredients	U.S.	
Weight	Volume		Weight	Volume
907 g	1.89 l	Celery, chopped	2 lb	2 qt
793 g	1.89 l	Bread Crumbs, whole wheat	1 lb, 12 oz	2 qt
2.72 kg	2.84 l	Milk	6 lb	3 qt
454 g	770 ml	Pecans, finely chopped	1 lb	3 ¼ cups
907 g	947 ml	Eggs (16 lge)	2 lb	1 qt
227 g	240 ml	Butter or Margarine, melted	8 oz	1 ½ cups
454 g	711 ml	Onions, chopped	1 lb	3 cups
43 g	45 ml	Salt	1 ½ oz	3 tbsp

Procedure

1. Combine all ingredients and divide into 2 greased serving pans (12 × 20 × 2 in).

2. Bake at 350°F/177°C for 40 to 45 minutes. Serve with mushroom sauce.

Corn Fritters

50 Servings (5.3 oz/155 g)

Fry, 360°F/182°C, 10 min

Metric		Ingredients	U.S.	
Weight	Volume		Weight	Volume
2.27 kg	4.73 l	Flour, pastry	5 lb	5 qt
18 g	20 ml	Salt	⅔ oz	1 ⅓ tbsp
114 g	150 ml	Baking Powder	4 oz	10 tbsp
57 g	60 ml	Sugar	2 oz	4 tbsp
756 g	829 ml	Eggs, beaten (14 lge)	1 lb, 12 oz	3 ½ cups
2.27 kg	2.37 l	Milk	5 lb	2 ½ qt
199 g	237 ml	Fat, melted	7 oz	1 cup
1.87 kg	1.95 l	Corn, drained	4 lb, 2 oz	8 ¼ cups

Procedure

1. Sift together twice flour, salt, baking powder, and sugar.
2. Combine eggs and milk. Mix into dry ingredients. Add melted fat and corn. Stir until blended.

3. Use a No. 20 scoop for dipping 100 fritters (2 per serving). Fry in deep fat at 360°F/182°C for 10 minutes.
4. Serve with syrup and/or crisp bacon.

Vegetable Casserole

50 Servings (6 oz/170 g)

Bake, 375°F/190°C, 15 min

Metric		Ingredients	U.S.		
Weight	Volume		Weight		Volume
1.14 kg	2.37 l	Celery, chopped	2 lb,	8 oz	2 ½ qt
1.14 kg	1.66 l	Carrots, chopped	2 lb,	8 oz	1 ¾ qt
2.72 kg	2.84 l	Beef Stock	6 lb		3 qt
454 g	711 ml	Onions, chopped	1 lb		3 cups
227 g	474 ml	Green Pepper, chopped		8 oz	2 cups
114 g	118 ml	Butter or Margarine		4 oz	½ cup
454 g	474 ml	Butter or Margarine	1 lb		2 cups
340 g	711 ml	Flour, bread		12 oz	3 cups
28 g	30 ml	Salt		1 oz	2 tbsp
	5 ml	Pepper			1 tsp
3.63 kg	3.79 l	Liquid (Beef Stock and Evaporated Milk)	8 lb		1 gal
907 g	1.89 l	Cheddar Cheese, grated	2 lb		2 qt
1.14 kg	1.42 l	Peas	2 lb,	8 oz	1 ½ qt
227 g	533 ml	Bread Crumbs		8 oz	2 ¼ cups
114 g	118 ml	Butter or Margarine, melted		4 oz	½ cup

Procedure

1. Cook celery and carrots in beef stock until tender. Drain, reserving stock. Sauté onions and green pepper in 4 oz/114 g of butter or margarine.
2. Melt 1 lb/454 g butter or margarine. Add flour and seasonings and blend. Cook over low heat 3 to 5 minutes. Stir while cooking.
3. Add stock and milk slowly, stirring constantly. Cook until sauce is smooth and thickened.

4. Blend in cheese. Add sautéed vegetables and peas.
5. Divide mixture into 2 greased serving pans (12 × 20 × 2 in). Sprinkle with crumbs mixed with melted butter or margarine and bake at 375°F/190°C for 15 minutes.

Note: 1 lb/454 g diced mushrooms may be sautéed with onions and added.

Chili Con Carne

50 Servings (8 oz/227 g)

Bake, 350°F/177°C, 2 hrs

Metric		Ingredients	U.S.		
Weight	Volume		Weight		Volume
2.04 kg	2.84 l	Red Kidney Beans	4 lb,	8 oz	3 qt
	3 cloves	Garlic, finely minced			3 cloves
907 g	1.89 l	Onions, sliced	2 lb		2 qt
114 g	118 ml	Bacon Fat or Margarine		4 oz	½ cup
3.18 kg	3.31 l	Ground Beef	7 lb		3 ½ qt
5.44 kg	5.68 l	Tomatoes	12 lb		6 qt
907 g	1.89 l	Green Pepper, chopped	2 lb		2 qt
46 g	75 ml	Chili Powder		1 ⅔ oz	5 tbsp
99 g	105 ml	Salt		3 ½ oz	7 tbsp
114 g	118 ml	Sugar		4 oz	½ cup
	7 ½ ml	Cayenne Pepper			1 ½ tsp

1. Wash beans and cover with boiling water. Soak overnight.
2. Cook until tender. Drain.
3. Sauté garlic and onions in bacon fat or margarine until tender. Add ground beef, brown, and separate. Mix all ingredients together.
4. Cook briskly for 30 minutes, then slowly, stirring occasionally. Put in serving pans and bake at 350°F/177°C for 2 hours.

Note: 1 lb/454 g pimiento may be substituted for green pepper if desired.

Weights During Preparation

Beans, raw   4 ½ lbs/2.04 kg   Beans, cooked   10 lbs/4.54 kg   Chili, cooked   25 lbs/11.35 kg

Onion Cheese Pie (Quiche)
48 Servings (⅛ 9-in pie)
Bake, 325°F/163°C, 30 min

Metric		Ingredients	U.S.	
Weight	Volume		Weight	Volume
	6 shells	Pie Shells, 9 in		6 shells
2.72 kg	5.68 l	Onions, thinly sliced	6 lb	6 qt
454 g	947 ml	Cheese, grated	1 lb	1 qt
2.27 kg	2.37 l	Milk, scalded	5 lb	2 ½ qt
14 g	15 ml	Salt	½ oz	1 tbsp
	10 ml	Nutmeg		2 tsp
	10 ml	Thyme		2 tsp
1.14 kg	1.18 l	Eggs, lightly beaten (20 lge)	2 lb, 8 oz	1 ¼ qt
396 g	947 ml	Bread Crumbs	14 oz	1 qt
454 g	947 ml	Cheese, grated	1 lb	1 qt

Procedure

1. Bake empty pie shells 7 minutes at 425°F/218°C. Lift sides of shells gently with fork to release steam and prevent puffing.
2. Steam onions 5 minutes.
3. Add 1 lb/454 g cheese to scalded milk and stir until melted. Add seasonings and lightly beaten eggs.
4. Sprinkle ¼ cup/59 ml of bread crumbs in the bottom of each baked crust. Distribute onions evenly over the bottom of the six crusts. Pour milk mixture over the onions. Mix 1 lb/454 g of cheese and remaining bread crumbs. Sprinkle over top of pies.
5. Bake at 325°F/163°C about 30 minutes or until the custard is set and the pies lightly browned.
6. Cut each pie into 8 servings.

Lentil Patties

50 Servings (5.9 oz/168 g)
Fry on hot griddle

Metric		Ingredients	U.S.	
Weight	Volume		Weight	Volume
907 g	1.89 l	Onions, chopped	2 lb	2 qt
227 g	237 ml	Oil	8 oz	1 cup
1.06 kg	1.39 l	Lentils, uncooked	2 lb, 5 1/3 oz	5 7/8 cups
1.82 kg	1.89 l	Eggs, beaten (32 lge)	4 lb	2 qt
	10 ml	Sage, powdered		2 tsp
57 g	60 ml	Salt	2 oz	4 tbsp
151 g	158 ml	Stock	5 1/3 oz	2/3 cup
340 g	1.42 l	Bread Crumbs	12 oz	6 cups
568 g	1.42 l	Oatmeal	1 lb, 4 oz	6 cups

Procedure

1. Braise onions in oil.
2. Cook lentils in 4 1/2 qts/4.26 l water. Drain.
3. Combine in following order: eggs, lentils, sage, salt, stock, bread crumbs, and oatmeal. Add onions. Mix well.
4. Dip patties with a No. 20 scoop and shape 100 patties.
5. Fry on a hot griddle, turning once.

Note: Serve with Béchamel Sauce or one of its modifications.

Carrot Loaf

50 Servings (7.2 oz/203 g)
Bake, 250°F/121°C, 1 hr

Metric		Ingredients	U.S.	
Weight	Volume		Weight	Volume
5.90 kg	9.22 l	Carrots	13 lb	9 3/4 qt
454 g	474 ml	Butter or Margarine	1 lb	2 cups
340 g	711 ml	Flour, bread	12 oz	3 cups
37 g	40 ml	Salt	1 1/3 oz	2 2/3 tbsp
	5 ml	Nutmeg		1 tsp
1.82 kg	1.89 l	Milk	4 lb	2 qt
793 g	829 ml	Eggs (16 med)	1 lb, 12 oz	3 1/2 cups
114 g	178 ml	Onions, chopped	4 oz	3/4 cup
28 g	178 ml	Parsley, chopped	1 oz	3/4 cup
681 g	1.42 l	Crumbs	1 lb, 8 oz	1 1/2 qt
133 g	158 ml	Butter or Margarine, melted	4 2/3 oz	2/3 cup

Procedure

1. Cook and mash carrots.
2. Melt butter or margarine. Add flour and seasonings. Blend. Cook over low heat 3 to 5 minutes. Stir while cooking. Add milk slowly, stirring constantly. Cook until smooth and thickened.
3. Beat eggs until light. Fold in vegetables, white sauce, crumbs, and melted margarine.
4. Divide into 2 greased serving pans (12 × 20 × 2 in).
5. Bake at 250°F/121°C for 1 hour or until set.

Scalloped Potatoes and Hamburger

50 Servings (8 oz/227 g)
Bake, 400°F/205°C, 1 hr

Metric		Ingredients	U.S.	
Weight	Volume		Weight	Volume
225 g	355 ml	Onions, chopped	8 oz	1 ½ cups
114 g	118 ml	Fat Drippings	4 oz	½ cup
2.27 kg	2.37 l	Ground Beef	5 lb	2 ½ qt
114 g	237 ml	Flour, bread	4 oz	1 cup
28 g	30 ml	Salt	1 oz	2 tbsp
	10 ml	Pepper		2 tsp
4.54 kg	40 med	Potatoes, raw, E.P.	10 lb	40 med
4.54 kg	4.74 l	Brown Gravy	10 lb	5 qt

Procedure

1. Sauté onions in drippings.
2. Mix ground beef, flour, salt, and pepper. Add to sautéed onion. Cook until lightly browned.
3. Slice potatoes thinly. Put layer of potatoes and then a layer of beef in greased pans (12 × 20 × 2 in). Repeat layers, finishing with potatoes on top. Use 5 lbs/2.27 kg potatoes and 3 lbs/1.36 kg meat per pan. Pour 2 ½ qts/2.37 l gravy over each pan.
4. Bake at 400°F/205°C for 1 hour or until potatoes are tender.

Note: The appearance is darker in color than in usual scalloped potatoes.

Spinach Soufflé

50 Servings (3 ½ oz/99 g)
Bake, 325°F/163°C, 30 min

Metric		Ingredients	U.S.	
Weight	Volume		Weight	Volume
340 g	355 ml	Butter or Margarine	12 oz	1 ½ cups
227 g	474 ml	Flour	8 oz	2 cups
28 g	30 ml	Salt	1 oz	2 tbsp
1.82 kg	1.89 l	Milk	4 lb	2 qt
340 g	316 ml	Egg Yolks (16 med)	12 oz	1 ⅓ cups
1.82 kg	1.89 l	Spinach, cooked, chopped	4 lb	2 qt
57 g	59 ml	Onions, grated	2 oz	¼ cup
227 g	474 ml	Bread Crumbs	8 oz	2 cups
28 g	30 ml	Lemon Juice or Vinegar	1 oz	2 tbsp
681 g	711 ml	Egg Whites (24 med)	1 lb, 8 oz	3 cups

Procedure

1. Melt butter or margarine. Add flour and salt. Blend. Cook over low heat 3 to 5 minutes. Stir while cooking. Add milk slowly, stirring constantly. Cook until smooth and thickened.
2. Beat egg yolks until creamy. Add a small amount of hot sauce to yolks, then add yolks to hot mixture. Cook until yolks are well-heated.
3. Spinach should be finely chopped. Add to cooked mixture. Add onions, bread crumbs, and lemon juice or vinegar.
5. Beat egg whites until stiff but not dry. Fold into hot spinach mixture. Divide mixture into 2 greased serving pans (12 × 20 × 2 in).
6. Bake at 325°F/163°C until inserted knife blade comes out clean.
7. Serve with cheese sauce.

Spinach and Eggs au Gratin

50 Servings (9.6 oz/272 g)

Bake, 350°F/177°C, 30 min

Metric		Ingredients	U.S.		
Weight	Volume		Weight		Volume
454 g	474 ml	Butter or Margarine, melted	1 lb		2 cups
227 g	474 ml	Flour, bread		8 oz	2 cups
3.63 kg	3.79 l	Milk, hot	8 lb		1 gal
43 g	45 ml	Salt		1 ½ oz	3 tbsp
	5 ml	White Pepper			1 tsp
454 g	947 ml	Cheddar Cheese, grated	1 lb		1 qt
5.90 kg	6.15 l	Spinach, cooked	13 lb		6 ½ qt
2.50 kg	50 med	Eggs, hard-cooked, sliced	5 lb,	8 oz	50 med
100 g	118 ml	Butter or Margarine, melted		3 ½ oz	½ cup
605 g	1.42 l	Bread Crumbs	1 lb, 5 ⅓ oz		1 ½ qt

Procedure

1. Make white sauce with butter or margarine, flour, and milk. Add salt, pepper, and cheese. Stir until cheese has melted.
2. Arrange a layer of spinach in each of 2 greased pans (12 × 20 × 2 in). Cover with a layer of sliced eggs.
3. Pour ¼ of white sauce over eggs in each pan. Repeat layers of spinach, eggs, and white sauce.
4. Add bread crumbs to melted butter or margarine and sauté until golden brown. Top pans with buttered crumbs.
5. Brown in oven at 350°F/177°C for about 3 minutes.

CHAPTER 5   *Fish*

Market supplies of fish are usually plentiful most of the year, with high and low seasonal supplies for specific species. The best method of preparation is influenced by the size, flavor, and the amount of fat contained in the fish. Those low in fat and that have firm flesh that will not break easily are best used for deep-fat frying. Others, such as salmon, that are high in fat, are more delicious when broiled or baked. When lean fish is baked or broiled, it is desirable to baste it with melted fat to prevent dryness. The flesh of fish is tender and delicate. It should be cooked just long enough to coagulate the muscle fibers. Fish flakes at the moment of doneness—when the heat has broken down the connective fibers just enough to allow the flesh to separate and fall into its natural divisions, when the thickest portion is probed gently with a fork. The fish will be most flavorful at this point. However, since fish needs little heat to cook, it will continue cooking when removed from the heat source through conduction of the internal heat. Therefore, it is better to remove the fish from the heat source just before this point is reached. The best test of "doneness" is the point at which the translucent flesh becomes opaque. The fish will flake by the time it is served. If using a thermometer, the internal temperature should be 140°F/60°C. At 150°F/66°C the flesh breaks down, allowing flavor and juices to escape.

Regardless of the preparation method, purchase the freshest fish possible. The flesh of fresh fish is springy and resilient when pressed lightly and should be moist and firm. The eyes of the fish should be bright, clear, and rounded. Salmon is an exception. The eyes of the salmon are relatively small and do not become significantly dull, cloudy, or sunken with age.

Table 2
Market Varieties and Cooking Methods for Fish

Species	Flavor	Fat	Size, lbs	Market	Cooking Method
Albacore Tuna	Rich	Medium	10–25	Gulf and Western	Barbecue, bake, poach
Bass, giant sea	Mild	V. Low	1–90	Eastern	Sauté, fry, broil
Grouper	Mild	Low	5–15	Whole US	Sauté, steam, bake
Bluefish	Mild	Low	1–7	Eastern	Sauté, steam, bake
Butterfish	Rich	High	¼–1	Eastern	Bake, poach, steam
Cod	Mild	V. Low	3–20	Whole US	Bake, fry, sauté
Flounder	Mild	V. Low	¼–5	Gulf and Eastern	Bake, steam, sauté
Haddock	Mild	Low	1½–7	Midwest and Eastern	Bake, fry, steam, sauté
Halibut	Mild	V. Low	10–75	Whole US	Broil, bake, fry, sauté
Ling Cod	Delicate	V. Low	5–30	Eastern, Western	Bake, fry, sauté, steam

Table 2
Market Varieties and Cooking Methods for Fish (cont.)

Species	Flavor	Fat	Size, lbs	Market	Cooking Method
Mackerel	Strong	Medium	1–2	Eastern, Midwest	Bake, fry, sauté, poach, barbecue
Perch	Mild	Medium	2–12	Midwest	Bake, pan-fry
Rockfish	Mild	V. Low	2–5	Whole US	Bake, poach, broil
Salmon	Rich	High	3–40	Whole US	Bake, poach, broil, sauté
Shad	Rich	High	1½–7	Gulf and Eastern	Bake, poach, sauté
Smelts	Mild	V. Low	¾–2 oz	Western	Sauté, bake
Snapper, red	Mild	V. Low	2–15	Gulf and Western	Bake, sauté, fry
Sole	Mild	V. Low	¾–7	Whole US	Bake, sauté, fry, poach
Sturgeon	Rich	Low	15–300	Western	Bake, poach, broil
Swordfish	Rich	Low	200–600	Western	Bake, poach, steam
Trout	Mild	V. Low	½–4	Western	Sauté, oven-fry
Whitefish	Mild	High	½–1½	Midwest	Poach, bake, sauté
Shellfish					
Clams	Mild	Low		Whole US	Fry, sauté, steam
Crabs	Mild	Low		Whole US	Boil
Lobsters	Mild	Low		Eastern	Boil
Oysters	Mild	Low		Whole US	Stew, sauté, bake
Scallops	Mild	Low		Whole US	Sauté, fry, bake
Shrimp	Mild	Low		Whole US	Boil, sauté, fry

Baked Whole Fish

50 Servings
Bake, 325°F/163°C, 2–3 hrs

Metric			US.	
Weight	Volume	Ingredients	Weight	Volume
9.08–10.89 kg	1-4 fish	Fish, whole, dressed	20–24 lb	1–4 fish
57 g	60 ml	Salt	2 oz	4 tbsp
227 g	237 ml	Bacon Fat or Oil	8 oz	1 cup
1.14 kg	50 slices	Bacon, sliced	2 lb, 8 oz	50 slices
		Bread Dressing		

Procedure

1. Wash and dry fish. Salt inside.
2. Make bread dressing (see recipe in Stuffing section).
3. Stuff fish loosely and lace closely with skewers and string. Place fish flat in baking pan and spread bacon fat generously over surface. Use additional fat if needed during baking.
4. Measure fish at thickest part after stuffing. Allow 10 minutes per inch of thickness. Bake at 450°F/232°C. Near the end of estimated cooking time, cut a slit in the center of the thickest part of the fish. If the flesh is slightly opaque, remove the fish from the oven. The fish will continue to cook from its own internal heat.

5. Serve, if desired, with slices of freshly broiled bacon.

Note: When preparing baked fish for buffet display, gently remove skin using care not to break the tender fish. Arrange garnish in a manner that will permit the fish to be cut and served easily. Sliced, stuffed olives, cucumber and lemon slices, hard-cooked egg, pimiento, parsley, or curly chicory are attractive items to use for garnishing. When serving, cut portions to bones running through center of fish and lift portions from above the bones. When the bones are bared (as in salmon) they can easily be removed and the lower half portioned and served. Cutting through the fish from top to bottom will cause the delicate fish to crumble.

Baked Fish Steak or Fillets

50 Servings (5 oz/142 g)
Bake, 350°F/177°C, 10–15 min

Metric		Ingredients	U.S.	
Weight	Volume		Weight	Volume
7.26 kg	50 pieces	Fish Steaks or Fillets	16 lb	50 pieces
907 g	947 ml	Milk	2 lb	1 qt
43 g	45 ml	Salt	1 ½ oz	3 tbsp
681 g	2.37 l	Bread Crumbs, fine, dry	1 lb, 8 oz	2 ½ qt
340 g	355 ml	Oil or Melted Fat	12 oz	1 ½ cups

Procedure

1. Combine milk and salt. Dip portions in milk and roll in crumbs until well covered.
2. Place on greased pan, baste lightly with oil or fat.
3. Bake at 350°F/177°C until flesh can be lightly flaked with fork (about 10 to 15 min).

Baked Fish Fillets with Puffy Cheese Sauce

50 Servings (4 oz/114 g)
Bake, 350°F/177°C, 30–40 min

Metric		Ingredients	U.S.	
Weight	Volume		Weight	Volume
5.68 kg	50 pieces	Fresh Red Snapper, Halibut, or Sole fillets, cut 4/lb	12 lb, 8 oz	50 pieces
114 g	118 ml	Sweet Pickle Relish	4 oz	½ cup
624 g	652 ml	Mayonnaise	1 lb, 6 oz	2 ¾ cups
255 g	533 ml	Cheddar Cheese, grated	9 oz	2 ¼ cups
21 g	22 ml	Salt	¾ oz	1 ½ tbsp
212 g	207 ml	Egg Yolks (10 med)	7 ½ oz	⅞ cup
	2 ½ ml	Cream of Tartar		½ tsp
283 g	296 ml	Egg Whites (10 med)	10 oz	1 ¼ cups

Procedure

1. Place fillets in a single layer in well-greased serving pans (12 × 20 × 2 in).
2. Drain the relish and combine relish, mayonnaise, cheese, salt, and egg yolks.
3. Beat egg whites until foamy. Add cream of tartar and continue beating until whites are stiff. Fold the sauce into the egg whites.
4. Cover the fish with the sauce and bake at 350°F/177°C for 30 to 40 minutes or until fish flakes easily when tested with a fork and the sauce is golden brown. Watch closely to prevent over browning.

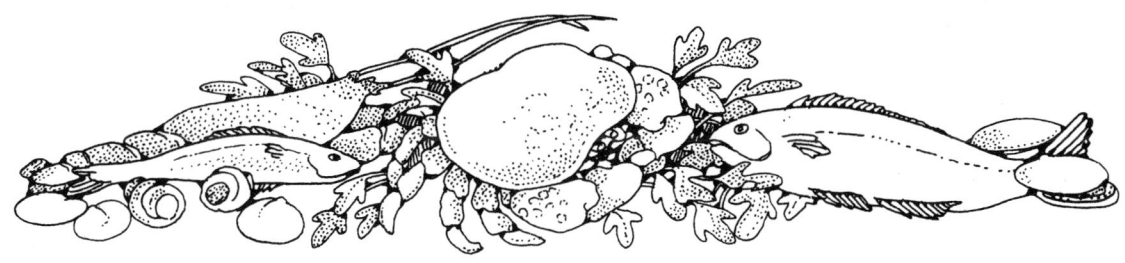

Baked Fish in Cheese Sauce

50 Servings (5 oz/142 g)
Bake, 350°F/177°C, 25 min

Metric		Ingredients	U.S.	
Weight	Volume		Weight	Volume
7.10 kg	50 pieces	Fish Fillets	15 lb, 10 oz	50 pieces
114 g	118 ml	Lemon Juice	4 oz	½ cup
340 g	355 ml	Butter or Margarine	12 oz	1 ½ cups
170 g	355 ml	Flour, all-purpose	6 oz	1 ½ cups
28 g	30 ml	Salt	1 oz	2 tbsp
	2 ½ ml	Mustard, dry		½ tsp
14 g	15 ml	Celery Salt	½ oz	1 tbsp
	10 ml	Pepper, white		2 tsp
156 g	237 ml	Onions, minced fine	5 ½ oz	1 cup
3.63 kg	3.79 l	Milk	8 lb	1 gal
681 g	1.42 l	Cheddar Cheese, grated	1 lb, 8 oz	1 ½ qt
454 g	947 ml	Cornflake Crumbs	1 lb	1 qt

Procedure

1. Arrange fillet portions in greased serving pans. Sprinkle with lemon juice.
2. Melt butter or margarine. Stir in flour, salt, dry mustard, celery salt, white pepper, and finely minced onions. Stir until smooth.
3. Cook over low heat 3 to 5 minutes. Stir while cooking. Add milk slowly, stirring constantly. Cook until smooth, glossy, and thickened, and flour is cooked.
4. Remove from heat and stir in grated cheese.
5. Pour only enough cheese sauce over fish portions to coat them. Sprinkle cornflake crumbs on top.
6. Bake at 350°F/177°C until fish is done (about 20 min).

Note: Too much cheese sauce on the fish will hide the portions and make fish difficult to serve.

Parmesan Baked Fish Fillets

50 Servings
Bake, 400°F/205°C, 10–15 min

Metric		Ingredients	U.S.	
Weight	Volume		Weight	Volume
567 g	1.89 l	Potato Chips, crushed	1 lb, 4 oz	2 qt
227 g	474 ml	Parmesan Cheese, grated	8 oz	2 cups
	5 ml	Thyme, crushed		2 tsp
5.67 kg	50 pieces	Fresh Fillets, cut 4/lb	12 lb, 8 oz	50 pieces
681 g	1.42 l	Flour, all-purpose	1 lb, 8 oz	1 ½ qt
454 g	415 ml	Milk, evaporated	1 lb	1 ¾ cups

Procedure

1. Mix potato chips, parmesan cheese, and thyme together.
2. Dip fish portions in flour, then milk, and finally in potato chip mixture. Work with small amount of potato chip mixture at a time.
3. Place portions in greased serving pans (12 × 20 × 2 in). Brush lightly with melted butter or margarine.
4. Bake at 400°F/205°C for 10 to 15 minutes.

Lemon Baked Fish

50 Servings (4 oz/114 g)
Bake, 400°F/205°C, 10–20 min

Metric		Ingredients	U.S.		
Weight	Volume		Weight		Volume
5.68 kg	50 pieces	Fish Fillets	12 lb,	8 oz	50 pieces
28 g	30 ml	Salt		1 oz	2 tbsp
255 g	267 ml	Lemon Juice		9 oz	1 1/8 cups
	15 ml	Paprika			1 tbsp
510 g	789 ml	Onions, chopped	1 lb,	2 oz	3 1/3 cups
255 g	267 ml	Butter or Margarine		9 oz	1 1/8 cups
71 g	444 ml	Parsley, chopped		2 1/2 oz	1 7/8 cups

Procedure

1. Combine lemon juice, salt, and paprika.
2. Dip each fillet into mixture, place in greased serving pan, and set aside for about 1 hour.
3. Sauté onion in margarine until transparent but not brown. Combine with chopped parsley.
4. Drain juices from serving pans of fish. Top each portion with a spoonful of onion and parsley mixture.
5. Bake fish at 400°F/205°C for about 10 minutes or until fish flesh becomes opaque.

Note: Red snapper, sole, cod, halibut, or other white fish may be used.

Rolled Stuffed Fish Fillets

50 Servings
Bake, 350°F/177°C, 20 min

Metric		Ingredients	U.S.		
Weight	Volume		Weight		Volume
283 g	395 ml	Onions, chopped		10 oz	1 2/3 cups
142 g	296 ml	Green Pepper, chopped		5 oz	1 1/4 cups
538 g	563 ml	Butter or Margarine	1 lb,	3 oz	2 3/8 cups
538 g	1.13 l	Celery, diced	1 lb,	3 oz	4 3/4 cups
1.25 kg	3.31 l	Bread Crumbs, soft	2 lb,	12 oz	3 1/2 qt
	11 ml	Salt			2 1/4 tsp
	2 1/2 ml	Pepper			1/2 tsp
114 g	118 ml	Lemon Juice		4 oz	1/2 cup
170 g	178 ml	Salad Oil		6 oz	3/4 cup
28 g	30 ml	Salt		1 oz	2 tbsp
	5 ml	Pepper			1 tsp
5.67 kg	50 pieces	Fish Fillets	12 lb,	8 oz	50 pieces

Procedure

1. Sauté onions and green pepper in butter or margarine until tender.
2. Add celery, bread crumbs, salt, and pepper. Blend.
3. Mix lemon juice, salad oil, salt, and pepper. Dip fillets in mixture.
4. Place a No. 30 scoop of stuffing on each fillet. Roll fillet around stuffing and skewer. Place in greased baking pan (12 × 20 × 2 in).
5. Bake at 350°F/177°C for 20 minutes or until fish tests done.

Note: Red snapper, sole, halibut, and cod are delicious to use.

Fish Fillets and Broccoli

50 Servings

Bake, 350°F/177°C, 25 min

Metric		Ingredients	U.S.		
Weight	Volume		Weight		Volume
5.67 kg	50 pieces	Fish Fillets	12 lb, 8 oz		50 pieces
3.63 kg	50 spears	Broccoli Spears	8 lb		50 spears
340 g	355 ml	Salad Dressing	12 oz		1 ½ cups
1.36 kg	1.42 l	Celery Soup, undiluted	3 lb		1 ½ qt
	5 ml	Thyme			1 tsp
14 g	15 ml	Salt	½ oz		1 tbsp
57 g	59 ml	Lemon Juice	2 oz		¼ cup
227 g	474 ml	Cornflake Crumbs	8 oz		2 cups

Procedure

1. Wrap a 4 oz/114 g portion of fish fillet around a spear of broccoli (about 2 ½ oz/71 g) and place in greased serving pans (12 × 20 × 2 in).
2. Combine salad dressing, soup, thyme, salt, and lemon juice and pour over fillets. Sprinkle lightly with cornflake crumbs.
3. Bake at 350°F/177°C until fish is done (about 25 minutes).

Note: Use a mild-flavored fish such as red snapper or sole.

Poached Fish

50 Servings

Procedure

1. Place fillets, thick slices, or whole fish on a perforated rack that can be used to raise the fish from the water after cooking. (A perforated steamer basket set inside a solid basket may be used, or the fish may be wrapped in cheesecloth.)
2. Sprinkle fish with salt, pepper, and lemon juice. Add just enough liquid to cover. The liquid may be hot water, milk, fish stock, or court bouillon. The poaching liquid should not be allowed to boil.
3. Cook in a moderate oven or steam cooker just until fish flakes when probed gently with a fork in thickest portion. Allow 10 min cooking time per inch of thickness (measure in thickest portion of fish).
4. Drain. Use liquid for sauce.

Barbecued or Broiled Fish

50 Servings

Procedure

1. Lay portions of fish steak, fillets, or whole fish prepared book style (bones in back removed to permit fish to open and lie flat), on a greased broiler rack. Brush with French dressing or mixture of melted butter or margarine, lemon juice, and salt.
2. Place rack 5 or 6 inches from heat source for small steaks and fillets. Thick, whole fish require longer to heat through and should be placed 7 to 9 inches or farther from the heat. Broil only until the surface can be flaked with a fork. Turn the fish and broil the other side.

Note: In barbecuing whole fish, to avoid breaking when turning, it helps to place a second greased broiler rack on top of fish. With the fish between the two racks, and held firmly, turn the whole fish at one time.

When broiling fish out-of-doors over an open fire and on a chicken wire rack, place the open side (inside of fish) down on rack to be broiled first. When the fish is ready to be turned, cover with heavy foil before placing second rack over the top. After the racks and fish are turned, the fish should be resting skin side down on the foil. When the cooking has been completed, the fish on the foil can be moved off the rack to the serving container with little danger of breaking.

Fish Cakes

50 Servings (5 oz/142 g)
Fry, 375°F/191°C

Metric		Ingredients	U.S.	
Weight	Volume		Weight	Volume
340 g	553 ml	Onions, chopped	12 oz	2 ⅓ cups
85 g	90 ml	Butter or Margarine	3 oz	6 tbsp
10 g	3 cloves	Garlic, minced	⅜ oz	3 cloves
4.77 kg	40 med	Potatoes, peeled	10 lb, 8 oz	40 med
2.95 kg	4.74 l	Fish, cooked, flaked	6 lb, 8 oz	5 qt
12 g	79 ml	Parsley, chopped		⅓ cup
454 g	474 ml	Eggs, beaten (8 lge)	1 lb	2 cups
43 g	45 ml	Salt	1 ½ oz	3 tbsp
7 g	15 ml	Pepper	¼ oz	1 tbsp

Procedure

1. Sauté onions and garlic in butter or margarine until golden.
2. Cook potatoes until tender. Drain and mash.
3. Combine and mix all ingredients: Form 100 cakes, using a No. 16 scoop. Flatten and chill.
4. Fry in deep fat at 375°F/191°C until fish cakes are golden brown.

Pan-Fried Fish

50 Servings (5 oz/142 g)

Metric		Ingredients	U.S.	
Weight	Volume		Weight	Volume
7.26 kg	50 pieces	Small Fish or Fillets	16 lb	50 pieces
907 g	1.42 l	Corn Meal	2 lb	1 ½ qt
85 g	90 ml	Salt	3 oz	6 tbsp
283 g	296 ml	Eggs, beaten (5 lge)	10 oz	1 ¼ cups
227 g	237 ml	Milk	8 oz	1 cup
57 g	59 ml	Lemon Juice	2 oz	¼ cup
454 g	474 ml	Fat for frying	1 lb	2 cups

Procedure

1. Blend corn meal and salt. Combine eggs, milk, and lemon juice.
2. Dip fish in egg-milk mixture. Roll in corn meal.
3. Heat fat to sizzling temperature but below smoking.
4. Brown fish from 3 to 5 minutes and reduce temperature.
5. Cover pan and steam fish a few minutes. Turn fish and brown the other side. Adjust cooking time to thickness of fish.

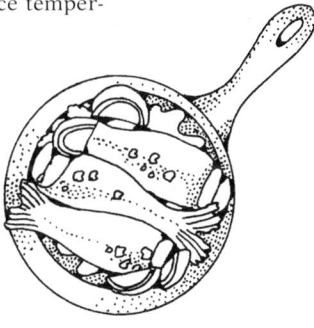

Fish Amandine

50 Servings (5 oz/142 g)
Bake, 450°F/232°C, 15 min

Metric		Ingredients	U.S.	
Weight	Volume		Weight	Volume
227 g	474 ml	Almonds, blanched, slivered	8 oz	2 cups
7.26 kg	50 pieces	Fish Fillets	16 lb	50 pieces
567 g	592 ml	Butter or Margarine	1 lb, 4 oz	2½ cups
28 g	30 ml	Salt	1 oz	2 tbsp
	10 ml	Pepper		2 tsp
57 g	59 ml	Lemon Juice	2 oz	¼ cup
28 g	45 ml	Lemon Rind, grated	1 oz	3 tbsp

Procedure

1. Toast almonds in 350°F/177°C oven or by sautéeing until lightly browned.
2. Arrange fish fillets on greased baking sheet.
3. Melt butter or margarine. Mix with almonds, seasonings, lemon juice, and rind. Spread over fish.
4. Bake at 450°F/232°C until done (about 15 min).

Seafood Fondue

64 Servings (4½ oz/128 g)
Bake, 325°F/163°C, 1¼ hrs

Metric		Ingredients	U.S.	
Weight	Volume		Weight	Volume
2.27 kg	66 slices	Bread Slices, crusts removed	5 lb	66 slices
1.02 kg	1.66 l	Crabmeat	2 lb, 4 oz	1¾ qt
1.02 kg	1.66 l	Halibut	2 lb, 4 oz	1¾ qt
510 g	790 ml	Mayonnaise	1 lb, 2 oz	3⅓ cups
156 g	237 ml	Onions, chopped	5½ oz	1 cup
567 g	1.81 l	Green Pepper, chopped	1 lb, 4 oz	5 cups
454 g	947 ml	Celery, chopped	1 lb	1 qt
1.53 kg	1.60 l	Eggs (27 lge)	3 lb, 6 oz	6¾ cups
4.54 kg	4.74 l	Milk	10 lb	5 qt
	5 ml	Salt		1 tsp
1.87 kg	1.89 l	Mushroom Soup	4 lb, 2 oz	2 qt
454 g	947 ml	Cheese, grated	1 lb	1 qt

Procedure

1. Place 16½ slices of trimmed bread (3 rows of 5½ slices) on bottom of each of 2 serving pans (12 × 20 × 2 in).
2. Steam, bone, and flake halibut.
3. Mix well-drained fish, mayonnaise, onions, green pepper, and celery. Spread over the bread.
4. Place remaining slices of trimmed bread on the top (3 rows of 5½ slices).
5. Mix eggs, milk, and salt together and pour over the fish mixture. Cover and place in refrigerator overnight.
6. Bake at 325°F/163°C for 15 minutes, then spoon mushroom soup over top. Sprinkle each pan with 8 oz/227 g of grated cheese and bake 1 hour at 325°F/163°C.
7. Cut pans 4 × 8 and serve.

Note: Shrimp and sole or red snapper may be substituted for crab and halibut.
Overcooking or long holding may result in syneresis-liquid bleeding out of the custard.

Crab Lorenzo

50 Servings (2/3 cup/158 ml)

Metric		Ingredients	U.S.	
Weight	Volume		Weight	Volume
2.95 kg	4.74 l	Crabmeat	6 lb, 8 oz	5 qt
454 g	474 ml	Butter or Margarine	1 lb	2 cups
227 g	355 ml	Onions, finely chopped	8 oz	1 ½ cups
681 g	1.42 l	Green Pepper, chopped	1 lb, 8 oz	1 ½ qt
227 g	474 ml	Flour, all-purpose	8 oz	2 cups
14 g	15 ml	Salt	½ oz	1 tbsp
	5 ml	Pepper, white		1 tsp
	5 ml	Paprika		1 tsp
3.63 kg	3.79 l	Milk	8 lb	1 gal
170 g	178 ml	Lemon Juice	6 oz	¾ cup
	2 ½ ml	Hot Pepper Sauce		½ tsp
340 g	711 ml	Swiss Cheese, shredded	12 oz	3 cups

Procedure

1. Remove shell particles from crabmeat.
2. Melt butter or margarine and sauté vegetables until tender. Blend in flour and seasonings. Slowly stir in milk and cook until mixture is smooth and thickened.
3. Remove from heat. Stir in lemon juice and pepper sauce.
4. Add crabmeat and divide mixture into two serving pans (12 × 20 × 2 in). Top with shredded Swiss cheese.
5. Bake at 350°F/177°C until cheese is melted (about 20 min). Serve on toast or in puff paste cups.

Crab or Lobster Newburg

50 Servings (2/3 cup/158 ml)

Metric		Ingredients	U.S.	
Weight	Volume		Weight	Volume
2.95 kg	3.79 l	Lobster Tails or Alaska Crabmeat	6 lb, 8 oz	4 qt
454 g	474 ml	Butter or Margarine	1 lb	2 cups
227 g	474 ml	Flour, bread	8 oz	2 cups
4.54 kg	4.74 l	Milk, hot	10 lb	5 qt
170 g	178 ml	Egg Yolks, beaten (8 med)	6 oz	¾ cup
	2 ½ ml	Paprika		½ tsp
21 g	22 ml	Salt	¾ oz	1 ½ tbsp
	5 ml	Pepper, white		1 tsp
283 g	395 ml	Pimiento, diced	10 oz	1 ⅔ cups
28 g	30 ml	Sherry	1 oz	2 tbsp

Procedure

1. Boil lobster tails or crabs. Remove from shells and cut into cubes.
2. Melt butter or margarine; add flour and blend. Slowly stir in milk and cook until sauce is smooth and thickened.
3. Add a little hot sauce to beaten eggs and then stir eggs into the hot sauce. Add remaining ingredients. Heat thoroughly. Serve on toast or in pastry or toast cups.

Deviled Crabmeat

50 Servings (4½ oz/128 g)
Bake, 350°F/177°C, 20 min

Metric		Ingredients	U.S.	
Weight	Volume		Weight	Volume
3.63 kg	5.68 l	Crabmeat	8 lb	1½ gal
340 g	355 ml	Butter or Margarine	12 oz	1½ cups
227 g	355 ml	Onions, chopped	8 oz	1½ cups
114 g	237 ml	Green Pepper, chopped	4 oz	1 cup
114 g	237 ml	Celery, finely chopped	4 oz	1 cup
170 g	355 ml	Flour, all-purpose	6 oz	1½ cups
1.36 kg	1.42 l	Milk	3 lb	1½ qt
14 g	15 ml	Salt	½ oz	1 tbsp
	5 ml	Pepper		1 tsp
7 g	15 ml	Mustard, dry	¼ oz	1 tbsp
	2½ ml	Cayenne Pepper		½ tsp
28 g	30 ml	Worcestershire Sauce	1 oz	2 tbsp
	15 ml	Sage		1 tbsp
114 g	118 ml	Lemon Juice	4 oz	½ cup
454 g	474 ml	Eggs, beaten (8 lge)	1 lb	2 cups
28 g	178 ml	Parsley, chopped	1 oz	¾ cup
227 g	711 ml	Buttered Crumbs	8 oz	3 cups

Procedure

1. Remove particles of shell or cartilage from crabmeat.
2. Sauté onions, green pepper, and celery lightly in butter or margarine. Blend in flour. Add milk gradually, stirring constantly. Cook until sauce is smooth and thickened. Add seasonings and lemon juice.
3. Add a little of the hot mixture to beaten eggs and then stir eggs into the sauce. Add parsley and crabmeat. Divide into two serving pans (12 × 20 × 2 in) and top with buttered crumbs.
4. Bake at 350°F/177°C until nicely browned (about 20 min).

Fried Oysters

50 Servings (approx. 3)
Fry, 360°F/182°C

Metric		Ingredients	U.S.	
Weight	Volume		Weight	Volume
3.18 kg	13 doz	Oysters	7 lb	13 doz
227 g	237 ml	Eggs, beaten (4 lge)	8 oz	1 cup
227 g	237 ml	Water	8 oz	1 cup
28 g	30 ml	Salt	1 oz	2 tbsp
	5 ml	Pepper		1 tsp
1.02 kg	3.19 l	Cracker Crumbs	2 lb, 4 oz	3⅜ qt

Procedure

1. Wash oysters and remove any foreign matter. Dry thoroughly.
2. Dip in mixture of egg and water, to which salt and pepper have been added. Roll in cracker crumbs.
3. Fry to golden brown in deep fat at 360°F/182°C. Serve immediately with tartar sauce.

Oysters Rockefeller

50 Servings (5 oysters)
Bake, 400°F/205°C, 10–15 min

Metric		Ingredients	U.S.	
Weight	Volume		Weight	Volume
4.54 kg	4.74 l	Oysters, drained (or 250 in shells)	10 lb	1 ¼ gal
227 g	355 ml	Onions, minced	8 oz	1 ½ cups
454 g	474 ml	Butter or Margarine	1 lb	2 cups
3.63 kg	3.79 l	Spinach, frozen, minced	8 lb	1 gal
21 g	22 ml	Salt	¾ oz	1 ½ tbsp
14 g	15 ml	Celery Salt	½ oz	1 tbsp
19 g	118 ml	Parsley, minced	⅔ oz	½ cup
	5 ml	Nutmeg		1 tsp
	10 ml	Thyme, dry, crushed		2 tsp
	2 ½ ml	Hot Pepper Sauce		½ tsp
397 g	947 ml	Bread Crumbs	14 oz	1 qt
907 g	50 slices	Lemon, sliced	2 lb	50 slices

Procedure

1. Arrange drained oysters in greased serving pans, or in deep half of shells.
2. Sauté onions in butter or margarine, add spinach and seasonings, and cook for 5 minutes. Add bread crumbs and mix well. Spread mixture on top of oysters.
3. Bake at 400°F/205°C for 10 or 15 minutes. Serve with lemon.

Fried Scallops

50 Servings (5 ½ oz/156 g)
Fry, 350°F/177°C, 2–3 min

Metric		Ingredients	U.S.	
Weight	Volume		Weight	Volume
7.26 kg	7.57 l	Scallops	16 lb	2 gal
454 g	474 ml	Eggs, beaten (8 lge)	1 lb	2 cups
170 g	178 ml	Milk	6 oz	¾ cup
28 g	30 ml	Salt	1 oz	2 tbsp
14 g	15 ml	Celery Salt	½ oz	1 tbsp
	5 ml	Pepper		1 tsp
	10 ml	Thyme (optional)		2 tsp
	5 ml	Marjoram (optional)		1 tsp
454 g	947 ml	Flour, all-purpose	1 lb	1 qt
397 g	947 ml	Bread Crumbs, fine, dry	14 oz	1 qt

Procedure

1. Wash scallops, removing any particles of shell. Drain well. Cut large scallops, if necessary, to make size uniform.
2. Combine eggs, milk, salt, and celery salt. Blend pepper, thyme, marjoram, flour, and bread crumbs.
3. Dip scallops in egg mixture, then in crumb mixture. Deep-fry at 350°F/177°C until nicely browned (about 2 to 3 min). Drain on absorbent paper. Serve immediately with a piquant sauce such as Tartar, Bacon, or Béarnaise.

Shrimp Creole
50 Servings (¾ cup/178 ml)

| Metric | | Ingredients | U.S. | |
Weight	Volume		Weight	Volume
454 g	711 ml	Onions, chopped	1 lb	3 cups
170 g	178 ml	Butter or Margarine	6 oz	¾ cup
	1 clove	Garlic, minced		1 clove
	5 ml	Pepper		1 tsp
28 g	30 ml	Salt	1 oz	2 tbsp
1.36 kg	1.42 l	Tomatoes, canned	3 lb	1 ½ qt
907 g	947 ml	Stock, chicken or fish, hot	2 lb	1 qt
340 g	474 ml	Pimiento, chopped	12 oz	2 cups
227 g	474 ml	Green Pepper, chopped	8 oz	2 cups
	3 cloves	Cloves, whole		3 cloves
114 g	178 ml	Cornstarch	4 oz	¾ cup
227 g	474 ml	Stock, chicken or fish, cold	8 oz	2 cups
1.36 kg	2.37 l	Shrimp, small, cooked, cleaned	3 lb	2 ½ qt
		Rice Custard		
114 g	158 ml	Rice, raw	4 oz	⅔ cup
907 g	947 ml	Eggs (16 lge)	2 lb	1 qt
2.72 kg	2.84 l	Milk	6 lb	3 qt
14 g	15 ml	Salt	½ oz	1 tbsp

Procedure

1. Sauté onions in butter or margarine. Add garlic and sauté.
2. Combine onions and garlic with remaining ingredients, except cornstarch, 2 cups/474 ml of cold stock, and shrimp. Simmer.
3. Mix cornstarch with cold stock and stir into hot stock and vegetable mixture. Cook until thickened.
4. Add shrimp and heat thoroughly just before serving.
5. Steam rice in boiling salted water until tender.
6. Beat eggs until lemon-colored. Add milk, rice, and salt. Bake in buttered molds or in 2 buttered serving pans (8 ½ × 15 × 2 ½ in) at 300°F/149°C for 45 to 60 min.
7. Serve Shrimp Creole in center of ring or over top of custard.

Shrimp Wiggle
50 Servings (¾ cup/178 ml)

| Metric | | Ingredients | U.S. | |
Weight	Volume		Weight	Volume
340 g	355 ml	Butter or Margarine	12 oz	1 ½ cups
170 g	355 ml	Flour, all-purpose	6 oz	1 ½ cups
28 g	30 ml	Salt	1 oz	2 tbsp
	5 ml	Pepper, white		1 tsp
4.54 kg	4.74 l	Milk, hot	10 lb	1 ¼ gal
	12 ½ ml	Worcestershire Sauce		2 ½ tsp
57 g	59 ml	Onion Juice	2 oz	¼ cup
2.04 kg	3.56 l	Shrimp	4 lb, 8 oz	3 ¾ qt
1.81 kg	2.84 l	Peas, fresh or frozen	4 lb	3 qt

1. Melt butter or margarine. Add flour, salt, and pepper. Blend. Cook over low heat 3 to 5 minutes. Stir while cooking.
2. Add milk slowly, stirring constantly. Cook until smooth and thickened. Add Worcestershire sauce and onion juice.

3. Fifteen minutes before serving, add shrimp and peas. Heat thoroughly. Serve over hot biscuits or in toast baskets.

Note: Very good served over rice custard.

Shrimp Parmesan

50 Servings (7 oz/198 g)
Bake, 350°F/177°C

Metric		Ingredients	U.S.	
Weight	Volume		Weight	Volume
57 g	59 ml	Salt	2 oz	¼ cup
28 g	30 ml	Oil	1 oz	2 tbsp
5.44 kg	5.68 l	Water, boiling	12 lb	1½ gal
907 g	1.89 l	Spaghetti, raw	2 lb	2 qt
340 g	1.24 l	Mushrooms, fresh, sliced	12 oz	5¼ cups
142 g	237 ml	Onions, grated	5 oz	1 cup
114 g	118 ml	Butter or Margarine	4 oz	½ cup
170 g	355 ml	Flour, all-purpose	6 oz	1½ cups
35 g	37 ml	Salt	1¼ oz	2½ tbsp
	2½ ml	Pepper, white		½ tsp
	3¾ ml	Paprika		¾ tsp
340 g	355 ml	Butter or Margarine, melted	12 oz	1½ cups
2.95 kg	3.08 l	Milk, hot	6 lb, 8 oz	3¾ qt
340 g	711 ml	Sharp Cheddar Cheese, grated	12 oz	3 cups
2.72 kg	4.74 l	Shrimp, Alaska	6 lb	5 qt
142 g	296 ml	Parmesan Cheese	5 oz	1¼ cups

Procedure

1. Add salt and oil to boiling water. Add spaghetti and cook 6 to 8 minutes or until tender. Drain, rinse with cold water. Drain well.
2. Sauté mushrooms and onions in 4 oz/114 g of butter or margarine.
3. Add flour and seasonings to melted butter or margarine. Blend.
4. Cook over low heat 3 to 5 minutes. Stir while cooking. Add milk slowly, stirring constantly. Cook until sauce is smooth and thickened.

5. Add cheddar cheese and blend into hot sauce.
6. Add mushrooms, onions, and shrimp to sauce. Mix well.
7. Combine spaghetti and sauce. Pour half into each of 2 serving pans (12 × 20 × 2 in). Sprinkle 2½ oz/71 g of Parmesan cheese over each pan of casserole.
8. Bake at 350°F/177°C until hot and browned.

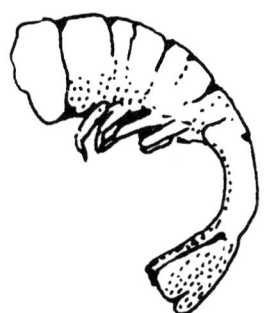

Salmon Croquettes

50 Servings (5¾ oz/177 g)
Bake, 350°F/177°C, 45 min

Metric		Ingredients	U.S.		
Weight	Volume		Weight		Volume
4.54 kg	4.74 l	Salmon, drained, boned, flaked	10 lb		5 qt
1.36 kg	2.84 l	Bread Crumbs	3 lb		3 qt
567 g	1.18 l	Celery, chopped	1 lb,	4 oz	1¼ qt
454 g	711 ml	Onions, chopped	1 lb		3 cups
37 g	40 ml	Salt		1⅓ oz	2⅔ tbsp
	5 ml	Pepper			1 tsp
114 g	118 ml	Lemon Juice		4 oz	½ cup
297 g	296 ml	Eggs, beaten (5 lge)		10 oz	1¼ cups
1.02 kg	1.07 l	Milk	2 lb,	4 oz	4½ cups
66 g	50 ml	Worcestershire Sauce		2⅓ oz	3⅓ tbsp

Procedure

1. Combine all ingredients. Shape into croquettes using a No. 16 scoop for sizing. Make 100 croquettes.
2. Bake in greased pans at 350°F/177°C for 45 minutes.
3. Serve with a favorite sauce such as creamed peas and pimiento, or chopped parsley and water chestnuts.

Scalloped Salmon and Peas

50 Servings (7 oz/198 g)
Bake, 350°F/177°C, 30 min

Metric		Ingredients	U.S.		
Weight	Volume		Weight		Volume
3.63 kg	3.79 l	Milk, hot	8 lb		1 gal
114 g	158 ml	Onions, chopped		4 oz	⅔ cup
14 g	80 ml	Parsley, chopped		½ oz	⅓ cup
	4 leaves	Bay Leaves			4 leaves
454 g	474 ml	Butter or Margarine	1 lb		2 cups
227 g	474 ml	Flour, bread		8 oz	2 cups
21 g	25 ml	Salt		¾ oz	1½ tbsp
	2½ ml	Paprika			½ tsp
681 g	1.42 l	Bread, soft, ½-in cubes	1 lb,	8 oz	1½ qt
4.54 kg	10 No. 1 cans	Salmon, drained, boned, flaked	10 lb		10 No. 1 cans
1.59 kg	2.37 l	Peas, frozen	3 lb,	8 oz	2½ qt
227 g	474 ml	Bread Crumbs, dry, fine		8 oz	2 cups
100 g	118 ml	Butter or Margarine, melted		3½ oz	½ cup

Procedure

1. Heat milk with onions, parsley, and bay leaves. Remove bay leaves.
2. Melt butter or margarine. Add flour, salt, and paprika. Blend. Cook over low heat 3 to 5 minutes. Stir while cooking. Add milk slowly, stirring constantly. Cook until sauce is smooth and thickened.
3. Spread bread cubes in 2 greased serving pans (12 × 20 × 2 in). Alternate layers of cream sauce, salmon, and peas, ending with sauce on top.
4. Stir bread crumbs into melted butter or margarine. Sprinkle buttered crumbs over casserole.
5. Bake at 350°F/177°C for 30 minutes or until nicely browned.

Salmon Patties

50 Servings (6 ½ oz/184 g)
Broil, 10 min

Metric		Ingredients	U.S.	
Weight	Volume		Weight	Volume
5.44 kg	6.39 l	Salmon, canned	12 lb	6 ¾ qt
851 g	2.13 l	Cracker Crumbs	1 lb, 14 oz	2 ¼ qt
1.19 kg	1.24 l	Eggs, beaten (21 lge)	2 lb, 10 oz	5 ¼ cups
14 g	15 ml	Salt	½ oz	1 tbsp
	10 ml	Pepper		2 tsp
340 g	355 ml	Lemon Juice	12 oz	1 ½ cups
2.04 kg	100 slices	Bacon	4 lb, 8 oz	100 slices

Procedure

1. Drain and flake salmon. Combine all ingredients except bacon.
2. Mix well and form into patties, using a No.16 scoop.
3. Wrap with slice of bacon, skewer with toothpick and broil for 5 minutes on each side. Allow 2 patties per serving.

Note: Serve with a modified Béchamel Sauce, such as Ravigote or Tomato.

Salmon Rice Casserole

50 Servings (4 oz/114 g)
Bake, 300°F/149°C, 30 min

Metric		Ingredients	U.S.	
Weight	Volume		Weight	Volume
1.14 kg	1.18 l	Rice, uncooked	2 lb, 8 oz	5 cups
2.72 kg	2.84 l	Water, boiling	6 lb	3 qt
19 g	20 ml	Salt	⅔ oz	1 ⅓ tbsp
2.72 kg	6 1-lb cans	Salmon, skinned, boned	6 lb	6 1-lb cans
114 g	118 ml	Eggs, beaten (2 lge)	4 oz	½ cup
227 g	711 ml	Cracker Crumbs	8 oz	3 cups
1.59 kg	1.66 l	Milk	3 lb, 8 oz	1 ¾ qt
28 g	30 ml	Salt	1 oz	2 tbsp
	2 ½ ml	Pepper		½ tsp
		Topping		
114 g	178 ml	Onions, finely chopped	4 oz	¾ cup
114 g	237 ml	Green Pepper, finely chopped	4 oz	1 cup
85 g	79 ml	Butter or Margarine	3 oz	⅓ cup
397 g	947 ml	Bread Crumbs	14 oz	1 qt

Procedure

1. Stir rice into boiling, salted water. Reduce heat. Cover tightly and continue cooking for 20 to 25 minutes, until water is absorbed and rice is tender.
2. Combine salmon, eggs, cracker crumbs, milk, and seasonings.
3. Place layer of cooked rice on bottom of 2 greased pans (12 × 20 × 2 in). Place salmon mixture as a second layer and a light layer of rice on top.
4. Sauté onions and green pepper in butter or margarine. Mix well with bread crumbs and sprinkle over rice. Bake at 300°F/149°C until browned (about 30 min).

Salmon Loaf

48 Servings (4 1/4 oz/120 g)
Bake, 350°F/177°C, 45 min

Metric		Ingredients	U.S.		
Weight	Volume		Weight		Volume
3.18 kg	4.98 l	Salmon, drained, boned, skinned	7 lb		5 1/4 qt
681 g	1.66 l	Bread Crumbs, dry	1 lb,	8 oz	1 3/4 qt
1.59 kg	1.66 l	Milk	3 lb,	8 oz	1 3/4 qt
681 g	711 ml	Eggs, beaten (12 lge)	1 lb,	8 oz	3 cups
114 g	158 ml	Pimiento, chopped		4 oz	2/3 cup
114 g	118 ml	Shortening, melted		4 oz	1/2 cup
47 g	35 ml	Worcestershire Sauce		1 2/3 oz	2 1/3 tbsp
85 g	90 ml	Lemon Juice		3 oz	6 tbsp
	5 ml	Pepper			1 tsp
14 g	15 ml	Salt		1/2 oz	1 tbsp

Procedure

1. Combine all ingredients and mix thoroughly. Scale 4 lbs, 6 oz/1.98 kg into each of 3 loaf pans (9 × 5 × 3 in).
2. Bake at 350°F/177°C for 45 minutes or until done.

3. Cut each loaf into 16 slices. Serve with a favorite sauce such as creamed pea and chopped, hard-cooked egg.

Scalloped Potatoes and Salmon

50 Servings (8 oz/227 g)
Bake, 400°F/205°C, 1 1/4 hrs

Metric		Ingredients	U.S.		
Weight	Volume		Weight		Volume
5.90 kg	9.24 l	Potatoes, pared	13 lb		9 3/4 qt
2.72 kg	2.84 l	Salmon, canned	6 lb		3 qt
114 g	118 ml	Onion Juice		4 oz	1/2 cup
43 g	45 ml	Salt		1 1/2 oz	3 tbsp
	10 ml	Pepper			2 tsp
454 g	504 ml	Bacon, diced	1 lb		2 1/8 cups
907 g	947 ml	Cream	2 lb		1 qt
907 g	947 ml	Milk	2 lb		1 qt
397 g	947 ml	Bread Crumbs		14 oz	1 qt

Procedure

1. Slice potatoes as for scalloping. Put 2 lb/907 g sliced potatoes in the bottom of 2 well-greased pans (12 × 20 × 2 in), then a layer of salmon, 1 1/2 lb/681 g, another 2 lb/907 g layer of potatoes and a second 1 1/2 lb/681 g layer of salmon, and a third layer of potatoes in each pan.
2. Sprinkle onion juice, salt, and pepper over top.

Spread diced bacon on top. Combine milk and cream and pour 1 qt/947 ml over each pan of salmon and potatoes. Sprinkle each pan with 2 cups/474 ml of crumbs.
3. Bake at 400°F/205°C until potatoes are tender (about 1 1/4 hrs).

Salmon Timbales

50 Servings (7 oz/198 g)
Bake, 350°F/177°C, 40–50 min

Metric		Ingredients	U.S.	
Weight	Volume		Weight	Volume
3.63 kg	8 1-lb cans	Salmon, boned, flaked	8 lb	8 1-lb cans
2.72 kg	6.63 l	Bread Crumbs, soft	6 lb	7 qt
2.27 kg	2.37 l	Milk	5 lb	2 ½ qt
198 g	237 ml	Butter or Margarine, melted	7 oz	1 cup
227 g	474 ml	Celery, finely chopped	8 oz	2 cups
114 g	178 ml	Onions, finely chopped	4 oz	¾ cup
57 g	59 ml	Lemon Juice	2 oz	¼ cup
681 g	711 ml	Eggs, beaten (12 lge)	1 lb, 8 oz	3 cups
14 g	15 ml	Salt	½ oz	1 tbsp
	2 ½ ml	Pepper		½ tsp

Procedure

1. Combine all ingredients and mix well. Pour half into each of 2 greased serving pans (12 × 20 × 2 in).
2. Bake at 350°F/177°C for 40 or 50 minutes or until set. Serve with Cheese, Green Pepper-Cheese, or Tomato Cheese Sauce.

Tuna Cashew Casserole

64 Servings
Bake, 350°F/177°C, 30 min

Metric		Ingredients	U.S.	
Weight	Volume		Weight	Volume
907 g	1.42 l	Onions, chopped	2 lb	1 ½ qt
1.70 kg	3.56 l	Celery, chopped	3 lb, 12 oz	3 ¾ qt
454 g	474 ml	Butter or Margarine	1 lb	2 cups
2.84 kg	2.84 l	Mushroom Soup	6 lb, 4 oz	3 qt
907 g	947 ml	Milk	2 lb	1 qt
454 g	711 ml	Cashews	1 lb	3 cups
1.28 kg	5.68 l	Chow Mein Noodles	2 lb, 13 oz	2 No. 10 cans
1.84 kg	2.13 l	Tuna, drained	4 lb, 1 oz	2 ¼ qt

Procedure

1. Sauté onions and celery in butter or margarine.
2. Combine sautéed vegetables, mushroom soup, and milk and heat.
3. Add remaining ingredients. Divide mixture into 2 greased serving pans (12 × 20 × 2 in).
4. Bake at 350°F/177°C for 30 minutes. Serve immediately as the noodles tend to lose their crispness.

Note: This casserole does not reheat well.

Tuna Chow Mein
50 Servings (¾ cup/178 ml)

Metric		Ingredients	U.S.	
Weight	Volume		Weight	Volume
3.63 kg	3.79 l	Fish or Chicken Stock	8 lb	1 gal
340 g	711 ml	Flour	12 oz	3 cups
907 g	977 ml	Fish or Chicken Stock, cold	2 lb	1 qt
567 g	889 ml	Onions, chopped	1 lb, 4 oz	3 ¾ cups
2.04 kg	4.26 l	Celery, chopped	4 lb, 8 oz	4 ½ qt
142 g	158 ml	Butter or Margarine	5 oz	⅔ cup
793 g	2.84 l	Mushrooms, sliced	1 lb, 12 oz	3 qt
170 g	178 ml	Soy Sauce	6 oz	¾ cup
793 g	2 ½ No. 2 cans	Bean Sprouts	1 lb, 12 oz	2 ½ No. 2 cans
1.93 kg	2.37 l	Tuna, drained, flaked	4 lb, 4 oz	2 ½ qt
170 g	237 ml	Pimiento	6 oz	1 cup

Procedure

1. Heat fish or chicken stock.
2. Make a paste of flour and cold stock. Add paste to hot stock, stirring until smooth and thick.
3. Sauté onions and celery in butter or margarine until almost tender. Add mushrooms.
4. Add vegetables, soy sauce, and bean sprouts to thickened stock. Mix well.
5. Add tuna and pimiento. Heat and serve on Chinese noodles.

Tuna Chop Suey
50 Servings (5 oz/142 g)

Metric		Ingredients	U.S.	
Weight	Volume		Weight	Volume
1.59 kg	3.31 l	Celery Rings	3 lb, 8 oz	3 ½ qt
454 g	947 ml	Green Pepper, chopped	1 lb	1 qt
1.36 kg	2.84 l	Onions, sliced	3 lb	3 qt
510 g	711 ml	Water Chestnuts, diced	1 lb, 2 oz	3 cups
114 g	118 ml	Butter or Margarine	4 oz	½ cup
21 g	22 ml	Salt	¾ oz	1 ½ tbsp
170 g	178 ml	Soy Sauce	6 oz	¾ cup
177 g	296 ml	Cornstarch	6 ¼ oz	1 ¼ cups
2.72 kg	2.84 l	Liquid from Sprouts, Tuna, Chestnuts, plus water	6 lb	3 qt
2.83 kg	4.26 l	Tuna, coarsely flaked	6 lb, 4 oz	4 ½ qt
681 g	1.42 l	Bean Sprouts, well-drained	1 lb, 8 oz	1 ½ qt

Procedure

1. Sauté vegetables and chestnuts in butter or margarine for 5 minutes. Add salt and soy sauce.
2. Stir cornstarch into liquid and combine with vegetables. Cover and cook for 5 minutes, stirring occasionally.
3. Add tuna and bean sprouts and simmer until well-heated.

Note: Serve ¾ cup/178 ml over ½ cup/118 ml cooked rice. 12 lb/5.44 kg or 1 ½ gal/5.63 l cooked rice required for 50 servings.

Tuna Pie

50 Servings (8 oz/227 g)
Bake, 425°F/218°C

Metric		Ingredients	U.S.	
Weight	Volume		Weight	Volume
1.59 kg	1.89 l	Tuna, white, flaked	3 lb, 8 oz	2 qt
4.54 kg	6.15 l	Potatoes, peeled, diced	10 lb	6½ qt
454 g	474 ml	Butter or Margarine	1 lb	2 cups
283 g	592 ml	Flour, bread	10 oz	2½ cups
28 g	30 ml	Salt	1 oz	2 tbsp
	2½ ml	Pepper, white		½ tsp
3.63 kg	3.79 l	Milk, hot	8 lb	1 gal
907 g	1.42 l	Peas, frozen	2 lb	1½ qt

Procedure

1. Drain tuna well. Steam potatoes until tender.
2. Melt butter or margarine. Add flour and seasonings. Blend. Cook over low heat 3 to 5 minutes. Stir while cooking. Add milk slowly, stirring constantly. Cook until sauce is smooth and thickened.
3. Combine potatoes, tuna, and peas. Pour sauce over mixture. Toss lightly to combine.
4. Put ¾ cup/178 ml of mixture into each of 50 casseroles or scale 13 lbs/5.90 kg into each of 2 greased serving pans (12 × 20 × 2 in). Top with pie crust and bake at 425°F/218°C until browned.

CHAPTER 6

Meats

Meat is a favorite food with the majority of people. It is likely to be the most costly item in menus and usually claims the largest share of food budgets. Managers who are truly concerned with pleasing customers with food quality and with the utilization of funds will be alert and informed in the selection, care, and preparation of meat.

When purchasing meat, indicate the desired total weight and weight of pieces, such as roasts, chops, and steaks. Specify the desired cut, grade, amount of trim, percentage of fat, and condition (whether fresh or frozen). Readers wishing fuller information are referred to chapters on "Selection and Preparation of Beef, Veal, Lamb, and Pork" in *Professional Food Preparation,* by Margaret E. Terrell, published by John Wiley & Sons, N. Y. (1979).

The browning of meat in roasting, broiling, and braising enriches its flavor. The meat's surface may be browned quickly at a high temperature and then cooked at much lower temperatures for tenderness and juiciness. Less tender cuts and grades may be cooked satisfactorily at 170°F/77°C to 250°F/121°C until the desired internal temperature is almost reached; then the oven temperature can be lowered and set at the desired internal temperature for the length of time needed for tenderizing. Allowances need to be made for the rise that occurs in internal temperature due to conduction of heat from the outer surface after the surrounding temperature has been lowered. The rise is greatest in very large roasts or those roasted at high temperatures. Meat will slice easier if removed from the heat 20 or 30 minutes before slicing. When placing a thermometer in meat to be roasted, the point of the thermometer should reach the thickest part of the roast, without touching bone at any point.

When tenderizers are used for meat, be alert to any unsatisfactory texture or flavor change in the meat.

Acids, such as those in lemon juice, vinegar, and tomatoes, combined with proper preparation techniques, are often adequate for producing palatable tenderness.

Boiling, stewing, braising, and steaming are the moist-heat methods of cooking. Sufficient liquid to cover the product is necessary when boiling and stewing. Braised meat is first browned, a little liquid is added, and the cooking pot is tightly covered to reduce evaporation. Steaming differs in that no water is added, but the product is cooked in a steam chamber or compartment, or in a pot, resting on a rack above boiling water that supplies the steam for cooking. Roasting, broiling, pan-frying, and grilling or griddling are dry-heat methods of cooking. Deep-fat frying is used for very few meat items, except those made into croquettes or cutlets.

Frozen meats may be completely or partially defrosted before cooking is begun. Complete defrosting is preferable. Defrosting in the refrigerator is best. If unwrapped and placed in the refrigerator, the majority of meat cuts and poultry, unless unusually large, can be defrosted sufficiently in 24 hours. Defrosting at room temperature requires 10 to 12 hours. In a waterproof package placed under cold, running water, defrosting requires 3 to 5 hours.

Care of meat in storage calls for protection, not only from spoilage, but also from dehydration and absorption of off-flavors. Meat can pick up flavors that may affect its fresh, sweet quality from knives, cutting boards, and other surfaces on which it is laid, and from refrigerator odors. The delicate flavor of lamb and veal is readily damaged by contact with off-flavors. There is less exchange of flavors when meat (or butter) is held at a temperature just above freezing. Recommended temperatures for meat storage are from 34°–36°F/1°–2°C, for the shortest possible holding time.

Use of Texturized Vegetable Protein Product. Protein from soybeans, cereal flours, and other plant foods may be used in ground meat dishes to extend the meat proteins. They are procurable in dry or frozen form and may be flavored or unflavored, colored or uncolored. The addition of the light-brown colored product is less apparent in meat dishes than the uncolored. In order to meet the U.S. Department of Agriculture standards for child-feeding programs, textured vegetable protein must meet the following conditions:

"(a) the textured vegetable protein must meet specifications listed in USDA,FNS Notice 219; (b) the hydrated product shall be served in combination with red meat, poultry, or fish; (c) meats used shall be ground and served as meat patties, meat loaves, meat sauce, chili, lasagna, pizza, or similar products; (d) the hydrated textured vegetable protein will have a moisture content of 60 to 65 percent; and (e) up to 30 percent of the meat may be replaced with hydrated vegetable protein."

Moisture content for the textured vegetable protein of 60 to 65 percent may be achieved by mixing one part of the product with 1.5 parts water (by weight). The following information published by the USDA may be used to guide calculation of the desired percentage.

Hydrated Vegetable Protein Product	Raw Meat	Dry Vegetable Protein	Water	Total Product
(percent)	(pound)	(pound)	(pound)	(pound)
30	0.70	0.12	0.18 (or .34 cup)	1.00
25	.75	.10	.15 (or .29 cup)	1.00
20*	.80	.08	.12 (or .23 cup)	1.00
15	.85	.06	.09 (or .17 cup)	1.00
10	.90	.04	.06 (or .11 cup)	1.00

"The following procedure may be used to determine the quantities of raw meat, dry textured vegetable protein, and water when the hydrated vegetable protein product replaces part (30%, 25%, 20%, 15%, 10%) of the raw meat in a recipe:

Directions
1. Convert quantity of raw meat in a recipe to pounds.
2. Choose the desired percentage of hydrated vegetable protein product from the first column in the table above.
3. Multiply the quantity (factor) of raw meat by the number on the same line in the table to obtain required pounds of raw meat, pounds of dry vegetable product, and water (pounds or cups).

Example
Assuming a recipe requires 4 lb, 8 oz. raw ground meat.
4 lb. 8 oz. = 4.5 lb. or a factor of 4.5.
*20 percent was chosen for this example:

4.5 × 0.80 lb. = 3.60 lb. (3 lb. 9¾ oz.) meat.
4.5 × 0.08 lb. = .36 lb. (5¾ oz.) dry textured vegetable protein product.

4.5 × 0.12 lb. = .54 lb. (8¾ oz.) water.
(or)   (or)
4.5 × 0.23 cups = 1.035 cups (1 cup) water."

Time and Temperature in the Cooking of Meat. The use of a meat thermometer helps to take the guesswork out of roasting meat. The desired degree of doneness will correspond with specific temperatures. For cooking to rare the internal temperature will be 140°F/60°C, medium 160°F/71°C and at 170°F/77°C the meat will be well done. After an initial browning of beef at a high temperature, the oven temperature may be reduced to equal the desired internal temperature and roasting continued until the desired internal temperature and degree of tenderness has been attained. Where shorter roasting time is required, 300°F to 325°F/140°C to 163°C may be used. These temperatures are most suitable for lamb. An internal temperature of 170°F/77°C will require from 25 to 30 minutes per pound of roast. A roasting temperature of 325°F/163°C is recommended for fresh pork, to an internal temperature of 170°F/77°C. Length of cooking time in roasting meat depends upon temperature used and size of the roast. Broiling time will depend on thickness of the chop or steak and distance from heat, as shown in the following tables.

Table 3
Time Required for Broiling Beef Steak

Steak Thickness (in)	Distance from Heat (in)	Cooking Time (min) per Side			Kind of Steak
		Rare	Medium Rare	Well Done	
1	2	5	6	7–8	Prime, choice, good,
1½	3	9	10	12–13	short loin, loin end,
2	4	16	18	20–22	and eye of rib.
1	3	10	12	14	Full sirloin cut,
1½	4	12–14	14–16	18–20	steaks from good, standard, and commercial grades.
1	3		9	10–11	Ground beef patties
1½	4		12	15–18	or hamburger.

Table 4
Time Required for Broiling Lamb

Cut	Thickness (in)	Distance from Heat (in)	Cooking Time (min) per Side	
			Medium	Well Done
Rib or Loin Chops	1	2	12 to 14	14 to 18
	1½	3	18 to 22	22 to 25
	2	3	25 to 30	30 to 35
Leg Steaks	1	2	12 to 15	14 to 18
Shoulder Chops	¾	2	14 to 16	16 to 18
Lamb Patties	¾	3	15 to 28	20 to 25
Riblets	1	3		20 to 25

Table 5
Cooking Schedule for Veal (Cooking at Approximately 325°F/163°C to 170°F/77°C Internal Temperature)

Cut	Size	Cooking Method	Approximate Time (hrs)
Leg, bone-in	5 lb/2.27 kg	Roasting	3½
	8 lb/3.63 kg	Roasting	4½
boned	20 lb/9.07 kg	Roasting	8
Loin, bone-in	5 lb/2.27 kg	Roasting	2¾
	8 lb/3.63 kg	Roasting	3½
Shoulder, bone-in	5 lb/2.27 kg	Roasting	3½
	8 lb/3.63 kg	Roasting	4
Boned-and-rolled	5 lb/2.27 kg	Roasting	3¾
	8 lb/3.63 kg	Roasting	4½
Boned-and-rolled	5 lb/2.27 kg	Braising	3
Chops, Steaks, Cutlets	½ to ¾ in	Braising	¾ to 2
	1 in	Braising	¾ to 2
Breast	¾ to 1 lb	Braising	1¾ to 2
Heart	¾ to 1 lb	Boiling	2½
Tongue	1¼ to 1½ lb	Boiling	2½
Stew Meat	1-in cubes	Stewing	2 to 3

Table 6
Time Required for Cooking Meat
with Moist Heat

Cut	Size	Approximate Total Time (hrs)
Beef Pot Roast	5 lb/2.27 kg	3 to 4
Swiss Steak	2½ × 4 in	2 to 3
Fricassee	2 in	1½ to 2½
Short Ribs	1½ × 2½ × 4 in	2 to 2½
Round Steak	¾ in	1 to 1½
Pork Spareribs	2 lb/907 g	1½ to 2
Braised Chops	¾ to 1½ in	1 to 1¼
Braised Steaks	¾ in	¾ to 1
Lamb Shanks	1 lb/454 g	1 to 1½
Lamb Stew	1½-in cubes	1½ to 2
Veal Chops	½ to ¾ in	¾ to 1
Broiled Ham (smoked)	12 lb/5.44 kg	3½ to 4
	8 lb/3.63 kg	3½ to 4
Boiled Picnic (smoked)	6 lb/2.72 kg	3 to 3½

Table 7
Baking or Braising Schedule for Pork at 325°F/163°C

Item	Approximate Weight	Approximate Time	Internal Temperature
Fresh Loin	3 lb/1.36 kg	2½ hr	170°F/77°C
	7 lb/3.18 kg	3 hr	170°F/77°C
Shoulder, bone-in	5 lb/2.27 kg	4 hr	170°F/77°C
Ham*	8 lb/3.63 kg	4¾ hr	170°F/77°C
	14 lb/6.35 kg	5½ hr	170°F/77°C
Spareribs	2 lb/907 g	1–1½ hr	170°F/77°C
Chops	6–8 oz/170–227 g	¾–1 hr	170°F/77°C
Canadian Bacon	1 lb/454 g	¾ hr	160°F/71°C
	4 lb/1.82 kg	2½ hr	160°F/71°C
Ham Slice, 2 in	2 lb/907 g	1½–1¾ hr	160°F/71°C
¾ in	1 lb/454 g	1–1½ hr	160°F/71°C
Ham, whole, bone-in	8 lb/3.63 kg	3¼ hr	160°F/71°C
	15 lb/6.81 kg	4½ hr	160°F/71°C
	24 lb/10.89 kg	6½ hr	160°F/71°C
Picnic, smoked	6 lb/2.72 kg	3 hr	170°F/77°C
Fully Cooked Ham	8 lb/3.63 kg	2¼ hr	130°F/54°C
	12 lb/5.44 kg	3 hr	130°F/54°C
	16 lb/7.26 kg	3¾ hr	130°F/54°C
Canned Ham or Picnic		20 minutes per lb	

*ROAST FRESH HAM (Uncured leg of pork) when roasted to 325°F/163°C will require 25 to 30 minutes per lb/454 g to reach an internal temperature of 170°F/77°C. Refer to the section on Sauces and Stuffings for a suitable dressing to serve with Roast Pork.

Beef Recipes

Roast Beef
Procedure

1. Determine size of portion and cut appropriate for budget allowance and patron needs. The ounce or gram allowance per portion may vary A.P. from 12 to 24 ounces/340 to 681 grams for prime rib to 4 or 5 ounces/114 to 142 grams for top round or clod.

The beef cuts commonly used for roasting, listed

in order of tenderness, are tenderloin, loin strip, rib, top round, sirloin tip (knuckle), chuck, and brisket, selected from the 3 or 4 top grades. The most tender cuts from lower grades are satisfactory when properly larded (wrapped in a layer of fat and/or fat distributed throughout the muscle area with a larding needle). It is advisable to prepare the less tender cuts of the lower grades by moist-heat methods and with suitable seasoning.

2. Choose roasting temperatures in terms of size of roast and desired degree of doneness. Very large roasts (standing ribs or cafeteria rounds, for example), especially those with a heavy fat covering, may be browned at 400°F/205°C for the first 20 or 30 minutes, then the temperature lowered to correspond with the desired degree of doneness (140°F/60°C rare, 160°F/71°C medium, 170°F/77°C well done) and roasting continued until the meat thermometer registers the appropriate internal temperature. If extra tenderness is desired, continue cooking at that oven temperature. Even a degree of rare can be maintained for 24 hours or longer if the temperature of roasting is held continuously, without variation, at the desired degree of doneness. Be aware that the temperature for roasting to a rare degree of doneness is close to that which permits bacterial growth. Special care and accuracy of thermostats are important for safety.

3. Place the meat thermometer with the bulb in the thickest center of the lean area. Place meat in the pan with the fat side uppermost.

4. Roasting temperature, size, and shape of the roast and the degree of tenderness desired will influence the length of cooking time. Allow approximately 3 or 4 hours as a minimum for less tender cuts of top grades and tender cuts of lower grades. If the temperature is evenly maintained at the desired internal temperature for degree of doneness, longer cooking will tenderize but not appreciably change the character of doneness.

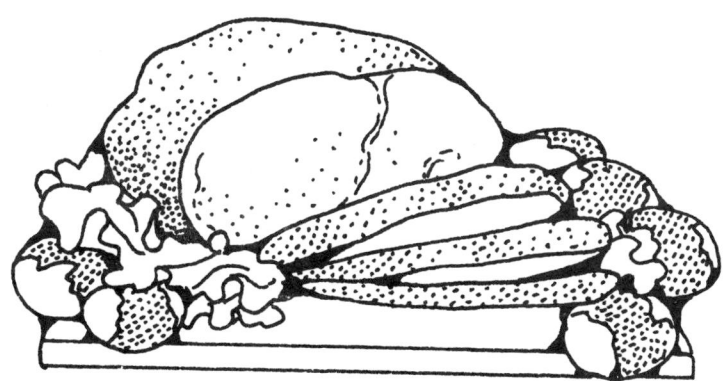

Broiled Steak

Steaks for broiling should never be less than ¾ inch thick, and 1 to 2 inches is preferable. When small pieces are required, select from cuts that are smallest in circumference, such as eye of rib, club, and tenderloin, or a loin strip steak that can be cut in half.

Procedure

1. Remove excess fat and cut covering fat at 1-inch intervals, to prevent curling during cooking. Use care not to cut into lean area.

2. Marinade steak if special flavor is desired (see marinades in Sauce section). A light flavor is imparted by allowing steak to stand for a short time before broiling in salad oil in which a garlic clove has been immersed.

3. Note Table 3 for broiling time and distance from heat according to thickness of steak.

4. Use care in turning steak to be sure that grill marks make a neat, attractive pattern on the steak, and do not look like a meandering plaid.

5. Season the steak after turning. 2 tbsp/30 ml vermouth per steak, added after the steak is on the plate, adds an appealing flavor.

Sauerbraten

50 Servings (4 oz/114 g)
Bake, 300°F/149°C

| Metric | | Ingredients | U.S. | |
Weight	Volume		Weight	Volume
		Marinade		
7.26 kg	7.57 l	Water	16 lb	2 gal
2.42 kg	2.53 l	Vinegar	5 lb, 5 ½ oz	2 ⅔ qt
595 g	829 ml	Brown Sugar	1 lb, 5 oz	3 ½ cups
	158 ml	Pickle Spices		⅔ cup
681 g	1.42 l	Onion, sliced	1 lb, 8 oz	1 ½ qt
227 g	474 ml	Celery, leaves and stalk, chopped	8 oz	2 cups
340 g	711 ml	Carrots, chopped	12 oz	3 cups
	1 clove	Garlic		1 clove
9.07 kg		Beef Roasts	20 lb	
		Sour Cream		

Procedure

1. Combine all marinade ingredients. Pour over meat and let stand 4 to 7 days, covered, in the refrigerator.
2. Remove roasts from marinade and place in roasting pans. Place onions from marinade on top of roasts. Add marinade to pans, cover, and bake at 300°F/149°C until internal temperature of meat registers 160°F/71°C.
3. Remove the meat. Thicken the stock for gravy. Add 2 cups/474 ml sour cream per gallon of stock.
4. Slice meat and serve with gravy.

Braised Flank Steak

50 Servings
Bake, 350°F/177°C, 1 ½ hrs

| Metric | | Ingredients | U.S. | |
Weight	Volume		Weight	Volume
7.71 kg	50 pieces	Flank Steaks, cubed	17 lb	50 pieces
567 g	1.18 l	Flour, all-purpose	1 lb, 4 oz	5 cups
85 g	90 ml	Salt	3 oz	6 tbsp
	10 ml	Pepper		2 tsp
	½ clove	Garlic		½ clove
1.36 kg	2.84 l	Onions, sliced	3 lb	3 qt
454 g	474 ml	Shortening	1 lb	2 cups
	4 leaves	Bay Leaves		4 leaves

Procedure

1. Cut flank steaks into 5 oz/142 g portions. Dredge steaks with mixture of flour, salt, and pepper.
2. Brown garlic and onions in 8 oz/227 g shortening. Remove. Add balance of shortening as needed and brown meat.
3. Place layers of meat and onions in baking pan. Add bay leaves. Cover.
4. Bake for 1 ½ hours at 350°F/177°C, or until tender.
5. To make gravy, remove meat and add liquid to make 4 qts/3.79 l. Thicken with 10 oz/283 g of flour mixed with 2 cups/474 ml cold water. Season with 2 tbsp/30 ml salt.

Note: If desired, gravy may be poured over meat and it may be served as Swiss steak; or 3 qts/2.84 l (1 No. 10 can) of tomato juice may be added to the meat when it is tender and then baking time increased 30 minutes.

Green Pepper Steak
50 Servings (9 oz/255 g)
Simmer, 2 hrs

Metric		Ingredients	U.S.	
Weight	Volume		Weight	Volume
5.44 kg	5.68 l	Round or Flank Steaks, cut into strips ½ × 3 in	12 lb	6 qt
21 g	6 cloves	Garlic, minced	¾ oz	6 cloves
170 g	355 ml	Onions, chopped	6 oz	1½ cups
114 g	118 ml	Shortening	4 oz	½ cup
3.63 kg	3.79 l	Beef Stock	8 lb	1 gal
57 g	59 ml	Soy Sauce	2 oz	¼ cup
14 g	15 ml	Seasoning Salt	½ oz	1 tbsp
681 g	1.42 l	Celery, sliced diagonally ½ inch	1 lb, 8 oz	1½ qt
2.27 kg	4.74 l	Green Pepper, large slices	5 lb	5 qt
212 g	355 ml	Cornstarch	7½ oz	1½ cups
907 g	947 ml	Water, cold	2 lb	1 qt

Procedure

1. Sauté steak, garlic, and onions in shortening until lightly browned. Add stock, soy sauce, and seasoning salt. Let simmer slowly for 1½ hours or until meat is tender.
2. Add celery and green pepper and cook until tender but firm (about 5 min).
3. Mix cornstarch with cold water and stir into the steak mixture. Cook until thickened, stirring.

Yankee Pot Roast
50 Servings
Simmer slowly, 4 hrs

Metric		Ingredients	U.S.	
Weight	Volume		Weight	Volume
7.36–9.07 kg		Beef, for pot roasting	16–20 lb	
227 g	237 ml	Shortening	8 oz	1 cup
43 g	45 ml	Salt	1½ oz	3 tbsp
	7½ ml	Pepper		1½ tsp
681 g	1.07 l	Onions, E.P., chopped	1 lb, 8 oz	4½ cups
7 g	2 cloves	Garlic, minced	¼ oz	2 cloves
114 g	4 bunches	Parsley, chopped	4 oz	4 bunches
	2 leaves	Bay Leaves		2 leaves
	5 ml	Thyme		1 tsp
1.36 kg	1.42 l	White Wine	3 lb	1½ qt
2.04 kg	2.13 l	Tomato Puree	4 lb, 8 oz	2¼ qt
1.82 kg	1.89 l	Water	4 lb	2 qt

Procedure

1. Brown meat in shortening. Add seasoning. When well-browned, add onions, garlic, parsley, bay leaves, and thyme. Simmer a few minutes.
2. Add wine, tomato puree, and sufficient water or broth to cover meat. Simmer slowly for about 4 hours, or until tender.
3. Remove meat and strain juice. Cook down to proper consistency for gravy.

Rolled Steak with Dressing
50 Servings (4 oz/114 g)
Bake, 275°F/135°C, 2 hrs

Metric		Ingredients	U.S.		
Weight	Volume		Weight		Volume
5.67 kg	50 steaks	Round Steak, sliced thin	12 lb,	8 oz	50 steaks
1.36 kg	2.84 l	Bread Crumbs, soft	3 lb		3 qt
454 g	711 ml	Onions, minced	1 lb		3 cups
170 g	237 ml	Bacon Fat		6 oz	1 cup
	20 ml	Sage or Poultry Seasoning			4 tsp
46 g	50 ml	Salt		1 2/3 oz	3 1/3 tbsp
14 g	25 ml	Pepper		1/2 oz	1 2/3 tbsp
681 g	711 ml	Milk, hot, to moisten	1 lb,	8 oz	3 cups, approx.

Procedure

1. Score thin slices of steak on one side. (Steak should be cut 4 servings per pound.)
2. Combine remaining ingredients for the dressing.
3. Spread dressing on the smooth side of the meat, using about 2 1/2 oz/71 g per serving. Roll, tie, or skewer with toothpicks.
4. Flour steak rolls and brown in hot fat.
5. Place steaks in serving pans (12 × 20 × 2 in) and add 1/2 cup/118 ml hot water to each pan. Cover pans and bake at 275°F/135°C for 2 hours or until tender.

Beefsteak Pie
48 Servings (7 1/2 oz/212 g)
Bake, 425°F/218°C, 15–20 min

Metric		Ingredients	U.S.		
Weight	Volume		Weight		Volume
6.81 kg	7.10 l	Boned Chuck, cubed	15 lb		7 1/2 qt
907 g	1.42 l	Carrots, diced	2 lb		1 1/2 qt
907 g	1.42 l	Rutabagas, diced	2 lb		1 1/2 qt
1.36 kg	2.13 l	Onions, chopped	3 lb		2 1/4 qt
114 g	118 ml	Steak Sauce		4 oz	1/2 cup
1.14 kg	1.18 l	Tomato Puree	2 lb,	8 oz	1 1/4 qt
2.27 kg	2.37 l	Beef Stock	5 lb		2 1/2 qt
	2 leaves	Bay Leaves			2 leaves
75 g	80 ml	Salt		2 2/3 oz	5 1/3 tbsp
	5 ml	Pepper			1 tsp
	1 1/4 ml	Garlic Salt			1/4 tsp
227 g	474 ml	Flour, all-purpose		8 oz	2 cups
454 g	474 ml	Water	1 lb		2 cups

Procedure

1. Brown cubed chuck on greased baking sheets.
2. Combine all ingredients except flour and water. Simmer until meat is tender. Stir flour into cold water until smooth. Stir mixture into meat mixture, stirring until thickened and flour has lost its raw taste.
3. Put in serving pans and cover with pie crust or biscuits. Bake at 425°F/218°C until crust or biscuits are browned.

Swiss Steak

50 Servings (6 oz/170 g)
Bake, 325°F/163°C, 2 hrs

Metric		Ingredients	U.S.	
Weight	**Volume**		**Weight**	**Volume**
340 g	711 ml	Flour, all-purpose	12 oz	3 cups
43 g	45 ml	Salt	1 ½ oz	3 tbsp
	10 ml	Pepper		2 tsp
8.40 kg	50 pieces	Round Steak	18 lb, 8 oz	50 pieces
227 g	237 ml	Shortening	8 oz	1 cup
907 g	1.42 l	Onions, sliced	2 lb	1 ½ qt
227 g	474 ml	Green Pepper, chopped	8 oz	2 cups
1.36 kg	1.42 l	Tomato Juice	3 lb	1 ½ qt

Procedure

1. Combine flour, salt, and pepper. Flour steak and brown in hot shortening.
2. Arrange steak in baking pan in alternate layers with onions and green pepper and pour tomato juice over it.
3. Bake at 325°F/163°C for 2 hours or until steak is tender.

Beef Stroganoff

50 Servings (6 oz/170 g)
Simmer, 2 hrs

Metric		Ingredients	U.S.	
Weight	**Volume**		**Weight**	**Volume**
4.54 kg	4.74 l	Beef Round, cut in strips	10 lb	5 qt
57 g	59 ml	Shortening	2 oz	¼ cup
170 g	178 ml	Beef Soup Base	6 oz	¾ cup
3.63 kg	3.79 l	Water, hot	8 lb	1 gal
227 g	237 ml	Tomato Puree	8 oz	1 cup
35 g	30 ml	Worcestershire Sauce	1 ¼ oz	2 tbsp
142 g	296 ml	Flour, all-purpose	5 oz	1 ¼ cups
9 g	10 ml	Salt	⅓ oz	2 tsp
227 g	237 ml	Water, cold	8 oz	1 cup
1.82 kg	6.63 l	Mushrooms, fresh, sliced	4 lb	1 ¾ gal
114 g	118 ml	Butter or Margarine	4 oz	½ cup
340 g	355 ml	Sherry	12 oz	1 ½ cups
1.14 kg	1.18 l	Sour Cream	2 lb, 8 oz	1 ¼ qt

Procedure

1. Brown meat in shortening. Dissolve beef base in hot water and add with puree and Worcestershire sauce to the meat. Simmer until the meat is tender (about 2 hrs).
2. Stir flour and salt into cold water until smooth. When meat is cooked, stir mixture into meat liquid to thicken gravy.
3. Sauté mushrooms in butter or margarine and add to meat mixture.
4. Stir in Sherry and sour cream shortly before serving.

Beef Burgundy
48 Servings (5 oz/142 g)

| Metric | | Ingredients | U.S. | |
Weight	Volume		Weight	Volume
1.36 kg	2.13 l	Onions, finely chopped	3 lb	2 ¼ qt
28 g	8 cloves	Garlic, minced	1 oz	8 cloves
454 g	474 ml	Shortening	1 lb	2 cups
6.81 kg	7.10 l	Beef Round, cubed	15 lb	7 ½ qt
681 g	711 ml	Beef Stock	1 lb, 8 oz	3 cups
907 g	947 ml	Mushrooms, canned, sliced	2 lb	1 qt
681 g	711 ml	Burgundy Wine	1 lb, 8 oz	3 cups
1.82 kg	1.89 l	Tomato Sauce	4 lb	2 qt
907 g	947 ml	Sour Cream	2 lb	1 qt
28 g	30 ml	Salt	1 oz	2 tbsp
	5 ml	Pepper		1 tsp
	5 ml	Basil, ground		1 tsp
57 g	59 ml	Worcestershire Sauce	2 oz	¼ cup
114 g	237 ml	Flour, all-purpose	4 oz	1 cup
227 g	237 ml	Water	8 oz	1 cup

Procedure

1. Sauté onions and garlic in shortening. Remove from fat and brown beef. Combine all ingredients except flour and water.
2. Simmer until meat is tender (about 2 hrs). Make a paste of flour and water. Stir this into the meat mixture, stirring until thickened and flour has lost its raw taste (about 10 min).

French Ragout
48 Servings (8 oz/227 g)
Bake, 300°F/149°C, 2–3 hrs

| Metric | | Ingredients | U.S. | |
Weight	Volume		Weight	Volume
3.63 kg	3.79 l	Boneless Chuck, cubed	8 lb	4 qt
340 g	711 ml	Flour	12 oz	3 cups
57 g	60 ml	Salt	2 oz	4 tbsp
	2 tsp	Pepper		2 tsp
227 g	237 ml	Shortening	8 oz	1 cup
907 g	947 ml	Tomato Puree	2 lb	1 qt
	2 leaves	Bay Leaves		2 leaves
	4 cloves	Cloves, whole		4 cloves
	1 ⅗ ml	Thyme, ground		⅓ tsp
14 g	15 ml	Salt	½ oz	1 tbsp
681 g	1.07 l	Carrots, diced	1 lb, 8 oz	4 ½ cups
567 g	1.07 l	Turnips, diced	1 lb, 4 oz	4 ½ cups
681 g	1.07 l	Onions, chopped	1 lb, 8 oz	4 ½ cups
907 g	1.07 l	Potatoes, diced	2 lb	4 ½ cups
907 g	1.42 l	Peas	2 lb	1 ½ qt
1.82 kg	1.89 l	Water	4 lb	2 qt

1. Dredge beef in mixture of flour, salt, and pepper. Brown in shortening.
2. Combine puree, bay leaves, cloves, thyme, and salt.
3. Combine vegetables except peas. Arrange layers of meat, vegetables, and sauce in baking pan. Add water.

4. Bake at 300°F/149°C until meat is tender. Add peas and cook 5 minutes longer.

Note: Attractive topped with small biscuits.

Norwegian Meatballs

58 Servings
Bake, 350°F/177°C, 30 min, 20 min

Metric		Ingredients	U.S.	
Weight	Volume		Weight	Volume
1.14 kg	1.18 l	Applesauce	2 lb, 8 oz	1 ¼ qt
567 g	592 ml	Eggs, beaten (10 lge)	1 lb, 4 oz	2 ½ cups
454 g	107 ml	Bread Crumbs, dry	1 lb	4 ½ cups
57 g	59 ml	Salt	2 oz	¼ cup
	12 ½ ml	Pepper		2 ½ tsp
4.54 kg	1.18 l	Ground Beef	10 lb	5 qt
		Sauce		
99 g	158 ml	Onion, finely chopped	3 ½ oz	⅔ cup
170 g	355 ml	Celery, finely chopped	6 oz	1 ½ cups
99 g	207 ml	Carrots, finely chopped	3 ½ oz	⅞ cup
142 g	148 ml	Butter or Margarine	5 oz	⅝ cup
71 g	148 ml	Flour	2 ½ oz	⅝ cup
2.27 kg	2.37 l	Tomato Juice	5 lb	2 ½ qt
43 g	45 ml	Sugar	1 ½ oz	3 tbsp
	12 ½ ml	Salt		2 ½ tsp

Procedure

1. Stir applesauce into eggs. Add bread crumbs, seasonings, and meat. Mix at low speed for 1 minute.
2. Shape balls, using a No. 16 dipper. Place in greased serving pans (12 × 20 × 2 in).
3. Bake at 350°F/177°C for 30 minutes. Drain drippings from meatballs and reserve.
4. Sauté onions, celery, and carrots in reserved drippings until tender.

5. Melt butter or margarine. Add flour and blend. Cook over low heat 3 to 5 minutes. Stir while cooking.
6. Add tomato juice slowly, stirring constantly. Cook until smooth and thickened. Add vegetables, sugar, and salt.
7. Pour sauce over meatballs and bake at 350°F/177°C for 20 minutes.

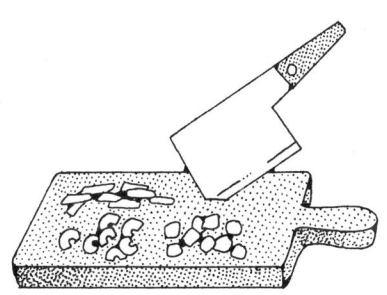

Teriyaki Steak Patties
60 Servings

Metric		Ingredients	U.S.	
Weight	Volume		Weight	Volume
4.54 kg	4.74 l	Ground Beef	10 lb	5 qt
681 g	1.66 l	Bread Crumbs	1 lb, 8 oz	1 ¾ qt
596 g	947 ml	Onions, chopped	1 lb, 5 oz	1 qt
567 g	592 ml	Egg (10 lge)	1 lb, 4 oz	2 ½ cups
170 g	178 ml	Sugar	6 oz	¾ cup
312 g	316 ml	Soy Sauce	11 oz	1 ⅓ cups
340 g	355 ml	Water	12 oz	1 ½ cups
21 g	6 cloves	Garlic, crushed	¾ oz	6 cloves
	20 ml	Ginger, dark		4 tsp
		Sauce		
2.27 kg	2.37 l	Water	5 lb	2 ½ qt
302 g	316 ml	Soy Sauce	10 ⅔ oz	1 ⅓ cups
151 g	158 ml	Sugar	5 ⅓ oz	⅔ cup
	10 ml	Garlic Salt		2 tsp
94 g	158 ml	Cornstarch	3 ⅓ oz	⅔ cup
	3 ¾ ml	Ginger		¾ tsp

Procedure

1. Combine all ingredients for steaks. Shape into patties using a No. 8 scoop.
2. Bake at 350°F/177°C for 30 minutes.

3. Mix all ingredients for sauce and cook until sauce is clear.
4. Pour sauce over steaks and serve.

Swedish Meatballs
65 Servings
Bake, 350°F/177°C, 1 hr

Metric		Ingredients	U.S.	
Weight	Volume		Weight	Volume
425 g	947 ml	Bread Crumbs	15 oz	1 qt
1.36 kg	1.42 l	Light Cream	3 lb	1 ½ qt
2.38 kg	2.48 l	Ground Beef	5 lb, 4 oz	2 ⅝ qt
2.38 kg	2.48 l	Ground Pork	5 lb, 4 oz	2 ⅝ qt
85 g	90 ml	Salt	3 oz	6 tbsp
	30 ml	Allspice, ground		2 tbsp
227 g	355 ml	Onions, finely chopped	8 oz	1 ½ cups
681 g	711 ml	Eggs, slightly beaten (12 lge)	1 lb, 8 oz	3 cups
		Gravy		
2.95 kg	3.08 l	Drippings and Water	6 lb, 8 oz	3 ¼ qt
99 g	79 ml	Beef Base	3 ½ oz	⅓ cup
151 g	158 ml	Skimmed Fat	5 ⅓ oz	⅔ cup
151 g	316 ml	Flour, all-purpose	5 ⅓ oz	1 ⅓ cups

1. Mix bread crumbs and cream.
2. Add ground beef and pork, salt, allspice, onions, and beaten eggs. Mix slowly until blended.
3. Shape 130 balls using a No. 16 dipper. Place meatballs in serving pans (12 × 20 × 2 in).
4. Bake at 300°F/149°C for 1½ hours.
5. After meatballs are cooked, drain off drippings. Skim off fat. Use fat and juices for gravy.
6. Heat drained juices and water to boiling. Dissolve soup base in water and juices.
7. Combine skimmed fat and flour to make a roux. Add to boiling stock and cook, stirring, until thickened, and raw starch taste has disappeared.
8. Ladle gravy over meatballs and serve 2 meatballs per portion.

Hamburger Creole with Cheese Biscuits

50 Servings (7½ oz/212 g)
Bake, 400°F/205°C, 20 min
Bake, 425°F/218°C, 20 min

Metric			U.S.	
Weight	Volume	Ingredients	Weight	Volume
4.54 kg	4.74 l	Hamburger	10 lb	5 qt
397 g	947 ml	Bread Crumbs	14 oz	1 qt
43 g	45 ml	Salt	1½ oz	3 tbsp
	5 ml	Pepper		1 tsp
227 g	237 ml	Onions, grated or shredded	8 oz	1 cup
283 g	296 ml	Eggs, well-beaten (5 lge)	10 oz	1¼ cups
		Soup		
1.82 kg	1.89 l	Tomatoes	4 lb	2 qt
227 g	355 ml	Onions, finely chopped	8 oz	1½ cups
14 g	15 ml	Sugar	½ oz	1 tbsp
	1 leaf	Bay Leaf		1 leaf
	3 sprigs	Parsley		3 sprigs
114 g	237 ml	Celery, chopped	4 oz	1 cup
170 g	178 ml	Butter or Margarine	6 oz	¾ cup
85 g	178 ml	Flour, all-purpose	3 oz	¾ cup
1.82 kg	1.89 l	Milk	4 lb	2 qt
14 g	15 ml	Salt	½ oz	1 tbsp
	5 ml	Pepper		1 tsp
		Biscuits		
1.03 kg	2.13 l	Flour, pastry	2 lb, 4 oz	2¼ qt
57 g	80 ml	Baking Powder	2 oz	5⅓ tbsp
14 g	15 ml	Salt	½ oz	1 tbsp
227 g	237 ml	Shortening	8 oz	1 cup
340 g	711 ml	Cheddar Cheese, grated	12 oz	3 cups
681 g	711 ml	Milk	1 lb, 8 oz	3 cups

Procedure

1. Combine meat, crumbs, salt, pepper, onions, and eggs. Mix well. Shape 100 balls, using a No. 20 scoop. Divide into 2 serving pans (12 × 20 × 2 in) and brown in oven at 400°F/205°C for about 20 minutes.
2. Cook tomatoes, onions, sugar, bay leaf, parsley, and celery together for 30 minutes.
3. Make white sauce with butter or margarine, flour, salt, pepper, and milk. Add tomato mixture to sauce and mix. Do not heat further. Pour over meatballs, using approximately 2¼ qts/2.13 l for each of 2 pans.
4. Make biscuits, roll to ⅜-inch thickness, cut with 1½-inch cutter, and place one on top of each meatball.
5. Bake at 425°F/218°C about 20 minutes until biscuits are done. Serve 2 meatballs and 2 biscuits per portion.

Savory Beef Stew

50 Servings

Simmer about 2 ½ hrs

| Metric | | Ingredients | U.S. | |
Weight	Volume		Weight	Volume
5.44 kg	5.68 l	Lean Beef, 1 ½-in cubes	12 lb	1 ½ gal
114 g	237 ml	Flour, all-purpose	4 oz	1 cup
57 g	59 ml	Shortening	2 oz	¼ cup
610 g	947 ml	Onions, diced	1 lb, 5 ½ oz	1 qt
28 g	30 ml	Salt	1 oz	2 tbsp
	5 ml	Pepper		1 tsp
227 g	237 ml	Vinegar	8 oz	1 cup
454 g	316 ml	Molasses	1 lb	1 ⅓ cups
2.95 kg	3.31 l	Tomatoes, canned	6 lb, 8 oz	1 No. 10 can
907 g	1.89 l	Celery, sliced	2 lb	2 qt
1.82 kg	2.84 l	Carrots, chunked	4 lb	3 qt
283 g	474 ml	Raisins	10 oz	2 cups
	10 ml	Ginger, ground		2 tsp

Procedure

1. Dredge beef with flour and brown in shortening. Add onions, salt, and pepper. Blend vinegar, molasses, and tomatoes and add to meat.
2. Cover and simmer until meat is tender (about 2 ½ hrs).
3. Add celery, carrots, raisins, and ginger. Cook until carrots are tender.

Meat Loaf

60 Servings

Bake, 325°F/163°C, 1 ½ hrs

| Metric | | Ingredients | U.S. | |
Weight	Volume		Weight	Volume
737 g	770 ml	Pork Sausage	1 lb, 10 oz	3 ¼ cups
3.80 kg	4.02 l	Ground Beef	8 lb, 6 oz	4 ¼ qt
681 g	1.07 l	Onions, chopped	1 lb, 8 oz	4 ½ cups
43 g	45 ml	Salt	1 ½ oz	3 tbsp
	10 ml	Pepper		2 tsp
340 g	355 ml	Eggs, beaten (6 lge)	12 oz	1 ½ cups
454 g	1.07 l	Bread Crumbs, dry	1 lb	4 ½ cups
567 g	592 ml	Milk	1 lb, 4 oz	2 ½ cups
	10 ml	Sage		2 tsp

Procedure

1. Mix all ingredients until blended. Do not overmix.
2. Scale 7 lb, 8 oz/3.40 kg for each loaf. Place 2 loaves lengthwise in serving pan (12 × 20 × 2 in).
3. Bake at 325°F/163°C for 1 ½ hours. Drain. Slice into 30 portions per loaf.

Note: Loaf may be varied by layering with bread dressing or by spreading mixture and rolling like jelly rolls to form loaves.

Hamburger Stroganoff
50 Servings

Metric		Ingredients	U.S.	
Weight	Volume		Weight	Volume
907 g	1.42 l	Onions, chopped	2 lb	1 ½ qt
14 g	4 cloves	Garlic, minced	½ oz	4 cloves
57 g	59 ml	Shortening, melted	2 oz	¼ cup
5.45 kg	5.68 l	Ground Beef	12 lb	1 ½ gal
142 g	296 ml	Flour, bread	5 oz	1 ¼ cups
907 g	947 ml	Mushrooms, canned, sliced	2 lb	1 qt
	5 ml	Basil, ground		1 tsp
	5 ml	Pepper		1 tsp
	15 ml	Paprika		1 tbsp
57 g	60 ml	Salt	2 oz	4 tbsp
907 g	947 ml	Water or Stock	2 lb	1 qt
1.36 kg	1.42 l	Sour Cream	3 lb	1 ½ qt
28 g	178 ml	Parsley, chopped	1 oz	¾ cup

Procedure

1. Sauté onions and garlic in shortening until tender. Add beef and brown evenly.
2. Stir in flour until absorbed. Stir in mushrooms, seasonings, and water or stock. Cook until thickened (about 5 min).
3. Fold in sour cream. Heat to serving temperature, but do not boil. Pour into serving pans and garnish with chopped parsley.

Cheese Meat Loaf
60 Servings
Bake, 325°F/163°C, 1 ½ hrs

Metric		Ingredients	U.S.	
Weight	Volume		Weight	Volume
454 g	14 slices	Bread Slices	1 lb	14 slices
907 g	947 ml	Milk	2 lb	1 qt
340 g	474 ml	Onions, finely chopped	12 oz	2 cups
340 g	711 ml	Celery, finely chopped	12 oz	3 cups
4.54 kg	4.74 l	Ground Beef	10 lb	5 qt
681 g	1.42 l	Cheddar Cheese, grated	1 lb, 8 oz	1 ½ qt
57 g	60 ml	Salt	2 oz	4 tbsp
57 g	60 ml	Worcestershire Sauce	2 oz	4 tbsp
18 g	118 ml	Parsley, chopped	⅔ oz	½ cup
567 g	592 ml	Eggs, slightly beaten (10 lge)	1 lb, 4 oz	2 ½ cups

Procedure

1. Beat bread and milk in mixer 2 minutes at low speed.
2. Combine bread mixture with remaining ingredients and mix well.
3. Form into loaves. Bake at 325°F/163°C for about 1 ½ hours. Pour off juices as they accumulate in the baking pan.
4. Slice into 60 portions.

Meat Loaf
(with 20% Textured Vegetable Protein)
50 Servings
Bake, 350°F/177°C, 1 ½ hrs

Metric		Ingredients	U.S.	
Weight	Volume		Weight	Volume
567 g	592 ml	Water, hot	1 lb, 4 oz	2 ½ cups
14 g	15 ml	Beef Soup Base	½ oz	1 tbsp
425 g	711 ml	Textured Vegetable Protein	15 oz	3 cups
454 g	14 slices	Bread, sliced	1 lb	14 slices
681 g	711 ml	Milk	1 lb, 8 oz	3 cups
227 g	355 ml	Onions, chopped	8 oz	1 ½ cups
114 g	237 ml	Celery, chopped	4 oz	1 cup
2.50 kg	2.60 l	Ground Beef	5 lb, 8 oz	2 ¾ qt
28 g	30 ml	Salt	1 oz	2 tbsp
28 g	30 ml	Worcestershire Sauce	1 oz	2 tbsp
	5 ml	Pepper		1 tsp
312 g	326 ml	Eggs, beaten (7 med)	11 oz	1 ⅜ cups

Procedure

1. Dissolve soup base in hot water. Cool. Stir in textured vegetable protein. Let stand 15 minutes.
2. Soak bread in milk and blend in mixer at low speed.
3. Combine all ingredients and continue mixing at low speed for 3 or 4 minutes.
4. Divide into 2 greased pans (12 × 20 × 2 in). Mold into loaves (2) lengthwise in each pan.
5. Bake at 350°F/177°C for 1 ½ hours. Drain. Slice ¾ inch thick.

Italian Meat Loaf Glacé
60 Servings
Bake, 325°F/163°C, 15 min

Metric		Ingredients	U.S.	
Weight	Volume		Weight	Volume
	2 loaves	Meat Loaves (60 servings)		2 loaves
	10 ml	Onion, finely chopped		2 tsp
907 g	947 ml	Tomato Puree	2 lb	1 qt
227 g	237 ml	Water	8 oz	1 cup
	3 ⅓ ml	Oregano		⅔ tsp
	3 ⅓ ml	Basil		⅔ tsp
	5 ml	Sugar		1 tsp
	5 ml	Salt		1 tsp
	1 ⅔ ml	Pepper		⅓ tsp
	1 ⅔ ml	Garlic Powder		⅓ tsp
227 g	474 ml	Mozzarella Cheese, grated	8 oz	2 cups

Procedure

1. Prepare and bake favorite meat loaves. Drain loaves.
2. Blend all of the glacé ingredients, except the cheese, and simmer. Spread glacé over the meat loaves. Sprinkle cheese over the loaves.
3. Bake at 325°F/163°C for 15 minutes or until loaves are heated through and cheese is melted and bubbly.

Meat Loaf, Cold
50 Servings

Metric		Ingredients	U.S.	
Weight	Volume		Weight	Volume
3.86 kg	4.98 l	Cooked Meat, ground	8 lb 8 oz	5 ¼ qt
681 g	1.07 l	Onions, ground	1 lb, 8 oz	4 ½ cups
340 g	711 ml	Green Pepper, ground	12 oz	3 cups
57 g	355 ml	Parsley, ground	2 oz	1 ½ cups
1.82 kg	1.89 l	Broth	4 lb	2 qt
114 g	237 ml	Gelatin, granulated	4 oz	1 cup
	10 ml	Salt		2 tsp
	7 ½ ml	Mustard, dry		1 ½ tsp
	⅝ ml	Cayenne Pepper		⅛ tsp
14 g	15 ml	Worcestershire Sauce	½ oz	1 tbsp

Procedure

1. Cook onions, green pepper, and parsley in broth until tender, reserving 2 cups of cold broth to soften gelatin.
2. Add softened gelatin to hot mixture and stir until dissolved.
3. Add salt, mustard, pepper, and Worcestershire sauce. Stir mixture into cooked ground meat.

4. Press 5 lb/2.27 kg of mixture into each of 3 greased loaf pans (5 × 9× 3 in).
5. Refrigerate until set.

Note: This loaf slices well and is delicious for sandwiches.

Spanish Meat Squares
48 Servings
Bake, 350°F/177°C, 1 hr

Metric		Ingredients	U.S.	
Weight	Volume		Weight	Volume
227 g	316 ml	Bacon Fat	8 oz	1 ⅓ cups
170 g	355 ml	Flour, all-purpose	6 oz	1 ½ cups
57 g	60 ml	Salt	2 oz	4 tbsp
	5 ml	Pepper		1 tsp
681 g	711 ml	Milk	1 lb, 8 oz	3 cups
3.18 kg	3.31 l	Ground Beef	7 lb	3 ½ qt
227 g	632 ml	Oatmeal, uncooked	8 oz	2 ⅔ cups
907 g	947 ml	Tomato Puree	2 lb	1 qt
227 g	237 ml	Eggs, beaten (4 lge)	8 oz	1 cup
227 g	533 ml	Bread Crumbs	8 oz	2 ¼ cups
340 g	711 ml	Celery, finely chopped	12 oz	3 cups
454 g	711 ml	Onions, finely chopped	1 lb	3 cups
227 g	474 ml	Green Pepper, finely chopped	8 oz	2 cups

Procedure

1. Melt bacon fat. Add flour and seasonings. Blend.
2. Cook over low heat 3 to 5 minutes. Stir while cooking. Add milk slowly, stirring constantly. Cook until sauce is smooth, glossy, and thickened.
3. Combine all ingredients and mix well.

4. Scale 4¾ lb/2.15 kg into each of 2 greased serving pans (12 × 20 × 2 in).
5. Bake at 350°F/177°C for 1 hour or until done. Cut each pan into 24 portions (4 × 6).

John Marzetti
50 Servings (1 cup/237 ml)
Bake, 325°F/163°C, 35–40 min

Metric		Ingredients	U.S.		
Weight	Volume		Weight		Volume
1.42 kg	2.60 l	Macaroni, uncooked	3 lb,	2 oz	2 ¾ qt
9.07 kg	9.46 l	Water, boiling	20 lb		2 ½ gal
85 g	90 ml	Salt		3 oz	6 tbsp
2.72 kg	2.84 l	Ground Beef	6 lb		3 qt
1.19 kg	1.89 l	Onions, chopped	2 lb,	10 oz	2 qt
510 g	1.89 l	Mushrooms, fresh, sliced	1 lb,	2 oz	2 qt
57 g	59 ml	Butter or Margarine		2 oz	¼ cup
43 g	45 ml	Salt		1 ½ oz	3 tbsp
	6 ml	Garlic Salt			1 ⅛ tsp
	2 ½ ml	Pepper			½ tsp
	6 ml	Basil			1 ⅛ tsp
1.70 kg	1.78 l	Tomato Puree	3 lb,	12 oz	7 ½ cups
1.14 kg	2.37 l	Cheddar Cheese, grated (for sauce)	2 lb,	8 oz	2 ½ qt
454 g	947 ml	Cheddar Cheese, grated (for topping)	1 lb		1 qt

Procedure

1. Cook macaroni in boiling salted water until tender. Drain and rinse in cold water. Drain.
2. Brown ground beef in baking pan in oven 350°F/177°C. Drain drippings from meat and use skimmed fat to sauté onions until tender.
3. Sauté sliced mushrooms in butter or margarine.
4. Combine beef, onions, mushrooms, salt, garlic salt, pepper, basil, and tomato puree. Simmer for 30 minutes.
5. Add 2 ½ lb/1.14 kg grated cheese and macaroni to tomato sauce. Blend well and pour into 2 greased serving pans (12× 20× 2 in). Sprinkle 4 oz/114 g of cheese on top of each casserole. Bake at 325°F/163°C for 35–40 minutes or until bubbly hot.

Baked Corned Beef Slices with Pineapple
48 slices
Bake, 450°F/232°C, 15 min

Metric		Ingredients	U.S.		
Weight	Volume		Weight		Volume
5.44 kg	7.10 l	Corned Beef, chilled, canned	12 lb		7 ½ qt
511 g	533 ml	Eggs, beaten (9 lge)		18 oz	2 ¼ cups
567 g	2.37 l	Cornflakes, crushed	1 lb,	4 oz	2 ½ qt
	50 slices	Pineapple Slices			50 slices
114 g	118 ml	Margarine, melted		4 oz	½ cup
170 g	178 ml	Brown Sugar		6 oz	¾ cup

Procedure

1. Slice corned beef in 48 portions (4 oz/114 g).
2. Dip in beaten egg and crushed cornflakes. Place on greased sheet, with a pineapple slice on top.
3. Brush pineapple with melted margarine and sprinkle with brown sugar.
4. Bake at 450°F/232°C until brown (about 15 min).

Note: Use a little pineapple juice on slices if they are too dry.

Corned Beef Hash with Poached Egg

48 Servings (5 ½ oz/156 g)
Bake, 400°F/205°C, 30 min

Metric		Ingredients	U.S.	
Weight	Volume		Weight	Volume
1.82 kg	2.37 l	Corned Beef, canned, chopped	4 lb	2 ½ qt
3.63 kg	4.26 l	Potatoes, cooked, chopped	8 lb	4 ½ qt
567 g	947 ml	Onions, finely chopped	1 lb, 4 oz	1 qt
227 g	947 ml	Cornflakes, slightly crumbled	8 oz	1 qt
1.82 kg	1.89 l	Meat Stock	4 lb	2 qt
	7 ½ ml	Pepper		1 ½ tsp
2.38 kg	48 eggs	Eggs	5 lb, 4 oz	48 eggs

Procedure

1. Combine all ingredients except eggs. Mix thoroughly but gently.
2. Divide into 2 greased serving pans (12 × 20 × 2 in).
3. Bake at 400°F/205°C for 30 minutes or until crusty on top.
4. Remove from oven and mark each pan in 24 servings. Make an indentation in center of each serving with a tablespoon or with a No. 12 scoop and break egg into indentation. Sprinkle with salt and pepper. Cover pan and replace in oven until eggs are set (about 15 to 20 min).

Note: If potatoes were not salted when cooked, add 1 tbsp of salt to recipe.

Beef Biscuit Roll

50 Servings
Bake, 450°F/232°C, 15 min

Metric		Ingredients	U.S.	
Weight	Volume		Weight	Volume
2.72 kg	4.26 l	Cooked Beef, ground	6 lb	4 ½ qt
7 g	7 ml	Salt	¼ oz	½ tbsp
	2 ½ ml	Pepper		½ tsp
170 g	237 ml	Onions, finely chopped	6 oz	1 cup
	5 ml	Mustard, dry		1 tsp
21 g	22 ml	Worcestershire Sauce	¾ oz	1 ½ tbsp
681 g	711 ml	Stock	1 lb, 8 oz	3 cups
170 g	355 ml	Flour	6 oz	1 ½ cups
		Biscuit Dough		
1.14 kg	2.37 l	Flour, pastry	2 lb, 8 oz	2 ½ qt
71 g	100 ml	Baking Powder	2 ½ oz	6 ⅔ tbsp
21 g	22 ml	Salt	¾ oz	1 ½ tbsp
142 g	158 ml	Shortening	5 oz	⅔ cup
793 g	829 ml	Milk (approx.)	1 lb, 12 oz	3 ½ cups

Procedure

1. Cook ground meat, if not already cooked; then combine all ingredients in meat mixture.
2. Sift together flour, baking powder, and salt. Cut in shortening and add milk slowly, enough to make a soft dough. Stir only enough to mix.
3. Yield: 8 lb, 5 oz/3.77 kg of meat mixture, 4 lbs, 12 oz/2.16 kg of biscuit dough.
4. Divide dough into two equal parts. Roll each into rectangular shape and spread with meat mixture. Roll like a jelly roll. Slice each into 25 rolls. Place sliced side up on greased baking sheets.
5. Bake at 450°F/232°C for 15 minutes.
6. Serve with gravy (1 gal/3.79 l).

Barbecued Hamburger (Sloppy Joe)
60 Servings

Metric		Ingredients	U.S.	
Weight	Volume		Weight	Volume
3.40 kg	3.56 l	Ground Beef	7 lb, 8 oz	3¾ qt
114 g	118 ml	Chili Sauce	4 oz	½ cup
1.59 kg	1.66 l	Tomato Puree	3 lb, 8 oz	1¾ qt
1.59 kg	1.66 l	Catsup	3 lb, 8 oz	1¾ qt
114 g	118 ml	Lemon Juice	4 oz	½ cup
227 g	316 ml	Brown Sugar	8 oz	1⅓ cups
454 g	474 ml	Water	1 lb	2 cups
21 g	45 ml	Mustard, dry	¾ oz	3 tbsp
454 g	947 ml	Celery, diced	1 lb	1 qt
227 g	474 ml	Green Pepper, diced	8 oz	2 cups
681 g	1.07 l	Onions, chopped	1 lb, 8 oz	4½ cups
227 g	237 ml	Vinegar	8 oz	1 cup
	15 ml	Pepper		1 tbsp
	7½ ml	Basil		1½ tsp
	7½ ml	Oregano		1½ tsp
28 g	30 ml	Salt	1 oz	2 tbsp
	15 ml	Chili Powder		1 tbsp
	30 buns	Hamburger Buns		30 buns

Procedure

1. Brown meat. Add remaining ingredients and simmer gently.

2. Toast halves of hamburger buns. Serve a 3 oz/85 g ladle of barbecued beef on half of hamburger bun.

Oriental Meatballs
50 Servings
Bake, 300°F/149°C, 50 min

Metric		Ingredients	U.S.	
Weight	Volume		Weight	Volume
1.82 kg	16 med	Potatoes, E.P.	4 lb	16 med
3.63 kg	3.79 l	Ground Beef	8 lb	4 qt
283 g	296 ml	Eggs, beaten (5 lge)	10 oz	1¼ cups
114 g	711 ml	Parsley, minced	4 oz	3 cups
114 g	178 ml	Onions, finely chopped	4 oz	¾ cup
43 g	45 ml	Salt	1½ oz	3 tbsp
2.95 kg	3.31 l	Tomato Puree	6 lb, 8 oz	1 No. 10 can
	5 ml	Paprika		1 tsp
18 g	30 ml	Salt	1 oz	2 tbsp

Procedure

1. Cook and mash potatoes. Combine with beef, eggs, parsley, onions, and salt.
2. Shape 100 balls, using a level No. 16 scoop. Place 50 meatballs in each of 2 greased serving pans (12 × 20 × 2 in). Bake at 300°F/149°C for 30 minutes.
3. Heat tomato puree, paprika, and salt. Drain off drippings from pans of meatballs and add to tomato mixture. Blend and pour over balls.
4. Return pans to oven and continue baking for 20 minutes.

Stuffed Cabbage Rolls

50 Servings (8 oz/227 g)
Bake, 300°F/149°C, 2 hrs

Metric		Ingredients	U.S.		
Weight	Volume		Weight		Volume
5.44 kg	50 leaves	Cabbage Leaves	12 lb		50 leaves
397 g	474 ml	Rice, uncooked		14 oz	2 cups
	12 ½ ml	Salt			2 ½ tsp
907 g	947 ml	Water	2 lb		1 qt
227 g	355 ml	Onions, finely chopped		8 oz	1 ½ cups
340 g	1 can	Evaporated Milk		12 oz	1 can
2.27 kg	2.37 l	Ground Beef	5 lb		2 ½ qt
28 g	30 ml	Salt		1 oz	2 tbsp
	10 ml	Pepper			2 tsp
149 g	178 ml	Butter or Margarine, melted		5 ¼ oz	¾ cup
1.82 kg	1.89 l	Tomato Soup, undiluted	4 lb		2 qt

Procedure

1. Select large, well-shaped cabbage leaves. Steam in steam cooker for 4 minutes, or until slightly tender. Remove and drain well.
2. Cook rice in salted water until tender.
3. Combine cooked rice, onions, milk, uncooked beef, salt, and pepper.
4. Roll 2 leaves with a scant No. 10 scoop of meat mixture in center. Place in well-greased serving pans (12 × 20 × 2 in).
5. Brush top of cabbage rolls with melted butter or margarine. Bake at 300°F/149°C for 2 hours. They should be golden brown on top.
6. Heat undiluted tomato soup. Drain off drippings from cabbage rolls and combine with soup. Ladle this mixture over cabbage rolls and serve.

Salisbury Steak

50 Servings (5 oz/142 g)
Bake, 325°F/163°C, 1 hr

Metric		Ingredients	U.S.		
Weight	Volume		Weight		Volume
454 g	1.42 l	Bread Crumbs, soft	1 lb		1 ½ qts
114 g	237 ml	Milk, nonfat, dry		4 oz	1 cup
794 g	828 ml	Water, warm	1 lb,	12 oz	3 ½ cups
5.68 kg	5.92 l	Ground Beef, lean	12 lb,	8 oz	6 ¼ qts
283 g	296 ml	Eggs, beaten (5 lge)		10 oz	1 ¼ cups
681 g	1.07 l	Onions, chopped	1 lb,	8 oz	4 ½ cups
	5 ml	Basil, dry, crushed			1 tsp
	5 ml	Pepper			1 tsp
57 g	60 ml	Salt		2 oz	4 tbsp
28 g	30 ml	Worcestershire Sauce		1 oz	2 tbsp

Procedure

1. Sprinkle dry milk on warm water and stir to reconstitute. Add soft bread crumbs and let stand 5 minutes.
2. Combine all ingredients and mix well, but handle lightly.
3. Dip slightly rounded No. 8 scoops and form oval-shaped patties 1 inch thick. Arrange on lightly greased baking sheets.
4. Bake at 325°F/163°C for 1 hour or until done.

Veal Recipes

Roast Leg of Veal
50–60 Servings
Bake, 300°F/149°C

Metric		Ingredients	U.S.	
Weight	Volume		Weight	Volume
11.34 kg	1 leg	Leg of Veal, A.P.	25 lb	1 leg

Procedure

1. Bone and roll in pieces that will roast and slice well.
2. Rub with beef fat or shortening.
3. Cover bottom of roasting pan with chopped onion and carrots. Place veal on vegetables, skin side up, and insert meat thermometer to center of roast.
4. Bake at 300°F/149°C until meat thermometer registers 170°F/77°C or bake 30 minutes per pound of roast.

Veal Scallopini
50 Servings
Bake, 375°F/190°C, 1½ hrs

Metric		Ingredients	U.S.	
Weight	Volume		Weight	Volume
		Marinade		
28 g	30 ml	Salt	1 oz	2 tbsp
21 g	22 ml	Sugar	¾ oz	1½ tbsp
	7½ ml	Nutmeg		1½ tsp
14 g	30 ml	Paprika	½ oz	2 tbsp
28 g	30 ml	Mustard, prepared	1 oz	2 tbsp
28 g	8 cloves	Garlic Cloves	1 oz	8 cloves
454 g	474 ml	Lemon Juice or Vinegar	1 lb	2 cups
907 g	947 ml	Salad Oil	2 lb	1 qt
6.35 kg	50 pieces	Veal Cutlets	14 lb	50 pieces
170 g	355 ml	Flour, all-purpose	6 oz	1½ cups
454 g	474 ml	Shortening	1 lb	2 cups
907 g	1.42 l	Onions, chopped or sliced	2 lb	1½ qt
907 g	1.89 l	Green Pepper, cut in strips	2 lb	2 qt
454 g	1.66 l	Mushrooms, fresh, sliced	1 lb	7 cups
1.82 kg	1.89 l	White Stock	4 lb	2 qt
14 g	15 ml	Salt	½ oz	1 tbsp

Procedure

1. Combine marinade ingredients. Marinate veal cutlets for 20 to 30 minutes; be sure that all pieces are coated. Remove garlic cloves.
2. Remove veal from marinade and dry well. Dredge with flour to coat all pieces. Brown in hot fat and place in serving pans (12 × 20 × 2 in).
3. Distribute onions, green pepper, and mushrooms over veal. Mix 2 cups/474 ml of marinade with white stock and salt. Pour mixture over veal.
4. Bake covered at 375°F/190°C for 1 hour. Remove cover and continue baking for another 30 minutes.
5. Pour off sauce in skillet. Boil it, stirring vigorously until smooth and concentrated enough to serve as a sauce for the scallopini.

Veal Cordon Bleu
50 Servings (5 oz/142 g)
Bake, 300°F/149°C, 1 hr

| Metric | | Ingredients | U.S. | |
Weight	Volume		Weight	Volume
7.71 kg	100 pieces	Veal Cutlets	17 lb	100 pieces
2.27 kg	50 slices	Ham, thin slices	5 lb	50 slices
1.42 kg	50 slices	Swiss Cheese, sliced	3 lb, 2 oz	50 slices
681 g	1.42 l	Flour	1 lb, 8 oz	1 ½ qt
	10 ml	Nutmeg, ground		2 tsp
	5 ml	Cloves		1 tsp
454 g	474 ml	Eggs, beaten (8 lge)	1 lb	2 cups
454 g	474 ml	Milk	1 lb	2 cups
1.36 kg	3.31 l	Bread Crumbs, fine, dry	3 lb	3 ½ qt
227 g	237 ml	Cooking Oil	8 oz	1 cup
227 g	237 ml	Butter, clarified	8 oz	1 cup
227 g	237 ml	White Wine, dry	8 oz	1 cup
114 g	118 ml	White Stock	4 oz	½ cup

Procedure

1. Pound cutlets with meat mallet to ⅛-inch thickness. Sprinkle with salt and pepper.
2. Place on each of 50 cutlets, one slice of ham and one slice of cheese. Top with another cutlet. Pound edges of cutlets together to encase ham and cheese.
3. Blend flour and spices. Mix eggs and milk. Coat cutlets with flour mixture, dip in egg mixture, and roll in crumbs until well covered.
4. Heat oil and butter together in a baking pan. Place cutlets in baking pans and turn cutlets to oil both sides. Brown for 20 minutes at 425°F/218°C. Turn cutlets and brown the other side. Lower the temperature to 300°F/149°C. Mix wine and stock, pour over cutlets, and continue baking until tender.

Brown Fricassee of Veal
50 Servings (6 oz/170 g)

| Metric | | Ingredients | U.S. | |
Weight	Volume		Weight	Volume
5.67 kg	5.68 l	Veal, cut in 2-in pieces	12 lb, 8 oz	1 ½ gal
227 g	474 ml	Flour, bread	8 oz	2 cups
14 g	15 ml	Salt	½ oz	1 tbsp
454 g	474 ml	Shortening	1 lb	2 cups
340 g	711 ml	Flour, bread	12 oz	3 cups
14 g	15 ml	Salt	½ oz	1 tbsp
	5 ml	Pepper		1 tsp
907 g	947 ml	Chili Sauce	2 lb	1 qt
907 g	947 ml	Water	2 lb	1 qt
1.36 kg	2.84 l	Onions, chopped	3 lb	3 qt
	5 ml	Basil		1 tsp

Procedure

1. Roll meat in flour; salt it. Brown in shortening.
2. Add water to cover and simmer ¾ hour.
3. Make an uncooked sauce of remaining ingredients. Pour over meat and cook for ¾ hour.
4. Yield: 50 servings (6 oz/170 g).

Hungarian Veal Goulash

50 Servings

Metric		Ingredients	U.S.	
Weight	Volume		Weight	Volume
1.82 kg	2.84 l	Onions, diced	4 lb	3 qt
14 g	4 cloves	Garlic, minced	½ oz	4 cloves
567 g	592 ml	Shortening	1 lb, 4 oz	2 ½ cups
9.07 kg	9.46 l	Veal, 2-oz pieces	20 lb	2 ½ gal
57 g	60 ml	Salt	2 oz	4 tbsp
	10 ml	Pepper		2 tsp
454 g	474 ml	Tomato Puree	1 lb	2 cups
170 g	355 ml	Paprika	6 oz	1 ½ cups
14 g	15 ml	Celery Salt	½ oz	1 tbsp
	5 ml	Caraway Seed		1 tsp
28 g	178 ml	Parsley	1 oz	¾ cup
4.54 kg	4.74 l	White Stock	10 lb	5 qt
340 g	711 ml	Flour, all-purpose	12 oz	3 cups
681 g	711 ml	Sour Cream	1 lb, 8 oz	3 cups

Procedure

1. Brown onions and garlic in shortening.
2. Add veal and remaining ingredients, except flour and sour cream. Cover and simmer for 2 hours. Thicken with flour that has been mixed with sufficient water to make a paste. Cook until flour has lost its raw taste.
3. Add sour cream. Heat to serving temperature but do not boil.

Wiener Schnitzel

50 Servings
Bake, 350°F/177°C, 40 min

Metric		Ingredients	U.S.	
Weight	Volume		Weight	Volume
10.89 kg	50 pieces	Veal Cutlets	24 lb	50 pieces
681 g	1.42 l	Flour, all-purpose	1 lb, 8 oz	1 ½ qt
43 g	45 ml	Salt	1 ½ oz	3 tbsp
	10 ml	Pepper		2 tsp
28 g	178 ml	Parsley, minced	1 oz	¾ cup
681 g	711 ml	Eggs, beaten (12 lge)	1 lb, 8 oz	3 cups
681 g	711 ml	Milk	1 lb, 8 oz	3 cups
114 g	118 ml	Lemon Juice	4 oz	½ cup
793 g	1.89 l	Bread Crumbs, fine, dry	1 lb, 12 oz	2 qt
454 g	474 ml	Shortening	1 lb	2 cups

Procedure

1. Pound cutlets with mallet to ¼-inch thickness. Clip edges to prevent curling. Blend flour, salt, pepper, and parsley. Combine eggs, milk, and lemon juice.
2. Coat cutlets with flour mixture. Dip into egg mixture and then into crumbs.
3. Place breaded cutlets on a greased baking sheet (18 × 26 × 1). Brush cutlets with melted butter or margarine and bake at 350°F/177°C, turning once to brown both sides, for about 40 minutes.
4. Garnish with slice of lemon.

Jellied Veal Loaf
50 Servings
Chill

| Metric | | Ingredients | U.S. | |
Weight	Volume		Weight	Volume
85 g	135 ml	Gelatin	3 oz	9 tbsp
340 g	355 ml	Water, cold	12 oz	1 ½ cups
1.36 kg	1.42 l	Veal Stock, hot	3 lb	1 ½ qt
1.36 kg	1.42 l	Veal Stock, cold	3 lb	1 ½ qt
114 g	118 ml	Onion Juice	4 oz	½ cup
1.82 kg	2.84 l	Veal, cooked, diced	4 lb	3 qt
170 g	178 ml	Lemon Juice	6 oz	¾ cup
510 g	789 ml	Carrots, cooked, diced	1 lb, 2 oz	3 ⅓ cups
340 g	1.07 l	Celery Rings	12 oz	4 ½ cups
567 g	711 ml	Green Peas	1 lb, 4 oz	3 cups
43 g	90 ml	Green Pepper, chopped	1 ½ oz	6 tbsp
14 g	15 ml	Worcestershire Sauce	½ oz	1 tbsp
28 g	30 ml	Salt	1 oz	2 tbsp
57 g	59 ml	Vinegar	2 oz	¼ cup

Procedure

1. Soak gelatin in cold water.
2. Add hot veal stock and stir until dissolved. Add cold stock.
3. When mixture begins to thicken, add remaining ingredients. Blend well.
4. Divide mixture into 3 oiled loaf pans (9 × 5 × 3). Chill.

Italian Stew
50 Servings (1 cup/237 ml)
Simmer, 1 ½–2 hrs

| Metric | | Ingredients | U.S. | |
Weight	Volume		Weight	Volume
2.72 kg	2.84 l	Veal, cubed	6 lb	3 qt
2.72 kg	2.84 l	Pork, cubed	6 lb	3 qt
907 g	1.42 l	Onions, ½-in pieces	2 lb	1 ½ qt
681 g	1.42 l	Green Pepper, chopped	1 lb, 8 oz	1 ½ qt
170 g	178 ml	Butter or Margarine	6 oz	¾ cup
2.95 kg	3.31 l	Tomatoes	6 lb, 8 oz	1 No. 10 can
57 g	60 ml	Salt	2 oz	4 tbsp
	5 ml	Pepper		1 tsp
1.82 kg	1.89 l	Water	4 lb	2 qt
340 g	711 ml	Flour, bread	12 oz	3 cups
454 g	474 ml	Water	1 lb	2 cups

Procedure

1. Brown meat well.
2. Sauté onions and green pepper in butter or margarine. Add to meat. Add tomatoes, seasonings, and 2 qt/1.89 l of water, to cover meat and vegetables. Simmer, covered, for 1 ½ to 2 hours.
3. Make paste of flour and 2 cups/474 ml of water. Add to stew to thicken. Cook until raw flavor disappears.

Veal Birds

50 Servings
Bake, 325°F/163°C, 1 hr

Metric		Ingredients	U.S.		
Weight	Volume		Weight		Volume
1.36 kg	2.84 l	Bread Crumbs	3 lb		3 qt
454 g	474 ml	Bacon, chopped	1 lb		2 cups
1.14 kg	1.89 l	Onions, finely chopped	2 lb,	8 oz	2 qt
681 g	711 ml	Eggs, well-beaten (12 lge)	1 lb,	8 oz	3 cups
7.72 kg	100 slices	Veal, sliced, 6 per lb/454 g	17 lb		100 slices
454 g	947 ml	Flour, bread	1 lb		1 qt
57 g	60 ml	Salt		2 oz	¼ cup
7 g	15 ml	Pepper		¼ oz	1 tbsp
681 g	711 ml	Butter or Margarine	1 lb,	8 oz	3 cups
340 g	711 ml	Flour, bread		12 oz	3 cups
43 g	45 ml	Salt		1½ oz	3 tbsp
	5 ml	Pepper, white			1 tsp
2.95 kg	3.08 l	Milk, hot	6 lb,	8 oz	3¼ qt

Procedure

1. Combine bread crumbs, bacon, onions, and eggs. Mix well.
2. Place 1 oz/28 g of dressing on each slice of veal. Roll and fasten with a toothpick.
3. Combine 1 lb/454 g flour, 4 tbsp/60 ml salt, and 1 tbsp pepper. Roll each "veal bird" in the mixture. Brown quickly in hot fat.
4. Melt butter or margarine. Add flour and seasonings.
   Blend. Cook over low heat 3 to 5 minutes. Stir while cooking. Add milk slowly, stirring constantly. Cook until sauce is smooth and thickened.
5. Place veal birds in serving pans (12 × 20 × 2 in) and pour white sauce over them. Bake at 325°F/163°C for about 1 hour.
6. Yield: 100 veal birds, or 2 per serving.

Veal and Bacon Patties

50 Servings (2 patties)
Bake, 325°F/163°C

Metric		Ingredients	U.S.		
Weight	Volume		Weight		Volume
756 g	789 ml	Cream, 20%	1 lb,	10⅔ oz	3⅓ cups
510 g	1.18 l	Bread Crumbs, soft	1 lb,	2 oz	1¼ qt
4.54 kg	4.74 l	Veal, ground	10 lb		5 qt
	7½ ml	Curry Powder			1½ tsp
368 g	770 ml	Onion, finely chopped		13 oz	3¼ cups
142 g	296 ml	Green Pepper, chopped		5 oz	1¼ cups
28 g	30 ml	Salt		1 oz	2 tbsp
1.14 kg	100 slices	Bacon	2 lb,	8 oz	100 slices

Procedure

1. Combine all ingredients except bacon. Mix well. Partially cook bacon.
2. Shape into 100 patties with a No. 16 dipper.
3. Wrap each patty with a slice of bacon and secure with a toothpick.
4. Bake at 325°F/163°C until brown.

Lamb Recipes

Roast Lamb

50 Servings
Bake, 325°F/163°C, 2½–3 hrs

Metric		Ingredients	U.S.	
Weight	Volume		Weight	Volume
10.89 kg	4 legs	Legs of Lamb, A.P.	24 lb	4 legs
28 g	30 ml	Salt	1 oz	2 tbsp
	5 ml	Pepper		1 tsp
14 g	4 cloves	Garlic	½ oz	4 cloves

Procedure

1. Insert garlic clove next to round bone in each leg.
2. Place in roasting pan, fat side up. Combine salt and pepper. Rub mixture over roasts.
3. Insert thermometer so that bulb is in center of the large muscle.
4. Roast at 325°F/163°C oven temperature until thermometer registers degree of doneness preferred. Allow about 25 min per pound for medium rare or medium (145°F/63°C to 160°F/71°C).
5. Remove from heat and let stand 15 to 20 minutes before slicing.

Barbecued Lamb Shanks

50 Servings
Bake, 325°F/163°C, 2 hrs

Metric		Ingredients	U.S.	
Weight	Volume		Weight	Volume
28.15 kg	50 shanks	Lamb Shanks	62 lb	50 shanks
610 g	947 ml	Onions, chopped	1 lb, 5½ oz	1 qt
28 g	8 cloves	Garlic, minced	1 oz	8 cloves
128 g	355 ml	Orange Rind, chopped	4½ oz	1½ cups
340 g	355 ml	Orange Juice	12 oz	1½ cups
907 g	947 ml	Catsup	2 lb	1 qt
114 g	118 ml	Vinegar	4 oz	½ cup
114 g	118 ml	Salad Oil	4 oz	½ cup
14 g	15 ml	Mustard, prepared	½ oz	1 tbsp
28 g	30 ml	Soy Sauce	1 oz	2 tbsp
14 g	15 ml	Worcestershire Sauce	½ oz	1 tbsp
340 g	474 ml	Brown Sugar	12 oz	2 cups
14 g	15 ml	Salt	½ oz	1 tbsp
	15 ml	Ginger, minced, fresh root		1 tbsp

Procedure

1. Brown lamb shanks in oven until lightly browned. Pour off excess fat.
2. Blend remaining ingredients for sauce and simmer 5 or 10 minutes.
3. Arrange shanks in serving pans and cover with barbecue sauce. Cover pans and bake at 325°F/163°C until lamb is tender (about 2 hrs).

Note: Sauce may be used for barbecued riblets or breast of lamb.

Lamb Stew

50 Servings (8 ½ oz/242 g)

| Metric | | Ingredients | U.S. | | |
Weight	Volume		Weight		Volume
3.41 kg	3.56 l	Lamb, 1 ½-in cubes	7 lb,	8 oz	3 ¾ qt
14 g	15 ml	Sugar		½ oz	1 tbsp
142 g	158 ml	Shortening		5 oz	⅔ cup
99 g	178 ml	Flour, all-purpose		3 ½ oz	¾ cup
57 g	60 ml	Salt		2 oz	4 tbsp
	5 ml	Pepper			1 tsp
454 g	947 ml	Onions, quartered	1 lb		1 qt
28 g	8 cloves	Garlic, minced		1 oz	8 cloves
1.36 kg	1.42 l	Water, hot	3 lb		1 ½ qt
454 g	474 ml	Wine, red cooking	1 lb		2 cups
14 g	15 ml	Worcestershire Sauce		½ oz	1 tbsp
2.04 kg	3.08 l	Carrots, diced	4 lb,	8 oz	3 ¼ qt
3.18 kg	4.98 l	Potatoes, diced	7 lb		5 ¼ qt
907 g	1.89 l	Celery, chopped	2 lb		2 qt
907 g	1.42 l	Peas, frozen	2 lb		1 ½ qt

Procedure

1. Sprinkle lamb with sugar. Brown in shortening on all sides. Drain off excess fat. Stir in flour, salt, and pepper, and brown slightly.
2. Add onions, garlic, water, wine, and Worcestershire sauce. Simmer for 45 minutes or until meat and vegetables are almost tender.
3. Add carrots, potatoes, and celery. Cook until tender (about 20 to 30 min). Add peas during last 5 minutes of cooking.

Note: Make Shepherd's Pie by adding mashed potato topping.

Lamb Curry

50 Servings

| Metric | | Ingredients | U.S. | | |
Weight	Volume		Weight		Volume
5.44 kg	5.68 l	Lamb, 1-in cubes	12 lb		6 qt
170 g	178 ml	Shortening		6 oz	¾ cup
907 g	1.42 l	Onions, chopped	2 lb		1 ½ qt
1.36 kg	2.84 l	Celery, chopped	3 lb		3 qt
1.82 kg	3.31 l	Apples, pared, chopped	4 lb		3 ½ qt
454 g	711 ml	Raisins	1 lb		3 cups
227 g	474 ml	Flour, bread		8 oz	2 cups
57 g	59 ml	Salt		2 oz	¼ cup
	5 ml	Pepper			1 tsp
57 g	118 ml	Curry Powder		2 oz	½ cup
28 g	59 ml	Ginger, fresh or ground		1 oz	¼ cup
	10 ml	Hot Pepper Sauce			2 tsp
114 g	118 ml	Worcestershire Sauce		4 oz	½ cup
1.82 kg	1.89 l	Water, hot	4 lb		2 qt
57 g	59 ml	Chicken Soup Base		2 oz	¼ cup
454 g	1.42 l	Coconut, shredded	1 lb		1 ½ qt

1. Brown lamb lightly in hot shortening. Add onions, celery, apples, and raisins and continue cooking.
2. Add flour, salt, spices, and sauces. Dissolve soup base in hot water and add to mixture, stirring until well-blended. Continue simmering until lamb is tender (about 1 hour).

3. Stir in shredded coconut and continue cooking for another 20 minutes.

Note: Flavors blend and are more delicious if this dish is allowed to stand several hours or overnight, then reheated for service.

French Lamb Stew
50 Servings

Metric		Ingredients	U.S.	
Weight	Volume		Weight	Volume
3.63 kg	3.79 l	Lamb Stew Meat	8 lb	4 qt
85 g	79 ml	Fat	3 oz	⅓ cup
43 g	79 ml	Flour, bread	1½ oz	⅓ cup
454 g	711 ml	Carrots, chopped	1 lb	3 cups
454 g	711 ml	Turnips, chopped	1 lb	3 cups
454 g	711 ml	Onions, chopped	1 lb	3 cups
	5 ml	Sugar		1 tsp
1.14 kg	1.18 l	Broth	2 lb, 8 oz	1¼ qt
1.14 kg	1.18 l	Tomatoes, canned	2 lb, 8 oz	1¼ qt
28 g	30 ml	Salt	1 oz	2 tbsp
	5 ml	Pepper		1 tsp
	5 ml	Garlic Salt		1 tsp
1.06 kg	1.66 l	Potatoes, quartered	2 lb, 5½ oz	1¾ qt
610 g	947 ml	Peas, fresh or frozen	1 lb, 5½ oz	1 qt

Procedure

1. Brown lamb in fat; add flour and continue to brown. Add carrots, turnips, onions, and sugar and brown.
2. Add broth, tomatoes, and seasonings and bring to boiling. Add potatoes and cook until tender.

3. Five minutes before serving, add peas and continue cooking.

Baked Lamb Steaks
50 Servings (5 oz/142 g)
Bake, 325°F/163°C, 1 hr

Metric		Ingredients	U.S.		
Weight	Volume		Weight		Volume
7.04 kg	50 cuts	Lamb Shoulder Steaks	15 lb,	8 oz	50 steaks
227 g	474 ml	Flour, bread		8 oz	2 cups
43 g	45 ml	Salt		1 ½ oz	3 tbsp
	10 ml	Pepper			2 tsp
	20 ml	Marjoram, ground			4 tsp
	10 ml	Mace, ground			2 tsp
114 g	118 ml	Shortening		4 oz	½ cup
21 g	6 cloves	Garlic, cloves		¾ oz	6 cloves
2.72 kg	2.84 l	Water	6 lb		3 qt
28 g	178 ml	Parsley		1 oz	¾ cup

Procedure

1. Dredge steaks with mixture of flour, salt, and spices. Lightly brown steaks on both sides in hot shortening in which garlic cloves have been browned and removed.

2. Arrange steaks in serving pans (12 × 20 × 2 in). Pour water over steaks, cover, and bake at 325°F/163°C until tender (about 1 hr).

3. Sprinkle parsley over steaks before service.

Shashlik
50 Servings
Broil

Metric		Ingredients	U.S.		
Weight	Volume		Weight		Volume
8.17 kg	9.46 l	Lamb, 1 ¼-in cubes	18 lb		2 ½ gal
28 g	30 ml	Salt		1 oz	2 tbsp
	10 ml	Pepper			2 tsp
28 g	8 cloves	Garlic, minced		1 oz	8 cloves
907 g	1.42 l	Onions, chopped	2 lb		1 ½ qt
227 g	237 ml	Lemon Juice		8 oz	1 cup
227 g	237 ml	Salad Oil		8 oz	1 cup
340 g	355 ml	Red Wine		12 oz	1 ½ cups
681 g	100 caps	Mushrooms, fresh	1 lb,	8 oz	100 caps
1.59 kg	100	Cherry Tomatoes	3 lb,	8 oz	100

Procedure

1. Make marinade with salt, pepper, garlic, onions, lemon juice, oil, and wine. Add lamb and marinate in the refrigerator for 8–24 hours.

2. Arrange on skewers, alternating lamb with mushrooms and tomatoes. Place far enough apart on broiler for heat to reach sides. Brush lamb and vegetables with some of the marinade or oil and baste as they cook.

3. Boil on one side until brown, turn over and broil until nicely browned. Total cooking time is about 10 to 15 minutes.

4. Heat the marinade and thicken it with a flour-and-water paste, to use as a sauce. Serve the shashlik and sauce with noodles or rice.

Lamb Pinwheels

50 Servings

Bake, 425°F/218°C, 35–40 min

| Metric | | Ingredients | U.S. | |
Weight	Volume		Weight	Volume
2.27 kg	2.37 l	Lamb Shoulder, ground	5 lb	2½ qt
340 g	474 ml	Carrots, ground	12 oz	2 cups
454 g	711 ml	Onions, ground	1 lb	3 cups
	5 ml	Worcestershire Sauce		1 tsp
	5 ml	Oregano		1 tsp
28 g	30 ml	Salt	1 oz	2 tbsp
1.48 kg	3.08 l	Flour, all-purpose	3 lb, 4 oz	3¼ qt
71 g	75 ml	Sugar	2½ oz	5 tbsp
71 g	100 ml	Baking Powder	2½ oz	6⅔ tbsp
14 g	15 ml	Salt	½ oz	1 tbsp
567 g	592 ml	Shortening	1 lb, 4 oz	2½ cups
851 g	889 ml	Milk	1 lb, 14 oz	3¾ cups

Procedure

1. Mix lamb, carrots, onions, Worcestershire sauce, oregano, and 2 tbsp/30 ml salt thoroughly.
2. Sift together flour, sugar, baking powder, and 1 tbsp/15 ml salt. Cut in shortening. Add milk and stir only enough to mix. Divide into 5 equal parts. Roll each into a rectangle and spread with 1 ⅓ lb/605 g of lamb mixture.
4. Roll each rectangle as for jelly roll and slice into 10 slices. Place on a greased baking sheet and bake at 425°F/218°C for 35 to 40 minutes.

Note: Serve with mushroom sauce.

Mixed Grill

50 Servings

| Metric | | Ingredients | U.S. | |
Weight	Volume		Weight	Volume
4.54 kg	50 chops	Lamb Rib Chops	10 lb	50 chops
1.36 kg	50 links	Pork Sausages, link	3 lb	50 links
3.86 kg	50 pieces	Calves' Liver	8 lb, 8 oz	50 pieces
681 g	1.42 l	Flour, all-purpose	1 lb, 8 oz	1½ qt
2.72 kg	50 slices	Tomatoes, fresh	6 lb	50 slices
907 g	1.89 l	Bread Crumbs	2 lb	2 qt
28 g	30 ml	Salt	1 oz	1 tbsp
	5 ml	Pepper		1 tsp

Procedure

1. Have lamb chops cut 5 per lb/454 g. Brown on both sides. Season.
2. Brown link sausages.
3. Dredge liver in flour and season. Fry to golden brown.
4. Dip tomatoes in bread crumbs, seasoned with salt and pepper. Broil. Garlic or onion salt may be substituted for plain salt if desired.
5. Serve one lamb chop, one pork sausage, one slice liver, and one tomato slice per portion.

Pork Recipes

Sweet and Sour Pork
50 Servings (¾ cup/178 ml)

Metric		Ingredients	U.S.	
Weight	Volume		Weight	Volume
28 g	30 ml	Sugar	1 oz	2 tbsp
340 g	355 ml	Soy Sauce	12 oz	1½ cups
10 g	10 ml	Salt		2 tsp
	5 ml	Pepper		1 tsp
340 g	355 ml	Pineapple Juice	12 oz	1½ cups
4.54 kg	4.73 l	Lean Pork, 1-in cubes	10 lb	5 qt
227 g	237 ml	Shortening	8 oz	1 cup
454 g	711 ml	Onions, cut in sections	1 lb	3 cups
454 g	1.66 l	Mushrooms, sliced	1 lb	1¾ qt
454 g	711 ml	Green Onions, cut diagonally	1 lb	3 cups
454 g	947 ml	Sweet Peppers, red or green, diced	1 lb	1 qt
255 g	355 ml	Brown Sugar	9 oz	1½ cups
170 g	316 ml	Cornstarch	6 oz	1⅓ cups
907 g	947 ml	Chicken Stock	2 lb	1 qt
227 g	237 ml	Vinegar	8 oz	1 cup
227 g	237 ml	Tomato Sauce	8 oz	1 cup
1.82 kg	1.89 l	Pineapple, tidbits	4 lb	2 qt

Procedure

1. Blend sugar, soy sauce, salt, pepper, and pineapple juice. Marinate pork in this mixture for 1 hour.
2. Remove pork from marinade. Sauté in hot shortening until nicely browned. Remove from fat and cook in stock until tender (about 1 hour).
3. Sauté onions in fat in which pork was sautéed until transparent. Add mushrooms, green onions, and sweet peppers. Sauté lightly.
4. Heat marinade to boiling. Blend sugar and cornstarch and thicken combined stock, marinade, vinegar, and tomato sauce. Combine all ingredients and heat thoroughly.

Note: Serve on crisp noodles.

Deviled Pork Chops
50 servings
Bake, 350°F/177°C, 1½ hrs

Metric		Ingredients	U.S.	
Weight	Volume		Weight	Volume
2.72 kg	2.84 l	Chili Sauce	6 lb	3 qt
	5 ml	Mustard, dry		1 tsp
43 g	40 ml	Worcestershire Sauce	1½ oz	2⅔ tbsp
43 g	40 ml	Lemon Juice	1½ oz	2⅔ tbsp
	5 ml	Onion Juice		1 tsp
7.72 kg	50 chops	Pork Chops	17 lb	50 chops
21 g	22 ml	Salt	¾ oz	1½ tbsp
	2½ ml	Pepper		½ tsp

1. Combine chili sauce, mustard, Worcestershire sauce, lemon, and onion juice. Mix thoroughly.
2. Dip each chop into the sauce and place in one layer in serving pan. Sprinkle with salt and pepper. Let stand for 30 minutes.

3. Cover and bake at 350°F/177°C for 1 ½ hours, or until tender.

Pork Sweet Potato Pie

50 Servings

Bake, 375°F/190°C, 30 min

Metric		Ingredients	U.S.	
Weight	Volume		Weight	Volume
14 g	4 cloves	Garlic, cloves, cut	½ oz	4 cloves
227 g	237 ml	Bacon Fat	8 oz	1 cup
5.44 kg	5.68 l	Lean Pork, cubed	12 lb	6 qt
454 g	947 ml	Flour, all-purpose	1 lb	1 qt
57 g	59 ml	Salt	2 oz	¼ cup
7 g	15 ml	Pepper	¼ oz	1 tbsp
907 g	1.42 l	Carrots, diced	2 lb	1 ½ qt
454 g	947 ml	Celery, coarsely chopped	1 lb	1 qt
610 g	947 ml	Onions, chopped	1 lb, 5 ½ oz	1 qt
227 g	237 ml	Vinegar, cider	8 oz	1 cup
14 g	30 ml	Mustard, dry	½ oz	2 tbsp
1.82 kg	1.89 l	Water, hot	4 lb	2 qt
		Topping		
3.63 kg	3.79 l	Sweet Potato, cooked, mashed	8 lb	4 qt
312 g	947 ml	Coconut, flaked	11 oz	1 qt
	5 ml	Nutmeg		1 tsp
14 g	15 ml	Salt	½ oz	1 tbsp
454 g	474 ml	Butter or Margarine	1 lb	2 cups

1. Sauté cloves of garlic in bacon fat; then remove from fat.
2. Dredge pork with flour, salt, and pepper. Brown in hot fat.
3. Add vegetables, vinegar, mustard, and water. Let simmer for 30 minutes.

4. Blend sweet potatoes, coconut, nutmeg, salt, and butter for topping. Arrange pork and vegetables in serving pans (12 × 20 × 2 in). Cover with sweet potato topping and bake at 375°F/190°C for 30 minutes.

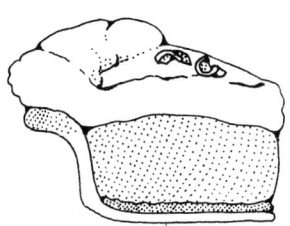

Barbecued Spareribs

50 Servings

Bake, 325°F/163°C, 2 ½ hrs

Metric		Ingredients	U.S.	
Weight	Volume		Weight	Volume
11.34 kg	100 pieces	Spareribs of Pork	25 lb	100 pieces
114 g	158 ml	Brown Sugar	4 oz	⅔ cup
4 g	15 ml	Garlic Powder		1 tbsp
6 g	15 ml	Paprika		1 tbsp
14 g	15 ml	Salt	½ oz	1 tbsp
	5 ml	Pepper		1 tsp
14 g	15 ml	Mustard, prepared	½ oz	1 tbsp
	⅝ ml	Cayenne Pepper		⅛ tsp
312 g	474 ml	Onions, minced	11 oz	2 cups
907 g	947 ml	Catsup or Chili Sauce	2 lb	1 qt
340 g	355 ml	Lemon Juice or Vinegar	12 oz	1 ½ cups
28 g	30 ml	Worcestershire Sauce	1 oz	2 tbsp

Procedure

1. Bake the spareribs at 325°F/163°C until partially cooked. Pour off excess fat.
2. Combine remaining ingredients and simmer until slightly thickened.
3. Pour sauce over spareribs and continue baking, basting often, until tender. Total cooking time: approximately 2 ½ hours.

Spanish Pork Chops

50 Servings

Bake, 325°F/163°C, 1 hr

Metric		Ingredients	U.S.	
Weight	Volume		Weight	Volume
28 g	30 ml	Salt	1 oz	2 tbsp
1.36 kg	1.66 l	Rice, uncooked	3 lb	1 ¾ qt
3.40 kg	3.56 l	Water, boiling	7 lb, 8 oz	3 ¾ qt
283 g	474 ml	Onions, chopped	10 oz	2 cups
227 g	474 ml	Celery, chopped	8 oz	2 cups
114 g	118 ml	Butter or Margarine	4 oz	½ cup
28 g	30 ml	Salt	1 oz	2 tbsp
	5 ml	Pepper		1 tsp
7.72 kg	50 chops	Pork Chops	17 lb	50 chops
5.44 kg	5.68 l	Tomato Juice	12 lb	6 qt

Procedure

1. Add salt and rice to boiling water. Stir and cover tightly. Cook on low heat 15 minutes. Remove from heat and let stand, covered, 10 minutes.
2. Sauté onions and celery in butter or margarine. Add seasonings and combine with rice.
3. Brown pork chops. Layer rice and vegetables in bottom of pans. Lay chops on top and cover with tomato juice. Baste occasionally.
4. Bake at 325°F/163°C for 1 hour.

Danish Pork Chops

50 Servings

Roast, 325°F/163°C, 1 hr

| Metric | | Ingredients | U.S. | |
Weight	Volume		Weight	Volume
454 g	474 ml	Eggs, beaten (8 lge)	1 lb	2 cups
21 g	22 ml	Salt	¾ oz	1 ½ tbsp
170 g	178 ml	Milk	6 oz	¾ cup
8.17 kg	50 chops	Pork Chops, ½ in thick	18 lb	50 chops
681 g	2.13 l	Cracker Crumbs	1 lb, 8 oz	2 ¼ qt
340 g	355 ml	Shortening	12 oz	1 ½ cups
2.72 kg	15 apples	Apples, red, cored, cut in rings	6 lb	15 apples
567 g	711 ml	Prunes, cooked, 30/40 size	1 lb, 4 oz	3 cups
681 g	711 ml	Prune Juice	1 lb, 8 oz	3 cups

Procedure

1. Combine eggs, salt, and milk. Beat slightly.
2. Dip pork chops in egg mixture, then in cracker crumbs.
3. Fry on one side only, using 11 oz/312 g fat.
4. Use 1 oz/28 g fat for greasing pans. Place in greased pan, uncooked side down, and place one apple ring on each chop, with a prune (pit removed) in the center of each ring.
5. Bake at 325°F/163°C for one hour. Baste with prune juice after chops have cooked for 15 minutes.

Pork Chops with Fruit Filling

48 Servings (7 oz/198 g)

Bake, 350°F/177°C, 1 hr

| Metric | | Ingredients | U.S. | |
Weight	Volume		Weight	Volume
7.26 kg	48 chops	Pork Chops, cut 3 per lb/454 g	16 lb	48 chops
57 g	59 ml	Salt	2 oz	¼ cup
		Filling		
142 g	237 ml	Onions, chopped	5 oz	1 cup
114 g	237 ml	Celery, chopped	4 oz	1 cup
85 g	79 ml	Bacon Fat or Drippings	3 oz	⅓ cup
340 g	1.42 l	Bread Crumbs, soft	12 oz	1 ½ qt
227 g	355 ml	Raisins	8 oz	1 ½ cups
907 g	1.66 l	Apples, pared, chopped	2 lb	1 ¾ qt
	10 ml	Poultry Seasonings		2 tsp
	10 ml	Salt		2 tsp
	1 ¼ ml	Pepper		¼ tsp

Procedure

1. Cut a pocket by splitting the meaty part of the chop. Sprinkle with salt on both sides.
2. Prepare filling by sautéeing onions and celery in hot bacon fat. Stir in remaining ingredients until well mixed.
3. Fill chop pockets with ¼ cup/59 ml filling and arrange in pans. Bake at 350°F/177°C until meat is tender and browned (about 1 hr).

Glazed Ham Loaf

48 Servings

Bake, 350°F/177°C, 1–1½ hrs

| Metric | | Ingredients | U.S. | |
Weight	Volume		Weight	Volume
28 g	30 ml	Mustard, prepared	1 oz	2 tbsp
	5 ml	Pepper		1 tsp
	5 ml	Allspice		1 tsp
	2½ ml	Thyme, powdered		½ tsp
	5 ml	Cinnamon		1 tsp
2.27 kg	2.37 l	Ham, ground	5 lb	2½ qt
1.36 kg	1.42 l	Beef, ground	3 lb	1½ qt
255 g	266 ml	Eggs, slightly beaten (5 med)	9 oz	1⅛ cups
454 g	474 ml	Beef Stock	1 lb	2 cups
567 g	1.42 l	Oatmeal, uncooked	1 lb, 4 oz	1½ qt
454 g	632 ml	Brown Sugar	1 lb	2⅔ cups
114 g	118 ml	Water	4 oz	½ cup

Procedure

1. Combine spices and seasonings. Mix well. Mix meat and eggs with beef stock, oatmeal, and spices.
2. Scale 3¾ lb/1.70 kg into each of 3 loaf pans (9 × 5 × 3 in).
3. Combine brown sugar and water. Pour equal amounts over loaves.
4. Bake at 350°F/177°C about 1 to 1½ hours. Cut each loaf into 16 slices.

Stuffed Ham Rolls

50 Servings

Bake, 300°F/149°C, 30 min

| Metric | | Ingredients | U.S. | |
Weight	Volume		Weight	Volume
283 g	395 ml	Onions, chopped	10 oz	1⅔ cups
142 g	296 ml	Green Pepper, chopped	5 oz	1¼ cups
538 g	563 ml	Butter or Margarine	1 lb, 3 oz	2⅜ cups
538 g	1.13 l	Celery, diced	1 lb, 3 oz	4¾ cups
1.25 kg	3.31 l	Bread Crumbs, soft	2 lb, 12 oz	3½ qt
	11 ml	Salt		2¼ tsp
	2½ ml	Pepper		½ tsp
2.83 kg	100 slices	Ham, cooked, 1-oz slices	6 lb, 4 oz	100 slices
340 g	296 ml	Mustard, prepared	12 oz	1¼ cups
3.18 kg	3.31 l	Béchamel Sauce with mushrooms	7 lb	3½ qt

Procedure

1. Sauté onions and green pepper in butter or margarine until tender.
2. Add celery, bread crumbs, salt, and pepper.
3. Spread ham slices evenly with mustard (very thinly). Place dressing on each slice with No. 30 scoop. Roll and lay seam down on greased serving pans.
4. Bake at 300°F/149°C for 30 minutes.
5. Ladle sauce over rolls and keep hot for service. (The sauce may be poured over the rolls before baking, if desired.)

Baked Cured Ham

50 Servings
Bake, 325°F/163°C, 3–6 hrs

Metric		Ingredients	U.S.	
Weight	Volume		Weight	Volume
6.81 kg	1 ham	Ham	15 lb	1 ham
	15 cloves	Cloves, whole		15 cloves
907 g	947 ml	Pineapple Juice	2 lb	1 qt
57 g	60 ml	Mustard, prepared	2 oz	4 tbsp
907 g	1.26 l	Brown Sugar	2 lb	5 1/3 cups
454 g	2 oranges	Oranges, slices, unpeeled	1 lb	2 oranges

Procedure

1. Stud ham with cloves.
2. Make a syrup of pineapple juice, prepared mustard, and brown sugar. Pour over ham and bake at 325°F/163°C (about 5 hrs or 20 min per lb/454 g). Baste often and during the last half hour of baking, place orange slices on top of ham.

Note: The pan syrup may be used in making a sauce to serve with the ham.

Ham Patties with Pineapple

50 Servings
Bake, 350°F/177°C, 40 min

Metric		Ingredients	U.S.	
Weight	Volume		Weight	Volume
2.15 kg	2.25 l	Ham, ground	4 lb, 12 oz	9 1/2 cups
2.10 kg	2.19 l	Beef, ground	4 lb, 10 oz	9 1/4 cups
170 g	415 ml	Bread Crumbs	6 oz	1 3/4 cups
793 g	829 ml	Milk	1 lb, 12 oz	3 1/2 cups
128 g	135 ml	Mustard, prepared	4 1/2 oz	9 tbsp
	50 slices	Pineapple Slices (120 ct), drained		50 slices
		Sauce		
43 g	75 ml	Cornstarch	1 1/2 oz	5 tbsp
170 g	178 ml	Water, cold	6 oz	3/4 cup
850 g	889 ml	Juice from Pineapple Slices	1 lb, 14 oz	3 3/4 cups
170 g	178 ml	Sugar	6 oz	3/4 cup
85 g	90 ml	Vinegar	3 oz	6 tbsp
7 g	7 1/2 ml	Salt	1/4 oz	1 1/2 tsp
340 g	474 ml	Brown Sugar	12 oz	2 cups
	5 ml	Mustard, dry		1 tsp
	7 1/2 ml	White Cloves		1 1/2 tsp

Procedure

1. Combine ground ham, ground beef, bread crumbs, milk, and mustard. Mix well, but handle lightly.
2. Dip slightly rounded No. 8 scoops of mixture and form patties. Indent a slice of pineapple on each patty. Arrange in serving pans (12 × 20 × 2 1/2 in).
3. Bake at 350°F/177°C for 25 minutes.
4. Add cornstarch to cold water and stir until smooth.
5. Combine remaining sauce ingredients and heat to boiling. Add cornstarch mixture and cook, stirring, until sauce is thickened and clear.
6. Pour sauce over patties and bake 15 minutes longer.

Ham Slices with Fruit Topping
50 Servings (6 oz/170 g)
Bake, 350°F/177°C, 30 min

Metric		Ingredients	U.S.		
Weight	Volume		Weight		Volume
5.67 kg	100 slices	Ham Slices, cooked pullman	12 lb,	8 oz	100 slices
2.04 kg	2.13 l	Apple Slices, canned	4 lb,	8 oz	2 ¼ qt
312 g	474 ml	Raisins or Chopped Prunes		11 oz	2 cups
	22 ½ ml	Orange Rind, grated			1 ½ tbsp
255 g	355 ml	Brown Sugar		9 oz	1 ½ cups
227 g	592 ml	Bread Crumbs		8 oz	2 ½ cups
133 g	158 ml	Butter or Margarine, melted		4 ⅔ oz	⅔ cup

Procedure

1. Arrange ham slices in serving pans. Mix fruit, orange rind, and brown sugar together. Place ¼ cup/ 59 ml of the mixture on each ham slice. Sprinkle with crumbs and drizzle melted butter or margarine over top.

2. Bake at 350°F/177°C for 30 minutes or until the food is thoroughly heated.

Ham Loaf, Jellied
51 Servings

Metric		Ingredients	U.S.		
Weight	Volume		Weight		Volume
114 g	178 ml	Gelatin		4 oz	¾ cup
681 g	711 ml	Water, cold	1 lb,	8 oz	3 cups
1.36 kg	1.42 l	Water, boiling	3 lb		1 ½ qt
4.42 kg	4.50 l	Ham, cooked, coarsely ground	9 lb,	12 oz	4 ¾ qt
128 g	135 ml	Mustard, prepared		4 ½ oz	9 tbsp
567 g	592 ml	Lemon Juice	1 lb,	4 oz	2 ½ cups
340 g	711 ml	Green Pepper, chopped		12 oz	3 cups
170 g	237 ml	Pimiento		6 oz	1 cup
	2 ½ ml	Red Pepper			½ tsp
43 g	45 ml	Vinegar		1 ½ oz	3 tbsp

Procedure

1. Soak gelatin in cold water. Add boiling water and stir until dissolved. Cool.
2. Add remaining ingredients before gelatin begins to set.
3. Scale 5 ¼ lb/2.39 g into each of 3 oiled loaf pans (9 × 5 × 3 in).
4. Chill until firmly set. Slice 17 slices per loaf.

Ham and Rice Loaf

48 Servings
Bake, 350°F/177°C, 1 hr

Metric		Ingredients	U.S.	
Weight	Volume		Weight	Volume
1.82 kg	1.89 l	Ham, ground	4 lb	2 qt
907 g	947 ml	Veal, ground	2 lb	1 qt
681 g	711 ml	Pork, ground	1 lb, 8 oz	3 cups
1.19 kg	1.54 l	Rice, cooked	2 lb, 10 oz	6 ½ cups
227 g	237 ml	Eggs, beaten (4 lge)	8 oz	1 cup
907 g	947 ml	Milk	2 lb	1 qt
170 g	533 ml	Cracker or Bread Crumbs	6 oz	2 ¼ cups
14 g	15 ml	Horseradish, prepared	½ oz	1 tbsp
	10 ml	Salt		2 tsp

Procedure

1. Combine all ingredients and mix well.
2. Press 4 ½ lb/2.04 kg into each of 3 loaf pans (9 × 5 × 3 in).
3. Bake at 350°F/177°C for 1 ½ hours or until done.

Note: Ground turkey may be substituted for the veal.

Ham à la King

50 Servings (⅔ cup/158 ml)

Metric		Ingredients	U.S.	
Weight	Volume		Weight	Volume
567 g	592 ml	Butter or Margarine	1 lb, 4 oz	2 ½ cups
681 g	1.42 l	Green Pepper, chopped	1 lb, 8 oz	1 ½ qt
340 g	711 ml	Flour, all-purpose	12 oz	3 cups
3.63 kg	3.79 l	Milk	8 lb	1 gal
28 g	30 ml	Salt	1 oz	2 tbsp
	2 ½ ml	White Pepper		½ tsp
793 g	16 lge	Eggs, hard-cooked, diced	1 lb, 12 oz	16 lge
227 g	316 ml	Pimiento, chopped	8 oz	1 ⅓ cups
2.50 kg	3.79 l	Ham, diced	5 lb, 8 oz	1 gal

Procedure

1. Sauté green pepper in butter or margarine. Add flour and blend. Add milk and seasonings, stirring constantly until sauce is thick and smooth.
2. Add remaining ingredients and heat thoroughly in a double boiler.
3. Serve on toast, toasted bun, in patty shells, or on cornbread.

Ham and Eggs au Gratin on Toast
50 Servings

| Metric | | Ingredients | U.S. | |
Weight	Volume		Weight	Volume
340 g	711 ml	Green Pepper, chopped	12 oz	3 cups
340 g	355 ml	Butter or Margarine	12 oz	1 ½ cups
170 g	355 ml	Flour, bread	6 oz	1 ½ cups
2.72 kg	2.84 l	Milk, hot	6 lb	3 qt
	5 ml	Paprika		1 tsp
	5 ml	Mustard		1 tsp
454 g	947 ml	Cheddar Cheese, ground	1 lb	1 qt
1.82 kg	2.84 l	Ham, cooked, chopped	4 lb	3 qt
907 g	18 lge	Eggs, hard-cooked, chopped	2 lb	18 lge
	50 slices	Toast		50 slices

Procedure

1. Sauté green pepper in butter or margarine. Add flour and blend. Add milk, stirring constantly until sauce is thick and smooth.
2. Add paprika, mustard, and cheese. Stir until well-blended.
3. Add ham and eggs and heat thoroughly.
4. Serve on toast, toasted bun, or in toast cups.

Caramel Ham Loaf
48 Servings
Bake, 350°F/177°C, 1 ½–2 hrs

| Metric | | Ingredients | U.S. | |
Weight	Volume		Weight	Volume
907 g	2.13 l	Bread, day-old	2 lb	2 ¼ qt
1.82 kg	1.89 l	Milk	4 lb	2 qt
397 g	415 ml	Eggs, slightly beaten (7 lge)	14 oz	1 ¾ cups
	15 ml	Mustard, dry		1 tbsp
18 g	20 ml	Salt		1 ⅓ tbsp
	5 ml	Pepper		1 tsp
3.63 kg	3.79 l	Beef, ground	8 lb	1 gal
1.36 kg	1.42 l	Ham, raw, ground	3 lb	1 ½ qt
340 g	474 ml	Brown Sugar	12 oz	2 cups
	15 ml	Cloves, whole		1 tbsp

Procedure

1. Break bread into pieces and soak in milk. Add eggs, mustard, salt, and pepper. Blend meats into mixture, mixing thoroughly.
2. Place 4 oz/114 g of brown sugar in the bottom of each of 3 loaf pans (9 × 5 × 3 in). Sprinkle 1 tsp/5 ml whole cloves over this and place 6 lb/2.72 kg meat mixture on top.
3. Bake at 350°F/177°C for 1 ½ to 2 hours, or until brown and well-done.

Ham Croquettes
50 Servings
Fry, 360°F/182°C

Metric		Ingredients	U.S.	
Weight	Volume		Weight	Volume
1.70 kg	1.78 l	Rice, uncooked	3 lb, 12 oz	7 ½ cups
85 g	90 ml	Salt	3 oz	6 tbsp
1.36 kg	1.42 l	Milk	3 lb	1 ½ qt
4.08 kg	4.26 l	Water	9 lb	4 ½ qt
1.82 kg	1.89 l	Eggs, beaten (36 med)	4 lb	2 qt
2.72 kg	5.68 l	Ham, coarsely ground	6 lb	6 qt
227 g	474 ml	Green Pepper, diced	8 oz	2 cups

Procedure

1. Cook rice in boiling liquid (milk and water combined).
2. Add beaten eggs, ham, and green pepper. Mix well. Place in refrigerator overnight and chill.
3. Shape 100 croquettes, using a No. 16 scoop. Fry in deep fat at 360°F/182°C until nicely browned.

Note: Croquettes may be dipped in beaten egg and rolled in bread crumbs before frying, if desired.

CHAPTER 7 _____ *Poultry*

Guard the delicate goodness of poultry by cooking it at a low temperature until it is thoroughly done. Temperatures of 300°F/149°C and 325°F/163°C are satisfactory for small birds, and 275°F/135°C and 300/°F/149°C for large ones. The minimum cooking time for the most tender young broilers is 45 minutes; older, larger birds require from 15 to 25 minutes per pound of total weight for good results. The proper time allowance depends to a considerable degree upon size and age.

Table 8
Approximate Time for Thawing and Roasting Poultry

Kind of Poultry	Ready-to-Cook Weight	Thawing (40°F/4°C) Frozen Birds (hr)	Roasting Time (325°F/163°C) Stuffed (hr)	Unstuffed (hr)
Cornish Hen	1½ lb /681 g	8–11	1½–2	1–1½
Broiler or Fryer	1½ lb /681 g	8–11	1½–2	¾–1½
Roaster	3½ lb /1.59 kg	10–12	2–3½	1½–2¾
Capon	6½ lb /2.95 kg	10–12	3–6	2–3
Duck	4½ lb /2.04 kg	13–18	2½–3	
Goose	8 lb /3.63 kg	13–18	3–3½	
	12 lb /5.44 kg	20–30	3½–5	
Turkey	8 lb /3.63 kg	10–12	3–4½	2–2¼
	12 lb /5.44 kg	12–15	3½–5	2½–3
	16 lb /7.26 kg	20–26	6–7½	3¾–4½
	24 lb /10.89 kg	22–30	7½–9	4½–5½
Turkey Parts—				
Halves	5 lb /2.27 kg	10–12	3–3½	
Quarters	7 lb /3.18 kg	12–15	3½–4	
Half Breast	10 lb /4.54 kg	12–15	4–5	

Chicken Recipes

Broiled Chicken
Procedure

1. Select birds weighing 1 ½ to 2 ½ lb/681 g to 1.14 kg each. Allow at least 12 oz/340 g per person for an adequate portion.
2. Cut birds in halves or quarters, choosing a size that will look well on the plate.
3. Brush with melted fat and sprinkle with salt.
4. Arrange on broiler rack to broil the inside first, then turn pieces and broil the outside. Place rack about 4 inches from flame or heating element.
5. Broil for 15 or 20 minutes on each side. Allow a total cooking time of 45 minutes for small birds and 60 minutes for larger ones. Give special attention to cooking the fleshy parts, such as breasts. Turn and place pieces at proper angle for browning on all sides.

Pan-Fried Chicken
Procedure

1. Birds may weigh from 1 ½ to 5 lb/681 g to 2.27 kg if young and tender. Allow 12 to 16 oz/340 to 454 g A.P. per portion.
2. Cut birds into attractive pieces (quarters or disjointed).
3. Pieces may be rolled in coating preferred—(a) bread or cracker crumbs and seasoning; (b) flour, corn meal, and seasoning; (c) flour and seasoning. Quantities of flour and seasoning required for 50 portions:

| Metric | | | U.S. | |
Weight	Volume	Ingredients	Weight	Volume
681 g	1.42 l	Flour, pastry or all-purpose	1 lb, 8 oz	6 cups
43 g	45 ml	Salt	1 ½ oz	3 tbsp
	5 ml	Pepper		1 tsp
681 g	711 ml	Fat for frying (sufficient for ¼-in-deep layer in pan)	1–1 lb, 8 oz	2–3 cups

4. Brown at moderate temperature. Small birds may be cooked in fat until done. Larger and older chickens are better when a small amount of liquid, either water or milk, is added to the browned chicken and cooking continued for an hour in the oven (until chicken is tender).

Chicken Timbales
50 Servings (4 oz/114 g)
Bake, 325°F/163°C, 1 hr

| Metric | | | U.S. | |
Weight	Volume	Ingredients	Weight	Volume
1.36 kg	3.31 l	Bread, cubed	3 lb	3 ½ qt
1.53 kg	1.60 l	Eggs (27 lge)	3 lb, 6 oz	6 ¾ cups
3.18 kg	3.31 l	Cream, 20%	7 lb	3 ½ qt
2.38 kg	6.63 l	Chicken, ground	5 lb, 4 oz	7 qt
49 g	52 ml	Salt	1 ¾ oz	3 ½ tbsp
	7 ½ ml	Pepper, white		1 ½ tsp

1. Soak bread cubes in mixture of slightly beaten eggs and cream.
2. Add chicken, salt, and pepper. Mix well.
3. Yield: About 20 lb/9.07 kg. Pour ¾ cup/178 ml into each of 50 lightly greased individual casseroles. Bake in pan of water at 325°F/163°C for 1 hour or until an inserted knife blade comes out clean.

Chicken Supreme

50 Servings
Bake, 350°F/177°C, 1 hr

Metric		Ingredients	U.S.	
Weight	Volume		Weight	Volume
5.67 kg	50 pieces	Chicken Breasts, 4 oz each	12 lb, 8 oz	50 pieces
1.82 kg	1.89 l	Cream of Mushroom Soup, undiluted	4 lb	2 qt
681 g	711 ml	Orange Juice	1 lb, 8 oz	3 cups
255 g	355 ml	Black Olives, chopped	9 oz	1 ½ cups
114 g	158 ml	Pimiento, chopped	4 oz	⅔ cup
14 g	15 ml	Salt	½ oz	1 tbsp
	5 ml	Pepper		1 tsp

Procedure

1. Place chicken breasts, skin side up, in serving pans (12 × 20 × 1 in).
2. Mix remaining ingredients and pour over chicken.
3. Bake at 350°F/177°C for 1 hour, or until tender. Chicken will become light brown on top. Sauce does not need to be stirred during baking.

Oven-Fried Chicken

50 Servings (8 oz/227 g)
Bake, 325°F/163°C, 1 ½ hrs

Metric		Ingredients	U.S.	
Weight	Volume		Weight	Volume
11.34 kg		Fryer Thighs and Breasts	25 lb	100 pieces
340 g	355 ml	Salad Oil	12 oz	1 ½ cups
114 g	118 ml	Lemon Juice	4 oz	½ cup
21 g	22 ml	Salt	¾ oz	1 ½ tbsp
	5 ml	Pepper		1 tsp
	5 ml	Poultry Seasoning		1 tsp
227 g	474 ml	Cornflake Crumbs	8 oz	2 cups

Procedure

1. Prepare chicken in pieces for frying.
2. Blend salad oil, lemon juice, and seasonings.
3. Place chicken pieces in seasoning mixture, being sure that all pieces are well covered with the seasoning. Let stand a few minutes.
4. Place on greased baking sheet, skin side up and with pieces far enough apart to allow browning on all sides. Sprinkle crumbs over the chicken generously.
5. Bake at 325°F/163°C until chicken is tender (about 1 ½ hrs).

Stewed Chicken

50 Servings

Simmer, 2 or 3 hrs

Many delicious dishes are made with chicken broth and diced stewed chicken. Qualities to aim for are good, rich chicken flavor, tenderness, and juiciness. Chicken pie, creamed chicken, chicken soufflé, and chicken salad are some of the favorite dishes for which stewing chicken is the first step in preparation.

Metric		Ingredients	U.S.	
Weight	Volume		Weight	Volume
15.87 kg	10 fowls	Chicken	35 lb	10 fowls
1.82 kg	1.89 l	Water (to cover)	4 lb	2 qt
43 g	45 ml	Salt	1 ½ oz	3 tbsp
907 g	8 small	Carrots	2 lb	8 small
907 g	6 med	Onions	2 lb	6 med
227 g	6 stalks	Celery	8 oz	6 stalks
	6 cloves	Cloves, whole		6 cloves
	5 ml	Peppercorns		1 tsp

Procedure

1. Chicken may be whole or disjointed for cooking.
2. Add water to barely cover and simmer until tender. Add vegetables and seasonings and cook for 30 to 45 minutes longer, or until meat will come off bones readily.
3. Let chicken stand in broth until cool. This will improve flavor and add juiciness to the chicken.
4. Refrigerate as soon as stock has cooled sufficiently, approximately 30 to 40 minutes longer.

Chicken Tahitian

50 Servings (4 oz/114 g)

Bake, 325°F/163°C, 1 hr

Metric		Ingredients	U.S.	
Weight	Volume		Weight	Volume
6.81 kg	50 pieces	Chicken Breasts	15 lb	50 pieces
340 g	711 ml	Flour, all-purpose	12 oz	3 cups
28 g	30 ml	Salt	1 oz	2 tbsp
	5 ml	Pepper		1 tsp
454 g	474 ml	Orange Juice Concentrate	1 lb	2 cups
300 g	355 ml	Margarine, melted	10 ½ oz	1 ½ cups
9 g	30 ml	Ginger, ground		2 tbsp
28 g	30 ml	Soy Sauce	1 oz	2 tbsp

Procedure

1. Remove bones and skin from chicken breasts. Dredge with mixture of flour, salt, and pepper. Place on greased baking pans, sufficiently apart to allow browning. Brush with melted butter or margarine.
2. Lightly brown in 325°F/163°C oven for 45 minutes.
3. Combine orange juice concentrate, margarine, ginger, and soy sauce. Brush on hot chicken generously.
4. Return to 325°F/163°C oven and bake for 20 minutes or until nicely browned and chicken is tender. Watch that it does not become too brown during baking.

Note: The drippings, thickened with flour, provide a good sauce to serve with the chicken.

Chicken Cacciatore
50 Servings (¾ cup/178 ml)

| Metric | | Ingredients | U.S. | |
Weight	Volume		Weight	Volume
28 g	8 cloves	Garlic, minced	1 oz	8 cloves
907 g	1.42 l	Onions, thinly sliced	2 lb	1½ qt
340 g	711 ml	Green Pepper, ½-in dices	12 oz	3 cups
1.36 kg	1.42 l	Mushrooms, canned, sliced	3 lb	1½ qt
114 g	118 ml	Butter or Margarine	4 oz	½ cup
7 g	15 ml	Oregano, dry, crushed	¼ oz	1 tbsp
114 g	118 ml	Lemon Juice	4 oz	½ cup
14 g	15 ml	Salt	½ oz	1 tbsp
681 g	711 ml	Mushroom Liquor (from can)	1 lb, 8 oz	3 cups
4.54 kg	4.74 l	Tomato Soup	10 lb	5 qt
1.82 kg	2.84 l	Chicken, cooked, cubed	4 lb	3 qt
227 g	474 ml	Cheddar Cheese, grated	8 oz	2 cups

Procedure

1. Sauté garlic, onions, green pepper, and mushrooms in butter or margarine until tender. Add oregano, lemon juice, salt, mushroom liquor, and tomato soup. Simmer for 15 minutes, stirring occasionally to prevent sticking.

2. Gently stir in cubed chicken and heat thoroughly. Add cheese and blend. Serve over cooked rice, bulgar wheat, spaghetti or noodles, and sprinkle with grated cheese.

Note: Cubed turkey breast may be substituted for chicken.

Chicken à la King
50 Servings (⅔ cup/158 ml)

| Metric | | Ingredients | U.S. | |
Weight	Volume		Weight	Volume
114 g	237 ml	Green Pepper, chopped	4 oz	1 cup
510 g	1.89 l	Mushrooms, sliced, fresh	1 lb, 2 oz	2 qt
227 g	237 ml	Butter or Margarine	8 oz	1 cup
454 g	947 ml	Flour, bread	1 lb	1 qt
2.27 kg	2.37 l	Chicken Broth, cold	5 lb	2½ qt
2.27 kg	2.37 l	Milk, hot	5 lb	2½ qt
28 g	30 ml	Salt	1 oz	2 tbsp
	2½ ml	Pepper		½ tsp
1.82 kg	2.84 l	Chicken, cooked, diced	4 lb	3 qt
57 g	79 ml	Pimiento, chopped	2 oz	⅓ cup

Procedure

1. Sauté green pepper and mushrooms in butter or margarine until tender.
2. Make a paste of flour and cold chicken broth. Add to green pepper and mushroom mixture. Blend.
3. Add hot milk and stir until thickened and smooth.
4. Add remaining ingredients. Heat in double boiler.
5. Serve on melba toast, in toast cups, or over cornbread.

Swiss Chicken Breasts

48 Servings (7 oz/198 g)
Bake, 325°F/163°C, 20 min

| Metric | | Ingredients | U.S. | |
Weight	Volume		Weight	Volume
5.44 kg	48 pieces	Chicken Breasts, skinned, boned	12 lb	48 pieces
2.72 kg	48 slices	Ham, boiled, sliced	6 lb	48 slices
1.36 kg	48 slices	Swiss Cheese, sliced	3 lb	48 slices
170 g	355 ml	Flour, all-purpose	6 oz	1 ½ cups
340 g	355 ml	Eggs, slightly beaten (6 lge)	12 oz	1 ½ cups
397 g	947 ml	Bread Crumbs, fine, dry	14 oz	1 qt
340 g	355 ml	Shortening	12 oz	1 ½ cups
681 g	711 ml	White Wine	1 lb, 8 oz	3 cups
340 g	355 ml	Butter or Margarine	12 oz	1 ½ cups
227 g	355 ml	Onions, finely chopped	8 oz	1 ½ cups
170 g	355 ml	Flour, all-purpose	6 oz	1 ½ cups
14 g	15 ml	Salt	½ oz	1 tbsp
	2 ½ ml	Pepper		½ tsp
2.72 kg	2.84 l	Milk, whole	6 lb	3 qt
28 g	178 ml	Parsley, chopped	1 oz	¾ cup

Procedure

1. Flatten chicken breasts by placing them between waxed paper and pounding with a mallet or rolling with a rolling pin, using a slightly pounding motion.
2. Place thin ham slice on chicken breast and top with slice of cheese. Roll the chicken breast around the ham and cheese and skewer with a toothpick.
3. Dip chicken rolls in flour, then in beaten egg, and roll in crumbs. Sauté in shortening at moderate temperature until lightly browned. Add wine and let simmer for 20 minutes. Place the chicken rolls in serving pans (12 × 20 × 2 in).
4. Melt butter or margarine, sauté onions lightly, and add flour and seasonings. Blend. Cook over low heat 3 to 5 minutes. Stir while cooking. Add milk and drippings from chicken, stirring constantly to make sauce. Cook until smooth and thickened.
5. Pour sauce over chicken rolls and bake at 325°F/163°C for 20 minutes. Garnish with chopped parsley.

Old-Fashioned Chicken Pie

50 Servings (4 ½ oz/128 g)
Bake, 400°F/205°C

| Metric | | Ingredients | U.S. | |
Weight	Volume		Weight	Volume
114 g	118 ml	Butter or Margarine	4 oz	½ cup
681 g	711 ml	Chicken Fat	1 lb, 8 oz	3 cups
397 g	829 ml	Flour, bread	14 oz	3 ½ cups
28 g	30 ml	Salt	1 oz	2 tbsp
	10 ml	Pepper, white		2 tsp
5.44 kg	5.68 l	Chicken Stock, heated	12 lb	1 ½ gal
1.81 kg	2.84 l	Chicken Meat, diced	4 lb	3 qt
1.14 kg	1.78 l	Carrots, cooked, diced	2 lb, 8 oz	7 ½ cups
2.27 kg	2.84 l	Potatoes, cooked, diced	5 lb	3 qt

1. Melt butter or margarine and chicken fat. Add flour, salt, and pepper. Blend. Cook over low heat 3 to 5 minutes. Stir while cooking. Add chicken stock slowly, stirring to form a smooth gravy. Cook until thickened.
2. Scale 2 lb/907 g chicken meat, (1 lb/454 g each of light and dark), into each of 2 serving pans (12 × 20 × 2 in). Add 1 ¼ lb/567 g carrots and 2 ½ lb/1.14 kg potatoes to each pan. Pour 3 qts/2.84 l of gravy over each pan.
3. Top with rich biscuit dough or pie crust (see Baking Powder Biscuits, p. 2). Bake at 400°F/205°C until brown.

Note: When made in individual casseroles, allow ¾ cup per casserole and cover with pie crust.

Chicken and Cornbread Casserole

50 Servings (12 oz/340 g)

Bake, 400°F/205°C, 45 min

| Metric | | | U.S. | |
Weight	Volume	Ingredients	Weight	Volume
340 g	355 ml	Shortening or Oil	12 oz	1 ½ cups
907 g	1.42 l	Onions, chopped	2 lb	1 ½ qt
1.36 kg	2.84 l	Celery, chopped	3 lb	3 qt
454 g	947 ml	Green Pepper, chopped	1 lb	1 qt
454 g	947 ml	Flour, all-purpose	1 lb	1 qt
1.36 kg	1.42 l	Chicken Broth	3 lb	1 ½ qt
5.90 kg	6.63 l	Tomato Sauce	13 lb	2 No. 10 cans
28 g	30 ml	Salt	1 oz	2 tbsp
	5 ml	Pepper		1 tsp
2.72 kg	4.26 l	Chicken, cooked, diced	6 lb	4 ½ qt
567 g	711 ml	Ripe Olives, quartered	1 lb, 4 oz	3 cups
		Cornbread Crust		
681 g	1.42 l	Flour, all-purpose	1 lb, 8 oz	1 ½ qt
793 g	1.42 l	Corn Meal	1 lb, 12 oz	1 ½ qt
43 g	60 ml	Baking Powder	1 ½ oz	4 tbsp
28 g	30 ml	Salt	1 oz	2 tbsp
340 g	355 ml	Eggs, beaten (6 lge)	12 oz	1 ½ cups
1.36 kg	1.42 l	Milk	3 lb	1 ½ qt
425 g	474 ml	Cooking Oil	15 oz	2 cups

Procedure

1. Heat shortening and sauté vegetables. Blend in flour and stir in broth and tomato sauce. Add salt and pepper and cook until thickened.
2. Gently stir in chicken and olives. Divide mixture into 2 pans (12 × 20 × 2 in).
3. Sift dry ingredients together. Blend beaten eggs, milk, and oil. Stir into dry ingredients until they are moistened. Cover pans with cornbread crust.
4. Bake at 400°F/205°C for 45 minutes.

Chicken Croquettes

50 Servings (4 oz/114 g)
Deep Fry, 375°F/190°C

Metric		Ingredients	U.S.	
Weight	Volume		Weight	Volume
227 g	711 ml	Mushrooms, fresh, chopped	8 oz	3 cups
14 g	15 ml	Butter or Margarine	½ oz	1 tbsp
454 g	474 ml	Eggs, beaten (8 lge)	1 lb	2 cups
2.04 kg	3.08 l	Chicken, cooked, chopped	4 lb, 8 oz	3 ¼ qt
879 g	2.37 l	Bread Crumbs, soft	1 lb, 15 oz	2 ½ qt
681 g	711 ml	Mayonnaise	1 lb, 8 oz	3 cups
170 g	237 ml	Pimiento, diced	6 oz	1 cup
57 g	355 ml	Parsley, chopped	2 oz	1 ½ cups
	5 ml	Mustard, dry		1 tsp
57 g	59 ml	Lemon Juice	2 oz	¼ cup
	10 ml	Salt		2 tsp
907 g	947 ml	Milk	2 lb	1 qt
227 g	474 ml	Flour, all-purpose	8 oz	2 cups
340 g	355 ml	Eggs, beaten (6 lge)	12 oz	1 ½ cups
298 g	711 ml	Bread Crumbs	8 oz	3 cups

Procedure

1. Sauté mushrooms in butter or margarine.
2. Combine all but last three ingredients. Mix well. Portion with a No. 20 scoop, and shape into 100 croquettes.
3. Roll croquettes in flour, dip into beaten egg, and roll in bread crumbs.
4. Fry in deep fat at 375°F/190°C until golden brown. Drain.

Note: Serve with Mushroom Sauce. Turkey or tuna fish may be used in place of the chicken.

Chicken Chow Mein

50 Servings (6 oz/170 g)

Metric		Ingredients	U.S.	
Weight	Volume		Weight	Volume
2.38 kg	4.98 l	Chicken, cut into strips	5 lb, 4 oz	5 ¼ qt
255 g	533 ml	Flour, bread	9 oz	2 ¼ cups
128 g	135 ml	Butter or Margarine	4 ½ oz	9 tbsp
567 g	592 ml	Soy Sauce	1 lb, 4 oz	2 ½ cups
1.70 kg	3.56 l	Celery, chopped	3 lb, 12 oz	3 ¾ qt
340 g	711 ml	Green Pepper, chopped	12 oz	3 cups
1.02 kg	1.60 l	Onions, chopped	2 lb, 4 oz	6 ¾ cups
4.42 kg	4.98 l	Bean Sprouts	9 lb, 12 oz	1 ½ No. 10 cans
1.59 kg	1.66 l	Chicken Stock	3 lb, 8 oz	1 ¾ qt
510 g	711 ml	Almonds, blanched	1 lb, 2 oz	3 cups
681 g	2.37 l	Mushrooms, sliced, fresh	1 lb, 8 oz	2 ½ qt
255 g	266 ml	Butter or Margarine	9 oz	1 ⅛ cups
1.51 kg	1.82 l	Rice, uncooked	3 lb, 5 ⅓ oz	7 ⅔ cups
3.63 kg	3.79 l	Water	8 lb	1 gal
28 g	30 ml	Salt	1 oz	2 tbsp

1. Cut chicken in strips, 1 in × ¾ in × ⅜ in. Dredge in flour and sauté in fat until golden brown.
2. Add soy sauce and blend.
3. Add vegetables and bean-sprout liquid. Add stock. Cook until vegetables are tender. Add sprouts.
4. Sauté almonds and sliced mushrooms in butter or margarine. Add to chow mein.
5. Add rice to boiling salted water. Stir and cover tightly. Cook over low heat for 20 minutes, until water is absorbed and rice is tender. Remove from heat and let stand covered 10 minutes.
6. Serve ¾ cup sauce per serving on rice.

Note: Crisp noodles (1 lb, 8 oz/681 g) may be substituted for the rice.

Little Red Hens

50 Turnovers (4 oz/114 g)
Bake, 425°F/218°C, 20 min

Metric		Ingredients	U.S.		
Weight	Volume		Weight		Volume
1.25 kg	1.89 l	Chicken, cooked, finely diced	2 lb,	12 oz	2 qt
454 g	947 ml	Celery, minced	1 lb		1 qt
170 g	355 ml	Green Pepper, finely chopped		6 oz	1 ½ cups
170 g	237 ml	Onions, minced		6 oz	1 cup
681 g	711 ml	Salad Dressing	1 lb,	8 oz	3 cups
57 g	59 ml	Worcestershire Sauce		2 oz	¼ cup
454 g	474 ml	Cottage Cheese, drained	1 lb		2 cups
	2 ½ ml	Mustard, dry			½ tsp
	5 ml	Pepper			1 tsp
	1 ¼ ml	Hot Pepper Sauce			¼ tsp
57 g	59 ml	Lemon Juice		2 oz	¼ cup
		Biscuit Crust			
1.36 kg	2.84 l	Flour, pastry or all-purpose	3 lb		3 qt
14 g	15 ml	Salt		½ oz	1 tbsp
64 g	68 ml	Sugar		2 ¼ oz	4 ½ tbsp
64 g	90 ml	Baking Powder		2 ¼ oz	6 tbsp
510 g	533 ml	Shortening	1 lb,	2 oz	2 ¼ cups
766 g	789 ml	Milk (approx.)	1 lb,	11 oz	3 ⅓ cups

Procedure

1. Blend filling ingredients thoroughly.
2. Mix flour, salt, sugar, and baking powder together and cut in fat for biscuit dough. Add milk, stirring and using caution to add only enough to form a soft dough that will be easy to roll out.
3. Roll dough to ⅛-inch thickness. Cut in circles 6 inches in diameter (use a No. 10 can for measuring).

Place a No. 16 scoop of filling on half of the biscuit circle and turn the other half over it. Moisten and crimp edges to seal in filling.
4. Arrange on baking sheet; brush tops lightly with milk. Bake at 425°F/218°C until nicely browned (about 20 min).

Chicken-Ham Roll-Ups

50/2-oz Servings

| Metric | | Ingredients | U.S. | |
Weight	Volume		Weight	Volume
1.08 kg	1.42 l	Rice, cooked	2 lb, 6 oz	1 ½ qt
28 g	178 ml	Parsley, minced	1 oz	¾ cup
283 g	474 ml	Almonds, chopped	10 oz	2 cups
	2 ½ ml	Pepper		½ tsp
	2 ½ ml	Poultry Seasoning		½ tsp
114 g	118 ml	Butter or Margarine, melted	4 oz	½ cup
2.84 kg	50 slices	Boiled Ham, sliced pullman	6 lb, 4 oz	50 slices
		Sauce		
454 g	474 ml	Butter or Margarine	1 lb	2 cups
227 g	474 ml	Flour, all-purpose	8 oz	2 cups
9 g	10 ml	Salt	⅓ oz	2 tsp
	5 ml	Pepper		1 tsp
	10 ml	Nutmeg		2 tsp
1.82 kg	1.89 l	Milk	4 lb	2 qt
1.82 kg	1.89 l	Chicken Broth	4 lb	2 qt
1.82 kg	2.84 l	Chicken, cooked, diced	4 lb	3 qt

Procedure

1. Mix well rice, parsley, almonds, seasonings, and melted butter or margarine. Spread a No. 30 scoop of mixture on ham slices. Roll slices around filling and place in serving pans (12 × 20 × 2 in).
2. Melt butter or margarine in sauce pan. Blend in flour and seasoning. Cook over low heat 3 to 5 minutes. Stir while cooking. Gradually stir in milk and chicken broth, stirring constantly. Cook until smooth and thickened. Add cooked, diced chicken. Heat thoroughly. Pour over the ham rolls, and heat 20 minutes at 350°F/177°C.

Note: The sauce and rolls may be kept separate if desired, and the sauce served over the rolls on the plate.

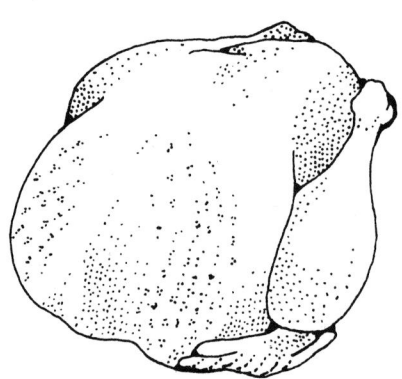

Chicken Loaf

48 Servings
Bake, 325°F/163°C, 1 hr

Metric		Ingredients	U.S.		
Weight	Volume		Weight		Volume
9.07 kg	4 hens	Chicken (cooked chicken, 3 lb/1.36 kg or 4 qt/3.79 l)	20 lb		4 hens
198 g	237 ml	Giblets, finely diced		7 oz	1 cup
454 g	947 ml	Celery, diced	1 lb		1 qt
156 g	237 ml	Onions, chopped		5 ½ oz	1 cup
114 g	237 ml	Green Pepper, diced		4 oz	1 cup
85 g	118 ml	Pimiento, diced		3 oz	½ cup
170 g	178 ml	Chicken Fat		6 oz	¾ cup
1.59 kg	2.84 l	Bread Cubes	3 lb,	8 oz	3 qt
425 g	947 ml	Bread Crumbs		15 oz	1 qt
28 g	30 ml	Salt		1 oz	2 tbsp
	5 ml	Pepper			1 tsp
28 g	30 ml	Worcestershire Sauce		1 oz	2 tbsp
2.72 kg	2.84 l	Chicken Broth	6 lb		3 qt
681 g	711 ml	Eggs, beaten (12 lge)	1 lb,	8 oz	3 cups

Procedure

1. Cook chicken the day before needed and reserve stock and fat. Add 2 tsp/10 ml salt, 1 cup/237 g of chopped onions, ½ cup/118 ml chopped parsley, and 1 cup/237 ml of chopped celery to water (sufficient to cover chickens) in which chicken is cooked.
2. Remove chicken from bones and cut into 1-inch cubes. Finely chop giblets.
3. Sauté celery, onions, green pepper, and pimiento in chicken fat. Add chicken, bread, and seasonings. Stir broth into beaten eggs and pour over the mixture. Toss lightly together until well mixed. Pour into 4 well-greased loaf pans (9 × 5 × 3 in). Set pans in shallow pan of warm water.
4. Bake at 325°F/163°C until lightly browned and set. Cut each loaf into 12 portions and serve with chicken gravy or mushroom soup.

Turkey Recipes

Mock Drumsticks
50 Servings
Bake, 300°F/149°C, 1 hr

| Metric | | Ingredients | U.S. | |
Weight	Volume		Weight	Volume
2.72 kg	2.84 l	Pork Sausage	6 lb	3 qt
2.72 kg	2.84 l	Ground Turkey	6 lb	3 qt
567 g	592 ml	Turkey or Chicken Stock	1 lb, 4 oz	2 ½ cups
255 g	592 ml	Bread Crumbs	9 oz	2 ½ cups
283 g	296 ml	Eggs, beaten (5 lge)	10 oz	1 ¼ cups
28 g	30 ml	Salt	1 oz	2 tbsp
	2 ½ ml	Poultry Seasoning		½ tsp
567 g	889 ml	Onions, finely chopped	1 lb, 4 oz	3 ¾ cups
681 g	1.66 l	Bread Crumbs	1 lb, 8 oz	1 ¾ qt

Procedure

1. Combine all ingredients except the last ingredient and mix well. Shape into drumsticks on skewers, using a No. 16 scoop (100 drumsticks).
2. Roll in 1 ½ lb/681 g bread crumbs. Sauté in fat until brown. Arrange in baking pan. Add 1 qt/947 ml boiling water.
3. Cover and bake at 300°F/149°C for 1 hour.

Turkey Brunswick Stew
50 Servings

| Metric | | Ingredients | U.S. | |
Weight	Volume		Weight	Volume
2.72 kg	2.84 l	Turkey Broth	6 lb	3 qt
1.36 kg	1.42 l	Tomatoes, canned	3 lb	1 ½ qt
766 g	1.18 l	Onions, chopped	1 lb, 11 oz	1 ¼ qt
	5 ml	Ginger, ground		1 tsp
14 g	15 ml	Salt	½ oz	1 tbsp
	5 ml	Pepper		1 tsp
28 g	178 ml	Parsley or Fresh Basil, chopped	1 oz	¾ cup
28 g	30 ml	Worcestershire Sauce	1 oz	2 tbsp
	5 ml	Garlic Salt		1 tsp
	5 ml	Celery Salt		1 tsp
1.81 kg	2.84 l	Lima Beans, frozen, cooked	4 lb	3 qt
1.81 kg	1.89 l	Corn, whole kernel, canned	4 lb	2 qt
1.81 kg	2.84 l	Turkey, cooked, diced	4 lb	3 qt

Procedure

1. Combine all ingredients except corn, lima beans, and turkey and simmer for 1 hour, stirring occasionally.
2. Add corn, cooked lima beans, and turkey. Cook 10 to 15 minutes longer.

Note: Stew should cook down until fairly thick.

Turkey Loaf

50 Servings
Bake, 300°F/149°C, 1 hr

Metric		Ingredients	U.S.	
Weight	Volume		Weight	Volume
2.72 kg	2.84 l	Turkey, cooked, ground	6 lb	3 qt
1.36 kg	1.42 l	Pork Sausage	3 lb	1 ½ qt
624 g	1.42 l	Bread Crumbs	1 lb, 6 oz	1 ½ qt
454 g	711 ml	Onions, finely chopped	1 lb	3 cups
14 g	15 ml	Salt	½ oz	1 tbsp
	5 ml	Pepper		1 tsp
28 g	178 ml	Parsley, chopped	1 oz	¾ cup
681 g	711 ml	Eggs, beaten (12 lge)	1 lb, 8 oz	3 cups
2.72 kg	2.84 l	Milk	6 lb	3 qt

Procedure

1. Combine ingredients in the order given. Pour into 4 greased loaf pans (5 × 9 × 3 in) or 2 serving pans (12 × 20 × 2 in).

2. Bake at 300°F/149°C until inserted knife blade comes out clean.

Note: Serve with a Béchamel Sauce or gravy.

Turkey Tamale Pie

50 Servings
Bake, 350°F/177°C, 1 ¼ hrs

Metric		Ingredients	U.S.	
Weight	Volume		Weight	Volume
4.08 kg	4.26 l	Turkey or Chicken Stock	9 lb	4 ½ qt
43 g	45 ml	Salt	1 ½ oz	3 tbsp
907 g	1.42 l	Corn Meal, yellow	2 lb	1 ½ qt
907 g	1.42 l	Onions, minced	2 lb	1 ½ qt
21 g	6 cloves	Garlic, minced	¾ oz	6 cloves
340 g	474 ml	Bacon or Salt Pork, diced	12 oz	2 cups
340 g	355 ml	Salad Oil	12 oz	1 ½ cups
1.36 kg	1.42 l	Tomatoes, canned	3 lb	1 ½ qt
1.36 kg	1.42 l	Corn, whole kernel	3 lb	1 ½ qt
19 g	60 ml	Chili Powder	⅔ oz	4 tbsp
	15 ml	Paprika		1 tbsp
	7 ½ ml	Pepper		1 ½ tsp
1.81 kg	2.84 l	Turkey, cooked, diced	4 lb	3 qt
681 g	711 ml	Eggs, beaten (12 lge)	1 lb, 8 oz	3 cups
340 g	711 ml	Cheddar Cheese, grated	12 oz	3 cups

Procedure

1. Heat stock to boiling. Add salt and slowly stir in corn meal. Cook until thick, stirring constantly.

2. Sauté onions, garlic, and pork in salad oil until lightly browned. Stir in vegetables and seasonings. Combine with corn meal. Fold in eggs and turkey.

3. Divide into 2 greased serving pans (12 × 20 × 2 in). Bake at 350°F/177°C for 1 hour.

4. Sprinkle cheese evenly over top of tamale pies and return to the oven to melt the cheese, approx. 15 min.

Turkey Tetrazzini

64 Servings (9 oz/255 g)
Bake, 425°F/218°C, 30 min

Metric		Ingredients	U.S.	
Weight	Volume		Weight	Volume
1.36 kg	2.84 l	Spaghetti, uncooked	3 lb	3 qt
8.17 kg	8.51 l	Water, boiling	18 lb	2 ¼ gal
85 g	89 ml	Salt	3 oz	⅜ cup
454 g	1.66 l	Mushrooms, fresh, sliced	1 lb	1 ¾ qt
454 g	711 ml	Onions, chopped	1 lb	3 cups
227 g	474 ml	Green Pepper, chopped	8 oz	2 cups
227 g	474 ml	Celery, chopped	8 oz	2 cups
114 g	118 ml	Butter or Margarine	4 oz	½ cup
227 g	474 ml	Flour, all-purpose	8 oz	2 cups
340 g	355 ml	Butter or Margarine, melted	12 oz	1 ½ cups
28 g	30 ml	Salt	1 oz	2 tbsp
	7 ½ ml	Pepper, white		1 ½ tsp
198 g	158 ml	Chicken Base	7 oz	⅔ cup
4.54 kg	4.74 l	Milk, hot	10 lb	1 ¼ gal
2.72 kg	4.26 l	Turkey, cooked, diced	6 lb	4 ½ qt
227 g	316 ml	Pimiento, chopped	8 oz	1 ⅓ cups
454 g	947 ml	Cheddar Cheese, grated	1 lb	1 qt

Procedure

1. Add spaghetti to boiling salted water. Stir. Reheat to boiling. Cook until tender. Drain and rinse. Drain well.
2. Sauté mushrooms, onions, green pepper, and celery in 4 oz butter or margarine.
3. Combine flour, melted butter or margarine, and seasonings to make a roux. Add roux with chicken base to hot milk and cook until thickened.
4. Add turkey, pimiento, and spaghetti to sauce.
5. Divide into 2 greased serving pans (12 × 20 × 2 in). Top with grated cheese (about 2 cups/474 ml per pan) and bake at 425°F/218°C for 30 minutes.

Turkey Chestnut Pie

50 Servings (8 oz/227 g)
Bake, 400°F/205°C, 15 min

Metric		Ingredients	U.S.	
Weight	Volume		Weight	Volume
2.38 kg	3.79 l	Turkey, cooked, diced	5 lb, 4 oz	1 gal
1.82 kg	2.84 l	Green Peas, frozen	4 lb	3 qt
340 g	474 ml	Pimiento, chopped	12 oz	2 cups
142 g	474 ml	Chives, chopped	5 oz	2 cups
907 g	1.42 l	Water Chestnuts, diced	2 lb	1 ½ qt
681 g	711 ml	Butter or Margarine	1 lb, 8 oz	3 cups
340 g	711 ml	Flour, all-purpose	12 oz	3 cups
28 g	30 ml	Salt	1 oz	2 tbsp
	10 ml	Pepper		2 tsp
5.44 kg	5.68 l	Milk	12 lb	1 ½ gal
	50	Baking Powder Biscuits		50

1. Combine turkey, peas, pimiento, chives, and water chestnuts.
2. Melt butter or margarine. Add flour and seasonings. Blend. Cook over low heat 3 to 5 minutes. Stir while cooking. Add milk slowly, stirring constantly. Cook until smooth and thickened.

3. Stir white sauce into turkey mixture and divide into 2 serving pans (12 × 20 × 2 in). Top with baking powder biscuits.
4. Bake at 400°F/205°C 15 minutes or until biscuits are done.

Turkey Pie

48 Servings

Bake, 400°F/205°C, 15 min

Metric		Ingredients	U.S.	
Weight	Volume		Weight	Volume
681 g	711 ml	Butter or Margarine	1 lb, 8 oz	3 cups
397 g	829 ml	Flour, all-purpose	14 oz	3 ½ cups
19 g	20 ml	Salt	⅔ oz	1 ⅓ tbsp
	7 ½ ml	Pepper, white		1 ½ tsp
	10 ml	Curry Powder		2 tsp
3.86 kg	4.02 l	Chicken Stock, hot	8 lb, 8 oz	4 ¼ qt
1.59 kg	2.37 l	Potatoes, diced	3 lb, 8 oz	2 ½ qt
1.59 kg	2.37 l	Carrots, diced	3 lb, 8 oz	2 ½ qt
1.02 kg	1.60 l	Peas, frozen	2 lb, 4 oz	6 ¾ cups
2.84 kg	4.42 l	Turkey, cooked, diced	6 lb, 4 oz	4 ⅔ qt
		Crust		
907 g	1.66 l	Biscuit Mix	2 lb	1 ¾ qt
510 g	533 ml	Milk	1 lb, 2 oz	2 ¼ cups
114 g	118 ml	Butter or Margarine, melted	4 oz	½ cup
312 g	592 ml	Biscuit Mix	11 oz	2 ½ cups

Procedure

1. Melt butter or margarine. Combine melted butter or margarine, flour, and seasonings to make a roux. Add to hot stock, stirring, and cook until gravy is smooth and thickened.
2. Steam potatoes and carrots until tender. Rinse frozen peas with hot water and drain.
3. Combine gravy, potatoes, carrots, peas, and diced turkey. Divide into 2 greased serving pans (12 × 20 × 1 in).

4. Combine the first three items for the crust to make a soft dough. Divide dough in half; turn out on board sprinkled with biscuit mix. Knead each half lightly 12 to 15 strokes.
5. Roll each half to fit top of serving pans. Place biscuit crust over turkey pie, seal edges, and bake at 400°F/205°C until crust is brown (about 15 min).

Hot Turkey Mousse

50 Servings
Bake, 300°F/149°C, 1 hr

Metric		Ingredients	U.S.		
Weight	Volume		Weight		Volume
510 g	533 ml	Butter or Margarine	1 lb,	2 oz	2 ¼ cups
255 g	533 ml	Flour, all-purpose		9 oz	2 ¼ cups
	5 ml	Pepper			1 tsp
	10 ml	Poultry Seasoning			2 tsp
	1 ¼ ml	Cloves, ground			¼ tsp
2.72 kg	2.84 l	Milk	6 lb		3 qt
2.72 kg	4.26 l	Turkey, finely chopped	6 lb		4 ½ qt
1.36 kg	2.13 l	Ham, minced	3 lb		2 ¼ qt
596 g	1.42 l	Bread Crumbs, soft	1 lb,	5 oz	1 ½ qt
1.19 kg	1.24 l	Eggs, beaten (21 lge)	2 lb,	10 oz	5 ¼ cups

Procedure

1. Melt butter or margarine. Add flour and seasonings. Blend. Cook over low heat 3 to 5 minutes. Stir while cooking. Add milk slowly, stirring constantly. Cook until smooth and thickened.

2. Cool slightly. Fold in turkey, ham, crumbs, and eggs.
3. Divide into 2 greased serving pans (12 × 20 × 2 in).
4. Bake at 300°F/149°C for 1 hour or until inserted knife comes out clean.

Harlequin Turkey

50 Servings (5 oz/142 g)
Bake, 425°F/218°C, 15 min

Metric		Ingredients	U.S.		
Weight	Volume		Weight		Volume
681 g	1.07 l	Onions, chopped	1 lb,	8 oz	4 ½ cups
340 g	711 ml	Green Pepper, chopped		12 oz	3 cups
227 g	237 ml	Butter or Margarine		8 oz	1 cup
170 g	355 ml	Flour, all-purpose		6 oz	1 ½ cups
28 g	30 ml	Salt		1 oz	2 tbsp
	2 ½ ml	Pepper			½ tsp
1.36 kg	1.42 l	Applesauce	3 lb		1 ½ qt
1.36 kg	1.42 l	Tomatoes, canned	3 lb		1 ½ qt
454 g	711 ml	Raisins, seedless	1 lb		3 cups
1.36 kg	1.42 l	Turkey Broth	3 lb		1 ½ qt
	30 ml	Parsley, chopped			2 tbsp
3.63 kg	5.68 l	Turkey, cooked, diced	8 lb		1 ½ gal
	50	Drop Biscuits			50

Procedure

1. Sauté onions and green pepper in butter or margarine until tender.
2. Add flour, salt, and pepper and mix well.
3. Heat to boiling applesauce, tomatoes, raisins, and turkey broth. Stir in flour and vegetable mixture.

4. Cook over low heat, stirring constantly until thickened.
5. Stir in parsley and turkey. Pour into serving pans (12 × 20 × 2 in) and top with drop biscuits. Bake at 425°F/218°C for 15 minutes.

Turkey Curry
50 Servings

| Metric | | Ingredients | U.S. | |
Weight	Volume		Weight	Volume
	3 cloves	Garlic, minced		3 cloves
907 g	1.42 l	Onions, chopped	2 lb	1 ½ qt
1.36 kg	2.84 l	Celery, chopped	3 lb	3 qt
340 g	355 ml	Butter or Margarine	12 oz	1 ½ cups
227 g	474 ml	Flour, bread	8 oz	2 cups
43 g	45 ml	Salt	1 ½ oz	3 tbsp
	5 ml	Pepper		1 tsp
57 g	118 ml	Curry Powder	2 oz	½ cup
28 g	59 ml	Ginger, fresh, minced	1 oz	¼ cup
	5 ml	Hot Pepper Sauce		1 tsp
57 g	59 ml	Worcestershire Sauce	2 oz	¼ cup
1.81 kg	1.89 l	Turkey Stock	4 lb	2 qt
1.81 kg	3.31 l	Apples, pared, chopped	4 lb	3 ½ qt
454 g	711 ml	Raisins	1 lb	3 cups
454 g	1.42 l	Coconut, shredded	1 lb	1 ½ qt
2.72 kg	4.26 l	Turkey, cooked, diced	6 lb	4 ½ qt

Procedure

1. Sauté garlic, celery, and onions in butter or margarine until tender. Stir in flour, salt, spices, and sauces. Add stock gradually while stirring and continue cooking until mixture has thickened. Add apples and raisins and cook until tender.

2. Stir in coconut and turkey. Cook for another 20 or 30 minutes.

Baked Turkey Patties
50 Servings (2 patties)
Bake, 325°F/163°C, 1 ½ hrs

| Metric | | Ingredients | U.S. | |
Weight	Volume		Weight	Volume
4.54 kg	4.74 l	Ground Turkey, dark meat	10 lb	5 qt
907 g	1.89 l	Carrots, raw, grated	2 lb	2 qt
326 g	474 ml	Onions, finely chopped	11 ½ oz	2 cups
681 g	711 ml	Eggs, slightly beaten (12 lge)	1 lb, 8 oz	3 cups
	15 ml	Curry Powder		1 tbsp
	5 ml	Pepper		1 tsp
	10 ml	Mustard		2 tsp
28 g	30 ml	Worcestershire Sauce	1 oz	2 tbsp
28 g	30 ml	Salt	1 oz	2 tbsp
1.25 kg	1.30 l	Tomato Soup, canned	2 lb, 12 oz	5 ½ cups

Procedure

1. Combine all ingredients, except tomato soup. Mix thoroughly. Shape into 100 patties using a No. 16 scoop and arrange in serving pans (12 × 20 × 2 in).

2. Pour undiluted tomato soup over the patties. Bake at 325°F/163°C for 1 ½ hours.

Stuffed Peppers

50 Servings
Bake, 450°F/232°C, 15–20 min

| Metric | | | U.S. | |
Weight	Volume	Ingredients	Weight	Volume
3.63 kg	25 lge	Green Peppers	8 lb	25 lge
567 g	1.18 l	Bread Crumbs, soft	1 lb, 4 oz	1 ¼ qt
227 g	237 ml	Shortening, melted	8 oz	1 cup
114 g	178 ml	Onions, chopped	4 oz	¾ cup
1.25 kg	1.42 l	Chicken or Turkey, chopped	2 lb, 12 oz	1 ½ qt
198 g	207 ml	Eggs, beaten (4 med)	7 oz	⅞ cup
340 g	355 ml	Milk	12 oz	1 ½ cups
21 g	22 ml	Salt	¾ oz	1 ½ tbsp
	2 ½ ml	Pepper		½ tsp

Procedure

1. Cut peppers into halves, crosswise. Remove seeds and tough white portions. Wash. Steam 5 to 8 minutes.
2. Mix remaining ingredients. With a No. 20 scoop, fill halves of green peppers.
3. Bake on a greased sheet at 450°F/232°C for 15 to 20 minutes.

Turkey and Sausage Casserole

50 Servings
Bake, 375°F/190°C, 25 min

| Metric | | | U.S. | |
Weight	Volume	Ingredients	Weight	Volume
1.81 kg	1.89 l	Pork Sausage, bulk	4 lb	2 qt
454 g	711 ml	Onions, chopped	1 lb	3 cups
454 g	947 ml	Green Pepper, chopped	1 lb	1 qt
227 g	474 ml	Flour, all-purpose	8 oz	2 cups
28 g	30 ml	Salt	1 oz	2 tbsp
	15 ml	Poultry Seasoning		1 tbsp
	5 ml	Pepper		1 tsp
1.82 kg	1.89 l	Milk	4 lb	2 qt
57 g	355 ml	Parsley, chopped	2 oz	1 ½ cups
2.41 kg	3.79 l	Turkey, cooked, diced	5 lb, 5 oz	1 gal
1.02 kg	2.37 l	Bread Cubes, dry	2 lb, 4 oz	2 ½ qt

Procedure

1. Fry out sausage. Strain meat from drippings. Use 2 cups/474 ml of drippings and cook onions and green pepper until tender.
2. Blend in flour and seasonings. Stir in milk and cook, stirring constantly until smooth and thickened. Fold in remaining ingredients.
3. Arrange in serving pans (12 × 20 × 2 in) and bake at 375°F/190°C until nicely browned (about 20 to 25 min).

Turkey-Mushroom Scallop
50 Servings
Bake, 350°F/177°C, 40 min

Metric		Ingredients	U.S.	
Weight	Volume		Weight	Volume
227 g	237 ml	Butter or Margarine	8 oz	1 cup
454 g	947 ml	Flour, all-purpose	1 lb	1 qt
	10 ml	Salt		2 tsp
3.63 kg	3.79 l	Milk	8 lb	1 gal
142 g	237 ml	Onions, chopped	5 oz	1 cup
227 g	474 ml	Green Pepper, chopped	8 oz	2 cups
454 g	1.66 l	Mushrooms, fresh, sliced	1 lb	1 ¾ qt
454 g	474 ml	Butter or Margarine	1 lb	2 cups
1.82 kg	2.84 l	Turkey, cooked, diced	4 lb	3 qt
227 g	237 ml	Butter or Margarine	8 oz	1 cup
2.39 kg	5.68 l	Bread cubes	5 lb, 4 oz	1 ½ gal
	22 ml	Poultry Seasoning		1 ½ tbsp
	5 ml	Pepper		1 tsp
	2 ½ ml	Mustard, dry		½ tsp
907 g	947 ml	Turkey Stock	2 lb	1 qt

Procedure

1. Melt 8 oz butter or margarine. Add flour and salt. Blend. Cook over low heat 3 to 5 minutes. Stir while cooking. Add milk slowly, stirring constantly. Cook until sauce is smooth and thickened.
2. Sauté onions, green pepper, and mushrooms in 1 lb/454 g of butter or margarine. Add vegetables and turkey to white sauce.
3. Melt 8 oz/227 g of butter or margarine and pour over bread cubes. Add seasonings to turkey stock and toss lightly with bread cubes to make a medium dry dressing.
4. Spread half of the dressing in the bottoms of 2 greased serving pans (12 × 20 × 2 in). Cover with turkey mixture and top with remaining dressing.
5. Bake at 350°F/177°C for 40 minutes.

CHAPTER 8 _Vegetables_

Table 9
Suggested Quantities and Cooking Times for Vegetables*

Vegetable	Amount A.P. 50 Portions ½ cup/118 ml	% Waste in Preparation	Cooking Time (min)			
			Boiling	Steaming	(psi)	Baking
				5	15	
Asparagus Spears	9.07 kg/20 lb	30–40	5–10	5–8	½–1 ½	
Beans, canned lima or kidney	5.90 kg/2 No. 10	—	10–15	5–8	3–4	
frozen	4.54 kg/10 lb	—	10–15	6–8	2–4	
Beans, green, fresh	4.54 kg/10 lb	0–15	10–20	10–12	1–3	
canned	5.90 kg/2 No. 10	—	10–15	5–8	3–4	
Bean Sprouts	5.90 kg/2 No. 10	—	10	5	2	
Beets, fresh	6.81 kg/15 lb	25	30–45	30–45	5–10	
canned	6.30 kg/2 ¼ No. 10	—	10–15	5–8	3–4	
Broccoli, fresh	8.17 kg/18 lb	30–40	10–15	7–10	2–4	
frozen, cut	4.54 kg/10 lb	—	10–15	4–6	1–2	
frozen, spears	5.44 kg/12 lb	—	10–15	10–15	5–10	
Brussel Sprouts, frozen	2.27 kg/5 lb	—	5–10	8–10	1–3	
Cabbage, fresh shredded	2.72 kg/6 lb	15–20	5–8	5–8	3–4	
Carrots, fresh sliced/diced	5.44 kg/12 lb	20–25	15–25	15–25	6–15	
Cauliflower, fresh	8.17 kg/18 lb	40–50	15–20	8–10	1 ½–3	
frozen	4.54 kg/10 lb	—	5–10	6–8	1 ½–3	
Celery, sliced	5.44 kg/12 lb	20–30	10–20	10–12	2–3	
Corn, frozen	4.54 kg/10 lb	—	3–5	2–3	2–3	
Eggplant, pieces	3.18 kg/7 lb	10–25	10–20	10–15	5–10	
Mixed Frozen Vegetables	4.54 kg/10 lb	—	10–20	8–15	2–4	
Onions, small, whole	6.81 kg/15 lb	8–15	15–25	12–15	3–5	40–45
Parsnips, quartered	6.81 kg/15 lb	25–30	10–20	15–20	4–8	
Peas, fresh	11.34 kg/25 lb	50–60	8–20	5–10	1–2	
frozen	4.54 kg/10 lb	—	4–7	3–4	1	
Potatoes, sweet, whole	8.17 kg/18 lb	20–25	25–35	30–40	5–8	30–45
Potatoes, white, whole	6.81 kg/15 lb	20–25	25–40	20–25	8–12	45–60
Rutabagas, cubed	6.81 kg/15 lb	15–20	20–30	15–25	4–7	
Spinach, fresh	7.26 kg/16 lb	25–30	3–10	8–10	1	
frozen	4.54 kg/10 lb	—	2–4	3–5	½–1	

*Age, size, condition of vegetables, and altitude will influence cooking time.

Table 9
Suggested Quantities and Cooking Times for Vegetables* *(cont.)*

Vegetable	Amount A.P. 50 Portions ½ cup/118 ml	% Waste in Prep-aration	Cooking Time (min)			
			Boiling	Steaming 5	(psi) 15	Baking
Squash, Summer	6.81 kg/15 lb	5–15	10–20	8–12	1½–3	
Acorn	11.34 kg/25 lb	10–20	20–30	15–20	6–12	40–60
Hubbard	11.34 kg/25 lb	10–20	15–20	15–20	6–12	40–60
Zucchini	6.81 kg/15 lb	5–15	6–8	5–8	1–2	30–45
Tomatoes, whole	6.81 kg/15 lb	5–10	7–15	—	½–1	15–30
Turnips	4.54 kg/10 lb	—	—	25–30	10–20	

*Age, size, condition of vegetables, and altitude will influence cooking time.

Vegetables taste best when they are harvested at their prime point of maturity and are used immediately. Color, texture, flavor, and nutrients deteriorate during storage. Important rules to remember for vegetable cookery are:

1. Procure fresh vegetables that have reached the stage of maturity when they are best quality.
2. Clean and refrigerate immediately until time for use.
3. Cook quickly to that point of tenderness which is most palatable.

4. Season well and serve immediately.

Timing is important. Cook vegetables in accordance with the speed of service so that a fresh supply will be ready every 15 or 20 minutes. Table 9 is given as an aid in scheduling vegetable cooking. Suggestions for seasoning and combinations of vegetables that add interest and variety are given in Table 11.

Table 10
Microwave Cooking of Vegetables

The time required for cooking vegetables by microwave varies in relation to weight and volume. The approximate time for small quantities is as follows:

	Amount	Time (min)		Amount	Time (min)
Beans, lima, fresh	454 g/1 lb	8–10	Onions, small, whole	681 g/1½ lb	6–7
frozen	283 g/10 oz	9–10	Parsnips, quartered	681 g/1½ lb	7–8
Broccoli, fresh	681 g/1½ lb	7–9	Peas, fresh	907 g/2 lb	7–8
Brussels Sprouts, frozen	454 g/1 lb	6–8	Potatoes, white, whole	454 g/1 lb	8–10
Cabbage, fresh	454 g/1 lb	5–6	frozen	283 g/10 oz	5–6
Carrots, fresh	454 g/1 lb	7–8	Potatoes, sweet, whole	227 g/½ lb	3–4
Cauliflower, fresh	681 g/1½ lb	6–7	Potatoes, sweet, whole	454 g/1 lb	5–6
frozen	283 g/10 oz	8–9	Spinach, fresh	454 g/1 lb	5–6
Celery, sliced	454 g/1 lb	8–10	frozen	283 g/10 oz	6–7
Corn, frozen	283 g/10 oz	5–6			

When handling larger quantities of frozen vegetables, heat for an initial period of time, allow to stand 1 or 2 minutes, then loosen and stir product. Continue heating until done. In a microwave cooker delivering 2,000 watts, the approximate time requirements are as follows:

Product Depth	Weight	Approximate Heating Time		
		Initial	Final	Total
2 ½ in	459 g/1 lb	80 sec	75 sec	2 min, 35 sec
2 ½ in	907 g/2 lb	2 ½ min	2 ⅓ min	4 min, 50 sec
2 ½ in	1.36 kg/3 lb	4 min	3 min, 10 sec	7 min, 10 sec
2 ½ in	1.82 kg/4 lb	5 ½ min	4 min	9 ½ min
1 ½ in	1.82 kg/4 lb	4 min	4 min	8 min
1 in	1.82 kg/4 lb	4 min	2 ½ min	6 ½ min
2 ½ in	2.27 kg/5 lb	7 min	5 min	12 min

Creole Eggplant
50 Servings (½ cup oz/118 ml)
Bake, 350°F/177°C, 30 min

Metric		Ingredients	U.S.	
Weight	Volume		Weight	Volume
3.63 kg	7.57 l	Eggplant, peeled, diced	8 lb	8 qt
5.44 kg	5.68 l	Water, boiling	12 lb	1 ½ gal
28 g	30 ml	Salt	1 oz	2 tbsp
454 g	947 ml	Green Pepper, chopped	1 lb	1 qt
681 g	1.07 l	Onions, chopped	1 lb, 8 oz	4 ½ cups
114 g	118 ml	Butter or Margarine	4 oz	½ cup
2.95 kg	3.31 l	Tomatoes, canned, chopped	6 lb, 8 oz	1 No. 10 can
227 g	474 ml	Flour, all-purpose	8 oz	2 cups
340 g	355 ml	Butter or Margarine, melted	12 oz	1 ½ cups
28 g	30 ml	Salt	1 oz	2 tbsp
	10 ml	Basil		2 tsp
114 g	158 ml	Brown Sugar	4 oz	⅔ cup
	5 ml	Marjoram		1 tsp
	10 ml	Oregano		2 tsp
	5 ml	Savory		1 tsp
	5 ml	Garlic Salt		1 tsp
198 g	474 ml	Bread Crumbs	7 oz	2 cups
142 g	148 ml	Butter or Margarine	5 oz	⅝ cup
454 g	947 ml	Cheddar Cheese, grated	1 lb	1 qt

Procedure

1. Cook eggplant 6 minutes in boiling, salted water. Drain thoroughly.
2. Sauté green pepper and onion in 4 oz/114 g butter or margarine until tender. Add tomatoes and seasonings to sautéed vegetables and bring to a boil.
3. Add flour to 12 oz/355 ml melted butter or margarine to make a roux. Add roux to tomato mixture and cook until mixture has thickened.
4. Divide eggplant into two greased serving pans (12 × 20 × 2 in) and pour vegetable mixture over it.
5. Toss bread crumbs in 5 oz/148 ml melted butter or margarine, combine with cheese, and sprinkle over vegetables.
6. Bake at 350°F/177°C for 30 minutes.

Crusty Eggplant

56 Servings
Bake, 400°F/205°C, 25 min

Metric		Ingredients	U.S.	
Weight	Volume		Weight	Volume
3.03 kg	56 slices	Eggplant	6 lb, 11 oz	56 slices
793 g	829 ml	Eggs (14 lge)	1 lb, 12 oz	3 ½ cups
265 g	553 ml	Parmesan Cheese, grated	9 ⅓ oz	2 ⅓ cups
397 g	947 ml	Bread Crumbs, fine	14 oz	1 qt
20 g	118 ml	Parsley, finely chopped	⅔ oz	½ cup
	10 ml	Salt		2 tsp
	5 ml	Pepper		1 tsp
283 g	592 ml	Flour, all-purpose	10 oz	2 ½ cups
170 g	178 ml	Butter or Margarine, melted	6 oz	¾ cup

Procedure

1. Cut unpeeled eggplant into ½-inch slices.
2. Place slices in salted water for a few minutes, then lay them between paper toweling to remove excess moisture.
3. In a shallow pan, beat eggs slightly.
4. In another pan, combine cheese, bread crumbs, parsley, salt, and pepper.
5. Dust slices of eggplant with flour, dip in egg to cover all over, and dredge in crumb mixture, shaking off excess. Work with only a small amount of crumb mixture at a time.
6. Arrange slices on a well-greased baking sheet. Brush with melted butter or margarine. Bake uncovered at 400°F/205°C for 25 minutes or until lightly browned.

Nut-Buttered Carrots

50 Servings (5 oz/140 g)

Metric		Ingredients	U.S.	
Weight	Volume		Weight	Volume
7.26 kg	11.36 l	Carrots, 3-in halves or quarters	16 lb	3 gal
28 g	30 ml	Salt	1 oz	2 tbsp
114 g	118 ml	Butter or Margarine	4 oz	½ cup
85 g	118 ml	Brown Sugar	3 oz	½ cup
21 g	59 ml	Orange Rind	¾ oz	¼ cup
340 g	711 ml	Almonds or Filberts, sliced, toasted	12 oz	3 cups

Procedure

1. Cook carrots in salted water until tender but firm. Drain well.
2. Melt butter. Add sugar, orange rind, and nuts. Add carrots and turn them until well-coated with sugar mixture.

Zucchini Fried in Cheese Batter
50 Servings (5 oz/142 g)
Fry, 360°F/182°C

Metric		Ingredients	U.S.	
Weight	Volume		Weight	Volume
5.44 kg	50 sm	Zucchini	12 lb	50 sm
227 g	237 ml	Eggs (4 lge)	8 oz	1 cup
	10 ml	Salt		2 tsp
	5 ml	Cayenne Pepper		1 tsp
907 g	947 ml	Milk	2 lb	1 qt
156 g	120 ml	Oil	5½ oz	8 tbsp
907 g	1.89 l	Flour, pastry	2 lb	2 qt
	20 ml	Baking Powder		1⅓ tbsp
340 g	947 ml	Cheese, grated	12 oz	1 qt

Procedure

1. Wash zucchini thoroughly. Cut in strips as for French-fried potatoes.
2. Combine eggs, salt, cayenne, milk, and oil. Mix well.
3. Sift flour and baking powder. Add grated cheese and mix. Add liquid and mix only enough to moisten. (Use immediately, because mixture becomes thick upon standing. This makes it hard to coat the zucchini.) Dip pieces of zucchini in batter.
4. Fry in deep fat at 360°F/182°C, until golden brown. Drain and serve.

Lyonnaise Carrots
50 Servings (5.5 oz/56 g)
Bake, 350°F/177°C

Metric		Ingredients	U.S.	
Weight	Volume		Weight	Volume
4.54 kg	7.10 l	Carrots, sliced	10 lb	7½ qt
2.27 kg	4.74 l	Onions, sliced	5 lb	5 qt
85 g	89 ml	Butter or Margarine, melted	3 oz	⅓ cup
9 g	10 ml	Salt		2 tsp
	2½ ml	Pepper		½ tsp
1.36 kg	1.42 l	Beef Stock	3 lb	1½ qt

Procedure

1. Alternate layers of carrots and onions in greased serving pans (12 × 20 × 2 in), ending with carrots.
2. Combine butter or margarine with salt, pepper, and beef stock. Pour one-half of mixture over each pan.
3. Bake at 350°F/177°C until most of stock is absorbed and carrots and onions are tender.

Baked Zucchini

50 Servings (4 oz/114 g)
Bake, 350°F/177°C, 1 hr

Metric		Ingredients	U.S.	
Weight	Volume		Weight	Volume
5.44 kg		Zucchini	12 lb	
170 g	237 ml	Onions, finely chopped	6 oz	1 cup
114 g	118 ml	Butter or Margarine	4 oz	½ cup
150 g	355 ml	Bread Crumbs	5 ¼ oz	1 ½ cups
	7 ½ ml	Worcestershire Sauce		1 ½ tsp
114 g	237 ml	Cheddar Cheese, grated	4 oz	1 cup
18 g	118 ml	Parsley	⅔ oz	½ cup
	10 ml	Salt		2 tsp

Procedure

1. Cut zucchini in half lengthwise and then into portion lengths. Hollow out slightly, brush with margarine and sprinkle with salt.
2. Sauté onions in melted butter or margarine. Stir in remaining ingredients. Sprinkle mixture over zucchini.
3. Bake in greased pans in 350°F/177°C oven until tender (about 1 hr).

Medley of Vegetables

50 Servings (5.7 oz/163 g)
Bake, 350°F/177°C, 1 ½ hrs

Metric		Ingredients	U.S.	
Weight	Volume		Weight	Volume
1.02 kg	2.13 l	Onions, sliced	2 lb, 4 oz	2 ¼ qt
1.02 kg	2.13 l	Celery, 1-in strips	2 lb, 4 oz	2 ¼ qt
1.02 kg	1.66 l	Carrots, 1-in strips	2 lb, 4 oz	1 ¾ qt
1.70 kg	3.16 l	String Beans	3 lb, 12 oz	3 ⅓ qt
681 g	1.42 l	Green Pepper, 1-in strips	1 lb, 8 oz	1 ½ qt
3.06 kg	3.16 l	Tomatoes	6 lb, 12 oz	3 ⅓ qt
255 g	296 ml	Butter or Margarine, melted	9 oz	1 ¼ cups
	3 ¾ ml	Pepper		¾ tsp
57 g	60 ml	Salt	2 oz	4 tbsp
57 g	60 ml	Sugar	2 oz	4 tbsp
170 g	178 ml	Tapioca, quick-cooking	6 oz	¾ cup

Procedure

1. Combine all ingredients.
2. Scale 9 lb, 6 oz into each of 2 pans (12 × 20 × 2 in). Cover tightly and bake for about 1 ½ hours, until vegetables are tender.

Celery and Carrots Amandine
50 Servings (5 oz/142 g)

Metric		Ingredients	U.S.	
Weight	Volume		Weight	Volume
3.63 kg	7.57 l	Celery, diagonal slices	8 lb	2 gal
3.63 kg	7.57 l	Carrot Strips	8 lb	2 gal
454 g	474 ml	Butter or Margarine	1 lb	2 cups
340 g	711 ml	Almonds, blanched, slivered	12 oz	3 cups
114 g	118 ml	Lemon Juice	4 oz	½ cup
28 g	30 ml	Salt	1 oz	2 tbsp

Procedure

1. Cook celery and carrots until tender but firm. Drain well. Place in serving pans (12 × 20 × 2 in).
2. Heat butter or margarine in skillet. Add almonds and brown lightly.
3. Remove from heat, add lemon juice, and pour mixture over vegetables. Stir carefully to mix seasoning with vegetables.

Mandarin Carrots
50 Servings (½ cup/118 ml)
Bake, 375°F/190°C, 15–20 min

Metric		Ingredients	U.S.	
Weight	Volume		Weight	Volume
3.18 kg	4.98 l	Carrots, sliced	7 lb	5 ¼ qt
907 g	947 ml	Mandarin Oranges	2 lb	1 qt
907 g	947 ml	Water, hot		1 qt
92 g	158 ml	Cornstarch	3 ¼ oz	⅔ cup
114 g	118 ml	Sugar	4 oz	½ cup
14 g	15 ml	Salt	½ oz	1 tbsp
	2 ½ ml	Nutmeg		½ tsp
114 g	118 ml	Butter or Margarine	4 oz	½ cup
114 g	118 ml	Lemon Juice	4 oz	½ cup

Procedure

1. Cook carrots in boiling, salted water. Drain.
2. Drain mandarin oranges. Combine juice with hot water and bring to boiling. Mix cornstarch with sugar, salt, and nutmeg. Add to hot juice, stirring until thick and cornstarch has lost its raw taste. Remove from heat and add butter or margarine and lemon juice.
3. Place carrots in greased serving pans (12 × 20 × 2 in) and spread oranges evenly over the top. Pour thickened sauce over the carrots and oranges.
4. Bake at 375°/190°C until heated through (about 15 to 20 min). Prevent breaking tender orange segments by stirring as little as possible.

Toasted Carrots

50 Servings

Broil, 350°F/177°C

Metric		Ingredients	U.S.	
Weight	Volume		Weight	Volume
567 g	1.18 l	Cornflakes, crushed	1 lb, 4 oz	5 cups
	10 ml	Salt		2 tsp
	5 ml	Pepper		1 tsp
	5 ml	Paprika		1 tsp
8.17 kg	100 med	Carrots, cooked, whole	18 lb	100 med
340 g	395 ml	Butter or Margarine, melted	12 oz	1 ⅔ cups

Procedure

1. Combine crushed cornflakes, salt, pepper, and paprika. Roll carrots in butter or margarine, then in cornflake mixture.

2. Place under a broiler at moderate temperature (350°F/177°C). Turn frequently to brown on all sides.
3. Yield: 50 servings, 2 carrots per serving.

Peas and Mushrooms, Creamed

50 Servings

Metric		Ingredients	U.S.	
Weight	Volume		Weight	Volume
567 g	1.89 l	Mushrooms, sliced	1 lb, 4 oz	2 qt
340 g	355 ml	Butter or Margarine	12 oz	1 ½ cups
170 g	355 ml	Green Pepper, chopped	6 oz	1 ½ cups
114 g	178 ml	Onions, chopped	4 oz	¾ cup
454 g	947 ml	Celery, diced	1 lb	1 qt
255 g	533 ml	Flour, bread	9 oz	2 ¼ cups
3.18 kg	3.31 l	Milk, hot	7 lb	3 ½ qt
28 g	30 ml	Salt	1 oz	2 tbsp
	5 ml	Pepper		1 tsp
1.14 kg	1.42 l	Peas, cooked	2 lb, 8 oz	1 ½ qt
454 g	947 ml	Cheese, grated	1 lb	1 qt

Procedure

1. Sauté mushrooms in melted butter or margarine until light brown. Remove mushrooms.
2. Sauté green peppers, onions, and celery in fat. When tender, add flour, and mix until smooth. Add hot milk. Cook until smooth and the flour has lost its raw taste, stirring constantly. Season with salt and

pepper. Add cheese and stir until melted. Add mushrooms and peas.
3. Yield: 1 ½ gal/5.68 l sauce. Serve on toast, ½ cup/118 ml per serving. Garnish each serving with grated cheese.

Creole Green Beans

50 Servings (4.5 oz/128 g)
Bake, 375°F/190°C, 30–45 min

Metric		Ingredients	U.S.	
Weight	Volume		Weight	Volume
227 g	237 ml	Bacon, diced	8 oz	1 cup
454 g	711 ml	Onions, chopped	1 lb	3 cups
170 g	355 ml	Flour, pastry	6 oz	1 ½ cups
28 g	30 ml	Salt	1 oz	2 tbsp
	5 ml	Pepper		1 tsp
2.50 kg	2.60 l	Tomatoes, canned	5 lb, 8 oz	2 ¾ qt
3.86 kg	6.63 l	Green Beans, drained	8 lb, 8 oz	2 No. 10 cans

Procedure

1. Slice bacon and dice finely. Sauté. Add onions and sauté until tender.
2. Add flour, salt, and pepper and stir until smooth. Add tomatoes, stirring. Cook until mixture is thick and smooth and the flour has lost its raw taste.
3. Combine drained beans and sauce and scale 8 lb into each of 2 greased pans (12 × 20 × 2 in). Bake at 375°F/190°C for about 30 to 45 minutes.

Green Bean Mushroom Casserole

50 Servings
Bake, 350°F/177°C, 30–40 min

Metric		Ingredients	U.S.	
Weight	Volume		Weight	Volume
5.90 kg	6.63 l	Green Beans, whole	13 lb	2 No. 10 cans
454 g	1.66 l	Mushrooms, fresh, sliced	1 lb	7 cups
114 g	118 ml	Butter or Margarine	4 oz	½ cup
907 g	947 ml	Milk, whole	2 lb	1 qt
1.48 kg	1 can	Mushroom Soup	3 lb, 4 oz	1 can (52 oz)
227 g	474 ml	Cheese, grated	8 oz	2 cups

Procedure

1. Drain beans and arrange in even rows in greased serving pans (12 × 20 × 2 in) for ease of service.
2. Wash and slice mushrooms. Sauté in butter or margarine.
3. Add milk to mushroom soup. Add sautéed mushrooms to soup mixture and pour over beans.
4. Sprinkle with grated cheese.
5. Bake at 350°F/177°C for 30 to 40 minutes, or until thoroughly heated and cheese is melted.

Oriental Green Beans

50 Servings

Metric		Ingredients	U.S.	
Weight	**Volume**		**Weight**	**Volume**
85 g	118 ml	Onion, chopped	3 oz	½ cup
15 g	4 cloves	Garlic, minced	½ oz	4 cloves
114 g	118 ml	Bacon Drippings	4 oz	½ cup
28 g	59 ml	Bacon Bits	1 oz	¼ cup
57 g	59 ml	Soy Sauce	2 oz	¼ cup
5.44 kg	5.92 l	Green Beans, cut	12 lb	6 ¼ qt

Procedure

1. Sauté onions and garlic in bacon drippings.
2. Add bacon bits and soy sauce.
3. Pour over green beans and toss lightly.
4. Heat through thoroughly.

Corn-Stuffed Tomatoes

50 Servings (1 tomato)
Bake, 375°F/190°C, 20 min

Metric		Ingredients	U.S.	
Weight	**Volume**		**Weight**	**Volume**
8.17 kg	50 med	Tomatoes	18 lb	50 med
1.82 kg	1.80 l	Corn, whole kernel	4 lb	2 qt
227 g	474 ml	Cheddar Cheese, grated	8 oz	2 cups
227 g	474 ml	Green Pepper, chopped	8 oz	2 cups
57 g	59 ml	Mustard, prepared	2 oz	¼ cup
	3 ¾ ml	Curry Powder		¾ tsp
312 g	474 ml	Onions, chopped	11 oz	2 cups
	5 ml	Sugar		1 tsp
	10 ml	Salt		2 tsp
135 g	355 ml	Bread Crumbs	4 ¼ oz	1 ½ cups
67 g	78 ml	Buter or Margarine, melted	2 ⅓ oz	⅓ cup
	7 ½ ml	Worcestershire Sauce		1 ½ tsp
18 g	118 ml	Parsley	⅔ oz	¼ cup

Procedure

1. Slice off tops of tomatoes and hollow them out. Invert to drain.
2. Mix corn, cheese, green pepper, mustard, curry powder, onions, sugar, and salt. Fill tomatoes with mixture.
3. Lightly brown crumbs in butter or margarine. Add Worcestershire sauce and parsley. Sprinkle over tomatoes.
4. Bake in greased pans at 375°/190°C until tomatoes are tender (about 20 min).

Corn Timbales

50 Servings (2.7 oz/78 g)
Bake, 300°F/149°C, 1 ½ hrs

Metric		Ingredients	U.S.		
Weight	Volume		Weight		Volume
2.27 kg	4.74 l	Corn, whole kernel	5 lb		5 qt
511 g	711 ml	Stuffed Olives, sliced	1 lb,	2 oz	3 cups
2.04 kg	2.13 l	Eggs, slightly beaten (36 lge)	4 lb,	8 oz	2 ¼ qt
2.72 kg	2.84 l	Milk, warm	6 lb		3 qt
114 g	158 ml	Onions, grated		4 oz	⅔ cup
28 g	158 ml	Parsley, minced		1 oz	⅔ cup
43 g	45 ml	Salt		1 ½ oz	3 tbsp

Procedure

1. If timbales are to be cooked in individual molds, arrange sliced olives in bottom of greased molds with well-drained corn on top. If cooked in greased serving pans, place corn on the bottom and the sliced olives distributed on the top, so that they will be on top of portions when cut and served.

2. Beat eggs slightly. Add milk, onions, and seasoning.
3. Pour liquid mixture over corn and olives carefully to avoid disarrangement.
4. Bake at 300°F/149°C for 1 ½ hours or until an inserted knife blade comes out clean.

Corn-Stuffed Peppers

50 Servings
Bake, 375°F/190°C, 20–30 min

Metric		Ingredients	U.S.		
Weight	Volume		Weight		Volume
3.18 kg	25 lge	Green Peppers	7 lb		25 lge
4.77 kg	4.98 l	Corn, whole kernel	10 lb,	8 oz	1 ½ No. 10 cans
737 g	770 ml	Eggs, beaten (15 med)	1 lb,	10 oz	3 ¼ cups
454 g	947 ml	Bread Crumbs	1 lb		1 qt
227 g	237 ml	Milk		8 oz	1 cup
43 g	45 ml	Salt		1 ½ oz	3 tbsp
142 g	158 ml	Butter or Margarine, melted		5 oz	⅔ cup
283 g	474 ml	Onions, finely chopped		10 oz	2 cups

Procedure

1. Wash peppers and cut in halves. Remove seeds and the tough white portion. Steam for 5 minutes.
2. Drain corn of most of liquid. Combine remaining ingredients with corn. Mix well.

3. Place filling, using a No. 12 dipper, in each pepper-half. Top with buttered crumbs. Bake in greased pans at 375°F/190°C for 20 to 30 minutes.

Spinach Timbales

50 Servings
Bake, 275°F/135°C, 45 min

Metric		Ingredients	U.S.	
Weight	**Volume**		**Weight**	**Volume**
1.82 kg	1.89 l	Spinach, cooked, chopped	4 lb	2 qt
170 g	178 ml	Butter or Margarine	6 oz	¾ cup
588 g	622 ml	Eggs (12 med)	1 lb, 5 oz	2 ⅝ cups
2.72 kg	2.84 l	Milk	6 lb	3 qt
28 g	30 ml	Salt	1 oz	2 tbsp
	5 ml	Pepper		1 tsp
14 g	15 ml	Onion Juice	½ oz	1 tbsp
57 g	59 ml	Vinegar	2 oz	¼ cup
2.84 kg	50 slices	Bread	6 lb, 4 oz	50 slices
3.63 kg	50 slices	Tomatoes	8 lb	50 slices

Procedure

1. Combine all ingredients, except for tomatoes and bread.
2. Scale into two greased pans (12 × 20 × 2 in). Bake at 275°F/135°C until an inserted knife comes out clean. Cut 5 by 10.
3. Cut slices of bread with round cookie cutter. Butter tops and toast in oven until golden brown.
4. Place a slice of tomato on top of bread and a serving of spinach on top of tomato. Serve with Hollandaise sauce or cheese sauce.

Note: If served as a luncheon dish, place a slice of bacon on top of spinach and then the sauce. Cheese sauce may be substituted.

Escalloped Onions

50 Servings (5 oz/140 g)
Bake, 350°F/177°C, 30 min

Metric		Ingredients	U.S.	
Weight	**Volume**		**Weight**	**Volume**
6.81 kg	75 med	Onions, whole, dry	15 lb	75 med
2.61 kg	2 cans	Mushroom Soup	5 lb, 12 oz	2 cans (46 oz)
454 g	1.42 l	Soda Crackers, crushed	1 lb	1½ qt
454 g	533 ml	Butter or Margarine, melted	1 lb	2¼ cups

Procedure

1. Peel onions, cut in half, and gently boil in salted water until almost tender, but firm. Drain well.
2. Arrange onions in greased serving pan (12 × 20 × 2 in). Cover with mushroom soup. Sprinkle with cracker crumbs mixed with the melted butter or margarine.
3. Bake at 350°F/177°C for 30 minutes or until onions are tender.

Savory Onions

50 Servings (5 oz/142 g)
Bake, 350°F/177°C, 30 min

| Metric | | Ingredients | U.S. | |
Weight	Volume		Weight	Volume
6.81 kg	50 lge	Onions, E.P.	15 lb	50 lge
255 g	316 ml	Brown Sugar	9 oz	1 ⅓ cups
43 g	45 ml	Salt	1 ½ oz	3 tbsp
	5 ml	Pepper		1 tsp
1.36 kg	1.42 l	Chili Sauce	3 lb	1 ½ qt
212 g	237 ml	Margarine or Butter, melted	7 ½ oz	1 cup

Procedure

1. Steam onions until almost tender. Drain. Arrange in greased serving pans (12 × 20 × 2 in).
2. Combine remaining ingredients and mix thoroughly.
3. Pour sauce over onions and bake at 350°F/177°C until glazed and tender (for about ½ hr).

Scalloped Corn

50 Servings (6 ¾ oz/191 g)
Bake, 350°F/177°C, to brown

| Metric | | Ingredients | U.S. | |
Weight	Volume		Weight	Volume
198 g	207 ml	Eggs (4 med)	7 oz	⅞ cup
114 g	237 ml	Green Pepper, chopped	4 oz	1 cup
170 g	237 ml	Pimiento, chopped	6 oz	1 cup
6.81 kg	7.10 l	Corn, cream-style	15 lb	7 ½ qt
454 g	474 ml	Milk	1 lb	2 cups
28 g	30 ml	Salt	1 oz	2 tbsp
	2 ½ ml	Pepper		½ tsp
454 g	474 ml	Butter or Margarine	1 lb	2 cups
397 g	947 ml	Cracker Crumbs	14 oz	1 qt

Procedure

1. Beat eggs slightly and add green pepper, pimientos, corn, milk, salt, pepper, and 8 oz/227 g melted butter or margarine. Mix well.
2. Add remaining 8 oz/227 g melted butter or margarine to cracker crumbs.
3. Yield: About 21 ½ lb/9.75 kg. Place alternate layers of corn mixture and cracker crumbs, ending with cracker crumbs, in each of 2 greased pans (12 × 20 × 2 in).
4. Bake at 350°F/177°C until crumbs are brown and mixture is set.

Escalloped Tomatoes

50 Servings (4 ½ oz/128 g)
Bake, 375°F/190°C, about 30 min

| Metric | | Ingredients | U.S. | |
Weight	Volume		Weight	Volume
5.90 kg	6.63 l	Tomatoes, solid pack	13 lb	2 No. 10 cans
76 g	118 ml	Onions, grated	2 ⅔ oz	½ cup
227 g	237 ml	Sugar	8 oz	1 cup
14 g	15 ml	Salt	½ oz	1 tbsp
454 g	947 ml	Bread, finely cubed	1 lb	1 qt
100 g	118 ml	Butter or Margarine, melted	3 ½ oz	½ cup
227 g	474 ml	Bread Crumbs	8 oz	2 cups
100 g	118 ml	Butter or Margarine, melted	3 ½ oz	½ cup

Procedure

1. Combine tomatoes and seasonings. Mix thoroughly.
2. Toast bread cubes and sprinkle with melted butter or margarine. Place in bottom of 2 greased pans (10 × 12 × 2 in). Pour equal amounts of tomato mixture over bread cubes. Sprinkle with bread crumbs and butter or margarine.
3. Bake at 375°F/190°C until browned.

Sweet Potato Soufflé

50 Servings (5 oz/140 g)
Bake, 300°F/149°C, 35 min

| Metric | | Ingredients | U.S. | |
Weight	Volume		Weight	Volume
5.44 kg	5.68 l	Sweet Potatoes, cooked, mashed	12 lb	1 ½ gal
1.02 kg	1.07 l	Milk, hot	2 lb, 4 oz	4 ½ cups
170 g	237 ml	Brown Sugar	6 oz	1 cup
1.36 kg	1.42 l	Eggs, separated (24 lge)	3 lb	1 ½ qt
28 g	75 ml	Orange Rind, grated	1 oz	⅓ cup
681 g	711 ml	Orange Juice	1 lb, 8 oz	3 cups
28 g	30 ml	Salt	1 oz	2 tbsp

Procedure

1. Fluff sweet potatoes with hot milk. Add brown sugar, egg yolks, orange rind, juice, and salt. Whip until well-blended.
2. Whip egg whites until stiff but moist. Fold into sweet potatoes. Divide into 2 serving pans (12 × 20 × 2 in). Raw sweet potato may be grated on top if desired.
3. Bake at 300°F/149°C for 30 to 40 minutes or until the soufflé tests done.

Note: May be varied by spreading marshmallows on top to brown during the last 5 minutes of baking.

Banana Yams

50 Servings (6 oz/170 g)
Bake, 350°F/177°C, 30 min

| Metric | | Ingredients | U.S. | |
Weight	Volume		Weight	Volume
5.44 kg	5.68 l	Yams, cooked, mashed	12 lb	6 qt
1.36 kg	1.89 l	Brown Sugar	3 lb	2 qt
567 g	592 ml	Bananas, mashed	1 lb, 4 oz	2 ½ cups
681 g	711 ml	Butter or Margarine	1 lb, 8 oz	3 cups
454 g	947 ml	Pecans, coarsely chopped	1 lb	1 qt
57 g	59 ml	Lemon Juice	2 oz	¼ cup
7 g	22 ½ ml	Cinnamon		1 ½ tbsp
14 g	15 ml	Salt	½ oz	1 tbsp

Procedure

1. Blend all of the ingredients and divide into 2 greased serving pans (12 × 20 × 2 in).
2. Bake at 350°F/177°C until nicely browned (about 30 min).

Note: If yams are too dry, add liquid before baking. The color of this dark dish may be brightened by topping with a simple meringue. The flavor is very nice, especially with ham or other pork dishes.

Turnip Soufflé

50 Servings
Bake, 300°F/149°C, 45 min

| Metric | | Ingredients | U.S. | |
Weight	Volume		Weight	Volume
7.26 kg	32 med	Turnips, yellow	16 lb	32 med
454 g	474 ml	Butter or Margarine	1 lb	2 cups
114 g	237 ml	Flour, bread	4 oz	1 cup
793 g	829 ml	Eggs, separated (16 med)	1 lb, 12 oz	3 ½ cups
38 g	40 ml	Salt		2 ⅔ tbsp
20 g	20 ml	Worcestershire Sauce		4 tsp
	5 ml	Pepper		1 tsp

Procedure

1. Cook turnips until tender. Drain and mash.
2. Melt butter or margarine and add flour. Blend. Add turnips and cool slightly.
3. Add yolks, by first adding some of hot mixture to yolks and then adding all to hot mixture. Beat with mixer until light.
4. Add remaining ingredients to turnips.
5. Beat egg whites until stiff. Fold into turnip mixture.
6. Scale 9 lbs/4.08 kg into each of 2 greased pans (12 × 20 × 2 in). Bake at 300°F/149°C until set.

French Fried Onions
50 Servings

Metric		Ingredients	U.S.	
Weight	**Volume**		**Weight**	**Volume**
3.18 g	6.63 l	Onions, Bermuda, E.P.	7 lb	7 qt
227 kg	237 ml	Eggs, beaten (4 lge)	8 oz	1 cup
75 g	79 ml	Salt	2⅔ oz	⅓ cup
907 g	947 ml	Milk	2 lb	1 qt
		Flour, for dredging		
		Fat, for deep frying		

Procedure

1. Peel onions, slice crosswise, and separate into rings.
2. Combine eggs, salt, and milk. Mix well. Dip onions in liquid, then in flour. Do not let stand. Dip immediately before frying.
3. Fry in deep fat, 375°F/190°C for 2 to 4 minutes.

Scalloped Potatoes
48 Servings
Bake, 350°F/177°C, 1 hr, 10 min

Metric		Ingredients	U.S.	
Weight	**Volume**		**Weight**	**Volume**
4.54 kg	2.37 l	Potatoes, thinly sliced	10 lb	2½ qt
1.14 kg	2.37 l	Onions, thinly sliced	2 lb, 8 oz	2½ qt
227 g	237 ml	Butter or Margarine	8 oz	1 cup
1.02 kg	237 ml	Flour, all-purpose	4 oz	1 cup
28 g	30 ml	Salt	1 oz	2 tbsp
	10 ml	Pepper, white		2 tsp
3.63 kg	3.79 l	Milk	8 lb	1 gal
227 g	474 ml	Wheat Germ	8 oz	2 cups

Procedure

1. Arrange potato slices in two greased serving pans (12 × 20 × 2 in). Sprinkle with salt and white pepper.
2. Arrange onion slices on top of the potatoes.
3. Melt butter or margarine. Add flour and seasonings. Blend. Cook over low heat 3 to 5 minutes. Stir while cooking. Add milk slowly, stirring constantly. Cook until sauce is smooth and thickened.
4. Pour enough thin white sauce over potatoes and onions to cover. Avoid having pan so full it will boil over.
5. Sprinkle wheat germ over top of each pan. Bake at 350°F/177°C for 1 hour, covered. Remove cover and brown lightly for 10 minutes.

Mashed Potatoes
50 Servings (5 oz/142 g)

| Metric | | Ingredients | U.S. | |
Weight	Volume		Weight	Volume
5.44 kg	48 med	Potatoes, pared	12 lb	48 (med)
283 g	295 ml	Butter or Margarine	10 oz	1 ¼ cups
1.81–2.04 kg	1.89–2.37 l	Milk, hot	4–4 ½ lb	2–2 ½ qt
42 g	90 ml	Salt	1 ½ oz	3 tbsp

Procedure

1. Steam or boil the potatoes until tender. Drain and place in the mixer.
2. Whip at low speed until evenly mashed. Increase speed to high and whip for 2 minutes.
3. Add remaining ingredients and whip until light and creamy.

Note: 2 to 2 ½ lb/907 to 1.14 kg dehydrated potatoes may be used. If milk solids are used in place of fresh milk use 8 oz/ 227 g and sprinkle over potatoes before mashing, and use 2 qt/1.89 l to 2 ½ qt/2.37 l of hot water for the liquid.

Sweet Potato and Apple Scallop
50 Servings
Bake, 350°F/177°C, 30 min

| Metric | | Ingredients | U.S. | |
Weight	Volume		Weight	Volume
6.81 kg	45 med	Sweet Potatoes, A.P.	15 lb	45 med
3.18 kg	6.63 l	Apples, peeled, sliced	7 lb	7 qt
454 g	632 ml	Brown Sugar	1 lb	2 ⅔ cups
227 g	237 ml	Sugar	8 oz	1 cup
43 g	45 ml	Salt	1 ½ oz	3 tbsp
227 g	237 ml	Butter or Margarine	8 oz	1 cup
907 g	947 ml	Water	2 lb	1 qt
114 g	118 ml	Orange Juice	4 oz	½ cup
454 g	1.89 l	Marshmallows	1 lb	2 qt

Procedure

1. Cook sweet potatoes in skins until almost done. Peel and slice ⅓ to ½ inch thick.
2. Place alternate layers of sweet potatoes and apples in each of 2 greased serving pans (12 × 20 × 2 in): Top layer should be sweet potatoes.
3. Combine brown sugar, granulated sugar, salt, butter, water, and orange juice and cook to make syrup.
4. Pour syrup over potatoes and apples. Bake at 350°F/ 177°C for 30 minutes or until done. Just before serving, place marshmallows on top and allow to brown lightly.

Note: Chopped ham may be used in place of marshmallows for a luncheon dish. Gingersnaps may be used in place of/or in addition to marshmallows.

Harvard Beets
50 Servings (scant 5 oz)

| Metric | | Ingredients | U.S. | |
Weight	Volume		Weight	Volume
5.44 kg	6.63 l	Beets, cooked or canned	12 lb	2 No. 10 cans
2.04 kg	2.13 l	Beet Juice	4 lb, 8 oz	2 ¼ qt
283 g	296 ml	Sugar	10 oz	1 ¼ cups
198 g	355 ml	Cornstarch	7 oz	1 ½ cups
28 g	30 ml	Salt	1 oz	2 tbsp
	5 ml	Pepper		1 tsp
	5 ml	Cloves		1 tsp
	2 ½ ml	Nutmeg		½ tsp
567 g	592 ml	Vinegar	1 lb, 4 oz	2 ½ cups
114 g	118 ml	Butter or Margarine	4 oz	½ cup

Procedure

1. Drain juice from beets and heat it to boiling point.
2. Mix together sugar, cornstarch, salt, pepper, cloves, nutmeg, and vinegar. Add to hot juice, stirring until thick and cornstarch has lost its raw taste. Remove from heat. Add butter or margarine.
3. Add sauce to preheated beets, 3 qt/2.84 l of sauce for 9 ½ lb/4.31 kg of drained beets.

Glazed Parsnips
50 Servings (6 oz/170 g)
Bake, 400°F/205°C, 20–30 min

| Metric | | Ingredients | U.S. | |
Weight	Volume		Weight	Volume
9.07 kg	80 ml	Parsnips, pared, cooked	20 lb	about 80
340 g	474 ml	Brown Sugar	12 oz	2 cups
454 g	474 ml	Water	1 lb	2 cups
	5 ml	Salt		1 tsp
227 g	237 ml	Butter or Margarine	8 oz	1 cup

Procedure

1. Cut parsnips lengthwise into pieces approximately 1 × 3 inches. Arrange in serving pans (12 × 20 × 2 in).
2. Boil remaining ingredients, stirring until sugar is dissolved. Pour over parsnips, being careful to cover all pieces with the syrup.
3. Bake at 400°F/205°C for 20 to 30 minutes or until parsnips are nicely browned.

Note: Sweet potatoes or carrots may be substituted for the parsnips.

Parsley Green Rice
50 Servings (4 oz/114 g)
Bake, 300°F/149°C, 45 min

Metric		Ingredients	U.S.	
Weight	Volume		Weight	Volume
2.27 kg	2.96 l	Rice, cooked	5 lb	3 ⅛ qt
340 g	355 ml	Butter or Margarine, melted	12 oz	1 ½ cups
1.14 kg	1.18 l	Milk	2 lb, 8 oz	1 ¼ qt
567 g	1.18 l	Cheddar Cheese, grated	1 lb, 4 oz	1 ¼ qt
14 g	15 ml	Salt	½ oz	1 tbsp
	2 ½ ml	Pepper		½ tsp
397 g	592 ml	Onions, minced	14 oz	2 ½ cups
227 g	2.37 l	Parsley, finely chopped	8 oz	2 ½ qt
425 g	395 ml	Egg Yolks, beaten (20 med)	15 oz	1 ⅔ cups
567 g	592 ml	Egg Whites, stiffly beaten (20 med)	1 lb, 4 oz	2 ½ cups

Procedure

1. Blend all ingredients, except egg whites.
2. Fold in whites. Pour into greased custard cups or servings pans (12 × 20 × 2 in).
3. Bake at 300°F/149°C until set and lightly browned (about 45 min).

Red Cabbage with Sour Sauce
50 Servings

Metric		Ingredients	U.S.	
Weight	Volume		Weight	Volume
5.44 kg	15.14 l	Red Cabbage, shredded	12 lb	4 gal
454 g	4 med	Apples, sour, peeled, or chopped	1 lb	4 med
28 g	30 ml	Lemon Juice	1 oz	2 tbsp
71 g	75 ml	Salt	2 ½ oz	5 tbsp
340 g	355 ml	Bacon Fat	12 oz	1 ½ cups
454 g	474 ml	Vinegar	1 lb	2 cups
227 g	316 ml	Brown Sugar	8 oz	1 ⅓ cups
	10 ml	Cloves, ground		2 tsp

Procedure

1. Combine cabbage, apples, and lemon juice. Cook in water to cover until tender.
2. Combine remaining ingredients and boil for 10 minutes.
3. Drain cabbage mixture and pour sauce over the mixture. Let stand for 10 to 15 minutes before serving. Toss lightly.

Ratatouille

50 Servings
Bake, 350°F/177°C, 50 min

Metric		Ingredients	U.S.	
Weight	Volume		Weight	Volume
340 g	355 ml	Salad Oil	12 oz	1 ½ cups
28 g	6–10 cloves	Garlic, minced	1 oz	6–10 cloves
907 g	8 med	Onions, sliced	2 lb	8 med
1.82 kg	3.79 l	Eggplant, cubed	4 lb	4 qt
2.27 kg	4.74 l	Zucchini, sliced	5 lb	5 qt
907 g	1.89 l	Green Pepper, 1-in chunks	2 lb	2 qt
114 g	118 ml	Salt	4 oz	½ cup
	45 ml	Sweet Basil		3 tbsp
85 g	533 ml	Parsley, chopped	3 oz	2 ¼ cups
3.63 kg	6.15 l	Tomato Wedges	8 lb	6 ½ qt

Procedure

1. Heat oil and garlic together and let simmer a few minutes.
2. Mix the rest of the ingredients equally, except for the tomatoes. Divide into 2 greased pans (12 × 20 × 2 in) or 4 pans (10 × 12 × 2 in).
3. Pour the oil/garlic mixture over the vegetables and bake in 350°F/177°C oven for ½ hour and stir. Taste for salt.
4. Put the tomato wedges on top and bake for another 20 min or until vegetables are tender.

Carrots and Green Grapes

50 Servings (5 oz/140 g)

Metric		Ingredients	U.S.	
Weight	Volume		Weight	Volume
5.44 kg	8.51 l	Carrots, cut finger-size	12 lb	2 ¼ gal
28 g	30 ml	Salt	1 oz	2 tbsp
	5 ml	Basil		1 tsp
227 g	237 ml	Butter or Margarine	8 oz	1 cup
	5 ml	Thyme		1 tsp
	5 ml	Celery Salt		¼ tsp
28 g	30 ml	Lemon Juice	1 oz	2 tbsp
	⅝ ml	Pepper		⅛ tsp
1.82 kg	2.84 l	Green Grapes	4 lb	3 qt

Procedure

1. Cook carrots in boiling water to which salt and basil have been added. Cook only until tender but firm. Drain well. Place in serving pans (12 × 20 × 2 in).
2. Melt butter or margarine. Add seasonings and lemon juice. Pour over carrots. Add green grapes and mix lightly, being careful not to break carrots. Let stand for a minute for green grapes to heat. (Avoid excess heat or standing so that grapes will not lose their green color.)

Stuffed Zucchini

50 Servings
Bake, 350°F/177°C, 15 min

Metric		Ingredients	U.S.	
Weight	Volume		Weight	Volume
5.44		Zucchini	12 lb	
114 g	118 ml	Butter or Margarine	4 oz	½ cup
340 g	474 ml	Onions, chopped	12 oz	2 cups
454 g	474 ml	Corn, whole kernel	1 lb	2 cups
227 g	474 ml	Green Pepper, chopped	8 oz	2 cups
227 g	237 ml	Chili Sauce	8 oz	1 cup
99 g	237 ml	Bread Crumbs	3 ½ oz	1 cup
	5 ml	Basil, powdered		1 tsp
18 g	118 ml	Parsley, finely chopped	⅔ oz	½ cup
	10 ml	Salt		2 tsp
	7 ½ ml	Worcestershire Sauce		1 ½ tsp
114 g	237 ml	Cheddar Cheese, grated	4 oz	1 cup
99 g	237 ml	Bread Crumbs	3 ½ oz	1 cup

Procedure

1. Cut zucchini in half lengthwise and then into portion lengths. Hollow out seed section to form boat-shaped pieces. Parboil 1 minute. Drain well.
2. Melt butter or margarine, sauté onions, corn, green pepper, and chopped centers of zucchini. Mix in chili sauce, 1 cup/237 ml bread crumbs, and seasonings.
3. Fill zucchini boats with mixture. Combine cheese and crumbs and sprinkle on top. Bake in greased pans at 350°F/177°C for 15 minutes.

Grilled Tomatoes

50 Servings
Bake, 375°F/190°C, ½ hr

Metric		Ingredients	U.S.	
Weight	Volume		Weight	Volume
6.35 kg	25 lge	Tomatoes, firm	14 lb	25 lge
100 g	118 ml	Butter or Margarine, melted	3 ½ oz	½ cup
227 g	474 ml	Bread Crumbs, fine, dry	8 oz	2 cups
	5 ml	Salt		1 tsp
	1 ¼ ml	Pepper		¼ tsp
	2 ½ ml	Seasoning Salt		½ tsp

Procedure

1. Cut tomatoes in half. Brush with melted butter or margarine and dip in bread crumbs mixed with seasonings.
2. Place in greased pans and brown in oven at 375°F/190°C for ½ hour.

Table 11
Vegetable Seasoning and Combination Suggestions

Asparagus

a. 12 lb/5.44 kg cooked spears served with crumb sauce (2 qt/1.89 l dry bread crumbs and 1 lb/454 g chopped mushrooms browned in 8 oz/227 g butter or margarine).

b. 10 lb/454 kg cut asparagus cooked and blended with 1 qt/947 ml white sauce, 1 qt/947 ml mayonnaise, and ½ c/118 ml lemon juice.

Beans, green

a. 12 lb/5.44 kg cooked, seasoned with 8 oz/227 g butter or margarine, 1 lb/454 g minced onion, and 2 tbsp/30 ml dill seed.

b. 10 lb/4.54 kg cooked, seasoned with 2 lb/907 g sliced mushrooms sautéed in 8 oz/227 g butter or margarine.

c. 1 No. 10 can each of green beans and kidney beans, drained and seasoned with 1 lb/454 g minced onion, and 8 oz/227 g chopped green pepper sautéed in 8 oz/227 g butter or margarine.

d. 10 lb/4.54 kg green beans seasoned with 2 lb/907 g tomato soup and 1 lb/454 g toasted, slivered almonds.

Broccoli

a. 12 lb/5.44 kg cooked, seasoned with 10 oz/283 g melted butter or margarine.

b. Cooked spears served with 2 qt/1.89 l Hollandaise or Mock Hollandaise sauce.

c. 10 lb/4.54 kg cut broccoli served with blend of 1 qt/947 ml sour cream, 2 cups/474 ml mayonnaise, ¼ cup/59 ml lemon juice and 2 tsp/10 ml salt.

Cabbage

a. 10 lb/4.54 kg shredded cabbage blanched 5 minutes then layered into serving pans with 3 qt/2.84 l white sauce and 12 oz/340 g grated Cheddar cheese. Sprinkle 2 cups/474 ml buttered bread crumbs on top. Bake at 350°F/177°C, 20 min.

b. Boil 12 lb/5.44 kg wedges until tender. Garnish portions with 1 qt/947 ml mayonnaise mixed with 3 cups/711 ml sour cream, 2 tbsp/30 ml lemon juice, and 2 tsp/10 ml salt.

Carrots

a. 9 lb/4.08 kg cooked carrots, 3 lb/1.36 kg cooked celery rings, 8 oz/227 g butter or margarine, and 1 tsp/5 ml nutmeg.

c. 10 lb/4.54 kg cooked carrots, 1 cup/237 ml minced onion, 3 cups/711 ml sliced ripe olives, 1 tbsp/15 ml sugar, 8 oz/227 g melted butter or margarine.

Corn

a. 10 lb/4.54 kg whole kernel, 2 cups/474 ml chopped green pepper, 1 cup/237 ml chopped pimiento, 2 cups/474 ml minced onion, 8 oz/227 g melted butter or margarine, 1 tbsp/15 ml salt, and 1 tbsp/15 ml chili powder.

b. 6 lb/2.72 kg whole kernel, 6 lb/2.72 kg Fordhook limas, 8 oz/227 g butter or margarine, 1 tbsp/15 ml salt, and 1 tsp/5 ml pepper.

Onions

a. 10 lb/4.54 kg small, whole onions, boiled in salted water, well-drained, with 3 qt/2.84 l Béchamel sauce and 3 qts/2.84 l cooked green peas.

b. 10 lb/4.54 kg small, whole boiled onions with 3 qt/2.84 l thin cheese sauce and 3 cups/711 ml slivered, toasted almonds.

c. 12 lb/5.44 kg boiled onions, 10 oz/283 g butter or margarine, and 2 cups/474 ml minced parsley.

Peas or Baby Lima Beans

a. 10 lb/4.54 kg peas or limas, 8 oz butter or margarine, and 2 lb/907 g coarsely chopped water chestnuts.

b. 10 lb/4.54 kg peas or limas, 2 qt/1.89 l white sauce, and 2 cups/474 ml snipped chives.

c. 10 lb/4.54 kg peas or limas, 8 oz/227 g butter or margarine, and 2 qt/1.89 l celery rings or cauliflowerets.

d. 8 lb/3.63 kg peas or limas, 2 ½ qt/2.38 l white sauce, and 4 lb/1.82 kg boiled small, new potatoes.

e. 8 lb/3.63 kg peas or limas, 8 oz/227 g butter or margarine, and 1 No. 10 can small onions, drained.

Potatoes—Use 16 to 20 lb/7.26 to 9.07 kg, according to desired portion size.

a. Dip portion-size, dry, pared potatoes in 2 cups/474 ml oil or melted margarine and 2 tbsp/30 ml salt, roll in 2 qt/1.89 l cornflake crumbs. Place on baking sheet, bake at 400°F/205°C until tender.

b. Boil or steam whole potatoes, place on baking sheet, pour 2 cups/474 ml melted margarine over them, sprinkle generously with paprika and brown at 350°F/177°C, 20 to 30 min.

c. Steamed, diced potatoes in 3 qt/2.84 l sauce (white, cheese, soubise, or Béchamel).

d. Spread frozen, thawed fried or browned balls of shredded potatoes on a baking sheet, sprinkle with salt, and heat in broiler, 10 to 15 minutes, stirring to heat and brown evenly.

e. Place freshly mashed, seasoned potatoes in serving pans and top with 1 qt/947 ml cream whipped until stiff, in which 1 lb/454 g grated Cheddar cheese has been folded, and 1 tbsp/15 ml salt. Brown at 350°F/177°C until cheese is melted.

Spinach—Use 8 lb/3.63 kg to 12 lb/5.44 kg, according to desired portion size.

a. Boil spinach 3 min, drain well, chop and serve with 2 ½ qt/2.37 l sauce (Mornay, white, or Béchamel) or with blend of 1 qt/947 ml sour cream, 2 cups/474 ml mayonnaise, and ⅓ cup/79 ml lemon or lime juice.

b. Boil spinach 3 minutes, drain well, chop, season with 8 oz/227 g melted butter or margarine and ⅓ cup/79 ml lemon or lime juice, or vinegar.

CHAPTER 9 — Sauces, Relishes, and Stuffings

Sauces are a form of seasoning used to enhance many foods. Some foods have certain characteristics that need to be strengthened and others that need to be masked for best enjoyment. A flavor may be too mild or strong and a texture may be too soft or dry. Richness may be added or diluted through the use of the proper sauce. Fame for culinary skill may result from knowing how and when to use the proper sauce or accompaniment to heighten palatability.

Relishes and stuffings, like sauces, are important additions to the flavor, interest, and texture appeal of the foods that they accompany. The tart, spicy quality of relishes stimulates the appetite. A well-made stuffing extends the rich, meaty flavor of a dish. Stuffings should be light and absorbent rather than firm, gluey, and wet. They should be tasty and harmonize with the foods with which they are served.

Modern practices in kitchens have forced many to depend upon commercial soup bases for sauce and soup making. The slowly simmering stockpot has been eliminated from most kitchens due to labor cost and market practice. The soup base should be carefully chosen to obtain a suitable degree of flavor quality.

Marinades are used to flavor and to tenderize meats. The ingredients should be well-mixed and allowed to stand for a few hours to season before meat is added to marinate or cook in the marinade. Allow at least 2 hours for the marinade to flavor and tenderize the tougher cuts of meat. Tender meats such as chicken and pork may be baked in or basted with the marinade without soaking. Due to the excess fat on pork spareribs, it is advisable to cook them for 45 minutes to 1 hour, then pour off the fat before adding the marinade and continuing the cooking.

Sauces

COCKTAIL SAUCES

Mayonnaise Cocktail Sauce
2 ¼ qt/2.20 l

| Metric | | Ingredients | U.S. | |
Weight	Volume		Weight	Volume
1.50 kg	1.60 l	Mayonnaise	3 lb, 8 oz	6 ½ cups
227 g	237 ml	Catsup	8 oz	1 cup
227 g	237 ml	Chili Sauce	8 oz	1 cup
60 g	60 ml	Tarragon Vinegar	2 oz	¼ cup
114 g	118 ml	Lemon Juice	4 oz	½ cup
	2 ½ ml	Hot Pepper Sauce		½ tsp
	10 ml	Salt		2 tsp
		Optional		
310 g	474 ml	Sweet Pickle, minced	11 oz	2 cups

Procedure

1. Combine ingredients and mix well.

Note: Use with meat or fish cocktails.

Celery and Onion Cocktail Sauce
2 qt/1.90 l

| Metric | | Ingredients | U.S. | |
Weight	Volume		Weight	Volume
454 g	947 ml	Celery, finely minced	1 lb	1 qt
114 g	237 ml	Green onions, minced	4 oz	1 cup
454 g	474 ml	Chili Sauce	1 lb	2 cups
454 g	474 ml	Catsup	1 lb	2 cups
227 g	237 ml	Lemon Juice	8 oz	1 cup
57 g	60 ml	Worcestershire Sauce	2 oz	¼ cup
	10 ml	Hot Pepper Sauce		2 tsp
114 g	237 ml	Horseradish, grated	4 oz	1 cup
	5 ml	Salt		1 tsp

Procedure

1. Combine all ingredients and mix well.

Note: This is a sharp sauce for use with meat or fish cocktails.

Pineapple and Green Pepper Sauce
2 1/4 qt/2.20 l

Metric		Ingredients	U.S.	
Weight	Volume		Weight	Volume
40 g	45 ml	Tarragon Vinegar	1 1/2 oz	3 tbsp
40 g	45 ml	Malt Vinegar	1 1/2 oz	3 tbsp
850 g	592 ml	Honey, strained	1 lb, 14 oz	2 1/2 cups
340 g	711 ml	Green Pepper, minced	12 oz	3 cups
450 g	711 ml	Pineapple, fresh, chopped	1 lb	3 cups

Procedure

1. Combine vinegars and honey and bring to rolling boil.
2. Pour boiling vinegar over pineapple. When cool, add green pepper.

Note: Sauce for Grapefruit-Tarragon Cocktail.

Pineapple-Lemon Cocktail Sauce
2 qt/1.90 l

Metric		Ingredients	U.S.	
Weight	Volume		Weight	Volume
967 g	1.00 l	Pineapple Juice	2 lb, 2 oz	4 1/4 cups
57 g	60 ml	Lemon Juice	2 oz	1/4 cup
800 g	828 ml	Carbonated Water or Ginger ale	1 lb, 12 oz	3 1/2 cups

Procedure

1. Combine and blend well immediately before serving.

Note: Use over fruit cocktails.

Cucumber-Tarragon Cocktail Sauce
2 qt/1.90 l

Metric		Ingredients	U.S.	
Weight	Volume		Weight	Volume
681 g	1.18 l	Cucumbers, grated	1 lb, 8 oz	1 1/4 qt
340 g	711 ml	Green Pepper, minced	12 oz	3 cups
311 g	237 ml	Honey	11 oz	1 cup
28 g	30 ml	Tarragon Vinegar	1 oz	2 tbsp
28 g	30 ml	Malt Vinegar	1 oz	2 tbsp

Procedure

1. Combine and blend well.

Note: Serve over pineapple and grapefruit sections.

Piquant Cocktail Sauce
2 qt/1.90 l

Metric		Ingredients	U.S.		
Weight	Volume		Weight		Volume
681 g	711 ml	Catsup	1 lb,	8 oz	3 cups
681 g	711 ml	Tomato Puree	1 lb,	8 oz	3 cups
340 g	355 ml	Horseradish		12 oz	1 ½ cups
85 g	90 ml	Lemon Juice		3 oz	6 tbsp
	7 ½–15 ml	Hot Pepper Sauce			1 ½–3 tsp
14 g	15 ml	Worcestershire Sauce		½ oz	1 tbsp

Procedure

1. Combine ingredients and mix well. Use Hot Pepper Sauce according to taste (3 tsp/15 ml makes a sharp sauce).

Note: Minced green pepper and celery may be added.

Catsup and Cream Cheese Cocktail Sauce
2 qt/1.89 l

Metric		Ingredients	U.S.		
Weight	Volume		Weight		Volume
340 g	355 ml	Cream Cheese		12 oz	1 ½ cups
340 g	355 ml	Catsup		12 oz	1 ½ cups
681 g	711 ml	Mayonnaise	1 lb,	8 oz	3 cups
227 g	237 ml	Chili Sauce		8 oz	1 cup
114 g	118 ml	Lemon Juice		4 oz	½ cup
	10 ml	Salt			2 tsp

Procedure

1. Soften cream cheese with catsup. Fold in mayonnaise and remaining ingredients. Blend well.

Note: A tart, rich sauce suitable for crab, fish, shrimp, and grapefruit.

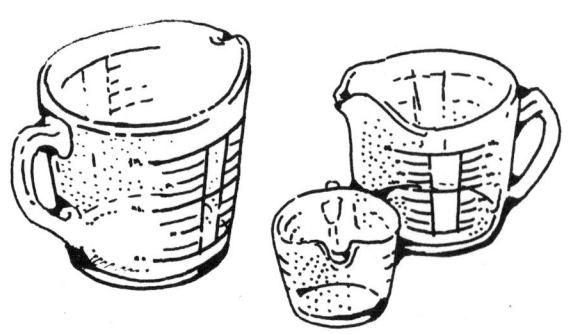

Tomato Sauce
1 gal / 3.79 l

| Metric | | Ingredients | U.S. | |
Weight	Volume		Weight	Volume
2.95 kg	3.31 l	Tomato Puree	6 lb, 8 oz	1 No. 10 can
170 g	237 ml	Onions, chopped	6 oz	1 cup
114 g	237 ml	Green Pepper, chopped	4 oz	1 cup
14 g	15 ml	Salt	½ oz	1 tbsp
	2 ½ ml	Pepper		½ tsp
	5 ml	Worcestershire Sauce		1 tsp

Procedure

1. Heat all ingredients to boiling. Simmer 20 minutes, uncovered.   2. Serve hot.

Barbecue Sauce
2 qt / 1.90 l

| Metric | | Ingredients | U.S. | |
Weight	Volume		Weight	Volume
114 g	158 ml	Brown Sugar	4 oz	⅔ cup
14 g	15 ml	Salt	½ oz	1 tbsp
	5 ml	Pepper		1 tsp
14 g	15 ml	Mustard, prepared	½ oz	1 tbsp
6 g	15 ml	Paprika		1 tbsp
	⅝ ml	Cayenne Pepper		⅛ tsp
312 g	474 ml	Onions, minced	11 oz	2 cups
907 g	947 ml	Catsup or Chili Sauce	2 lb	1 qt
340 g	355 ml	Lemon Juice or Vinegar	12 oz	1 ½ cups
28 g	30 ml	Worcestershire Sauce	1 oz	2 tbsp
4 g	15 ml	Garlic Powder		1 tbsp

Procedure

1. Blend dry ingredients. Add remaining ingredients and mix well.

Orange Barbecue Sauce
1 ¾ qt/1.66 l

Metric		Ingredients	U.S.	
Weight	Volume		Weight	Volume
42 g	118 ml	Orange Rind, chopped	1 ½ oz	½ cup
114 g	118 ml	Orange Juice	4 oz	½ cup
454 g	474 ml	Catsup	1 lb	2 cups
57 g	60 ml	Vinegar	2 oz	¼ cup
57 g	60 ml	Salad Oil	2 oz	¼ cup
596 g	474 ml	Molasses, light	1 lb, 5 oz	2 cups
340 g	474 ml	Onions, chopped	12 oz	2 cups
14 g	4 cloves	Garlic, minced	½ oz	4 cloves
7 g	7 ml	Mustard, prepared	¼ oz	1 ½ tsp
	2 ½ ml	Cloves, whole		½ tsp
	5 ml	Salt		1 tsp
	2 ½ ml	Cayenne Pepper		½ tsp
14 g	15 ml	Soy Sauce	½ oz	1 tbsp
9 g	10 ml	Worcestershire Sauce		2 tsp

Procedure

1. Blend ingredients and simmer 10 minutes. Let stand for seasonings to blend.   Note: Use with lamb shanks or spareribs.

Epicurean Sauce
1 ½ qt/1.42 l

Metric		Ingredients	U.S.	
Weight	Volume		Weight	Volume
511 g	533 ml	Whipping Cream	1 lb, 2 oz	2 ¼ cups
170 g	178 ml	Mayonnaise	6 oz	¾ cup
114 g	118 ml	Horseradish	4 oz	½ cup
21 g	22 ml	Mustard, prepared	¾ oz	1 ½ tbsp
	7 ½ ml	Salt		1 ½ tsp
	few grains	Cayenne Pepper		few grains

Procedure

1. Combine seasonings with mayonnaise. Fold in whipped cream.   Note: Use with roast beef or lamb.

Hamburger or Frankfurter Sauce
4 qt/3.79 l

| Metric | | Ingredients | U.S. | |
Weight	Volume		Weight	Volume
907 g	947 ml	Catsup	2 lb	1 qt
1.13 kg	1.18 l	Salad Dressing, cooked	2 lb, 8 oz	1 ¼ qt
1.36 kg	1.42 l	Pickle Relish	3 lb	1 ½ qt
283 g	237 ml	Mustard, prepared	10 oz	1 cup
	5 ml	Salt		1 tsp

Procedure

1. Combine all ingredients and mix well.

Béarnaise Sauce
3 cups/711 ml

| Metric | | Ingredients | U.S. | |
Weight	Volume		Weight	Volume
340	355 ml	Butter or Margarine	12 oz	1 ½ cups
114 g	118 ml	White Wine	4 oz	½ cup
114 g	118 ml	Wine Vinegar	4 oz	½ cup
	10 ml	Tarragon, dry leaves, minced		2 tsp
72 g	118 ml	Green Onions, minced	2 ½ oz	½ cup
	1 ¼ ml	Salt		¼ tsp
		Pepper to Taste		
340 g	316 ml	Egg Yolks (16 med)	12 oz	1 ⅓ cups
114 g	118 ml	Butter	4 oz	½ cup

Procedure

1. Melt 12 oz/340 g butter over low heat and set aside.
2. Boil wine, vinegar, tarragon, onions, salt, and pepper until reduced to 4 tbsp/60 ml.
3. Whip egg yolks in top of double boiler until thick. Beat in the wine and vinegar mixture. Add 1 oz/28 g cold butter.
4. Heat mixture over slowly simmering water. Beat with wire whip until mixture becomes thick as heavy cream. Do not let eggs thicken too quickly or become firm.
5. Remove from heat when mixture begins to coat wires of whip. Slice and beat in 1 oz/28 g more of cold butter.
6. Beat in melted butter or margarine in small droplets (¼ tsp/1 ¼ ml) at a time at the beginning, beating continuously. The mixture will thicken as the butter is added. Butter may be added more rapidly toward the end. Do not add milky residue at the bottom of the melted butter.

Mock Hollandaise Sauce

4 qt/3.79 l

Metric		Ingredients	U.S.	
Weight	Volume		Weight	Volume
227 g	237 ml	Butter or Margarine	8 oz	1 cup
114 g	237 ml	Flour, all-purpose	4 oz	1 cup
1.82 kg	1.89 l	Milk	4 lb	2 qt
10 g	10 ml	Salt	⅓ oz	2 tsp
	5 ml	Pepper		1 tsp
	1 ¼ ml	Cayenne Pepper		¼ tsp
57 g	60 ml	Sugar	2 oz	¼ cup
255 g	237 ml	Egg Yolks (12 med)	9 oz	1 cup
454 g	474 ml	Lemon Juice	1 lb	2 cups
907 g	947 ml	Mayonnaise	2 lb	1 qt

Procedure

1. Melt shortening. Add flour and blend. Add milk slowly, stirring constantly. Cook until thick. Add salt pepper, cayenne, and sugar.
2. Beat egg yolks and add to hot mixture, by first adding some of hot mixture to yolks. Stir constantly and cook for 2 minutes. Remove from heat.
3. Add lemon juice and mayonnaise. Blend.

Note: A good sauce for vegetables.

Tart Bacon Sauce for Vegetables

1 ¾ qt/1.66 l

Metric		Ingredients	U.S.	
Weight	Volume		Weight	Volume
227 g	237 ml	Bacon, cubed	8 oz	1 cup
57 g	118 ml	Flour, all-purpose	2 oz	½ cup
340 g	355 ml	Sugar	12 oz	1 ½ cups
28 g	30 ml	Salt	1 oz	2 tbsp
681 g	711 ml	Vinegar (40 grain)	1 lb, 8 oz	3 cups
681 g	711 ml	Water	1 lb, 8 oz	3 cups

Procedure

1. Fry bacon until light brown. Add flour and blend.
2. Combine sugar, salt, vinegar, and water. Add to bacon mixture, stirring until thickened.

Note: Serve with wilted lettuce, spinach, or hot potato salad, or poured over cooked green beans, broccoli, or boiled potatoes.

Hollandaise Sauce
3 cups/711 ml

Metric		Ingredients	U.S.	
Weight	Volume		Weight	Volume
340 g	355 ml	Butter or Margarine	12 oz	1 ½ cups
28 g	30 ml	Lemon Juice	1 oz	2 tbsp
28 g	30 ml	Water, cold	1 oz	2 tbsp
	1 ¼ ml	Salt		¼ tsp
340 g	316 ml	Egg Yolks (16 med)	12 oz	1 ⅓ cups
114 g	118 ml	Butter or Margarine	4 oz	½ cup

Procedure

1. Melt 12 oz/340 g butter or margarine over low heat and set aside.
2. Blend lemon juice with cold water and salt.
3. Whip egg yolks in top of double boiler until thick. Beat in lemon juice mixture. Add 1 oz/28 g cold butter.
4. Heat over slowly simmering water. Beat with wire whip until mixture becomes as thick as heavy cream. Do not let eggs thicken too rapidly or become firm.
5. Remove from heat when mixture begins to coat wires of whip. Slice and beat in 1 oz/28 g more of cold butter or margarine.
6. Beat in melted butter or margarine in small droplets (¼ tsp/1 ¼ ml) at a time at the beginning, beating continuously. The mixture will thicken as butter is added. Butter may be added more rapidly toward the end. Do not add milky residue at the bottom of melted butter or margarine.

Caper Sauce
1 ½ qt/1.42 l

Metric		Ingredients	U.S.	
Weight	Volume		Weight	Volume
142 g	237 ml	Capers	5 oz	1 cup
907 g	947 ml	Mayonnaise	2 lb	1 qt
85 g	118 ml	Onions, chopped	3 oz	½ cup
14 g	15 ml	Lemon Juice	½ oz	1 tbsp
14 g	15 ml	Caper liquid, from can	½ oz	1 tbsp
14 g	79 ml	Parsley	½ oz	⅓ cup
57 g	118 ml	Almonds, slivered (optional)	2 oz	½ cup

Procedure

1. Fold capers into mayonnaise with remaining ingredients.
2. Serve with fish or vegetables.

Note: Very good with fish.

Mushroom Sauce (Fresh)
4 qt/3.79 l

| Metric | | | U.S. | |
Weight	Volume	Ingredients	Weight	Volume
1.36 kg	4.74 l	Mushrooms, fresh	3 lb	5 qt
454 g	474 ml	Butter or Margarine	1 lb	2 cups
114 g	237 ml	Flour, all-purpose	4 oz	1 cup
57 g	59 ml	Onion Juice	2 oz	½ cup
1.82 kg	1.89 l	Cream	4 lb	2 qt
14 g	15 ml	Salt	½ oz	1 tbsp
	⅝ ml	Pepper		⅛ tsp

Procedure

1. Slice and sauté mushrooms in 8 oz/227 g of butter or margarine until light brown.
2. Melt remaining butter or margarine. Add flour and stir until smooth. Add onion juice. Gradually add cream, stirring until thick. Cook until flour loses its raw taste.
3. Add sautéed mushrooms and seasonings.

Mushroom Sauce (Canned)
4 qt/3.79 l

| Metric | | | U.S. | |
Weight	Volume	Ingredients	Weight	Volume
454 g	947 ml	Green Pepper, chopped	1 lb	1 qt
114 g	158 ml	Pimientos, chopped	4 oz	⅔ cup
907 g	947 ml	Mushrooms, canned, sliced	2 lb	1 qt
283 g	296 ml	Butter or Margarine	10 oz	1 ¼ cups
142 g	296 ml	Flour, all-purpose	5 oz	1 ¼ cups
36 g	37 ml	Salt	1 ¼ oz	2 ½ tbsp
2.27 kg	2.37 l	Milk and Mushroom Liquid, combined	5 lb	2 ½ qt
	⁵⁄₁₆ ml	Cayenne Pepper		¹⁄₁₆ tsp
	5 ml	Pepper		1 tsp

Procedure

1. Sauté green pepper, pimiento, and drained mushrooms in butter or margarine until tender.
2. Add flour and salt. Stir in milk, cayenne, and pepper. Cook until flour is cooked and sauce thickened.

Note: Serve with spaghetti or cheese loaf.

Mustard Sauce
1 ½ qt/1.42 l

| Metric | | Ingredients | U.S. | |
Weight	Volume		Weight	Volume
57 g	118 ml	Flour, all-purpose	2 oz	½ cup
57 g	59 ml	Sugar	2 oz	¼ cup
28 g	59 ml	Mustard, dry	1 oz	¼ cup
9 g	10 ml	Salt		2 tsp
283 g	296 ml	Vinegar (50 grain)	10 oz	1 ¼ cups
170 g	158 ml	Egg Yolks, beaten (8 med)	6 oz	⅔ cup
907 g	947 ml	Cream	2 lb	1 qt
57 g	59 ml	Butter or Margarine	2 oz	¼ cup

Procedure

1. Combine flour, sugar, mustard, and salt. Add vinegar slowly to make a smooth paste. Heat to boiling.
2. Pour mixture slowly over beaten egg yolks and continue beating. Add cream gradually, stirring constantly. Add melted butter or margarine.

Note: Use a sweet, not a bitter mustard. Serve on ham or tongue.

Tartar Sauce
1 gal/3.79 l

| Metric | | Ingredients | U.S. | |
Weight	Volume		Weight	Volume
2.50 kg	2.60 l	Mayonnaise, heavy	5 lb, 8 oz	2 ¾ qt
340 g	355 ml	Evaporated Milk	12 oz	1 ½ cups
340 g	355 ml	Vinegar	12 oz	1 ½ cups
	5 ml	Salt		1 tsp
170 g	237 ml	Sweet Pickles, chopped	6 oz	1 cup
85 g	178 ml	Green Pepper, chopped	3 oz	¾ cup
28 g	178 ml	Parsley, chopped	1 oz	¾ cup
85 g	178 ml	Celery, chopped	3 oz	¾ cup
170 g	237 ml	Green Onions, chopped	6 oz	1 cup

Procedure

1. Blend mayonnaise and evaporated milk, vinegar, and salt.

2. Add remaining ingredients and mix well.
Note: Chives may be substituted for the green onions.

Spaghetti Sauce

2 ¼ gal/8 ½ l

Metric		Ingredients	U.S.		
Weight	Volume		Weight		Volume
1.82 kg	1.89 l	Hamburger	4 lb		2 qt
454 g	711 ml	Onions, chopped	1 lb		3 cups
227 g	474 ml	Green Pepper, chopped		8 oz	2 cups
14 g	4 cloves	Garlic, minced		½ oz	4 cloves
28 g	178 ml	Parsley, chopped		1 oz	¾ cup
2.95 kg	3.31 l	Tomatoes, canned	6 lb,	8 oz	1 No. 10 can
3.18 kg	3.31 l	Tomato Puree	7 lb		1 No. 10 can
170 g	237 ml	Brown Sugar		6 oz	1 cup
76 g	79 ml	Salt		2 ⅔ oz	⅓ cup
4 g	15 ml	Chili Powder			1 tbsp
7 g	15 ml	Pepper			1 tbsp
	⅝ ml	Cayenne Pepper			⅛ tsp
4 g	10 ml	Basil			2 tsp
	2 ½ ml	Rosemary			½ tsp
28 g	30 ml	Worcestershire Sauce		1 oz	2 tbsp

Procedure

1. Brown ground beef. Add onions, green peppers, and garlic, and sauté until tender.
2. Add remaining ingredients and let simmer 3 or 4 hours, stirring occasionally, until concentrated and well blended in flavor.

Note: Flavor is improved by standing overnight. Ground lean pork may be substituted for part of the ground beef.

Mustard and Currant Jelly Sauce

2 qt/1.89 l

Metric		Ingredients	U.S.		
Weight	Volume		Weight		Volume
255 g	266 ml	Butter or Margarine		9 oz	1 ⅛ cups
85 g	178 ml	Flour, all-purpose		3 oz	¾ cup
57 g	60 ml	Mustard, prepared		2 oz	4 tbsp
57 g	60 ml	Horseradish		2 oz	4 tbsp
170 g	178 ml	Vinegar		6 oz	¾ cup
1.02 kg	1.07 l	Water, boiling	2 lb,	4 oz	4 ½ cups
9 g	10 ml	Salt			2 ¼ tsp
	1 ⅔ ml	Cayenne Pepper			⅓ tsp
	6 ⅔ ml	Pepper			1 ⅓ tsp
454 g	316 ml	Currant Jelly		1 lb	1 ⅓ cups

Procedure

1. Melt butter or margarine, add flour, and blend. Add remaining ingredients, except jelly. Cook until thick and smooth. Stir frequently.

2. Remove from heat. Add jelly. Blend.
Note: Serve with hot or cold meat.

Raisin Sauce
3 qt/2.84 l

Metric		Ingredients	U.S.	
Weight	Volume		Weight	Volume
454 g	474 ml	Water, boiling	1 lb	2 cups
454 g	711 ml	Raisins, soaked	1 lb	3 cups
530 g	553 ml	Water	1 lb, 2⅔ oz	2⅓ cups
142 g	1 lemon	Lemon, finely chopped	5 oz	1 lemon
170 g	1 orange	Orange, finely chopped	6 oz	1 orange
170 g	237 ml	Brown Sugar	6 oz	1 cup
71 g	118 ml	Cornstarch	2½ oz	½ cup
227 g	237 ml	Water, cold	8 oz	1 cup
227 g	237 ml	Butter or Margarine	8 oz	1 cup
605 g	632 ml	Pineapple Juice	1 lb, 5 oz	2⅔ cups

Procedure

1. Pour boiling water over raisins and let them soak until plump and tender.
2. Combine raisins with 2⅓ cups/553 ml water, lemon, orange, and brown sugar. Cook until tender.
3. Dissolve cornstarch in cold water and stir into hot raisin mixture. Stir and cook until mixture has thickened and cornstarch is clear.
4. Add butter and pineapple juice. When butter has melted, remove from heat.

Note: Serve with ham, pork, or smoked tongue.

Cherry Sauce
4½ qt/4.26 l

Metric		Ingredients	U.S.	
Weight	Volume		Weight	Volume
2.95 kg	3.31 l	Cherries, red pie	6 lb, 8 oz	1 No. 10 can
567 g	592 ml	Orange Juice	1 lb, 4 oz	2½ cups
567 g	592 ml	Sugar	1 lb, 4 oz	2½ cups
71 g	118 ml	Cornstarch	2½ oz	½ cup
	5 ml	Salt		1 tsp
	2 5.08-cm	Cinnamon Sticks		2 2-in
	12 cloves	Cloves, whole		12 cloves
	5 ml	Red Food Coloring		1 tsp
57 g	59 ml	Lemon Juice	2 oz	¼ cup
57 g	59 ml	Butter or Margarine	2 oz	¼ cup

Procedure

1. Drain juice from cherries and reserve. Combine cherry and orange juices.
2. Blend sugar, cornstarch, and salt. Gradually add juices. Add spices. Heat to boiling and cook, stirring, until mixture thickens and cornstarch is cooked. Remove whole spices.
3. Add red coloring and cherries. Heat to boiling, then remove from heat. Add butter or margarine and lemon juice.

Note: Will add interest and flavor to simple puddings.

Simple Marinade
1 qt/947 ml

Metric		Ingredients	U.S.	
Weight	Volume		Weight	Volume
340 g	355 ml	Salad Oil	12 oz	1 ½ cups
340 g	355 ml	Vinegar	12 oz	1 ½ cups
227 g	237 ml	Catsup	8 oz	1 cup
	5 ml	Worcestershire Sauce		1 tsp
	1 clove	Garlic, minced		1 clove
	⅝ ml	Hot Pepper Sauce (optional)		⅛ tsp

Procedure

1. Combine ingredients. Let stand for flavors to blend.   2. Let less-tender meats marinate for 2 hours or longer.

Wine Marinade
1 qt/947 ml

Metric		Ingredients	U.S.	
Weight	Volume		Weight	Volume
28 g	30 ml	Sugar	1 oz	2 tbsp
14 g	15 ml	Salt	½ oz	1 tbsp
	10 ml	Thyme		2 tsp
	10 ml	Basil		2 tsp
	5 ml	Marjoram		1 tsp
170 g	237 ml	Onions, chopped	6 oz	1 cup
7 g	2 cloves	Garlic, minced	¼ oz	2 cloves
340 g	355 ml	Salad Oil	12 oz	1 ½ cups
170 g	178 ml	Lemon Juice	6 oz	¾ cup
340 g	355 ml	Wine, dry	12 oz	1 ½ cups
	⅝ ml	Hot Pepper Sauce		⅛ tsp

Procedure

1. Combine ingredients and let stand to blend flavors.
2. Let food marinate for at least 2 hours, except for very tender meats, fish, or poultry that do not require the tenderizing effect of the marinade.

Teriyaki Marinade

1 qt/947 ml

| Metric | | Ingredients | U.S. | |
Weight	Volume		Weight	Volume
454 g	474 ml	Soy Sauce	1 lb	2 cups
340 g	355 ml	Pineapple Juice	12 oz	1 ½ cups
114 g	118 ml	Lemon Juice	4 oz	½ cup
114 g	118 ml	Sugar	4 oz	½ cup
85 g	118 ml	Onions, chopped	3 oz	½ cup
14 g	4 cloves	Garlic, minced	½ oz	4 cloves
	5 ml	Basil Leaves, crushed		1 tsp
	5 ml	Ginger, ground (or 1 tbsp fresh root, chopped)		1 tsp

Procedure

1. Combine ingredients and let stand to blend flavors.
2. To flavor and tenderize meat, let it remain in marinade 2 hours or longer.

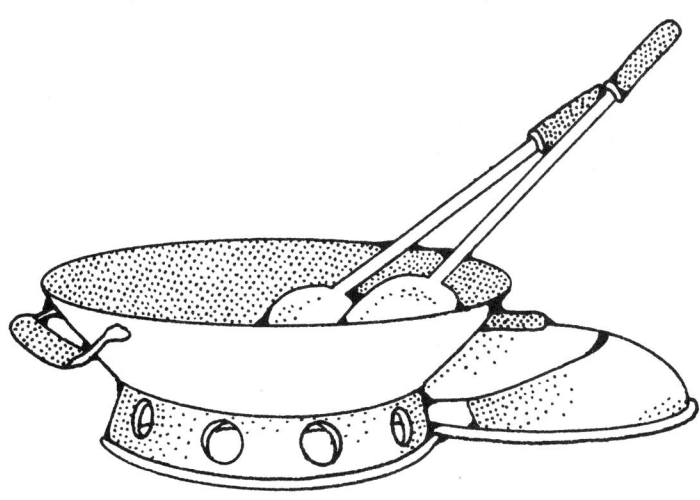

BUTTER SAUCES

See the descriptions and modifications given in the section on Canapé Butters. A slice or teaspoonful of these flavorful butters may be used as a sauce to enrich bland meats, poultry, fish, and vegetables.

STARCH-THICKENED SAUCES

The starches used for thickening sauces differ in their effectiveness. Comparable thickening of a gallon of liquid can be obtained with 8 oz/227 g pastry flour, 5 ½ oz/ 156 g cornstarch, 4 oz/114 g waxy-maize starch, and with 7 oz/198 g tapioca. Waxy-maize starch can be frozen and reheated and will retain its smooth texture, but thins when heated above 195°F/92°C.

White Sauce
1 gal/3.79 l

Metric			U.S.	
Weight	**Volume**	**Ingredients**	**Weight**	**Volume**
		Thin Sauce		
227 g	237 ml	Fat	8 oz	1 cup
114 g	237 ml	Flour	4 oz	1 cup
		Medium Sauce		
454 g	474 ml	Fat	1 lb	2 cups
227 g	474 ml	Flour	8 oz	2 cups
		Thick Sauce		
681 g	711 ml	Fat	1 lb, 8 oz	3 cups
340 g	711 ml	Flour	12 oz	3 cups
		Liquid and Seasoning for Sauce		
28 g	30 ml	Salt	1 oz	2 tbsp
5 g	10 ml	Pepper		2 tsp
3.63 kg	3.79 l	Milk	8 lb	1 gal

Procedure

1. Melt fat in large skillet. Add flour and seasonings. Blend.
2. Cook over low heat 3 to 5 minutes. Stir while cooking.
3. Add milk slowly, stirring constantly (if roux is cold, use hot milk).
4. Cook until smooth, glossy, thickened and flour is cooked.

Note: Fat may be butter, margarine, rendered chicken fat, or shortening.

Table 12
Modifications for White Sauce
(Approx. 1 gal/3.79 l)

Name	Ingredients	Use
Cheese	3 qt/2.84 l white sauce, 2 lb/907 g grated sharp cheese, 1 tbsp/15 ml dry mustard, 1 tbsp/15 ml Worcestershire sauce, 1 tsp/5 ml paprika.	Eggs, fish, croquettes, rice, vegetables
Cream	Substitute 2 qt/1.89 l cream for 2 qt/1.89 l milk in white sauce.	Chicken, fish, vegetables
Caper-Cucumber	3 qt/2.84 l white sauce, 1 cup/237 ml drained capers, 3 cups/711 ml grated cucumber, ⅛ tsp/⅝ ml hot pepper sauce.	Fish
Curry	1 gal/3.79 l white sauce, ⅓ cup/79 ml curry powder.	Eggs, poultry, lamb
Dill	1 gal/3.79 l white sauce, 1 tsp/5 ml nutmeg, 4 tbsp/60 ml dill seed.	Vegetables
Egg	3 qt/2.84 l white sauce, 2 lb/907 g diced hard-cooked eggs, 1 tsp/5 ml mustard.	Cornbread, fish
Green Grape and Almond	2½ qt/2.36 l white sauce, 3 cups/711 ml seedless grapes, cut in half, 2 cups/474 ml slivered almonds. Just before serving, add ¼ cup/59 ml lemon juice and 1 cup/237 ml Sherry.	Fish, pork, poultry
Mustard	1 gal/3.79 l white sauce, ½ cup/118 ml prepared mustard.	Cauliflower, fish, poultry

Table 12
Modifications for White Sauce *(cont.)*
(Approx. 1 gal/3.79 l)

Name	Ingredients	Use
Parsley	3 ½ qt/3.31 l white sauce, 3 cups/711 ml chopped parsley, 2 cups/474 ml minced onion, ¼ cup/59 ml lemon juice.	Meat or fish loaves
Peas and Pimiento	3 qt/2.84 l white sauce, 1 qt/947 ml cooked peas, 1 cup/237 ml chopped pimiento.	Salmon loaf, omelet, fish
Peas and Shrimp	2 ½ qt/2.36 l white sauce, 3 cups/711 ml cooked green peas, 3 cups/711 ml small shrimp, 1 tsp/5 ml Worcestershire sauce, ½ cup/118 ml minced pimiento.	Toast cups, croquettes, fish
Green Pepper and Cheese	3 qt/3.31 l white sauce, 3 cups/711 ml grated Cheddar, 2 cups/474 ml cooked diced green peppers, ½ cup/118 ml minced onion.	Fish, poultry, vegetables
Salmon and Parsley	3 qt/2.84 l white sauce, 1 qt/947 ml flaked, cooked salmon, 1 cup/237 ml chopped parsley (or green peas), ½ cup/118 ml minced chives.	Rice, toast, spaghetti, or noodles
Tomato-Cheese	3 qt/2.84 l white sauce, 1 qt/947 ml grated Cheddar, 2 tbsp/30 ml Worcestershire sauce, 1 tbsp/15 ml prepared mustard, and 2 cups/474 ml tomato puree.	Fish, rice, macaroni

Béchamel Sauce
5 qt/4.73 l

Metric		Ingredients	U.S.	
Weight	Volume		Weight	Volume
2.72 kg	2.84 l	Chicken Broth	6 lb	3 qt
227 g	355 ml	Onions, chopped	8 oz	1 ½ cups
28 g	60 ml	Peppercorns	1 oz	4 tbsp
227 g	355 ml	Carrots, chopped	8 oz	1 ½ cups
	4 leaves	Bay Leaves		4 leaves
227 g	474 ml	Celery, chopped	8 oz	2 cups
454 g	474 ml	Shortening	1 lb	2 cups
283 g	592 ml	Flour, all-purpose	10 oz	2 ½ cups
1.82 kg	1.89 l	Milk, hot	4 lb	2 qt
38 g	40 ml	Salt	1 ⅓ oz	2 ⅔ tbsp
	5 ml	Pepper		1 tsp
	⅝ ml	Cayenne Pepper		⅛ tsp

Procedure

1. Combine stock, bay leaves, and vegetables. Simmer 30 minutes. Strain. Save liquid.
2. Melt shortening in top of double boiler. Add flour and stir until smooth. Add 2 qt/1.89 l of strained stock, stirring constantly until mixture is thickened and the flour has lost its raw taste.

3. Add hot milk and seasonings.

Note: 6 oz/170 g Chicken Soup Base and 3 qt/2.84 l water may be used in place of the chicken broth.

Table 13
Modifications for Béchamel Sauce
(1 gal/3.79 l)

Name	Ingredients	Use
à la King	2 ½ qt/2.36 l Béchamel sauce, 1 qt/947 ml sliced, sautéed mushrooms, 1 cup/237 ml minced green peppers, ⅔ cup/158 ml pimiento cut in strips, ½ cup/118 ml slightly beaten egg yolks, 1 cup/237 ml cream. Cook until thickened. Remove from heat.	Chicken, ham, eggs, seafood
Almond	3 qt/2.84 l Béchamel sauce, 1 qt/947 ml blanched, slivered almonds (toasted), ¼ cup/59 ml lemon juice, ¼ tsp/1 ¼ ml nutmeg.	Chicken, fish, vegetables
Asparagus	3 qt/2.84 l Béchamel sauce, 1 qt/947 ml fresh asparagus cut into ⅜-in/.95 cm slices and cooked until crisp and tender.	Eggs, omelets, timbales
Bacon	3 qt/2.84 l Béchamel sauce, 1 qt/947 ml chopped cooked bacon.	Eggs, fish, vegetables
Carrot-Chive	3 qt/2.84 l Béchamel sauce, 1 cup/237 ml chopped, sautéed young onions, 3 cups/711 ml minced carrots, 1 cup/237 ml chopped chives.	Meat or fish loaves
Celery-Corn-Pepper	2 ½ qt/2.37 l Béchamel sauce, 1 qt/947 ml finely diced celery sautéed with 2 cups/474 ml chopped green pepper. Add 2 cups/474 ml drained whole kernel corn.	Meat or fish loaves
Eggs and Ham	2 ½ qt/2.37 l Béchamel sauce, 1 qt/947 ml chopped hard-cooked eggs, 1 tbsp/15 ml Worcestershire sauce, and 2 cups/474 ml diced ham.	Biscuits, cornbread, rice, toast
Ham and Peas	3 qt/2.84 l Béchamel sauce, 3 cups/711 ml diced ham, and 3 cups/711 ml cooked green peas.	Corn fritters, rice
Meat	3 qt/2.84 l Béchamel sauce, 2 tbsp/30 ml Worcestershire sauce, and one of the following: 1 qt/947 ml chipped beef, diced; 1 ½ qt/1.42 l cooked beef, diced; 1 qt/947 ml cooked ham, diced; 1 ½ qt/ 1.42 l cooked ground beef; 2 cups/474 ml chopped cooked crisp bacon and 2 cups/474 ml crisp sautéed chicken livers; 1 qt/947 ml sliced frankfurters; 1qt/947 ml diced salami; or 1 qt/947 ml browned sausage	Good meat extender with rice, biscuits, and pastas, or on toast
Mushroom	2 ½ qt/2.37 l Béchamel sauce and 2 qt/1.89 l sliced, sautéed fresh mushrooms.	Meats, fish, poultry
Mornay	3 qt/2.84 l Béchamel sauce, 2 cups/474 ml shredded Swiss cheese, 2 cups/474 ml grated Parmesan cheese, ¼ tsp/1 ¼ ml nutmeg.	Eggs, fish, poultry
Newburg	2 ½ qt/2.37 l Béchamel sauce, 1 ½ qt/1.43 l crabmeat, lobster, or shrimp, 1 cup/237 ml Sherry wine. Heat well, then add 8 beaten egg yolks mixed with 1 cup/237 ml cream. Stir and cook slowly until thickened. Remove from heat.	Toast, pastry cups, rice
Ravigote	3 ½ qt/3.31 l Béchamel sauce, ⅓ cup/79 ml chopped chives, ⅓ cup/79 ml chopped parsley, ⅓ cup/79 ml chopped green onion, and ¾ cup/178 ml tarragon vinegar.	Chicken, fish, crabmeat
Tomato	3 ¾ qt/3.56 l Béchamel sauce, 1 cup/237 ml tomato paste, ¼ cup/59 ml minced fresh basil or tarragon.	Eggs, veal

VELOUTÉ SAUCE

Velouté sauces are made in the same manner as white sauce, except that light-colored meat or chicken stock is substituted for milk in the recipe. The stock may be made with 4 to 6 ounces (114 to 170 grams) soup base and 1 gallon (3.79 liters) of hot water, if regular stock is not available.

Table 14
Modifications for Velouté Sauce
Approx. 1 gal/3.79 l

Name	Ingredients	Use
Allemande	3 ½ qt/3.31 l velouté sauce, 12 slightly beaten egg yolks mixed with 1 ½ cups/355 ml cream. Cook until thickened and add ¼ cup/59 ml lemon juice. Remove from heat.	Fish, poultry, vegetables
Caper	3 ¾ qt/3.56 l velouté sauce, 1 ½ cups/355 ml capers.	Fish, veal, lamb
Supreme	3 ½ qt/3.31 l velouté sauce, 2 cups/474 ml whipping cream beaten in until sauce is of desired consistency. Add 3 tbsp/45 ml lemon juice.	Eggs, fish, poultry, vegetables
Soubise	2 qt/1.89 l velouté sauce. Cook 3 qt/2.84 l sliced white onions until soft. Drain and put through sieve. Add pulp to sauce.	Pork, lamb, veal

BROWN SAUCE (ESPAGNOLE)

Brown Sauce has the rich flavor of well-browned meat, mixed with vegetables (mirepoix) and seasonings (bouquet garni or sachet). The mixed vegetables may include carrots, onions, turnips, celery, green peppers, and leeks. Parsley, thyme, basil, bay leaf, marjoram, and sometimes rosemary are popular herbs suitable for flavoring brown stock. A sweet-flavored fat (roast drippings or hydrogenated shortening) may be used for the roux. The flour is blended with the melted fat and allowed to cook until it becomes a uniform nut-brown in color. The proportions of fat, flour, liquid, and seasonings plus the procedures given for white sauce may be followed when making brown sauce.

Table 15
Modifications for Brown Sauce
Approx. 1 gal/3.79 l

Name	Ingredients	Use
Almond Gravy	3 qt/2.84 l brown sauce, 1 qt/947 ml sliced almonds.	Roast veal or turkey
Bacon Gravy	3 qt/2.84 l brown sauce, 1 qt/947 ml chopped crisp bacon.	Roast pork, chicken
Bordelaise	3 ½ qt/3.31 l brown sauce, 1 cup/237 ml sautéed minced onion, 1 cup/237 ml chopped mushrooms, 1 tbsp/15 ml chopped tarragon leaves, ½ cup/118 ml lemon juice, 1 cup/237 ml red wine.	Steak, roasts
Giblet Gravy	2 qt/1.89 l brown sauce, 2 qt/1.89 l chopped poultry livers and gizzards	Roast poultry
Mexican	2 ½ qt/2.37 l brown sauce, 1 ½ cups/355 ml minced onion, 1 cup/237 ml minced green pepper, 3 cloves minced garlic, 1 cup/237 ml minced celery, 1 qt/947 ml tomato catsup. Bring to boiling and simmer slowly until vegetables are cooked.	Fish, meats, omelets
Piquant	3 ½ qt/3.31 l brown sauce, 1 ½ cups/355 ml chopped sweet pickles, ¾ cup/178 ml capers, ¼ cup/59 ml vinegar, ½ cup/118 ml minced onion.	Pork, fish, tongue, boiled beef
Provençale	3 qt/2.84 l brown sauce, 1 qt/947 ml chopped fresh tomatoes, 6 cloves of garlic, minced.	Meats, rice, pastas, vegetables
Robert	3 ¼ qt/3.08 l brown sauce, 1 ½ cups/355 ml minced onion, ¾ cup/178 ml prepared mustard, 1 cup/237 ml hamburger relish, 3 tbsp/45 ml vinegar.	Hamburgers, pork, ham

SWEET SAUCES

Warm Spiced Cream
1 gal/3.79 l

Metric		Ingredients	U.S.	
Weight	Volume		Weight	Volume
3.63 kg	3.79 l	Heavy Cream	8 lb	4 qt
114 g	118 ml	Sugar	4 oz	½ cup
	12 cloves	Cloves, whole		12 cloves
7 g	20 ml	Cinnamon, ground		4 tsp
4 g	10 ml	Nutmeg, ground		2 tsp
9 g	10 ml	Vanilla		2 tsp

Procedure

1. Combine all ingredients except vanilla and heat to boiling.

2. Remove from heat. Add vanilla and remove cloves.
Note: Serve hot on apple pie, cobbler, or dumplings.

Fresh Peach Foamy Sauce
1 gal/3.79 l

Metric		Ingredients	U.S.	
Weight	Volume		Weight	Volume
1.82 kg	2.84 l	Peaches, fresh, E. P.	4 lb	3 qt
454 g	474 ml	Butter or Margarine	1 lb	2 cups
1.36 kg	1.54 l	Sugar	3 lb	6 ½ cups
255 g	237 ml	Egg Yolks, beaten (12 med)	9 oz	1 cup
	2 ½ ml	Salt		½ tsp
28 g	30 ml	Vanilla	1 oz	2 tbsp
340 g	355 ml	Egg Whites, stiffly beaten (12 med)	12 oz	1 ½ cups

Procedure

1. Pare peaches and steam them without water until soft. Mash peaches and save all liquid.
2. Put butter or margarine, sugar, egg yolks, and salt in top of double boiler. Cook, stirring constantly, until thick.

3. Remove from heat. Add vanilla. Cool slightly and fold in beaten egg whites and peaches.

Melba Sauce
1 gal/3.79 l

| Metric | | Ingredients | U.S. | |
Weight	Volume		Weight	Volume
1.82 kg	3.08 l	Raspberries, fresh	4 lb	3 ¼ qt
114 g	118 ml	Sugar	4 oz	½ cup
36 g	60 ml	Cornstarch	1 ¼ oz	¼ cup
681 g	711 ml	Currant Jelly	1 lb, 8 oz	3 cups

Procedure

1. Crush berries. Heat berries and juice. Blend sugar and cornstarch. Add a little of the juice to mix, then stir into hot berries. Cook, stirring, until thickened and cornstarch is clear.

2. Stir or crush the jelly. Stir into the hot mixture until melted.

Mandarin Apricot Sauce
6 qt/5.68 l

| Metric | | Ingredients | U.S. | |
Weight	Volume		Weight	Volume
454 g	947 ml	Apricots, dried	1 lb	1 qt
1.82 kg	1.89 l	Water	4 lb	2 qt
4.08 kg	3.79 l	Apricot Nectar	9 lb	4 qt
907 g	947 ml	Mandarin Oranges	2 lb	1 qt
567 g	592 ml	Sugar	1 lb, 4 oz	2 ½ cups
71 g	118 ml	Cornstarch	2 ½ oz	½ cup
	2 ½ ml	Salt		½ tsp
	2 ½ ml	Nutmeg		½ tsp
114 g	118 ml	Lemon Juice	4 oz	½ cup
57 g	59 ml	Butter	2 oz	¼ cup

Procedure

1. Simmer apricots in water until soft and tender. Chop fine or put through a sieve.
2. Heat nectar, sieved or chopped apricots, and orange sections, finely chopped, to boiling. Blend sugar, cornstarch, salt, and nutmeg. Stir in enough nectar to liquify, then add to hot mixture. Stir and cook until thickened and cornstarch is clear.

3. Remove from heat. Stir in lemon juice and butter.

Note: ½ cup/118 ml orange Curaçao added to the sauce just before serving adds to flavor for use on fruit cocktails or fruit cup desserts.

Apricot Almond Sauce
5 qt/4.74 l

Metric		Ingredients	U.S.		
Weight	Volume		Weight		Volume
2.95 kg	3.08 l	Apricots, pie-pack	6 lb,	8 oz	3 ¼ qt
681 g	711 ml	Orange Juice	1 lb,	8 oz	3 cups
907 g	947 ml	Sugar	2 lb		1 qt
71 g	118 ml	Cornstarch		2 ½ oz	½ cup
	2 ½ ml	Salt			½ tsp
57 g	59 ml	Butter or Margarine		2 oz	¼ cup
114 g	118 ml	Lemon Juice		4 oz	½ cup
283 g	474 ml	Almonds, blanched, slivered		10 oz	2 cups

Procedure

1. Chop or sieve the apricots. Add orange juice and heat to boiling.
2. Blend sugar, cornstarch, and salt. Add a little of the juice to liquify sugar and cornstarch. Stir into hot mixture. Cook, stirring constantly, until mixture thickens and cornstarch is clear.
3. Remove from heat. Stir in butter, lemon juice, and almonds.

Note: Delicious over cottage pudding, Spanish cream, or vanilla blancmange.

Marshmallow Sauce
3 qt/2.84 l

Metric		Ingredients	U.S.		
Weight	Volume		Weight		Volume
14 g	30 ml	Gelatin		½ oz	2 tbsp
114 g	118 ml	Water, cold		4 oz	½ cup
1.25 kg	1.36 l	Sugar	2 lb,	12 oz	5 ¾ cups
454 g	395 ml	Corn Syrup	1 lb		1 ⅔ cups
340 g	355 ml	Water, hot		12 oz	1 ½ cups
9 g	10 ml	Vanilla		⅓ oz	2 tsp

Procedure

1. Soften gelatin in cold water.
2. Combine sugar, corn syrup, and hot water. Heat to 220°F/104°C, or until it will form a soft ball in cold water. Add gelatin and stir until it is dissolved.
3. Transfer to beater bowl and beat until light (about 10 min). Add vanilla and blend.

Note: If sauce becomes too stiff, it may be thinned with hot water.

Orange Sauce
3 qt/2.84 l

Metric		Ingredients	U.S.		
Weight	Volume		Weight		Volume
1.36 kg	1.42 l	Water	3 lb		1 ½ qt
1.13 kg	1.24 l	Sugar	2 lb,	8 oz	5 ¼ cups
114 g	177 ml	Cornstarch		4 oz	¾ cup
	2 ½ ml	Cinnamon			½ tsp
	2 ½ ml	Salt			½ tsp
681 g	711 ml	Water, cold	1 lb,	8 oz	3 cups
567 g	592 ml	Orange Juice	1 lb,	4 oz	2 ½ cups
21 g	58 ml	Orange Rind, grated		¾ oz	¼ cup
76 g	79 ml	Lemon Juice		2 ⅔ oz	⅓ cup
227 g	237 ml	Butter or Margarine		8 oz	1 cup

Procedure

1. Heat water to boiling.
2. Mix sugar, cornstarch, cinnamon, and salt. Stir in cold water and add mixture to boiling water. Cook, stirring, until thickened and the cornstarch is clear.
3. Add butter or margarine. Remove from heat. Add juices and orange rind.

Butterscotch Sauce
1 gal/3.79 l

Metric		Ingredients	U.S.		
Weight	Volume		Weight		Volume
1.47 kg	2.37 l	Brown Sugar	3 lb,	4 oz	2 ½ qt
1.59 kg	1.23 l	Corn Syrup, dark	3 lb,	8 oz	4 ¾ cups
283 g	296 ml	Butter or Margarine		10 oz	1 ¼ cups
9 g	10 ml	Salt		⅓ oz	2 tsp
1.47 kg	1.54 l	Evaporated Milk	3 lb,	4 oz	6 ½ cups

Procedure

1. Boil sugar, syrup, butter or margarine, and salt until a drop will form a firm ball in cold water.
2. Remove from heat and partially cool. Gradually add milk, stirring constantly. Cool.

Note: Use on puddings and ice cream.

Ginger Fruit Sauce
1 gal/3.79 l

| Metric | | Ingredients | U.S. | |
Weight	Volume		Weight	Volume
2.27 kg	2.37 l	Sugar	5 lb	2 ½ qt
1.82 kg	1.89 l	Water	4 lb	2 qt
	10 ml	Salt		2 tsp
85 g	178 ml	Lemon Rind, in fine strips	3 oz	¾ cup
170 g	474 ml	Orange Rind, in fine strips	6 oz	2 cups
57 g	59 ml	Ginger, crystallized, chopped	2 oz	¼ cup
227 g	237 ml	Maraschino Cherries, chopped	8 oz	1 cup
57 g	118 ml	Cornstarch	2 oz	½ cup
227 g	237 ml	Maraschino Cherry Juice	8 oz	1 cup
170 g	178 ml	Lemon Juice	6 oz	¾ cup
340 g	355 ml	Orange Juice	12 oz	1 ½ cups

Procedure

1. Combine sugar, water, salt, and lemon and orange rinds. Cook slowly until rinds are clear and tender. Add ginger and simmer 15 minutes. Add cherries.
2. Blend cornstarch with maraschino cherry juice. Add to hot mixture. Cook until thickened and the cornstarch is clear.
3. Remove from heat. Add lemon and orange juices. Chill and serve with ice cream or puddings.

Note: 12 oz/340 g slivered, blanched almonds may be added.

Scotch Sauce
3 qt/2.84 l

| Metric | | Ingredients | U.S. | |
Weight	Volume		Weight	Volume
567 g	789 ml	Brown Sugar	1 lb, 4 oz	3 ⅓ cups
1.24 kg	1.07 l	Corn Syrup	2 lb, 12 oz	4 ½ cups
170 g	178 ml	Butter or Margarine	6 oz	¾ cup
1.02 kg	1.07 l	Light Cream	2 lb, 4 oz	4 ½ cups

Procedure

1. Combine brown sugar, corn syrup, and butter or margarine. Boil for 5 minutes, stirring until sugar is dissolved.
2. Add cream and bring to a brisk boil.

Note: Serve hot or cold on ice cream. Sauce thickens as it stands. It may be thinned with milk or water.

Hawaiian Fruit Sauce
1 gal/3.79 l

Metric		Ingredients	U.S.		
Weight	Volume		Weight		Volume
681 g	1.07 l	Dates, pitted, chopped	1 lb,	8 oz	4 ½ cups
681 g	711 ml	Sugar	1 lb,	8 oz	3 cups
454 g	474 ml	Water	1 lb		2 cups
907 g	1.18 l	Oranges, finely cubed	2 lb		5 cups
454 g	711 ml	Bananas, finely cubed	1 lb		3 cups
681 g	711 ml	Pineapple, crushed	1 lb,	8 oz	3 cups
76 g	79 ml	Lemon Juice		2 ⅔ oz	⅓ cup
	2 ½ ml	Salt			½ tsp

Procedure

1. Combine dates, sugar, and water. Cook until dates are tender. Cool.
2. Add remaining ingredients, including juice from pineapple and cubing of oranges. Mix well.

Note: May be used as pudding or ice cream sauce or filling for cake.

Brown Sugar Sauce
3 qt/2.84 l

Metric		Ingredients	U.S.		
Weight	Volume		Weight		Volume
1.36 kg	1.89 l	Brown Sugar	3 lb		2 qt
57 g	97 ml	Cornstarch		2 oz	6 ½ tbsp
567 g	474 ml	Corn Syrup, light	1 lb	4 oz	2 cups
1.36 kg	1.42 l	Water, boiling	3 lb		1 ½ qt
454 g	474 ml	Butter or Margarine	1 lb		2 cups
	5 ml	Salt			1 tsp
37 g	30 ml	Vinegar		1 ⅓ oz	2 tbsp
9 g	10 ml	Vanilla		⅓ oz	2 tsp

Procedure

1. Mix brown sugar and cornstarch. Combine corn syrup and boiling water and heat to boiling. Stir in sugar and cornstarch. Continue cooking for 8 minutes.

2. Remove from heat. Stir in remaining ingredients.

Tutti-Frutti Sauce
2 ½ qt/2.36 l

| Metric | | Ingredients | U.S. | |
Weight	Volume		Weight	Volume
1.02 kg	1.07 l	Water	2 lb, 4 oz	4 ½ cups
964 g	1.07 l	Sugar	2 lb, 2 oz	4 ½ cups
793 g	889 ml	Pineapple, crushed	1 lb, 12 oz	1 no. 2 ½ can
340 g	355 ml	Maraschino Cherries, chopped	12 oz	1 ½ cups
227 g	355 ml	Raisins, chopped or ground	8 oz	1 ½ cups
227 g	474 ml	Pecans, chopped	8 oz	2 cups
	2 ½ ml	Salt		½ tsp

Procedure

1. Boil water and sugar for 15 minutes.
2. Drain pineapple and add with remaining ingredients to the sugar mixture.

3. Simmer for 2 minutes.

Note: A good sauce for cottage pudding, cake, or ice cream.

Nutmeg Sauce
1 gal/3.79 l

| Metric | | Ingredients | U.S. | |
Weight	Volume		Weight	Volume
907 kg	1.26 l	Brown Sugar	2 lb	5 ⅓ cups
454 g	474 ml	Granulated Sugar	1 lb	2 cups
92 g	178 ml	Cornstarch	3 ¼ oz	¾ cup
	7 ½ ml	Salt		1 ½ tsp
907 g	947 ml	Water, cold	2 lb	1 qt
1.82 kg	1.89 l	Water, boiling	4 lb	2 qt
454 g	474 ml	Butter or Margarine	1 lb	2 cups
	10 ml	Nutmeg		2 tsp
57 g	59 ml	Vanilla	2 oz	¼ cup

Procedure

1. Blend sugars, cornstarch, and salt. Add cold water and mix. Add to boiling water. Cook, stirring, until cornstarch is done. Add butter or margarine and nutmeg.

2. Remove from heat and add vanilla.

Note: A good sauce for apple deserts such as cobbler.

Hard Sauce
3 qt/2.84 l

Metric		Ingredients	U.S.	
Weight	Volume		Weight	Volume
567 g	592 ml	Butter or Margarine	1 lb, 4 oz	2 ½ cups
2.27 kg	3.56 l	Powdered Sugar	5 lb	3 ¾ qt
170 g	178 ml	Water, boiling	6 oz	¾ cup
510 g	533 ml	Eggs, separated (9 lge)	1 lb, 2 oz	2 ¼ cups
14 g	15 ml	Vanilla	½ oz	1 tbsp
	10 ml	Lemon Extract		2 tsp

Procedure

1. Cream butter or margarine and powdered sugar.
2. Add boiling water slowly to beaten egg yolks and continue beating until light and lemon colored. Add to creamed mixture.

3. Fold in egg whites, beaten stiff but not dry. Add extracts.

Note: This has a lighter consistency than regular hard sauce.

Custard Sauce
1 gal/3.79 l

Metric		Ingredients	U.S.	
Weight	Volume		Weight	Volume
681 g	711 ml	Sugar	1 lb, 8 oz	3 cups
106 g	178 ml	Cornstarch	3 ¾ oz	¾ cup
	5 ml	Salt		1 tsp
2.72 kg	2.84 l	Milk	6 lb	3 qt
283 g	267 ml	Egg Yolks, slightly beaten (14 med)	10 oz	1 ⅛ cups
454 g	474 ml	Cream	1 lb	2 cups
170 g	178 ml	Butter or Margarine	6 oz	¾ cup
14 g	15 ml	Vanilla	½ oz	1 tbsp

Procedure

1. Blend sugar, cornstarch, and salt. Gradually stir in milk. Cook at medium heat, stirring until mixture begins to bubble. Continue cooking, stirring, for 2 minutes. Remove from heat.
2. Stir a little of the hot mixture into slightly beaten egg yolks, then stir yolks into hot mixture and continue cooking for 2 minutes.
3. Stir in cream and continue beating for 1 minute. Remove from heat. Add butter or margarine and vanilla. Stir until butter is melted.

Note: A sauce to add rich flavor to whipped desserts, such as prune whip.

Pineapple Sauce
1 gal/3.79 l

| Metric | | Ingredients | U.S. | |
Weight	Volume		Weight	Volume
142 g	237 ml	Cornstarch	5 oz	1 cup
793 g	829 ml	Sugar	1 lb, 12 oz	3 ½ cups
	5 ml	Salt		1 tsp
2.04 kg	2.13 l	Pineapple Juice	4 lb, 8 oz	2 ¼ qt
227 g	237 ml	Butter or Margarine	8 oz	1 cup
1.51 kg	1.42 l	Pineapple, crushed	3 lb, 5 ½ oz	1 ½ qt
	5 ml	Lemon Rind, grated		1 tsp
114 g	118 ml	Lemon Juice	4 oz	½ cup

Procedure

1. Blend cornstarch, sugar, and salt. Mix with pineapple juice. Cook until cornstarch is done and mixture thickened. Add butter or margarine.

2. Remove from heat. Add pineapple, lemon rind, and juice.

Note: Good on puddings but not sweet enough for ice cream.

Lemon Sauce
1 gal/3.79 l

| Metric | | Ingredients | U.S. | |
Weight	Volume		Weight	Volume
2.72 kg	2.84 l	Water	6 lb	3 qt
907 g	947 ml	Sugar	2 lb	1 qt
	5 ml	Salt		1 tsp
85 g	158 ml	Cornstarch	3 oz	⅔ cup
18 g	30 ml	Lemon Rind, grated	⅔ oz	2 tbsp
227 g	237 ml	Eggs, beaten (4 lge)	8 oz	1 cup
340 g	355 ml	Lemon Juice	12 oz	1 ½ cups
57 g	59 ml	Butter or Margarine	2 oz	¼ cup

Procedure

1. Heat water to boiling. Blend sugar, salt, and cornstarch. Moisten with the hot water and add to the boiling water, stirring constantly until mixture is thick and cornstarch has lost its raw taste. Add lemon rind.

2. Add beaten eggs, first adding a small amount of hot mixture to the eggs, stirring constantly. Cook for 5 minutes.

3. Remove from heat. Add lemon juice and butter or margarine.

Chocolate Sauce I

1 gal/3.79 l

Metric		Ingredients	U.S.	
Weight	Volume		Weight	Volume
681 g	711 ml	Chocolate, unsweetened	1 lb, 8 oz	3 cups
681 g	711 ml	Butter or Margarine	1 lb, 8 oz	3 cups
425 g	355 ml	Corn Syrup	15 oz	1 ½ cups
1.82 kg	3.55 l	Powdered Sugar	4 lb	3 ¾ qt
681 g	711 ml	Evaporated Milk	1 lb, 8 oz	3 cups
	5 ml	Salt		1 tsp
28 g	30 ml	Vanilla	1 oz	2 tbsp

Procedure

1. Melt chocolate and butter or margarine in double boiler over hot water. Stir in corn syrup. Add sugar and stir until smooth.
2. Add milk and salt. Heat and stir until well-blended and smooth. Remove from heat and add vanilla.

Note: This sauce may be used either hot or cold, and may be stored in refrigerator. Reheat over hot water to serve hot, and if thicker than desired, dilute with cream, syrup, or hot water.

Chocolate Sauce II

1 gal/3.79 l

Metric		Ingredients	U.S.	
Weight	Volume		Weight	Volume
2.72 kg	2.84 l	Sugar	6 lb	3 qt
340 g	711 ml	Cocoa, unsweetened	12 oz	3 cups
	10 ml	Salt		2 tsp
	7 ½ ml	Cream of Tartar		1 ½ tsp
454 g	474 ml	Milk	1 lb	2 cups
1.36 kg	1.42 l	Cream	3 lb	1 ½ qt
170 g	118 ml	Corn Syrup, dark	6 oz	½ cup
21 g	22 ml	Vanilla	¾ oz	1 ½ tbsp

Procedure

1. Blend sugar, cocoa, salt, and cream of tartar. Add milk, cream, and corn syrup gradually until well blended. Heat.
2. Boil until thick. Remove from heat. Cool. Add vanilla.

Relishes

Philadelphia Relish
1 gal/3.79 l

Metric		Ingredients	U.S.		
Weight	Volume		Weight		Volume
1.36 kg	2.84 l	Cabbage, chopped medium fine	3 lb		3 qt
454 g	829 ml	Green Pepper, chopped	1 lb		3 ½ cups
227 g	296 ml	Pimiento, chopped		8 oz	1 ¼ cups
681 g	1.07 l	Celery, chopped	1 lb,	8 oz	4 ½ cups
5 g	11 ml	Celery Seed			2 ¼ tsp
3 g	5 ml	Mustard Seed			1 tsp
28 g	30 ml	Salt		1 oz	2 tbsp
397 g	533 ml	Brown Sugar		14 oz	2 ¼ cups
227 g	237 ml	Vinegar		8 oz	1 cup

Procedure

1. Combine and chill all chopped vegetables.
2. Combine remaining ingredients and pour over vegetables just before serving.

Tomato-Cucumber Relish
1 gal/3.79 l

Metric		Ingredients	U.S.		
Weight	Volume		Weight		Volume
1.24 kg	1.42 l	Tomatoes, E.P.	2 lb, 12 oz		1 ½ qt
227 g	474 ml	Celery, E.P.		8 oz	2 cups
1.47 kg	2.36 l	Cucumbers, E.P.	3 lb, 4 oz		2 ½ qt
114 g	158 ml	Brown Sugar		4 oz	⅔ cup
57 g	60 ml	Salt		2 oz	4 tbsp
737 g	889 ml	Vinegar	1 lb, 10 oz		3 ¾ cups
19 g	60 ml	Mustard Seed		⅔ oz	2 tbsp

Procedure

1. Pare and dice vegetables in ¼-in pieces. Add remaining ingredients. Mix well.

Note: Relish will keep for a month under refrigeration.

Cucumber Relish

1 gal/3.79 l

| Metric | | Ingredients | U.S. | | |
Weight	Volume		Weight		Volume
2.04 kg	2.37 l	Cucumbers, finely chopped	4 lb,	8 oz	2 ½ qt
1.36 kg	1.89 l	Onions, finely chopped	3 lb		2 qt
227 g	474 ml	Celery, finely chopped		8 oz	2 cups
681 g	828 ml	Red and Green Peppers, finely chopped	1 lb,	8 oz	3 ½ cups
35 g	37 ml	Flour, pastry		1 ¼ oz	2 ½ tbsp
510 g	533 ml	Sugar	1 lb,	2 oz	2 ¼ cups
3 g	6 ¼ ml	Celery Seed			1 ¼ tsp
	6 ¼ ml	Turmeric			1 ¼ tsp
	5 ml	Salt			1 tsp
1.02 kg	1.07 l	Vinegar	2 lb,	4 oz	4 ½ cups

Procedure

1. Mix finely chopped vegetables together. Cover with salt water (1 tbsp/15 ml salt to 1 qt/947 ml water). Let stand overnight.
2. Let vegetables drain while preparing remainder of recipe.
3. Combine dry ingredients. Add vinegar and boil 5 minutes. Add well-drained vegetables and boil for 10 minutes. Cool.

Note: A tasty relish for hamburgers.

Rhode Island Tomato Relish

1 gal/3.79 l

| Metric | | Ingredients | U.S. | | |
Weight	Volume		Weight		Volume
1.70 kg	1.89 l	Tomatoes, ripe, peeled, chopped, and drained	3 lb,	12 oz	2 qt
227 g	355 ml	Onions, chopped		8 oz	1 ½ cups
454 g	947 ml	Celery, chopped	1 lb		1 qt
114 g	237 ml	Green Pepper, chopped		4 oz	1 cup
227 g	237 ml	Sugar		8 oz	1 cup
64 g	70 ml	Salt		2 ¼ oz	4 ⅔ tbsp
	2 ½ ml	White Pepper			½ tsp
28 g	50 ml	Mustard Seed		1 oz	3 ⅓ tbsp
567 g	592 ml	Vinegar	1 lb,	4 oz	2 ½ cups

Procedure

1. Combine all ingredients. Put in sterilized containers.
2. Let stand at least 24 hours before using.

Spiced Prunes
1 gal/3.79 l

Metric		Ingredients	U.S.	
Weight	Volume		Weight	Volume
2.04 kg	2.60 l	Prunes, dried	4 lb, 8 oz	2¾ qt
454 g	474 ml	Vinegar	1 lb	2 cups
114 g	118 ml	Water	4 oz	½ cup
	2½ ml	Salt		½ tsp
907 g	1.26 l	Brown Sugar	2 lb	5⅓ cups
28 g	5 5.08-cm	Cinnamon Sticks	1 oz	5 2-in
14 g	30 ml	Cloves, whole	½ oz	2 tbsp
283 g	2	Lemons, thinly sliced	10 oz	2

Procedure

1. Soak prunes overnight. Combine vinegar, water, salt, and sugar and heat to slow boil.
2. Add prunes and other ingredients. Cook slowly until tender (about 30 min). Pack in jars.

Note: Excellent garnish for meats.

Hot Buttered Apples
50 Servings (4¾ oz/135 g)
Bake, 400°F/205°C, 15 min

Metric		Ingredients	U.S.	
Weight	Volume		Weight	Volume
5.90 kg	6.15 l	Apples, pie-pack, drained	13 lb	6½ qt
283 g	296 ml	Butter or Margarine	10 oz	1¼ cups
283 g	296 ml	Sugar, granulated	10 oz	1¼ cups
283 g	395 ml	Brown Sugar	10 oz	1⅔ cups
	5 ml	Cinnamon		1 tsp
	2½ ml	Salt		½ tsp

Procedure

1. Place apples in serving pans (12 × 20 × 2 in).
2. Combine remaining ingredients and sprinkle over the apples.
3. Bake at 400 °F/205°C until heated through.

Corn Relish
1 gal/3.79 l

Metric		Ingredients	U.S.	
Weight	Volume		Weight	Volume
1.24 kg	1.30 l	Corn, whole kernel	2 lb, 12 oz	5 ½ cups
793 g	2.21 l	Cabbage, finely chopped	1 lb, 12 oz	2 ⅓ qt
454 g	947 ml	Green Pepper, chopped	1 lb	1 qt
114 g	157 ml	Pimiento, chopped	4 oz	⅔ cup
1.02 kg	1.07 l	Vinegar (50 grain)	2 lb, 4 oz	4 ½ cups
21 g	22 ml	Salt	¾ oz	1 ⅓ tbsp
681 g	947 ml	Brown Sugar	1 lb, 8 oz	1 qt
21 g	45 ml	Mustard, dry	¾ oz	3 tbsp

Procedure

1. Combine all ingredients and mix well. Let stand an hour in refrigerator to season. It is perishable and should be used at once.

Note: In order to keep relish, add 1 cup/237 ml more vinegar and boil for 30 minutes. Seal in sterilized jars.

Cooked Cranberry Relish
l gal/3.79 l

Metric		Ingredients	U.S.	
Weight	Volume		Weight	Volume
1.36 kg	1.42 l	Cranberry, pulp	3 lb	1 ½ qt
1.21 kg	1.42 l	Sugar	2 lb, 11 oz	1 ½ qt
170 g	179 ml	Orange Juice	6 oz	¾ cup
	5 ml	Orange Rind, grated		1 tsp
	2 ½ ml	Lemon Rind, grated		½ tsp
43 g	45 ml	Lemon Juice	1 ½ oz	3 tbsp
170 g	355 ml	Nuts, chopped	6 oz	1 ½ cups
340 g	355 ml	Pineapple, diced, drained	12 oz	1 ½ cups

Procedure

1. Cook cranberries until skins pop; sieve. Add sugar and heat to boiling. Add remaining ingredients and simmer for 3 minutes.

2. Remove from heat and cool thoroughly.

Raw Cranberry Relish
1 gal/3.79 l

Metric		Ingredients	U.S.	
Weight	Volume		Weight	Volume
1.98 kg	4.26 l	Cranberries	4 lb, 6 oz	4½ qt
1.02 kg	7 med	Oranges	2 lb, 4 oz	7 med
1.47 kg	1.66 l	Sugar	3 lb, 4 oz	7 cups

Procedure

1. Quarter oranges and grind with cranberries.
2. Add sugar and allow to stand overnight.

Note: Chopped walnuts (12 oz/340 g) may be added if desired.

Stuffings (or Dressings) for Meat, Fish, and Poultry

Dressing is an accompaniment and should blend well in flavor and texture with the meat, fish, or poultry with which it is served. Turkey, chicken, and veal may have a richer dressing, for example, than pork or goose. Fruit and savory dressings are appetizing with fatty or mild-flavored meats, fish, and poultry. A dry, mealy dressing may be used if a generous amount of sauce or gravy is to be served. Dryness in meat may be offset by using a fluffy (not soggy), moist dressing. When stuffing poultry, meat rolls, and chops, allow for the stuffing to swell during cooking.

It is a good practice to bake dressing separately rather than as stuffing in poultry. When cooked and frozen poultry rolls are used, the rolls maybe sawed into portion slices before thawing. When reheated, scoops of dressing may be arranged in serving pans (12 × 20 × 2 in) and the poultry slices placed on top of the scoops of dressing. Cover the pans with a lid or foil and heat thoroughly in oven at 325°F/163°C. Use a well-flavored soup base for making the gravy. The addition of onion and celery, fruit, or nuts to the stuffing may be desirable if the poultry tends to be too weak in flavor. Bacon, broiled and chopped, may be used to add both crisp texture and flavor.

Table 16
Modifications for Bread Dressing
(Quantities to be used with one recipe of Bread Dressing)

Name	Ingredients	Use
Almond	Add 1 qt/947 ml sliced almonds	Turkey
Almond-Water Chestnut	Add 2 cups/474 ml sliced, toasted almonds and 2 cups/474 ml sliced water chestnuts.	Poultry, veal, pork
Almond-Bacon	Add 2 cups/474 ml sliced almonds and 2 cups/474 ml chopped crisp bacon.	Poultry, veal
Cranberry	Grind 1 qt/947 ml raw cranberries; mix with ½ cup/118 ml sugar. Omit onion and poultry seasoning from dressing recipe.	Pork, veal, poultry
Crabmeat	Omit poultry seasoning and add 1 qt/947 ml flaked crabmeat, 2 cups/474 ml slightly beaten eggs, 2 tbsp/30 ml lemon juice, and 1 tbsp/15 ml Worcestershire sauce.	Fish
English Chestnut	Add 3 cups/711 ml cooked, chopped English chestnuts.	Beef, poultry
Giblet	Add 1 qt/947 ml cooked, chopped giblets.	Poultry
Mushroom	Add 1 qt/947 ml sautéed, sliced mushrooms.	Meats, fish, poultry
Oyster	Drain and chop 3 cups/711 ml oysters, and use with oyster liquor as part of broth.	Poultry

Bread Dressing
12 lb/5.44 kg

| Metric | | Ingredients | U.S. | |
Weight	Volume		Weight	Volume
2.27 kg	10.41 l	Bread, day-old, diced	5 lb	11 qt
454 g	474 ml	Butter or Margarine	1 lb	2 cups
14 g	15 ml	Salt	½ oz	1 tbsp
	10 ml	Pepper		2 tsp
7 g	30 ml	Poultry Seasoning	¼ oz	2 tbsp
454 g	711 ml	Onions, finely chopped	1 lb	3 cups
454 g	947 ml	Celery, finely chopped	1 lb	1 qt
1.82 kg	1.89 l	Broth	4 lb	2 qt

Procedure

1. Sauté onions and celery in butter or margarine until tender.
2. Combine bread, seasonings, and vegetables. Toss lightly together, moistening with broth until well mixed and with a satisfactory degree of moistness.

Note: If crusts are used, chop them very fine. Bacon fat may be substituted for part of the butter or margarine. Broth may be made with 2 qt/1.89 l water and 4 oz/114 g of chicken soup base.

Wild Rice Stuffing
2 gal/7.57 l

| Metric | | Ingredients | U.S. | |
Weight	Volume		Weight	Volume
283 g	474 ml	Onions, finely chopped	10 oz	2 cups
114 g	237 ml	Green Pepper, finely chopped	4 oz	1 cup
142 g	474 ml	Mushrooms (optional)	5 oz	2 cups
454 g	474 ml	Butter or Margarine	1 lb	2 cups
3.63 kg	5.68 l	Wild Rice, cooked	8 lb	6 qt
454 g	947 ml	Giblets, cooked, chopped	1 lb	1 qt
28 g	30 ml	Salt	1 oz	2 tbsp

Procedure

1. Sauté onions, green pepper, and mushrooms in butter or margarine until tender.
2. Mix all ingredients together thoroughly.

Note: Long-grain rice may be substituted for part of wild rice, or this recipe mixed half-and-half with bread dressing. Serve with game or poultry.

Sweet Potato Stuffing
1 gal/3.79 l

Metric		Ingredients	U.S.	
Weight	Volume		Weight	Volume
2.27 kg	2.84 l	Sweet Potatoes, cooked, mashed	5 lb	3 qt
907 g	1.42 l	Apples, pared, chopped	2 lb	1 ½ qt
312 g	355 ml	Brown Sugar	11 oz	1 ½ cups
	5 ml	Salt		1 tsp
33 g	15 ml	Orange Rind, grated		1 tbsp

Procedure

1. Combine all ingredients. Mix well.

Note: Use as stuffing for pork chops.

Cornbread Dressing
8 lb/3.63 kg

Metric		Ingredients	U.S.	
Weight	Volume		Weight	Volume
907 g	2.84 l	Cornbread Crumbs	2 lb	3 qt
681 g	2.84 l	Bread Crumbs, soft	1 lb, 8 oz	3 qt
454 g	474 ml	Butter or Margarine, melted	1 lb	2 cups
14 g	15 ml	Salt	½ oz	1 tbsp
	5 ml	Pepper		1 tsp
	15 ml	Poultry Seasoning		1 tbsp
227 g	237 ml	Eggs, beaten (4 lge)	8 oz	1 cup
454–681 g	474–711 ml	Stock	1–1 ½ lb	2–3 cups
227 g	474 ml	Celery, chopped	8 oz	2 cups
142 g	237 ml	Onions, chopped	5 oz	1 cup
114 g	237 ml	Green Pepper, chopped	4 oz	1 cup
454 g	474 ml	Butter or Margarine	1 lb	2 cups

Procedure

1. Combine bread crumbs, melted butter or margarine, seasonings, and beaten eggs. Add stock to desired degree of moisture.
2. Sauté vegetables in butter or margarine until tender. Mix into dressing, with a tossing rather than a stirring motion.
3. Bake at 350°F/177°C until nicely browned (about 25 to 30 min).

Sausage Stuffing
13 lb/5.90 kg

| Metric | | Ingredients | U.S. | |
Weight	Volume		Weight	Volume
907 g	947 ml	Sausage	2 lb	1 qt
454 g	711 ml	Onions, chopped	1 lb	3 cups
454 g	947 ml	Celery, chopped	1 lb	1 qt
2.27 kg	10.41 l	Bread Crumbs, day-old	5 lb	11 qt
14 g	15 ml	Salt	½ oz	1 tbsp
	15 ml	Poultry Seasoning		1 tbsp
1.82 kg	1.89 l	Broth	4 lb	2 qt

Procedure

1. Sauté sausage until browned. Add onions and celery and cook until tender.

2. Combine crumbs, sausage, and seasonings. Moisten with broth.

Apple and Raisin Stuffing
9 lb/4.08 kg

| Metric | | Ingredients | U.S. | |
Weight	Volume		Weight	Volume
907 g	1.89 l	Apples, pared, diced	2 lb	2 qt
605 g	947 ml	Raisins, small, seedless	1 lb, 5 ⅓ oz	1 qt
1.22 kg	5.68 l	Bread Crumbs	2 lb, 11 oz	6 qt
454 g	711 ml	Onions, finely chopped	1 lb	3 cups
14 g	15 ml	Salt	½ oz	1 tbsp
170 g	178 ml	Sugar	6 oz	¾ cup
	5 ml	Pepper		1 tsp
454 g	474 ml	Butter or Margarine	1 lb	2 cups
454 g	474 ml	Broth	1 lb	2 cups
	10 ml	Cinnamon, ground		2 tsp
	5 ml	Nutmeg, ground		1 tsp
	1 ¼ ml	Cloves, ground		¼ tsp

Procedure

1. Mix ingredients together well.

Note: Apples will add moisture in cooking; therefore, add less broth.

CHAPTER 10 _____ *Salads and Salad Dressings*

Salads are best when made of materials that are garden fresh and freshly dressed to insure crispness and piquancy. They should possess qualities that refresh and stimulate the appetite. Keep the salad materials refrigerated and serve them well-chilled.

Salad Greens Lettuce is a favorite salad green and the several varieties offer choice in both texture and flavor. Iceberg, butter types, loose leaf, and romaine are among the most common. There are other greens, also, that may be used alone or in combination with lettuce. The most popular kinds are cabbage, Chinese cabbage, tender celery leaves, curly chicory, Belgian and French endive, escarole, dandelion greens, nasturtium leaves and stems, parsley, fennel, basil, spinach, and watercress.

Wash all greens thoroughly and drain well. It helps in cleaning and in crisping greens to wash them in warm water. A strong spray of water is useful in cleaning fine indentations in leaves. Loose leaf greens should be separated and washed in a large amount of water. Shake off as much water as possible and let them drain. Store greens for refrigeration so they can continue to drain, with a rack underneath to prevent their standing in water. Cover well to prevent dehydration (in a crisper or with a plastic cover or damp cloth over them).

Protect the crispness of salad greens. Finely shredded lettuce loses crispness quickly and the long shreds are stringy and awkward to eat. Dressing tends to wilt greens and should be added just before serving. Keep salad materials and containers well-refrigerated.

Salad Arrangement Ensure an attractive appearance by arranging the salad to look fresh, crisp, and natural. Simple arrangements are best. Complicated ones create an impression of overhandling of the food. Choose an appropriate container for service and keep the salad in suitable proportion to the container, neither too large nor too small. Clever use of garnishes can make the simplest salads more interesting.

When selecting service containers for salads, consider the type of salad to be served, and choose those that will be appropriate in size, material, and design with other service containers used. Some people favor bowls, and others prefer plates. Salads requiring cutting with a fork are difficult to manage in a bowl. Tossed salads, made of small particles, need to be confined. Bowls are a less formal type of service than plates. Arranged salads look better on plates. Refrigerate containers!

Add interest and color with a decorative garnish. Bright-colored fruits and vegetables, pickles, olives, capers, egg-cuts, shredded meats or poultry, and salad dressings offer much variety from which to choose. A plump, fresh berry, orange segment, or peach slice will give an extra appeal to an ordinary fruit salad. A carrot curl, radish rose, or sprig of watercress may add interest to colorless salads, such as those made of winter cabbage.

Salads

FRUIT SALADS

Ambrosia Salad
50 Servings (4 oz/114 g)

| Metric | | Ingredients | U.S. | |
Weight	Volume		Weight	Volume
1.36 kg	2.13 l	Bananas, chunked	3 lb	2 ¼ qt
114 g	118 ml	Lemon Juice	4 oz	½ cup
2.27 kg	2.84 l	Oranges, diced	5 lb	3 qt
907 g	1.42 l	Grapes, seedless	2 lb	1 ½ qt
907 g	1.42 l	Cooked Fruit Dressing	2 lb	1 ½ qt
170 g	474 ml	Coconut, flaked	6 oz	2 cups

Procedure

1. Sprinkle bananas with lemon juice. Combine fruit and fold into dressing.

2. Arrange on lettuce cups and garnish with coconut.

Apple Knickerbocker
50 Servings (5.25 oz/150 g)

| Metric | | Ingredients | U.S. | |
Weight	Volume		Weight	Volume
1.82 kg	3.79 l	Apples, julienne cut	4 lb	4 qt
1.82 kg	1.89 l	Pineapple Tidbits, drained	4 lb	2 qt
1.36 kg	1.42 l	French Dressing	3 lb	1 ½ qt
1.48 kg	1.89 l	Orange Segments	3 lb, 4 oz	2 qt
1.82 kg	1.89 l	Grapefruit Segments	4 lb	2 qt
454 g	947 ml	Green Pepper, chopped	1 lb	1 qt
340 g	711 ml	Sweet Red Pepper, chopped	12 oz	3 cups

Procedure

1. Combine apple, pineapple, and French dressing. Let stand while sectioning citrus fruit. Drain.
2. Arrange apple and pineapple on lettuce with segments of orange and grapefruit alternately arranged on top.
3. Garnish with mixture of red and green pepper.

Cranberry and Pineapple
48 Servings

Metric		Ingredients	U.S.	
Weight	Volume		Weight	Volume
1.36 kg	3 No. 1 cans	Cranberry Sauce	3 lb	3 No. 1 cans
1.03 kg	3 No. 2 cans	Pineapple, 8-slice can	2 lb, 4 oz	3 No. 2 cans
907 g	4 11-oz cans	Mandarin Oranges	2 lb	4 11-oz cans
1.03 kg	3 No. 2 cans	Grapefruit Segments	2 lb, 4 oz	3 No. 2 cans
1.14 kg	50 cups	Lettuce Cups	2 lb, 8 oz	50 cups
681 g	947 ml	Fruit Salad Dressing	1 lb, 8 oz	1 qt

Procedure

1. Drain fruit. Carefully slide cranberry jelly from cans and slice each into 8 slices.
2. Arrange fruit on salad greens using 2 quarter slices of pineapple and cranberry jelly per portion. Serve with fruit salad dressing.

Carrot Almondine Salad
64 Servings

Metric		Ingredients	U.S.	
Weight	Volume		Weight	Volume
1.02 kg	7–8 apples	Apples, A.P.	2 lb, 4 oz	7–8 apples
227 g	237 ml	Lemon Juice	8 oz	1 cup
2.84 kg	5.92 l	Carrots, shredded	6 lb, 4 oz	6 ¼ qt
510 g	800 ml	Almonds, slivered and toasted	1 lb, 2 oz	3 ⅜ cups
255 g	533 ml	Green Pepper, chopped	9 oz	2 ¼ cups
624 g	652 ml	Salad Dressing	1 lb, 6 oz	2 ¾ cups
454 g	474 ml	Cream	1 lb	2 cups
198 g	207 ml	Vinegar	7 oz	⅞ cup
198 g	207 ml	Sugar	7 oz	⅞ cup
114 g	178 ml	Onion, chopped fine	4 oz	¾ cup
28 g	30 ml	Salt	1 oz	2 tbsp
	20 ml	Poppy Seeds		1 ⅓ tbsp
	⅝ ml	Pepper		⅛ tsp

Procedure

1. Core and chop apples coarsely. Toss with lemon juice to prevent browning. Combine apples, carrots, almonds, and green pepper.
2. Blend salad dressing, cream, vinegar, sugar, onion, salt, poppy seeds, and pepper.
3. Toss carrot mixture lightly with dressing. Scoop salad into lettuce cups with a No. 10 scoop.

Waldorf Salad
50 Servings (3.5 oz/99 g)

| Metric | | Ingredients | U.S. | |
Weight	Volume		Weight	Volume
3.41 kg	6.63 l	Apples, diced	7 lb, 8 oz	7 qt
907 g	1.89 l	Celery, chopped	2 lb	2 qt
681 g	711 ml	Combination Dressing	1 lb, 8 oz	3 cups
57 g	59 ml	Lemon Juice	2 oz	¼ cup
114 g	237 ml	Walnuts, chopped	4 oz	1 cup

Procedure

1. Wash, core, and dice tart, flavorful apples (peeled or unpeeled according to desired color and tenderness of skin). Marinate in salted water. Drain well.
2. Mix with celery, using care not to mash apple dices.
3. Combine salad dressing and lemon juice. Fold into salad.
4. Scoop salad into lettuce cups with a No. 12 dipper. Garnish with nuts, salad cherry, or fresh fruit.

Apple, Orange, and Pineapple
50 Servings (4 oz/114 g)

| Metric | | Ingredients | U.S. | |
Weight	Volume		Weight	Volume
1.82 kg	3.31 l	Apple, diced	4 lb	3 ½ qt
1.48 kg	1.89 l	Oranges, diced	3 lb, 4 oz	2 qt
1.82 kg	1.89 l	Pineapple Tidbits, drained	4 lb	2 qt
681 g	1.89 l	Fruit Salad Dressing	1 lb, 8 oz	2 qt
596 g	947 ml	Dates, cut in strips	1 lb, 5 oz	1 qt

Procedure

1. Combine fruit and fold into salad dressing.
2. Scoop into lettuce cups and garnish with date strips.

Avocado, Grapefruit, and Pineapple
50 Servings (5 oz/142 g)

| Metric | | Ingredients | U.S. | |
Weight	Volume		Weight	Volume
2.72 kg	50 slices	Pineapple, sliced	6 lb	50 slices
1.82 kg	100 slices	Avocado, sliced	4 lb	100 slices
1.82 kg	50 sections	Grapefruit Segments	4 lb	50 sections
907 g	1.89 l	Kumquat, sliced	2 lb	2 qt

Procedure

1. Cut pineapple slice in half and arrange on lettuce cups. Place a slice of avocado on each side of grapefruit segment and arrange between half slices of pineapple.

2. Garnish with sprinkling of kumquat slices. Serve with favorite dressing.

Note: Kiwi slices make an attractive garnish also.

Carrot and Pineapple Salad
50 Servings

| Metric | | Ingredients | U.S. | |
Weight	Volume		Weight	Volume
2.95 kg	3.31 l	Pineapple, sliced	6 lb, 8 oz	50 slices
454 g	474 ml	Mayonnaise	1 lb	2 cups
85 g	90 ml	Lemon Juice	3 oz	6 tbsp
	7 ½ ml	Salt		1 ½ tsp
1.36 kg	2.84 l	Carrots, shredded	3 lb	3 qt
71 g	118 ml	Almonds, blanched and slivered	2 ½ oz	½ cup
	¼ bunch	Parsley, sprigs		¼ bunch

Procedure

1. Arrange pineapple slices on salad greens.
2. Combine mayonnaise, lemon juice, and salt. Mix thoroughly with carrots.

3. Place a No. 30 scoopful of carrots on each pineapple slice. Garnish with slivered almonds and a sprig of parsley.

Carolina Salad
50 Servings (4 oz/114 g)

| Metric | | Ingredients | U.S. | |
Weight	Volume		Weight	Volume
567 g	947 ml	Raisins, seedless	1 lb, 4 oz	1 qt
681 g	711 ml	Sour Cream	1 lb, 8 oz	3 cups
2.16 kg	6.00 l	Cabbage, shredded	4 lb, 12 oz	6 ⅓ qt
1.82 kg	2.84 l	Apples, tart, unpeeled, chopped	4 lb	3 qt
907 g	947 ml	Mayonnaise or Salad Dressing	2 lb	1 qt
28 g	30 ml	Salt	1 oz	2 tbsp

Procedure

1. Mix raisins and sour cream and let stand.
2. Combine all ingredients and chill.

Note: If apples are not tart, add 2 oz/57 g lemon juice.

Frozen Fruit Salad
50 Servings (2 ½ × 2 ¾ in)

Metric		Ingredients	U.S.	
Weight	Volume		Weight	Volume
425 g	474 ml	Cherries, sweet or tart, drained	15 oz	2 cups
1.21 kg	1.42 l	Apricots, canned, chopped	2 lb, 11 oz	6 cups
1.14 kg	1.18 l	Peaches, canned, chopped	2 lb, 8 oz	5 cups
605 g	711 ml	Pears, canned, chopped	1 lb, 5⅓ oz	3 cups
1.36 kg	1.42 l	Pineapple Tidbits	3 lb	6 cups
114 g	474 ml	Marshmallows, chopped	4 oz	2 cups
57 g	59 ml	Lemon Juice	2 oz	¼ cup
454 g	474 ml	Mayonnaise	1 lb	2 cups
227 g	237 ml	Whipping Cream	8 oz	1 cup

Procedure

1. Mix well-drained fruits. Add marshmallows, lemon juice, and mayonnaise.
2. Whip cream until stiff and glossy. Fold into fruit mixture.
3. Place in mold or pour into pudding pans (10 × 16 × 2 ¼ in). Freeze.

Frozen Fruit with Cheese
50 Servings (2 ½ × 2 ¾ in)
Freeze

Metric		Ingredients	U.S.	
Weight	Volume		Weight	Volume
907 g	947 ml	Peaches, diced	2 lb	4 cups
454 g	474 ml	Oranges, diced	1 lb	2 cups
907 g	1.42 l	Bananas, diced	2 lb	1 ½ qt
227 g	474 ml	Nuts, chopped	8 oz	2 cups
454 g	474 ml	Maraschino Cherries, sliced	1 lb	2 cups
454 g	474 ml	Cream Cheese	1 lb	2 cups
227 g	237 ml	Lemon Juice	8 oz	1 cup
454 g	474 ml	Sugar	1 lb	2 cups
681 g	1.42 l	Cooked Fruit Dressing	1 lb, 8 oz	1 ½ qt

Procedure

1. Blend well-drained peaches, oranges, bananas, nuts, and cherries.
2. Cream the cheese with lemon juice. Add sugar. Slowly add salad dressing, blending mixture well.
3. Add to mixed fruits.
4. Pour into molds or into 2 pudding pans (10 × 16 × 2 ¼ in). Freeze.

GELATIN FRUIT SALADS

Lime Jelly Salad
50 Servings

Metric		Ingredients	U.S.		
Weight	Volume		Weight		Volume
567 g	681 ml	Lime Gelatin	1 lb,	4 oz	2 ⅞ cups
2.50 kg	2.60 l	Water, boiling	5 lb,	8 oz	2 ¾ qt
454 g	474 ml	Pineapple Juice	1 lb		2 cups
227 g	237 ml	Lemon Juice		8 oz	1 cup
1.36 kg	1.89 l	Pineapple, crushed, drained	3 lb		2 qt
283 g	889 ml	Coconut		10 oz	3 ¾ cups
340 g	355 ml	Cream Cheese, cubed		12 oz	1 ½ cups

Procedure

1. Dissolve gelatin in boiling water. Add cold juices. Cool.
2. When mixture begins to thicken, fold in crushed pineapple, coconut, and cream cheese.
3. Pour into molds and refrigerate until firm.

Lime Pear Mold
50 Servings

Metric		Ingredients	U.S.		
Weight	Volume		Weight		Volume
681 g	829 ml	Lime Gelatin	1 lb,	8 oz	3 ½ cups
1.82 kg	1.89 l	Water, boiling	4 lb		2 qt
1.82 kg	1.89 l	Pear Syrup and Cold Water	4 lb		2 qt
2.95 kg	3.31 l	Pears, drained and diced	6 lb,	8 oz	1 No. 10 can
114 g	118 ml	Candied Ginger, finely chopped		4 oz	½ cup
340 g	355 ml	Cream Cheese		12 oz	1 ½ cups

Procedure

1. Dissolve gelatin in boiling water. Add remaining syrup and cold water.
2. Chill until gelatin begins to thicken, and pour half of it into a serving pan (12 × 20 × 2 in). Arrange diced pear on top. Sprinkle chopped ginger evenly over the fruit.
3. Soften cream cheese with pear juice or milk. Fold it into the remaining gelatin and pour it over the fruit. Refrigerate until fully set.

Pineapple and Cottage Cheese Salad
50 Servings

| Metric | | Ingredients | U.S. | |
Weight	Volume		Weight	Volume
64 g	135 ml	Gelatin	2 ¼ oz	9 tbsp
1.02 kg	1.07 l	Pineapple Juice	2 lb, 4 oz	4 ½ cups
964 g	1.01 l	Whipping Cream	2 lb, 2 oz	4 ¼ cups
397 g	415 ml	Sugar	14 oz	1 ¾ cups
681 g	711 ml	Cottage Cheese	1 lb, 8 oz	3 cups
510 g	533 ml	Mayonnaise	1 lb, 2 oz	2 ¼ cups
340 g	553 ml	Pecans, chopped	12 oz	2 ⅓ cups
	10 ml	Salt		2 tsp
227 g	474 ml	Green Pepper, diced	8 oz	2 cups
340 g	711 ml	Celery, diced	12 oz	3 cups
142 g	197 ml	Pimiento, finely diced	5 oz	⅝ cup
567 g	1.07 l	Pineapple, crushed, drained	1 lb, 4 oz	4 ½ cups
510 g	533 ml	Lemon Juice	1 lb, 2 oz	2 ¼ cups

Procedure

1. Soak gelatin in 2 cups/474 ml cold pineapple juice. Heat remainder of pineapple juice. Dissolve soaked gelatin in hot juice.
2. Whip cream and whip in sugar. Combine cottage cheese and mayonnaise.
3. Fold whipped cream into cottage cheese mixture. Add pecans, salt, pepper, celery, pimientos, pineapple, lemon juice, and gelatin.
4. Pour into molds and refrigerate until firm.

Raspberry-Applesauce Salad
48 Servings

| Metric | | Ingredients | U.S. | |
Weight	Volume		Weight	Volume
4.08 kg	4.26 l	Applesauce, smooth, thick	9 lb	4 ½ qt
1.14 kg	1.36 l	Raspberry Gelatin	2 lb, 8 oz	5 ¾ cups
681 g	711 ml	Orange Juice	1 lb, 8 oz	3 cups
2.27 kg	2.37 l	7-Up	5 lb	2 ½ qt
681 g	1.42 l	Celery, chopped	1 lb, 8 oz	1 ½ qt
340 g	711 ml	Nuts, chopped (almonds)	12 oz	3 cups

Procedure

1. Heat half of the applesauce and dissolve the gelatin in it. Cool. Add remaining applesauce, orange juice, and 7-Up.
2. Combine celery and nuts and arrange in molds.
3. Pour gelatin mixture over celery and nuts. Refrigerate until firm.

Jellied Grapefruit and Apple Salad
50 Servings

| Metric | | Ingredients | U.S. | |
Weight	Volume		Weight	Volume
567 g	681 ml	Lemon Gelatin	1 lb, 4 oz	2 ⅞ cups
1.36 kg	1.42 l	Grapefruit Juice, boiling	3 lb	1 ½ qt
681 g	711 ml	Water, cold	1 lb, 8 oz	3 cups
454 g	474 ml	Lemon Juice	1 lb	2 cups
340 g	355 ml	Sugar	12 oz	1 ½ cups
9 g	10 ml	Salt	⅓ oz	2 tsp
9 g	15 ml	Lemon Rind, grated	⅓ oz	1 tbsp
1.36 kg	1.42 l	Grapefruit Segments	3 lb	1 ½ qt
454 g	711 ml	Apples, peeled or unpeeled, diced	1 lb	3 cups
227 g	474 ml	Walnuts, chopped	8 oz	2 cups

Procedure

1. Dissolve gelatin in hot grapefruit juice. Add cold water, lemon juice, sugar, salt, and lemon rind. Cool.
2. When mixture begins to thicken, add remaining ingredients.
3. Pour into molds and refrigerate.
4. Garnish with a bright fruit.

Jewel Salad
50 Servings

| Metric | | Ingredients | U.S. | |
Weight	Volume		Weight	Volume
567 g	681 ml	Lime Gelatin	1 lb, 4 oz	2 ⅞ cups
681 g	711 ml	Water, boiling	1 lb, 8 oz	3 cups
340 g	355 ml	Sugar	12 oz	1 ½ cups
170 g	178 ml	Vinegar	6 oz	¾ cup
170 g	178 ml	Lemon Juice	6 oz	¾ cup
793 g	889 ml	Pineapple Juice	1 lb, 12 oz	3 ¾ cups
	10 ml	Salt		2 tsp
765 g	1.42 l	Cucumbers, diced	1 lb, 11 oz	1 ½ qt
1.59 kg	1.66 l	Pineapple, crushed, drained	3 lb, 8 oz	1 ¾ qt

Procedure

1. Dissolve gelatin in boiling water. Add sugar, vinegar, lemon juice, pineapple juice, and salt. Chill until slightly thickened.
2. Add cucumbers and crushed pineapple.
3. Pour into molds and refrigerate until firm.

Note: 6 oz/170 g of slivered almonds added with cucumbers and pineapple is a delicious extra.

Cranberry Salad
50 Servings

Metric		Ingredients	U.S.	
Weight	Volume		Weight	Volume
681 g	829 ml	Cherry Gelatin	1 lb, 8 oz	3 ½ cups
1.82 kg	1.89 l	Water, boiling	4 lb	2 qt
114 g	118 ml	Lemon Juice	4 oz	½ cup
9 g	15 ml	Lemon Rind, grated	⅓ oz	1 tbsp
	10 ml	Salt		2 tsp
1.36 kg	1.42 l	Cranberries, canned, whole	3 lb	1 ½ qt
793 g	711 ml	Pineapple, crushed, undrained	1 lb, 12 oz	3 cups
227 g	474 ml	Walnuts, coarsely chopped	8 oz	2 cups

Procedure

1. Dissolve gelatin in boiling water. Add lemon juice, lemon rind, and salt. Cool.
2. When mixture begins to thicken, add cranberries, pineapple, and walnuts.
3. Pour into molds or pudding pans (10 × 16 × 2 ¼ in). Refrigerate.
4. Unmold or cut into portions and serve on salad greens with fruit salad dressing.

Avocado Cheese Mold
50 Servings

Metric		Ingredients	U.S.	
Weight	Volume		Weight	Volume
76 g	118 ml	Gelatin, granulated	2 ⅔ oz	½ cup
454 g	474 ml	Water, cold	1 lb	2 cups
340 g	415 ml	Lemon Gelatin	12 oz	1 ¾ cups
340 g	415 ml	Lime Gelatin	12 oz	1 ¾ cups
2.72 kg	2.84 l	Water, boiling	6 lb	3 qt
1.82 kg	1.89 l	Cottage Cheese, fine curds	4 lb	2 qt
1.36 kg	1.42 l	Combination Dressing	3 lb	1 ½ qt
1.36 kg	1.42 l	Avocado, ripe, mashed	3 lb	1 ½ qt
681 g	1.42 l	Celery, finely chopped	1 lb, 8 oz	1 ½ qt
85 g	118 ml	Onions, minced	3 oz	½ cup
170 g	355 ml	Green Pepper, finely chopped	6 oz	1 ½ cups
511 g	711 ml	Stuffed, Olives, sliced	1 lb, 2 oz	3 cups
	1 ¼ ml	Hot Pepper Sauce		¼ tsp

Procedure

1. Soften granulated gelatin in cold water. Add flavored gelatin and boiling water. Stir until completely dissolved. Cool.
2. Grind or crush cottage cheese until very fine. Blend with dressing and mashed avocado.
3. When gelatin is slightly thickened, combine all ingredients. Pour into molds and chill until set.

Raw Cranberry Salad
50 Servings (½ cup/118 ml)

| Metric | | Ingredients | U.S. | |
Weight	Volume		Weight	Volume
1.59 kg	3.08 l	Cranberries, fresh	3 lb, 8 oz	3 ¼ qt
1.14 kg	6 oranges	Oranges, whole	2 lb, 8 oz	6 oranges
681 g	711 ml	Sugar	1 lb, 8 oz	3 cups
595 g	711 ml	Cherry Gelatin	1 lb, 5 oz	3 cups
1.59 kg	1.66 l	Water, boiling	3 lb, 8 oz	7 cups
454 g	947 ml	Celery, finely diced	1 lb	1 qt

Procedure

1. Wash cranberries and coarsely grind them. Wash and coarsely grind oranges, including rinds.
2. Add sugar to fruit. Let stand for several hours for flavors to blend.
3. Dissolve gelatin in boiling water. Cool until it begins to thicken. Add cranberry and orange mixture and diced celery.
4. Mold and refrigerate until firm.

Custard Fruit Salad
50 Servings (3 oz/85 g)

| Metric | | Ingredients | U.S. | |
Weight	Volume		Weight	Volume
57 g	90 ml	Gelatin	2 oz	6 tbsp
793 g	829 ml	Water, cold	1 lb, 12 oz	3 ½ cups
14 g	30 ml	Cornstarch	½ oz	2 tbsp
227 g	237 ml	Sugar	8 oz	1 cup
7 g	7 ml	Salt	¼ oz	1 ½ tsp
170 g	158 ml	Egg Yolks (8 med)	6 oz	⅔ cup
454 g	474 ml	Orange Juice	1 lb	2 cups
	5 ml	Orange Rind, grated		1 tsp
198 g	207 ml	Lemon Juice	7 oz	⅞ cup
	5 ml	Lemon Rind, grated		1 tsp
793 g	829 ml	Cream, 40%	1 lb, 12 oz	3 ½ cups
793 g	829 ml	Pineapple, pieces	1 lb, 12 oz	3 ½ cups
227 g	415 ml	Apples, diced	8 oz	1 ¾ cups
397 g	415 ml	Maraschino Cherries, chopped	14 oz	1 ¾ cups
170 g	355 ml	Walnuts, chopped	6 oz	1 ½ cups

Procedure

1. Soak gelatin in cold water for 10 minutes.
2. Blend cornstarch, sugar, and salt. Beat egg yolks lightly. Mix with cornstarch and sugar. Add juices and rinds. Cook in double boiler until of custard consistency. Remove from heat and add gelatin. Cool.
3. Whip cream. When mixture begins to thicken, fold in whipped cream, fruit, and nuts.
4. Mold and chill.

Note: This is a dessert-type salad.

Apricot Pineapple Mold
50 Servings (5.5 oz/156 g)

| Metric | | Ingredients | U.S. | |
Weight	Volume		Weight	Volume
1.45 kg	1.66 l	Apricot Halves	3 lb, 3 oz	1 ¾ qt
1.02 kg	1.07 l	Pineapple Tidbits	2 lb, 4 oz	4 ½ cups
681 g	711 ml	Fruit Juice	1 lb, 8 oz	3 cups
114 g	118 ml	Vinegar	4 oz	½ cup
	2 ½ ml	Nutmeg		½ tsp
340 g	415 ml	Orange Gelatin	12 oz	1 ¾ cups
800 g	829 ml	Ginger ale	1 lb, 12 oz	3 ½ cups
340 g	415 ml	Orange Gelatin	12 oz	1 ¾ cups
681 g	711 ml	Water, boiling	1 lb, 8 oz	3 cups
681 g	711 ml	Apricot Juice, cold	1 lb, 8 oz	3 cups
454 g	474 ml	Sour Cream	1 lb	2 cups

Procedure

1. Drain apricots and pineapple, reserving juice. Heat juice, vinegar, and nutmeg to boiling. Pour over 12 oz/340 g gelatin and stir until dissolved. Cool. Stir in ginger ale and fruit before gelatin begins to thicken.

2. Fill molds half full. Chill until set.
3. Dissolve 12 oz/340 g gelatin in boiling water. Add cold apricot juice. Chill until gelatin begins to thicken. Stir in sour cream. Pour mixture on top of fruit mold. Chill until set.

Molded Cherry and Almond Salad
50 Servings

| Metric | | Ingredients | U.S. | |
Weight	Volume		Weight	Volume
7.26 kg	7.57 l	Drained Cherry Juice and Water	16 lb	2 gal
1.36 kg	1.66 l	Cherry Gelatin	3 lb	7 cups
907 g	947 ml	Sugar	2 lb	1 qt
1.81 kg	1.89 l	Cherries, red sour, pitted, drained	4 lb	2 qt
605 g	947 ml	Almonds, slivered	1 lb, 5 ⅓ oz	1 qt
907 g	1.89 l	Celery, diced	2 lb	2 qt

Procedure

1. Heat half of the cherry syrup and water to boiling and pour over gelatin. Stir until gelatin is dissolved. Add sugar and dissolve.
2. Add remainder of cold syrup and water.
3. Chill until it begins to congeal.

4. Arrange fruit, almonds, and celery in two serving pans (12 × 20 × 2 in).
5. Pour gelatin over the fruit. Stir gently to distribute fruit. Chill until set.

Jellied Carrot and Pineapple Salad
50 Servings

Metric		Ingredients	U.S.	
Weight	Volume		Weight	Volume
567 g	681 ml	Lemon Gelatin	1 lb, 4 oz	2 7/8 cups
2.04 kg	2.13 l	Water, boiling	4 lb, 8 oz	2 1/4 qt
	5 ml	Salt		1 tsp
681 g	711 ml	Pineapple Juice	1 lb, 8 oz	3 cups
114 g	118 ml	Lemon Juice	4 oz	1/2 cup
681 g	1.07 l	Carrots, shredded	1 lb, 8 oz	4 1/2 cups
1.36 kg	1.42 l	Pineapple, crushed, drained	3 lb	1 1/2 qt
9 g	15 ml	Lemon Rind, grated	1/3 oz	1 tbsp

Procedure

1. Dissolve gelatin in boiling water. Add salt. Stir in pineapple and lemon juice. Cool.
2. When mixture begins to thicken, add carrots, pineapple, and lemon rind.
3. Pour into molds and refrigerate until firm.

Grapefruit and Olive Mold
50 Servings (3.6 oz/106 g)

Metric		Ingredients	U.S.	
Weight	Volume		Weight	Volume
283 g	355 ml	Lemon Gelatin	10 oz	1 1/2 cups
283 g	355 ml	Lime Gelatin	10 oz	1 1/2 cups
681 g	711 ml	Water, hot	1 lb, 8 oz	3 cups
	5 ml	Salt		1 tsp
1.48 g	1.54 l	Grapefruit Juice	3 lb, 4 oz	6 1/2 cups
340 g	355 ml	Lemon Juice	12 oz	1 1/2 cups
1.36 kg	1.42 l	Grapefruit Segments	3 lb	1 1/2 qt
454 g	947 ml	Celery, chopped	1 lb	1 qt
340 g	474 ml	Stuffed Olives, sliced	12 oz	2 cups

Procedure

1. Dissolve gelatin in hot water. Add salt and juices. Chill until it begins to thicken.
2. Add remaining ingredients. Pour into molds. Chill.

Vegetable Medley Salad
50 Servings (4 oz/114 g)

Metric		Ingredients	U.S.	
Weight	Volume		Weight	Volume
907 g	1.89 l	Baby Lima Beans, cooked	2 lb	2 qt
907 g	1.66 l	String Beans, cooked	2 lb	1 ¾ qt
454 g	474 ml	Peas, cooked	1 lb	2 cups
454 g	947 ml	Carrot Curls	1 lb	1 qt
681 g	2.84 l	Lettuce, chopped	1 lb, 8 oz	3 qt
227 g	237 ml	Radishes, thinly sliced	8 oz	1 cup
28 g	30 ml	Salt	1 oz	2 tbsp
	5 ml	Pepper		1 tsp
2.27 kg	2.37 l	Tomato Wedges	5 lb	2 ½ qt
	50	Avocado Strips or Artichoke Hearts		50
	50	Cauliflowerets		50

Procedure

1. Combine lima beans, string beans, peas, carrots, chopped lettuce, radishes, salt, pepper, and tomato wedges, reserving 50 wedges. Toss together lightly. Set up in lettuce cups, 4 oz/114 g per serving. Garnish with tomato wedge, avocado strip, and caulifloweret.
2. Serve with French dressing.

Mixed Green Salad
50 Servings (3 oz/85 g)

Metric		Ingredients	U.S.	
Weight	Volume		Weight	Volume
1.82 kg	18.92 l	Spinach, tender, young, chopped	4 lb	5 gal
1.14 kg	4.74 l	Lettuce, chopped	2 lb, 8 oz	5 qt
907 g	2.60 l	Cabbage, chopped	2 lb	2 ¾ qt
30 g	30 ml	Onion Juice	1 oz	2 tbsp
170 g	178 ml	Vinegar	6 oz	¾ cup
14 g	15 ml	Salt	½ oz	1 tbsp
454 g	474 ml	French Dressing	1 lb	2 cups
454 g	474 ml	Bacon, diced, fried, and drained	1 lb	2 cups

Procedure

1. Mix all ingredients together lightly.

Note: Fresh basil, fennel, or watercress adds interest to this salad.

Green Goddess Salad
50 Servings (4 oz/114 g)

| Metric | | Ingredients | U.S. | |
Weight	Volume		Weight	Volume
7 g	2 cloves	Garlic	¼ oz	2 cloves
1.82 kg	7.59 l	Lettuce, heads	4 lb	2 gal
907 g	3.79 l	Romaine	2 lb	1 gal
681 g	1.89 l	Curly Chicory or Spinach	1 lb, 8 oz	3 qt
1.82 kg	1.89 l	Green Goddess Dressing	4 lb	2 qt
454 g	474 ml	Anchovy Fillets (or other seafood)	1 lb	2 cups

Procedure

1. Rub salad bowl with cut cloves of garlic. Break lettuce and chicory into bite-size pieces.
2. Moisten salad greens well with dressing. Portion. Garnish with anchovy fillets or other seafood. Serve at once.

Caesar Salad
50 Servings (7 oz/198 g)

| Metric | | Ingredients | U.S. | |
Weight	Volume		Weight	Volume
681 g	711 ml	Salad Oil	1 lb, 8 oz	3 cups
43 g	12 cloves	Garlic, minced	1 ½ oz	12 cloves
340 g	355 ml	Eggs (6 lge)	12 oz	1 ½ cups
1.59 kg	3.79 l	Bread, ½-in cubes	3 lb, 8 oz	1 gal
3.63 kg	15.14 l	Romaine	8 lb	4 gal
28 kg	30 ml	Salt	1 oz	2 tbsp
	10 ml	Pepper		2 tsp
170 g	178 ml	Wine Vinegar	6 oz	¾ cup
14 g	15 ml	Worcestershire Sauce	½ oz	1 tbsp
227 g	237 ml	Lemon Juice	8 oz	1 cup
340 g	711 ml	Parmesan Cheese, grated	12 oz	3 cups
454 g	474 ml	Anchovy Fillets	1 lb	2 cups

Procedure

1. Prepare garlic oil by placing sliced garlic in salad oil. Let remain 15 minutes, then remove.
2. Coddle eggs for 1 minute and set aside to cool.
3. Brown bread cubes in ¾ cup/178 ml garlic oil. (If this is done in 250°F/121°C oven, it will require approximately 1 ½ to 2 hrs.)
4. Break chilled romaine into bite-sized pieces. Sprinkle with salt and pepper and 2 ¼ cups/533 ml garlic oil. Toss lightly to mix.
5. Break eggs over salad. Combine vinegar, Worcestershire sauce, and lemon juice. Sprinkle over salad. Toss lightly again.
6. Sprinkle with bread croutons and cheese. Toss.
7. Serve portions and garnish with anchovy fillets.

Bean Sprout and Chestnut Salad
50 Servings (4 oz/114 g)

| Metric | | Ingredients | U.S. | |
Weight	Volume		Weight	Volume
2.27 kg	3.79 l	Bean Sprouts, drained	5 lb	1 gal
907 g	1.42 l	Water Chestnuts, diced	2 lb	1 ½ qt
454 g	947 ml	Celery, thin diagonal cuts	1 lb	1 qt
454 g	947 ml	Green Pepper, slivered	1 lb	1 qt
907 g	947 ml	Savory Dressing	2 lb	1 qt
340 g	711 ml	Almonds, salted	12 oz	3 cups

Procedure

1. Drain well sprouts and chestnuts. Combine with celery, green pepper, and salad dressing. Let marinate and chill for at least an hour.

2. Portion onto salad greens and garnish with almonds.

Carrot and Raisin Salad
50 Servings (4 oz/114 g)

| Metric | | Ingredients | U.S. | |
Weight	Volume		Weight	Volume
681 g	1.07 l	Raisins	1 lb, 8 oz	4 ½ cups
3.89 kg	6.00 l	Carrots, raw, grated	8 lb, 8 oz	6 ⅓ qt
14 g	15 ml	Salt	½ oz	1 tbsp
1.14 kg	1.18 l	Combination Dressing	2 lb, 8 oz	1 ¼ qt

Procedure

1. Soften raisins by pouring boiling water over them. Allow them to stand for a few minutes, then drain well. Chill.

2. Toss all ingredients together lightly to mix well. Chill.

Cucumber and Tomato Salad
50 Servings (5 oz/142 g)

| Metric | | Ingredients | U.S. | |
Weight	Volume		Weight	Volume
2.39 kg	5.68 l	Cucumbers, peeled and diced	5 lb, 4 oz	6 qt
2.04 kg	4.26 l	Celery, chopped	4 lb, 8 oz	4 ½ qt
2.72 kg	2.84 l	Tomato Wedges	6 lb	3 qt
28 g	237 ml	Basil or Watercress, fresh, chopped	1 oz	1 cup
28 g	30 ml	Salt	1 oz	1 tbsp
1.82 kg	1.89 l	French Dressing	4 lb	2 qt
567 g	50 rings	Green Pepper, rings	1 lb, 4 oz	50 rings

Procedure

1. Combine vegetables, except green pepper rings. Chill thoroughly.
2. Sprinkle with salt and toss together with French dressing just before service.
3. Garnish with green pepper rings.

Cabbage Slaw
50 Servings (4 oz/114 g)

Metric		Ingredients	U.S.	
Weight	Volume		Weight	Volume
4.08 kg	11.36 l	Cabbage, shredded	9 lb	3 gal
793 g	829 ml	Salad Dressing	1 lb, 12 oz	3 ½ cups
114 g	118 ml	Vinegar	4 oz	½ cup
454 g	474 ml	Sour Cream	1 lb	2 cups
57 g	60 ml	Salt	2 oz	4 tbsp
	5 ml	White Pepper		1 tsp
114 g	118 ml	Sugar	4 oz	½ cup

Procedure

1. Shred cabbage; crisp in cold water for an hour. Drain well.
2. Mix remaining ingredients thoroughly. Pour over cabbage and toss lightly.
3. Garnish with paprika, green pepper rings, slice of orange, or sprig of parsley.

Green Pepper Slaw
50 Servings (3.3 oz/94 g)

Metric		Ingredients	U.S.	
Weight	Volume		Weight	Volume
1.36 kg	3.79 l	Cabbage, finely shredded	3 lb	1 gal
681 g	1.42 l	Celery, chopped	1 lb, 8 oz	1 ½ qt
793 g	1.66 l	Green Pepper, finely chopped	1 lb, 12 oz	1 ¾ qt
1.36 kg	1.42 l	Pineapple, crushed, drained	3 lb	1 ½ qt
567 g	592 ml	Combination Dressing	1 lb, 4 oz	2 ½ cups
14 g	15 ml	Salt	½ oz	1 tbsp
	2 ½ ml	Pepper		½ tsp
340 g	474 ml	Stuffed Olives, sliced	12 oz	2 cups

Procedure

1. Combine cabbage, celery, green pepper, and pineapple.
2. Mix with combination dressing, salt, and pepper.
3. Chill and serve on lettuce cups. Garnish with olive slices.

Bean Salad
50 Servings (4 oz/114 g)

Metric		Ingredients	U.S.	
Weight	Volume		Weight	Volume
1.36 kg	2.37 l	Green Beans, cut	3 lb	2 ½ qt
907 g	1.66 l	Wax Beans, cut	2 lb	1 ¾ qt
907 g	1.18 l	Garbanzo Beans	2 lb	5 cups
907 g	1.18 l	Red Kidney Beans	2 lb	5 cups
454 g	711 ml	Onions, chopped	1 lb	3 cups
454 g	947 ml	Green Pepper, chopped	1 lb	1 qt
340 g	711 ml	Celery, chopped	12 oz	3 cups
28 g	178 ml	Fresh Basil or Parsley, chopped	1 oz	¾ cup
14 g	15 ml	Salt	½ oz	1 tbsp
681 g	711 ml	French Dressing	1 lb, 8 oz	3 cups

Procedure

1. Use cooked or canned beans. Drain well and blend with remaining ingredients.

2. Refrigerate and let vegetables marinate in French dressing for at least an hour.

Zucchini Salad
50 Servings (5 oz/142 g)

Metric		Ingredients	U.S.	
Weight	Volume		Weight	Volume
2.72 kg	5.68 l	Zucchini, 1 ½ to 2 in-diameter	6 lb	6 qt
1.36 kg	2.13 l	Baby Lima Beans, cooked	3 lb	2 ¼ qt
340 g	355 ml	Green Onions, minced	12 oz	1 ½ cups
170 g	237 ml	Pimiento, chopped	6 oz	1 cup
28 g	30 ml	Salt	1 oz	2 tbsp
28 g	30 ml	Sugar	1 oz	2 tbsp
57 g	355 ml	Parsley or Chives, chopped	2 oz	1 ½ cups
1.36 kg	1.42 l	Chiffonade Dressing	3 lb	1 ½ qt
1.36 kg	50	Cherry Tomatoes	3 lb	50

Procedure

1. Slice zucchini into 3/16-inch slices. Drop into boiling water and cook for 1 minute. Drain well and chill.
2. Combine all ingredients except tomatoes and chill for 2 hours.

3. Scald tomatoes and remove skins. Chill well and use for garnishing salads.

Hot Vegetable Salad
50 Servings (5.5 oz/156 g)

Metric		Ingredients	U.S.	
Weight	Volume		Weight	Volume
2.72 kg	7.57 l	Cabbage, finely shredded	6 lb	2 gal
1.36 kg	2.13 l	Onions, very finely chopped	3 lb	2 ¼ qt
907 g	1.89 l	Green Pepper, finely chopped	2 lb	2 qt
2.72 kg	5.68 l	Celery, very finely chopped	6 lb	6 qt
28 g	30 ml	Butter or Margarine	1 oz	2 tbsp
37 g	30 ml	Olive Oil	1 ⅓ oz	2 tbsp
57 g	60 ml	Salt	2 oz	4 tbsp
	7 ½ ml	Pepper		1 ½ tsp
283 g	296 ml	Vinegar	10 oz	1 ¼ cups

Procedure

1. Combine vegetables and toss lightly.
2. Place butter or margarine, olive oil, seasonings, and vinegar in heavy skillet. Heat and add vegetables. Cook over high heat for from 5 to 7 minutes, tightly covered.
3. Serve immediately.

Pea, Pickle, and Cheese Salad
Yield: 25 #10 Scoops;
50 #20 Scoops

Metric		Ingredients	U.S.	
Weight	Volume		Weight	Volume
2.27 kg	2.37 l	Peas, cooked, drained	5 lb	2 ½ qt
907 g	1.89 l	American Cheese, cubed	2 lb	2 qt
454 g	474 ml	Pickle Relish, drained	1 lb	2 cups
907 g	1.89 l	Celery, chopped	2 lb	2 qt
454 g	1.42 l	Onions, thinly sliced	1 lb	1 ½ qt
9 g	10 ml	Salt	⅓ oz	2 tsp
454 g	474 ml	Salad Dressing	1 lb	2 cups

Procedure

1. Combine all ingredients.
2. Serve with a No. 10 scoop on lettuce cup.
3. Salad may be garnished with onion ring, pimiento, or tomato wedge.

Cottage Cheese and Carrot Salad
50 Servings (2 in × 2 in)

Metric		Ingredients	U.S.	
Weight	Volume		Weight	Volume
567 g	681 ml	Lemon Gelatin	1 lb, 4 oz	2 7/8 cups
1.14 kg	1.18 l	Water, boiling	2 lb, 8 oz	1 1/4 qt
1.14 kg	1.18 l	Water, cold	2 lb, 8 oz	1 1/4 qt
142 g	158 ml	Vinegar	5 oz	2/3 cup
	7 1/2 ml	Salt		1 1/2 tsp
43 g	59 ml	Onions, minced	1 1/2 oz	1/4 cup
1.14 kg	1.18 l	Cottage Cheese, creamed	2 lb, 8 oz	1 1/4 qt
283 g	592 ml	Carrots, shredded	10 oz	2 1/2 cups
9 g	59 ml	Parsley, chopped	1/3 oz	1/4 cup

Procedure

1. Dissolve gelatin in boiling water. Add cold water, vinegar, salt, and onions. Chill.
2. When mixture begins to thicken, add cottage cheese, carrots, and parsley.
3. Pour into flat pans. Let set in refrigerator.
4. Cut into 2-inch squares and serve on lettuce.

Perfection Salad
64 Servings

Metric		Ingredients	U.S.	
Weight	Volume		Weight	Volume
3.63 kg	3.79 l	Water, boiling	8 lb	1 gal
1.36 kg	1.66 l	Lemon Gelatin	3 lb	1 3/4 qt
3.18 kg	3.31 l	Water, cold	7 lb	3 1/2 qt
454 g	474 ml	Vinegar	1 lb	2 cups
9 g	10 ml	Salt	1/3 oz	2 tsp
681 g	1.42 l	Celery, diced	1 lb, 8 oz	1 1/2 qt
907 g	2.52 l	Cabbage, shredded	2 lb	2 2/3 qt
283 g	592 ml	Green Pepper, chopped fine	10 oz	2 1/2 cups
198 g	277 ml	Pimiento, chopped	7 oz	1 1/6 cups

Procedure

1. Pour boiling water over gelatin. Stir until dissolved. Add cold water, vinegar, and salt. Cool.
2. When mixture begins to thicken, add remaining ingredients.
3. Pour into 2 serving pans (12 × 20 × 2 in) and refrigerate until firm.
4. Cut pans into 64 portions (4 × 8).

Jellied Beet Salad
50 Servings (5 oz/142 g)

| Metric | | Ingredients | U.S. | |
Weight	Volume		Weight	Volume
681 g	829 ml	Orange Gelatin	1 lb, 8 oz	3 ½ cups
1.82 kg	1.89 l	Water, boiling	4 lb	2 qt
907 g	947 ml	Beet Juice	2 lb	1 qt
227 g	237 ml	Vinegar	8 oz	1 cup
	5 ml	Hot Pepper Sauce		1 tsp
28 g	30 ml	Salt	1 oz	2 tbsp
907 g	1.18 l	Oranges, diced	2 lb	5 cups
1.36 kg	1.66 l	Beets, diced	3 lb	7 cups
1.14 kg	2.37 l	Celery, finely diced	2 lb, 8 oz	2 ½ qt

Procedure

1. Dissolve gelatin in boiling water. Add beet juice, vinegar, pepper sauce, and salt.
2. When gelatin begins to thicken, stir in remaining ingredients.
3. Pour into molds and refrigerate until set.

Thousand Island Mold
50 Servings (2 in × 2 in)

| Metric | | Ingredients | U.S. | |
Weight	Volume		Weight	Volume
567 g	681 ml	Lemon Gelatin	1 lb, 4 oz	2 ⅞ cups
1.36 kg	1.42 l	Water, boiling	3 lb	1 ½ qt
14 g	15 ml	Salt	½ oz	1 tbsp
	5 ml	Pepper		1 tsp
681 g	711 ml	Catsup	1 lb, 8 oz	3 cups
681 g	711 ml	Mayonnaise	1 lb, 8 oz	3 cups
340 g	711 ml	Celery, chopped	12 oz	3 cups
567 g	1.18 l	Green Pepper, chopped	1 lb, 4 oz	1 ¼ qt
227 g	355 ml	Stuffed Olives, chopped	8 oz	1 ½ cups
681 g	2.84 l	Lettuce, shredded	1 lb, 8 oz	3 qt

Procedure

1. Dissolve gelatin in boiling water. Add salt and pepper. Chill until mixture begins to thicken. Combine catsup with mayonnaise. Blend with thickened gelatin.
2. Add vegetables and mix.
3. Pour into individual molds or into flat plans. When set, cut into servings and arrange on lettuce cups. Garnish with slices of egg.

Molded Cucumber Salad
50 Servings

Metric		Ingredients	U.S.	
Weight	Volume		Weight	Volume
3.63 kg	3.79 l	Water, boiling	8 lb	1 gal
1.36 kg	1.66 l	Lemon Gelatin	3 lb	1 ¾ qt
3.63 kg	3.79 l	Water, cold	8 lb	1 gal
681 g	711 ml	Sour Cream	1 lb, 8 oz	3 cups
681 g	711 ml	Salad Dressing	1 lb, 8 oz	3 cups
156 g	237 ml	Onions, finely chopped	5 ½ oz	1 cup
1.36 kg	2.21 l	Cucumbers, peeled, diced	3 lb	2 ⅓ qt
198 g	276 ml	Pimientos, chopped	7 oz	1 ⅙ cups

Procedure

1. Pour boiling water over gelatin. Stir until dissolved. Add cold water and chill until partly coagulated.
2. Mix sour cream and salad dressing together.
3. Combine all of the ingredients with the gelatin and stir to mix well.
4. Pour into individual molds or serving pans (12 × 20 × 2 in) to be cut into individual portions. Refrigerate until firm.
5. Garnish with pepper ring or ripe olive.

Gazpacho Mold
50 Servings (4 oz/114 g)

Metric		Ingredients	U.S.	
Weight	Volume		Weight	Volume
57 g	118 ml	Gelatin, granulated	2 oz	½ cup
454 g	474 ml	Tomato Juice, cold	1 lb	2 cups
1.59 kg	1.66 l	Tomato Juice, hot	3 lb, 8 oz	1 ¾ qt
21 g	6 cloves	Garlic, minced	¾ oz	6 cloves
	10 ml	Hot Pepper Sauce		2 tsp
14 g	15 ml	Worcestershire Sauce	½ oz	1 tbsp
28 g	30 ml	Salt	1 oz	2 tbsp
28 g	30 ml	Sugar	1 oz	2 tbsp
454 g	474 ml	Vinegar or Pickle Juice	1 lb	2 cups
340 g	711 ml	Green Pepper, chopped	12 oz	3 cups
454 g	947 ml	Celery, chopped	1 lb	1 qt
1.14 kg	1.89 l	Tomatoes, diced	2 lb, 8 oz	2 qt
624 g	947 ml	Onions, chopped	1 lb, 6 oz	1 qt
255 g	474 ml	Cucumber, diced	9 oz	2 cups

Procedure

1. Soften gelatin in cold juice for 10 minutes. Stir into hot juice until completely dissolved.
2. Combine with garlic, sauces, salt, sugar, and vinegar. Cool.
3. When gelatin is slightly thickened, stir in chopped vegetables. Pour into molds and refrigerate until firm.

Cottage Cheese and Vegetable Mold
50 Servings (5 oz/142 g)

| Metric | | Ingredients | U.S. | |
Weight	Volume		Weight	Volume
737 g	889 ml	Lemon Gelatin	1 lb, 10 oz	3 ¾ cups
1.36 kg	1.42 l	Water, boiling	3 lb	1 ½ qt
1.36 kg	1.42 l	Water, cold	3 lb	1 ½ qt
454 g	474 ml	Vinegar	1 lb	2 cups
227 g	237 ml	Lemon Juice	8 oz	1 cup
14 g	15 ml	Salt	½ oz	1 tbsp
227 g	237 ml	Sugar	8 oz	1 cup
170 g	355 ml	Green Pepper, chopped	6 oz	1 ½ cups
340 g	947 ml	Green Cabbage, shredded	12 oz	1 qt
170 g	237 ml	Onions, finely chopped	6 oz	1 cup
340 g	711 ml	Celery, diced	12 oz	3 cups
340 g	474 ml	Pimiento, chopped	12 oz	2 cups
1.36 kg	1.42 l	Cottage Cheese	3 lb	1 ½ qt

Procedure

1. Dissolve gelatin in boiling water. Add cold water, vinegar, lemon juice, salt, and sugar. Chill until mixture begins to thicken.
2. Stir in chopped vegetables and divide half of mixture into two serving pans (12 × 20 × 2 in) and chill until it thickens.
3. Before gelatin is firm, layer cottage cheese on top of it. Divide the remaining gelatin mixture over top of cottage cheese. Chill until set.

Cucumber and Cottage Cheese Mold
50 Servings (5 ¼ oz/150 g)

| Metric | | Ingredients | U.S. | |
Weight	Volume		Weight	Volume
454 g	553 ml	Lemon Gelatin	1 lb	2 ⅓ cups
567 g	592 ml	Water, hot	1 lb, 4 oz	2 ½ cups
567 g	592 ml	Water, cold	1 lb, 4 oz	2 ½ cups
1.14 kg	1.18 l	Mayonnaise	2 lb, 8 oz	1 ¼ qt
2.27 kg	2.37 l	Cottage Cheese	5 lb	2 ½ qt
1.82 kg	6 lge	Cucumber, diced ¼-in	4 lb	6 lge
312 g	474 ml	Onions, finely chopped	11 oz	2 cups
14 g	15 ml	Salt	½ oz	1 tbsp
340 g	711 ml	Almonds, blanched, slivered	12 oz	3 cups
114 g	118 ml	Vinegar	4 oz	½ cup

Procedure

1. Dissolve gelatin in hot water and add cold water. Let cool. Stir in remaining ingredients.
2. Pour into molds and refrigerate until set.

Tomato Aspic, Clear
50 Servings (4 oz/114 g)

| Metric | | Ingredients | U.S. | |
Weight	Volume		Weight	Volume
151 g	237 ml	Gelatin	5 ⅓ oz	1 cup
454 g	474 ml	Water, cold	1 lb	2 cup
1.82 kg	1.89 l	Tomato Juice	4 lb	2 qt
1.82 kg	1.89 l	Tomato Puree	4 lb	2 qt
340 g	553 ml	Onions, grated or finely chopped	12 oz	2 ⅓ cups
454 g	947 ml	Celery, finely chopped	1 lb	1 qt
227 g	474 ml	Green Pepper, finely chopped	8 oz	2 cups
57 g	355 ml	Parsley, chopped	2 oz	1 ½ cups
	2 leaves	Bay Leaves		2 leaves
	10 ml	Paprika		2 tsp
7 g	15 ml	Mustard, dry	¼ oz	1 tbsp
28 g	30 ml	Worcestershire Sauce	1 oz	2 tbsp
	⅝ ml	Cayenne Pepper		⅛ tsp
28 g	30 ml	Salt	1 oz	2 tbsp
227 g	237 ml	Sugar	8 oz	1 cup
28 g	30 ml	Horseradish	1 oz	2 tbsp
454 g	474 ml	Vinegar	1 lb	2 cups

Procedure

1. Soak gelatin in 2 cups/474 ml of cold water.
2. Simmer the remaining ingredients together for 20 minutes. Add soaked gelatin and stir until dissolved.
3. Pour into flat pans. Chill until set.
4. Cut into servings. Serve on lettuce garnished with green pepper or celery rings.

Variation

1. Add 2 cups/474 ml sliced stuffed olives and 1 qt/947 ml diced celery when mixture begins to thicken.
2. Do not cook the celery, onions, green pepper, and parsley, but add them to the aspic when it begins to thicken.

MEAT, FISH, EGG, AND CHEESE SALADS

Shrimp and Avocado
50 Servings (6 ¼ oz/177 g)

| Metric | | Ingredients | U.S. | |
Weight	Volume		Weight	Volume
2.72 kg	4.74 l	Shrimp, small	6 lb	5 qt
1.36 kg	1.42 l	French Dressing, Fashion	3 lb	1 ½ qt
907 g	1.89 l	Celery, diced	2 lb	2 qt
4.54 kg	50 halves	Avocado	10 lb	50 halves

Procedure

1. Marinate cooked, cleaned shrimp in dressing for 1 hour.
2. Drain shrimp and combine with celery. Pile into halves of avocado set on crisp greens.
3. Garnish with hard-cooked egg, tomato, or lemon wedge.

Crab Ravigote
50 Servings (4 oz/114 g)

| Metric | | Ingredients | U.S. | |
Weight	Volume		Weight	Volume
454 g	474 ml	Mayonnaise	1 lb	2 cups
907 g	1.89 l	Celery, chopped	2 lb	2 qt
57 g	355 ml	Parsley, chopped fine	2 oz	1 ½ cups
114 g	75 ml	Onion Juice	4 oz	5 tbsp
28 g	30 ml	Salt	1 oz	2 tbsp
	5 ml	Pepper		1 tsp
1.14 kg	1.89 l	Eggs, hard-cooked, diced	2 lb, 8 oz	2 qt
3.18 kg	4.74 l	Crabmeat	7 lb	5 qt
114 g	158 ml	Pimiento, diced	4 oz	⅔ cup

Procedure

1. Blend mayonnaise, celery, parsley, and seasonings.
2. Combine all ingredients and toss lightly to mix.
3. Place on bed of shredded lettuce, in crab shells, or on lettuce cups, serving a No. 16 scoop of ravigote. Garnish with strips of pimiento and mayonnaise.

Salmon Salad
50 Servings (5 oz/142 g)

| Metric | | Ingredients | U.S. | |
Weight	Volume		Weight	Volume
3.18 kg	4.98 l	Salmon, flaked	7 lb	5 ¼ qt
1.82 kg	3.79 l	Celery, diced	4 lb	4 qt
614 g	12 eggs	Eggs, hard-cooked, diced	1 lb, 6 oz	12 eggs
454 g	1.26 l	Cabbage, shredded	1 lb	1 ⅓ qt
14 g	15 ml	Salt	½ oz	1 tbsp
454 g	711 ml	Sweet Pickles, chopped	1 lb	3 cups
681 g	711 ml	Mayonnaise	1 lb, 8 oz	3 cups
57 g	59 ml	Vinegar	2 oz	¼ cup

Procedure

1. Drain salmon and flake.
2. Add celery, eggs, cabbage, salt, and pickles.
3. Combine mayonnaise and vinegar. Mix with other ingredients and chill.
4. Serve on lettuce, using a No. 12 scoop.

Tuna Fish Mold

50 Servings (4 ½ oz/128 g)

Metric		Ingredients	U.S.	
Weight	Volume		Weight	Volume
681 g	829 ml	Lemon Gelatin	1 lb, 8 oz	3 ½ cups
907 g	947 ml	Water, boiling	2 lb	1 qt
681 g	711 ml	Chili Sauce	1 lb, 8 oz	3 cups
170 g	178 ml	Lemon Juice	6 oz	¾ cup
907 g	947 ml	Mayonnaise	2 lb	1 qt
14 g	15 ml	Worcestershire Sauce	½ oz	1 tbsp
	⅝ ml	Hot Pepper Sauce		⅛ tsp
14 g	15 ml	Salt	½ oz	1 tbsp
2.04 kg	2.37 l	Tuna, drained, flaked	4 lb, 8 oz	2 ½ qt
114 g	178 ml	Onions, minced	4 oz	¾ cup
454 g	947 ml	Celery, chopped	1 lb	1 qt
454 g	8 eggs	Eggs, hard-cooked, sliced	1 lb	8 eggs

Procedure

1. Dissolve gelatin in boiling water.
2. Combine chili sauce, lemon juice, mayonnaise, sauces, and salt. Add to gelatin.
3. When gelatin is slightly thickened, fold in tuna, onions, and celery.
4. Pour into mold and refrigerate until set. Portion and garnish with egg slices.

Tuna Fish Salad

50 Servings (4 ½ oz/128 g)

Metric		Ingredients	U.S.	
Weight	Volume		Weight	Volume
681 g	711 ml	Mayonnaise	1 lb, 8 oz	3 cups
454 g	474 ml	Sour Cream	1 lb	2 cups
340 g	355 ml	Sweet Pickle Relish	12 oz	1 ½ cups
14 g	15 ml	Salt	½ oz	1 tbsp
	5 ml	Pepper		1 tsp
	5 ml	Paprika		1 tsp
3.18 kg	3.79 l	Tuna, flaked	7 lb	4 qt
454 g	8 eggs	Eggs, hard-cooked, chopped	1 lb	8 eggs
1.14 kg	2.37 l	Celery, chopped	2 lb, 8 oz	2 ½ qt
340 g	474 ml	Stuffed Olives, sliced	12 oz	2 cups

Procedure

1. Blend mayonnaise, sour cream, relish, and seasonings. Combine with tuna fish, eggs, and celery, tossing together lightly. Use care to prevent breaking tuna and eggs.
2. Serve on crisp greens and garnish with sliced olives.

Seafood Salad
50 Servings (4 ¼ oz/121 g)

Metric		Ingredients	U.S.	
Weight	Volume		Weight	Volume
907 g	1.89 l	Celery, diced	2 lb	2 qt
454 g	829 ml	Cucumber, diced	1 lb	3 ½ cups
312 g	474 ml	Onions, minced	11 oz	2 cups
114 g	118 ml	Lemon Juice	4 oz	½ cup
681 g	711 ml	Mayonnaise	1 lb, 8 oz	3 cups
14 g	15 ml	Salt	½ oz	1 tbsp
907 g	1.42 l	Crabmeat	2 lb	6 cups
907 g	1.54 l	Shrimp, small	2 lb	6 ½ cups
1.82 kg	2.84 l	Sole, poached, flaked	4 lb	3 qt

Procedure

1. Combine celery, cucumber, onions, lemon juice, mayonnaise, and salt.
2. Combine seafood and dressing mixture, using care to avoid breaking tender fish.
3. Serve on crisp greens and garnish with slices of cucumber or shrimp.

Chef's Salad
50 Servings (6 oz/170 g)

Metric		Ingredients	U.S.	
Weight	Volume		Weight	Volume
1.82 kg	7.58 l	Iceberg Lettuce	4 lb	2 gal
907 g	3.79 l	Romaine	2 lb	1 gal
454 g	711 ml	Green Onions, sliced	1 lb	3 cups
681 g	1.42 l	Celery, sliced	1 lb, 8 oz	1 ½ qt
454 g	947 ml	Green Pepper, strips	1 lb	1 qt
28 g	30 ml	Salt	1 oz	2 tbsp
	5 ml	Pepper		1 tsp
	10 ml	Garlic Salt		2 tsp
681 g	711 ml	French Dressing	1 lb, 8 oz	3 cups
907 g	1.42 l	Chicken, cooked, julienne	2 lb	1 ½ qt
907 g	1.42 l	Ham, cooked, julienne	2 lb	1 ½ qt
907 g	1.42 l	Swiss Cheese, julienne	2 lb	1 ½ qt
681 g	12 eggs	Eggs, hard-cooked, sliced	1 lb, 8 oz	12 eggs
454 g	474 ml	Anchovy Fillets (optional)	1 lb	2 cups

Procedure

1. Break lettuce and romaine into bite-sized pieces. Toss lightly together with other vegetables, seasonings, and French dressing.
2. Portion and garnish with julienne strips of meat and cheese. Add sliced egg and anchovy fillets if desired. Serve immediately.

Rice Curry with Prawns
50 Servings (6 oz/170 g)

Metric Weight	Metric Volume	Ingredients	U.S. Weight	U.S. Volume
3.63 kg	4.74 l	Rice, cooked	8 lb	5 qt
681 g	1.07 l	Green Onions, chopped	1 lb, 8 oz	4 ½ cups
57 g	355 ml	Parsley, chopped	2 oz	1 ½ cups
681 g	1.42 l	Celery, chopped	1 lb, 8 oz	1 ½ qt
454 g	947 ml	Green Pepper, chopped	1 lb	1 qt
28 g	8 cloves	Garlic, minced	1 oz	8 cloves
454 g	711 ml	Water Chestnuts, diced	1 lb	3 cups
1.82 kg	2.84 l	Prawns, cooked, cleaned	4 lb	3 qt
681 g	711 ml	French Dressing	1 lb, 8 oz	3 cups
	22 ½ ml	Curry Powder		1 ½ tbsp
114 g	118 ml	Sugar	4 oz	½ cup
28 g	30 ml	Salt	1 oz	2 tbsp

Procedure

1. Toss rice, vegetables, and water chestnuts together lightly to mix. Chill well.
2. Marinate prawns in French dressing. Drain off dressing, combine it with seasonings, and pour over the rice and vegetables. Mix thoroughly.
3. Portion with a No. 8 scoop onto crisp greens. Garnish with prawns.

Potato Salad with Shrimp
50 Servings (6 ½ oz/184 g)

Metric Weight	Metric Volume	Ingredients	U.S. Weight	U.S. Volume
1.25 kg	2.13 l	Shrimp, cooked	2 lb, 12 oz	2 ¼ qt
3.86 kg	4.50 l	Potatoes, cooked, diced	8 lb, 8 oz	4 ¾ qt
1.22 kg	24 eggs	Eggs, hard-cooked, diced	2 lb, 11 oz	24 eggs
142 g	237 ml	Onions, chopped	5 oz	1 cup
907 g	1.66 l	Cucumbers, chopped, E.P.	2 lb	7 cups
227 g	474 ml	Green Pepper, chopped	8 oz	2 cups
	2 ½ ml	Pepper		½ tsp
28 g	30 ml	Salt	1 oz	2 tbsp
	1 ¼ ml	Garlic Salt		¼ tsp
28 g	30 ml	Lemon Juice	1 oz	2 tbsp
737 g	770 ml	Boiled Dressing	1 lb, 10 oz	3 ¼ cups

Procedure

1. Cut the shrimp into small pieces.
2. Mix all ingredients with boiled salad dressing. Cool thoroughly before serving. Garnish with slices of egg and shrimp.

Note: 8 lb/3.63 kg cooked rice may be substituted for potatoes.

Potato Salad
50 Servings (6¼ oz/177 g)

| Metric | | Ingredients | U.S. | |
Weight	Volume		Weight	Volume
5.67 kg	7.10 l	Potatoes, cooked	12 lb, 8 oz	7½ qt
227 g	237 ml	Salad Oil	8 oz	1 cup
227 g	237 ml	Vinegar	8 oz	1 cup
454 g	947 ml	Onions, green or white, sliced	1 lb	1 qt
43 g	45 ml	Salt	1½ oz	3 tbsp
	5 ml	Pepper		1 tsp
21 g	22 ml	Sugar	¾ oz	1½ tbsp
	⅝ ml	Cayenne Pepper		⅛ tsp
	5 ml	Mustard, dry		1 tsp
	5 ml	Paprika		1 tsp
681 g	711 ml	Boiled Dressing	1 lb, 8 oz	3 cups
340 g	355 ml	Light Cream	12 oz	1½ cups
907 g	18 eggs	Eggs, hard-cooked, sliced	2 lb	18 eggs
454 g	947 ml	Celery, chopped	1 lb	1 qt
28 g	178 ml	Parsley, chopped	1 oz	¾ cup

Procedure

1. Slice potatoes.
2. Mix oil, vinegar, onions, salt, pepper, sugar, cayenne, mustard, and paprika as for French Dressing. Pour over potatoes. Allow to marinate for at least 1 hour.
3. Mix boiled dressing and light cream.
4. Add mixed dressing, eggs, celery, and parsley to potatoes. Mix lightly, but thoroughly enough for slices of potatoes to be covered with dressing.
5. Garnish with paprika and parsley. Chill and serve.

Creamy Chicken Salad
50 Servings (4 oz/114 g)

| Metric | | Ingredients | U.S. | |
Weight	Volume		Weight	Volume
907 g	947 ml	Combination Dressing	2 lb	1 qt
340 g	711 ml	Whipped Cream	12 oz	3 cups
14 g	15 ml	Salt	½ oz	1 tbsp
114 g	118 ml	Lemon Juice	4 oz	½ cup
2.44 kg	3.79 l	Chicken, cooked, cubed	5 lb, 6 oz	4 qt
907 g	1.89 l	Celery, diced	2 lb	2 qt
454 g	474 ml	Pickles, sweet, chopped	1 lb	2 cups
681 g	12 eggs	Eggs, hard-cooked, diced	1 lb, 8 oz	12 eggs

Procedure

1. Blend salad dressing, whipped cream, salt, and lemon juice.
2. Fold in chicken, celery, pickles, and eggs, using care to prevent breaking pieces of chicken and eggs.
3. Serve 4 oz/114 g on salad greens garnished with salted almonds, tomato wedges, or pepper rings.

Chinese Chicken Salad

50 Servings (4.5 oz/128 g)

Metric		Ingredients	U.S.		
Weight	Volume		Weight		Volume
64 g	135 ml	Gelatin		2 ¼ oz	9 tbsp
283 g	296 ml	Water, cold		10 oz	1 ¼ cups
1.48 kg	1.54 l	Chicken Stock, boiling	3 lb,	4 oz	6 ½ cups
964 g	1.00 l	Pineapple Juice	2 lb,	2 oz	4 ¼ cups
	5 ml	Paprika			1 tsp
28 g	30 ml	Salt		1 oz	2 tbsp
1.36 kg	2.13 l	Chicken, cooked, diced	3 lb		2 ¼ qt
1.48 kg	1.54 l	Pineapple, drained, diced	3 lb,	4 oz	6 ½ cups
681 g	1.07 l	Almonds, blanched, shredded	1 lb,	8 oz	4 ½ cups
114 g	237 ml	Green Pepper, chopped		4 oz	1 cup
114 g	158 ml	Pimiento, chopped		4 oz	⅔ cup
		Green Grapes			

Procedure

1. Soak gelatin in cold water. Dissolve in boiling chicken stock. Add pineapple juice, paprika, and salt. Cool.
2. When mixture begins to thicken, fold in chicken, pineapple, almonds, green pepper, and pimiento.
3. Pour into flat pans. Refrigerate until set.
4. Cut into portions. Serve in lettuce cups. Garnish with small green grape clusters.

Molded Chicken Salad

50 Servings (4 oz/114 g)

Metric		Ingredients	U.S.		
Weight	Volume		Weight		Volume
71 g	150 ml	Gelatin, plain		2 ½ oz	10 tbsp
681 g	711 ml	Water, cold	1 lb,	8 oz	3 cups
1.14 kg	1.18 l	Chicken Stock, hot	2 lb,	8 oz	1 ¼ qt
340 g	355 ml	Lemon Juice		12 oz	1 ½ cups
142 g	158 ml	Sugar		5 oz	⅔ cup
1.14 kg	1.18 l	Salad Dressing	2 lb,	8 oz	1 ¼ qt
9 g	10 ml	Salt, to taste		⅓ oz	2 tsp
1.14 kg	1.78 l	Chicken, diced	2 lb,	8 oz	7 ½ cups
567 g	1.18 l	Celery, chopped	1 lb,	4 oz	1 ¼ qt
454 g	711 ml	Tokay Grapes, halved	1 lb		3 cups

Procedure

1. Soften gelatin in cold water, then add hot stock and stir until dissolved. Add lemon juice and sugar. Chill.
2. When mixture begins to thicken, fold in salad dressing, and salt. Add remaining ingredients. Mix.
3. Pour into flat pans. Place in refrigerator.
4. Cut into portions. Serve in lettuce cups.

Layer Tomato and Cheese Salad
50 Servings (3.75 oz/106 g)

Metric		Ingredients	U.S.	
Weight	Volume		Weight	Volume
737 g	770 ml	Lemon-Flavored Gelatin	1 lb, 10 oz	3 ¼ cups
3.63 kg	3.79 l	Tomato Juice	8 lb	1 gal
	5 ml	Salt		1 tsp
340 g	355 ml	Cream Cheese	12 oz	1 ½ cups
114 g	118 ml	Mayonnaise	4 oz	½ cup
	5 ml	Salt		1 tsp
227 g	474 ml	American Cheese, grated	8 oz	2 cups
454 g	474 ml	Whipping Cream	1 lb	1 pint

Procedure

1. Dissolve lemon gelatin in 2 qt/1.89 l of hot tomato juice. Add salt and 2 qt/1.89 l of cold tomato juice.
2. Reserve 1 qt/947 ml of mixture and pour remainder into pans or molds. Chill.
3. Combine cream cheese, mayonnaise, and salt. When the 1 qt/947 l of mixture begins to thicken, beat in the cream cheese mixture. Fold in American cheese and whipped cream.
4. Pour the cream cheese mixture on top of "set" tomato juice mixture. Chill.
5. Arrange cuts or molds on lettuce cups. Garnish with sprig of parsley and dressing or with a green pepper ring.

Note: Layers tend to separate when cut if first layer is allowed to set too firmly before second layer is added.

Country Ham Salad
50 Servings (6 oz/170 g)

Metric		Ingredients	U.S.	
Weight	Volume		Weight	Volume
1.36 kg	1.42 l	Mayonnaise	3 lb	1 ½ qt
227 g	237 ml	Vinegar	8 oz	1 cup
71 g	75 ml	Salt, to taste	2 ½ oz	5 tbsp
	10 ml	Pepper		2 tsp
2.50 kg	3.79 l	Ham, cooked, diced	5 lb, 8 oz	4 qt
907 g	1.07 l	Potatoes, cooked, diced	2 lb	4 ½ cups
907 g	1.42 l	Carrots, cooked, diced	2 lb	1 ½ qt
907 g	947 ml	Peas, cooked	2 lb	1 qt
454 g	947 ml	Celery, diced	1 lb	1 qt
511 g	10 eggs	Eggs, hard-cooked, diced	1 lb, 2 oz	10 eggs
227 g	474 ml	Green Pepper, diced	8 oz	2 cups
227 g	355 ml	Onions, diced fine	8 oz	1 ½ cups

Procedure

1. Combine mayonnaise, vinegar, salt, and pepper and toss together with remaining ingredients.
2. Chill before serving.

Ham Salad
50 Servings (5 oz/142 g)

Metric		Ingredients	U.S.	
Weight	Volume		Weight	Volume
2.44 kg	3.79 l	Ham, cooked, diced	5 lb, 6 oz	4 qt
681 g	12 eggs	Eggs, hard-cooked, diced	1 lb, 8 oz	12 eggs
1.59 kg	2.37 l	Baby Limas, cooked	3 lb 8 oz	2 ½ qt
681 g	1.42 l	Celery, diced	1 lb, 8 oz	1 ½ qt
454 g	711 ml	Onions, chopped	1 lb	3 cups
454 g	474 ml	Sweet Pickles, chopped	1 lb	2 cups
1.36 kg	1.42 l	Combination Dressing	3 lb	1 ½ qt
14 g	15 ml	Salt	½ oz	1 tbsp
340 g	474 ml	Ripe Olives	12 oz	2 cups

Procedure

1. Combine all ingredients, except olives, tossing lightly to mix. Avoid breaking pieces of ham and eggs.

2. Serve portions on crisp greens garnished with ripe olives.

Cheese and Ham in Aspic
50 Servings (5.75 oz/164 g)

Metric		Ingredients	U.S.	
Weight	Volume		Weight	Volume
4.54 kg	4.74 l	Tomato Aspic, clear	10 lb	5 qt
907 g	947 ml	Cream Cheese	2 lb	1 qt
1.36 kg	1.42 l	Cottage Cheese	3 lb	1 ½ qt
14 g	15 ml	Salt	½ oz	1 tbsp
	2 ½ ml	Pepper, white		½ tsp
21 g	45 ml	Gelatin	¾ oz	3 tbsp
170 g	178 ml	Water, cold	6 oz	¾ cup
793 g	829 ml	Ham, ground	1 lb, 12 oz	3 ½ cups
340 g	355 ml	Mayonnaise	12 oz	1 ½ cups
114 g	237 ml	Green Pepper, chopped	4 oz	1 cup
7 g	15 ml	Mustard, dry	¼ oz	1 tbsp
114 g	237 ml	Celery, finely chopped	4 oz	1 cup

Procedure

1. Prepare clear tomato aspic. Cool.
2. Pour one-third of the aspic mixture into two pans (10 × 16 × 2 ¼ in). Chill until firm.
3. Mix cream cheese and cottage cheese well, adding salt and pepper. Spread cheese over firm aspic.
4. Carefully pour another third of the aspic over the cheese and allow to set.
5. Soak gelatin in cold water and dissolve over hot water. Mix dissolved gelatin with remaining ingredients. Spread over second layer of firm aspic.
6. Cover with last third of aspic and chill until set.
7. Serve on lettuce, cutting contents of each pan into 25 servings.

Note: This should be made a day before it is to be served.

Molded Egg Salad
50 Servings (3 oz/85 g)

| Metric | | Ingredients | U.S. | |
Weight	Volume		Weight	Volume
57 g	118 ml	Gelatin	2 oz	½ cup
227 g	237 ml	Water, cold	8 oz	1 cup
454 g	474 ml	Water, hot	1 lb	2 cups
454 g	474 ml	Mayonnaise	1 lb	2 cups
1.48 kg	30 eggs	Eggs, hard-cooked, sliced	3 lb, 4 oz	30 eggs
851 g	889 ml	Salad Dressing	1 lb, 14 oz	3 ¾ cups
454 g	947 ml	Celery, chopped	1 lb	1 qt
114 g	237 ml	Green Pepper, chopped	4 oz	1 cup
114 g	118 ml	Lemon Juice	4 oz	½ cup
170 g	178 ml	Pickle Relish	6 oz	¾ cup
43 g	59 ml	Pimiento, chopped	1 ½ oz	¼ cup
14 g	15 ml	Salt	½ oz	1 tbsp
85 g	237 ml	Cabbage, chopped	3 oz	1 cup

Procedure

1. Soak gelatin in 1 cup/237 ml of cold water and dissolve in 2 cups/474 ml of hot water.
2. Add mayonnaise and mix thoroughly. Combine remaining ingredients with gelatin mixture.
3. Pour into flat pans and chill.
4. Cut into portions and serve in lettuce cups.

Pineapple Macaroni Salad
48 Servings (No. 10 Scoop)

| Metric | | Ingredients | U.S. | |
Weight	Volume		Weight	Volume
638 g	1.18 l	Macaroni, uncooked	1 lb, 6 ½ oz	1 ¼ qt
3.63 kg	3.79 l	Water, boiling	8 lb	1 gal
58 g	59 ml	Salt	2 oz	¼ cup
1.02 kg	1.18 l	Pineapple Tidbits, drained	2 lb, 4 oz	1 ¼ qt
340 g	474 ml	Green Pepper, chopped	12 oz	2 cups
425 g	474 ml	Dill Pickles, chopped	15 oz	2 cups
106 g	178 ml	Green Onions, chopped	3 ¾ oz	¾ cup
340 g	711 ml	Cheddar Cheese, diced	12 oz	3 cups
567 g	592 ml	Salad Dressing	1 lb, 4 oz	2 ½ cups
	22 ½ ml	Seasoning Salt		1 ½ tbsp
	7 ½ ml	Dill Weed		1 ½ tsp

Procedure

1. Cook macaroni in boiling, salted water 10 minutes, or until barely tender. Drain, rinse with cold water, and cool.
2. Add well-drained pineapple tidbits, green pepper, pickle, onion, and cheese. Toss well with salad dressing that has been blended with seasonings.
3. Chill and using a No. 10 scoop, portion salad into lettuce cups. Garnish with pineapple or pepper rings.

Club Salad
50 Servings (6 oz/170 g)

Metric		Ingredients	U.S.		
Weight	Volume		Weight		Volume
1.14 kg	2.13 l	Macaroni	2 lb,	8 oz	2 ¼ qt
9.07 kg	9.47 l	Water	20 lb		2 ½ gal
85 g	90 ml	Salt		3 oz	6 tbsp
511 g	10 eggs	Eggs, hard-cooked, diced	1 lb,	2 oz	10 eggs
227 g	474 ml	Ripe Olives, chopped		8 oz	2 cups
454 g	711 ml	Sweet Pickles, chopped	1 lb		3 cups
1.14 kg	2.37 l	Celery, diced	2 lb,	8 oz	2 ½ qt
227 g	316 ml	Pimiento, chopped		8 oz	1 ⅓ cups
227 g	474 ml	Green Pepper, chopped		8 oz	2 cups
43 g	266 ml	Parsley, chopped		1 ½ oz	1 ⅛ cups
114 g	178 ml	Onions, grated		4 oz	¾ cup
57 g	60 ml	Salt		2 oz	4 tbsp
114 g	118 ml	Vinegar		4 oz	½ cup
454 g	474 ml	Mayonnaise	1 lb		2 cups

Procedure

1. Drop macaroni into 2 ½ gal/9.46 l of water, vigorously boiling, to which 3 oz/85 g of salt has been added. Cook until tender. Drain, wash, and cool.

2. Combine macaroni with other ingredients in order listed.
3. Chill and serve on lettuce.

Turkey Salad
50 Servings (5 oz/142 g)

Metric		Ingredients	U.S.		
Weight	Volume		Weight		Volume
3.18 kg	4.98 l	Turkey, cooked, diced	7 lb		5 ¼ qt
907 g	1.42 l	Eggs, hard-cooked, diced	2 lb		18 med
2.27 kg	4.74 l	Celery, finely chopped	5 lb		5 qt
43 g	45 ml	Salt		1 ½ oz	3 tbsp
	5 ml	Pepper, white			1 tsp
255 g	355 ml	Stuffed Olives, chopped		9 oz	1 ½ cups
793 g	829 ml	Mayonnaise	1 lb,	12 oz	3 ½ cups

Procedure

1. Combine all ingredients. Chill thoroughly.

2. Serve on lettuce. A No. 12 scoop may be used.

Table 17
Suggested Salad Combinations

Ingredients	Dressings	Garnish
Fruit		
Apple, diced, celery rings, pecans	Orange Cheese	Salad cherry
Apple slices, grapefruit and orange segments	French	Chopped pimiento and green pepper
Apple slices and pineapple	Cooked fruit	Mandarin oranges
Apple slices, grapes, pineapple	Blue cheese	Avocado wedge
Apple, celery, and orange, diced	Poppyseed	Green pepper
Apricot halves, jellied crushed pineapple	Orange cheese	Blueberries or sliced kumquat
Apricot halves, orange segments	Cooked fruit	Banana chunk rolled in nuts
Avocado, grapefruit segments	French	Peeled cherry tomato
Avocado, pineapple tidbits, and tart apple wedges	Lemon cream	Sliced stuffed olives
Banana, diced, orange segments, pineapple tidbits	Avocado	Fresh berries
Cranberry and orange mold	Cooked fruit	Green grapes
Dark cherry mold, Bing cherries, pineapple tidbits	Golden pineapple	Slivered almonds
Cherries, pineapple, and banana	Lemon honey	Mandarin oranges
Grapefruit and cucumber	Celery Seed	Green pepper ring
Grapefruit and pineapple	Honey French	Pomegranate seed or avocado
Grapefruit and orange segments	French	Fresh grapes
Honeydew melon, pineapple, and grapes	Apricot cream	Salad cherry
Honeydew melon, canteloupe, and watermelon	Lemon or lime juice	Green grapes
Peach half and pineapple	Cooked fruit	Date strips
Pineapple slice and orange	Lemon honey	Prune filled with plum butter
Pineapple, fresh pear, and orange	Orange cheese	Cherry
Pineapple, grape and celery rings	Blue cheese	Toasted, salted almonds
Vegetable		
Asparagus spear and tomato slice	Piquant	Sieved egg yolk
Asparagus cuts, celery rings, tomato	Thousand Island	Sliced stuffed olive
Cabbage, celery, green pepper, onion	Nippy	Radish slices
Carrot, chopped, raisins, celery	Combination	Spanish peanuts
Carrot, chopped, pineapple tidbits, and celery	Pineapple mayonnaise	Mandarin oranges
Whole kernel corn, green pepper, sliced green onion, celery	French	Pimiento
Corn kernels, diced cucumber, and onion rings	Sour cream	Sliced radish
Cucumber slices and onion rings	French	Tomato wedge
Kidney beans, cut green beans, chopped onion, and celery	Fashion French	Bacon bits
Lima beans, chopped parsley, sliced green onion, celery	French	Cherry tomato
Lima beans, kidney beans, whole kernel corn, celery, and onion	Piquant	Sliced, hard-cooked egg
Green beans, minced onion, celery rings	Creole	Shredded cheese
Green beans (asparagus pack) with tomato slice	Mayonnaise	Celery rings
Fresh spinach, iceberg lettuce, sliced celery, and young onion	Piquant	Shredded ham
Tomato and cucumber slices	Combination	Cauliflowerets
Tomato aspic cubes, green beans, celery rings	Mayonnaise	Sliced green onions
Sliced zucchini, tomato, and celery	French	Hard-cooked egg
Diced zucchini, onion, and celery	Savory	Carrot curls
Main Dish Salads		
	Cheese	
Cottage cheese and pineapple mold	Mayonnaise	Malaga grapes
Cottage cheese, minced herbs in tomato	French	Salted almonds
Cheese and nut balls, pineapple	Honey French	Green pepper
Frozen fruit and cream cheese	Cooked fruit	Cherry
Diced Cheddar, celery rings, and pineapple	Combination	Cherry tomato
Green peas, diced Cheddar, chopped pickle	French	Onion rings

Table 17
Suggested Salad Combinations
(cont.)

Ingredients	Dressings	Garnish
Egg		
Egg and celery salad, tomato wedges	Mayonnaise	Green pepper
Stuffed eggs with cucumber slices	Mayonnaise	Tomato wedge
Egg salad and ripe olives	Cooked	Julienne ham
Hard-cooked egg, club salad	Combination	Sliced stuffed olives
Egg and potato salad	Mayonnaise	Salami or wiener slices
Fish		
Crab Louis—Crabmeat, tomato, hard-cooked egg, shredded lettuce	Thousand Island	Ripe olives
Lobster, celery, minced onion, chopped egg	Mayonnaise	Tomato
Shrimp, spinach, and lettuce salad	French	Chopped, hard-cooked egg
Shrimp, diced celery, cucumber	French	Stuffed olive
Salmon flakes, diced celery, chopped egg, and pickle	Mayonnaise	Cucumber slices
Tuna flakes, celery rings, cucumber	Combination	Sliced egg
Tomato aspic ring filled with shrimp or tuna salad	Mayonnaise	Celery curls
Avocado filled with fish or poultry salad	Mayonnaise	Lemon wedge
Meat		
Chicken salad and grapefruit	Mayonnaise	Toasted almonds
Ham salad and pineapple slice	Combination	Spanish peanuts
Frankfurter and potato salad	Combination	Julienne cheese
Ham salad with asparagus tips	Combination	Stuffed egg-half

Salad Dressings

COOKED SALAD DRESSINGS

Cooked Fruit Dressing
1 gal/3.79 l

Metric			U.S.		
Weight	**Volume**	**Ingredients**	**Weight**		**Volume**
681 g	711 ml	Pineapple Juice	1 lb,	8 oz	3 cups
681 g	711 ml	Orange Juice	1 lb,	8 oz	3 cups
114 g	118 ml	Lemon Juice		4 oz	½ cup
35 g	60 ml	Cornstarch		1¼ oz	4 tbsp
85 g	90 ml	Sugar		3 oz	6 tbsp
	5 ml	Salt			1 tsp
511 g	533 ml	Eggs, beaten (10 med)	1 lb,	2 oz	2¼ cups
907 g	947 ml	Whipping Cream	2 lb		1 qt

1. Heat fruit juices to boiling. Thoroughly blend cornstarch, sugar, and salt. Add to hot mixture, stirring constantly until mixture thickens and cornstarch loses its raw taste.
2. Add small portion of hot mixture to beaten eggs, stirring. Then add egg mixture to hot mixture. Cook for 5 minutes. Cool thoroughly.
3. Whip cream and fold into cold mixture shortly before serving.

Boiled Dressing
1 gal/3.79 l

| Metric | | Ingredients | U.S. | |
Weight	Volume		Weight	Volume
28 g	30 ml	Salt	1 oz	2 tbsp
	7 ½ ml	Paprika		1 ½ tsp
35 g	75 ml	Mustard, dry	1 ¼ oz	5 tbsp
	½ ml	Cayenne Pepper		1/10 tsp
454 g	474 ml	Sugar	1 lb	2 cups
454 g	947 ml	Flour, pastry	1 lb	1 qt
907 g	947 ml	Milk, cold	2 lb	1 qt
1.36 kg	1.42 l	Water, boiling	3 lb	1 ½ qt
907 g	947 ml	Vinegar	2 lb	1 qt
142 g	148 ml	Butter or Margarine	5 oz	5/8 cup
340 g	316 ml	Egg Yolks (16 med)	12 oz	1 ⅓ cups (16 med)

Procedure

1. Mix dry ingredients thoroughly. Add cold milk and blend.
2. Add boiling water and mix. Place in double boiler and heat, stirring, until flour is thoroughly cooked.
3. Add vinegar and butter or margarine.
4. Beat egg yolks until creamy. Add some of the hot mixture to the egg yolks, then stir egg yolks into cooked mixture, beating constantly. Cook for 3 minutes.

Mustard Dressing
1 qt/947 ml

| Metric | | Ingredients | U.S. | |
Weight	Volume		Weight	Volume
3 g	10 ml	Mustard, dry		2 tsp
9 g	10 ml	Salt	⅓ oz	2 tsp
793 g	829 ml	Condensed Milk	1 lb, 12 oz	3 ½ cups
170 g	158 ml	Egg Yolks, slightly beaten (8 med)	6 oz	⅔ cup
227 g	237 ml	Vinegar	8 oz	1 cup

Procedure

1. Make a paste of mustard, salt, and 2 tbsp/30 ml of the milk.
2. Heat milk in double boiler. Combine paste with condensed milk.
3. Add yolks to the hot mixture by first adding a portion of hot mixture to the eggs, stirring. Stir until well-blended. Cook until thickened.
4. When cold, add vinegar, stirring until mixture thickens.
5. Yield: 1 quart. Good served with ham.

Golden Pineapple Dressing
1 gal/3.79 l

Metric		Ingredients	U.S.		
Weight	Volume		Weight		Volume
1.59 kg	1.66 l	Pineapple Juice	3 lb,	8 oz	1 ¾ qt
114 g	118 ml	Lemon Juice		4 oz	½ cup
57 g	105 ml	Cornstarch		2 oz	7 tbsp
340 g	355 ml	Sugar		12 oz	1 ½ cups
9 g	10 ml	Salt		⅓ oz	2 tsp
255 g	237 ml	Egg Yolks, slightly beaten (12 med)		9 oz	1 cup
340 g	355 ml	Butter or Margarine		12 oz	1 ½ cups
681 g	711 ml	Heavy Cream (32%)	1 lb,	8 oz	3 cups

Procedure

1. Heat fruit juices in double boiler.
2. Combine cornstarch, sugar, and salt. Blend. Add to hot juice, stirring until thick.
3. Add egg yolks by first adding portion of hot mixture to the yolks, stirring constantly.
4. Remove from heat at once. Add butter and stir until melted. Cool.
5. Whip cream and fold into the thickened mixture when it is cold.

Buttercup Dressing
1 gal/3.79 l

Metric		Ingredients	U.S.		
Weight	Volume		Weight		Volume
71 g	158 ml	Flour		2 ½ oz	⅔ cup
567 g	632 ml	Sugar	1 lb,	4 oz	2 ⅔ cups
9 g	10 ml	Salt		⅓ oz	2 tsp
567 g	592 ml	Pineapple Juice	1 lb,	4 oz	2 ½ cups
170 g	178 ml	Lemon Juice		6 oz	¾ cup
510 g	533 ml	Eggs, separated (10 med)	1 lb,	2 oz	2 ¼ cups
170 g	711 ml	Marshmallows		6 oz	3 cups
567 g	592 ml	Whipping Cream	1 lb,	4 oz	2 ½ cups

Procedure

1. Mix flour, sugar, and salt with enough of the fruit juice to make a smooth paste.
2. Boil remainder of juice and add flour mixture. Place in double boiler and cook until thick, or until the flour has lost its raw taste, stirring constantly.
3. Add small portion of hot mixture to slightly beaten egg yolks, stirring. Add to hot mixture and cook for 5 minutes.
4. Remove from heat. Add marshmallows while hot.
5. When cool, fold in stiffly beaten egg whites. Whip cream and fold into dressing before serving.

Basic French Dressing
1 gal/3.79 l

Metric		Ingredients	U.S.	
Weight	Volume		Weight	Volume
3 g	10 ml	Mustard, dry		2 tsp
340 g	355 ml	Sugar	12 oz	1 ½ cups
57 g	60 ml	Salt	2 oz	4 tbsp
28 g	60 ml	Paprika	1 oz	4 tbsp
28 g	30 ml	Onion Juice	1 oz	2 tbsp
2.27 kg	2.37 l	Salad Oil	5 lb	2 ½ qt
907 g	947 ml	Vinegar	2 lb	4 cups
99 g	89 ml	Eggs, unbeaten (2 med)	3 ½ oz	⅜ cup

Procedure

1. Combine mustard, sugar, salt, paprika, and onion juice. Mix well.
2. Add 1 cup oil slowly, beating. Add 1 cup vinegar, beating. Continue to alternate, adding liquids slowly and beating continuously.
3. Drop eggs into mixture and beat thoroughly.

Vinaigrette Dressing
1 gal/3.79 l

Metric		Ingredients	U.S.	
Weight	Volume		Weight	Volume
170 g	158 ml	Egg Yolks, hard-cooked (8 med)	6 oz	⅔ cup
10 g	22 ml	Mustard, dry	⅜ oz	1 ½ tbsp
14 g	30 ml	Paprika	½ oz	2 tbsp
28 g	30 ml	Salt	1 oz	2 tbsp
9 g	22 ml	Curry Powder	⅓ oz	1 ½ tbsp
1.02 kg	1.07 l	Vinegar	2 lb, 4 oz	4 ½ cups
2.27 kg	2.37 l	Oil	5 lb	2 ½ qt
	30 ml	Chives, minced		2 tbsp
43 g	30 ml	Onions, minced	1 ½ oz	2 tbsp
	30 ml	Parsley, finely chopped		2 tbsp
18 g	30 ml	Pimiento, finely chopped	⅔ oz	2 tbsp

Procedure

1. Mash yolks with mustard, paprika, salt, and curry powder. Stir in vinegar and gradually blend in oil.
2. Mix in remaining ingredients.

Note: A ½ cup/118 ml of chopped pickle may be added if desired.

Tomato French Dressing
1 gal/3.79 l

Metric		Ingredients	U.S.	
Weight	Volume		Weight	Volume
1.82 kg	1.89 l	Tomato Soup	4 lb	2 qt
85 g	90 ml	Worcestershire Sauce	3 oz	6 tbsp
340 g	355 ml	Sugar	12 oz	1 ½ cups
227 g	237 ml	Tarragon Vinegar	8 oz	1 cup
340 g	355 ml	Cider Vinegar	12 oz	1 ½ cups
1.14 kg	1.18 l	Salad Oil	2 lb, 8 oz	1 ¼ qt
18 g	20 ml	Salt	⅔ oz	4 tsp
7 g	15 ml	Mustard, dry	¼ oz	1 tbsp
9 g	10 ml	Onion Juice	⅓ oz	2 tsp

Procedure

1. Combine all ingredients and mix. Shake well before using.

Note: Appetizing with head-of-lettuce salad or with cucumber and tomato salad.

Savory Dressing
1 gal/3.79 l

Metric		Ingredients	U.S.	
Weight	Volume		Weight	Volume
2.72 kg	2.84 l	Oil	6 lb	3 qt
907 g	947 ml	Vinegar	2 lb	1 qt
227 g	237 ml	Sugar	8 oz	1 cup
114 g	118 ml	Salt	4 oz	½ cup
28 g	90 ml	Mustard, dry	1 oz	6 tbsp
14 g	30 ml	Paprika	½ oz	2 tbsp
	2–4 cloves	Garlic, finely minced		2–4 cloves
	5⁄16 ml	Cayenne Pepper		1⁄16 tsp

Procedure

1. Combine all ingredients. Beat until thoroughly blended.

THYME   PARSLEY   BASIL

Fashion French Dressing

1 gal/3.79 l

Metric		Ingredients	U.S.	
Weight	Volume		Weight	Volume
1.36 kg	1.42 l	Salad Oil	3 lb	1 ½ qt
454 g	474 ml	Vinegar	1 lb	2 cups
681 g	711 ml	Catsup	1 lb, 8 oz	3 cups
85 g	79 ml	Worcestershire	3 oz	⅓ cup
28 g	8 cloves	Garlic, halved	1 oz	8 cloves
907 g	1.42 l	Onions, minced	2 lb	1 ½ qt
567 g	592 ml	Sugar	1 lb, 4 oz	2 ½ cups
28 g	30 ml	Salt	1 oz	2 tbsp

Procedure

1. Blend ingredients. Let stand 4 days to ripen.
2. Strain, if a smooth dressing is desired, or merely remove garlic cloves.

Piquant Dressing

1 gal/3.79 l

Metric		Ingredients	U.S.	
Weight	Volume		Weight	Volume
2.04 kg	2.13 l	Salad Oil	4 lb, 8 oz	2 ¼ qt
1.14 kg	1.18 l	Vinegar	2 lb, 8 oz	1 ¼ qt
57 g	60 ml	Salt	2 oz	¼ cup
7 g	15 ml	Pepper	¼ oz	1 tbsp
57 g	59 ml	Egg Whites (2 med)	2 oz	¼ cup
312 g	474 ml	Sweet Pickles, finely chopped	11 oz	2 cups
7 g	15 ml	Paprika	¼ oz	1 tbsp
	⅝ ml	Cayenne Pepper		⅛ tsp

Procedure

1. Combine salad oil, vinegar, salt, pepper, and egg white. Beat until oil is in suspension.

2. Add remaining ingredients and mix.

TARRAGON   SAGE   MINT

Chiffonade Dressing
1 gal/3.79 l

| Metric | | | U.S. | |
Weight	Volume	Ingredients	Weight	Volume
227 g	355 ml	Onions, grated	8 oz	1 ½ cups
227 g	316 ml	Pimiento, chopped	8 oz	1 ⅓ cups
57 g	355 ml	Parsley, chopped	2 oz	1 ½ cups
397 g	8 eggs	Eggs, hard-cooked, chopped	14 oz	8 eggs
227 g	474 ml	Celery, chopped	8 oz	2 cups
114 g	178 ml	Dill Pickle, chopped	4 oz	¾ cup
227 g	237 ml	Chili Sauce	8 oz	1 cup
2.27 kg	2.37 l	French Dressing	5 lb	2 ½ qt

Procedure

1. Combine all ingredients. Mix well and serve.

Honey Dressing
1 gal/3.79 l

| Metric | | | U.S. | |
Weight	Volume	Ingredients	Weight	Volume
907 g	947 ml	Sugar	2 lb	1 qt
14 g	30 ml	Mustard, dry	½ oz	2 tbsp
	30 ml	Paprika		2 tbsp
	7 ½ ml	Salt		1 ½ tsp
14 g	30 ml	Celery Seed	½ oz	2 tbsp
793 g	592 ml	Honey, strained	1 lb, 12 oz	2 ½ cups
567 g	592 ml	Vinegar	1 lb, 4 oz	2 ½ cups
114 g	118 ml	Lemon Juice	4 oz	½ cup
18 g	30 ml	Onions, grated	⅔ oz	2 tbsp
1.36 kg	1.42 l	Salad Oil	3 lb	1 ½ qt

Procedure

1. Mix dry ingredients. Add honey, vinegar, lemon juice, and grated onions.

2. Pour oil into mixture very slowly, beating constantly.

Celery Seed Dressing
3 ½ qt/3.31 l

| Metric | | Ingredients | U.S. | |
Weight	Volume		Weight	Volume
793 g	829 ml	Sugar	1 lb, 12 oz	3 ½ cups
6 g	20 ml	Mustard, dry		4 tsp
19 g	20 ml	Salt	⅔ oz	4 tsp
596 g	632 ml	Vinegar	1 lb, 5 oz	2 ⅔ cups
1.82 kg	1.89 l	Oil	4 lb	2 qt
57 g	118 ml	Celery Seed	2 oz	½ cup

Procedure

1. Mix dry ingredients. Add small amount of vinegar. Beat well.

2. Add oil and remaining vinegar alternately while beating. Add celery seed.

MAYONNAISE AND VARIATIONS

Mayonnaise
1 gal/3.79 l

| Metric | | Ingredients | U.S. | |
Weight	Volume		Weight	Volume
114 g	118 ml	Egg Yolks (6 med)	4 oz	½ cup
28 g	30 ml	Salt	1 oz	2 tbsp
	⅝ ml	Cayenne Pepper		⅛ tsp
	2 ½ ml	Paprika		½ tsp
	10 ml	Mustard		2 tsp
28 g	30 ml	Sugar	1 oz	2 tbsp
227 g	237 ml	Vinegar	8 oz	1 cup
3.41 kg	3.56 l	Salad Oil	7 lb, 8 oz	3 ¾ qt

Procedure

1. Beat egg yolks on second speed of mixer until well-beaten.
2. Mix dry ingredients with one half the vinegar and add to the beaten egg yolks.

3. Add oil slowly to eggs. Toward the last, oil may be added more rapidly. Continue beating constantly. After all oil is added, add remainder of vinegar and continue beating for 5 minutes.

Mayonnaise with Cooked Base

1 gal/3.79 l

Metric		Ingredients	U.S.	
Weight	Volume		Weight	Volume
		Part 1		
	20 ml	Flour		1 ⅓ tbsp
	2 ½ ml	Salt		½ tsp
	5 ml	Mustard, dry		1 tsp
	1 ¼ ml	Sugar		¼ tsp
	40 ml	Water, cold		2 ⅔ tbsp
		Part 2		
	2 ½ ml	Butter or Margarine, melted		½ tsp
49 g	1 egg	Egg, beaten	1 ¾ oz	1 egg
35 g	37 ml	Vinegar, hot	1 ¼ oz	2 ½ tbsp
99 g	105 ml	Water, hot	3 ½ oz	7 tbsp
		Part 3		
198 g	207 ml	Eggs, beaten (4 med)	7 oz	⅞ cup
18 g	20 ml	Sugar	⅔ oz	1 ⅓ tbsp
18 g	20 ml	Salt	⅔ oz	1 ⅓ tbsp
	5 ml	Paprika		1 tsp
	5 ml	Mustard, dry		1 tsp
2.84 kg	2.96 l	Oil	6 lb, 4 oz	3 ⅛ qt
170 g	178 ml	Vinegar	6 oz	¾ cup

Procedure

1. Combine ingredients of Part 1. Stir until smooth.
2. Add Part 2 to Part 1, stirring well.
3. Heat and cook mixture until it thickens. Cool.
4. In Part 3, combine eggs, sugar, salt, paprika, and dry mustard. Beat in mixing machine, adding oil and vinegar very slowly.
5. Combine Part 3 with Parts 1 and 2, stirring continually.
6. Yield: 1 gallon.

Persian Dressing

1 gal/3.79 l

Metric		Ingredients	U.S.	
Weight	Volume		Weight	Volume
283 g	296 ml	Eggs, hard-cooked, chopped (5 lge)	10 oz	1 ¼ cups
128 g	178 ml	Olives, crushed	4 ½ oz	¾ cup
142 g	237 ml	Dill Pickles, chopped	5 oz	1 cup
114 g	118 ml	Catsup	4 oz	½ cup
3.18 kg	3.31 l	Mayonnaise	7 lb	3 ½ qt

Procedure

1. Combine eggs, olives, pickles, and catsup. Fold mixture into mayonnaise.

Combination Dressing
1 gal/3.79 l

Metric		Ingredients	U.S.		
Weight	Volume		Weight		Volume
681 g	711 ml	Vinegar	1 lb,	8 oz	3 cups
907 g	947 ml	Water	2 lb		1 qt
454 g	474 ml	Sugar	1 lb		2 cups
227 g	474 ml	Flour, pastry		8 oz	2 cups
28 g	59 ml	Mustard, dry		1 oz	¼ cup
28 g	30 ml	Salt		1 oz	2 tbsp
	7½ ml	Paprika			1½ tsp
	½ ml	Cayenne Pepper			1/10 tsp
340 g	355 ml	Water, cold		12 oz	1½ cups
170 g	178 ml	Eggs (3 lge)		6 oz	¾ cup
1.36 kg	1.42 l	Mayonnaise	3 lb		1½ qt

Procedure

1. Heat vinegar and water to boiling.
2. Mix dry ingredients together. Add cold water. Stir into boiling liquid. Cook in double boiler for about 45 minutes or until done.
3. Beat eggs well. Pour hot mixture over eggs slowly. Allow to cool.
4. When cool, add mayonnaise and mix well.

Green Goddess Dressing
1 gal/3.79 l

Metric		Ingredients	U.S.		
Weight	Volume		Weight		Volume
227 g	237 ml	Tarragon Vinegar		8 oz	1 cup
227 g	237 ml	Lemon Juice		8 oz	1 cup
283 g	296 ml	Anchovy Paste		10 oz	1¼ cups
2.72 kg	2.84 l	Mayonnaise	6 lb		3 qt
156 g	237 ml	Capers, chopped		5½ oz	1 cup
71 g	237 ml	Chives, chopped		2½ oz	1 cup
28 g	8 cloves	Garlic, mixed		1 oz	8 cloves
151 g	237 ml	Onions, chopped		5⅓ oz	1 cup
28 g	178 ml	Parsley, chopped		1 oz	¾ cup

Procedure

1. Blend vinegar and lemon juice into anchovy paste and then into mayonnaise.
2. Add remaining ingredients.
3. Serve on lettuce or tossed green salad.

Creole Dressing
1 gal/3.79 l

Metric		Ingredients	U.S.	
Weight	Volume		Weight	Volume
227 g	474 ml	Green Pepper, finely chopped	8 oz	2 cups
114 g	158 ml	Sweet Pickles, finely chopped	4 oz	⅔ cup
114 g	158 ml	Olives, finely chopped	4 oz	⅔ cup
114 g	158 ml	Onions, finely chopped	4 oz	⅔ cup
227 g	237 ml	Chili Sauce	8 oz	1 cup
227 g	237 ml	Catsup	8 oz	1 cup
2.72 kg	2.84 l	Mayonnaise	6 lb	3 qt
57 g	60 ml	Salt	2 oz	4 tbsp
28 g	60 ml	Paprika	1 oz	4 tbsp

Procedure

1. Combine all ingredients. Mix thoroughly.

Thousand Island Dressing
1 gal/3.79 l

Metric		Ingredients	U.S.	
Weight	Volume		Weight	Volume
454 g	474 ml	Chili Sauce	1 lb	2 cups
766 g	1.18 l	Eggs, hard-cooked, chopped (14 lge)	1 lb, 11 oz	1 ¼ qt
85 g	118 ml	Pimiento, chopped	3 oz	½ cup
57 g	79 ml	Green Olives or Pickles, chopped	2 oz	⅓ cup
57 g	79 ml	Onions, chopped	2 oz	⅓ cup
	⅝ ml	Cayenne Pepper		⅛ tsp
2.27 kg	2.37 l	Mayonnaise	5 lb	2 ½ qt

Procedure

1. Combine seasonings and fold into mayonnaise.

Horseradish Dressing
1 gal/3.79 l

Metric		Ingredients	U.S.	
Weight	Volume		Weight	Volume
3.41 kg	3.56 l	Mayonnaise	7 lb, 8 oz	3 ¾ qt
283 g	296 ml	Horseradish	10 oz	1 ¼ cups
	10 ml	Mustard, dry		2 tsp

1. Combine all ingredients and mix thoroughly. Good served with ham, perfection salad, or salads with cabbage base.

Russian Dressing
1 gal/3.79 l

Metric		Ingredients	U.S.	
Weight	Volume		Weight	Volume
227 g	237 ml	Lemon Juice	8 oz	1 cup
567 g	592 ml	Chili Sauce	1 lb, 4 oz	2 ½ cups
28 g	30 ml	Onion Juice or Grated Onion	1 oz	2 tbsp
142 g	118 ml	Worcestershire Sauce	5 oz	½ cup
	⅝ ml	Cayenne Pepper		⅛ tsp
2.72 kg	2.84 l	Mayonnaise	6 lb	3 qt

Procedure

1. Combine all ingredients. Chill thoroughly and serve with head-of-lettuce salad.

CHEESE AND CREAM DRESSINGS

Fruit Salad Dressing
1 gal/3.79 l

Metric		Ingredients	U.S.	
Weight	Volume		Weight	Volume
907 g	947 ml	Orange Juice	2 lb	1 qt
454 g	474 ml	Lemon Juice	1 lb	2 cups
907 g	947 ml	Eggs, slightly beaten (16 lge)	2 lb	1 qt
340 g	632 ml	Powdered Sugar	12 oz	2 ⅔ cups
	2 ½ ml	Salt		½ tsp
907 g	947 ml	Heavy Cream	2 lb	1 qt

Procedure

1. Heat juice in double boiler.
2. Combine eggs, powdered sugar, and salt. Beat slightly, or until blended.
3. Add eggs to hot mixture by first adding some of hot mixture to eggs, stirring. Cook for 2 minutes or until spoon is coated. Remove from heat immediately. Cool.
4. Whip the cream and fold into the chilled dressing just before serving.

Apricot Dressing
1 gal/3.79 l

Metric		Ingredients	U.S.	
Weight	Volume		Weight	Volume
1.82 kg	1.89 l	Mayonnaise	4 lb	2 qt
170 g	237 ml	Almonds, blanched and chopped	6 oz	1 cup
114 g	118 ml	Lemon Juice	4 oz	½ cup
340 g	355 ml	Apricot Juice	12 oz	1 ½ cups
454 g	474 ml	Whipping Cream	1 lb	2 cups

Procedure

1. Combine mayonnaise, almonds, lemon juice, and enough apricot juice to make good consistency.

2. Whip cream and fold into dressing mixture.

Sour Cream Dressing
1 gal/3.79 l

Metric		Ingredients	U.S.	
Weight	Volume		Weight	Volume
681 g	711 ml	Lemon Juice or Vinegar	1 lb, 8 oz	3 cups
28 g	30 ml	Onions, grated	1 oz	2 tbsp
57 g	60 ml	Salt	2 oz	4 tbsp
340 g	355 ml	Sugar	12 oz	1 ½ cups
	⅝ ml	Cayenne Pepper		⅛ tsp
2.72 kg	2.84 l	Sour Cream	6 lb	3 qt

Procedure

1. Combine lemon juice, onions, and seasonings.
2. Gradually beat mixture into sour cream, beating until mixture is stiff.

Orange Cheese Dressing
1 gal/3.79 l

| Metric | | Ingredients | U.S. | |
Weight	Volume		Weight	Volume
1.14 kg	1.18 l	Cottage Cheese, low fat	2 lb, 8 oz	1 ¼ qt
454 g	474 ml	Orange Concentrate, undiluted	1 lb	2 cups
57 g	59 ml	Lemon Juice	2 oz	¼ cup
	7 ½ ml	Salt		1 ½ tsp
1.14 kg	1.18 l	Salad Dressing	2 lb, 8 oz	1 ¼ qt
454 g	947 ml	Whipped Cream	1 lb	1 qt

Procedure

1. Grind cottage cheese until particles are fine. Stir in undiluted orange juice concentrate, lemon juice, salt, and salad dressing.

2. Fold in whipped cream. Chill.

Avocado Dressing
1 gal/3.79 l

| Metric | | Ingredients | U.S. | |
Weight	Volume		Weight	Volume
1.82 kg	1.89 l	Avocado, ripe, mashed	4 lb	2 qt
170 g	178 ml	Lemon Juice	6 oz	¾ cup
681 g	1.07 l	Onions, minced	1 lb, 8 oz	4 ½ cups
907 g	947 ml	Sour Cream	2 lb	1 qt
	1 ¼ ml	Hot Pepper Sauce		¼ tsp
28 g	30 ml	Salt	1 oz	2 tbsp

Procedure

1. Blend lemon juice with mashed avocado. Stir in remaining ingredients.

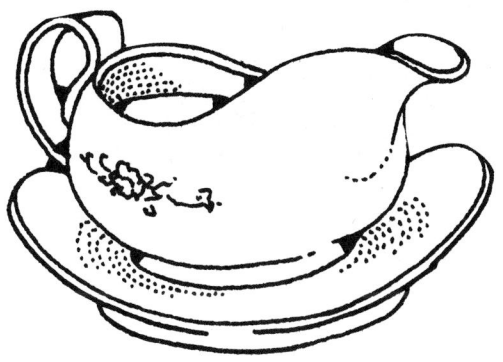

Roquefort Cheese Dressing
1 gal/3.79 l

Metric		Ingredients	U.S.	
Weight	Volume		Weight	Volume
454 g	474 ml	Roquefort Cheese	1 lb	2 cups
1.14 kg	1.18 l	Vinegar	2 lb, 8 oz	1 ¼ qt
2.27 kg	2.37 l	Salad Oil	5 lb	2 ½ qt
14 g	30 ml	Mustard, dry	½ oz	2 tbsp
14 g	30 ml	Paprika	½ oz	2 tbsp
28 g	30 ml	Salt	1 oz	2 tbsp
66 g	79 ml	Catsup	2 ⅓ oz	⅓ cup
28 g	37 ml	Sugar	1 oz	2 ½ tbsp

Procedure

1. Mash cheese (not too finely.)
2. Beat all other ingredients together well.

3. Add cheese and beat.

Blue Cheese Dressing
1 gal/3.79 l

Metric		Ingredients	U.S.	
Weight	Volume		Weight	Volume
340 g	355 ml	Eggs (6 lge)	12 oz	1 ½ cups
1.82 kg	2.01 l	Salad Oil	4 lb	8 ½ cups
28 g	30 ml	Salt	1 oz	2 tbsp
57 g	118 ml	Paprika	2 oz	½ cup
57 g	60 ml	Celery Salt	2 oz	4 tbsp
	15 ml	Pepper		1 tbsp
454 g	474 ml	Vinegar	1 lb	2 cups
28 g	30 ml	Mustard, prepared	1 oz	2 tbsp
28 g	30 ml	Horseradish, prepared	1 oz	2 tbsp
21 g	6 cloves	Garlic, minced	¾ oz	6 cloves
227 g	474 ml	Blue Cheese, grated	8 oz	2 cups

Procedure

1. Beat eggs. Add oil, slowly beating until an emulsion is formed.
2. Add dry ingredients. Alternately beat in oil and vinegar.

3. Add mustard, horseradish, finely chopped garlic, and cheese. Add additional vinegar if needed for desired consistency.

Lemon Honey Dressing
3 qt/2.84 l

Metric		Ingredients	U.S.	
Weight	Volume		Weight	Volume
907 g	947 ml	Cream Cheese	2 lb	1 qt
510 g	355 ml	Honey	1 lb, 2 oz	1 ½ cups
567 g	592 ml	Lemon Juice	1 lb, 4 oz	2 ½ cups
7 g	22 ml	Grated Lemon Rind	¼ oz	1 ½ tbsp
14 g	15 ml	Salt	½ oz	1 tbsp
	⅝ ml	Cayenne Pepper		⅛ tsp
907 g	947 ml	Salad Oil	2 lb	1 qt

Procedure

1. Blend cream cheese and honey with lemon juice, lemon rind, salt, and pepper.

2. Beat oil in slowly. Chill. Stir well before serving.

Honey Cream Dressing
1 gal/3.79 l

Metric		Ingredients	U.S.	
Weight	Volume		Weight	Volume
681 g	711 ml	Cream Cheese	1 lb, 8 oz	3 cups
681 g	474 ml	Honey, strained	1 lb, 8 oz	2 cups
151 g	158 ml	Lemon Juice or Pineapple Juice	5 ⅓ oz	⅔ cup
	6 ¼ ml	Salt		1 ¼ tsp
2.27 kg	2.37 l	Mayonnaise	5 lb	2 ½ qt

Procedure

1. Blend cream cheese and honey. Add fruit juice and salt.

2. Fold in mayonnaise.

CHAPTER 11   *Sandwiches and Canapés*

Sandwiches

Sandwiches may be a triumph of good eating or a poor excuse to sustain the appetite until mealtime. Their place on menus may range from main dining room specialities to box-lunch fillers. When well-made, sandwiches rate among the most popular foods. Sandwiches have nutritional significance when they serve as the main part of daily lunches. The use of enriched bread and fillings that provide adequate protein is strongly recommended. The combination of bread and filling needs to be full-bodied enough to be satisfying, and sufficiently moist, flavorful, and piquant to be appetizing.

Use care to avoid a too-smooth texture and a flat, insipid flavor. Avoid dryness, stale flavors, soaking of bread, loss of crisp texture, absorption of off-flavors, (from cutting board or knife), and lack of sanitation. Proper refrigeration of the perishable materials and clean handling are prerequisites for safety. Quality is best when sandwiches are made to order, but this is often impossible. Prompt wrapping helps to preserve freshness. Clear plastic or waxed paper, which permit sandwiches to be seen, are best for display.

Eye appeal adds to enjoyment, whether sandwiches are wrapped or served on a plate. The appearance should be neat and attractive. Consumer interest is directed first and most strongly to the filling. It is important, therefore, to cut and arrange portions so that fillings can be seen. Relish accompaniments may be used to add color and good texture. Crisp vegetables or fruit or spicy pickles add considerably to both eye and appetite appeal.

Spreads Butter or margarine, mayonnaise, or other salad dressings are commonly used to spread the bread before adding a filling. (See Canapé Spreads for suggestions.) A coating of butter or margarine on bread helps to keep the moist fillings from soaking into the bread and adds richness to the flavor. Ease of spreading butter or margarine, as well as volume, can be increased by whipping evaporated milk into it. The amount to use is 8 oz/227 g of evaporated milk to 1 lb/454 g of butter or margarine. Add the milk gradually while the butter or margarine is being beaten in a mixer or with a rotary beater. This quantity is sufficient for spreading 100 bread slices for 50 sandwiches. Savory Butter (accompanying recipe) is an appetizing spread for use with meat or poultry sandwiches.

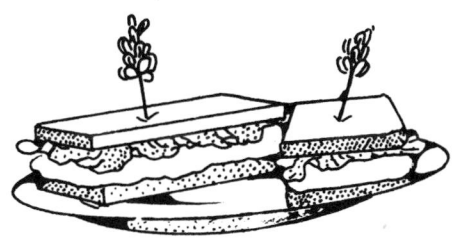

Savory Butter

2 cups/474 ml

| Metric | | Ingredients | U.S. | |
Weight	Volume		Weight	Volume
340 g	355 ml	Butter or Margarine	12 oz	1 ½ cups
	37 ½ ml	Lemon juice		2 ½ tbsp
	2 ½ ml	Mustard, prepared		½ tsp
	2 ½ ml	Horseradish, prepared		½ tsp
	1 ¼ ml	Salt		¼ tsp

Procedure

1. Cream butter or margarine. Slowly add lemon juice, beating until juice is entirely blended.
2. Add seasonings and beat until light and fluffy.
3. Yield: 2 cups/474 ml or 96 tsp/480 ml. One teaspoon of spread covers one slice of bread.

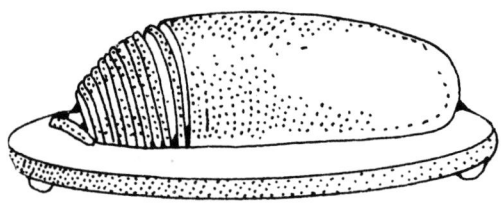

Bread There are many kinds of breads and rolls suitable for sandwich-making. It is a good idea to study local markets for those varieties popular with a specific clientele. Thickness of bread slices and sizes of buns and rolls differ. Examination, pricing, and testing will help in determining the best selection for specific use. Table 18 indicates weights, number of slices per loaf, and thickness of slices of common commercial varieties.

Table 18
Slices in Common Commercial Bread Loaves
(not including ends)

Variety	Grams/Ounces per Loaf	Slices in Loaf	Thickness of Slice (in)
Egg Sesame	638/22½	23	⅜
Egg Sesame	425/15	15	⅜
Honey Wheat	638/22½	22	⅜
Raisin	425/15	16	½
Rye, regular	454/16	23	⅜
Rye, regular	907/32	33	⅜
White, pullman	907/32	28	½
White, pullman	907/32	36	⅜
White, pullman	1.36 kg/48	44	½
White, pullman	1.36 kg/48	56	⅜
White, pullman	567/20	19	⅝
White, pullman	681/24	24	⅝
Whole Wheat, regular	454/16	16	⅝
Whole Wheat, regular	907/32	28	½
Whole Wheat, regular	1.36 kg/48	44	½
Whole Wheat, regular	1.36 kg/48	56	⅜

SANDWICH FILLINGS

Cheese Sandwich
50 Sandwiches (1 ⅔ oz/46 g)

Metric		Ingredients	U.S.	
Weight	Volume		Weight	Volume
1.36 kg	2.84 l	Cheddar Cheese, ground	3 lb	3 qt
14 g	30 ml	Mustard, dry	½ oz	2 tbsp
14 g	15 ml	Worcestershire Sauce	½ oz	1 tbsp
681 g	711 ml	Combination Dressing	1 lb, 8 oz	3 cups
9 g	10 ml	Salt	⅓ oz	2 tsp

Procedure

1. Blend ingredients thoroughly.
2. Yield: 3 ¾ qt/3.56 l or filling for 50 sandwiches, portioned with a No. 24 scoop.

Variations

Flavor may be varied by adding one of the following:

142 g	296 ml	Bacon Bits	5 oz	1 ¼ cups
170 g	474 ml	Bacon, cooked and crumbed	6 oz	2 cups
156 g	237 ml	Capers	5 ½ oz	1 cup
227 g	474 ml	Celery, finely chopped	8 oz	2 cups
227 g	237 ml	Chili Sauce	8 oz	1 cup
170 g	355 ml	Green Pepper, finely chopped	6 oz	1 ½ cups
170 g	237 ml	Pimiento, finely chopped	6 oz	1 cup
57 g	474 ml	Watercress	2 oz	2 cups

Tuna Salad Sandwich
50 Sandwiches (2 oz/57 g)

Metric		Ingredients	U.S.	
Weight	Volume		Weight	Volume
1.42 kg	1.66 l	Tuna	3 lb, 2 oz	7 cups
340 g	711 ml	Celery, finely chopped	12 oz	3 cups
255 g	355 ml	Pickles, finely chopped	9 oz	1 ½ cups
43 g	45 ml	Mustard, prepared	1 ½ oz	3 tbsp
28 g	30 ml	Lemon Juice	1 oz	2 tbsp
793 g	829 ml	Boiled Dressing	1 lb, 12 oz	3 ½ cups

Procedure

1. Combine drained and flaked tuna with remaining ingredients. Mix thoroughly.

2. Yield: 4 ½ lb/2.04 kg or 50 No. 24 scoops.

Tuna and Cheese Filling
55 Sandwiches (2 oz/57 g)

| Metric | | Ingredients | U.S. | |
Weight	Volume		Weight	Volume
1.82 kg	2.13 l	Tuna, drained and flaked	4 lb	2 ¼ qt
567 g	1.18 l	Cheddar Cheese, shredded	1 lb, 4 oz	5 cups
567 g	533 ml	Salad Dressing	1 lb, 4 oz	2 ¼ cups
283 g	296 ml	Pickle Relish	10 oz	1 ¼ cups

Procedure

1. Combine ingredients and mix thoroughly.   2. Use a No. 24 scoop to measure filling.

Tuna and Egg Salad Sandwich
50 Sandwiches (1 ¾ oz/49 g)

| Metric | | Ingredients | U.S. | |
Weight	Volume		Weight	Volume
1.42 kg	1.66 l	Tuna, drained and flaked	3 lb, 2 oz	7 cups
568 g	10 eggs	Eggs, hard-cooked, chopped	1 lb, 4 oz	10 eggs
397 g	395 ml	Salad Dressing	14 oz	1 ⅔ cups
161 g	158 ml	Pickle Relish	5 ⅔ oz	⅔ cup
198 g	415 ml	Celery, finely chopped	7 oz	1 ¾ cups

Procedure

1. Combine all ingredients.   2. Use a No. 24 scoop.

Egg and Ham Sandwich
53 Sandwiches (2 oz/57 g)

| Metric | | Ingredients | U.S. | |
Weight	Volume		Weight	Volume
2.04 kg	3.08 l	Eggs, hard-cooked, diced (36 lge)	4 lb, 8 oz	3 ¼ qt
567 g	592 ml	Ham, cooked, ground	1 lb, 4 oz	2 ½ cups
114 g	178 ml	Green Pepper, finely chopped	4 oz	¾ cup
	3 ¾ ml	Salt		¾ tsp
	3 ¾ ml	Pepper, white		¾ tsp
114 g	178 ml	Onions, minced	4 oz	¾ cup
340 g	355 ml	Salad Dressing	12 oz	1 ½ cups

Procedure

1. Combine ingredients and mix thoroughly.   2. Use a No. 24 scoop.

Egg Sandwich
50 Sandwiches (2 oz/57 g)

| Metric | | Ingredients | U.S. | |
Weight	Volume		Weight	Volume
1.82 kg	2.84 l	Eggs, hard-cooked (36 med)	4 lb	3 qt
114 g	118 ml	Pimiento, minced	4 oz	½ cup
454 g	711 ml	Sweet Relish	1 lb	3 cups
454 g	474 ml	Cooked Dressing	1 lb	2 cups
14 g	30 ml	Mustard, prepared	½ oz	2 tbsp

Procedure

1. Finely chop eggs.
2. Combine ingredients and mix thoroughly.

3. Portion with a No. 24 scoop.

Pimiento Cheese Filling
67 Sandwiches (1 ¾ oz/49 g)

| Metric | | Ingredients | U.S. | |
Weight	Volume		Weight	Volume
1.59 kg	3.31 l	Cheddar Cheese, grated	3 lb, 8 oz	3 ½ qt
397 g	2 cans	Pimiento, chopped	14 oz	2 cans (7 oz)
567 g	592 ml	Salad Dressing	1 lb, 4 oz	2 ½ cups

Procedure

1. Combine filling ingredients.

2. Portion filling with No. 24 scoop.

Egg Salad with Bacon Bits
65 Sandwiches (2 ¼ oz/64 g)

| Metric | | Ingredients | U.S. | |
Weight	Volume		Weight	Volume
170 g	296 ml	Bacon Bits	6 oz	1 ¼ cups
3.12 kg	55 lge	Eggs, hard-cooked, chopped	6 lb, 14 oz	55 lge
283 g	296 ml	Salad Dressing	10 oz	1 ¼ cups
454 g	947 ml	Celery, chopped	1 lb	1 qt
9 g	10 ml	Salt	⅓ oz	2 tsp
	5 ml	Pepper		1 tsp

Procedure

1. Combine all ingredients.

2. Portion filling with a No. 24 scoop.

Date and Nut Sandwich
50 Sandwiches (1 ⅔ oz/46 g)

Metric		Ingredients	U.S.	
Weight	Volume		Weight	Volume
1.59 kg	2.37 l	Dates, ground	3 lb, 8 oz	2 ½ qt
227 g	237 ml	Water	8 oz	1 cup
454 g	947 ml	Walnuts, chopped	1 lb	1 qt
114 g	118 ml	Orange Juice	4 oz	½ cup
21 g	59 ml	Orange Rind, grated	¾ oz	¼ cup

Procedure

1. Combine dates and water. Cook to make a paste. Cool.
2. Add remaining ingredients and mix.

3. Yield: 50 level No. 24 scoops or 5 ½ lb/2.50 kg.

Note: If necessary, moisten with more orange juice.

Cream Cheese and Chili Sauce Sandwich Spread
50 Sandwiches (1 ¾ oz/49 g)

Metric		Ingredients	U.S.	
Weight	Volume		Weight	Volume
1.59 kg	1.66 l	Cream Cheese	3 lb, 8 oz	1 ¾ qt
454 g	474 ml	Chili Sauce	1 lb	2 cups
9 g	10 ml	Salt	⅓ oz	2 tsp
	1 ¼ ml	Pepper		¼ tsp
	10 ml	Onion Juice		2 tsp
454 g	474 ml	Mayonnaise	1 lb	2 cups

Procedure

1. Combine all ingredients and mix until smooth and well-blended.
2. Scoop with a No. 24 scoop. This is a smooth mixture.

Note: Chopped stuffed olives or celery, or combination of vegetables, may be added to give texture.

Green Pepper and Cream Cheese Sandwich
50 Sandwiches (1 ½ oz/43 g)

Metric		Ingredients	U.S.	
Weight	Volume		Weight	Volume
1.36 kg	1.42 l	Cream Cheese	3 lb	1 ½ qt
57 g	90 ml	Chives, finely chopped	2 oz	6 tbsp
340 g	711 ml	Green Pepper, finely chopped	12 oz	3 cups
340 g	355 ml	Milk (approx.)	12 oz	1 ½ cups
9 g	10 ml	Salt	⅓ oz	2 tsp
	2 ½ ml	Pepper		½ tsp
	1 ¼ ml	Tabasco Sauce		¼ tsp

Procedure

1. Combine cream cheese, chives, and green pepper and mix on mixing machine, slowly adding enough milk to obtain a spreading consistency. Add seasonings and blend.

2. Yield: 50 No. 24 scoops.

Chipped Beef Sandwich
50 Sandwiches (1 ⅔ oz/46 g)

Metric			U.S.	
Weight	Volume	Ingredients	Weight	Volume
1.02 kg	1.89 l	Chipped Beef	2 lb, 4 oz	2 qt
198 g	4 eggs	Eggs, hard-cooked	7 oz	4 eggs
114 g	237 ml	Celery	4 oz	1 cup
114 g	237 ml	Stuffed Olives	4 oz	1 cup
907 g	947 ml	Boiled Dressing	2 lb	1 qt
57 g	60 ml	Lemon Juice	2 oz	4 tbsp
28 g	30 ml	Vinegar	1 oz	2 tbsp

Procedure

1. Grind chipped beef.
2. Finely chop eggs, celery, and olives. Combine with chipped beef and add to boiled dressing, lemon juice, and vinegar. Blend thoroughly.

3. Yield: 4 ½ lb/2.04 kg or 50 No. 24 scoops.

Corned Beef Sandwich
50 Sandwiches (2 oz/57 g)

Metric			U.S.	
Weight	Volume	Ingredients	Weight	Volume
907 g	1.42 l	Corned Beef, cooked or canned	2 lb	1 ½ qt
681 g	12 eggs	Eggs, hard-cooked	1 lb, 8 oz	12 eggs
227 g	355 ml	Onions	8 oz	1 ½ cups
9 g	10 ml	Salt	⅓ oz	2 tsp
681 g	711 ml	Salad Dressing	1 lb, 8 oz	3 cups
	few drops	Tabasco Sauce		few drops
	2 ½ ml	Mustard, dry		½ tsp

Procedure

1. Grind corned beef, hard-cooked eggs, and onions.
2. All salad dressing mixed with seasonings.

3. Use a No. 24 scoop, slightly rounded. Total weight 4 ¼ lb/1.93 kg.

Meat Salad Sandwich
64 Sandwiches (1 ½ oz/43 g)

| Metric | | Ingredients | U.S. | |
Weight	Volume		Weight	Volume
2.04 kg	3.08 l	Meat, cooked, finely chopped	4 lb, 8 oz	3 ¼ qt
57 g	59 ml	Mustard, prepared	2 oz	¼ cup
57 g	59 ml	Pickle Relish	2 oz	¼ cup
9 g	10 ml	Worcestershire Sauce	⅓ oz	2 tsp
567 g	533 ml	Salad Dressing	1 lb, 4 oz	2 ¼ cups

Procedure

1. Combine filling ingredients.

2. Portion filling with a No. 24 scoop.

Meat and Egg Salad Sandwich
50 Sandwiches (2 oz/57 g)

| Metric | | Ingredients | U.S. | |
Weight	Volume		Weight	Volume
1.48 kg	1.89 l	Meat (Beef, Veal, Pork), cooked, chopped	3 lb, 4 oz	2 qt
454 g	8 eggs	Eggs, hard-cooked, chopped	1 lb	8 eggs
227 g	355 ml	Sweet Pickles, chopped	8 oz	1 ½ cups
227 g	474 ml	Celery, chopped	8 oz	2 cups
454 g	474 ml	Combination Dressing	1 lb	2 cups
9 g	10 ml	Salt	⅓ oz	2 tsp

Procedure

1. Combine ingredients and mix well.

2. Yield: 3 ¾ qt/3.56 l or filling for 50 sandwiches.

Shrimp Salad Sandwich
50 Sandwiches (2 oz/57 g)

| Metric | | Ingredients | U.S. | |
Weight	Volume		Weight	Volume
397 g	829 ml	Celery, finely diced	14 oz	3 ½ cups
1.22 kg	2.01 l	Shrimp, drained, chopped	2 lb, 11 oz	8 ½ cups
907 g	16 eggs	Eggs, hard-cooked, diced	2 lb	16 eggs
85 g	178 ml	Green Pepper, chopped	3 oz	¾ cup
567 g	395 ml	Salad Dressing	1 lb, 4 oz	1 ⅔ cups
38 g	40 ml	Lemon Juice	1 ⅓ oz	2 ⅔ tbsp
	10 ml	Salt		2 tsp
	⅝ ml	Pepper, white		⅛ tsp

Procedure

1. Combine all of the ingredients. Mix lightly.

2. Portion filling with a No. 20 scoop.

Salmon Salad Sandwich
50 Sandwiches (2 oz/57 g)

| Metric | | Ingredients | U.S. | |
Weight	Volume		Weight	Volume
1.42 kg	1.66 l	Salmon, drained, flaked	3 lb, 2 oz	1 ¾ qt
454 g	8 eggs	Eggs, hard-cooked, chopped	1 lb	8 eggs
227 g	237 ml	Pickle Relish	8 oz	1 cup
14 g	15 ml	Lemon Juice	½ oz	1 tbsp
9 g	10 ml	Salt	⅓ oz	2 tsp
681 g	711 ml	Salad Dressing	1 lb, 8 oz	3 cups

Procedure

1. Combine salmon with remaining ingredients. Mix well.

2. Portion with a No. 24 scoop.

Ham Salad Sandwich
50 Sandwiches (1 ¾ oz/49 g)

| Metric | | Ingredients | U.S. | |
Weight	Volume		Weight	Volume
907 g	1.42 l	Ham, cooked, chopped	2 lb	1 ½ qt
454 g	8 eggs	Eggs, hard-cooked, chopped	1 lb	8 eggs
227 g	474 ml	Celery, finely chopped	8 oz	2 cups
255 g	355 ml	Sweet Pickles, finely chopped	9 oz	1 ½ cup
7 g	15 ml	Mustard, prepared	¼ oz	1 tbsp
681 g	711 ml	Cooked Dressing	1 lb, 8 oz	3 cups
	5 ml	Salt		1 tsp

Procedure

1. Combine all ingredients and mix well.

2. Yield: 50 No. 24 scoops.

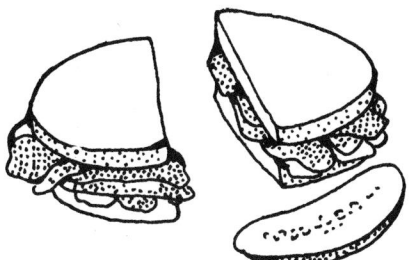

Vegetarian Sandwich
50 Sandwiches (2 ½ oz/71 g)

Metric		Ingredients	U.S.	
Weight	Volume		Weight	Volume
1.36 kg	1.42 l	Cream Cheese	3 lb	1 ½ qt
340 g	711 ml	Carrot, grated	12 oz	3 cups
340 g	592 ml	Sweet Pickles	12 oz	2 ½ cups
340 g	474 ml	Black Olives, chopped	12 oz	2 cups
340 g	711 ml	Celery, chopped	12 oz	3 cups
	11 ¼ ml	Salt		2 ¼ tsp

Procedure

1. Soften cream cheese. Mix in remaining ingredients.
2. Portion filling with a No. 20 scoop.
3. Add layer of *one* of the following:
   a. Fresh mushrooms, sliced.

b. Tomato slices and lettuce.
c. Swiss cheese, sliced.
d. Cucumber slices.
e. Red leaf lettuce.

Tomato, Cheese, and Sprout Sandwich
54 Sandwiches (2 oz/57 g)

Metric		Ingredients	U.S.	
Weight	Volume		Weight	Volume
850 g	1.42 l	Cheddar Cheese, cut in small cubes	1 lb, 14 oz	1 ½ qt
850 g	1.42 l	Tomatoes, diced	1 lb, 14 oz	1 ½ qt
638 g	1.34 l	Celery, chopped fine	1 lb, 6 ½ oz	5 ⅔ cups
212 g	1.34 l	Alfalfa Sprouts	7 ½ oz	5 ⅔ cups
340 g	355 ml	Salad Dressing	12 oz	1 ½ cups
	1 ⅞ ml	Salt		⅜ tsp
	1 ⅞ ml	Pepper, white		⅜ tsp

Procedure

1. Combine all of the ingredients.

2. Portion filling with a No. 20 scoop.

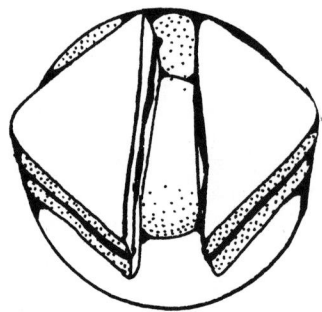

Chicken Salad Sandwich
50 Sandwiches (2 oz/57 g)

| Metric | | Ingredients | U.S. | |
Weight	Volume		Weight	Volume
1.36 kg	2.13 l	Chicken, finely chopped	3 lb	2 ¼ qt
227 g	474 ml	Celery, finely chopped	8 oz	2 cups
227 g	316 ml	Sweet Pickles, finely chopped	8 oz	1 ⅓ cups
43 g	45 ml	Mustard, prepared	1 ½ oz	3 tbsp
681 g	711 ml	Salad Dressing	1 lb, 8 oz	3 cups
28 g	30 ml	Lemon Juice	1 oz	2 tbsp
9 g	10 ml	Salt	⅓ oz	2 tsp
114 g	178 ml	Onions, minced	4 oz	¾ cup

Procedure

1. Combine all ingredients and mix thoroughly.
2. Yield: About 5 lb, 14 oz/2.67 kg or 50 No. 24 scoops.

Note: Chicken salad sandwich filling is superior when chicken, celery, and pickles are chopped rather than ground.

Turkey Salad Sandwich
50 Sandwiches (1 ½ oz/43 g)

| Metric | | Ingredients | U.S. | |
Weight	Volume		Weight	Volume
1.14 kg	1.78 l	Turkey, cooked, chopped	2 lb, 8 oz	7 ½ cups
454 g	8 eggs	Eggs, hard-cooked, chopped	1 lb	8 eggs
198 g	296 ml	Celery, finely diced	7 oz	1 ¼ cups
	6 ¼ ml	Salt		1 ¼ tsp
283 g	296 ml	Salad Dressing	10 oz	1 ¼ cups
	⅝ ml	Pepper		⅛ tsp

Procedure

1. Combine filling ingredients.

2. Portion filling with a No. 24 scoop.

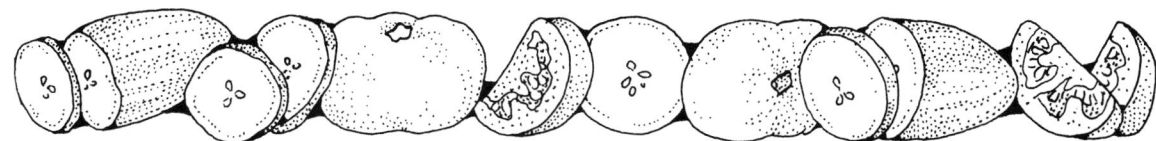

Table 19
Sandwich Filling Suggestions

Almonds, celery, chicken, and sweet pickle.

Crisp bacon, chili sauce, ground baked beans, and chopped celery.

Ground baked beans, Cheddar cheese, and pepperoni, mixed with minced celery and crushed potato chips.

Bacon and peanut butter.

Banana and peanut butter.

Carrot, raisins, mayonnaise, and pickles.

Cabbage, peanuts, carrot, crisp bacon, and mayonnaise.

Cheddar cheese, sweet pickles, and bacon.

Cheddar cheese, salad dressing, and tomato.

Cheddar cheese, chili sauce, and chipped beef.

Sharp Cheddar cheese blended with softened butter or margarine, minced hot peppers, pimiento, and dehydrated onion soup mix.

Cream cheese, marmalade, and pecans.

Cream cheese, chopped olives, and pimiento.

Ground cottage cheese, peanuts, and sweet pickle.

Cheese and salad dressing with sliced cucumbers.

Cheese, grated pineapple, salad dressing, and chopped carrot.

Chicken salad and crisp bacon.

Corned beef hash mixed with pickle relish and mayonnaise, and slice of Swiss cheese.

Crab salad and tomato slices.

Dates, nuts, cream cheese, and lemon juice.

Chopped egg, chives, dressing, and cooked bacon.

Chopped egg, corned beef, mustard dressing, pickle.

Chopped egg, bologna, cooked dressing, and celery.

Sliced egg and sliced ham, with pickle relish and dressing.

Figs, lemon juice, cream cheese, and nuts.

Figs, raisins, orange, nuts, and cream cheese.

Sliced beef, lettuce, and mustard dressing.

Flaked cooked fish, chopped celery, pickle relish, and mayonnaise.

Beef, celery, mayonnaise, and chili sauce.

Ham, egg, celery, pickle, and cooked dressing.

Ham, cheese, pickle, and cooked dressing.

Chopped ham, shredded carrot, green onion, mayonnaise, prepared mustard.

Meat loaf, sliced, with pickle relish.

Ground meat, chopped celery, pickle, and cooked dressings.

Sliced tongue and relish, mixed with salad dressing.

Liverwurst, celery, green pepper, and salad dressing.

Sliced tongue, minced pickle, cooked dressing, and horseradish.

Pork, sliced dill pickle, and cooked dressing.

Salmon flakes, lemon juice, celery, sweet pickle, and salad dressing.

Sardines, lemon juice, catsup, salad dressing, and tomato slices.

Shrimp paste, lemon juice, salad dressing, and cucumber slices.

Swiss cheese grated and mixed with chopped ripe olives, green peppers, and mayonnaise.

Sliced tomato and bacon with lettuce and mayonnaise.

Tuna, chopped egg, pickle, cooked dressing, and tomato slice.

Tuna, minced celery, chili sauce, cooked dressing, and sliced cucumber.

Watercress, cheese, celery, crisp bacon, and salad dressing.

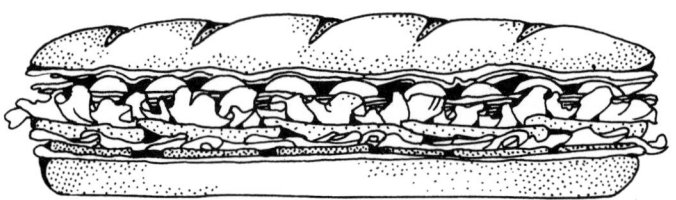

Grilled Pizza Sandwich
50 Sandwiches
Grill

Metric			U.S.	
Weight	Volume	Ingredients	Weight	Volume
227 g	316 ml	Ripe Olives, chopped	8 oz	1 ⅓ cups
	1 ¼ ml	Pepper		¼ tsp
	5 ml	Oregano		1 tsp
	5 ml	Salt		1 tsp
99 g	178 ml	Chives or Green Onions, minced	3 ½ oz	¾ cup
1.02 kg	1.07 l	Ground Beef, cooked	2 lb, 4 oz	4 ½ cups
114 g	237 ml	Parmesan Cheese, grated	4 oz	1 cup
737 g	770 ml	Tomato Puree	1 lb, 10 oz	3 ¼ cups
3.63 g	100 slices	French Bread sliced ⅜-in thick	8 lb	100 slices
2.10 kg	100 slices	Tomato Slices	4 lb, 10 oz	100 slices
1.42 kg	50 slices	Cheddar Cheese, sliced	3 lb, 2 oz	50 slices
681 g	711 ml	Butter or Margarine, melted	1 lb, 8 oz	3 cups

Procedure

1. Combine olives, pepper, oregano, salt, chives, beef, Parmesan cheese, and tomato puree.
2. Put a No. 24 scoop of meat mixture on alternate slices of bread.
3. Arrange 2 tomato slices over top of meat mixture. Cover tomato slices with 1 slice of cheese.
4. Cover with top slice of bread. Brush sandwich with butter or margarine. Grill.

Hamburgers
50 Servings (4 oz/114 g meat)
Grill

Metric			U.S.	
Weight	Volume	Ingredients	Weight	Volume
5.67 kg	5.92 l	Ground Beef (20% fat)	12 lb, 8 oz	6 ¼ qt
454 g	474 ml	Catsup	1 lb	2 cups
340 g	355 ml	Combination Salad Dressing	12 oz	1 ½ cups
511 g	533 ml	Hamburger Relish	1 lb, 2 oz	2 ¼ cups
94 g	79 ml	Mustard, prepared	3 ⅓ oz	⅓ cup
	2 ½ ml	Salt		½ tsp
1.35 kg	50 buns	Hamburger Buns	3 lb	50 buns
681 g	50 pieces	Lettuce	1 lb, 8 oz	50 pieces

Procedure

1. Shape hamburger into 4 oz/114 g patties. Grill on medium hot (350°F/177°C) griddle. Brown on both sides according to degree of doneness desired.
2. Combine catsup, dressing, relish, mustard, and salt.
3. Slice buns and toast on slow section of griddle while hamburger is cooking.
4. Place grilled hamburger in buns with approximately 1 oz/28 g sauce and lettuce.

Hamburgers

(with Textured Vegetable Protein) 50 Servings

Grill

Metric		Ingredients	U.S.	
Weight	Volume		Weight	Volume
		30% Textured Vegetable Protein Product		
928 g	1.30 l	Vegetable Protein Product	2 lb, ¾ oz	5 ½ cups
681 g	711 ml	Water	1 lb, 8 oz	3 cups
2.78 kg	3.00 l	Ground Beef	6 lb, 2 oz	3 ⅙ qt
28 g	30 ml	Salt	1 oz	2 tbsp
		20% Textured Vegetable Protein Product		
319 g	889 ml	Vegetable Protein Product	11 ¼ oz	3 ¾ cups
454 g	474 ml	Water	1 lb	2 cups
3.18 kg	3.31 l	Ground Beef	7 lb	3 ½ qt
28 g	30 ml	Salt	1 oz	2 tbsp
		10% Textured Vegetable Protein Product		
156 g	444 ml	Vegetable Protein Product	5 ½ oz	1 ⅞ cups
227 g	237 ml	Water	8 oz	1 cup
3.58 kg	3.67 l	Ground Beef	7 lb, 14 oz	3 ⅞ qt
28 g	30 ml	Salt	1 oz	2 tbsp

Procedure

1. Combine water and Vegetable Protein Product and let stand for 15 minutes.
2. Mix with meat and salt at low mixer speed for 3 minutes.
3. Portion into ⅓ cup/79 ml patties using a No. 12 scoop. Flatten to size desired, allowing for ¾-inch shrinkage in cooking.
4. Grill on a hot griddle or bake on sheet pans in oven at 400°F/205°C for 10 minutes.

Persian Crab Sandwich

50 Servings

Metric		Ingredients	U.S.	
Weight	Volume		Weight	Volume
2.72 kg	100 slices	Bread	6 lb	100 slices
2.27 kg	100 slices	Tomato Slices	5 lb	100 slices
2.13 kg	3.31 l	Crabmeat	4 lb, 11 oz	3 ½ qt
2.84 kg	100 slices	Cheddar Cheese, sliced	6 lb, 4 oz	100 slices
2.27 kg	100 slices	Bacon, cooked slices	5 lb	100 slices

Procedure

1. Toast bread lightly. Arrange slice of tomato on each slice with ¾ oz/21 g of crabmeat placed loosely on top of tomato slices.
2. Place slice of cheese over the crabmeat and broil until cheese is softened.
3. Garnish with bacon slice.
4. Serve two per portion.

Toasted Cheese Sandwich
50 Sandwiches (2 oz/57 g)

| Metric | | Ingredients | U.S. | |
Weight	Volume		Weight	Volume
1.82 kg	3.79 l	Cheddar Cheese, ground	4 lb	4 qt
567 g	1.18 l	Aged Cheddar Cheese, ground	1 lb, 4 oz	1 ¼ qt
605 g	632 ml	Buttermilk	1 lb, 5 ⅓ oz	2 ⅔ cups
50 g	118 ml	Mustard, dry	1 ¾ oz	½ cup
43 g	45 ml	Worcestershire Sauce	1 ½ oz	3 tbsp
	8 ¾ ml	Salt		1 ¾ tsp
	1 ¼ ml	Pepper		¼ tsp

Procedure

1. Blend the cheese and buttermilk together. Add remaining ingredients and mix well.
2. Yield: About 6 ½ lb/2.95 kg. Spread 2 oz/57 g of mixture on a slice of fresh dry toast. Brown under broiler to order.

Cheese and Bacon
50 Servings

| Metric | | Ingredients | U.S. | |
Weight	Volume		Weight	Volume
1.36 kg	75 slices	Bacon slices, cooked, cut in half	3 lb	150 (½ slices)
1.42 kg	50 slices	Cheddar Cheese, sliced	3 lb, 2 oz	50 slices
3.63 kg	100 slices	Bread	8 lb	100 slices
595 g	711 ml	Butter or Margarine, melted	1 lb, 5 oz	3 cups

Procedure

1. Arrange slice of cheese on bread slice with 3 halves of bacon on top. Cover with bread.
2. Brush sandwich on both sides with butter.
3. Grill until lightly browned on one side, turn and brown the second side until cheese has softened and bread is lightly browned.

Cheese Dreams
50 Servings
Bake, 450°F/232°C, 10 min

French bread, split lengthwise, then each length cut on the diagonal into 5 pieces	5 loaves	
Cheese, cut square slice diagonally to fit the bread	50 slices	1 slice per serving
Tomato, sliced thinly	150 slices	3 slices per serving
Bacon, cooked and drained	100 slices	2 slices per serving

Procedure

1. Butter bread. Place cheese, then tomato, and bacon on bread slices.
2. Bake in oven at 450°F/232°C about 10 minutes, or until cheese is melted.

Baked Cheeseburgers
50 Servings (4 oz/114 g)
Bake, 400°F/205°C, 15 min

| Metric | | Ingredients | U.S. | |
Weight	Volume		Weight	Volume
1.36 kg	2.84 l	Cheddar Cheese, ground	3 lb	3 qt
151 g	158 ml	Butter, melted	5 ⅓ oz	⅔ cup
397 g	415 ml	Eggs, beaten (7 lge)	14 oz	1 ¾ cups
	15 ml	Mustard, dry		1 tbsp
	7 ½ ml	Salt		1 ½ tsp
	5 ml	Paprika		1 tsp
99 g	105 ml	Worcestershire Sauce	3 ½ oz	7 tbsp
	50 buns	Hamburger Buns		50 buns
2.27 kg	50 slices	Bacon, partially cooked	5 lb	50 slices

Procedure

1. Combine all ingredients except buns and bacon. Mix to spreading consistency.
2. Split buns. Spread, using a scant No. 40 scoop of mixture on each bun-half. Top with half a slice of partially cooked bacon.
3. Bake at 400°F/205°C for 15 minutes.

Barbecued Beef on a Bun
50 Servings

| Metric | | Ingredients | U.S. | |
Weight	Volume		Weight	Volume
907 g	1.89 l	Celery, chopped	2 lb	2 qt
312 g	474 ml	Onions, chopped	11 oz	2 cups
151 g	158 ml	Vinegar	5 ⅓ oz	⅔ cup
1.82 kg	1.89 l	Water	4 lb	2 qt
1.82 kg	1.89 l	Catsup	4 lb	2 qt
170 g	237 ml	Brown Sugar	6 oz	1 cup
28 g	59 ml	Mustard, dry	1 oz	¼ cup
57 g	59 ml	Salt	2 oz	¼ cup
	10 ml	Smoke Flavoring		2 tsp
2.72 kg	2.84 l	Ground Beef, lightly cooked	6 lb	3 qt

Procedure

1. Combine all ingredients except hamburger and heat to simmering temperature. Do not cook enough to soften vegetables.
2. Add hamburger, combine well with sauce, and serve over 2 halves of hamburger bun that has been toasted in a hot oven.

Note: For approximately 30% TVP use 4 ¼ lb/1.94 kg meat, 12 oz/340 g TVP, and 1 lb/454 g water in place of 6 lbs hamburger.

Tuna Burgers

50 Servings

Metric		Ingredients	U.S.	
Weight	Volume		Weight	Volume
567 g	1.18 l	Cheddar Cheese, grated	1 lb, 4 oz	1 ¼ qt
850 g	1.30 l	Eggs, hard-cooked, chopped (15 lge)	1 lb, 14 oz	5 ½ cups
1.36 kg	1.60 l	Tuna, drained, flaked	3 lb	6 ¾ cups
85 g	178 ml	Green Pepper, chopped	3 oz	¾ cup
114 g	178 ml	Onions, chopped	4 oz	¾ cup
567 g	592 ml	Salad Dressing	1 lb, 4 oz	2 ½ cups
71 g	75 ml	Lemon Juice	2 ½ oz	5 tbsp
14 g	15 ml	Salt	½ oz	1 tbsp

Procedure

1. Combine all ingredients.
2. Split buns (hamburger or frankfurter) and place tops cut side down on a buttered pan. Place bottoms, cut side up, on the tops.
3. Place a No. 12 scoop of tuna mixture on each bun. Spread.
4. Place in oven until cheese melts.

Hot Barbecued Frankfurters

50 Servings (4 ¼ oz/121 g)
Simmer

Metric		Ingredients	U.S.	
Weight	Volume		Weight	Volume
907 g	1.42 l	Onions, chopped	2 lb	1 ½ qt
227 g	237 ml	Butter or Margarine	8 oz	1 cup
340 g	355 ml	Catsup	12 oz	1 ½ cups
907 g	947 ml	Applesauce	2 lb	1 qt
114 g	118 ml	Vinegar	4 oz	½ cup
	⅝ ml	Hot Pepper Sauce		⅛ tsp
57 g	79 ml	Brown Sugar	2 oz	⅓ cup
14 g	15 ml	Salt	½ oz	1 tbsp
3.18 kg	4.97 l	Frankfurters, sliced	7 lb	5 ¼ qt
1.59 kg	100 slices	French Bread, sliced	3 lb, 8 oz	100 slices
567 g	592 ml	Butter or Margarine	1 lb, 4 oz	2 ½ cups

Procedure

1. Sauté onions in butter or margarine. Add catsup, applesauce, vinegar, pepper sauce, sugar, and salt. Simmer uncovered for 15 minutes.
2. Slice frankfurters at an angle ¼ inch thick. Add to sauce and let simmer for 15 minutes.
3. Butter French bread slices and toast lightly on grill or in oven.
4. Ladle 4 ¼ oz/121 g filling into each sandwich.

Bean and Frank Burgers
50 Servings (2 oz/57 g filling)

Metric		Ingredients	U.S.	
Weight	Volume		Weight	Volume
454 g	711 ml	Hamburger Relish	1 lb	3 cups
340 g	355 ml	Boiled Dressing	12 oz	1 ½ cups
312 g	474 ml	Onions, minced	11 oz	2 cups
312 g	474 ml	Bacon, crisp, chopped	11 oz	2 cups
907 g	947 ml	Baked Beans	2 lb	1 qt
681 g	1.07 l	Frankfurters, ⅛-in slices	1 lb, 8 oz	4 ½ cups

Procedure

1. Blend relish, dressing, onions, and bacon. Blend lightly with beans and frankfurters.

2. Serve on buttered hamburger buns (may be either hot or cold).

Bacon, Lettuce, and Tomato
50 Servings

Metric		Ingredients	U.S.	
Weight	Volume		Weight	Volume
2.10 kg	100 strips	Bacon (22 slices per lb/454 g)	4 lb, 10 oz	100 strips
4.54 kg	50 slices	Tomato, large, sliced	10 lb	50 slices
	50 leaves	Lettuce (crisp)		50 leaves
3.63 kg	100 slices	Bread, white or whole wheat	8 lb	100 slices
454 g	474 ml	Butter or Margarine, whipped	1 lb	2 cups

Procedure

1. Grill bacon.
2. Toast bread and butter lightly.
3. Assemble lettuce leaf (to fit bread slice), tomato slice, and 2 strips of bacon (cut in half, if necessary, to fit sandwich).
4. Place between bread slices and cut as desired.

Reuben Sandwich
50 Servings (5 oz/114 g filling)
Grill

Metric		Ingredients	U.S.	
Weight	Volume		Weight	Volume
681 g	1.07 l	Sauerkraut	1 lb, 8 oz	4 ½ cups
2.27 kg	100 slices	Rye Bread, Russian	5 lb	100 slices
681 g	711 ml	Thousand Island Dressing	1 lb, 8 oz	3 cups
1.59 kg	50 slices	Swiss Cheese	3 lb, 8 oz	50 slices
2.27 kg	50 slices	Corned Beef, sliced	5 lb	50 slices
454 g	474 ml	Butter or Margarine	1 lb	2 cups

1. Drain sauerkraut well, squeezing out extra moisture.
2. Spread bread slices with dressing. Place cheese, sauerkraut, and corned beef in each sandwich. Close sandwich and spread butter or margarine on both sides of sandwich.
3. Grill sandwich on both sides until lightly toasted and thoroughly heated through and the cheese softened.

Table 20
Hot Meat Sandwich Suggestions

Hot sliced meat sandwiches may be made by arranging slices of cooked meat on bread and serving a hot sauce or gravy over them. (See sauce and gravy variations.) They may be served easily from a steam table. Suggested combinations are:

Beef, with mustard or vegetable sauce or brown gravy

Corned beef, with mustard, egg, or vegetable sauce

Ham, baked or boiled, with horseradish added to ham gravy

Chicken or turkey, with giblet or mushroom gravy

Lamb, with parsley or peas, and pimiento sauce, or gravy

Tongue, with vegetable, mustard, or tomato sauce

Veal, with parsley, or with vegetable sauce, or mushroom gravy

Spiced ham or meat loaves, with egg, or tomato sauce or gravy

Table 21
Club Sandwich Combinations

Club sandwiches are made with 3 slices of toast and assorted fillings. They are popular, although they tend to fall apart and are difficult to eat. Skewering with toothpicks helps to hold them in place and makes them easier to handle. Suggestions of combinations for the two "decks" are:

Cheddar cheese and tomato, plus ham, and lettuce

Cheddar cheese and lettuce, plus bacon, and tomato

Swiss cheese and lettuce, plus ham, and thinly sliced dill pickle

Chicken slices and lettuce, plus bacon, and tomato

Sautéed chicken livers, chopped, and lettuce, plus bacon, and tomato

Chicken salad, plus sliced ham, and lettuce

Chicken slices and lettuce, plus egg salad, and tomato

Beef slices and lettuce, plus dill pickle slices, and tomato

Beef tongue and lettuce, plus egg salad, and tomato

Smoked beef tongue and lettuce, plus sliced chicken, and tomato

Crab salad and bacon, plus tomato, and lettuce

Egg slices and lettuce, plus salmon salad, and tomato

Egg salad and lettuce, plus sardine fillets, and tomato

Egg salad and anchovy, plus tomato, and lettuce

Ham and lettuce, plus turkey, and pickle slices

Ham and lettuce, plus egg salad, and fresh cucumber slices

Tuna salad and egg slices, plus tomato, and lettuce

Turkey and lettuce, plus bacon, and tomato

Turkey and lettuce, plus spiced ham, or bologna, and sliced pickle

Canapés and Fancy Sandwiches

Canapés and fancy sandwiches are tasty morsels of appetizing food arranged on bases of bread, pastry, or wafers. Meticulous handling is required to make them trim and beautiful. The rewards are gratifying. When skillfully prepared, they create an impression of painstaking care that adds to the enjoyment of food. Appeal is enhanced by choosing flavors harmonious with beverages or foods with which they are served, and by bright, varied, and attractive forms and colors. Sticky, limp, or crumbly canapés are difficult to handle and should be avoided.

Either small assorted canapés and hors d'oeuvres or one large canapé may be served at the table as a first course. Large canapés are especially good as appetizers for serving large groups. They require less handwork than the small ones and may be served on a flat plate, thus eliminating a need for cocktail glasses or soup bowls.

When refrigerating canapés, place them on waxed paper on a tray or baking sheet. Cover completely with light plastic or waxed paper. If waxed paper is used, place a damp cloth over the canapés. This will help keep them fresh and attractive for several hours. It is important that the consistency of the spread be firm enough for covering without disarranging the sandwiches. When catering for a large number, it is advisable to prepare some of the ribbon or pinwheel type which can be prepared well in advance and frozen. These can be sliced and thawed as needed.

Pinwheel and ribbon sandwiches are attractive as part of an assortment and require less handwork than many of the open-faced sandwiches.

Pinwheels may be made by slicing day-old bread ⅛-inch to ¼-inch thick, lengthwise through the loaf. Trim off the crusts to form a rectangle. Using a rolling pin, roll bread lightly from one end to the other to make it easier to handle without breaking. Spread with softened butter or margarine and then with bright-colored spreads having cream cheese as their base. Across one end of the rectangle place stuffed olives, arranged end-to-end, or a strip of pickle, pimiento, minced ham or bologna, or other food that will blend with filling and make an attractive center for the sandwich. Roll bread tightly over this center filling as in making jelly roll. Wrap roll tightly in plastic or wax paper and twist ends to hold it firmly in place. Put roll in the refrigerator for several hours, or until set. (Pinwheels may be frozen and kept for several days.) Slice with a sharp knife.

Ribbon sandwiches require light and dark bread and bright fillings made with a base of cream cheese. Slice day-old bread ¼-inch to ⅓-inch thick, lengthwise through the loaf, and trim to form rectangles. Spread lightly with butter, one white rectangle and one dark one. Spread the white one with filling and place piece of dark bread, butter-side down, on top. Spread this piece of dark bread with butter and with filling. Spread a white rectangle with butter and place on top. Continue as before, alternating white and dark bread, with filling between, until sandwich is as wide as desired, ending with a white slice on top. Wrap tightly with wax paper and refrigerate for several hours, or until firm enough for slicing. Slice to measure approximately ½ inch × 1¾ inches × 2½ inches. Use a broad spatula for handling.

Delicious, small sandwiches may be made with fancy breads. (See section on Breads.) These may be spread with butter and softened cream cheese. Nut and fruit breads are especially suitable.

BASES FOR CANAPÉS

Bread Use day-old bread to supply satisfactory firmness. Select texture and flavor that will be in harmony with the spread. Many of the yeast or quick breads are suitable—fruit, nut, oatmeal, orange, prune, raisin, rye, white, and whole wheat. Slice and cut bread into neat, attractive forms for an appealing assortment—crescent, diamond, finger, rectangle, square, star, and triangle. Large canapés may have a base approximately 3 inches in diameter. Small ones for assortments should be 2 inches or less.

Chips Corn and potato chips are favorites.

Pastry Crisp texture, varied shape, and rich flavor are possible if pastry is baked and spread shortly before serving.

Wafers Numerous varieties are available. New ones are continually being introduced on the market to reward alert shoppers.

Puff Shells Tender, crisp, golden brown shells about 1¼ inches in diameter are appealing in an assortment. Shells may be prepared in advance and filled shortly before serving.

CANAPÉ BUTTERS

A thin coating of butter or margarine on bread adds richness and helps prevent bread from absorbing excess moisture from the spread. A quarter pound (114 g) whipped butter or margarine will spread 50 small canapes (2 inches in diameter). It may be blended with a flavoring substance, if desired, which is in paste, liquid, or finely minced form. Suggested flavors are listed below with quantities required to flavor 4 oz/114 g of butter or margarine:

Anchovy 2 tbsp/30 ml anchovy paste and 1 tsp/5 ml lemon juice.

Avocado 2 oz/57 g avocado puree, 1 tsp/5 ml lemon juice, salt to taste, and green coloring if needed. (Good with nuts or pineapple.)

Catsup 2 oz/57 g catsup. (Appetizing for meat or fish spreads.)

Cheese 2 oz/57 g grated sharp Cheddar cheese.

Chive 2 tbsp/30 ml minced chives and 2 tsp/10 ml lemon juice.

Egg Yolk 4 tbsp/60 ml sieved hard-cooked egg yolks, 1 tsp/5 ml lemon juice, ⅛ tsp/1⅝ ml mustard, ¼ tsp/1¼ ml salt.

Garlic ¼ tsp/1¼ finely minced, or 1 clove split and allowed to remain in soft butter 30 minutes and then removed.

Herb 2 tsp/10 ml of the following herb mixture: ¼ lemon, grated rind, and juice mixed with finely minced or ground

6 needles rosemary

1 tsp/5 ml chopped parsley

1 tsp/5 ml ground basil

⅓ tsp/1⅔ ml ground thyme

½ tsp/2½ ml tarragon

1 small clove garlic

1 tsp/5 ml minced onion

Horseradish 2 tsp/10 ml powdered horseradish, ½ tsp/2½ ml mustard, 1 tsp/5 ml lemon juice. (Very good for ham or tongue sandwiches.)

Lemon 1½ tbsp/2½ ml lemon juice and ¼ tsp/1¼ ml grated rind.

Mint 4 tbsp/60 ml minced mint leaves, 2 tsp/10 ml lemon juice, and a tiny bit green coloring. (Refreshing flavor with orange, pineapple, or lamb sandwiches.)

Mustard 2 tbsp/30 ml prepared mustard.

Nasturtium 4 tbsp/60 ml minced nasturtium stems, 1 tsp/5 ml lemon juice, and a tiny bit green coloring. (Spicy with meat sandwiches.)

Parsley (Maître d'Hôtel) 4 tbsp/60 ml minced parsley and 2 tsp/10 ml lemon juice.

Pimiento 4 tbsp/60 ml sieved pimiento and 1 tsp/5 ml lemon juice. Good color and flavor with cucumber, celery, or olive.

Sardine 2 tbsp/30 ml sardine paste, 1 tsp/5 ml lemon juice, ¼ tsp/1¼ ml onion juice.

Shrimp 1 cup/237 ml shrimp puree, 1 tsp/5 ml lemon juice, ¼ tsp/1¼ ml salt.

Tomato ½ cup/118 ml tomato paste, 1 tbsp/15 ml lemon juice, ½ tsp/2½ ml Worcestershire sauce.

Worcestershire ½ tsp/2½ ml Worcestershire sauce, drop of hot pepper sauce. (Good for meat spreads.)

CANAPÉ SPREADS AND ARRANGEMENTS

Cheese

Almond, Pickle, Cheese Soften cream cheese with cream and blend with finely chopped almonds. Remove crusts from bread slices (either white or whole wheat). Spread generously with cheese mixture and roll a slice around a large sweet pickle until edges meet. Chill until firm. Slice ½ inch thick and garnish with pimiento.

*Blue and Cream Cheese Blend cheeses with sufficient cream to soften enough for spreading. Use a base of rye, whole wheat, or fruit bread and garnish with walnut or pecan half.

Caraway Cheese Slice slender loaf of caraway rye bread about ¼ inch thick. Spread with cheese butter and place in a hot oven until cheese melts into the bread.

Cucumber Cheese Place ³⁄₁₆-inch-thick slice of fresh cucumber in center of lemon-buttered square or star-shaped canapé. Brush cucumber with mayonnaise and place slice of stuffed olive in center. Garnish points with softened cream cheese put through star tip of pastry tube. Garnish with pimiento.

*Sherry Cheddar Soften aged Cheddar and cream cheese with Sherry wine and cream until easy to spread. Use on base of fruit or nut bread and garnish with salted almond or walnut half.

Tomato Cheese Use tomatoes 1½ to 1¾ inches in diameter. Slice ⁵⁄₁₆ inch thick. Remove seeds from pockets. Place slice on 2-inch round of lemon-buttered bread. Fill seed pockets and pipe edge with softened cream cheese put through the star tip of a pastry tube. Garnish with minced chives

or watercress.

Fish

Caviar Place a cucumber slice ¼ inch thick on lemon-buttered bread. Arrange caviar on center. Garnish with tiny pickled onion. Pipe mayonnaise around edge of cucumber and cover mayonnaise with sieved hard-cooked egg yolk.

Egg Anchovy Place slice of hard-cooked egg on circle of lemon-buttered bread. Brush egg slice with mayonnaise. Place a curled anchovy fillet in center. Pipe edge with cream cheese and dust cheese with minced green pepper.

Smoked Oysters or Clams Place smoked fish on center of catsup-buttered rectangle of bread. Pipe edge with softened cheese. Garnish with small bits of sweet pickle.

*Shrimp Butter Blend shrimp puree with finely chopped and well-drained cucumber. Spread on lemon-buttered rye or whole wheat bread, using a fork. Garnish with parsley, pimiento, or watercress.

Shrimp and Cheese Use either large shrimp split lengthwise or small Alaska shrimp. Marinate shrimp in garlic French dressing. Drain well. If using large shrimp, arrange cut side down on lemon-buttered crescents of bread. Pipe edge with cream cheese and dust with sieved egg yolk or finely chopped green pepper.

---

* Starred items may be softened sufficiently with cream or salad dressing to be used as dips.

Smoked or Kippered Salmon Place thin slices of smoked or kippered salmon on lemon-buttered bread. Garnish with mayonnaise and green celery rings, or stuffed olive.

Tuna Finely mince celery and tuna fish. Blend with cooked salad dressing. Season to taste with lemon juice, salt, and pepper. Spread bread generously, using a fork. Garnish with slices of small sweet pickle and pimiento.

Fruit

Fresh Fruit Spread crisp pastry with blend of cream cheese and powdered sugar. Arrange fresh berries or other fresh fruit chunks on top.

Dried Fruit (Apricot, fig, prune, pear, raisin) Blend finely ground dried fruit with cream cheese and lemon juice. Spread on nut bread and garnish with kumquat slice, maraschino cherry, or pineapple tidbit. Pipe softened cream cheese around the edge.

Maraschino Cherry Mince cherries and blend with cream cheese. Spread on fruit or nut bread, using a fork. Garnish with a salted almond.

Avocado Blend 4 oz/114 g avocado puree with 2 oz/ 57 g cream cheese, 2 tsp/10 ml lemon juice, salt to taste, and a drop of hot pepper sauce. Add tiny bit of green coloring if needed for appealing color. Garnish with kumquat or fresh pineapple.

Meat

Beef, Corned Soften cream cheese with Thousand Island Dressing. Add chopped sauerkraut. Spread on bread with a fork and decorate with bits of corned beef and Swiss cheese.

Beef, Dried Blend finely chopped dried beef, horseradish, mustard, and chives with cream cheese. Moisten with dressing. Spread on bread and garnish with pickle or olive.

Chicken Season finely minced chicken and celery with lemon juice, mustard, and salt. Blend with salad dressing. Arrange on bread and garnish with pickle, olive, or almond.

Egg and Devilled Ham Blend minced hard-cooked egg and pickle with devilled ham and cooked salad dressing. Spread on whole-grain bread. Garnish with bits of ham, pickle, stuffed olive, or celery rings.

Ham and Pickle Blend minced ham and finely minced pickle with mayonnaise. Spread on bread with a fork. Pipe edge with softened cream cheese. Dust edging with sieved egg yolk. Garnish with ripe olive.

Smoked Liver Sausage Spread bread with catsup butter. Soften liver sausage with salad dressing until smooth enough to spread on bread with a fork. Garnish with slice of stuffed olive or dill pickle.

Peanut Butter and Bacon Spread bread with peanut butter softened with salad dressing. Sprinkle generously with chopped crisp bacon.

Nut

Almond and Cheddar Soften Cheddar cheese with cream and blend with finely chopped almonds. Garnish spread with—candied fruit, candied ginger, nut, or maraschino cherry.

Pecan and Ripe Olive Soften cream cheese with cream, add lemon juice, and salt. Blend with chopped ripe olives and pecans. Spread on bread with a fork. Garnish with green pepper, crisp bacon, or sweet pickle slice.

---

* Starred items may be softened sufficiently with cream or salad dressing to be used as dips.

SAVORY GARNISHES FOR CANAPÉS

Cream Cheese Soften with cream or salad dressing to consistency easy to press through pastry tip, yet firm enough to retain sharpness of form.

Egg, Hard-Cooked Sliced or quartered; minced white; sieved yolk.

Fish Anchovy fillet or paste; crab legs or shreds; small chunks of herring or sardine; lobster pieces; small oysters or smoked oysters or clams; cooked salmon flakes or thin slices of smoked or kippered salmon; shrimp.

Fruit Apricot, dried or fresh; berries; kumquat slices; maraschino cherries, green cherries, fresh sweet cherries; candied orange or grapefruit peel; candied ginger; pineapple chunks or tidbits, fresh, frozen, canned, candied.

Meat Strips of chicken, ham, pork, or beef.

Pickles Capers; strips, slices, or minced sweet, dill, or mustard cucumber pickles; strips, slices, and minced ripe, green, and stuffed olives; pearl onions; green pepper and pimiento.

Nuts Whole, slivered, sliced, or chopped almonds or Brazil nuts; filberts; pecan, cashew, and walnuts, whole, halves, or pieces.

Vegetables Carrot curls; chicory; chives; green onion; cucumber slices or strips; mint, parsley, watercress; red or green pepper, radish, tomato.

Anchovy, Egg, and Tomato
50 Servings (3 in)

Metric		Ingredients	U.S.		
Weight	Volume		Weight		Volume
2.04 kg	3 loaves	Bread, whole wheat	4 lb, 8 oz		50 slices
227 g	237 ml	Cream Cheese	8 oz		1 cup
1.14 kg	25 eggs	Eggs, hard-cooked, small	2 lb, 8 oz		25 eggs
	5 ml	Mustard, prepared			1 tsp
57 g	60 ml	Cream	2 oz		¼ cup
	5 ml	Salt			1 tsp
227 g	50 fillets	Anchovy, rolled fillets	8 oz		50 fillets
1.82 kg	15 sm	Tomatoes, 2-in diameter	4 lb		15 sm
71 g	237 ml	Chives, minced	2 ½ oz		1 cup

Procedure

1. Cut 3-inch rounds in ½-inch-thick bread slices. Spread with softened cream cheese.
2. Cut eggs in half crosswise. Trim tips of white so egg half sits level. Remove yolk, keeping white intact.
3. Mix yolks with mustard, cream, and salt. Fill whites with egg mixture put through star tip of pastry tube. Decorate with rolled anchovy fillet.
4. Place ½-inch-thick slice of peeled tomato on top of bread round. Place egg on top of tomato. Decorate around edge of tomato and egg with frill of softened cream cheese. Sprinkle cheese with chopped chives.

Aspic and Shrimp
50 Servings

Metric		Ingredients	U.S.	
Weight	Volume		Weight	Volume
2.04 kg	50 slices	Bread, white	4 lb, 8 oz	50 slices
		Tomato Aspic (⅔ recipe—see Tomato Aspic, Clear)		
1.36 kg	3.79 l	Shrimp, small or Alaska	3 lb	4 qt
340 g	355 ml	Garlic French Dressing	12 oz	1 ½ cups
14 g	15 ml	Lemon Juice	½ oz	1 tbsp
85 g	79 ml	Cream Cheese	3 oz	⅓ cup
340 g	50 sprigs	Curly Chicory or Watercress	12 oz	50 sprigs
	50	Lemon Wedges		50

Procedure

1. Make bread rounds ½ inch thick and size to fit top of muffin cups.
2. Dip bread rounds in aspic mixture until slightly soaked.
3. Fill muffin cups within ¾ inch of top with aspic. Place bread rounds on top. Chill until aspic is set.
4. Unmold and place on plates with bread side down.
5. Marinate shrimp in garlic French dressing and lemon juice until well-seasoned. Drain thoroughly. Heap shrimp on top of aspic and decorate with cream cheese. Garnish plate with curly chicory or watercress, and lemon wedge.

Hot Seafood Canapé
50 Servings

| Metric | | Ingredients | U.S. | |
Weight	Volume		Weight	Volume
2.04 kg	3 loaves	Bread, white or whole wheat	4 lb, 8 oz	50 slices
227 g	237 ml	Butter	8 oz	1 cup
1.82 kg	50 slices	Tomatoes, fresh, sliced	4 lb	50 slices
340 g	474 ml	Shrimp	12 oz	2 cups
312 g	474 ml	Crabmeat	11 oz	2 cups
227 g	474 ml	Celery, minced	8 oz	2 cups
454 g	474 ml	Mayonnaise	1 lb	2 cups
227 g	474 ml	Green Pepper, minced	8 oz	2 cups
85 g	118 ml	Onions, minced	3 oz	½ cup
	⅝ ml	Pepper		⅛ tsp
	2 ½ ml	Salt		½ tsp
28 g	30 ml	Worcestershire Sauce	1 oz	2 tbsp

Procedure

1. Brush rounds of bread with butter and brown in hot oven. Place tomato slice on top of each round.
2. Blend remaining ingredients. Place a No. 40 scoop of mixture on top of tomato slice. Spread with fork to cover tomato. Sprinkle with buttered crumbs.
3. Bake at 350°F/177°C until nicely browned. Serve at once.

Hot Chicken Liver Canapé
50 Servings

| Metric | | Ingredients | U.S. | |
Weight	Volume		Weight	Volume
		Pastry, plain (use ½ Plain Pie Crust recipe)		
170 g	237 ml	Chicken Livers, minced	6 oz	1 cup
198 g	4 med	Eggs, hard-cooked, minced	7 oz	4 med
20 g	120 ml	Parsley, minced	⅔ oz	½ cup
	2 ½ ml	Mustard		½ tsp
14 g	15 ml	Cream	½ oz	1 tbsp
	5 ml	Lemon Juice		1 tsp
85 g	120 ml	Crisp Bacon, chopped	3 oz	½ cup
	2 ½ ml	Salt		½ tsp

Procedure

1. Roll pastry ⅛ inch thick and cut into 4-inch squares.
2. Blend remaining ingredients. Place rounded teaspoonful of mixture on center of each square.
3. Lightly moisten pastry edges with water. Fold to form a triangle over mixture. Press edges firmly with floured fork.
4. Fry in deep fat at 370°F/188°C or brush with milk and bake at 450°F/232°C until golden brown.

CHAPTER 12 _____ *Cakes and Frostings*

Cakes

Cakes are generally classified according to ingredients, such as butter or sponge, and according to shape: cup, layer, sheet, loaf, or sponge (tube cake-pan). Qualities desired in cakes are fine grain, moist, even texture, good volume and contour, tenderness, and flavors that are an appealing blend of good materials and tastes. Materials, temperatures, and mixing methods influence quality and should be tested carefully in the specific setting where cakes are to be made. Cake flours yield better volume and texture than pastry or all-purpose flours, although good quality cakes can be made with all-purpose flours. Individual bakers must determine whether it is worthwhile to procure cake flour if cakes are made infrequently. Temperatures should be gauged as accurately as possible. If ovens are not ac-

curate, calculation should be made to offset the degree of inaccuracy, including speed of temperature recovery when a cold load of cake is put in.

The method of mixing ingredients influences the quality of cakes. Four methods are in common use, namely, a) the conventional cake method, b) muffin method, c) quick-mix, high-ratio, or simplified method, and d) the pastry-blend method. High-ratio method refers to a higher proportion of sugar to flour and proper balance of other ingredients. It is recommended that recipes be followed according to method indicated or that appropriate adjustment be made in ingredient quantities. The majority of the recipes for butter cakes follow the conventional cake method.

Table 22
Cooking Temperatures and Times for Desserts (Approx.)

Food	Temperature	Time (minutes)
Cakes with Fat		
Cupcakes	350°F/177°C	30
Sheet or Layer Cakes	350°F/177°C	25–35
Loaf Cakes	325°–350°F/163°–177°C	50–60
Cakes without Fat		
Sponge or Angel Cakes	300°–325°F/149°–163°C	1½ hrs
Jelly Rolls	375°F/190°C	12–14
Fruit Cakes	300°F/149°C	2–3 hrs
Cookies		
Balls	325°–350°F/163°–177°C	12–20
Bars and Squares	325°–350°F/163°–177°C	20–45
Shortbread	400°F/205°C	15
Macaroons	300°–325°F/149°–163°C	30
Pressed Cookies	350°F/177°C	15
Dropped Cookies	350°–400°F/177°–205°C	8–15
Rolled Cookies	375°F/190°C	8–10
Sliced Cookies	400°F/205°C	10–12
Meringues		
Dry Meringues	275°F/135°C	90
Chewy Meringues	325°F/163°C	50
Cream Puffs	450°F/232°C	15
	Then 350°F/177°C	20–30
Pies		
Pastry	425°–450°F/218°–232°C	10
Puff Paste	450°F/232°C	5–8
Custard-type Pies	450°F/232°C	15
	Then 350°F/177°C	25–30
Meringue Topping	350°F/177°C	15
Two-Crust Fruit Pies	450°F/232°C	10
	Then 350°F/177°C	20–30
Baked Apples	375°/190°C	60
Puddings		
Betties	350°F/177°C	60
Cobblers	350°F/177°C	45
Custards	300°F/149°C	30
Baked Fruit Desserts	350°–375°F/177°–190°C	30–60
Indian Puddings	300°F/149°C	120
Steamed Puddings (5 lb/2.27 kg pressure)	280°F/138°C	60
Deep-Fat Fried Desserts		
Cake Doughnuts	375°–380°F/190°–193°C	2–3
Raised Doughnuts	360°–375°F/182°–190°C	2–3
Fritters	370°–380°F/188°–193°C	2–5

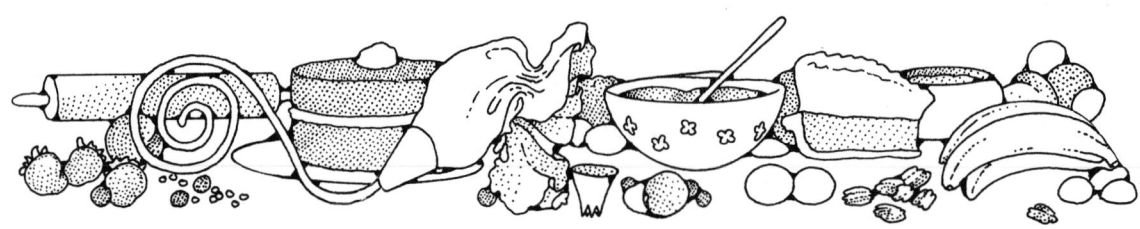

SHORTENED OR BUTTER CAKES

Oatmeal Cake
60 Servings
Bake, 350°F/177°C, 35–40 min

Metric		Ingredients	U.S.	
Weight	Volume		Weight	Volume
368 g	1.03 l	Oatmeal, quick-cooking	13 oz	4 ⅓ cups
1.14 kg	1.18 l	Water, boiling	2 lb, 8 oz	1 ¼ qt
454 g	474 ml	Butter or Margarine	1 lb	2 cups
907 g	947 ml	Granulated Sugar	2 lb	1 qt
681 g	947 ml	Brown Sugar	1 lb, 8 oz	1 qt
19 g	20 ml	Vanilla	⅔ oz	4 tsp
454 g	474 ml	Eggs (8 lge)	1 lb	2 cups
605 g	1.42 l	Flour	1 lb, 8 oz	1 ½ qt
9 g	20 ml	Cinnamon	⅓ oz	4 tsp
9 g	20 ml	Nutmeg	⅓ oz	4 tsp
9 g	10 ml	Salt	⅓ oz	2 tsp
16 g	20 ml	Soda		4 tsp
		Broiled Topping		
340 g	355 ml	Butter or Margarine	12 oz	1 ½ cups
454 g	632 ml	Brown Sugar	1 lb	2 ⅔ cups
454 g	1.42 l	Coconut, shredded	1 lb	1 ½ qt
255 g	237 ml	Evaporated Milk	9 oz	1 cup
19 g	20 ml	Vanilla	⅔ oz	4 tsp
454 g	947 ml	Chopped Nuts	1 lb	1 qt

Procedure

1. Gradually stir oatmeal into boiling water. Let stand 20 minutes.
2. Cream butter or margarine; gradually add sugars and vanilla and beat until light and fluffy. Beat in eggs.
3. Blend flour, cinnamon, nutmeg, salt, and soda. Add dry ingredients to creamed mixture alternately with oatmeal, beating after each addition.
4. Scale 3 lb, 4 oz/1.47 kg into each of 3 well-greased pudding pans (12 × 16 × 2 ½ in).
5. Bake at 350°F/177°C for 35 to 40 minutes.
6. Combine topping ingredients. Spread 1 lb, 6 oz/624 g on each hot cake and place under broiler until slightly brown. (Cakes may be placed in oven at 350°F/177°C until topping is lightly browned.)
7. When cake has cooled, cut each pan into 20 portions (4 × 5).

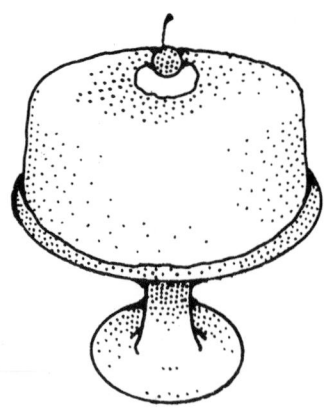

Applesauce Cake

50 Servings (2.5 oz/71 g)
Bake, 350°F/177°C, 30–35 min

| Metric | | Ingredients | U.S. | |
Weight	Volume		Weight	Volume
454 g	474 ml	Butter or Margarine	1 lb	2 cups
1.02 kg	1.42 l	Brown Sugar	2 lb, 4 oz	1 ½ qt
227 g	237 ml	Eggs (4 lge)	8 oz	1 cup
16 g	20 ml	Soda		4 tsp
907 g	947 ml	Applesauce, thick, unsweetened	2 lb	1 qt
19 g	20 ml	Salt	⅔ oz	4 tsp
	10 ml	Cloves		2 tsp
9 g	20 ml	Cinnamon	⅓ oz	4 tsp
793 g	1.66 l	Flour	1 lb, 12 oz	1 ¾ qt
312 g	474 ml	Raisins	11 oz	2 cups

Procedure

1. Cream butter or margarine thoroughly. Add sugar gradually and cream until light and fluffy. Beat in eggs.
2. Add soda to applesauce.
3. Sift dry ingredients together. Add alternately ¾ of dry ingredients and applesauce to creamed mixture. Combine remaining ¼ of dry ingredients with raisins. Add to cake mixture and mix well.
4. Pour into well-greased sheet pan (18×26×1 in). Bake at 350°F/177°C for 30 to 35 minutes or until cake tests done.
5. When cake has cooled, frost with Minute or Brown Sugar Frosting and cut each cake into 50 pieces (5×10).

Pound Cake

50 Servings
Bake, 325°F/163°C, 1 hr

| Metric | | Ingredients | U.S. | |
Weight	Volume		Weight	Volume
681 g	1.42 l	Flour, cake	1 lb, 8 oz	1 ½ qt
	7 ½ ml	Baking Powder		1 ½ tsp
7 g	15 ml	Nutmeg	¼ oz	1 tbsp
681 g	711 ml	Butter or Margarine	1 lb, 8 oz	3 cups
681 g	711 ml	Sugar	1 lb, 8 oz	3 cups
114 g	118 ml	Lemon Juice	4 oz	½ cup
681 g	711 ml	Eggs, separated (12 lge)	1 lb, 8 oz	3 cups
	3 ¾ ml	Salt		¾ tsp

Procedure

1. Sift flour, baking powder, and nutmeg together.
2. Cream butter or margarine well and add sugar gradually, beating constantly. Add lemon juice and continue beating.
3. Beat egg yolks until light and lemon-colored. Add to creamed mixture.
4. Beat egg whites and salt until stiff but not dry. Fold into creamed mixture. Fold in flour and mix only enough to blend.
5. Scale 2 lb/907 kg batter into each of 3 loaf pans (9×5×3 in) greased on bottom only. Bake at 325°F/163°C for 1 hour.
6. Cool and cut each cake into 17 servings.

Burnt Sugar Cake

50 Servings

Bake, 350°F/177°C, 35–40 min

Metric			U.S.	
Weight	Volume	Ingredients	Weight	Volume
312 g	316 ml	Butter or Margarine	11 oz	1 ⅓ cups
907 g	947 ml	Sugar	2 lb	1 qt
9 g	10 ml	Vanilla	⅓ oz	2 tsp
454 g	474 ml	Eggs (8 lge)	1 lb	2 cups
170 g	178 ml	Caramel Syrup	6 oz	¾ cup
907 g	1.89 l	Flour, cake, sifted	2 lb	2 qt
28 g	37 ml	Baking Powder	1 oz	2 ½ tbsp
7 g	7 ½ ml	Salt		1 ½ tsp
567 g	592 ml	Milk	1 lb, 4 oz	2 ½ cups

Procedure

1. Cream thoroughly butter or margarine, sugar, and vanilla. Add eggs, one at a time, beating after each addition. Add caramel syrup and blend.
2. Sift together cake flour, baking powder, and salt.
3. Add dry ingredients alternately with milk to the creamed mixture. Start with dry ingredients and blend after each addition. Mix for 1 minute on medium speed, or until smooth.
4. Yield: 7 ¼ lb/3.30 kg. Pour into greased baking sheet (18×26×1 in).
5. Bake at 350°F/177°C for 35 to 40 minutes.
6. When cool, frost with Brown Sugar Frosting or Seafoam Icing. Cut cake into 50 pieces (5×10).

Note: To make caramel syrup, melt 1 lb/454 g granulated sugar in a heavy skillet over medium heat. Stir constantly until melted and dark. Cool slightly. Add ¾ cup/178 ml hot water and stir until caramel is dissolved. Boil for about 10 minutes to a thick syrup, 220°F/104°C. Cool. This may be stored in refrigerator and used as needed.

White Cake

50 Servings

Bake, 350°F/177°C, 35 min

Metric			U.S.	
Weight	Volume	Ingredients	Weight	Volume
397 g	415 ml	Butter or Margarine	14 oz	1 ¾ cups
1.02 kg	1.07 l	Sugar	2 lb, 4 oz	4 ½ cups
19 g	20 ml	Vanilla	⅔ oz	1 ⅓ tbsp
1.08 kg	2.25 l	Flour, cake, sifted	2 lb, 6 oz	9 ½ cups
39 g	55 ml	Baking Powder		3 ⅔ tbsp
9 g	10 ml	Salt	⅓ oz	2 tsp
793 g	829 ml	Milk	1 lb, 12 oz	3 ½ cups
340 g	355 ml	Egg Whites, unbeaten (12 med)	12 oz	1 ½ cups

Procedure

1. Cream butter or margarine, sugar, and vanilla until light and fluffy.
2. Sift flour, baking powder, and salt together. Add alternately with milk to creamed mixture, starting with dry ingredients and blending after each addition.
3. Slowly pour in unbeaten egg whites, mixing on medium speed until well-blended.
4. Pour into a greased baking sheet (18×26×1 in).
5. Bake at 350°F/177°C for 35 minutes.
6. When cake is cool, frost with a favorite frosting, and cut into 50 pieces (5×10).

Pineapple Glacé Cake

50 Servings

Bake, 350°F/177°C, 35–40 min

Metric		Ingredients	U.S.	
Weight	Volume		Weight	Volume
		Topping		
2.04 kg	1.89 l	Pineapple, crushed	4 lb, 8 oz	2 qt
340 g	395 ml	Butter or Margarine, melted	12 oz	1 ⅔ cups
567 g	789 ml	Brown Sugar	1 lb, 4 oz	3 ⅓ cups
340 g	355 ml	Butter or Margarine	12 oz	1 ½ cups
907 g	947 ml	Sugar	2 lb	1 qt
14 g	15 ml	Vanilla	½ oz	1 tbsp
397 g	415 ml	Eggs, beaten (7 lge)	14 oz	1 ¾ cups
907 g	1.89 l	Flour, cake	2 lb	2 qt
28 g	45 ml	Baking Powder	1 oz	3 tbsp
	5 ml	Salt		1 tsp
567 g	592 ml	Milk	1 lb, 4 oz	2 ½ cups

Procedure

1. Combine pineapple, melted butter or margarine, and brown sugar. Pour into greased baking sheet (18×26×1 in).
2. Cream butter or margarine and add sugar slowly. Beat until light and fluffy.
3. Add vanilla and beaten eggs. Continue beating.
4. Sift dry ingredients and add alternately with milk to the creamed mixture, starting with dry ingredients.
5. Pour batter from dipper onto topping. Do not try to spread.
6. Bake at 350°F/177°C for 35 to 40 minutes, or until done.
7. Let cool for 10 minutes and turn upside down on another sheet pan, so that glacé is on top.
8. When cool, cut cake into 50 portions (5×10).

Chocolate Cake

50 Servings

Bake, 375°F/190°C, 25 min

Metric		Ingredients	U.S.	
Weight	Volume		Weight	Volume
340 g	355 ml	Butter or Margarine	12 oz	1 ½ cups
1.02 kg	1.07 l	Sugar	2 lb, 4 oz	4 ½ cups
14 g	15 ml	Vanilla	½ oz	1 tbsp
170 g	178 ml	Chocolate, unsweetened, melted	6 oz	¾ cup
283 g	296 ml	Eggs (5 lge)	10 oz	1 ¼ cups
681 g	1.42 l	Flour, cake	1 lb, 8 oz	1 ½ qt
14 g	22 ½ ml	Cream of Tartar	½ oz	4 ½ tsp
7 g	7 ½ ml	Salt	¼ oz	1 ½ tsp
340 g	355 ml	Milk	12 oz	1 ½ cups
12 g	15 ml	Soda		1 tbsp
43 g	45 ml	Water, cold	1 ½ oz	3 tbsp
454 g	474 ml	Water, boiling	1 lb	2 cups

Procedure

1. Cream butter or margarine, sugar, and vanilla until light and fluffy. Add melted chocolate and continue beating. Add eggs, a few at a time, beating after each addition.
2. Sift flour, cream of tarter, and salt together. Add alternately with milk, starting with dry ingredients and ending with dry ingredients.
3. Dissolve soda in cold water and add to batter.
4. Add boiling water last, and stir only enough to mix thoroughly.
5. Pour into greased baking sheet (18×26×1 in.). Bake at 375°F/190°C for 25 minutes.
6. When cake has cooled, ice with Chocolate Frosting or Mocha Butter Cream Icing and cut cake into 50 pieces (5×10).

Chocolate Devil's Food Cake
50 Servings
Bake, 325°F/163°C, 45 min

| Metric | | | U.S. | |
Weight	Volume	Ingredients	Weight	Volume
510 g	533 ml	Water, boiling	1 lb, 2 oz	2 ¼ cups
227 g	237 ml	Chocolate, unsweetened, melted	8 oz	1 cup
340 g	355 ml	Butter or Margarine	12 oz	1 ½ cups
14 g	15 ml	Vanilla	½ oz	1 tbsp
1.08 kg	1.18 l	Sugar	2 lb, 6 oz	4 ¾ cups
510 g	533 ml	Eggs (9 lge)	1 lb, 2 oz	2 ¼ cups
793 g	1.66 l	Flour, cake, sifted	1 lb, 12 oz	1 ¾ qt
7 g	7 ½ ml	Salt		1 ½ tsp
8 g	10 ml	Soda		2 tsp
7 g	10 ml	Baking Powder		2 tsp
454 g	474 ml	Buttermilk	1 lb	2 cups

Procedure

1. Add boiling water to melted chocolate. Mix well and bring to a boil, stirring. Cool.
2. Cream butter or margarine, vanilla, and sugar until light and fluffy. Add chocolate paste. Add eggs a few at a time, beating well after each addition.
3. Sift dry ingredients and add alternately with buttermilk, starting with dry ingredients and blending after each addition.
4. Pour into a greased baking sheet (18×26×1 in). Bake at 325°F/163°C for 45 minutes or until cake tests done.
5. When cake has cooled, frost with Chocolate Frosting, Chocolate Wonder Frosting, or Minute Icing. Cut cake into 50 portions (5×10).

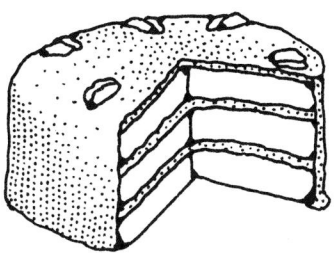

Buttermilk Chocolate Cake

50 Servings
Bake, 375°F/190°C, 35 min

| Metric | | Ingredients | U.S. | |
Weight	Volume		Weight	Volume
454 g	474 ml	Butter or Margarine	1 lb	2 cups
1.02 kg	1.12 l	Sugar	2 lb, 4 oz	4 ¾ cups
21 g	22 ml	Vanilla	¾ oz	1 ½ tbsp
312 g	326 ml	Eggs (6 med)	11 oz	1 ⅜ cups (6 med)
283 g	296 ml	Chocolate, unsweetened, melted	10 oz	1 ¼ cups
681 g	1.42 l	Flour, cake, sifted	1 lb, 8 oz	1 ½ qt
	15 ml	Soda		1 tbsp
	10 ml	Salt		2 tsp
681 g	711 ml	Buttermilk	1 lb, 8 oz	3 cups

Procedure

1. Cream butter or margarine, sugar, and vanilla until light and fluffy.
2. Add eggs one at a time, beating after each addition. Add melted chocolate, which has been cooled. Blend well.
3. Sift flour, soda, and salt together. Add alternately with buttermilk, starting with dry ingredients and blending after each addition. Mix 1 minute at medium speed, or until smooth.
4. Pour into greased baking sheet (18×26×1 in). Bake at 375°F/190°C for 35 minutes.
5. When cake has cooled, ice with Chocolate Frosting or Mocha Butter Cream Frosting and cut cake into 50 pieces (5×10).

Banana Cake

50 Servings
Bake, 325°F/163°C, 45–60 min

| Metric | | Ingredients | U.S. | |
Weight	Volume		Weight	Volume
340 g	355 ml	Butter or Margarine	12 oz	1 ½ cups
907 g	947 ml	Sugar	2 lb	4 cups
14 g	15 ml	Vanilla	½ oz	1 tbsp
283 g	296 ml	Eggs (5 lge)	10 oz	1 ¼ cups
567 g	592 ml	Banana Pulp	1 lb, 4 oz	2 ½ cups
793 g	1.66 l	Flour, cake, sifted	1 lb, 12 oz	1 ¾ qt
10 g	15 ml	Baking Powder		1 tbsp
	5 ml	Soda		1 tsp
	7 ½ ml	Salt		1 ½ tsp
340 g	355 ml	Buttermilk	12 oz	1 ½ cups

Procedure

1. Cream butter or margarine, sugar, and vanilla until light and fluffy.
2. Add eggs one at a time, beating constantly. Add banana pulp and continue beating.
3. Sift flour, baking powder, soda, and salt. Add alternately with buttermilk to creamed mixture, starting with dry ingredients.
4. Pour into a greased baking sheet (18×26×1 in). Bake at 325°F/163°C for 45 to 60 minutes or until cake tests done.
5. When cake has cooled, frost with Chocolate Malt or Minute Icing. Butterscotch Cream Filling and Chocolate Whipped-Cream Frosting are suggested also. Cut cake into 50 pieces (5×10).

Butter Cake

60 Servings
Bake, 350°F/177°C, 35 min

| Metric | | | U.S. | |
Weight	Volume	Ingredients	Weight	Volume
1.36 kg	3.08 l	Flour, cake	3 lb	3 ¼ qt
47 g	67 ml	Baking Powder	1 ⅔ oz	4 ½ tbsp
11 g	11 ml	Salt		2 ¼ tsp
624 g	652 ml	Butter or Margarine	1 lb, 6 oz	2 ¾ cups
1.36 kg	1.42 l	Sugar	3 lb	1 ½ qt
28 g	30 ml	Vanilla	1 oz	2 tbsp
510 g	533 ml	Eggs (9 lge)	1 lb, 2 oz	2 ¼ cups
1.02 kg	1.07 l	Milk	2 lb, 4 oz	4 ½ cups

Procedure

1. Sift together flour, baking powder, and salt.
2. Cream butter or margarine, sugar, and vanilla until light and fluffy.
3. Beat eggs until light and lemon-colored. Add to creamed mixture and blend well.
4. Add all of the flour mixture, then all of the milk. Mix at low speed for 2 minutes. Scrape down sides of bowl and beat at medium speed for 10 seconds.
5. Scale 3 lb, 10 oz/1.64 kg of batter into each of 3 greased pans (10×16×2¼ in) and bake at 350°F/177°C for 35 to 40 minutes.
6. When cake is cool, frost with a favorite frosting and cut cake into 20 portions (4×5).

Carrot Cake

60 Servings
Bake, 350°F/177°C, 40 min

| Metric | | | U.S. | |
Weight	Volume	Ingredients	Weight	Volume
567 g	593 ml	Eggs, beaten (10 lge)	1 lb, 4 oz	2 ½ cups
936 g	947 ml	Sugar	2 lb, 1 oz	1 qt
510 g	533 ml	Oil	1 lb, 2 oz	2 ¼ cups
681 g	1.42 l	Flour, cake	1 lb, 8 oz	1 ½ qt
5 g	11 ¼ ml	Cinnamon		2 ¼ tsp
14 g	15 ml	Salt	½ oz	1 tbsp
24 g	30 ml	Soda		2 tbsp
255 g	800 ml	Coconut, flaked	9 oz	3 ⅜ cups
596 g	947 ml	Carrots, finely grated	1 lb, 5 oz	1 qt
510 g	533 ml	Pineapple, crushed, undrained	1 lb, 2 oz	2 ¼ cups
255 g	533 ml	Walnuts, chopped	9 oz	2 ¼ cups

Procedure

1. Beat eggs, sugar, and oil together. Sift dry ingredients together; add to eggs. Beat until well-blended.
2. Add coconut, grated carrots, pineapple, and nuts. Mix to blend.
3. Scale 3 lb/1.36 kg into each of 3 greased pudding pans (10×16×2¼ in).
4. Bake at 350°F/177°C for 40 minutes or until done.
5. When cake has cooled, ice with Cream Cheese Frosting. Cut each cake into 20 pieces (5×4).

Mild Gingerbread
50 Servings (2 ½ × 3 ¼ in)
Bake, 350°F/177°C, 30 min

| Metric | | Ingredients | U.S. | |
Weight	Volume		Weight	Volume
340 g	355 ml	Butter or Margarine	12 oz	1 ½ cups
340 g	355 ml	Sugar	12 oz	1 ½ cups
227 g	237 ml	Eggs (4 lge)	8 oz	1 cup
567 g	415 ml	Molasses	1 lb, 4 oz	1 ¾ cups
737 g	1.54 l	Flour, cake, sifted	1 lb, 10 oz	6 ½ cups
24 g	30 ml	Soda		2 tbsp
	6 ¼ ml	Salt		1 ¼ tsp
	6 ¼ ml	Cinnamon		1 ¼ tsp
	6 ¼ ml	Ginger		1 ¼ tsp
	2 ½ ml	Cloves		½ tsp
907 g	947 ml	Sour Milk or Buttermilk	2 lb	1 qt

Procedure

1. Cream butter or margarine and sugar thoroughly. Add eggs one at a time, beating after each addition. Add molasses and blend.
2. Sift together flour, soda, salt, and spices. Add alternately with sour milk to creamed mixture. Start with dry ingredients and blend well after each addition.
3. Pour into a greased baking sheet (18×26×1 in).
4. Bake at 350°F/177°C for 30 minutes. When cool, cut cake into 50 servings (5×10). Portions may be garnished with whipped cream.

Dark, Spicy Gingerbread
50 Servings (2 ½ × 3 ¼ in)
Bake, 350°F/177°C, 30 min

| Metric | | Ingredients | U.S. | |
Weight	Volume		Weight	Volume
340 g	355 ml	Butter or Margarine	12 oz	1 ½ cups
340 g	355 ml	Sugar	12 oz	1 ½ cups
936 g	711 ml	Molasses	2 lb, 1 oz	3 cups
851 g	1.78 l	Flour, cake, sifted	1 lb, 14 oz	7 ½ cups
7 g	15 ml	Cinnamon		1 tbsp
	10 ml	Cloves		2 tsp
7 g	15 ml	Ginger		1 tbsp
14 g	15 ml	Salt	½ oz	1 tbsp
454 g	474 ml	Water, hot	1 lb	2 cups
28 g	35 ml	Soda	1 oz	2 ⅓ tbsp
312 g	326 ml	Eggs, beaten (6 med)	11 oz	1 ⅜ cups

1. Cream butter or margarine and sugar thoroughly. Add molasses and blend.
2. Sift together flour, spices, and salt. Add alternately with combined hot water and soda. Start with dry ingredients and blend well after each addition.
3. Mix in beaten eggs.
4. Pour into greased baking sheet (18×26×1 in). Bake at 350°F/177°C for 30 minutes.
5. When cake is cool, cut into 50 pieces (5×10) and garnish with whipped cream.

Pumpkin Cake

50 Servings
Bake, 375°F/190°C, 15 min
then 325°F/163°C, 15–20 min

Metric		Ingredients	U.S.	
Weight	Volume		Weight	Volume
340 g	355 ml	Butter or Margarine	12 oz	1½ cups
907 g	947 ml	Sugar	2 lb	1 qt
21 g	22 ml	Vanilla		1½ tbsp
283 g	296 ml	Eggs, beaten (5 lge)	10 oz	1¼ cups
255 g	355 ml	Pumpkin, cooked	9 oz	1½ cups
737 g	1.54 l	Flour, cake	1 lb, 10 oz	6½ cups
9 g	11¼ ml	Soda		2¼ tsp
11 g	15 ml	Baking Powder		1 tbsp
	3¾ ml	Cinnamon		¾ tsp
	3¾ ml	Cloves		¾ tsp
	3¾ ml	Allspice		¾ tsp
340 g	355 ml	Buttermilk	12 oz	1½ cups

Procedure

1. Cream butter or margarine, sugar, and vanilla. Add eggs and pumpkin. Mix well.
2. Sift together flour, baking powder, and spices. Add alternately with buttermilk to the creamed mixture, starting with dry ingredients.
3. Pour into greased baking sheet pan (18×26×1 in). Bake at 375°F/190°C for 15 minutes; then reduce temperature to 325°F/163°C until cake is done (about 15 or 20 min).
4. When cake has cooled, frost with Brown Sugar Frosting, Minute Icing, or Seafoam Icing. Cut cake into 50 pieces (5×10).

Note: This is a moist cake with a very good flavor.

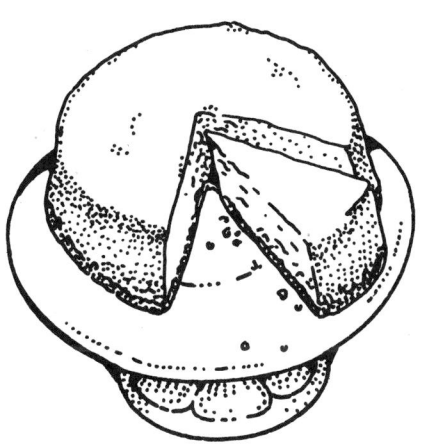

Plain Cake

50 Servings

Bake, 350°F/177°C, 35 min

Metric		Ingredients	U.S.		
Weight	Volume		Weight		Volume
340 g	355 ml	Butter or Margarine		12 oz	1½ cups
793 g	829 ml	Sugar	1 lb,	12 oz	3½ cups
19 g	20 ml	Vanilla			1⅓ tbsp
340 g	355 ml	Eggs (6 lge)		12 oz	1½ cups
907 g	1.89 l	Flour, cake, sifted	2 lb		2 qt
43 g	60 ml	Baking Powder		1½ oz	4 tbsp
9 g	10 ml	Salt		⅓ oz	2 tsp
737 g	770 ml	Milk	1 lb,	10 oz	3¼ cups

Procedure

1. Cream butter or margarine, sugar, and vanilla thoroughly. Add eggs one at a time, beating after each addition.
2. Sift together flour, baking powder, and salt.
3. Add dry ingredients alternately with milk to creamed mixture. Start with dry ingredients and blend after each addition. Mix 1 minute at medium speed, or until smooth, after last addition has been made.
4. Pour into greased baking sheet (18×26×1 in). Bake at 350°F/177°C for 35 minutes.
5. When cake has cooled, frost with your favorite frosting and cut into 50 servings (5×10).

Light Christmas Cake

2 Loaves

Bake, 300°F/149°C, 2 hrs

Metric		Ingredients	U.S.		
Weight	Volume		Weight		Volume
397 g	415 ml	Butter or Margarine		14 oz	1¾ cups
510 g	533 ml	Sugar	1 lb,	2 oz	2¼ cups
9 g	10 ml	Vanilla		⅓ oz	2 tsp
340 g	355 ml	Eggs (6 lge)		12 oz	1½ cups
255 g	266 ml	Milk or Orange Juice		9 oz	1 cup + 2 tbsp
510 g	1.07 l	Flour, cake	1 lb,	2 oz	4½ cups
	10 ml	Baking Powder			2 tsp
454 g	711 ml	Bleached Raisins	1 lb		3 cups
255 g	415 ml	Almonds, blanched		9 oz	1¾ cups
510 g	533 ml	Candied Cherries	1 lb,	2 oz	2¼ cups
255 g	533 ml	Candied Orange Peel		9 oz	2¼ cups

Procedure

1. Cream butter or margarine, sugar, and vanilla until light and fluffy.
2. Add eggs one at a time, beating thoroughly after each addition.
3. Add milk or orange juice alternately with sifted flour and baking powder, reserving a small amount of flour for fruit.
4. Chop all fruit and nuts. Sprinkle with remaining flour. Add to mixture, stirring until mixed.
5. Yield: 7½ lb/3.41 kg. Scale 3¾ lb/1.70 kg into each of 2 paper-lined loaf pans (5×9×3 in).
6. Bake at 300°F/149°C for about 2 hours. Cool before removing from pans and paper.
7. Cut each loaf into 18 slices.

Tea Cake

50 Servings

Bake, 350°F/177°C, 30 min

Metric		Ingredients	U.S.	
Weight	Volume		Weight	Volume
510 g	533 ml	Butter or Margarine	1 lb, 2 oz	2 ¼ cups
1.02 kg	1.07 l	Sugar	2 lb, 4 oz	4 ½ cups
198 g	178 ml	Egg Yolks, beaten (9 med)	7 oz	¾ cup
9 g	10 ml	Lemon Juice	⅓ oz	2 tsp
9 g	10 ml	Vanilla	⅓ oz	2 tsp
	2 ½ ml	Almond Extract		½ tsp
14 g	15 ml	Brandy (optional)	½ oz	1 tbsp
793 g	1.66 l	Flour, cake	1 lb, 12 oz	1 ¾ qt
	30 ml	Baking Powder		2 tbsp
	1 ¼ ml	Salt		¼ tsp
510 g	533 ml	Milk	1 lb, 2 oz	2 ¼ cups
255 g	267 ml	Egg Whites (9 med)	9 oz	1 ⅛ cups

Procedure

1. Cream butter or margarine. Add sugar gradually and cream until light and fluffy. Add beaten egg yolks, lemon juice, vanilla, and almond extract (and brandy, if used).
2. Sift flour, baking powder, and salt. Add alternately with milk in three parts, starting with dry ingredients.
3. Beat egg whites until stiff but moist. Fold into cake batter.
4. Pour into greased baking sheet (18×26×1 in). Bake at 350°F/177°C for 25 minutes.

Note: This cake may be baked in loaf pans by scaling 1 ¾ lb/ 793 g into each of 4 greased loaf pans. Allow 1 hour for baking.

Nut Cake

50 Servings

Bake, 350°F/177°C, 25 min

Metric		Ingredients	U.S.	
Weight	Volume		Weight	Volume
510 g	533 ml	Butter or Margarine	1 lb, 2 oz	2 ¼ cups
1.02 kg	1.12 l	Sugar	2 lb, 4 oz	4 ¾ cups
851 g	1.78 l	Flour, cake	1 lb, 14 oz	7 ½ cups
32 g	45 ml	Baking Powder	1 ⅛ oz	3 tbsp
	7 ½ ml	Salt		1 ½ tsp
	7 ½ ml	Cream of Tartar		1 ½ tsp
340 g	355 ml	Milk	12 oz	1 ½ cups
681 g	711 ml	Egg Whites, beaten (24 med)	1 lb, 8 oz	3 cups
340 g	711 ml	Nut Meats, chopped	12 oz	3 cups

Procedure

1. Cream butter or margarine. Add sugar gradually and beat until light.
2. Sift dry ingredients, and add alternately with milk, starting with dry ingredients.
3. Fold in stiffly beaten egg whites. Add nuts.
4. Pour into a greased baking sheet (18×26×1 in). Bake at 350°F/177°C, for 25 minutes.
5. When cool, cut cake into 50 pieces (5×10).

Note: Butterscotch Cream Filling and Seafoam Icing or Chocolate Filling and Frosting are suggested.

Date and Nut Sheet Cake

50 Servings

Bake, 325°F/163°C, 40–60 min

Metric		Ingredients	U.S.	
Weight	**Volume**		**Weight**	**Volume**
	5 ml	Soda		1 tsp
510 g	533 ml	Water, hot	1 lb, 2 oz	2 ¼ cups
907 g	1.42 l	Dates, pitted, chopped	2 lb	1 ½ qt
283 g	296 ml	Butter or Margarine	10 oz	1 ¼ cups
681 g	711 ml	Sugar	1 lb, 8 oz	3 cups
14 g	15 ml	Vanilla	½ oz	1 tbsp
255 g	267 ml	Eggs (5 med)	9 oz	1 ⅛ cups
681 g	1.42 l	Flour, cake	1 lb, 8 oz	1 ½ qt
10 g	15 ml	Baking Powder		1 tbsp
14 g	15 ml	Salt	½ oz	1 tbsp
227 g	474 ml	Nuts, chopped	8 oz	2 cups

Procedure

1. Dissolve soda in hot water and pour over dates.
2. Cream butter or margarine, sugar, and vanilla until light and fluffy. Add eggs one at a time, beating after each addition.
3. Sift flour, baking powder, and salt, saving a portion to flour nuts. Add dry ingredients to creamed mixture, alternately with date mixture, blending after each addition. Add floured nuts. Mix.
4. Yield: 8 lb/3.63 kg. Pour into greased baking sheet (18×26×1 in).
5. Bake at 325°F/163°C for 40 to 60 minutes or until it tests done.
6. When cool, frost with Lemon-Orange or Orange Frosting and cut cake into 50 pieces (5×10).

Date Sandwich Cake

50 Servings

Bake, 350°F/177°C, 35–40 min

Metric		Ingredients	U.S.	
Weight	**Volume**		**Weight**	**Volume**
624 g	652 ml	Butter or Margarine	1 lb, 6 oz	2 ¾ cups
454 g	474 ml	Granulated Sugar	1 lb	2 cups
340 g	474 ml	Brown Sugar	12 oz	2 cups
397 g	415 ml	Eggs (7 lge)	14 oz	1 ¾ cups
907 g	1.89 l	Flour, cake	2 lb	2 qt
6 g	10 ml	Cream of Tartar		2 tsp
8 g	10 ml	Soda		2 tsp
9 g	10 ml	Salt	⅓ oz	2 tsp
227 g	237 ml	Cream	8 oz	1 cup
227 g	237 ml	Sour Milk or Buttermilk	8 oz	1 cup
681 g	1.89 l	Rolled Oats	1 lb, 8 oz	2 qt
		Filling		
1.82 kg	2.84 l	Dates, chopped	4 lb	3 qt
170 g	237 ml	Brown Sugar	6 oz	1 cup
227 g	237 ml	Water, boiling	8 oz	1 cup
227 g	237 ml	Orange Juice Concentrate	8 oz	1 cup

1. Cream butter or margarine and sugars until light and fluffy. Add eggs one at a time, beating well after each addition.
2. Sift flour, cream of tartar, soda, and salt. Add alternately with cream and sour milk to the creamed mixture, starting with dry ingredients. Blend after each addition. Mix in rolled oats.
3. Combine dates, brown sugar, and boiling water. Cook until dates are soft. Stir well to make a paste. Add orange juice concentrate and cool.
4. Scale 5 lb/2.27 kg cake batter into a greased baking sheet (18×26×1 in). Spread all of filling over batter and top with remaining cake batter.
5. Bake at 350°F/177°C for 35 to 40 minutes or until a toothpick piercing cake comes out clean.
6. Cut cake 10×5. Serve with lemon sauce or whipped cream.

Raisin Cake
48 Servings
Bake, 350°F/177°C, 35–40 min

Metric		Ingredients	U.S.		
Weight	Volume		Weight		Volume
312 g	474 ml	Raisins		11 oz	2 cups
907 g	947 ml	Water	2 lb		1 qt
227 g	237 ml	Butter or Margarine		8 oz	1 cup
454 g	632 ml	Brown Sugar	1 lb		2⅔ cups
198 g	207 ml	Eggs (4 med)		7 oz	⅞ cup
681 g	1.42 l	Flour, cake, sifted	1 lb,	8 oz	1½ qt
	10 ml	Salt			2 tsp
	20 ml	Cinnamon			4 tsp
	5 ml	Cloves			1 tsp
	10 ml	Nutmeg			2 tsp
	10 ml	Soda			2 tsp
454 g	474 ml	Raisin Liquid	1 lb		2 cups
212 g	474 ml	Walnuts, chopped		7½ oz	2 cups

Procedure

1. Simmer raisins in water for 10 minutes. Drain, reserving 2 cups of liquid.
2. Cream butter or margarine and sugar. Add eggs and beat until light.
3. Sift together flour, salt, and spices. Add soda to raisin liquid. Add dry ingredients and liquid alternately to creamed mixture, mixing until smooth after each addition. Stir in raisins and nuts.
4. Pour into greased baking sheet (18×26×1 in). Bake at 350°F/177°C until it tests done (about 35 or 40 min).
5. When cake is cool, frost with Lemon-Orange or Brown Sugar Frosting and cut in 50 pieces (5×10).

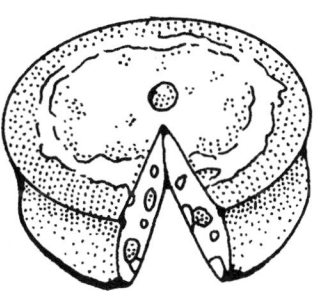

Raisin and Nut Cake

8 layers, 9-inch
Bake, 375°F/190°C, 30–35 min

Metric		Ingredients	U.S.	
Weight	Volume		Weight	Volume
1.82 kg	2.84 l	Raisins, coarsely ground	4 lb	3 qt
1.14 kg	1.18 l	Water, boiling	2 lb, 8 oz	1 ¼ qt
454 g	474 ml	Butter or Margarine	1 lb	2 cups
681 g	947 ml	Brown Sugar	1 lb, 8 oz	1 qt
397 g	415 ml	Eggs, well-beaten (7 lge)	14 oz	1 ¾ cups
14 g	15 ml	Vanilla	½ oz	1 tbsp
907 g	1.89 l	Flour, all-purpose	2 lb	2 qt
14 g	15 ml	Salt	½ oz	1 tbsp
	20 ml	Soda		1 ⅓ tbsp
425 g	947 ml	Walnuts, coarsely chopped	15 oz	1 qt

Procedure

1. Pour boiling water over raisins and let cool.
2. Cream butter or margarine and sugar. Add eggs and vanilla. Whip until well blended.
3. Sift flour, salt, and soda together. Add alternately with raisins to creamed mixture. Add nuts. Scale 22 oz/623 g of batter into 8 well-greased and floured 9-inch cake pans.
4. Bake at 375°F/190°C until it tests done (about 30 to 35 min).
5. When cake has cooled, frost with Brown Sugar Frosting.

Plantation Spice Cake

50 Servings
Bake, 375°F/190°C, 30 min

Metric		Ingredients	U.S.	
Weight	Volume		Weight	Volume
454 g	474 ml	Butter or Margarine	1 lb	2 cups
907 g	947 ml	Sugar	2 lb	1 qt
340 g	355 ml	Eggs (6 lge)	12 oz	1 ½ cups
793 g	1.66 l	Flour, cake, sifted	1 lb, 12 oz	1 ¾ qt
	5 ml	Salt		1 tsp
21 g	30 ml	Baking Powder	¾ oz	2 tbsp
7 g	15 ml	Cinnamon	¼ oz	1 tbsp
7 g	15 ml	Nutmeg	¼ oz	1 tbsp
340 g	533 ml	Raisins, chopped	12 oz	2 ¼ cups
624 g	652 ml	Water, cold	1 lb, 6 oz	2 ¾ cups

Procedure

1. Cream butter or margarine and sugar until light and fluffy. Add eggs one at a time, beating after each addition.
2. Sift together flour, salt, baking powder, and spices. Use a small amount of mixture to flour raisins.
3. Add dry ingredients alternately with cold water, blending after each addition. Add raisins and mix for a minute on medium speed or until smooth.
4. Pour into greased baking sheet (18×26×1 in).
5. Bake at 375°F/190°C for 30 minutes or until done.
6. When cool, frost with whipped cream or Minute Icing. Cut cake into 50 pieces (5×10).

Southern Peanut Butter Cake

50 Servings
Bake, 350°F/177°C, 25–30 min

| Metric | | Ingredients | U.S. | |
Weight	Volume		Weight	Volume
283 g	296 ml	Butter or Margarine	10 oz	1 ¼ cups
965 g	1.01 l	Sugar	2 lb, 2 oz	4 ¼ cups
38 g	40 ml	Vanilla	1 ⅓ oz	2 ⅔ tbsp
312 g	296 ml	Peanut Butter	11 oz	1 ¼ cups
283 g	296 ml	Eggs (5 lge)	10 oz	1 ¼ cups
851 g	1.78 l	Flour, all-purpose	1 lb, 14 oz	7 ½ cups
28 g	35 ml	Soda	1 oz	2 ⅓ tbsp
1.14 kg	1.18 l	Sour Milk	2 lb, 8 oz	1 ¼ qt

Procedure

1. Cream butter or margarine, sugar, and vanilla (medium speed) 10 minutes or until light and fluffy.
2. Add peanut butter and blend well.
3. Add eggs one at a time, blending well after each addition.
4. Add sifted dry ingredients alternately with sour milk, beginning and ending with dry ingredients.
5. Pour into greased baking sheet (18×26×1 in). Bake at 350°F/177°C for 25 to 30 minutes.
6. When cake has cooled, frost with Chocolate Frosting or Brown Sugar Frosting and cut into 50 pieces (5×10).

Louisiana Spice Cake

50 Servings
Bake, 375°F/190°C, 30 min

| Metric | | Ingredients | U.S. | |
Weight	Volume		Weight	Volume
454 g	474 ml	Margarine	1 lb	2 cups
907 g	947 ml	Sugar	2 lb	1 qt
340 g	355 ml	Eggs (7 med)	12 oz	1 ½ cups
793 g	1.66 l	Flour, cake, sifted	1 lb, 12 oz	1 ¾ qt
	30 ml	Baking Powder		2 tbsp
	5 ml	Salt		1 tsp
	10 ml	Ginger		2 tsp
	15 ml	Cinnamon		1 tbsp
	5 ml	Cloves		1 tsp
	5 ml	Nutmeg		1 tsp
312 g	237 ml	Molasses	11 oz	1 cup
567 g	592 ml	Coffee, cold	1 lb, 4 oz	2 ½ cups

Procedure

1. Cream margarine and sugar until light and fluffy. Add eggs one at a time, beating after each addition.
2. Sift flour, baking powder, salt, and spices together.
3. Add dry ingredients alternately with combined molasses and cold coffee to creamed mixture. Blend until smooth.
4. Pour into a greased baking sheet (18×26×1 in).
5. Bake at 375°F/190°C for 30 minutes or until it tests done.
6. When cake has cooled, frost with a fluffy white frosting and sprinkle with nuts. Cake may be cut into 50 pieces (5×10).

Orange Date Cake

50 Servings

Bake, 350°F/177°C, 35–40 min

Metric		Ingredients	U.S.		
Weight	**Volume**		**Weight**		**Volume**
567 g	592 ml	Butter or Margarine	1 lb,	4 oz	2 ½ cups
1.14 kg	1.18 l	Sugar	2 lb,	8 oz	5 cups
19 g	20 ml	Vanilla		⅔ oz	4 tsp
57 g	158 ml	Orange Rind, grated		2 oz	⅔ cup
510 g	533 ml	Eggs (9 lge)	1 lb,	2 oz	2 ¼ cups
1.14 kg	2.37 l	Flour, cake	2 lb,	8 oz	2 ½ qt
	25 ml	Soda			5 tsp
681 g	711 ml	Sour Milk or Buttermilk	1 lb,	8 oz	3 cups
567 g	889 ml	Dates, pitted, chopped	1 lb,	4 oz	3 ¾ cups
283 g	592 ml	Nuts, chopped		10 oz	2 ½ cups

Procedure

1. Cream butter or margarine, sugar, vanilla, and grated orange rind until light and fluffy. Add eggs one at a time, beating after each addition.
2. Mix and sift flour and soda. Add alternately ¾ of flour with sour milk or buttermilk, blending well.
3. Combine remaining ¼ of flour with dates and nuts. Add to cake mixture. Mix.
4. Yield: 10 ½ lb/4.77 kg. Scale into greased sheet cake pan (18×26×1 in).
5. Bake at 350°F/177°C for 35 to 40 minutes.
6. When cake has cooled, ice with Orange Frosting and cut into 50 pieces (5×10).

Cupcakes

5 dozen

Bake, 350°F/177°C, 30 min

Metric		Ingredients	U.S.		
Weight	**Volume**		**Weight**		**Volume**
737 g	770 ml	Sugar	1 lb,	10 oz	3 ¼ cups
454 g	474 ml	Butter or Margarine	1 lb		2 cups
19 g	20 ml	Vanilla		⅔ oz	4 tsp
454 g	474 ml	Eggs (8 lge)	1 lb		2 cups
793 g	1.66 l	Flour, cake, sifted	1 lb,	12 oz	1 ¾ qt
43 g	60 ml	Baking Powder		1 ½ oz	4 tbsp
	10 ml	Salt			2 tsp
567 g	592 ml	Milk	1 lb,	4 oz	2 ½ cups

Procedure

1. Cream sugar and butter or margarine with vanilla until light and fluffy.
2. Add eggs, one at a time, beating well after each addition.
3. Sift together flour, baking powder, and salt. Add alternately with milk to the creamed mixture, starting with dry ingredients and blending well after each addition.
4. Portion into well-greased muffin pans (paper baking cups may be used instead) with a No. 20 scoop. Bake at 350°F/177°C for 30 minutes.
5. When cakes have cooled, frost with any favorite frosting.

CAKES AND FROSTINGS

SPONGE CAKES

Angel Food Cake
48 Servings
Bake, 300°F/149°C, 1–1 ½ hrs

| Metric | | Ingredients | U.S. | |
Weight	Volume		Weight	Volume
1.36 kg	1.42 l	Egg Whites (48 med)	3 lb	1 ½ qt
	5 ml	Salt		1 tsp
	25 ml	Cream of Tartar		5 tsp
1.14 kg	1.18 l	Sugar, sifted	2 lb, 8 oz	5 cups
57 g	60 ml	Lemon Juice	2 oz	¼ cup
19 g	20 ml	Vanilla		1 ⅓ tbsp
	5 ml	Almond Extract		1 tsp
397 g	947 ml	Flour, cake	14 oz	1 qt

Procedure

1. Beat egg whites and salt until they "peak." Add cream of tartar and half the sugar gradually. Beat until stiff but not dry. Add lemon juice, vanilla, and almond extract.
2. Sift flour and remaining sugar together several times. Fold into batter.
3. Yield: 8 lb/3.63 kg. Scale 2 lb/907 g into each of 4 ungreased angel cake pans.
4. Bake at 300°F/149°C for from 1 to 1 ½ hours. Cool in inverted pans.
5. Frost with Chocolate Whipped Cream Frosting or Minute Icing. Fresh Strawberry Whip served on this cake is especially good.
6. Cut each cake into 12 servings.

Chocolate Peppermint Roll

50 Servings
Bake, 375°F/190°C, 20 min

Metric		Ingredients	U.S.	
Weight	**Volume**		**Weight**	**Volume**
170 g	355 ml	Flour, cake	6 oz	1 ½ cups
170 g	355 ml	Cocoa, unsweetened	6 oz	1 ½ cups
	22 ml	Baking Powder		1 ½ tbsp
	5 ml	Salt		1 tsp
907 g	947 ml	Eggs, separated (16 lge)	2 lb	1 qt
1.02 g	1.13 l	Sugar	2 lb, 4 oz	4 ¾ cups
128 g	135 ml	Water	4 ½ oz	9 tbsp
21 g	22 ml	Vanilla	¾ oz	1 ½ tbsp

Procedure

1. Sift flour, cocoa, baking powder, and salt together.
2. Beat egg whites until they peak. Fold in half of sugar (using low speed).
3. Add water to yolks and beat until light. Add remaining half of sugar gradually, beating until fluffy. Fold into beaten egg whites. Fold in sifted dry ingredients. Add vanilla.
4. Lightly grease 2 baking sheets (18×26×1 in). Line them with wax paper and grease the wax paper. Scale 2 lb, 13 oz/1.27 kg of batter into each paper-lined baking sheet.
5. Bake at 375°F/190°C for 20 minutes. Immediately invert cake onto a cloth sprinkled with powdered sugar. Remove wax paper from bottom of cake, trim edges, and immediately roll cake and cloth with cloth inside and covering the outside. When cool, unroll cake and spread with Peppermint Frosting (1 qt/947 ml per roll). Then, reroll and refrigerate.
6. Cut each roll into 25 slices (¾ in).

Note: Rolls may also be filled with whipped cream and crushed peppermint candy.

Jelly Roll

50 Servings (2 Sheet Cakes)
Bake, 375°F/190°C, 12–14 min

Metric		Ingredients	U.S.	
Weight	**Volume**		**Weight**	**Volume**
368 g	355 ml	Egg Yolks (18 med)	13 oz	1 ½ cups
397 g	415 ml	Eggs, whole (7 med)	14 oz	1 ¾ cups
935 g	978 ml	Sugar	2 lb, 1 oz	4 ⅛ cups
28 g	30 ml	Vanilla	1 oz	2 tbsp
198 g	207 ml	Milk, warmed	7 oz	⅞ cup
	11 ml	Salt		2 ¼ tsp
765 g	1.60 l	Flour, cake	1 lb, 11 oz	6 ¾ cups
32 g	45 ml	Baking Powder	1 ⅛ oz	3 tbsp
2.27 kg	2.37 l	Raspberry Jam	5 lb	2 ½ qt

1. Beat yolks and whole eggs at high speed until light and lemon colored (about 10 minutes).
2. Gradually add sugar, beating constantly. Add vanilla.
3. Sift salt, flour, and baking powder together. Add alternately with the warm milk to the creamed mixture.
4. Scale 2 lb, 14 oz/1.30 kg to each of 2 greased wax paper-lined baking sheets (18×26×1 in). Bake at 375°F/190°C for 12 to 14 minutes.
5. Quickly invert the cakes onto clean towels sprinkled heavily with sifted powdered sugar. Remove wax paper from the bottoms of the cakes. Trim edges of cakes. Immediately roll the cakes and towels with the towels inside and covering the outside of the cakes.
6. When cooled, unroll cakes. Spread with raspberry jam (2 ½ lb/1.14 kg per cake) and reroll. Sprinkle top with powdered sugar.
7. Cut each cake into 25 portions.

Mocha Roll
50 Servings
Bake, 375°F/190°C, 12–14 min

Metric			U.S.	
Weight	Volume	Ingredients	Weight	Volume
510 g	474 ml	Egg Yolks (24 med)	1 lb, 2 oz	2 cups
510 g	533 ml	Eggs, whole (10 med)	1 lb, 2 oz	2 ¼ cups
793 g	889 ml	Sugar	1 lb, 12 oz	3 ¾ cups
9 g	10 ml	Vanilla	⅓ oz	2 tsp
14 g	15 ml	Salt	½ oz	1 tbsp
1.02 kg	2.49 l	Flour, cake	2 lb, 4 oz	10 ½ cups
43 g	60 ml	Baking Powder	1 ½ oz	4 tbsp
142 g	148 ml	Milk, lukewarm	5 oz	⅝ cup
114 g	118 ml	Coffee	4 oz	½ cup
227 g	355 ml	Filberts, roasted, ground	8 oz	1 ½ cups

Procedure

1. Beat egg yolks and whole eggs on high speed until light.
2. Add sugar gradually, beating at medium speed constantly. Add vanilla.
3. Combine salt, flour, and baking powder and sift. Add alternately with lukewarm milk (98°F/37°C) and coffee. Fold in filberts.
4. Lightly grease 2 baking sheets (18×26×1 in). Line with wax paper, then grease wax paper. Scale 3 lb, 4 oz/1.48 kg into each of the 2 baking sheets. Bake at 375°F/190°C for 12 to 14 minutes.
5. Quickly invert cake onto clean towel heavily sprinkled with sifted powdered sugar. Remove wax paper from the bottoms of the cakes. Trim edges of cakes. Immediately roll the cakes and towels with the towels inside and covering the outside.
6. When cooled, unroll cakes. Spread with filling (1 qt/947 ml per cake) and reroll (see Fillings and Frostings).

Fillings and Frostings

Minute Icing
1 Sheet Cake

Metric		Ingredients	U.S.	
Weight	**Volume**		**Weight**	**Volume**
1.14 kg	2.07 l	Powdered Sugar, sifted	2 lb, 8 oz	8 ¾ cups
	2 ½ ml	Salt		½ tsp
170 g	178 ml	Milk	6 oz	¾ cup
227 g	237 ml	Butter or Margarine, melted	8 oz	1 cup
	7 ½ ml	Vanilla		1 ½ tsp

Procedure

1. Combine sugar and salt. Add half of milk. Mix. Add melted butter or margarine and mix. Add vanilla and remaining milk.
2. Mix until smooth. Spread on cake.
3. Yield: 3 lb/1.36 kg.

Butterscotch Cream Filling
4 lb/1.81 kg

Metric		Ingredients	U.S.	
Weight	**Volume**		**Weight**	**Volume**
567 g	789 ml	Brown Sugar	1 lb, 4 oz	3 ⅓ cups
227 g	474 ml	Flour, all-purpose	8 oz	2 cups
	5 ml	Salt		1 tsp
1.14 kg	1.18 l	Water, hot	2 lb, 8 oz	5 cups
283 g	316 ml	Butter or Margarine	10 oz	1 ⅓ cups
35 g	37 ml	Vanilla	1 ¼ oz	2 ½ tbsp
681 g	711 ml	Whipping Cream, whipped	1 lb, 8 oz	3 cups

Procedure

1. Combine brown sugar, flour, salt, and water in double boiler. Heat, stirring constantly, until thick, and then cook 8 minutes longer.
2. Add butter or margarine. Cool. Add vanilla.
3. Fold in whipped cream.
4. Yield: 4 lb/1.81 kg or filling for 2 sheet cakes.

Seafoam Icing
1 Sheet Cake

Metric		Ingredients	U.S.	
Weight	**Volume**		**Weight**	**Volume**
567 g	789 ml	Brown Sugar	1 lb, 4 oz	3 ⅓ cups
170 g	178 ml	Water	6 oz	¾ cup
198 g	207 ml	Egg Whites, beaten	7 oz	⅞ cup
	2 ½ ml	Salt		½ tsp
	5 ml	Vanilla		1 tsp

1. Boil brown sugar and water to 235°F/113°C or soft-ball stage.
2. Beat egg whites with salt until stiff but moist.
3. Add hot syrup slowly to egg whites, beating until smooth and of nice spreading consistency.

4. Add vanilla at end of beating.
5. Yield: 1 lb, 10 oz/737 g.

Note: Sprinkle chopped nuts over icing.

Brown Sugar Frosting
For 2 Sheet Cakes

Metric		Ingredients	U.S.	
Weight	Volume		Weight	Volume
454 g	474 ml	Butter or Margarine	1 lb	2 cups
681 g	947 ml	Brown Sugar	1 lb, 8 oz	1 qt
	5/16 ml	Salt		1/16 tsp
227 g	237 ml	Milk	8 oz	1 cup
1.30 kg	2.37 l	Powdered Sugar, sifted	2 lb, 14 oz	2 1/2 qt
	10 ml	Vanilla		2 tsp

Procedure

1. Melt butter or margarine. Add brown sugar and salt. Cook for 2 minutes over low heat.
2. Add milk gradually, stirring constantly, and heat until mixture comes to a boil.

3. Remove from heat. Add sifted powdered sugar and vanilla. Beat to spreading consistency.

Note: Increase powdered sugar if needed for desired consistency.

Boston Cream Pie Filling
1 1/2 qt/1.42 l

Metric		Ingredients	U.S.	
Weight	Volume		Weight	Volume
212 g	355 ml	Cornstarch	7 1/2 oz	1 1/2 cups
454 g	474 ml	Sugar	1 lb	2 cups
	5 ml	Salt		1 tsp
454 g	474 ml	Milk, cold	1 lb	2 cups
1.82 kg	1.89 l	Milk, scalded	4 lb	2 qt
255 g	237 ml	Egg Yolks, beaten (12 med)	9 oz	1 cup
114 g	118 ml	Butter or Margarine	4 oz	1/2 cup
14 g	15 ml	Vanilla	1/2 oz	1 tbsp

Procedure

1. Blend dry ingredients. Add cold milk, and then stir into scalded milk. Stir and cook until thick and smooth.
2. Add a little hot mixture to beaten egg yolks, stirring, and then stir yolks into hot mixture. Cook 2 minutes. Remove from heat.
3. Add butter or margarine and vanilla. Cool.

Chocolate Frosting
1 Sheet Cake

Metric		Ingredients	U.S.	
Weight	Volume		Weight	Volume
114 g	118 ml	Butter or Margarine	4 oz	½ cup
737 g	1.30 l	Powdered Sugar	1 lb, 10 oz	5 ½ cups
170 g	158 ml	Evaporated Milk	6 oz	⅔ cup
	1 ¼ ml	Salt		¼ tsp
9 g	10 ml	Vanilla	⅓ oz	2 tsp
170 g	158 ml	Chocolate, unsweetened, melted	6 oz	⅔ cup

Procedure

1. Cream butter or margarine and powdered sugar.
2. Add milk and mix well.

3. Add salt, vanilla, and melted chocolate. Beat until fluffy, at least 2 minutes.

Chocolate Wonder Frosting
1 Sheet Cake

Metric		Ingredients	U.S.	
Weight	Volume		Weight	Volume
170 g	178 ml	Cream Cheese	6 oz	¾ cup
57 g	59 ml	Milk	2 oz	¼ cup
454 g	829 ml	Powdered Sugar	1 lb	3 ½ cups
128 g	118 ml	Chocolate, unsweetened, melted	4 ½ oz	½ cup
	⅝ ml	Salt		⅛ tsp

Procedure

1. Beat cream cheese on high speed until soft. Add milk gradually and continue beating.
2. Add powdered sugar slowly, beating well. Add chocolate and salt and beat until smooth.

3. Yield: About 3 cups/711 ml, or enough frosting for one sheet cake.

Note: If frosting seems too stiff, warm over hot water until thin enough to spread.

Chocolate Whipped-Cream Frosting
4 Angel Food Cakes

Metric		Ingredients	U.S.	
Weight	Volume		Weight	Volume
907 g	947 ml	Whipping Cream	2 lb	1 qt
114 g	237 ml	Chocolate, unsweetened, grated	4 oz	1 cup
28 g	40 ml	Confectioner's Sugar	1 oz	8 tsp
19 g	20 ml	Vanilla	⅔ oz	4 tsp
	5 ml	Salt		1 tsp

1. Scald 1 cup/237 ml of the cream and the chocolate in the top of a double boiler. Cool.
2. Beat remaining cream to spreading consistency. Add sugar, vanilla, and salt.
3. Fold in cooled chocolate mixture.
4. Spread lightly on cake.
5. Yield: Enough for 4 chocolate angel food cakes.

Chocolate Malt Icing
1 Sheet Cake

Metric		Ingredients	U.S.	
Weight	Volume		Weight	Volume
227 g	237 ml	Butter or Margarine	8 oz	1 cup
	3¾ ml	Salt		¾ tsp
85 g	158 ml	Malted Milk Powder	3 oz	⅔ cup
	7½ ml	Vanilla		1½ tsp
1.02 kg	1.87 l	Powdered Sugar	2 lb, 4 oz	7⅞ cups
114 g	237 ml	Cocoa, unsweetened	4 oz	1 cup
340 g	355 ml	Milk (approx.)	12 oz	1½ cups

Procedure

1. Cream shortening and add salt, malted milk, and vanilla. Cream well.
2. Add sifted powdered sugar and cocoa and enough milk to make good spreading consistency. Beat until smooth.
3. Yield: About 3¾ lb/1.70 kg. Spread on cool cake.

Peppermint Frosting
3 qt/2.84 l

Metric		Ingredients	U.S.	
Weight	Volume		Weight	Volume
907 g	947 ml	Sugar	2 lb	1 qt
340 g	355 ml	Water	12 oz	1½ cups
	2½ ml	Cream of Tartar		½ tsp
397 g	415 ml	Egg Whites (14 med)	14 oz	1¾ cups
283 g	533 ml	Powdered Sugar	10 oz	2¼ cups
	2½ ml	Oil of Peppermint		½ tsp
	5 ml	Salt		1 tsp

Procedure

1. Combine sugar and water. Bring to boil. Add cream of tartar and continue cooking until mixture spins long firm threads (3-in threads).
2. Beat egg whites until foamy and add half the powdered sugar slowly. Beat just until whites "peak."
3. Beating on high speed, slowly add syrup to egg whites. When well-mixed, add remaining powdered sugar, salt, and oil of peppermint. Beat thoroughly.
4. Yield: 3 qt/2.84 l or 4½ lb/2.04 kg.

Note: This is a fluffy boiled frosting that may be varied in many ways, by using other flavorings and by adding chopped fruit or nuts.

Mocha Chocolate Icing
1 Sheet Cake

Metric		Ingredients	U.S.	
Weight	Volume		Weight	Volume
681 g	1.24 l	Powdered Sugar	1 lb, 8 oz	5 ¼ cups
57 g	59 ml	Butter or Margarine, melted	2 oz	¼ cup
85 g	79 ml	Chocolate, unsweetened, melted	3 oz	⅓ cup
	7 ½ ml	Vanilla		1 ½ tsp
57 g	59 ml	Milk	2 oz	¼ cup
57 g	59 ml	Coffee	2 oz	¼ cup

Procedure

1. Combine sugar, butter or margarine (melted), chocolate, and vanilla. Mix thoroughly.
2. Add milk and coffee, stirring constantly.
3. Yield: 2 ¼ lb/1.02 kg, or icing for 1 sheet cake (18×26×1 in).

Mocha Butter-Cream Icing
1 Sheet Cake

Metric		Ingredients	U.S.	
Weight	Volume		Weight	Volume
227 g	237 ml	Butter or Margarine	8 oz	1 cup
907 g	1.66 l	Powdered Sugar	2 lb	7 cups
	5 ml	Vanilla		1 tsp
	2 ½ ml	Salt		½ tsp
71 g	158 ml	Cocoa, unsweetened	2 ½ oz	⅔ cup
142 g	158 ml	Coffee, cold	5 oz	⅔ cup

Procedure

1. Cream butter or margarine, slowly adding powdered sugar and vanilla. Cream thoroughly.
2. Combine salt, cocoa, and cold coffee, making a smooth mixture. Slowly add to creamed mixture, beating until mixture is smooth and of spreading consistency.
3. Yield: 2 lb, 15 oz/1.33 kg.

Orange Icing
1 Sheet Cake

Metric		Ingredients	U.S.	
Weight	Volume		Weight	Volume
114 g	118 ml	Orange Juice Concentrate	4 oz	½ cup
	22 ½ ml	Orange Rind		1 ½ tbsp
1.14 kg	2.07 l	Powdered Sugar	2 lb, 8 oz	8 ¾ cups
21 g	22 ml	Butter or Margarine	¾ oz	1 ½ tbsp
	2 ½ ml	Salt		½ tsp

1. Combine all ingredients and beat at high speed until of a spreading consistency.

2. Yield: 2¾ lb/1.25 kg, or icing for 1 sheet cake.

Orange Frosting
3 lb/1.36 kg

Metric		Ingredients	U.S.	
Weight	Volume		Weight	Volume
227 g	237 ml	Butter or Margarine, soft	8 oz	1 cup
1.14 kg	2.07 l	Powdered Sugar	2 lb, 8 oz	8¾ cups
21 g	59 ml	Orange Rind, grated	¾ oz	¼ cup
9 g	15 ml	Lemon Rind, grated	⅓ oz	1 tbsp
	2½ ml	Salt		½ tsp
57 g	59 ml	Lemon Juice	2 oz	¼ cup
142 g	158 ml	Orange Juice	5 oz	⅔ cup

Procedure

1. Cream butter or margarine. Slowly add powdered sugar, creaming thoroughly. Add orange rind, lemon rind, and salt.

2. Slowly add juices, mixing until smooth.
3. Yield: 3 lb/1.36 kg.

Lemon-Orange Frosting
1 Sheet Cake

Metric		Ingredients	U.S.	
Weight	Volume		Weight	Volume
227 g	237 ml	Butter or Margarine	8 oz	1 cup
907 g	1.66 l	Powdered Sugar	2 lb	7 cups
	10 ml	Orange Rind, grated		2 tsp
114 g	118 ml	Orange Juice	4 oz	½ cup
28 g	30 ml	Lemon Juice	1 oz	2 tbsp
	1¼ ml	Salt		¼ tsp

Procedure

1. Blend butter or margarine and powdered sugar.
2. Stir in remaining ingredients and beat until smooth and creamy.

Note: Add additional orange juice concentrate and powdered sugar for desired flavor and consistency.

Lemon Nut Frosting
1 Sheet Cake

Metric		Ingredients	U.S.		
Weight	Volume		Weight		Volume
76 g	79 ml	Lemon Juice		2 ⅔ oz	⅓ cup
	1 ¼ ml	Vanilla			¼ tsp
1.02 kg	1.89 l	Powdered Sugar	2 lb,	4 oz	2 qt
114 g	118 ml	Cream		4 oz	½ cup
114 g	237 ml	Nuts, chopped		4 oz	1 cup
	5 ml	Lemon Rind			1 tsp

Procedure

1. Mix lemon juice, lemon rind, vanilla, and half the powdered sugar together.
2. Add cream. Stir until smooth. Gradually mix in remaining sugar, to make of spreading consistency.
3. Yield: 3 lb/1.36 kg. Frost cool cake and sprinkle with chopped nuts.

Apricot Frosting
2 ½ qt/2.37 l

Metric		Ingredients	U.S.		
Weight	Volume		Weight		Volume
340 g	711 ml	Apricots, dried		12 oz	3 cups
1.14 kg	1.18 l	Water	2 lb,	8 oz	5 cups
227 g	237 ml	Butter or Margarine		8 oz	1 cup
1.59 kg	2.84 l	Powdered Sugar	3 lb,	8 oz	3 qt
57 g	59 ml	Lemon Juice		2 oz	¼ cup
		Milk or Cream			

Procedure

1. Boil apricots in water for 30 minutes. Sieve. Yield: 9 oz/255 g (1 cup/237 ml).
2. Combine puree with butter or margarine and cream thoroughly. Add sugar gradually, beating constantly. Add lemon juice and cream or milk to make a spreading consistency.
3. Yield: 2 ½ qt/2.37 l or frosting for 1 sheet cake.

Note: Coconut may be sprinkled over the top.

CHAPTER 13 _____ Cookies

Cookies are a favorite sweet that afford considerable variety in terms of richness, shape, flavor, and consistency. Most cookies are simple to make. Mixing time is approximately the same as that for cake. The time variation tends to be greatest for shaping, depending on the amount of handwork or individual handling required. For this reason, the cookie recipes in this chapter have been divided according to the type of shaping that is required for them:

Ball Cookies   The dough is firm enough to form into balls and flatten with a fork.

Bars and Squares   The dough is soft and may be poured into a baking pan, baked, and cut into different sizes and shapes.

Pressed Cookies   A smooth dough, firm enough to hold a sharp form, is pressed through a cookie tube.

Drop Cookies   The dough is soft enough to drop from a spoon or scoop onto a baking sheet.

Sliced Cookies   Firm dough is formed in long rolls (approximately 2 inches in diameter). It is refrigerated to be stiff enough for slicing.

Rolled Cookies   Soft dough, stiff enough to roll, is rolled out with a rolling pin to desired thickness, and cut into desired shape and size with a cutter.

When baking cookies, a shiny aluminum sheet should be used to insure even distribution of heat. Each batch of cookies should be started on a cold baking sheet. If placed on a warm cookie sheet, the cookies will begin to spread and lose their shape before they reach the oven.

Unless otherwise specified, it is best to remove cookies from the cookie sheet while still warm. If cookies are allowed to cool on the baking sheet, they will be difficult to remove, whether the pan has been greased or not. The baking sheet retains heat, and the cookies overbake. They may crack and split. Cookies high in sugar and fat should be removed from the cookie sheet immediately after being taken from the oven, to lower the temperature of the cookies quickly so they will become crisp. Crisp cookies will not retain their crispness if stored with moist cookies. Cookies tend to stick together if stacked before they are cool.

Ball Cookies

Brown Sugar Cookies
96 Cookies (2 ½ in)
Bake, 350°F/177°C, 10–12 min

Metric		Ingredients	U.S.		
Weight	Volume		Weight		Volume
510 g	533 ml	Butter or Margarine	1 lb,	2 oz	2 ¼ cups
510 g	711 ml	Brown Sugar	1 lb,	2 oz	3 cups
170 g	178 ml	Eggs (3 lge)		6 oz	¾ cup
681 g	1.42 l	Flour, all-purpose	1 lb,	8 oz	1 ½ qt
	7 ½ ml	Soda			1 ½ tsp
	7 ½ ml	Baking Powder			1 ½ tsp
	5 ml	Salt			1 tsp
227 g	355 ml	Raisins, white		8 oz	1 ½ cups
85 g	178 ml	Walnuts, chopped		3 oz	¾ cup

Procedure

1. Cream butter or margarine. Add brown sugar and cream well. Beat in eggs.
2. Mix together flour, soda, baking powder, salt, raisins, and nuts. Add to creamed mixture and blend.

Form into balls the size of a walnut, place on a greased baking sheet and flatten with a fork.
3. Bake at 350°F/177°C for 10 to 12 minutes.

Cherry Balls
50 Cookies (1 ½ in)
Bake, 325°F/163°C, 16 min

Metric		Ingredients	U.S.	
Weight	Volume		Weight	Volume
227 g	237 ml	Butter or Margarine	8 oz	1 cup
114 g	118 ml	Sugar	4 oz	½ cup
	5 ml	Vanilla		1 tsp
85 g	79 ml	Egg Yolks (4 med)	3 oz	⅓ cup
19 g	30 ml	Orange Rind, grated	⅔ oz	2 tbsp
	30 ml	Lemon Juice		2 tbsp
	1 ¼ ml	Salt		¼ tsp
227 g	474 ml	Flour, cake	8 oz	2 cups
114 g	118 ml	Egg Whites (4 med)	4 oz	½ cup
283 g	474 ml	Pecans, chopped	10 oz	2 cups
114 g	118 ml	Maraschino Cherries	4 oz	½ cup

Procedure

1. Cream butter or margarine and sugar. Add vanilla, egg yolks, orange rind, lemon juice, and salt. Cream thoroughly.
2. Add flour and blend. Chill 1 hour. Beat egg whites until they "peak."
3. Mold dough into balls 1 inch in diameter. Dip balls into beaten egg whites, roll in chopped pecans, and place on well-greased baking sheet. Place ¼ cherry on top of each cookie.
4. Bake at 325°F/163°C for 16 minutes.

Coconut Rum Balls
50 Servings

Metric		Ingredients	U.S.	
Weight	Volume		Weight	Volume
595 g	1.42 l	Chocolate Wafers, finely rolled	1 lb, 5 oz	1 ½ qt
397 g	711 ml	Confectioner's Sugar, sifted	14 oz	3 cups
340 g	711 ml	Pecans or Walnuts, finely chopped	12 oz	3 cups
212 g	178 ml	Corn Syrup, light	7 ½ oz	¾ cup
170 g	178 ml	Dark Rum	6 oz	¾ cup
227 g	711 ml	Coconut, flaked	8 oz	3 cups

Procedure

1. Blend chocolate wafers, sugar, nuts, syrup, and rum. (Mixture will be stiff and sticky.)
2. Form balls 1 inch in diameter and roll in coconut.
3. Refrigerate until firm (overnight) and roll again in coconut (if balls are sticky).

Bars and Squares

Apricot Dream Bars
96 Bars (1 ½ × 3 in)
Bake, 350°F/177°C, 15 min, 25 min

Metric		Ingredients	U.S.	
Weight	Volume		Weight	Volume
454 g	947 ml	Apricots, dried	1 lb	1 qt
681 g	711 ml	Butter or Margarine	1 lb, 8 oz	3 cups
340 g	355 ml	Granulated Sugar	12 oz	1 ½ cups
681 g	1.42 l	Flour, all-purpose	1 lb, 8 oz	1 ½ qt
1.02 kg	1.42 l	Brown Sugar	2 lb, 4 oz	1 ½ qt
596 g	622 ml	Eggs, beaten (12 med)	1 lb, 5 oz	2 ⅝ cups
227 g	474 ml	Flour, all-purpose	8 oz	2 cups
	15 ml	Baking Powder		1 tbsp
	7 ½ ml	Salt		1 ½ tsp
340 g	711 ml	Nuts, chopped	12 oz	3 cups
14 g	15 ml	Vanilla	½ oz	1 tbsp
		Confectioner's Sugar		

Procedure

1. Wash, cover with water, and boil apricots 10 minutes. Drain, cool, and chop them.
2. Combine butter or margarine, granulated sugar, and flour. Blend until crumbly. Press into a greased baking sheet (18 × 26 × 1 in). Bake at 350°F/177°C for 15 minutes.
3. Beat brown sugar into beaten eggs. Add flour, baking powder, and salt. Blend. Stir in nuts, vanilla, and apricots. Spread mixture over baked layer. Bake at 350°F/177°C for 25 minutes. Cool.
4. Cut 8 × 12 into 96 pieces, 1 ½ × 3 inches. Sprinkle generously with, or roll bars in, confectioner's sugar.

Dream Bars

100 Bars (2 ½ × 1 ¾ in)

Bake, 350°F/177°C, 15 min, 25 min

Metric		Ingredients	U.S.		
Weight	Volume		Weight		Volume
681 g	711 ml	Margarine	1 lb,	8 oz	3 cups
510 g	711 ml	Brown Sugar	1 lb,	2 oz	3 cups
9 g	10 ml	Salt		⅓ oz	2 tsp
681 g	1.42 l	Flour, all-purpose	1 lb,	8 oz	1 ½ qt
		Second Layer			
567 g	592 ml	Eggs (10 lge)	1 lb,	4 oz	2 ½ cups
1.02 kg	1.42 l	Brown Sugar	2 lb,	4 oz	1 ½ qt
85 g	178 ml	Flour		3 oz	¾ cup
	10 ml	Baking Powder			2 tsp
43 g	45 ml	Vanilla		1 ½ oz	3 tbsp
907 g	2.84 l	Coconut	2 lb		3 qt
340 g	711 ml	Nuts, chopped		12 oz	3 cups

Procedure

1. Cream margarine and brown sugar (medium speed) until light and fluffy.
2. Add flour and salt. Blend. Pack into baking sheet (18 × 26 × 1 in). Bake at 350°F/177°C for 15 minutes or until light brown.
3. Beat eggs. Add brown sugar and beat. Stir in remaining ingredients. Spread over first layer and bake for 25 minutes or until mixture is firm in the middle of the pan.
4. When cool, cut 10 × 10 into 100 pieces.

Coconut Orange Squares

100 Bars (2 ½ × 1 ¾ in)

Bake, 350°F/177°C, about 35 min

Metric		Ingredients	U.S.		
Weight	Volume		Weight		Volume
340 g	355 ml	Butter or Margarine		12 oz	1 ½ cups
1.36 kg	1.42 l	Sugar	3 lb		1 ½ qt
43 g	118 ml	Orange Rind, grated		1 ½ oz	½ cup
340 g	355 ml	Eggs, beaten (6 lge)		12 oz	1 ½ cups
114 g	118 ml	Milk		4 oz	½ cup
454 g	947 ml	Flour, all-purpose, sifted	1 lb		1 qt
	15 ml	Baking Powder			1 tbsp
	10 ml	Salt			2 tsp
850 g	2.60 l	Coconut, flaked	1 lb,	14 oz	2 ¾ qt

Procedure

1. Cream butter or margarine and sugar until light and fluffy. Add orange rind, eggs, and milk. Mix until well-blended.
2. Blend flour, baking powder, and salt. Add with coconut to liquid mixture. Stir only enough to blend.
3. Spread onto a greased and floured baking sheet (18 × 26 × 1).
4. Bake at 350°F/177°C for about 35 minutes or until it tests done.
5. Cut 10 × 10 into 100 pieces while warm.

Orange Spice Bars

50 Servings (2.3 oz/65 g)
Bake, 350°F/177°C, 20 min

Metric		Ingredients	U.S.		
Weight	Volume		Weight		Volume
454 g	474 ml	Butter or Margarine	1 lb		2 cups
681 g	947 ml	Brown Sugar	1 lb,	8 oz	1 qt
340 g	355 ml	Eggs (6 lge)		12 oz	1 ½ cups
114 g	118 ml	Orange Juice		4 oz	½ cup
	15 ml	Orange Peel, grated			1 tbsp
681 g	1.42 l	Flour, all-purpose, sifted	1 lb,	8 oz	1 ½ qt
	15 ml	Soda			1 tbsp
	7 ½ ml	Salt			1 ½ tsp
	15 ml	Cinnamon			1 tbsp
	7 ½ ml	Nutmeg			1 ½ tsp
	3 ¾ ml	Cloves			¾ tsp
340 g	711 ml	Walnuts, chopped		12 oz	3 cups
114 g	355 ml	Coconut, shredded		4 oz	1 ½ cups
		Orange Glaze			
596 g	1.42 l	Powdered Sugar	1 lb,	5 oz	1 ½ qt
114 g	118 ml	Orange Juice		4 oz	½ cup
	30 ml	Orange Peel, grated			2 tbsp

Procedure

1. Cream butter or margarine and sugar until light and fluffy. Add eggs, orange juice, and peel. Mix well.
2. Sift together flour, soda, salt, and spices. Blend into sugar mixture. Stir in chopped nuts.
3. Pour into greased baking sheet (18 × 26 × 1 in). Bake at 350°F/177°C for 20 minutes or until it tests done. Cool in pan.
4. Mix powdered sugar, orange juice, and grated peel together and spread cake with glaze. Sprinkle with coconut.
5. Cut into 50 portions (5 × 10).

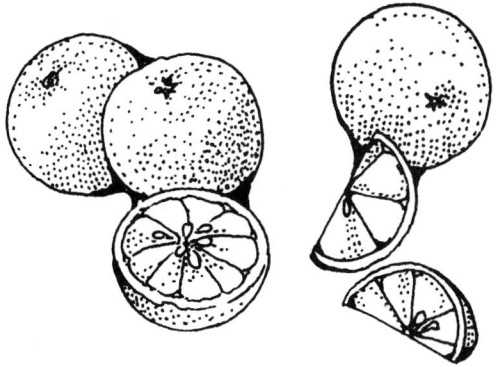

Date Oat Bars

96 Bars (1 ½ × 3 in)

Bake, 375°F/190°C, 15 or 20 min

Metric		Ingredients	U.S.	
Weight	Volume		Weight	Volume
907 g	1.42 l	Dates, chopped	2 lb	1 ½ qt
255 g	355 ml	Brown Sugar	9 oz	1 ½ cups
624 g	652 ml	Water	1 lb, 6 oz	2 ¾ cups
	45 ml	Flour, cake		3 tbsp
14 g	15 ml	Vanilla	½ oz	1 tbsp
57 g	59 ml	Lemon Juice	2 oz	¼ cup
340 g	711 ml	Flour, cake	12 oz	3 cups
	15 ml	Soda		1 tbsp
340 g	947 ml	Oatmeal	12 oz	1 qt
510 g	711 ml	Brown Sugar	1 lb, 2 oz	3 cups
510 g	533 ml	Butter or Margarine, melted	1 lb, 2 oz	2 ¼ cups

Procedure

1. Cook dates, brown sugar, water, and 3 tbsp/45 ml of flour until thick, stirring to prevent sticking. Add vanilla and lemon juice.
2. Combine flour and soda. Blend in oatmeal, brown sugar, and melted butter or margarine. Divide mixture in half. Spread one half evenly onto a greased baking sheet (18 × 26 × 1 in).
3. Spread date mixture evenly on top of crumb mixture. Cover date mixture with remaining crumb mixture.
4. Bake at 375°F/190°C for 15 or 20 minutes.
5. Cool and cut 8 × 12 into 96 pieces, 1 ½ × 3 inches.

Note: Filling remains soft.

Brownies

70 Servings (1.6 oz/76 g)

Bake, 350°F/177°C, 35 min

Metric		Ingredients	U.S.	
Weight	Volume		Weight	Volume
283 g	296 ml	Butter or Margarine	10 oz	1 ½ cups
1.14 kg	1.18 l	Sugar	2 lb, 8 oz	5 cups
	25 ml	Vanilla		5 tsp
283 g	296 ml	Chocolate, unsweetened, melted	10 oz	1 ¼ cups
567 g	592 ml	Eggs, well-beaten (10 lge)	1 lb, 4 oz	2 ½ cups
397 g	829 ml	Flour, cake	14 oz	3 ½ cups
21 g	30 ml	Baking Powder	¾ oz	2 tbsp
	5 ml	Salt		1 tsp
681 g	1.42 l	Walnuts, chopped	1 lb, 8 oz	1 ½ qt

Procedure

1. Cream butter or margarine, sugar, and vanilla thoroughly. Stir in melted chocolate and eggs.
2. Sift together flour, baking powder, and salt. Stir into creamed mixture. Add chopped nuts.
3. Spread onto a greased baking sheet (18 × 26 × 1 in). Bake at 350°F/177°C for about 35 minutes or until it tests done.
4. Cut 7 × 10 into 70 pieces, 2 ⅓ × 2 ½ × 1 inches.

Peanut Butter Bars

64 Bars (2 × 2½ in)

Bake, 350°F/177°C, 25–30 min

| Metric | | | U.S. | |
Weight	Volume	Ingredients	Weight	Volume
277 g	237 ml	Butter or Margarine	8 oz	1 cup
510 g	474 ml	Peanut Butter	1 lb, 2 oz	2 cups
907 g	947 ml	Sugar	2 lb	1 qt
	5 ml	Salt		1 tsp
454 g	474 ml	Eggs (8 lge)	1 lb	2 cups
14 g	15 ml	Vanilla	½ oz	1 tbsp
454 g	947 ml	Flour, all-purpose	1 lb	1 qt
	20 ml	Baking Powder		4 tsp
340 g	947 ml	Coconut	12 oz	1 qt
		Confectioner's Sugar		

Procedure

1. Blend butter or margarine, peanut butter, sugar, salt, eggs, and vanilla.
2. Sift together flour and baking powder. Stir in coconut. Combine mixtures. Spread half of the batter in each of 2 greased bake pans (10 × 16 × 2¼ in).
3. Bake at 350°F/177°C for 25 to 30 minutes.
4. Cut (4 × 8) while warm and sprinkle with confectioner's sugar.

Fudge Bars

60 Bars (2¼ oz/64 g)

Bake, 350°F/177°C, 45 min

| Metric | | | U.S. | |
Weight	Volume	Ingredients	Weight	Volume
1.02 kg	1.13 l	Sugar	2 lb, 4 oz	4¾ cups
283 g	296 ml	Butter or Margarine	10 oz	1¼ cups
340 g	355 ml	Chocolate, unsweetened, melted	12 oz	1½ cups
227 g	207 ml	Egg Yolks (12 med)	8 oz	⅞ cup
	7½ ml	Salt		1½ tsp
	10 ml	Vanilla		2 tsp
227 g	237 ml	Milk	8 oz	1 cup
340 g	711 ml	Flour, all-purpose	12 oz	3 cups
681 g	1.42 l	Nuts, chopped	1 lb, 8 oz	1½ qt
340 g	355 ml	Egg Whites, stiffly beaten (12 med)	12 oz	1½ cups

Procedure

1. Cream sugar and butter or margarine until light and fluffy.
2. Add melted chocolate and blend.
3. Beat in egg yolks, salt, and vanilla.
4. Add milk alternately with sifted flour, beginning and ending with flour.
5. Add nuts and blend.
6. Carefully fold in stiffly beaten egg whites.
7. Pour into greased baking sheet (18 × 26 × 1 in). Bake at 350°F/177°C for 45 minutes. Cut (6×10) into 60 portions.

Oatmeal Shortbread
48 Strips (2 × 2 ½ in)
Bake, 400°F/205°C, 15 min

| Metric | | Ingredients | U.S. | |
Weight	Volume		Weight	Volume
397 g	1.07 l	Oats, rolled, quick-cooking	14 oz	4 ½ cups
	7 ½ ml	Baking Powder		1 ½ tsp
114 g	355 ml	Coconut, shredded	4 oz	1 ½ cups
340 g	355 ml	Sugar	12 oz	1 ½ cups
	2 ½ ml	Salt		½ tsp
340 g	355 ml	Butter	12 oz	1 ½ cups

Procedure

1. Mix rolled oats with baking powder.
2. Add coconut, sugar, and salt.
3. Mix in butter, as in making pie crust.
4. Press mixture into pan (12 × 20 × 2 in). Bake at 400°F/205°C, for 15 minutes or until a golden brown.
5. Cut shortbread in strips. Make 8 × 6 cuts across pan.

Blarney Stones
60 Servings (2 ½ oz/71 g)
Bake, 325°F/163°C, 30 min

| Metric | | Ingredients | U.S. | |
Weight	Volume		Weight	Volume
624 g	652 ml	Eggs (11 lge)	1 lb, 6 oz	2 ¾ cups
1.36 kg	1.48 l	Sugar	3 lb	6 ¼ cups
681 g	1.42 l	Flour	1 lb, 8 oz	6 cups
	5 ml	Salt		1 tsp
21 g	30 ml	Baking Powder		2 tbsp
681 g	711 ml	Water, hot	1 lb, 8 oz	3 cups
		Topping		
397 g	711 ml	Powdered Sugar	14 oz	3 cups
340 g	355 ml	Butter or Margarine	12 oz	1 ½ cups
114 g	237 ml	Nuts or Fruit, chopped	4 oz	1 cup

Procedure

1. Beat eggs until thick and lemon-colored. Add sugar, a tablespoon at a time, beating continually.
2. Sift flour, salt, and baking powder. Add to egg mixture, to make a smooth, light batter. Add hot water and mix until smooth.
3. Quickly pour on a greased baking sheet (18 × 26 × 1 in). Bake at 325°F/163°C for 30 minutes.
4. Cut in squares and cover while warm with a mixture of powdered sugar and butter or margarine, thoroughly creamed. Sprinkle with nuts or candied fruit.

Butterscotch Squares

60 Servings (2 ½ × 3 in)
Bake, 350°F/177°C, 20 min

| Metric | | Ingredients | U.S. | |
Weight	Volume		Weight	Volume
454 g	474 ml	Butter or Margarine	1 lb	2 cups
1.36 kg	1.89 l	Brown Sugar	3 lb	2 qt
397 g	415 ml	Eggs (7 lge)	14 oz	1 ¾ cups
18 g	20 ml	Vanilla	⅔ oz	4 tsp
605 g	1.26 l	Flour, cake, sifted	1 lb, 5 ⅓ oz	1 ⅓ qt
14 g	15 ml	Salt	½ oz	1 tbsp
28 g	40 ml	Baking Powder	1 oz	2 ⅔ tbsp
454 g	947 ml	Walnuts, chopped	1 lb	1 qt

Procedure

1. Combine butter or margarine and sugar. Cook slowly until smooth. Cool.
2. Add eggs one at a time, beating after each addition. Add vanilla.
3. Sift flour, salt, and baking powder together. Add to mixture and blend.
4. Add half of chopped nuts. Mix.
5. Pour onto a greased baking sheet (18 × 26 × 1 in). Sprinkle top with remaining nuts.
6. Bake at 350°F/177°C for 20 minutes. While warm, cut 6 × 10 into 60 pieces.

Cocoa Squares

60 Servings (2 ½ × 3 in)
Bake, 350°F/177°C, 20 min

| Metric | | Ingredients | U.S. | |
Weight	Volume		Weight	Volume
681 g	711 ml	Butter or Margarine	1 lb, 8 oz	3 cups
1.25 kg	1.30 l	Sugar	2 lb, 12 oz	5 ½ cups
14 g	15 ml	Vanilla	½ oz	1 tbsp
567 g	592 ml	Eggs (10 lge)	1 lb, 4 oz	2 ½ cups
340 g	711 ml	Flour, all-purpose	12 oz	3 cups
170 g	355 ml	Cocoa, unsweetened	6 oz	1 ½ cups
14 g	15 ml	Salt	½ oz	1 tbsp
340 g	711 ml	Nuts, chopped	12 oz	3 cups

Procedure

1. Cream butter or margarine, add sugar and cream thoroughly. Add vanilla.
2. Beat in eggs.
3. Sift flour, cocoa, and salt together. Mix with creamed mixture. Mix in nuts.
4. Pour into a greased baking sheet (18 × 26 × 1 in).
5. Bake at 350°F/177°C for about 20 minutes. Cut 6 × 10 into 60 pieces.

Chocolate Cereal Bars
96 Bars (1 ½ × 3 in)

Metric		Ingredients	U.S.		
Weight	Volume		Weight		Volume
425 g	355 ml	Corn Syrup, light		15 oz	1 ½ cups
128 g	178 ml	Brown Sugar		4 ½ oz	¾ cup
	1 ¼ ml	Salt			¼ tsp
511 g	711 ml	Peanut Butter	1 lb,	2 oz	3 cups
14 g	15 ml	Vanilla		½ oz	1 tbsp
170 g	1.42 l	Rice Cereal, crisp		6 oz	1 ½ qt
114 g	711 ml	Cornflakes, lightly crushed		4 oz	3 cups
511 g	711 ml	Chocolate Pieces, semi-sweet	1 lb,	2 oz	3 cups

Procedure

1. Heat syrup, sugar, and salt to full boil. Stir in peanut butter and remove from heat. Stir in vanilla, cereals, and chocolate.

2. Press mixture into greased baking sheet (18 × 26 × 1 in). Chill for 1 hour.
3. Cut 8 × 12 into 96 pieces, 1 ½ × 3 inches.

Molasses Date Squares
100 Bars (2 ½ × 1 ¾ in)
Bake, 350°F/177°C, 35 min

Metric		Ingredients	U.S.		
Weight	Volume		Weight		Volume
454 g	474 ml	Butter or Margarine	1 lb		2 cups
454 g	474 ml	Sugar	1 lb		2 cups
624 g	474 ml	Molasses	1 lb,	6 oz	2 cups
198 g	207 ml	Eggs (4 med)		7 oz	⅞ cup
454 g	947 ml	Flour, all-purpose	1 lb		1 qt
	10 ml	Salt			2 tsp
	5 ml	Cinnamon			1 tsp
	2 ½ ml	Ginger			½ tsp
	2 ½ ml	Soda			½ tsp
340 g	711 ml	Walnuts		12 oz	3 cups
907 g	1.42 l	Dates, pitted, chopped	2 lb		1 ½ qt
142 g	237 ml	Raisins		5 oz	1 cup
454 g	829 ml	Confectioner's Sugar	1 lb		3 ½ cups
114 g	118 ml	Milk, hot		4 oz	½ cup
	10 ml	Cinnamon			2 tsp
114 g	237 ml	Walnuts, chopped		4 oz	1 cup

Procedure

1. Cream butter or margarine and sugar. Add molasses and eggs and beat until light and well-blended.
2. Add dry ingredients sifted together. Add nuts and fruit. Mix well.
3. Pour into greased and floured baking sheet (18 × 26 × 1 in) and bake at 350°F/177°C, for 35 minutes.

4. Combine last 4 ingredients for frosting. Dribble frosting over bars while warm. Cut (10 × 10) into 100 pieces while warm, and let cool in pan.

Date Squares

70 Squares (2 ½ × 2 ½ in)
Bake, 350°F/177°C, 35 min

| Metric | | Ingredients | U.S. | |
Weight	Volume		Weight	Volume
340 g	711 ml	Flour, cake	12 oz	3 cups
510 g	553 ml	Sugar	1 lb, 2 oz	2 ⅓ cups
21 g	22 ml	Salt	¾ oz	1 ½ tbsp
14 g	22 ml	Baking Powder	½ oz	1 ½ tbsp
1.51 kg	2.37 l	Dates, chopped	3 lb, 5 ½ oz	2 ½ qt
510 g	1.07 l	Walnuts, chopped	1 lb, 2 oz	4 ½ cups
454 g	474 ml	Eggs, well-beaten, 8 lge	1 lb	2 cups
21 g	22 ml	Vanilla	¾ oz	1 ½ tbsp

Procedure

1. Sift flour, sugar, salt, and baking powder together. Add chopped dates and nuts.
2. Add beaten eggs and vanilla. Mix.
3. Spread into a greased baking sheet (18 × 26 × 1 in). Bake at 350°F/177°C for 35 minutes. Cut 7 × 10 into squares 2 ½ × 2 ½ inches.

Date Torte

70 Servings (2 ½ oz/71 g)
Bake, 350°F/177°C, 35 min

| Metric | | Ingredients | U.S. | |
Weight	Volume		Weight	Volume
567 g	592 ml	Eggs (10 lge)	1 lb, 4 oz	2 ½ cups
1.02 kg	1.13 l	Sugar	2 lb, 4 oz	4 ¾ cups
595 g	1.42 l	Bread Crumbs, ground	1 lb, 5 oz	1 ½ qt
	5 ml	Salt		1 tsp
28 g	30 ml	Vanilla	1 oz	2 tbsp
1.02 kg	1.60 l	Dates, chopped	2 lb, 4 oz	6 ¾ cups
1.02 kg	2.13 l	Walnuts, chopped	2 lb, 4 oz	2 ¼ qt

Procedure

1. Beat eggs and gradually add sugar.
2. Add bread crumbs, salt, and vanilla. Blend. Add dates and nuts. Mix.
3. Spread into baking sheet (18 × 26 × 1 in). Bake at 350°F/177°C for 35 minutes.
4. Cut while warm into 70 pieces (7 × 10). Serve with whipped cream.

Pineapple Date Bars

64 Bars (2 × 2 ½ in)

Bake, 350°F/177°C, 20 min

Metric		Ingredients	U.S.	
Weight	Volume		Weight	Volume
454 g	474 ml	Pineapple, crushed	1 lb	2 cups
610 g	947 ml	Dates, chopped	1 lb, 5 ½ oz	1 qt
454 g	947 ml	Nuts, chopped	1 lb	1 qt
397 g	415 ml	Eggs, separated (7 lge)	14 oz	1 ¾ cups
454 g	474 ml	Sugar	1 lb	2 cups
227 g	237 ml	Evaporated Milk	8 oz	1 cup
14 g	15 ml	Vanilla	½ oz	1 tbsp
340 g	711 ml	Flour, all-purpose	12 oz	3 cups
	30 ml	Baking Powder		2 tbsp
	10 ml	Salt		2 tsp
		Confectioner's Sugar		

Procedure

1. Mix pineapple, dates, and nuts.
2. Beat egg yolks. Add sugar gradually. Add milk and vanilla.
3. Sift dry ingredients and combine with egg mixture. Add fruit mixture.
4. Beat egg whites until stiff but not dry. Fold into batter.
5. Divide into 2 greased bake pans (10 × 16 × 2 ¼ in). Bake at 350°F/177°C for 20 minutes.
6. Cut while warm (4 × 8) and sprinkle with confectioner's sugar.

Luscious Lemon Bars

100 Bars (2 ½ × 1 ¾ in)

Bake, 350°F/177°C, 15 min, 35 min

Metric		Ingredients	U.S.	
Weight	Volume		Weight	Volume
907 g	947 ml	Butter or Margarine	2 lb	1 qt
	1 ¼ ml	Salt		¼ tsp
312 g	563 ml	Powdered Sugar	11 oz	2 ⅜ cups
907 g	1.89 l	Flour	2 lb	2 qt
1.81 kg	1.89 l	Sugar	4 lb	2 qt
114 g	237 ml	Flour, all-purpose	4 oz	1 cup
907 g	947 ml	Eggs, lightly beaten (16 lge)	2 lb	1 qt
340 g	355 ml	Lemon Juice	12 oz	1 ½ cups
		Powdered Sugar		

Procedure

1. Combine the first four items and press the mixture into lightly greased baking sheet (18 × 26 × 1 in). Bake at 350°F/177°C for 15 minutes.
2. Combine sugar and flour. Mix in beaten eggs and lemon juice.
3. Pour mixture into slightly cooled crust.
4. Bake at 350°F/177°C for 35 minutes or until set.
5. Cool and sprinkle with powdered sugar. Cut 10 × 10 into 100 bars.

Pressed Cookies

Creole Wafers
4 dozen Cookies (3 in)
Bake, 325°F/163°C, 12 min

Metric		Ingredients	U.S.		
Weight	Volume		Weight		Volume
681 g	711 ml	Sugar	1 lb,	8 oz	3 cups
340 g	355 ml	Butter or Margarine		12 oz	1 ½ cups
170 g	178 ml	Eggs (3 lge)		6 oz	¾ cup
227 g	237 ml	Chocolate, unsweetened, melted		8 oz	1 cup
255 g	533 ml	Flour, cake		9 oz	2 ¼ cups
	5 ml	Salt			1 tsp
227 g	395 ml	Pecans, chopped		8 oz	1 ⅔ cups

Procedure

1. Cream butter or margarine and sugar well.
2. Add eggs gradually and cream.
3. Add chocolate.
4. Blend in sifted flour and salt. Add nuts. Mix.
5. Yield: 4 lb/1.82 kg of batter.

6. Press through a pastry tube, to the diameter of a half-dollar, on lightly greased baking sheets.
7. Bake at 325°F/163°C for 12 minutes.

Note: Cookies may be dropped with a No. 40 scoop if desired and flattened on pan.

Spritz
4 dozen Cookies
Bake, 350°F/177°C, 15 min

Metric		Ingredients	U.S.	
Weight	Volume		Weight	Volume
227 g	237 ml	Butter or Margarine	8 oz	1 cup
170 g	178 ml	Sugar	6 oz	¾ cup
21 g	1 med	Egg Yolk	¾ oz	1 med
	2 ½ ml	Orange Juice		½ tsp
	5 ml	Orange Rind		1 tsp
283 g	592 ml	Flour, cake	10 oz	2 ½ cups
	1 ¼ ml	Salt		¼ tsp
	2 ½ ml	Baking Powder		½ tsp

Procedure

1. Cream butter or margarine. Add sugar gradually and cream until light and fluffy.
2. Add unbeaten egg yolk and cream well. Blend in orange juice and rind.
3. Sift cake flour, salt, and baking powder together.

Add slowly to creamed mixture and blend well. Batter will be stiff.
4. Press through a Swedish cookie tube onto a greased sheet pan. Bake at 350°F/177°C for about 15 minutes.

Drop Cookies

Chocolate Cookies
10 dozen Cookies
Bake, 300°F/149°C, 25 min

| Metric | | Ingredients | U.S. | |
Weight	Volume		Weight	Volume
227 g	237 ml	Butter or Margarine	8 oz	1 cup
340 g	533 ml	Brown Sugar	12 oz	2 ¼ cups
99 g	89 ml	Eggs (2 med)	3 ½ oz	⅜ cup
114 g	118 ml	Chocolate, unsweetened, melted	4 oz	½ cup
	5 ml	Soda		1 tsp
227 g	237 ml	Milk	8 oz	1 cup
283 g	592 ml	Flour, cake	10 oz	2 ½ cups
	5 ml	Salt		1 tsp
	7 ½ ml	Vanilla		1 ½ tsp
170 g	355 ml	Walnuts, chopped	6 oz	1 ½ cups

Procedure

1. Cream butter or margarine and sugar thoroughly. Beat in eggs. Add melted chocolate.
2. Dissolve soda in milk. Sift flour and salt together. Add alternately with milk to creamed mixture. Stir in vanilla and nuts. Chill.
3. Drop onto greased baking sheet with a No. 30 scoop.
4. Bake at 300°F/149°C for 25 minutes.

Note: These are very nice lightly iced.

Chocolate Crinkles
6 dozen large Cookies
Bake, 350°F/177°C, 10–12 min

| Metric | | Ingredients | U.S. | |
Weight	Volume		Weight	Volume
198 g	207 ml	Butter or Margarine	7 oz	⅞ cup
198 g	7 squares	Chocolate, unsweetened	7 oz	7 squares
793 g	829 ml	Sugar	1 lb, 12 oz	3 ½ cups
340 g	355 ml	Eggs (6 lge)	12 oz	1 ½ cups
	18 ml	Vanilla		3 ½ tsp
397 g	829 ml	Flour, all-purpose	14 oz	3 ½ cups
	18 ml	Baking Powder		3 ½ tsp
	5 ml	Salt		1 tsp
		Confectioner's Sugar		

Procedure

1. Melt butter or margarine and chocolate. Add to sugar and mix.
2. Blend in eggs and vanilla. Mix well.
3. Mix flour, baking powder, and salt together. Add to chocolate mixture.
4. Chill for 2 hours.
5. Drop on greased baking sheet with No. 40 scoop. Flatten. Sprinkle with confectioner's sugar.
6. Bake at 350°F/177°C for 10 to 12 minutes.

Rocks

100 Cookies (2 ½ in)
Bake, 350°F/177°C, 20 min

Metric		Ingredients	U.S.		
Weight	Volume		Weight		Volume
454 g	474 ml	Butter or Margarine	1 lb		2 cups
681 g	711 ml	Sugar	1 lb,	8 oz	3 cups
	10 ml	Vanilla			2 tsp
297 g	296 ml	Eggs (6 med)		10 ½ oz	1 ¼ cups
	10 ml	Soda			2 tsp
57 g	59 ml	Water, hot		2 oz	¼ cup
681 g	1.42 l	Flour, all-purpose	1 lb,	8 oz	1 ½ qt
	10 ml	Salt			2 tsp
	10 ml	Cinnamon			2 tsp
	10 ml	Nutmeg			2 tsp
454 g	947 ml	Walnuts, chopped	1 lb		1 qt
227 g	355 ml	Dates, chopped		8 oz	1 ½ cups

Procedure

1. Cream butter or margarine and sugar. Add vanilla. Beat in eggs.
2. Combine soda and hot water. Add.
3. Sift flour, salt, and spices together. Add to mixture and blend.
4. Add chopped dates and nuts. Mix well. Drop with a No. 30 scoop onto a greased baking sheet.
5. Bake at 350°F/177°C for 20 minutes.

Chocolate Chip Cookies

5 ½ dozen Cookies
Bake, 375°F/190°C, 8–10 min

Metric		Ingredients	U.S.		
Weight	Volume		Weight		Volume
454 g	474 ml	Butter or Margarine	1 lb		2 cups
454 g	474 ml	Granulated Sugar	1 lb		2 cups
368 g	513 ml	Brown Sugar		13 oz	2 ⅙ cups
227 g	237 ml	Eggs (4 lge)		8 oz	1 cup
	12 ½ ml	Vanilla			2 ½ tsp
681 g	1.42 l	Flour, all-purpose	1 lb,	8 oz	1 ½ qt
	12 ½ ml	Soda			2 ½ tsp
14 g	15 ml	Salt		½ oz	1 tbsp
	10 ml	Water, hot			2 tsp
567 g	789 ml	Chocolate Chips, semi-sweet	1 lb,	4 oz	3 ⅓ cups

Procedure

1. Cream butter or margarine and gradually add sugars. Cream until light and fluffy.
2. Add eggs and vanilla. Mix well.
3. Sift together flour, soda, and salt. Add gradually, blending after each addition.
4. Add hot water. Stir in chocolate bits.
5. Drop on greased baking sheet with a No. 30 scoop.
6. Bake at 375°F/190°C for 8 or 10 minutes.

Chocolate Meringue Cookies

50 Cookies (1 ½ oz/43 g)
Bake, 300°F/149°C, 25 min

| Metric | | Ingredients | U.S. | |
Weight	Volume		Weight	Volume
198 g	207 ml	Egg Whites (7 med)	7 oz	⅞ cup
454 g	829 ml	Confectioner's Sugar	1 lb	3 ½ cups
	5 ml	Salt		1 tsp
425 g	1.30 l	Coconut	15 oz	5 ½ cups
170 g	1.42 l	Cornflakes	6 oz	1 ½ qt
511 g	711 ml	Chocolate Pieces, semi-sweet	1 lb, 2 oz	3 cups
14 g	15 ml	Vanilla	½ oz	1 tbsp
300 g	50 cherries	Cherries, candied	10 ½ oz	50 cherries

Procedure

1. Beat egg whites at low speed. Gradually add sugar and salt. Continue beating until egg whites are stiff and satiny in appearance.
2. Fold in all ingredients except cherries. Drop with a No. 40 scoop onto a well-greased and floured baking sheet. Put a cherry on top of each cookie.
3. Bake at 300°F/149°C until done (about 25 min).

Coconut Macaroons

6 dozen Macaroons
Bake, 350°F/177°C, 10 min

| Metric | | Ingredients | U.S. | |
Weight	Volume		Weight	Volume
907 g	2.84 l	Coconut	2 lb	3 qt
312 g	326 ml	Egg Whites (11 med)	11 oz	1 ⅜ cups
681 g	711 ml	Sugar	1 lb, 8 oz	3 cups
	5 ml	Vanilla		1 tsp

Procedure

1. Heat coconut, unbeaten egg whites, and sugar until warm. Stir constantly. Add vanilla.
2. Using a No. 40 scoop, drop onto heavily greased and floured baking sheets (18 × 26 × 1 in) or sheets lined with waxed paper. Allow cookies to dry a little before baking.
3. Bake at 350°F/177°C for 10 minutes or until cookies are lightly browned.
4. Remove immediately from baking sheet.

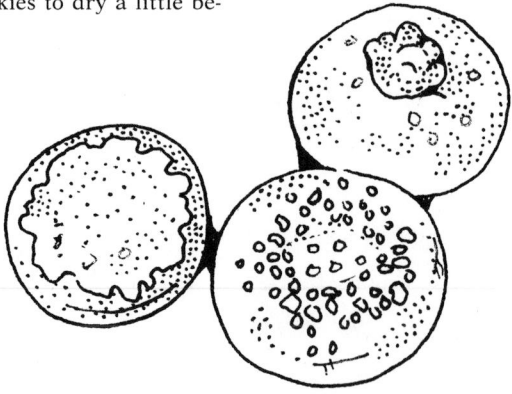

Pumpkin Nut Cookies
8 dozen large Cookies
Bake, 350°F/177°C, 15 min

Metric		Ingredients	U.S.	
Weight	Volume		Weight	Volume
227 g	237 ml	Butter or Margarine	8 oz	1 cup
454 g	474 ml	Sugar	1 lb	2 cups
227 g	237 ml	Eggs, beaten (4 lge)	8 oz	1 cup
368 g	474 ml	Pumpkin, solid pack	13 oz	2 cups
454 g	947 ml	Flour, all-purpose	1 lb	1 qt
28 g	40 ml	Baking Powder	1 oz	2 ⅔ tbsp
9 g	10 ml	Salt	⅓ oz	2 tsp
	25 ml	Cinnamon		5 tsp
	5 ml	Nutmeg		1 tsp
	2 ½ ml	Ginger		½ tsp
227 g	474 ml	Nuts, chopped	8 oz	2 cups
312 g	474 ml	Raisins	11 oz	2 cups

Procedure

1. Cream butter or margarine and gradually add sugar. Mix until light and fluffy. Beat in eggs and pumpkin.
2. Sift dry ingredients together and blend into pumpkin mixture. Stir in raisins and nuts.
3. Drop on greased baking sheet with a No. 40 scoop. Bake at 350°F/177°C for 15 minutes.

Soft Molasses Cookies
7 dozen Cookies (No. 30 Scoop)
Bake, 400°F/205°C, 10–12 min

Metric		Ingredients	U.S.	
Weight	Volume		Weight	Volume
340 g	355 ml	Butter or Margarine	12 oz	1 ½ cups
681 g	947 ml	Brown Sugar	1 lb, 8 oz	1 qt
624 g	474 ml	Molasses	1 lb, 6 oz	2 cups
99 g	89 ml	Eggs (2 med)	3 ½ oz	⅜ cup
1.19 kg	2.49 l	Flour, all-purpose	2 lb, 10 oz	10 ½ cups
	10 ml	Salt		2 tsp
	10 ml	Cinnamon		2 tsp
	5 ml	Ginger		1 tsp
340 g	355 ml	Water, hot	12 oz	1 ½ cups
	10 ml	Soda		2 tsp

Procedure

1. Cream butter or margarine. Add sugar gradually and cream well. Add molasses. Beat in eggs, blending well.
2. Sift flour, salt, and spices together. Stir soda into hot water and add alternately with dry ingredients to creamed mixture.
3. Drop onto greased, lightly floured baking sheets with a No. 30 scoop.
4. Bake at 400°F/205°C for 10 to 12 minutes.

Molasses Crumb Cookies

54 Cookies (1⅔ oz/47 g)
Bake, 350°F/177°C, 15 min

| Metric | | Ingredients | U.S. | |
Weight	Volume		Weight	Volume
283 g	296 ml	Butter or Margarine	10 oz	1¼ cups
454 g	474 ml	Sugar	1 lb	2 cups
149 g	158 ml	Eggs (3 med)	5¼ oz	⅔ cup
454 g	355 ml	Molasses	1 lb	1½ cups
681 g	1.42 l	Flour, cake	1 lb, 8 oz	1½ qt
	10 ml	Baking Powder		2 tsp
	15 ml	Soda		1 tbsp
	7½ ml	Salt		1½ tsp
	7½ ml	Ginger		1½ tsp
	15 ml	Cinnamon		1 tbsp
	7½ ml	Cloves		1½ tsp
340 g	711 ml	Cake Crumbs, ground	12 oz	3 cups
114 g	118 ml	Water	4 oz	½ cup

Procedure

1. Cream butter or margarine and sugar until light and fluffy. Beat in eggs. Add molasses and mix.
2. Sift flour, baking powder, soda, salt, and spices together. Add ground cake crumbs.
3. Add dry ingredients, alternately with water, to the creamed mixture.
4. Drop onto greased baking sheet with a No. 40 scoop.
5. Bake at 350°F/177°C for 15 minutes.

Oatmeal Date Cookies

5 dozen Cookies (1¼ oz/35 g)
Bake, 350°F/177°C, 17 min

| Metric | | Ingredients | U.S. | |
Weight	Volume		Weight	Volume
340 g	355 ml	Butter or Margarine	12 oz	1½ cups
510 g	711 ml	Brown Sugar	1 lb, 2 oz	3 cups
170 g	178 ml	Eggs (3 lge)	6 oz	¾ cup
	15 ml	Lemon Rind, grated		1 tbsp
71 g	75 ml	Lemon Juice	2½ oz	5 tbsp
340 g	533 ml	Dates, chopped	12 oz	2¼ cups
340 g	711 ml	Flour, all-purpose	12 oz	3 cups
	7½ ml	Salt		1½ tsp
	7½ ml	Soda		1½ tsp
510 g	1.42 l	Oatmeal, quick-cooking	1 lb, 2 oz	1½ qt
170 g	355 ml	Walnuts, chopped	6 oz	1½ cups

Procedure

1. Cream butter or margarine and sugar. Beat in eggs, lemon rind, and juice. Blend in chopped dates.
2. Blend flour, salt, soda, oatmeal, and nuts. Stir into creamed mixture until well-mixed. Drop onto ungreased baking sheet with a No. 40 scoop and flatten slightly.
3. Bake at 350°F/177°C for about 17 minutes or until center is dry to the touch.

Applesauce Cookies

50 Cookies

Bake, 375°F/190°C, 15 min

Metric		Ingredients	U.S.	
Weight	Volume		Weight	Volume
227 g	237 ml	Butter or Margarine	8 oz	1 cup
454 g	474 ml	Sugar	1 lb	2 cups
681 g	711 ml	Applesauce, sweetened	1 lb, 8 oz	3 cups
	10 ml	Soda		2 tsp
605 g	1.26 l	Flour, all-purpose	1 lb, 5⅓ oz	5⅓ cups
	10 ml	Cinnamon		2 tsp
	2½ ml	Cloves		½ tsp
	7½ ml	Salt		1½ tsp
170 g	237 ml	Raisins	6 oz	1 cup
114 g	237 ml	Walnuts, chopped	4 oz	1 cup

Procedure

1. Cream butter or margarine and sugar until light and fluffy.
2. Add applesauce in which soda has been dissolved.
3. Sift flour, salt, and spices together. Add to creamed mixture (reserving a little flour for raisins and walnuts). Add raisins and walnuts. Chill.
4. Drop on greased baking sheets with a No. 30 scoop.
5. Bake at 375°F/190°C for 15 minutes.

Oatmeal Drop Cookies

50 Cookies (1½ oz/43 g)

Bake 350°F/177°C, 15 min

Metric		Ingredients	U.S.	
Weight	Volume		Weight	Volume
283 g	296 ml	Butter or Margarine	10 oz	1¼ cups
340 g	355 ml	Sugar	12 oz	1½ cups
149 g	158 ml	Eggs (3 med)	5¼ oz	⅔ cup
340 g	711 ml	Oats, rolled	12 oz	3 cups
340 g	711 ml	Flour	12 oz	3 cups
	7½ ml	Cinnamon		1½ tsp
	7½ ml	Ginger		1½ tsp
	7½ ml	Salt		1½ tsp
	15 ml	Soda		1 tbsp
340 g	355 ml	Sour Milk or Buttermilk	12 oz	1½ cups
340 g	533 ml	Raisins or Dates	12 oz	2¼ cups
170 g	355 ml	Walnuts, chopped	6 oz	1½ cups

Procedure

1. Cream butter or margarine. Add sugar and cream well.
2. Beat in eggs. Add rolled oats and mix.
3. Sift flour, spices, and salt together. Combine sour milk and soda. Then add flour mixture, alternately with liquid ingredients, to the creamed mixture.
4. Add raisins, or chopped dates, and chopped walnuts.
5. Yield: 3½ lb/1.59 kg. Drop on greased baking sheet using a No. 30 scoop and bake at 350°F/177°C for 15 minutes.

Spicy Oatmeal Cookies
50 Cookies (3 in)
Bake, 375°F/190°C, 8 min

| Metric | | Ingredients | U.S. | |
Weight	Volume		Weight	Volume
227 g	237 ml	Butter or Margarine	8 oz	1 cup
340 g	474 ml	Brown Sugar	12 oz	2 cups
198 g	207 ml	Eggs, slightly beaten (4 med)	7 oz	7/8 cup
227 g	474 ml	Flour, all-purpose	8 oz	2 cups
	10 ml	Baking Soda		2 tsp
	5 ml	Salt		1 tsp
	2½ ml	Cinnamon		½ tsp
	2½ ml	Nutmeg		2½ ml
	½ tsp	Cloves		½ tsp
227 g	355 ml	Raisins	8 oz	1½ cups
227 g	474 ml	Nuts, chopped	8 oz	2 cups
114 g	118 ml	Milk	4 oz	½ cup
340 g	947 ml	Oats, rolled	12 oz	1 qt

Procedure

1. Cream butter or margarine and sugar until light and fluffy. Add slightly beaten eggs.
2. Sift together flour, soda, salt, and spices. Flour raisins and nuts with part of mixture.
3. Add sifted dry ingredients alternately with milk to the creamed mixture. Stir in oatmeal, raisins, and nuts. Mix well.
4. Drop with a No. 40 scoop onto well-greased baking sheets and bake at 375°F/190°C for 10 to 12 minutes.

Cashew Crunch Cookies
5 dozen Large Cookies
Bake, 350°F/177°C, 12–15 min

| Metric | | Ingredients | U.S. | |
Weight	Volume		Weight	Volume
340 g	355 ml	Butter or Margarine	12 oz	1½ cups
170 g	178 ml	Granulated Sugar	6 oz	¾ cup
170 g	237 ml	Brown Sugar	6 oz	1 cup
85 g	89 ml	Eggs (2 med)	3 oz	3/8 cup
	7½ ml	Vanilla		1½ tsp
382 g	800 ml	Flour, all-purpose	13½ oz	3 3/8 cups
	3¾ ml	Soda		¾ tsp
	3¾ ml	Cream of Tartar		¾ tsp
85 g	178 ml	Cashews, unsalted, chopped	3 oz	¾ cup

Procedure

1. Cream butter or margarine and sugars at medium speed for 5 minutes or until light and fluffy.
2. Add eggs and vanilla. Blend with creamed mixture.
3. Combine dry ingredients and add at low speed. Mix well.
4. Add nuts and blend. Drop on greased baking sheet with No. 40 scoop.
5. Bake at 350°F/177°C for 12 to 15 minutes.

Ginger Cookies

6 ½ dozen large Cookies
Bake, 375°F/190°C, 10–12 min

Metric		Ingredients	U.S.	
Weight	Volume		Weight	Volume
397 g	415 ml	Butter or Margarine	14 oz	1 ¾ cups
681 g	711 ml	Sugar	1 lb, 8 oz	3 cups
114 g	118 ml	Eggs (2 lge)	4 oz	½ cup
198 g	158 ml	Molasses	7 oz	⅔ cup
624 g	1.30 l	Flour, all-purpose	1 lb, 6 oz	5 ½ cups
	11 ml	Soda		2 ¼ tsp
	2 ½ ml	Salt		½ tsp
7 g	15 ml	Ginger, ground	¼ oz	1 tbsp
7 g	15 ml	Cinnamon	¼ oz	1 tbsp
		Granulated Sugar for Topping		

Procedure

1. Cream butter or margarine and sugar at medium speed for 5 minutes or until light and fluffy.
2. Add eggs. Continue beating until blended. Add molasses.
3. Combine dry ingredients. Add to creamed mixture. Mix at low speed until well-blended.
4. Form into balls using a No. 40 scoop.
5. Dip top of cookies in granulated sugar.
6. Bake on greased baking sheet at 375°F/190°C for 10 to 12 minutes.

Almond Crunch Cookies

8 dozen Cookies
Bake, 400°F/205°C, 8–10 min

Metric		Ingredients	U.S.	
Weight	Volume		Weight	Volume
681 g	711 ml	Margarine	1 lb, 8 oz	3 cups
737 g	770 ml	Granulated Sugar	1 lb, 10 oz	3 ¼ cups
595 g	829 ml	Brown Sugar	1 lb, 5 oz	3 ½ cups
454 g	474 ml	Eggs, beaten (8 lge)	1 lb	2 cups
14 g	15 ml	Almond Extract	½ oz	1 tbsp
1.36 g	2.84 l	Flour, all-purpose	3 lb	3 qt
	20 ml	Soda		4 tsp
	10 ml	Cream of Tartar		2 tsp
14 g	15 ml	Salt	½ oz	1 tbsp
312 g	474 ml	Almonds, slivered	11 oz	2 cups

Procedure

1. Cream margarine and sugars (medium speed for 5 min) until light and fluffy.
2. Add eggs and almond extract to creamed mixture. Blend.
3. Add combined dry ingredients to creamed mixture (low speed). Mix well until blended. Blend in almonds.
4. Drop on greased baking sheet with a No. 30 scoop.
5. Bake at 400°F/205°C for 8 to 10 minutes.

Peanut Chocolate Drops

60 Cookies (1¼ oz/35 g)
Bake, 400°F/205°C, 8–10 min

Metric		Ingredients	U.S.	
Weight	Volume		Weight	Volume
85 g	3 squares	Chocolate, unsweetened	3 oz	3 squares
227 g	237 ml	Butter or Margarine	8 oz	1 cup
340 g	355 ml	Sugar	12 oz	1½ cups
114 g	118 ml	Eggs (2 lge)	4 oz	½ cup
	10 ml	Vanilla		2 tsp
114 g	118 ml	Buttermilk	4 oz	½ cup
340 g	711 ml	Flour, all-purpose	12 oz	3 cups
	3¾ ml	Soda		¾ tsp
340 g	711 ml	Peanuts, Spanish, salted	12 oz	3 cups
		Frosting		
43 g	45 ml	Butter or Margarine	1½ oz	3 tbsp
85 g	3 squares	Chocolate, unsweetened	3 oz	3 squares
64 g	67 ml	Water	2¼ oz	4½ tbsp
368 g	711 ml	Powdered Sugar	13 oz	3 cups
	3⅓ ml	Vanilla		⅔ tsp

Procedure

1. Melt chocolate and let cool.
2. Cream butter or margarine and sugar until light and fluffy. Blend in eggs, vanilla, and chocolate. Stir in buttermilk.
3. Blend flour and soda. Add to creamed mixture. Stir in peanuts.
4. Drop cookies 2 inches apart on a greased baking sheet using a No. 40 scoop.
5. Bake at 400°F/205°C for 8 to 10 minutes.
6. Frost while warm with chocolate frosting made by melting butter or margarine and chocolate over low heat. Add water and vanilla. Blend in powdered sugar until smooth and spreadable.

Potato Chip Cookies

6 dozen large Cookies
Bake, 350°F/177°C, 15 min

Metric		Ingredients	U.S.	
Weight	Volume		Weight	Volume
425 g	444 ml	Butter or Margarine	15 oz	1⅞ cups
227 g	237 ml	Sugar	8 oz	1 cup
	10 ml	Vanilla		2 tsp
425 g	889 ml	Flour, all-purpose	15 oz	3¾ cups
106 g	355 ml	Crushed Potato Chips	3¾ oz	1½ cups
114 g	237 ml	Walnuts, chopped	4 oz	1 cup

Procedure

1. Cream butter or margarine, gradually adding sugar. Cream until light and fluffy. Add vanilla and blend.
2. Add flour and blend. Add potato chips and walnuts. Mix well.
3. Drop on greased baking sheets with a No. 40 scoop. Flatten cookies with tines of a fork.
4. Bake at 350°F/177°C for 15 minutes.

Coconut Krispies

10 dozen Cookies

Bake, 375°F/190°C, 10 min

Metric		Ingredients	U.S.		
Weight	Volume		Weight		Volume
681 g	711 ml	Butter or Margarine	1 lb,	8 oz	3 cups
681 g	711 ml	Granulated Sugar	1 lb,	8 oz	3 cups
340 g	474 ml	Brown Sugar		12 oz	2 cups
14 g	15 ml	Vanilla		½ oz	1 tbsp
298 g	296 ml	Eggs, beaten (6 med)		10 ½ oz	1 ¼ cups
766 g	1.66 l	Flour, cake	1 lb,	11 oz	1 ¾ qt
10 g	15 ml	Baking Powder			1 tbsp
12 g	15 ml	Baking Soda			1 tbsp
	7 ½ ml	Salt			1 ½ tsp
681 g	1.89 l	Oats, rolled	1 lb,	8 oz	2 qt
170 g	1.42 l	Rice Krispies		6 oz	1 ½ qt
425 g	1.33 l	Coconut, shredded		15 oz	5 ⅝ cups

Procedure

1. Cream butter or margarine, sugars, and vanilla until light and fluffy. Add eggs gradually and beat until well-blended.
2. Blend flour, baking powder, soda, salt, and rolled oats. Stir into creamed mixture. Add Rice Krispies and coconut and mix.
3. Drop onto greased baking sheet with a No. 30 scoop. Bake at 375°F/190°C until lightly browned or about 10 minutes.

Norwegian Cookies

5 dozen cookies

Bake, 325°F/163°C, 20 min

Metric		Ingredients	U.S.		
Weight	Volume		Weight		Volume
907 g	947 ml	Sugar	2 lb		1 qt
340 g	355 ml	Butter or Margarine		12 oz	1 ½ cups
149 g	158 ml	Eggs, beaten (3 med)		5 ¼ oz	⅔ cup
340 g	474 ml	Raisins		12 oz	2 cups
340 g	711 ml	Oatmeal, quick-cooking		12 oz	3 cups
454 g	947 ml	Flour, all-purpose	1 lb		1 qt
	10 ml	Soda			2 tsp
	2 ½ ml	Salt			½ tsp
	45 ml	Orange Rind, grated			3 tbsp

Procedure

1. Cream sugar and butter or margarine. Add beaten eggs and beat until light.
2. Coarsely grind raisins and oatmeal. Beat into creamed mixture.
3. Sift dry ingredients together and stir in orange rind. Stir into creamed mixture to form a stiff dough.
4. Drop onto greased baking sheet with a No. 30 scoop and flatten with a fork.
5. Bake at 325°F/163°C until cookies are a light, golden brown (about 20 min). Remove from pan immediately.

Note: Flavoring which may be substituted for orange rind: 1 teaspoon of nutmeg, or 1 teaspoon of allspice, or ¼ teaspoon of ground cardamom.

Chocolate Coconut Macaroons

4 dozen Cookies (3 in)
Bake, 350°F/177°C, 15 min

| Metric | | Ingredients | U.S. | |
Weight	Volume		Weight	Volume
170 g	178 ml	Butter or Margarine	6 oz	¾ cup
340 g	355 ml	Sugar	12 oz	1 ½ cups
198 g	207 ml	Eggs (4 med)	7 oz	⅞ cup
14 g	15 ml	Vanilla	½ oz	1 tbsp
114 g	118 ml	Chocolate, unsweetened, melted	4 oz	½ cup
283 g	592 ml	Flour, cake	10 oz	2 ½ cups
	15 ml	Baking Powder		1 tbsp
	5 ml	Salt		1 tsp
57 g	59 ml	Milk	2 oz	¼ cup
454 g	1.42 l	Coconut	1 lb	1 ½ qt

Procedure

1. Cream butter or margarine and sugar until light and fluffy. Beat in eggs and vanilla. Stir in chocolate.
2. Sift flour, baking powder, and salt together. Add alternately with milk to creamed mixture. Stir in coconut.
3. Drop on a greased baking sheet (18 × 26 × 1 in) with a No. 40 scoop.
4. Bake at 350°F/177°C for 15 minutes.

Snickerdoodle Cookies

5 ½ dozen large Cookies
Bake, 350°F/177°C, 10 min

| Metric | | Ingredients | U.S. | |
Weight	Volume		Weight	Volume
340 g	355 ml	Butter or Margarine	12 oz	1 ½ cups
510 g	533 ml	Sugar	1 lb, 2 oz	2 ¼ cups
170 g	178 ml	Eggs (3 lge)	6 oz	¾ cup
567 g	1.18 l	Flour, all-purpose	1 lb, 4 oz	1 ¼ qt
14 g	22 ml	Cream of Tartar	½ oz	1 ½ tbsp
12 g	15 ml	Soda		1 tbsp
	2 ½ ml	Salt		½ tsp
		Topping		
21 g	22 ml	Sugar	¾ oz	1 ½ tbsp
	7 ½ ml	Cinnamon		1 ½ tsp

Procedure

1. Cream butter or margarine and sugar at medium speed 5 minutes or until light and fluffy.
2. Add eggs. Blend well.
3. Combine dry ingredients. Add to creamed mixture at low speed until well-blended.
4. Chill dough until easy to handle.
5. Form balls using No. 40 scoop. Dip tops of cookies in topping mixture and place on an ungreased baking sheet.
6. Bake at 350°F/177°C for 10 minutes or until lightly browned.

Pineapple Coconut Cookies
8 dozen large Cookies
Bake, 375°F/190°C, 15 min

| Metric | | Ingredients | U.S. | |
Weight	Volume		Weight	Volume
454 g	474 ml	Butter or Margarine	1 lb	2 cups
454 g	632 ml	Brown Sugar	1 lb	2 ⅔ cups
454 g	474 ml	Granulated Sugar	1 lb	2 cups
	5 ml	Vanilla		1 tsp
198 g	207 ml	Eggs (4 med)	7 oz	⅞ cup
510 g	533 ml	Pineapple, crushed, drained	1 lb, 2 oz	2 ¼ cups
1.14 kg	2.37 l	Flour, all-purpose	2 lb, 8 oz	2 ½ qt
	5 ml	Soda		1 tsp
28 g	40 ml	Baking Powder	1 oz	2 ⅔ tbsp
	5 ml	Salt		1 tsp
151 g	474 ml	Coconut, shredded	5 ⅓ oz	2 cups
213 g	474 ml	Walnuts, chopped (optional)	7 ½ oz	2 cups
		Confectioner's Sugar		

Procedure

1. Cream butter or margarine. Add sugars and mix (medium speed) until light and fluffy. Add vanilla. Blend in eggs. Add pineapple.
2. Sift dry ingredients together and add to creamed mixture. Mix until well-blended. Add coconut and nuts. Mix thoroughly.
3. Drop with a No. 30 scoop onto greased baking sheets. Bake at 350°F/177°C for 15 minutes.
4. When cookies are completely cool, sift confectioner's sugar liberally over tops. Cookies do not store well.

Peanut Butter Cookies
10 dozen large Cookies
Bake, 350°F/177°C, 10–12 min

| Metric | | Ingredients | U.S. | |
Weight	Volume		Weight	Volume
822 g	869 ml	Butter or Margarine	1 lb, 13 oz	3 ⅔ cups
793 g	829 ml	Granulated Sugar	1 lb, 12 oz	3 ½ cups
567 g	789 ml	Brown Sugar	1 lb, 4 oz	3 ⅓ cups
964 g	889 ml	Peanut Butter	2 lb, 2 oz	3 ¾ cups
567 g	592 ml	Eggs (10 lge)	1 lb, 4 oz	2 ½ cups
1.05 kg	2.19 l	Flour, all-purpose	2 lb, 5 oz	9 ¼ cups
	10 ml	Salt		2 tsp
	15 ml	Baking Soda		1 tbsp

Procedure

1. Cream butter or margarine, gradually adding sugars, and cream until light and fluffy.
2. Add peanut butter. Blend well. Add eggs.
3. Add dry ingredients, sifted together, mixing slowly. Blend well.
4. Drop on greased baking sheet with a No. 30 scoop. Flatten cookies with tines of a fork.
5. Bake at 350°F/177°C from 10 to 12 minutes.

Nut Delights
50 Cookies (2 in)
Bake, 350°F/177°C, 20–25 min

| Metric | | Ingredients | U.S. | |
Weight	Volume		Weight	Volume
	2½ ml	Salt		½ tsp
511 g	533 ml	Eggs Whites, stiffly beaten (18 med)	1 lb, 2 oz	2¼ cups
1.02 kg	1.07 l	Sugar	2 lb, 4 oz	4½ cups
454 g	60 crackers	Graham Crackers	1 lb	60 crackers
387 g	829 ml	Nuts, chopped	14 oz	3½ cups

Procedure

1. Beat salt and egg whites. Gradually add sugar and beat until stiff.
2. Fold in graham crackers, broken in large pieces, and chopped nuts.
3. Fill paper soufflé cups placed in muffin pans with a No. 20 scoop of batter.
4. Bake at 350°F/177°C for 20 to 25 minutes.

Sliced Cookies

Lemon Slices
4 dozen Cookies
Bake, 375°F/190°C, 10–12 min

| Metric | | Ingredients | U.S. | |
Weight	Volume		Weight	Volume
114 g	118 ml	Butter or Margarine	4 oz	½ cup
227 g	237 ml	Sugar	8 oz	1 cup
57 g	59 ml	Egg (1 lge)	2 oz	¼ cup
	15 ml	Lemon Rind, grated		1 tbsp
14 g	15 ml	Lemon Juice	½ oz	1 tbsp
241 g	474 ml	Flour, all-purpose, sifted	8½ oz	2 cups
	5 ml	Baking Powder		1 tsp
	1¼ ml	Salt		¼ tsp
	⅝ ml	Nutmeg		⅛ tsp
28 g	1 lge	Egg White	1 oz	1 lge
57 g	118 ml	Almonds or Brazil Nuts, shaved	2 oz	½ cup

Procedure

1. Cream butter or margarine and sugar. Beat in egg, lemon rind, and juice.
2. Sift together dry ingredients and stir into sugar mixture to form a smooth dough. Chill dough for a half hour, or until easy to handle.
3. Shape dough into rolls 2½ inches in diameter. Wrap tightly in waxed paper and chill overnight.
4. Slice rolls ½ inch thick and place on ungreased baking sheet. Brush slices with egg white and sprinkle with shaved nuts or chopped almonds.
5. Bake at 375°F/190°C for 10 to 12 minutes or until lightly browned.

Butterscotch Cookies

50–60 Cookies

Bake, 375°F/190°C, 10 min

Metric		Ingredients	U.S.	
Weight	Volume		Weight	Volume
340 g	474 ml	Brown Sugar	12 oz	2 cups
227 g	237 ml	Butter or Margarine	8 oz	1 cup
114 g	118 ml	Eggs (2 lge)	4 oz	½ cup
397 g	829 ml	Flour, all-purpose	14 oz	3 ½ cups
	5 ml	Soda		1 tsp
	2 ½ ml	Salt		½ tsp
114 g	237 ml	Nuts, chopped	4 oz	1 cup

Procedure

1. Cream sugar and butter or margarine. Beat in eggs.
2. Blend dry ingredients and add to creamed mixture. Beat until well-blended. Stir in nuts.
3. Form into rolls 3 inches in diameter. Wrap in waxed paper and refrigerate overnight.
4. Slice ³/₁₆ inch thick and place on a greased baking sheet. Bake at 375°F/190°C for 10 minutes.

Orange and Nut Cookies

10 dozen Cookies

Bake, 375°F/190°C, 10–15 min

Metric		Ingredients	U.S.		
Weight	Volume		Weight		Volume
227 g	237 ml	Butter or Margarine		8 oz	1 cup
170 g	237 ml	Brown Sugar		6 oz	1 cup
227 g	237 ml	Granulated Sugar		8 oz	1 cup
142 g	148 ml	Eggs (3 med)		5 oz	⅝ cup
9 g	15 ml	Orange Rind, grated		⅓ oz	1 tbsp
43 g	45 ml	Orange Juice		1 ½ oz	3 tbsp
510 g	1.07 l	Flour, all-purpose, sifted	1 lb,	2 oz	4 ½ cups
	5 ml	Baking Soda			1 tsp
	2 ½ ml	Salt			½ tsp
57 g	118 ml	Nuts, chopped		2 oz	½ cup

Procedure

1. Cream butter or margarine and sugars until light and fluffy. Add eggs one at a time. Beat well after each addition. Add orange rind and juice.
2. Sift together flour, soda, and salt, reserving a little flour for nuts. Add to creamed mixture. Mix well. Blend in floured nuts. Divide dough in half and press into rolls about 2 inches in diameter. Chill thoroughly.
3. Slice 60 cookies per roll and place on greased sheet. Bake at 375°F/190°C for 10 to 15 minutes or until lightly browned.

Oatmeal Refrigerator Cookies

5 dozen Cookies
Bake, 350°F/177°C, 10–12 min

| Metric | | Ingredients | U.S. | |
Weight	Volume		Weight	Volume
227 g	237 ml	Butter or Margarine	8 oz	1 cup
227 g	237 ml	Granulated Sugar	8 oz	1 cup
170 g	237 ml	Brown Sugar	6 oz	1 cup
114 g	118 ml	Eggs (2 lge)	4 oz	½ cup
	5 ml	Vanilla		1 tsp
	15 ml	Orange Rind, grated		1 tbsp
170 g	355 ml	Flour, sifted, all-purpose	6 oz	1 ½ cups
	2 ½ ml	Salt		½ tsp
	5 ml	Soda		1 tsp
340 g	711 ml	Oats, rolled, quick-cooking	12 oz	3 cups
114 g	237 ml	Walnuts, chopped	4 oz	1 cup
114 g	118 ml	Citron or Candied Cherries, chopped	4 oz	½ cup
71 g	237 ml	Coconut, flaked	2 ½ oz	1 cup
71 g	118 ml	Raisins, chopped or ground	2 ½ oz	½ cup
57 g	118 ml	Oats, rolled, quick-cooking	2 oz	½ cup

Procedure

1. Cream butter or margarine and sugars. Beat in eggs, vanilla, and orange rind.
2. Sift together flour, salt, and soda. Add gradually to sugar mixture.
3. Add remaining ingredients except ½ cup/118 ml rolled oats. Mix well and form into rolls about 2 ½ inches in diameter.
4. Spread reserved ½ cup/118 ml dry oatmeal on sheets of heavy waxed paper and press cookie dough in it to uniformly cover rolls. Wrap the rolls tightly in the waxed paper and chill overnight.
5. Cut chilled dough ¼ inch thick and place on un-greased baking sheet.
6. Bake at 350°F/177°C for 10 to 12 minutes. Cool slightly before removing from pan.

Rolled Cookies

Pecan Lace Cookies

4 dozen Cookies
Bake, 400°F/205°C, 7–9 min

| Metric | | Ingredients | U.S. | |
Weight	Volume		Weight	Volume
28 g	30 ml	Butter or Margarine	1 oz	2 tbsp
312 g	432 ml	Brown Sugar	11 oz	1 5/6 cup
99 g	89 ml	Eggs, well-beaten (2 med)	3 ½ oz	3/8 cup
	5 ml	Vanilla		1 tsp
57 g	118 ml	Flour, pastry	2 oz	½ cup
	5 ml	Baking Powder		1 tsp
	5/16 ml	Salt		1/16 tsp
227 g	474 ml	Pecans, coarsely chopped	8 oz	2 cups

1. Cream butter or margarine and sugar. Add eggs and vanilla. Mix.
2. Sift flour, baking powder, and salt, reserving a small amount to flour the nuts. Add to creamed mixture and mix thoroughly. Add floured nuts. Blend.

3. Yield: 1 lb, 4 oz/567 g. Drop 1 ½ tsp/7 ½ ml of batter well apart onto buttered and floured baking sheets. Bake at 400°F/205°C for 7 to 9 minutes. Cool slightly before removing from pans.

Note: Do not attempt to make these in hot weather.

Butter Cookies
100 Cookies (3 in)
Bake, 375°F/190°C, 15 min

Metric		Ingredients	U.S.		
Weight	Volume		Weight		Volume
510 g	533 ml	Butter or Margarine	1 lb,	2 oz	2 ¼ cups
510 g	533 ml	Sugar	1 lb,	2 oz	2 ¼ cups
14 g	15 ml	Vanilla		½ oz	1 tbsp
170 g	178 ml	Egg Yolks (8 med)		6 oz	¾ cup
681 g	1.42 l	Flour, cake	1 lb,	8 oz	1 ½ qt
32 g	45 ml	Baking Powder			3 tbsp
	5 ml	Salt			1 tsp
114 g	118 ml	Water		4 oz	½ cup

Procedure

1. Cream butter or margarine. Add sugar, creaming thoroughly. Add vanilla. Beat in egg yolks.
2. Sift together flour, baking powder, and salt. Add alternately with water to creamed mixture.

3. Roll dough to ¼-inch thickness and cut with 2 ½-inch cutter.
4. Bake at 375°F/190°C for about 15 minutes.

Note: This is a brittle cookie that should be removed from pan while hot.

Sugar Cookies
100 Cookies (3 in)
Bake, 350°F/177°C, 15 min

Metric		Ingredients	U.S.		
Weight	Volume		Weight		Volume
454 g	474 ml	Butter or Margarine	1 lb		2 cups
737 g	770 ml	Sugar	1 lb,	10 oz	3 ¼ cups
9 g	10 ml	Vanilla		⅓ oz	2 tsp
297 g	296 ml	Eggs (6 med)		10 ½ oz	1 ¼ cups
793 g	1.66 l	Flour, cake	1 lb,	12 oz	7 cups
15 g	20 ml	Baking Powder		½ oz	4 tsp
	5 ml	Salt			1 tsp
57 g	59 ml	Milk		2 oz	¼ cup

Procedure

1. Cream butter or margarine. Add sugar and cream well. Add vanilla.
2. Beat in eggs.
3. Sift flour, baking powder, and salt; then add, alternately with milk, to first mixture. Mix well. Chill 1 hour.

4. Yield: 5 lb/2.27 kg. Roll ¼ inch thick, cut with 2 ½-inch-diameter cutter, and place on greased sheet. Sprinkle with sugar.
5. Bake at 350°F/177°C for 15 minutes.

CHAPTER 14 _____ *Puddings*

Egg and Milk Desserts

Butterscotch Pudding
50 Servings (4.5 oz/128 g)

Metric		Ingredients	U.S.	
Weight	**Volume**		**Weight**	**Volume**
3.18 kg	3.31 l	Milk	7 lb	3 ½ qt
1.36 kg	1.89 l	Brown Sugar	3 lb	2 qt
283 g	474 ml	Cornstarch	10 oz	2 cups
9 g	10 ml	Salt	⅓ oz	2 tsp
907 g	947 ml	Milk, cold	2 lb	1 qt
340 g	316 ml	Egg Yolks (16 med)	12 oz	1 ⅓ cups
227 g	237 ml	Butter or Margarine	8 oz	1 cup
14 g	15 ml	Vanilla	½ oz	1 tbsp
	2 ½ ml	Maple Extract		½ tsp

Procedure

1. Scald 3 ½ qt/3.31 l milk in double boiler.
2. Mix dry ingredients. Add cold milk and blend. Add to hot milk, stirring constantly. Cook until cornstarch is well-cooked and mixture thickens.
3. Beat egg yolks. Add a little hot mixture to yolks, then stir yolks into hot mixture. Stir and cook for 3 minutes.
4. Remove from heat and add butter and flavorings. Cool thoroughly.
5. Spoon into serving dishes; garnish with whipped cream and nuts.

Note: Whole eggs may be used in place of yolks only, but the pudding will be less smooth.

Variation

Chopped nuts may be stirred into pudding when flavorings are added.

Rice Custard

50 Servings (4⅔ oz/132 g)

Bake, 300°F/149°C, 1 hr

Metric			U.S.	
Weight	**Volume**	**Ingredients**	**Weight**	**Volume**
567 g	592 ml	Rice (uncooked)	1 lb, 4 oz	2 ½ cups
1.51 kg	1.97 l	Rice (cooked)	3 lb, 5 ⅓ oz	8 ⅓ cups
4.08 kg	4.26 l	Milk	9 lb	4 ½ qt
454 g	474 ml	Sugar	1 lb	2 cups
14 g	15 ml	Salt	½ oz	1 tbsp
793 g	829 ml	Eggs (14 lge)	1 lb, 12 oz	3 ½ cups
21 g	22 ml	Vanilla	¾ oz	1 ½ tbsp
	10 ml	Nutmeg		2 tsp
43 g	45 ml	Butter	1 ½ oz	3 tbsp

Procedure

1. Wash rice and cook in 5 qt/4.74 l of water, seasoned with 3 tbsp/45 ml of salt. Drain and rinse with cold water.
2. Scald milk and add rice, sugar, and salt.
3. Beat eggs slightly and add a small amount of milk mixture to the beaten eggs, stirring. Then add all to hot milk mixture.
4. Add vanilla. Divide mixture into 2 greased baking pans (10 × 16 × 2 ¼ in).
5. Sprinkle the tops with nutmeg and dot with butter.
6. Bake in a slow oven, 300°F/149°C, for about an hour, or until a silver knife inserted in the center of the custard comes out clean.

Macaroon Creams

50 Servings (5 oz/142 g)

Metric			U.S.	
Weight	**Volume**	**Ingredients**	**Weight**	**Volume**
4.54 kg	4.74 l	Milk, scalded	10 lb	5 qt
907 g	947 ml	Sugar	2 lb	1 qt
170 g	296 ml	Cornstarch	6 oz	1 ¼ cups
	5 ml	Salt		1 tsp
454 g	474 ml	Eggs, slightly beaten (8 lge)	1 lb	2 cups
	7 ½ ml	Almond Flavoring		1 ½ tsp
454 g	947 ml	Macaroons, crushed	1 lb	1 qt
907 g	947 ml	Heavy Cream	2 lb	1 qt

Procedure

1. Mix sugar, cornstarch, and salt and add to scalded milk. Cook in double boiler until thickened.
2. Add a small amount of hot mixture to slightly beaten eggs, stirring while adding. Then add all to hot mixture. Cook for 5 minutes, or until eggs are cooked. Chill.
3. Add almond flavoring. Stir in crushed macaroons. Divide into 2 bake pans (10 × 16 × 2 ¼ in). Spread whipped cream over the top. Chill.

Fresh Peach Rice Pudding

50 Servings (5 ½ oz/156 g)
Bake, 350°F/177°C, 30 min

Metric		Ingredients	U.S.		
Weight	Volume		Weight		Volume
681 g	829 ml	Rice, uncooked	1 lb,	8 oz	3 ½ cups
3.63 kg	3.79 l	Water	8 lb		1 gal
28 g	30 ml	Salt		1 oz	2 tbsp
1.36 kg	1.42 l	Milk	3 lb		1 ½ qt
793 g	829 ml	Sugar	1 lb,	12 oz	3 ½ cups
28 g	30 ml	Salt		1 oz	2 tbsp
19 g	30 ml	Lemon Rind		⅔ oz	2 tbsp
283 g	267 ml	Egg Yolks (13 med)		10 oz	1 ⅛ cups
151 g	158 ml	Lemon Juice		5 ⅓ oz	⅔ cup
5.44 kg	5.68 l	Peaches, fresh, sliced, E.P.	12 lb		6 qt
170 g	237 ml	Almonds, blanched and shredded		6 oz	1 cup
114 g	118 ml	Butter or Margarine, melted		4 oz	½ cup
454 g	829 ml	Confectioner's Sugar	1 lb		3 ½ cups

Procedure

1. Add rice and 2 tbsp/30 ml of salt to 1 gal/3.79 l of vigorously boiling water. Cook until very soft. Drain, throwing away water.
2. Add milk to rice and cook in double boiler until mushy.
3. Add sugar, 2 tbsp/30 ml of salt, and lemon rind.
4. Pour rice mixture over beaten egg yolks. Add lemon juice.
5. Divide into 2 greased pans (10 × 16 × 2 ¼ in).
6. Cover with sliced peaches and sprinkle tops with slivered almonds, brush with melted butter, and sift confectioner's sugar on top.
7. Bake at 350°F/177°C for 30 minutes, or until set but not dry.
8. Serve with whipped cream or Fresh Peach Foamy Sauce.

Baked Custard

50 Servings (4 oz/114 g)
Bake, 300°F/149°C, 30 min

Metric		Ingredients	U.S.		
Weight	Volume		Weight		Volume
4.31 kg	4.50 l	Milk	9 lb,	8 oz	4 ¾ qt
907 g	947 ml	Eggs, slightly beaten (16 lge)	2 lb		1 qt
397 g	415 ml	Sugar		14 oz	1 ¾ cups
9 g	10 ml	Salt		⅓ oz	2 tsp
14 g	15 ml	Vanilla		½ oz	1 tbsp
	7 ½ ml	Nutmeg			1 ½ tsp

Procedure

1. Heat milk.
2. Beat eggs slightly (avoid foam). Stir in sugar, salt, and flavoring.
3. Gradually add hot milk to egg mixture, stirring constantly.
4. Fill 50 custard cups or bake in pudding pans (10 × 16 × 2 ¼ in).
5. Bake at 300°F/149°C for about 30 minutes, or until an inserted knife blade comes out clean. Avoid overbaking as the custards will continue to cook from contained heat after removal from oven.

Blancmange
50 Servings (4 oz/114 g)

Metric		Ingredients	U.S.	
Weight	Volume		Weight	Volume
4.08 kg	4.26 l	Milk	9 lb	4 ½ qt
319 g	533 ml	Cornstarch	11 ¼ oz	2 ¼ cups
510 g	533 ml	Sugar	1 lb, 2 oz	2 ¼ cups
9 g	10 ml	Salt	⅓ oz	2 tsp
454 g	474 ml	Water, cold	1 lb	2 cups
340 g	355 ml	Eggs (6 lge)	12 oz	1 ½ cups
114 g	118 ml	Butter or Margarine	4 oz	½ cup
21 g	22 ml	Vanilla	¾ oz	1 ½ tbsp

Procedure

1. Heat milk. Blend cornstarch, sugar, salt, and cold water and add to hot milk, stirring constantly. Continue boiling for 2 minutes, or until mixture is thickened.
2. Beat eggs lightly. Add part of the hot mixture to eggs, then stir eggs into hot mixture. Cook for about 3 minutes.
3. Remove from heat and add butter or margarine. Cool slightly. Add vanilla.
4. When cool, stir thoroughly, then spoon into sherbet glasses using a No. 12 scoop. Garnish with whipped cream and nuts or fruit.

Chocolate Pudding
50 Servings (4.5 oz/128 g)

Metric		Ingredients	U.S.	
Weight	Volume		Weight	Volume
3.18 kg	3.31 l	Milk	7 lb	3 ½ qt
793 g	829 ml	Sugar	1 lb, 12 oz	3 ½ cups
227 g	415 ml	Cornstarch	8 oz	1 ¾ cups
283 g	296 ml	Chocolate, unsweetened, melted	10 oz	1 ¼ cups
9 g	10 ml	Salt	⅓ oz	2 tsp
1.36 kg	1.42 l	Milk, cold	3 lb	1 ½ qt
340 g	316 ml	Egg Yolks (16 med)	12 oz	1 ⅓ cups
114 g	118 ml	Butter or Margarine	4 oz	½ cup
21 g	22 ml	Vanilla	¾ oz	1 ½ tbsp

Procedure

1. Heat 3 ½ qt/3.31 l milk in double boiler.
2. Blend sugar, cornstarch, and salt. Add cold milk and mix. Stir into hot milk. Stirring constantly, cook until the mixture is thickened.
3. Add melted chocolate. Beat egg yolks, add a small amount of hot mixture to yolks, then stir into hot mixture. Cook for 3 minutes.
4. Remove from heat and add butter or margarine and flavoring. Cool.
5. Spoon into dessert dishes and garnish with whipped cream.

Note: Whole eggs may be substituted for yolks, but pudding will not be as smooth. 8 oz/227 g cocoa plus 2 oz/57 g butter or margarine may be substituted for the chocolate, but flavor will be less rich. Add the cocoa with the other dry ingredients.

Chocolate Soufflé

50 Servings (2 oz/57 g)

Bake, 325°F/163°C, 1 hr

Metric		Ingredients	U.S.	
Weight	Volume		Weight	Volume
227 g	237 ml	Margarine	8 oz	1 cup
156 g	326 ml	Flour, pastry	5 ½ oz	1 ⅜ cups
	5 ml	Salt		1 tsp
1.36 kg	1.42 l	Milk	3 lb	1 ½ qt
227 g	237 ml	Chocolate, unsweetened, melted	8 oz	1 cup
302 g	316 ml	Sugar	10 ⅔ oz	1 ⅓ cups
283 g	267 ml	Egg Yolks (13 med)	10 oz	1 ⅛ cups
510 g	533 ml	Egg Whites (18 med)	1 lb, 2 oz	2 ¼ cups
302 g	316 ml	Sugar	10 ⅔ oz	1 ⅓ cups
21 g	22 ml	Vanilla	¾ oz	1 ½ tbsp

Procedure

1. Melt margarine in double boiler. Mix in flour and salt well. Add milk and cook until flour is done. Add melted chocolate.
2. Beat egg yolks until creamy. Add ⅔ lb/316 g sugar gradually. Add small amount of hot mixture to yolks, then add yolks to hot mixture. Cook for 1 minute.
3. Beat egg whites, adding sugar gradually as for meringue. Beat until quite stiff. Add vanilla.
4. Fold whites into chocolate mixture, thoroughly but gently.
5. Scale 3 lb, 10 oz/1.64 kg into each of 2 pudding pans (10 × 16 × 2 ¼ in).
6. Bake at 325°F/163°C for 1 hour. (Inserted knife blade should come out clean.) Cut while warm and serve immediately, garnished with whipped cream.

Eggless Chocolate Pudding

50 Servings (4.5 oz/128 g)

Metric		Ingredients	U.S.	
Weight	Volume		Weight	Volume
3.63 kg	3.79 l	Milk	8 lb	1 gal
793 g	829 ml	Sugar	1 lb, 12 oz	3 ½ cups
283 g	474 ml	Cornstarch	10 oz	2 cups
9 g	10 ml	Salt	⅓ oz	2 tsp
907 g	947 ml	Milk, cold	2 lb	1 qt
283 g	296 ml	Chocolate, unsweetened, melted	10 oz	1 ¼ cups
227 g	237 ml	Margarine	8 oz	1 cup
21 g	22 ml	Vanilla	¾ oz	1 ½ tbsp

Procedure

1. Heat 1 gal/3.79 l milk in double boiler.
2. Blend sugar, cornstarch, and salt. Add cold milk and mix. Add to hot milk, stirring constantly. Cook until mixture is thickened.
3. Melt chocolate. Add to cooked mixture. Continue cooking a few minutes.
4. Remove from heat. Add margarine and vanilla. Cool.
5. Spoon into glasses and serve with whipped cream.

Note: This pudding is less rich than one using eggs. 8 oz/227 g cocoa may be substituted for the chocolate. It may be added with the dry ingredients. Pudding with chocolate has the richer flavor.

Eggless Butterscotch Pudding
50 Servings (4.5 oz/128 g)

Metric			U.S.	
Weight	Volume	Ingredients	Weight	Volume
4.31 kg	4.50 l	Milk	9 lb, 8 oz	4¾ qt
1.36 kg	1.89 l	Brown Sugar	3 lb	2 qt
340 g	592 ml	Cornstarch	12 oz	2½ cups
9 g	10 ml	Salt	⅓ oz	2 tsp
907 g	947 ml	Milk, cold	2 lb	1 qt
227 g	237 ml	Margarine	8 oz	1 cup
14 g	15 ml	Vanilla	½ oz	1 tbsp
	2½ ml	Maple Extract		½ tsp

Procedure

1. Heat 4¾ qt/4.50 l milk in double boiler.
2. Mix dry ingredients. Add cold milk and mix well. Stir into hot milk and cook, stirring constantly until the mixture is thickened.
3. Remove from heat and add margarine and flavoring. Cool.
4. Spoon into serving glasses and garnish with whipped cream and nuts.

Note: Nuts may be added to the mixture (8 oz/227 g) along with the flavoring, if desired.

Lemon-Cream Rice Pudding
50 Servings (4.5 oz/128 g)

Metric			U.S.	
Weight	Volume	Ingredients	Weight	Volume
4.08 kg	4.26 l	Milk	9 lb	4½ qt
681 g	829 ml	Rice	1 lb, 8 oz	3½ cups
21 g	22 ml	Salt	¾ oz	1½ tbsp
681 g	711 ml	Sugar	1 lb, 8 oz	3 cups
14 g	22 ml	Lemon Rind, grated	½ oz	1½ tbsp
191 g	178 ml	Egg Yolks, beaten (9 med)	6¾ oz	¾ cup
283 g	296 ml	Lemon Juice	10 oz	1¼ cups
340 g	355 ml	Egg Whites (12 med)	12 oz	1½ cups
	5 ml	Salt		1 tsp
454 g	474 ml	Sugar	1 lb	2 cups
57 g	59 ml	Lemon Juice	2 oz	¼ cup

Procedure

1. Scald milk in double boiler. Add rice and salt and cook until rice is done.
2. Blend sugar, grated rind, and egg yolks. Add a small amount of hot mixture, stirring, then stir yolk mixture into hot rice. Cook for about 2 minutes. Remove from heat and add lemon juice.
3. Divide mixture into 2 greased pudding pans (10 × 16 × 2¼ in).
4. Make meringue by beating egg whites and salt until foamy, then slowly beating in sugar until stiff but not dry. Beat in lemon juice.
5. Spread meringue over mixture and brown at 350°F/177°C.

Brownie Pudding

50 Servings
Bake, 350°F/177°C, 40 min

| Metric | | Ingredients | U.S. | |
Weight	Volume		Weight	Volume
793 g	1.66 l	Flour, all-purpose	1 lb, 12 oz	1 ¾ qt
57 g	80 ml	Baking Powder	2 oz	5 ⅓ tbsp
38 g	40 ml	Salt	1 ⅓ oz	2 ⅔ tbsp
1.02 kg	1.07 l	Granulated Sugar	2 lb, 4 oz	4 ½ cups
114 g	237 ml	Cocoa, unsweetened	4 oz	1 cup
114 g	237 ml	Milk Solids, nonfat	4 oz	1 cup
199 g	237 ml	Shortening, melted	7 oz	1 cup
737 g	770 ml	Water	1 lb, 10 oz	3 ¼ cups
28 g	30 ml	Vanilla	1 oz	2 tbsp
340 g	711 ml	Nuts, chopped	12 oz	3 cups
		Topping		
1.02 kg	1.58 l	Brown Sugar	2 lb, 4 oz	6 ⅔ cups
170 g	355 ml	Cocoa, unsweetened	6 oz	1 ½ cups
2.72 kg	2.84 l	Water, hot	6 lb	3 qt

Procedure

1. Mix dry ingredients.
2. Add shortening, water, vanilla, and nuts. Mix well.
3. Pour batter into 2 pans (12 × 20 × 2 in). Blend brown sugar and cocoa and sprinkle over batter.
4. Place pans on oven door and pour hot water over topping before placing in oven.
5. Bake at 350°F/177°C for 40 minutes. Cut into portion sizes. Lift cake into serving dish and spoon sauce over it from bottom of pan.

Tapioca Cream Pudding

50 Servings (4 ½ oz/128 g)
Chill

| Metric | | Ingredients | U.S. | |
Weight	Volume		Weight	Volume
4.54 kg	4.74 l	Milk, scalded	10 lb	5 qt
397 g	553 ml	Tapioca, minute	14 oz	2 ⅓ cups
9 g	10 ml	Salt	⅓ oz	2 tsp
681 g	711 ml	Sugar	1 lb, 8 oz	3 cups
567 g	592 ml	Eggs, slightly beaten (10 lge)	1 lb, 4 oz	2 ½ cups
9 g	10 ml	Vanilla	⅓ oz	2 tsp

Procedure

1. Mix tapioca, salt, and sugar. Add to scalded milk. Cook in double boiler until tapioca is clear. Stir to prevent lumpiness.
2. Add a small amount of hot mixture to eggs, stirring, and then add all to hot mixture. Cook for 2 minutes.
3. Remove from heat. Add vanilla. Divide into 2 bake pans (10 × 16 × 2 ¼ in). Chill
4. Serve with whipped cream or fresh fruit, or both.

Bread Pudding
50 Servings (4 oz/114 g)
Bake, 325°F/163°C, 30 min

Metric		Ingredients	U.S.	
Weight	Volume		Weight	Volume
567 g	1.81 l	Bread	1 lb, 4 oz	5 cups
198 g	237 ml	Margarine, melted	7 oz	1 cup
3.63 kg	3.79 l	Milk	8 lb	1 gal
737 g	770 ml	Eggs (13 lge)	1 lb, 10 oz	3 ¼ cups
454 g	474 ml	Sugar	1 lb	2 cups
9 g	10 ml	Salt	⅓ oz	2 tsp
9 g	10 ml	Vanilla	⅓ oz	2 tsp
	7 ½ ml	Nutmeg		1 ½ tsp

Procedure

1. Break bread into pieces. Pour melted margarine over it, tossing lightly.
2. Heat milk in double boiler.
3. Beat eggs slightly. Add sugar, salt, and flavoring. Stir hot milk slowly into egg mixture. Stir until sugar is dissolved. Pour over bread.
4. Pour into 2 pudding pans (10 × 16 × 2 ¼ in). Bake at 325°F/164°C until custard is set (about 30 min). Cut and lift custard into serving dishes and serve with or without whipped cream.

Variations

1. Add 12 oz/340 g raisins
2. Add 12 oz/340 g coconut.

Lemon Sponge Pudding
50 Servings
Bake, 325°F/163°C, 45 min

Metric		Ingredients	U.S.	
Weight	Volume		Weight	Volume
9 g	10 ml	Salt	⅓ oz	2 tsp
2.38 kg	2.53 l	Sugar	5 lb, 4 oz	2 ⅔ qt
227 g	474 ml	Flour, all-purpose	8 oz	2 cups
454 g	474 ml	Lemon Juice	1 lb	2 cups
57 g	59 ml	Lemon Rind, grated	2 oz	¼ cup
142 g	178 ml	Butter or Margarine, melted	5 oz	¾ cup
1.14 kg	1.18 l	Eggs, separated (20 lge)	2 lb, 8 oz	1 ¼ qt
2.42 kg	2.53 l	Milk	5 lb, 5 ⅓ oz	2 ⅔ qt

Procedure

1. Blend salt, sugar, and flour. Add lemon juice, grated rind, and melted butter or margarine.
2. Beat yolks and add milk. Blend with lemon mixture.
3. Beat egg whites until stiff but not dry. Fold into batter.
4. Scale 7 lb, 8 oz/3.41 kg into each greased serving pan

(12 × 20 × 2 in). Place in pan of hot water and bake at 325°F/163°C for 45 minutes or until inserted toothpick comes out clean.

Note: The servings are most attractive when the pudding is cut and the cake carefully lifted into serving dishes on top of sauce from bottom.

Lemon Pudding

50 Servings (4.5 oz/128 g)

Metric		Ingredients	U.S.	
Weight	**Volume**		**Weight**	**Volume**
2.72 kg	2.84 l	Water	6 lb	3 qt
1.82 kg	1.89 l	Sugar	4 lb	2 qt
14 g	15 ml	Salt	½ oz	1 tbsp
297 g	533 ml	Cornstarch	10½ oz	2¼ cups
681 g	711 ml	Water, cold	1 lb, 8 oz	3 cups
18 g	30 ml	Lemon Rind	⅔ oz	2 tbsp
397 g	355 ml	Egg Yolks (19 med)	14 oz	1½ cups
227 g	237 ml	Butter or Margarine	8 oz	1 cup
454 g	474 ml	Lemon Juice	1 lb	2 cups

Procedure

1. Heat 3 qt/2.84 l of water to boiling.
2. Mix dry ingredients. Add 3 cups/711 ml of cold water and mix.
3. Add mixed dry ingredients and lemon rind to boiling water, stirring constantly. Cook until mixture is thick and smooth and there is no starchy flavor.
4. Beat egg yolks well. Add small amount of hot mixture to yolks; mix. Stir yolks into hot mixture. Cook a minute longer, until egg yolk is cooked. Remove from heat.
5. Add butter or margarine and lemon juice. Cool.
6. Using a No. 10 scoop, portion into dessert dishes and serve with cake or cookie crumbs, or a fruit sauce, and whipped cream.

Cottage Pudding

48 Servings (2 × 3⅓ in)
Bake, 350°F/177°C, 35 min

Metric		Ingredients	U.S.	
Weight	**Volume**		**Weight**	**Volume**
283 g	296 ml	Butter or Margarine	10 oz	1¼ cups
737 g	770 ml	Sugar	1 lb, 10 oz	3¼ cups
14 g	15 ml	Vanilla	½ oz	1 tbsp
297 g	296 ml	Eggs (6 med)	10½ oz	1¼ cups
793 g	1.66 l	Flour, cake	1 lb, 12 oz	1¾ qt
	5 ml	Salt		1 tsp
28 g	40 ml	Baking Powder	1 oz	2⅔ tbsp
624 g	652 ml	Milk	1 lb, 6 oz	2¾ cups

Procedure

1. Cream butter or margarine. Gradually add sugar, creaming thoroughly. Add vanilla.
2. Add eggs one at a time, beating well after each addition.
3. Sift together flour, salt, and baking powder and then add alternately with milk to the creamed mixture. Mix well after each addition.
4. Divide into two greased bake pans (10 × 16 × 2¼ in). Bake at 350°F/177°C for 35 minutes, or until cake tests done.
5. When cool, cut each pan into 24 portions, Serve topped with a favorite sauce, such as orange custard sauce, fruit sauce, or chocolate sauce.

Indian Pudding

50 Servings (5 oz/142 g)
Bake, 300°F/149°C, 2 hrs

Metric		Ingredients	U.S.	
Weight	Volume		Weight	Volume
9.53 kg	9.93 l	Milk	21 lb	10½ qt
1.22 kg	947 ml	Molasses, dark	2 lb, 11 oz	1 qt
681 g	711 ml	Sugar	1 lb, 8 oz	3 cups
624 g	947 ml	Corn Meal, yellow	1 lb, 6 oz	1 qt
14 g	30 ml	Cinnamon	½ oz	2 tbsp
	7½ ml	Nutmeg		1½ tsp
43 g	45 ml	Salt	1½ oz	3 tbsp
454 g	474 ml	Butter or Margarine	1 lb	2 cups

Procedure

1. Heat 2 gal/7.58 l of milk in a double boiler. Add molasses.
2. Mix sugar, corn meal, spices, and salt and stir into hot mixture. Cook, stirring, until it thickens. Add butter or margarine.
3. Pour half of the pudding into each of 2 serving pans (12 × 20 × 2 in). Pour half of the remaining cold milk over each pan of pudding. Do not stir.
4. Bake in a slow oven, 300°F/149°C, for about 2 hours or until an inserted knife blade comes out clean.
5. Serve with cream, hard sauce, or ice cream.

Mock Indian Pudding

50 Servings (4⅓ oz/123 g)
Bake, 300°F/149°, 1 hr

Metric		Ingredients	U.S.	
Weight	Volume		Weight	Volume
4.08 kg	4.26 l	Milk	9 lb	4½ qt
283 g	12 biscuits	Shredded Wheat Biscuits	10 oz	12 biscuits
454 g	474 ml	Sugar	1 lb	2 cups
283 g	237 ml	Molasses	10 oz	1 cup
7 g	15 ml	Cinnamon	¼ oz	1 tbsp
	5 ml	Ginger		1 tsp
14 g	15 ml	Salt	½ oz	1 tbsp
681 g	711 ml	Eggs, slightly beaten (12 lge)	1 lb, 8 oz	3 cups
227 g	355 ml	Raisins	8 oz	1½ cups

Procedure

1. Heat milk in double boiler and soak biscuits in the milk.
2. Add sugar, molasses, spices, and salt.
3. Add a small amount of hot mixture to slightly beaten eggs; stir. Then add all to hot mixture. Add raisins.
4. Divide mixture into 2 greased baking pans (10 × 16 × 2¼ in).
5. Bake in a slow oven at 300°F/149°C for about an hour, or until a silver knife inserted in center comes out clean.
6. Serve hot with hard sauce or cold with whipped cream.

Farina Pudding

50 Servings (4⅔ oz/132 g)

Metric		Ingredients	U.S.	
Weight	Volume		Weight	Volume
114 g	158 ml	Almonds, sliced	4 oz	⅔ cup
5.22 kg	5.44 l	Milk	11 lb, 8 oz	5¾ qt
454 g	632 ml	Farina	1 lb	2⅔ cups
33 g	35 ml	Salt		2⅓ tbsp
595 g	622 ml	Eggs, separated (12 med)	1 lb, 5 oz	2⅝ cups
567 g	592 ml	Sugar	1 lb, 4 oz	2½ cups
	7½ ml	Almond Extract		1½ tsp

Procedure

1. Pour boiling water over almonds. Permit them to stand for 5 minutes. Drain. Then slip off the skins and slice.
2. Heat milk in double boiler as hot as possible. Then add farina and cook until done. Add salt and almonds.
3. Beat egg yolks and add sugar. Remove a small amount of hot milk mixture and stir into yolk mixture. Then add all to milk mixture and cook until eggs thicken. Cool

4. Add 1 tsp/5 ml of salt to the egg whites and beat until stiff but still moist.
5. Add almond flavoring to the pudding and then fold in the beaten egg whites.
6. Serve with a No. 12 scoop and top with whipped cream and a maraschino cherry. Yield: 50 servings (4⅔ oz/132 g).

Floating Island

50 Servings (4 oz/114 g)

Metric		Ingredients	U.S.	
Weight	Volume		Weight	Volume
3.63 kg	3.79 l	Milk	8 lb	1 gal
454 g	474 ml	Sugar	1 lb	2 cups
9 g	10 ml	Salt	⅓ oz	2 tsp
71 g	148 ml	Cornstarch	2½ oz	⅝ cup
510 g	474 ml	Egg Yolks, beaten (24 med)	1 lb, 2 oz	2 cups
7 g	7 ml	Vanilla	¼ oz	1½ tsp
681 g	711 ml	Egg Whites (24 med)	1 lb, 8 oz	3 cups
9 g	10 ml	Salt	⅓ oz	2 tsp
340 g	355 ml	Sugar	12 oz	1½ cups

Procedure

1. Heat milk to boiling point. Blend sugar, salt, and cornstarch and stir into hot milk. Cook and stir constantly until thickened and starch is cooked.
2. Add a little hot mixture to beaten yolks, then add yolks to hot mixture. Cook, stirring, for 3 minutes. Remove from heat and add vanilla. Chill. Serve in sherbet glasses and top with meringue.

3. Prepare meringue by beating egg whites until frothy. Add salt and sugar gradually and beat until stiff but not dry. Drop with a No. 60 scoop or tablespoon on top of boiling water in shallow pan (12 × 20 × 2 in) and place in oven at 350°F/177°C for about 10 minutes or until set.

Grapenuts Custard

50 Servings (4 ⅓ oz/123 g)
Bake, 300°F/149°C, 1 hr

Metric		Ingredients	U.S.	
Weight	Volume		Weight	Volume
4.31 kg	4.50 l	Milk, scalded	9 lb, 8 oz	4 ¾ qt
454 g	504 ml	Sugar	1 lb	2 ⅛ cups
9 g	10 ml	Salt	⅓ oz	2 tsp
907 g	947 ml	Eggs, slightly beaten (16 lge)	2 lb	1 qt
14 g	15 ml	Vanilla	½ oz	1 tbsp
198 g	415 ml	Grapenuts	7 oz	1 ¾ cups
170 g	295 ml	Raisins	6 oz	1 ¼ cups

Procedure

1. Add sugar and salt to scalded milk. Add to slightly beaten eggs. Add vanilla.
2. Yield: 6 quarts. Put raisins into 2 greased dessert pans (10 × 16 × 2 ¼ in). Pour half of custard into each pan.
3. Sprinkle the top with Grapenuts.
4. Bake at 300°F/149°C for 1 hour or until a silver knife comes out clean.

Boston Cream Pie

50 Servings
Bake, 350°F/177°C, 30 min

Metric		Ingredients	U.S.	
Weight	Volume		Weight	Volume
510 g	533 ml	Butter or Margarine	1 lb, 2 oz	2 ¼ cups
1.02 kg	1.07 l	Sugar	2 lb, 4 oz	4 ½ cups
198 g	178 ml	Egg Yolks, beaten (9 med)	7 oz	¾ cup
	10 ml	Lemon Juice		2 tsp
	15 ml	Vanilla		1 tbsp
793 g	1.66 l	Flour, cake	1 lb, 12 oz	1 ¾ qt
	30 ml	Baking Powder		2 tbsp
	1 ¼ ml	Salt		¼ tsp
510 g	533 ml	Milk	1 lb, 2 oz	2 ¼ cups
255 g	267 ml	Egg Whites, beaten (9 med)	9 oz	1 ⅛ cups

Procedure

1. Cream butter or margarine. Add sugar gradually. Add egg yolks, lemon juice, and vanilla.
2. Sift together flour, baking powder, and salt. Add alternately with milk to creamed mixture, starting with dry ingredients. Add in 3 parts.
3. Beat egg whites stiff but moist. Fold into batter.
4. Pour batter into greased baking sheet (18 × 26 × 1 in). Bake at 350°F/177°C for 30 minutes or until done.
5. Cut cake in half lengthwise and in thirds crosswise.

Place layer of Boston Cream Pie Filling (see recipe p. 000) on one half of cake. Place alternate corner pieces on either end, and opposite center pieces on center section. Dot top with powdered sugar. Slice 17 cuts per section.

Note: Cake may be made in round cake pans. Scale 1 ¼ lb/567 g batter into each of 5 pans. Layer by cutting in half and placing filling between halves.

Fruit Desserts

Apple Betty

50 Servings (5 oz/142 g)
Bake, 350°F/177°C, 1 hr

Metric		Ingredients	U.S.		
Weight	Volume		Weight		Volume
4.54 kg	7.10 l	Apples, pie pack, chopped	10 lb		7 ½ qt
454 g	474 ml	Water	1 lb		2 cups
57 g	59 ml	Lemon Juice		2 oz	¼ cup
	5 ml	Lemon Rind, grated			1 tsp
681 g	947 ml	Brown Sugar	1 lb,	8 oz	1 qt
7 g	13 ml	Nutmeg		¼ oz	2 ½ tsp
	7 ½ ml	Cinnamon			1 ½ tsp
		Crumb topping			
681 g	1.42 l	Bread Crumbs	1 lb,	8 oz	1 ½ qt
300 g	355 ml	Margarine, melted		10 ½ oz	1 ½ cups
14 g	15 ml	Salt		½ oz	1 tbsp
227 g	237 ml	Granulated Sugar		8 oz	1 cup
340 g	711 ml	Peanuts, chopped		12 oz	3 cups
		Graham Cracker Topping			
567 g	1.66 l	Graham Crackers, fine crumbs	1 lb,	4 oz	1 ¾ qt
227 g	474 ml	Walnuts, chopped		8 oz	2 cups
454 g	474 ml	Margarine, melted	1 lb		2 cups
	2 ½ ml	Salt			½ tsp
227 g	474 ml	Granulated Sugar		8 oz	2 cups

Procedure

1. Mix apples thoroughly with water, lemon juice, lemon rind, brown sugar, and seasonings. Divide into 2 greased pudding pans (10 × 16 × 2 ¼ in).
2. Mix all ingredients together for chosen topping and sprinkle over apple mixture.

3. Bake at 350°F/177°C for about 1 hour, or until apples are tender and crust is brown. Serve with whipped cream or nutmeg sauce.

Note: Use either crumb or graham cracker topping.

Apricot Whip

50 Servings (3 ⅔ oz/103 g)

Metric		Ingredients	U.S.		
Weight	Volume		Weight		Volume
2.04 kg	4.26 l	Apricots (dried)	4 lb,	8 oz	4 ½ qt
3.63 kg	8.98 l	Apricots (cooked and drained)	8 lb		9 ½ qt
14 g	15 ml	Salt		½ oz	1 tbsp
510 g	533 ml	Egg Whites (18 lge)	1 lb,	2 oz	2 ¼ cups
1.02 kg	1.07 l	Sugar	2 lb,	4 oz	4 ½ cups
64 g	67 ml	Lemon Juice		2 ¼ oz	4 ½ tbsp
9 g	15 ml	Lemon Rind, grated		⅓ oz	1 tbsp

Procedure

1. Cook apricots, drain, and grind coarsely.
2. Add salt to egg whites and beat until foamy. Gradually add sugar, beating until egg whites are stiff but not dry.
3. Add lemon juice and grated rind to apricots and carefully fold in meringue.
4. Yield: 11 ¼ lb/5.10 kg. Serve with a No. 12 scoop.

Apple Goodie

50 Servings (5 ⅔ oz/163 g)
Bake, 350°F/177°C, 1 hr

Metric		Ingredients	U.S.		
Weight	Volume		Weight		Volume
4.45 kg	7.10 l	Apples, peeled and sliced	10 lb		7 ½ qt
454 g	474 ml	Water	1 lb		2 cups
57 g	59 ml	Lemon Juice		2 oz	¼ cup
	5 ml	Lemon Rind, grated			1 tsp
1.14 kg	1.18 l	Granulated Sugar	2 lb,	8 oz	5 cups
57 g	118 ml	Flour, pastry		2 oz	½ cup
	2 ½ ml	Salt			½ tsp
	7 ½ ml	Cinnamon			1 ½ tsp
7 g	12 ½ ml	Nutmeg		¼ oz	2 ½ tsp
		Topping			
454 g	947 ml	Flour, pastry	1 lb		1 qt
	5 ml	Salt			1 tsp
	5 ml	Baking Powder			1 tsp
	5 ml	Soda			1 tsp
605 g	869 ml	Brown Sugar	1 lb, 5 ⅓ oz		3 ⅔ cups
340 g	947 ml	Oatmeal, raw		12 oz	1 qt
567 g	592 ml	Butter or Margarine	1 lb,	4 oz	2 ½ cups

Procedure

1. Mix apples, water, lemon juice, and rind. Blend dry ingredients and add to apples. Mix well. Divide mixture into 2 pudding pans (10 × 16 × 2 ¼ in).
2. Sift flour, salt, baking powder, and soda together. Add remainder of topping ingredients and mix together as for pastry. Mix only until crumbly. Divide and spread over apples in the 2 pans.
3. Bake at 350°F/177°C for 1 hour, or until apples are tender and crust is brown. Cut into portions and serve with whipped cream.

Apple Crisp

60 Servings

Bake, 400°F/205°C, 30 min

Metric		Ingredients	U.S.		
Weight	Volume		Weight		Volume
907 g	947 ml	Apple juice	2 lb		1 qt
170 g	285 ml	Cornstarch		6 oz	1 ⅕ cup
1.22 kg	1.36 l	Granulated Sugar	2 lb,	11 oz	5 ¾ cup
	10 ml	Salt			2 tsp
	10 ml	Cinnamon			2 tsp
	2 ½ ml	Nutmeg			½ tsp
340 g	355 ml	Fruit Juice, cold		12 oz	1 ½ cups
170 g	178 ml	Margarine		6 oz	¾ cup
85 g	90 ml	Lemon Juice		3 oz	⅜ cup
5.90 kg	6.63 l	Apples, pie pack, drained	13 lb		2 No. 10 cans
		Topping			
255 g	267 ml	Margarine		9 oz	1 ⅛ cup
793 g	1.10 l	Brown Sugar	1 lb,	12 oz	4 ⅔ cups
382 g	1.07 l	Oatmeal		13 ½ oz	4 ½ cups
382 g	790 ml	Flour		13 ½ oz	3 ⅓ cups

Procedure

1. Heat apple juice. Blend cornstarch, sugar, salt, and spices. Combine with cold juice and stir into hot apple juice. Cook, stirring, until thickened and starch is cooked.
2. Remove from heat and add margarine and lemon juice.
3. Combine apples with hot mixture. Divide into 2 greased 12 × 20 × 2 in pans.

4. Thoroughly mix ingredients for topping and sprinkle over the apples.
5. Bake at 400°F/205°C for 30 minutes or until topping is light brown. Serve in sherbet glasses using a No. 10 scoop. Garnish with whipped cream or warm spiced cream.

Apple Dumpling

50 Dumplings

Bake, 400°F/205°C, 30 min

Metric		Ingredients	U.S.		
Weight	Volume		Weight		Volume
1.19 kg	2.49 l	Flour, all-purpose	2 lb,	10 oz	10 ½ cups
57 g	80 ml	Baking Powder		2 oz	5 ⅓ tbsp
28 g	30 ml	Salt		1 oz	2 tbsp
28 g	30 ml	Sugar		1 oz	2 tbsp
567 g	592 ml	Shortening	1 lb,	4 oz	2 ½ cups
1.66 kg	1.59 l	Milk	3 lb,	10 ⅔ oz	6 ⅔ cups
	50 apples	Apples, small, tart, peeled, cored			50 apples
681 g	741 ml	Sugar	1 lb,	8 oz	3 ⅛ cups
	15 ml	Cinnamon			1 tbsp
	5 ml	Salt			1 tsp

1. Sift together flour, baking powder, salt, and sugar.
2. Blend in shortening. Add milk a little at a time, distributing it as in making pastry, using only enough for dough to hold together.
3. Roll dough thin, cut in squares, and place an apple in center of each.
4. Blend sugar, cinnamon, and salt. Place 1 tbsp/15 ml of mixture on each apple. Bring up four corners of pastry around apple and seal with milk.
5. Brush tops with thin cream and sprinkle with sugar. Bake at 400°F/205°C for 30 minutes or until apples are tender and crust is brown.
6. Serve with Warm Spiced Cream, or Lemon Sauce, and whipped cream.

Note: Chopped apples may be used instead of whole apples. Use 2 oz/57 g per dumpling.

Apple Pan Dowdy

50 Servings (5 ½ oz/156 g)
Bake, 400°F/205°C, 45 min

Metric		Ingredients	U.S.	
Weight	Volume		Weight	Volume
907 g	1.89 l	Flour	2 lb	2 qt
57 g	80 ml	Baking Powder	2 oz	5 ⅓ tbsp
14 g	15 ml	Salt	½ oz	1 tbsp
85 g	79 ml	Granulated Sugar	3 oz	⅓ cup
170 g	178 ml	Lard or Shortening	6 oz	¾ cup
605 g	632 ml	Milk	1 lb, 5 ⅓ oz	2 ⅔ cups
		Apple Mixture		
5.44 kg	8.51 l	Apples, E.P.	12 lb	9 qt
1.25 kg	1.74 l	Brown Sugar	2 lb, 12 oz	7 ⅓ cups
	5 ml	Cinnamon		1 tsp
	5 ml	Nutmeg		1 tsp
	10 ml	Salt	⅓ oz	2 tsp
170 g	178 ml	Butter or Margarine	6 oz	¾ cup

Procedure

Crust
1. Sift together flour, baking powder, salt, and sugar.
2. Blend in lard or shortening.
3. Add milk slowly to make a stiff dough.
4. Roll dough to fit pans. Yield: 4 lbs.

Apple Mixture

1. Line 2 bake pans (10 × 16 × 2 ¼ in) with sliced apples.
2. Combine brown sugar, cinnamon, nutmeg, and salt; sprinkle over top of apples.
3. Cover with crust.
4. Bake at 400°F/205°C for 45 minutes or until apples are tender.
5. Remove from oven immediately and turn upside down on trays.
6. Dot with butter or margarine. Cut and serve with whipped cream.

Apple Cheese Crisp

50 Servings (5.5 oz/156 g)
Bake, 350°F/177°C, 1 hr

| Metric | | Ingredients | U.S. | | |
Weight	Volume		Weight		Volume
4.54 kg	7.10 l	Apples, pie pack slices	10 lb		7 ½ qt
454 g	474 ml	Water	1 lb		2 cups
57 g	59 ml	Lemon Juice		2 oz	¼ cup
	5 ml	Lemon Rind, grated			1 tsp
681 g	711 ml	Granulated Sugar	1 lb,	8 oz	3 cups
7 g	12 ml	Nutmeg		¼ oz	2 ½ tsp
	7 ½ ml	Cinnamon			1 ½ tsp
	2 ½ ml	Salt			½ tsp
		Topping			
454 g	947 ml	Flour, pastry	1 lb		1 qt
	5 ml	Salt			1 tsp
454 g	474 ml	Butter or Margarine	1 lb		2 cups
756 g	1.07 l	Brown Sugar	1 lb, 10⅔ oz		4 ½ cups
681 g	1.42 l	American Cheese, grated	1 lb,	8 oz	1 ½ qt

Procedure

1. Mix apples, water, lemon juice, and rind. Divide into 2 pudding pans (10 × 16 × 2 ¼ in). Mix sugar, spices, and salt and sprinkle over apples.
2. Combine all of the ingredients for the topping, except cheese. Blend as for pastry, until crumbly. Lightly work in cheese. Divide topping in half and spread one half over each pan.
3. Bake at 350°F/177°C for 1 hour, or until apples are tender and crust is brown.
4. Spoon into serving dishes and serve hot or cold with whipped cream.

Butterscotch Apple Dessert

50 Servings (3.5 oz/99 g)
Bake, 350°F/177°C, 1 hr

| Metric | | Ingredients | U.S. | | |
Weight	Volume		Weight		Volume
170 g	355 ml	Flour, all-purpose		6 oz	1 ½ cups
170 g	355 ml	Bread Crumbs, ground		6 oz	1 ½ cups
1.02 kg	1.42 l	Brown Sugar	2 lb,	4 oz	1 ½ qt
	3 ¾ ml	Salt			¾ tsp
340 g	355 ml	Butter or Margarine		12 oz	1 ½ cups
170 g	355 ml	Nuts, chopped		6 oz	1 ½ cups
4.66 kg	8.51 l	Apples, sliced	10 lb,	4 oz	9 qt

Procedure

1. Mix flour, bread crumbs, sugar, and salt. Cut in butter or margarine, Add nuts.
2. Peel and slice apples. Spread about half of the apples in 2 greased pudding pans (10 × 16 × 2 ¼ in). Sprinkle them with part of the crumb mixture. Add remaining apple slices and sprinkle with remaining crumb mixture.
3. Bake at 350°F/177°C for 1 hour. Serve warm with or without cream.

Apricot Custard
50 Servings (4 oz/114 g)
Bake, 300°F/149°C, 1 hr, 10 min

Metric		Ingredients	U.S.	
Weight	Volume		Weight	Volume
3.00 kg	3.08 l	Apricots, pie pack	6 lb, 10 oz	3 ¼ qt (1 No. 10 can)
454 g	474 ml	Sugar	1 lb	2 cups
	2 ½ ml	Salt		½ tsp
151 g	237 ml	Almonds, shredded	5 ⅓ oz	1 cup
756 g	789 ml	Eggs, slightly beaten (15 med)	1 lb, 10 ⅔ oz	3 ⅓ cups
340 g	355 ml	Sugar	12 oz	1 ½ cups
	5 ml	Salt		1 tsp
2.72 kg	2.84 l	Milk	6 lb	3 qt
28 g	30 ml	Vanilla Extract	1 oz	2 tbsp
	7 ½ ml	Lemon Extract		½ tbsp
	1 ¼ ml	Almond Extract		¼ tsp

Procedure

1. Mix apricots, sugar, and salt thoroughly, mashing apricots as much as possible. Divide into 2 pans (10 × 16 × 2 ¼ in).
2. Sprinkle almonds on top of apricots.
3. Mix remainder of ingredients together: eggs, sugar, salt, milk, and flavoring. Carefully divide and pour over almonds and apricots.
4. Bake at 300°F/149°C until firm (for about 1 hr, 10 min).
5. Cool and serve.

Baked Apple Tapioca
50 Servings (6 oz/170 g)
Bake, 375°F/190°C, 1 hr

Metric		Ingredients	U.S.	
Weight	Volume		Weight	Volume
4.54 kg	7.10 l	Apples, peeled and sliced	10 lb	7 ½ qt
2.72 kg	2.84 l	Water, hot	6 lb	3 qt
76 g	79 ml	Lemon Juice	2 ⅔ oz	⅓ cup
	5 ml	Lemon Rind		1 tsp
340 g	415 ml	Tapioca, quick-cooking	12 oz	1 ¾ cups
907 g	1.26 l	Brown Sugar	2 lb	5 ⅓ cups
793 g	829 ml	Granulated Sugar	1 lb, 12 oz	3 ½ cups
	7 ½ ml	Salt		1 ½ tsp
	12 ½ ml	Nutmeg		2 ½ tsp
	7 ½ ml	Cinnamon		1 ½ tsp
114 g	118 ml	Butter or Margarine	4 oz	½ cup

Procedure

1. Combine apples, hot water, lemon juice, and rind in deep pan and bake at 375°F/190°C for about 30 minutes.
2. Mix tapioca, sugars, salt, and spices and add to apples. Add butter or margarine.
3. Continue baking until apples are tender and tapioca is cooked.
4. Cooked yield: about 2 gal/7.57 l.
5. Serve hot or cold with hard sauce or whipped cream.

Blueberry Pudding

50 Servings

Bake, 350°F/177°C, 25 min

Metric		Ingredients	U.S.	
Weight	Volume		Weight	Volume
454 g	474 ml	Butter or Margarine	1 lb	2 cups
907 g	947 ml	Sugar	2 lb	1 qt
397 g	415 ml	Eggs (8 med)	14 oz	1 ¾ cups
170 g	178 ml	Blueberry Juice	6 oz	¾ cup
510 g	1.07 l	Flour, all-purpose	1 lb, 2 oz	4 ½ cups
	5 ml	Salt		1 tsp
	10 ml	Nutmeg		2 tsp
	10 ml	Cinnamon		2 tsp
	10 ml	Soda		2 tsp
114 g	118 ml	Water, hot	4 oz	½ cup
1.14 kg	1.42 l	Blueberries, canned, drained	2 lb, 8 oz	1 ½ qt

Procedure

1. Cream butter or margarine and sugar until light and fluffy.
2. Add eggs, a few at a time, beating constantly. Add blueberry juice and mix well.
3. Sift flour, salt, nutmeg, and cinnamon.
4. Dissolve soda in ½ cup/118 ml of hot water. Add alternately with flour to creamed mixture.
5. Stir in blueberries. Pour into 2 greased baking pans (10 × 16 × 2 ¼ in).
6. Bake at 350°F/177°C for 25 minutes.
7. Sprinkle with powdered sugar upon removing from oven.

FRUIT COBBLERS

Crust for Fruit Cobblers

50 Servings

Bake, 450°F/232°C, 12–15 min

Metric		Ingredients	U.S.	
Weight	Volume		Weight	Volume
907 g	1.89 l	Flour, all-purpose	2 lb	2 qt
227 g	237 ml	Sugar	8 oz	1 cup
57 g	80 ml	Baking Powder	2 oz	5 ⅓ tbsp
14 g	15 ml	Salt	½ oz	1 tbsp
340 g	355 ml	Margarine	12 oz	1 ½ cups
681 g	711 ml	Milk	1 lb, 8 oz	3 cups

Procedure

1. Sift dry ingredients into mixer bowl. Add shortening and mix with flat beater for 3 minutes at low speed.
2. Add milk. Mix for 30 minutes at medium speed.
3. Portion onto greased baking sheet with a No. 30 scoop. Brush tops with milk and sprinkle with granulated sugar.
4. Bake at 450°F/232°C for 12 to 15 minutes until nicely browned.

Note: Biscuits may be baked on top of fruit if preferred. If baked on the fruit, bake at 450°F/232°C for 10 minutes, then lower the temperature to 350°F/177°C, and continue baking until fruit is tender.

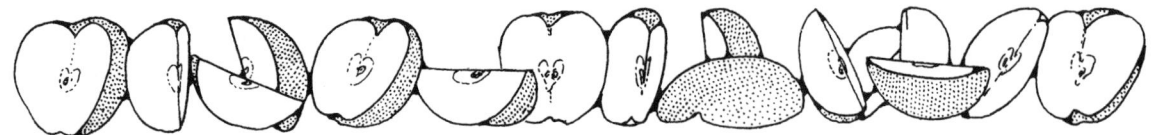

FILLINGS FOR COBBLERS

Apple

| Metric | | Ingredients | U.S. | |
Weight	Volume		Weight	Volume
	12½ ml	Nutmeg		2½ tsp
	7½ ml	Cinnamon		1½ tsp
	7½ ml	Salt		1½ tsp
1.36 kg	1.42 l	Sugar	3 lb	1½ qt
170 g	355 ml	Flour, all-purpose	6 oz	1½ cups
114 g	118 ml	Lemon Juice	4 oz	½ cup
5.44 kg	8.51 l	Apples, peeled and sliced	12 lb	9 qt

Procedure

1. Combine dry ingredients.
2. Mix dry ingredients and lemon juice with apples.
3. Divide into 2 pudding pans (10 × 16 × 2¼ in).
4. Top with crust.

Rhubarb

| Metric | | Ingredients | U.S. | |
Weight	Volume		Weight	Volume
57 g	59 ml	Lemon Juice	2 oz	¼ cup
	15 ml	Lemon Rind, grated		1 tbsp
4.54 kg	9.46 l	Rhubarb, fresh, diced	10 lb	10 qt
2.04 kg	2.13 l	Sugar	4 lb, 8 oz	2¼ qt
9 g	10 ml	Salt	⅓ oz	2 tsp
212 g	355 ml	Cornstarch	7½ oz	1½ cups

Procedure

1. Combine lemon juice and rind with rhubarb.
2. Divide into 2 pudding pans. Mix dry ingredients and sprinkle on top.
3. Top with crust.

Bake all cobblers until fruit is tender. Crusts may be spread evenly over the fruit, dropped in portions on top of the fruit, or baked separately as drop biscuits. When serving, spoon the fruit into the serving dish and top with crust.

Apricot, Berry, Cherry, or Peach

Metric		Ingredients	U.S.	
Weight	Volume		Weight	Volume
283 g	474 ml	Cornstarch	10 oz	2 cups
1.14 kg	1.18 l	Sugar	2 lb, 8 oz	5 cups
	10 ml	Salt		2 tsp
340 g	355 ml	Fruit Juice, cold	12 oz	1 ½ cups
1.36 kg	1.42 l	Fruit Juice, hot	3 lb	1 ½ qt
170 g	178 ml	Butter or Margarine	6 oz	¾ cup
57 g	59 ml	Lemon Juice	2 oz	¼ cup
5.90 kg	6.63 l	Fruit, drained	13 lb	2 No. 10 cans

Procedure

1. Combine dry ingredients with cold juice and stir into hot juice. Cook until thick and clear.
2. Remove from heat and add butter or margarine and lemon juice.
3. Add fruit and divide into 2 pudding pans.
4. Top with crust.

Note: 2 tbsp/30 ml cinnamon and ½ tsp/2 ½ ml nutmeg may be added if desired.

Date Delight

50–60 Servings
Bake, 350°F/177°C, 30 min

Metric		Ingredients	U.S.	
Weight	Volume		Weight	Volume
2.27 kg	2.96 l	Dates, pitted, chopped	5 lb	3 ⅛ qt
1.14 kg	1.18 l	Water, boiling	2 lb, 8 oz	5 cups
681 g	711 ml	Granulated Sugar	1 lb, 8 oz	3 cups
	5 ml	Salt		1 tsp
9 g	15 ml	Lemon Rind, grated	⅓ oz	1 tbsp
85 g	90 ml	Lemon Juice	3 oz	6 tbsp
454 g	1.26 l	Oatmeal, raw	1 lb	5 ⅓ cups
907 g	1.89 l	Flour, pastry	2 lb	2 qt
1.14 kg	1.58 l	Brown Sugar	2 lb, 8 oz	6 ⅔ cups
	22 ½ ml	Soda		1 ½ tbsp
14 g	15 ml	Salt	½ oz	1 tbsp
850 g	889 ml	Butter or Margarine	1 lb, 14 oz	3 ¾ cups

Procedure

1. Boil dates, water, granulated sugar, salt, and lemon rind until thick, stirring constantly. Remove from heat and add lemon juice.
2. Mix oatmeal, flour, brown sugar, soda, salt, and butter together as for pastry. Mix only until crumbly.
3. Spread ⅔ of crumb mixture into a well-greased baking sheet (18 × 26 × 1 in). Spread date filling on top and top with remaining crumb mixture.
4. Bake at 350°F/177°C for about 30 minutes.

Variation

Mincemeat (7 lb/3.18 kg) may be used in place of date filling.

Date Nut Pudding

50 Servings (3 ½ oz/99 g)
Bake, 300°F/149°C, 45–60 min

| Metric | | Ingredients | U.S. | |
Weight	Volume		Weight	Volume
907 g	947 ml	Water, boiling	2 lb	1 qt
1.82 kg	2.84 l	Dates, pitted and chopped	4 lb	3 qt
14 g	20 ml	Soda	½ oz	4 tsp
57 g	59 ml	Butter or Margarine	2 oz	¼ cup
907 g	947 ml	Sugar	2 lb	1 qt
170 g	178 ml	Eggs, well-beaten (3 lge)	6 oz	¾ cup
454 g	947 ml	Flour, pastry	1 lb	1 qt
	7 ½ ml	Salt		1 ½ tsp
454 g	947 ml	Walnuts, chopped	1 lb	1 qt
57 g	59 ml	Lemon Juice	2 oz	¼ cup
9 g	15 ml	Lemon Rind, grated	⅓ oz	1 tbsp

Procedure

1. Pour boiling water over dates; cool. Add soda to cooled dates.
2. Cream butter or margarine and sugar thoroughly. Add eggs and blend well.
3. Mix flour, salt, and chopped nuts. Add flour mixture to creamed mixture alternately with the date mixture, blending after each addition.
4. Stir in grated lemon rind and juice.
5. Divide into 2 greased pudding pans (10 × 16 × 2 ¼ in).
6. Bake at 300°F/149°C for 45 minutes or until it tests done. Serve with whipped cream.

Lemon Meringue Pudding

50 Servings (4 oz/114 g)
Bake, 350°F/177°C, 30 min

| Metric | | Ingredients | U.S. | |
Weight	Volume		Weight	Volume
283 g	296 ml	Butter or Margarine	10 oz	1 ¼ cups
283 g	592 ml	Flour, pastry	10 oz	2 ½ cups
1.70 kg	1.77 l	Sugar	3 lb, 12 oz	7 ½ cups
	7 ½ ml	Salt		1 ½ tsp
510 g	474 ml	Egg Yolks, beaten (24 med)	1 lb, 2 oz	2 cups
510 g	533 ml	Lemon Juice	1 lb, 2 oz	2 ¼ cups
76 g	118 ml	Lemon Rind, grated	2 ⅔ oz	½ cup
1.82 kg	1.89 l	Milk	4 lb	2 qt
681 g	711 ml	Egg Whites (24 med)	1 lb, 8 oz	3 cups

Procedure

1. Cream butter or margarine thoroughly. Blend flour, sugar, and salt. Add to butter or margarine and mix until creamy.
2. Add egg yolks beaten until creamy and blend thoroughly.
3. Mix in lemon juice, rind, and milk.
4. Beat egg whites until stiff (but not dry) and fold into batter.
5. Divide into 2 greased pudding pans (10 × 16 × 2 ¼ in). Bake at 350°F/177°C for about 30 minutes.
6. Chill and serve with whipped cream.

Cranberry Tortoni
48 Servings
Freeze Overnight

Metric		Ingredients	U.S.	
Weight	Volume		Weight	Volume
907 g	947 ml	Milk, evaporated, undiluted	2 lb	1 qt
170 g	178 ml	Lemon Juice	6 oz	¾ cup
340 g	1.42 l	Marshmallows, cut up	12 oz	1½ qt
1.59 kg	1.66 l	Pineapple Tidbits	3 lb, 8 oz	1¾ qt
454 g	474 ml	Pineapple Juice	1 lb	2 cups
1.82 kg	1.89 l	Cranberry Sauce, whole	4 lb	2 qt
71 g	237 ml	Graham Cracker Crumbs	2½ oz	1 cup

Procedure

1. Chill evaporated milk in freezer for 30 minutes. Whip until it begins to thicken. Add lemon juice and whip until stiff.
2. Fold in marshmallows, pineapple and juice, and cranberry sauce.
3. Pour into serving pan (12 × 20 × 2 in) and freeze until firm.
4. Cut portions and serve with sprinkling of graham crackers on top.

Rhubarb Betty
50 Servings (4 oz/114 g)
Bake, 375°F/190°C, 50 min

Metric		Ingredients	U.S.	
Weight	Volume		Weight	Volume
57 g	59 ml	Lemon Juice	2 oz	¼ cup
	5 ml	Lemon Rind, grated		1 tsp
4.54 kg	9.46 l	Rhubarb, frozen (containing 6 parts water to 1 part sugar)	10 lb	10 qt
340 g	355 ml	Granulated Sugar	12 oz	1½ cups
	7½ ml	Salt		1½ tsp
99 g	178 ml	Cornstarch	3½ oz	¾ cup
		Topping		
567 g	1.18 l	Bread Crumbs	1 lb, 4 oz	5 cups
	5 ml	Salt		1 tsp
454 g	632 ml	Brown Sugar	1 lb	2⅔ cups
7 g	15 ml	Nutmeg	¼ oz	1 tbsp
198 g	237 ml	Butter or Margarine, melted	7 oz	1 cup

Procedure

1. Add lemon juice and rind to rhubarb.
2. Mix together thoroughly sugar, salt, and cornstarch. Add to rhubarb and mix well.
3. Divide into 2 greased pudding pans (10 × 16 × 2¼ in), carefully distributing fruit and juice evenly.
4. Mix dry ingredients for topping and pour melted butter or margarine over mixture and blend well. Sprinkle evenly over top of rhubarb.
5. Bake at 375°F/190°C for about 50 minutes or until rhubarb is done and betty nicely browned. Serve with whipped cream or topping.

Rhubarb Torte

50 Servings

Bake, 350°F/177°C, 45 min

Metric		Ingredients	U.S.	
Weight	Volume		Weight	Volume
		Crust		
681 g	711 ml	Butter or Margarine	1 lb, 8 oz	3 cups
340 g	355 ml	Sugar	12 oz	1 ½ cups
128 g	118 ml	Egg Yolks (6 med)	4 ½ oz	½ cup
	2 ½ ml	Salt		½ tsp
1.02 kg	2.13 l	Flour, all-purpose	2 lb, 4 oz	2 ¼ qt
114 g	118 ml	Half and Half	4 oz	½ cup
		Filling		
2.27 kg	4.74 l	Rhubarb, sliced ¼ in	5 lb	5 qt
595 g	622 ml	Eggs (12 med)	1 lb, 5 oz	2 ⅝ cups
170 g	178 ml	Egg Whites (left from crust: 6 med)	6 oz	¾ cup
1.02 kg	1.07 l	Sugar	2 lb, 4 oz	4 ½ cups
1.36 kg	1.42 l	Evaporated Milk	3 lb	1 ½ qt
	2 ½ ml	Salt		½ tsp

Procedure

1. Cream butter or margarine and sugar. Blend in egg yolks. Add salt, flour, and milk and mix well.
2. Divide dough in half and press into two greased baking pans (12 × 20 × 2 in). Cover bottom of pans evenly and build up sides 1 ½ inches.
3. Spread sliced rhubarb evenly in crusts.
4. Beat eggs and egg whites and stir in sugar, milk, and salt. Pour mixture over the rhubarb.
5. Bake at 350°F/177°C for 45 minutes or until custard is set.

Prune Mousse

50 Servings

Metric		Ingredients	U.S.	
Weight	Volume		Weight	Volume
1.14 kg	1.89 l	Prunes, uncooked	2 lb, 8 oz	2 qt
907 g	947 ml	Eggs (16 lge)	2 lb	1 qt
605 g	947 ml	Powdered Sugar	1 lb, 5 ⅓ oz	1 qt
	5 ml	Salt		1 tsp
454 g	474 ml	Whipping Cream	1 lb	2 cups
23 g	25 ml	Vanilla		1 ⅔ tbsp
454 g	474 ml	Lemon Juice	1 lb	2 cups
227 g	237 ml	Pineapple Juice	8 oz	1 cup
624 g	474 ml	Pineapple, crushed, drained	1 lb, 6 oz	2 cups

Procedure

1. Cook prunes in water to cover until tender. Drain, pit, and cut in fourths.
2. Beat eggs on high speed until light and thick. Add powdered sugar and salt slowly, beating constantly.
3. Add prunes and continue beating on medium speed.
4. Whip cream. Fold prune mixture, vanilla, lemon juice, pineapple juice, and crushed pineapple into whipped cream.
5. Divide mixture into 2 servings pans (12 × 20 × 2 in). Chill.

Prune Crunch

50 Servings (3 oz/85 g)
Bake, 350°F/177°C, 40 min

Metric		Ingredients	U.S.	
Weight	Volume		Weight	Volume
1.82 kg	1.89 l	Prunes, cooked, coarsely chopped	4 lb	2 qt
340 g	355 ml	Prune Juice	12 oz	1 ½ cups
	30 ml	Orange Rind, grated		2 tbsp
454 g	474 ml	Granulated Sugar	1 lb	2 cups
170 g	355 ml	Walnuts or Pecans, chopped	6 oz	1 ½ cups
227 g	474 ml	Flour, all-purpose	8 oz	2 cups
	10 ml	Soda		2 tsp
	5 ml	Salt		1 tsp
340 g	474 ml	Brown Sugar	12 oz	2 cups
454 g	947 ml	Oats, rolled	1 lb	1 qt
283 g	296 ml	Butter or Margarine	10 oz	1 ¼ cup
114 g	118 ml	Egg Whites, unbeaten (4 med)	4 oz	½ cup

Procedure

1. Cook prunes, juice, orange rind, and granulated sugar over low heat until thick (about 10 min). Let cool, then stir in nuts.
2. Sift together flour, soda, and salt. Add brown sugar and oats. Cut butter or margarine into this mixture until fairly well blended. Stir in egg whites.
3. Spread 2 cups/474 ml of flour–oat mixture on bottom of 2 baking pans (10 × 16 × 2 ¼ in). Spread half of prune mixture over flour–oat mixture. Spread remaining flour–oat mixture over top of prune filling.
4. Bake at 350°F/177°C for 40 minutes.

Norwegian Prune Pudding

50 Servings (4.3 oz/123 g)
Simmer

Metric		Ingredients	U.S.	
Weight	Volume		Weight	Volume
1.59 kg	2.60 l	Prunes, dried	3 lb, 8 oz	2 ¾ qt
3.18 kg	3.31 l	Water, hot	7 lb	3 ½ qt
1.59 kg	1.66 l	Sugar	3 lb, 8 oz	7 cups
	7 ½ ml	Salt		1 ½ tsp
7 g	2 4-in	Cinnamon Sticks	¼ oz	2 4-in
161 g	267 ml	Cornstarch	5 ⅔ oz	1 ⅛ cups
340 g	355 ml	Water, cold	12 oz	1 ½ cups
9 g	15 ml	Lemon Rind, grated	⅓ oz	1 tbsp
114 g	118 ml	Lemon Juice	4 oz	½ cup

Procedure

1. Soak prunes for an hour in hot water. Cook until very soft. Cool and stone. Heat juice (add water if necessary to make 2 ½ qt/2.37 l).
2. Add sugar, salt, and cinnamon sticks. Simmer for 15 minutes. Remove cinnamon.
3. Mix cornstarch and cold water. Stir into hot mixture and cook, stirring, until thickened and starch is cooked. Add lemon rind and prune pulp.
4. Remove from heat and add lemon juice. Chill.
5. Serve with custard sauce or whipped cream.

Oatmeal Apple Torte

60 Servings (2 ½ × 3 ⅓ in)
Bake, 375°F/190°C, 25 min

| Metric | | Ingredients | U.S. | |
Weight	Volume		Weight	Volume
454 g	474 ml	Butter or Margarine	1 lb	2 cups
793 g	829 ml	Sugar	1 lb, 12 oz	3 ½ cups
340 g	355 ml	Eggs (6 lge)	12 oz	1 ½ cups
454 g	947 ml	Flour, all-purpose	1 lb	1 qt
14 g	20 ml	Baking Powder	½ oz	4 tsp
	10 ml	Soda		2 tsp
14 g	15 ml	Salt	½ oz	1 tbsp
9 g	20 ml	Cinnamon	⅓ oz	4 tsp
	10 ml	Nutmeg		2 tsp
	5 ml	Cloves, ground		1 tsp
28 g	59 ml	Cocoa, unsweetened (optional)	1 oz	¼ cup
1.82 kg	1.89 l	Apples, pie pack, drained	4 lb	2 qt
114 g	237 ml	Walnuts, chopped	4 oz	1 cup
	10 ml	Lemon Rind, grated		2 tsp
340 g	711 ml	Wheat or Oats, rolled	12 oz	3 cups

Procedure

1. Cream butter or margarine and sugar (medium speed) 10 minutes or until light and fluffy.
2. Add eggs one at a time, blending well after each addition.
3. Sift flour, baking powder, soda, salt, and spices (and cocoa if used).
4. Add dry ingredients to sugar mixture and mix until smooth.
5. Chop apples into ½-inch pieces. Add apples, nuts, lemon rind, and cereal. Blend well.
6. Divide mixture into 2 greased pans (12 × 20 × 2 in) and bake at 375°F/190°C for 25 minutes.
7. Cool and cut each pan into 30 portions (5 × 6).

Raisin Pudding

50 Servings (4.5 oz/128 g)
Bake, 375°F/190°C, 30 min

| Metric | | Ingredients | U.S. | |
Weight	Volume		Weight	Volume
142 g	148 ml	Shortening or Margarine	5 oz	⅝ cup
340 g	355 ml	Granulated Sugar	12 oz	1 ½ cups
28 g	45 ml	Orange Rind, grated	1 oz	3 tbsp
454 g	711 ml	Raisins	1 lb	3 cups
1.02 kg	2.13 l	Flour, pastry	2 lb, 4 oz	2 ¼ qt
	7 ½ ml	Salt		1 ½ tsp
	48 ¾ ml	Baking Powder		3 ¼ tbsp
907 g	947 ml	Milk	2 lb	1 qt
1.36 kg	1.89 l	Brown Sugar	3 lb	2 qt
2.27 kg	2.37 l	Water, boiling	5 lb	2 ½ qt
	2 ½ ml	Salt		½ tsp

Procedure

1. Cream shortening. Add granulated sugar and orange rind. Cream well. Mix in raisins.
2. Sift together flour, salt, and baking powder. Add alternately with milk. Beat until smooth.
3. Divide mixture into 2 greased pudding pans (10 × 16 × 2 ¼ in).
4. Boil brown sugar, water, and salt for 3 minutes. Pour half of the syrup over each pan of batter.
5. Bake at 375°F/190°C for 30 minutes or until batter is done.

Gelatin Desserts

Apricot Bavarian Cream

50 Servings

| Metric | | Ingredients | U.S. | |
Weight	Volume		Weight	Volume
340 g	711 ml	Apricots, dried	12 oz	3 cups
1.36 kg	1.42 l	Water	3 lb	1 ½ qt
425 g	474 ml	Orange Gelatin	15 oz	2 cups
1.36 kg	1.42 l	Water and Apricot Juice, hot	3 lb	1 ½ qt
340 g	355 ml	Sugar	12 oz	1 ½ cups
454 g	474 ml	Apricots, canned, crushed	1 lb	2 cups
43 g	45 ml	Lemon Juice	1 ½ oz	3 tbsp
	5 ml	Salt		1 tsp
510 g	533 ml	Whipping Cream	1 lb, 2 oz	2 ¼ cups

Procedure

1. Cook dried apricots in 1 ½ qt/1.42 l water until tender. Drain, saving juice. Put apricots through coarse grinder, or chop.
2. Dissolve orange gelatin in 1 ½ qt/1.42 l hot liquid.
3. Add sugar, apricot pulp, lemon juice, and salt.
4. Let stand until thick but not set. Beat on mixer at high speed until light and fluffy. Whip cream and fold in. Chill.

Bavarian Cream
50 Servings (3 oz/85 g)

Metric		Ingredients	U.S.	
Weight	Volume		Weight	Volume
57 g	118 ml	Gelatin	2 oz	½ cup
454 g	474 ml	Water, cold	1 lb	2 cups
1.82 kg	1.89 l	Milk	4 lb	2 qt
170 g	158 ml	Egg Yolks (8 med)	6 oz	⅔ cup
567 g	592 ml	Sugar	1 lb, 4 oz	2 ½ cups
28 g	30 ml	Butter or Margarine	1 oz	2 tbsp
7 g	7 ½ ml	Salt	¼ oz	1 ½ tsp
283 g	296 ml	Egg Whites (10 med)	10 oz	1 ¼ cups
681 g	711 ml	Whipping Cream	1 lb, 8 oz	3 cups
21 g	22 ml	Vanilla	¾ oz	1 ½ tbsp

Procedure

1. Soak gelatin in cold water for 5 or 10 minutes.
2. Scald milk in double boiler.
3. Beat egg yolks. Add sugar gradually and beat well.
4. Slowly add part of scalded milk to egg yolks and sugar, stirring constantly. Return to double boiler.
5. Add gelatin, butter or margarine, and salt. Cook until mixture will coat a silver spoon lightly.
6. Remove from heat and cool until it begins to thicken.
7. Beat egg whites until stiff (not dry) and fold into mixture.
8. Whip cream until thick and glossy. Add vanilla. Fold into mixture and chill. Serve with fresh fruit sauce or whipped cream and nuts.

Spanish Cream
48 Servings (3 oz/85 g)
Refrigerate

Metric		Ingredients	U.S.	
Weight	Volume		Weight	Volume
43 g	90 ml	Gelatin	1 ½ oz	6 tbsp
227 g	237 ml	Water, cold	8 oz	1 cup
2.72 kg	2.84 l	Milk	6 lb	3 qt
302 g	316 ml	Sugar	10 ⅔ oz	1 ⅓ cup
9 g	10 ml	Salt	⅓ oz	2 tsp
28 g	45 ml	Cornstarch	1 oz	3 tbsp
227 g	237 ml	Water, cold	8 oz	1 cup
151 g	158 ml	Egg Yolks (8 lge)	5 ⅓ oz	⅔ cup
302 g	316 ml	Egg Whites (8 lge)	10 ⅔ oz	1 ⅓ cup
21 g	22 ml	Vanilla	¾ oz	1 ½ tbsp

Procedure

1. Soak gelatin in cold water.
2. Scald milk. Add sugar and salt.
3. Mix cornstarch with cold water. Add to hot milk and cook until cornstarch is done.
4. Beat egg yolks. Add small amount of hot mixture to egg yolks, mixing constantly. Add all to hot mixture. Cook. Remove from heat.
5. Beat egg whites until stiff (not dry). Add vanilla to cream mixture and fold in egg whites. Pour equal amounts into 2 pans (10 × 16 × 2 ¼ in).
6. Chill (requires about 6 hrs).
7. Serve with whipped cream and garnish or a fruit sauce.

Orange Spanish Cream

50 Servings (3 oz/85 g)

Refrigerate

Metric		Ingredients	U.S.	
Weight	Volume		Weight	Volume
57 g	120 ml	Gelatin	2 oz	8 tbsp
454 g	474 ml	Milk, cold	1 lb	2 cups
1.36 kg	1.42 l	Milk, scalded	3 lb	1 ½ qt
454 g	474 ml	Sugar	1 lb	2 cups
7 g	7 ½ ml	Salt	¼ oz	1 ½ tsp
255 g	237 ml	Egg Yolks (12 med)	9 oz	1 cup
907 g	947 ml	Orange Juice	2 lb	1 qt
227 g	237 ml	Lemon Juice	8 oz	1 cup
9 g	15 ml	Orange Rind, grated	⅓ oz	1 tbsp
	5 ml	Lemon Rind, grated		1 tsp
454 g	474 ml	Egg Whites (16 med)	1 lb	2 cups

Procedure

1. Soak gelatin in cold milk for 5 or 10 minutes.
2. Dissolve soaked gelatin in scalding milk. Add sugar and salt and dissolve.
3. Beat egg yolks. Add small amount of hot liquid to egg yolks, stirring, then add yolks to hot liquid. Cook until somewhat thickened (thin).
4. Remove from heat and add juices and rinds.
5. Beat egg whites until stiff and carefully fold in. Chill.
6. Serve with colorful fruit sauce or garnish of sliced orange.

Raspberry Currant Bavarian

50 Servings (4.7 oz/135 g)

Refrigerate

Metric		Ingredients	U.S.	
Weight	Volume		Weight	Volume
1.36 kg	2.84 l	Currants, fresh	3 lb	3 qt
1.67 kg	2.84 l	Raspberries, fresh	3 lb, 11 oz	3 qt
1.36 kg	1.42 l	Water	3 lb	1 ½ qt
114 g	237 ml	Gelatin	4 oz	1 cup
454 g	474 ml	Water	1 lb	2 cups
907 g	947 ml	Sugar	2 lb	1 qt
	5 ml	Salt		1 tsp
227 g	237 ml	Egg Whites, stiffly beaten (8 med)	8 oz	1 cup
907 g	947 ml	Whipping Cream, whipped	2 lb	1 qt

Procedure

1. Clean currants. Boil raspberries and currants in 1 ½ qt/1.42 l of water until tender. Press through a sieve.
2. Soak gelatin in 2 cups/474 ml cold water for 5 minutes. Dissolve in hot juice. Add sugar and salt and stir until dissolved. Refrigerate until slightly thick.
3. Fold in stiffly beaten egg whites and whipped cream. Pour into molds or pans. Chill.
4. Serve with or without whipped cream and whole berries.

Caramel Sponge
50 Servings (3 oz/85 g)

| Metric | | Ingredients | U.S. | |
Weight	Volume		Weight	Volume
1.14 kg	1.18 l	Sugar	2 lb, 8 oz	5 cups
1.36 kg	1.42 l	Water	3 lb	1 ½ qt
7 g	7 ½ ml	Salt	¼ oz	1 ½ tsp
43 g	90 ml	Gelatin	1 ½ oz	6 tbsp
227 g	237 ml	Water, cold	8 oz	1 cup
1.59 kg	1.66 l	Whipping Cream	3 lb, 8 oz	1 ¾ qt
21 g	22 ml	Vanilla	¾ oz	1 ½ tbsp

Procedure

1. Caramelize sugar (be careful not to caramelize too much—sugar burns easily).
2. Add water and salt slowly to caramelized sugar (it boils over quickly). Boil until thoroughly dissolved.
3. Soak gelatin in cold water for 5 to 10 minutes. Remove syrup from heat and add soaked gelatin.
4. Volume at this point should be 2 qt/1.89 l. If less add water to make that amount. Chill.
5. When mixture thickens, add cream that has been whipped until thick and glossy, with vanilla added. Mix well. Chill.

Banana Cream Dessert
50 Servings (No. 16 Scoop)

| Metric | | Ingredients | U.S. | |
Weight	Volume		Weight	Volume
198 g	237 ml	Lemon Gelatin	7 oz	1 cup
850 g	889 ml	Water, boiling	1 lb, 14 oz	3 ¾ cups
567 g	592 ml	Whipping Cream	1 lb, 4 oz	2 ½ cups
1.42 kg	13	Bananas, peeled (approx.)	3 lb, 2 oz	13
57 g	65 ml	Sugar	2 oz	4 ⅓ tbsp

Procedure

1. Dissolve gelatin in boiling water.
2. Whip cream. Mash bananas and add sugar. Combine whipped cream with bananas and sugar.
3. When gelatin begins to thicken, stir in banana-cream mixture. Chill.
4. Serve with a No. 16 scoop into sherbet glasses. Garnish with sliced banana or fruit sauce such as strawberry or pineapple.

Pineapple Bavarian

50 Servings (2.5 oz/71 g)

Refrigerate

Metric		Ingredients	U.S.	
Weight	Volume		Weight	Volume
227 g	237 ml	Milk, cold	8 oz	1 cup
35 g	75 ml	Gelatin	1¼ oz	5 tbsp
907 g	947 ml	Milk, hot	2 lb	1 qt
9 g	10 ml	Salt	⅓ oz	2 tsp
170 g	267 ml	Powdered Sugar	6 oz	1⅛ cups
1.02 kg	947 ml	Pineapple, crushed (as is)	2 lb, 4 oz	1 qt
114 g	118 ml	Lemon Juice	4 oz	½ cup
	5 ml	Lemon Rind, grated		1 tsp
340 g	355 ml	Whipping Cream	12 oz	1½ cups
340 g	355 ml	Egg Whites (12 med)	12 oz	1½ cups
227 g	355 ml	Powdered Sugar	8 oz	1½ cups

Procedure

1. Soak gelatin in cold milk for 5 or 10 minutes.
2. Add hot milk, salt, and powdered sugar. Stir until dissolved. Cool until mixture begins to thicken.
3. Add pineapple, lemon juice, and rind to partially thickened mixture. (If pineapple or lemon juice is added before milk has begun to thicken, the acid will cause the milk to curdle.) Cool.
4. Whip cream until thick and glossy. Fold into mixture.
5. Beat egg whites, adding powdered sugar as for meringue. Fold into gelatin mixture and chill.

Note: Delicious served with apricot sauce.

Pineapple Date Bavarian

50 Servings (3.6 oz/103 g)

Refrigerate

Metric		Ingredients	U.S.	
Weight	Volume		Weight	Volume
43 g	90 ml	Gelatin	1½ oz	6 tbsp
454 g	474 ml	Water, cold	1 lb	2 cups
2.95 kg	3.08 l	Pineapple, crushed	6 lb, 8 oz	3¼ qt
793 g	829 ml	Dates, chopped	1 lb, 12 oz	3½ cups
302 g	316 ml	Sugar	10⅔ oz	1⅓ cups
7 g	7½ ml	Salt	¼ oz	1½ tsp
76 g	79 ml	Lemon Juice	2⅔ oz	⅓ cup
	5 ml	Lemon Rind, grated		1 tsp
567 g	592 ml	Whipping Cream	1 lb, 4 oz	2½ cups

Procedure

1. Soak gelatin in cold water for 10 minutes.
2. Drain pineapple. Heat juice and dates, add soaked gelatin, and stir until dissolved. Stir in sugar and salt until dissolved.
3. Add lemon juice, rind, and pineapple. Chill until mixture begins to thicken.
4. Whip cream until thick and glossy. Fold into partially thickened gelatin. Chill.

Note: Attractive garnished with fresh fruit or maraschino cherry.

Pineapple Rice Bavarian
50 Servings (4 oz/114 g)
Refrigerate

Metric		Ingredients	U.S.	
Weight	Volume		Weight	Volume
454 g	553 ml	Rice, uncooked	1 lb	2 ⅓ cups
3.63 kg	3.79 l	Water	8 lb	1 gal
14 g	15 ml	Salt	½ oz	1 tbsp
28 g	60 ml	Gelatin	1 oz	4 tbsp
454 g	474 ml	Water, cold	1 lb	2 cups
681 g	711 ml	Sugar	1 lb, 8 oz	3 cups
9 g	10 ml	Salt	⅓ oz	2 tsp
297 g	316 ml	Orange Juice	10 ½ oz	1 ⅓ cups
297 g	316 ml	Lemon Juice	10 ½ oz	1 ⅓ cups
297 g	316 ml	Water	10 ½ oz	1 ⅓ cups
28 g	45 ml	Orange Rind, grated	1 oz	3 tbsp
1.51 kg	1.42 l	Pineapple, crushed, undrained	3 lb, 5 ⅓ oz	6 cups
907 g	947 ml	Whipping Cream	2 lb	1 qt

Procedure

1. Cook rice in boiling salted water until tender. Drain and rinse well.
2. Soak gelatin in cold water for 5 minutes. Heat slowly until dissolved, stirring. Add sugar and salt and dissolve.
3. Add remaining ingredients, except cream. Chill until it begins to thicken.
4. Whip cream until thick and glossy. Fold into partially thickened mixture.
5. Chill. Serve garnished with colorful fruit and whipped cream.

Rhubarb, Jellied
48 Servings (4 ⅔ oz/132 g)
Refrigerate

Metric		Ingredients	U.S.	
Weight	Volume		Weight	Volume
2.72 kg	5.68 l	Rhubarb, frozen (containing 6 parts rhubarb to 1 part sugar)	6 lb	6 qt
283 g	296 ml	Sugar	10 oz	1 ¼ cups
7 g	7 ½ ml	Salt	¼ oz	1 ½ tsp
1.25 kg	1.30 l	Water, boiling	2 lb, 12 oz	5 ½ cups
737 g	770 ml	Strawberry Gelatin	1 lb, 10 oz	3 ¼ cups
1.36 kg	1.42 l	Water, cold	3 lb	1 ½ qt

Procedure

1. Cook rhubarb, sugar, salt, and hot water together, until rhubarb is tender.
2. Add strawberry gelatin and dissolve.
3. Add cold water.
4. Yield: 14 lb/6.35 kg or 1 ½ gal/5.68 l. Divide into 2 pans (10 × 16 × 2 ¼ in). Chill.
5. Cut contents of each pan into 24 portions.
6. Approximate size of servings 2 ½ × 2 ¾ in × 1 in.
7. Serve with whipped cream.

Note: Nice with ice cream also.

Applesauce Bavarian Cream
50 Servings (4.3 oz/120 g)

Metric		Ingredients	U.S.	
Weight	Volume		Weight	Volume
85 g	178 ml	Gelatin, granulated	3 oz	¾ cup
681 g	711 ml	Water, cold	1 lb, 8 oz	3 cups
2.04 kg	2.13 l	Applesauce	4 lb, 8 oz	2 ¼ qt
340 g	355 ml	Lemon Juice	12 oz	1 ½ cups
	30 ml	Lemon Rind, grated		2 tbsp
681 g	711 ml	Sugar	1 lb, 8 oz	3 cups
	15 ml	Cinnamon, ground		1 tbsp
	15 ml	Ginger, ground		1 tbsp
	15 ml	Nutmeg, ground		1 tbsp
14 g	15 ml	Salt	½ oz	1 tbsp
340 g	355 ml	Egg Whites (12 med)	12 oz	1 ½ cups
1.36 kg	1.42 l	Heavy Cream, whipped	3 lb	1 ½ qt
766 g	1.42 l	Ginger Snaps, crushed	1 lb, 11 oz	1 ½ qt

Procedure

1. Sprinkle gelatin on cold water and let hydrate for a few minutes.
2. Heat applesauce, lemon juice, and rind with half of the sugar. Dissolve gelatin in hot applesauce. Add spices. Chill until partly set.
3. Add salt to egg whites and whip until stiff. Add remaining sugar slowly, beating until glossy.
4. Fold whipped cream, egg white, and half of the crushed ginger snaps into the gelatin mixture. Pour into molds. Chill until firm. Sprinkle remaining ginger snap crumbs on top before serving.

Fresh Strawberry Whip
50 Servings (¾ cup/178 ml)
Refrigerate

Metric		Ingredients	U.S.	
Weight	Volume		Weight	Volume
14 g	30 ml	Gelatin	½ oz	2 tbsp
114 g	118 ml	Water, cold	4 oz	½ cup
1.02 kg	1.42 l	Strawberries, crushed	2 lb, 4 oz	1 ½ qt
681 g	711 ml	Sugar	1 lb, 8 oz	3 cups
85 g	89 ml	Egg Whites, unbeaten (3 med)	3 oz	⅜ cup
	2½ ml	Salt		½ tsp
18 g	15 ml	Lemon Juice	½ oz	1 tbsp

Procedure

1. Soften gelatin in cold water. Melt, stirring over low heat or hot water. Cool.
2. Combine crushed strawberries, sugar, unbeaten egg whites, and salt. Put in mixer. Begin to beat at medium speed. Increase to high speed and beat for 10 minutes.
3. Fold lemon juice and gelatin into strawberries.
4. Serve piled in sherbet glasses and garnished with whole strawberries.

Note: This strawberry whip is especially good served on angel food cake.

Prune Whip

50 Servings (No. 12 Scoop)

Metric		Ingredients	U.S.		
Weight	Volume		Weight		Volume
1.14 kg	1.89 l	Prunes, dried	2 lb,	8 oz	2 qt
	8 ¾ ml	Salt			1 ¾ tsp
567 g	592 ml	Egg Whites (20 med)	1 lb,	4 oz	2 ½ cups
340 g	355 ml	Sugar		12 oz	1 ½ cups
47 g	50 ml	Lemon Juice		1 ⅔ oz	3 ½ tbsp
	10 ml	Lemon Rind, grated			2 tsp

Procedure

1. Cover prunes with water and cook until tender. Drain, cool, pit, and chop.
2. Add salt to egg whites and beat until frothy. Gradually add sugar and beat until egg whites are stiff but moist.
3. Add lemon juice and grated rind to prunes, and then carefully fold in meringue.
4. Serve with a No. 12 scoop.

Note: Delicious served with Custard Sauce.

Strawberry Bavarian

50 Servings (3 oz/85 g)
Refrigerate

Metric		Ingredients	U.S.		
Weight	Volume		Weight		Volume
368 g	395 ml	Strawberry Flavored Gelatin		13 oz	1 ⅔ cups
227 g	237 ml	Sugar		8 oz	1 cup
1.36 kg	1.42 l	Water, boiling	3 lb		1 ½ qt
1.36 kg	1.42 l	Whipping Cream	3 lb		1 ½ qt
681 g	947 ml	Strawberries, crushed	1 lb,	8 oz	1 qt

Procedure

1. Mix gelatin and sugar. Dissolve in boiling water.
2. Refrigerate until mixture begins to thicken. Beat until foamy.
3. Whip cream. Fold in whipped cream and crushed strawberries.
4. Serve with whipped cream and whole strawberries.

Note: Raspberries may be substituted for the strawberries.

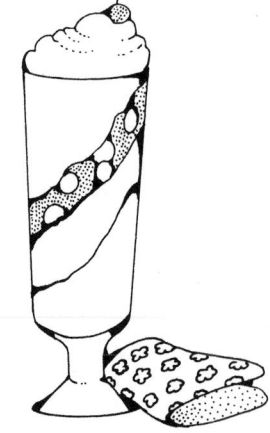

Refrigerator Puddings

Danish Apple Pudding
50 Servings (3.75 oz/106 g)
Refrigerate

| Metric | | Ingredients | U.S. | |
Weight	Volume		Weight	Volume
298 g	355 ml	Butter or Margarine, melted	10 ½ oz	1 ½ cups
1.14 kg	2.84 l	Cake Crumbs	2 lb, 8 oz	3 qt
227 g	316 ml	Brown Sugar	8 oz	1 ⅓ cups
	7 ½ ml	Cinnamon		1 ½ tsp
	7 ½ ml	Nutmeg		1 ½ tsp
	7 ½ ml	Salt		1 ½ tsp
2.95 kg	3.08 l	Applesauce	6 lb, 8 oz	3 ¼ qt
76 g	79 ml	Lemon Juice	2 ⅔ oz	⅓ cup
9 g	15 ml	Lemon Rind, grated	⅓ oz	1 tbsp
454 g	1.42 l	Coconut, toasted	1 lb	6 cups

Procedure

1. Mix butter or margarine with cake crumbs. Combine brown sugar, cinnamon, nutmeg, and salt. Mix with crumbs.
2. Combine applesauce, lemon juice, and rind.
3. Place layers of crumbs, coconut, then applesauce, next crumbs, and top with coconut in 2 pudding pans (10 × 16 × 2 ¼ in).
4. Chill overnight in refrigerator. Serve with whipped cream.

Fruit and Marshmallow Cream
50 Servings (3 ¼ oz/92 g)
Refrigerate Overnight

| Metric | | Ingredients | U.S. | |
Weight	Volume		Weight	Volume
510 g	474 ml	Peaches, pieces	1 lb, 2 oz	2 cups
1.02 kg	1.18 l	Pineapple, pieces	2 lb, 4 oz	1 ¼ qt
1.02 kg	1.42 l	Orange Sections	2 lb, 4 oz	1 ½ qt
510 g	947 ml	Bananas, sliced	1 lb, 2 oz	1 qt
907 g	3.79 l	Marshmallows, miniature	2 lb	4 qt
9 g	10 ml	Salt	⅓ oz	2 tsp
907 g	947 ml	Whipping Cream	2 lb	1 qt
227 g	355 ml	Pecans, chopped	8 oz	1 ½ cups

Procedure

1. Prepare fruit. Drain thoroughly.
2. Mix fruit, marshmallows, and salt together. Refrigerate overnight.
3. Just before serving, whip cream and fold into fruit. Also add nuts.
4. Yield: 9 ¼ lb/4.20 kg.
5. Serve with a No. 12 scoop.

Note: Other fruit may be substituted for peaches, if desired.

Pineapple Refrigerator Cake

48 Servings (4 oz/114 g)

Refrigerate 24 hrs

| Metric | | Ingredients | U.S. | |
Weight	Volume		Weight	Volume
283 g	267 ml	Egg Yolks (14 med)	10 oz	1 ⅛ cups
907 g	947 ml	Sugar	2 lb	1 qt
454 g	474 ml	Butter or Margarine	1 lb	2 cups
227 g	237 ml	Cream	8 oz	1 cup
850 g	1.42 l	Pineapple, crushed, drained	1 lb, 14 oz	1 ½ qt
9 g	10 ml	Salt	⅓ oz	2 tsp
	5 ml	Lemon Rind		1 tsp
114 g	118 ml	Lemon Juice	4 oz	½ cup
907 g	1.89 l	Vanilla Wafers or Dry Cake	2 lb	2 qt
681 g	1.11 l	Pecans, chopped	1 lb, 8 oz	4 ⅔ cups
255 g	296 ml	Maraschino Cherries, chopped	9 oz	1 ¼ cups

Procedure

1. Beat egg yolks thoroughly. Add sugar, butter or margarine, cream, pineapple, salt, and lemon rind. Cook in double boiler until of custard consistency. Remove from heat and add lemon juice.
2. Crush wafers or cake into crumbs. Mix with chopped pecans.
3. Divide half of crumb mixture into bottom of 2 pans (10 × 16 × 2 ¼ in), reserving half to sprinkle on top of filling.
4. Filling yield: 7 ¼ lb/3.30 kg. Spread half of filling over crumbs in each pan.
5. Sprinkle remaining crumbs over filling. Distribute ¾ cup/178 ml of maraschino cherry pieces over each pan. Refrigerate.
6. Cut contents of each pan into 24 pieces. Serve with whipped cream.

Steamed Puddings

Carrot Pudding

48 Servings (5 oz/142 g)

Steam, 2 hrs

Metric		Ingredients	U.S.	
Weight	Volume		Weight	Volume
907 g	947 ml	Sugar	2 lb	1 qt
454 g	474 ml	Margarine	1 lb	2 cups
681 g	1.07 l	Carrots, raw, grated	1 lb, 8 oz	4 ½ cups
567 g	947 ml	Potatoes, raw, grated	1 lb, 4 oz	1 qt
454 g	947 ml	Flour, sifted	1 lb	1 qt
	20 ml	Soda		1 ⅓ tbsp
	20 ml	Cinnamon		1 ⅓ tbsp
	20 ml	Salt		1 ⅓ tbsp
	10 ml	Cloves		2 tsp
567 g	947 ml	Raisins	1 lb, 4 oz	1 qt
227 g	355 ml	Currants, dried	8 oz	1 ½ cups
1.82 kg	1.89 l	Fruit Cake Mix	4 lb	2 qt

Procedure

1. Cream sugar and margarine until light and fluffy.
2. Mix in grated carrots and potatoes.
3. Sift together flour, soda, cinnamon, salt, and cloves.
4. Add raisins, currants, and fruit cake mix to dry ingredients. Add to creamed mixture and blend well.
5. Yield: 12 lb, 10 oz/5.72 kg.
6. Scale 6 lb, 5 oz/2.86 kg into each of 2 pans (12 × 20 × 2 in). Cover tightly and steam for 2 hours.
7. Cut contents of each pan into 24 portions. Serve with hard sauce.

Steam Pudding

48 Servings

Steam, 1 hr

Metric		Ingredients	U.S.	
Weight	Volume		Weight	Volume
454 g	474 ml	Butter or Margarine	1 lb	2 cups
681 g	711 ml	Sugar	1 lb, 8 oz	3 cups
312 g	326 ml	Eggs (6 med)	11 oz	1 ⅜ cups
850 g	711 ml	Corn Syrup	1 lb, 14 oz	3 cups
1.21 kg	2.84 l	Bread Crumbs	2 lb, 10 ⅔ oz	3 qt
170 g	355 ml	Flour, all-purpose	6 oz	1 ½ cups
	15 ml	Soda		1 tbsp
	15 ml	Cloves		1 tbsp
	30 ml	Cinnamon		2 tbsp
681 g	711 ml	Buttermilk or Sour Milk	1 lb, 8 oz	3 cups
1.14 kg	1.42 l	Fruit Mix	2 lb, 8 oz	1 ½ qt
		or Raisins and	1 lb	3 cups
		Nuts	12 oz	3 cups

Procedure

1. Cream shortening and sugar until light.
2. Add eggs one at a time. Add corn syrup and blend.
3. Add bread crumbs and mix well.
4. Sift flour, soda, cloves, and cinnamon. Add alternately with buttermilk.
5. Reserve some of flour to mix with fruit or raisins and nuts, depending upon which is used. Add fruit and blend.
6. Yield: About 12 lb/5.44 kg. Scale 6 lb/2.72 kg into each of 2 ungreased pans (12 × 20 × 2 in). Cover tightly and steam for 1 hour. Cut 6 × 4.

Devil's Food Pudding

48 Servings (3 ½ oz/99 g)

Steam, 1 hr, or Bake, 250°F/121°C, 1 ½ hrs

Metric		Ingredients	U.S.	
Weight	Volume		Weight	Volume
454 g	474 ml	Sugar	1 lb	2 cups
454 g	474 ml	Milk	1 lb	2 cups
340 g	711 ml	Chocolate, unsweetened, grated	12 oz	3 cups
454 g	474 ml	Butter or Margarine	1 lb	2 cups
907 g	947 ml	Sugar	2 lb	1 qt
340 g	355 ml	Eggs (6 lge)	12 oz	1 ½ cups
907 g	1.89 l	Flour, pastry	2 lb	2 qt
9 g	10 ml	Salt	⅓ oz	2 tsp
907 g	947 ml	Milk	2 lb	1 qt
21 g	21 ml	Vanilla	¾ oz	1 ½ tbsp
14 g	20 ml	Soda	½ oz	4 tsp
57 g	59 ml	Water, cold	2 oz	¼ cup

Procedure

1. Cook sugar, milk, and chocolate together until thick. Cool thoroughly.
2. Cream butter or margarine and sugar thoroughly.
3. Beat eggs well and add to creamed mixture. Beat until fluffy. Add cooled chocolate mixture and blend well.
4. Sift flour and salt. Add alternately with milk (⅓ of flour and ½ of the milk at a time). Add vanilla.
5. Mix soda and water and add last. Mix in well.
6. Yield: 10 ½ lb/4.77 kg. Divide into 2 pans (10 × 16 × 2 ¼ in). Cover pans tightly.
7. Steam pudding for 1 hour or bake at 250°F/121°C for 1 ½ hours.
8. Cut contents of each pan into 24 portions (2 ½ × 2 ¾ × 2 in).
9. Serve hot with whipped cream or ice cream.

Note: This is a popular pudding.

Date Pudding

48 Servings (3⅔ oz/103 g)
Steam, 2 hrs

Metric		Ingredients	U.S.	
Weight	Volume		Weight	Volume
283 g	296 ml	Butter or Margarine	10 oz	1¼ cups
907 g	1.26 l	Brown Sugar	2 lb	5⅓ cups
14 g	15 ml	Vanilla	½ oz	1 tbsp
255 g	267 ml	Eggs (5 med)	9 oz	1⅛ cups
793 g	1.66 l	Flour, all-purpose	1 lb, 12 oz	1¾ qt
57 g	80 ml	Baking Powder	2 oz	5⅓ tbsp
9 g	10 ml	Salt	⅓ oz	2 tsp
1.14 kg	1.18 l	Milk	2 lb, 8 oz	1¼ qt
793 g	1.18 l	Dates, chopped	1 lb, 12 oz	1¼ qt
567 g	1.18 l	Nuts, chopped	1 lb, 4 oz	1¼ qt

Procedure

1. Cream butter or margarine. Gradually add brown sugar, creaming well. Add vanilla.
2. Add eggs one at a time, beating well after each addition.
3. Sift together flour, baking powder, and salt. Reserve ½ cup/118 ml for flouring dates and nuts. Add alternately with milk to creamed mixture, starting with dry ingredients, and blending well after each addition.
4. Stir in floured chopped dates and nuts.
5. Yield: 11⅛ lb/5.05 kg.
6. Divide mixture into 2 pans (10 × 16 × 2¼ in). Cover tightly and steam for 2 hours.
7. Serve with hard sauce or whipped cream.

Persimmon Pudding

48 Servings (3 oz/85 g)
Steam, 2 hrs

Metric		Ingredients	U.S.	
Weight	Volume		Weight	Volume
1.36 kg	1.42 l	Sugar	3 lb	1½ qt
85 g	90 ml	Butter or Margarine	3 oz	6 tbsp
28 g	30 ml	Vanilla	1 oz	2 tbsp
681 g	1.42 l	Flour, all-purpose	1 lb, 8 oz	1½ qt
32 g	45 ml	Baking Powder		3 tbsp
	30 ml	Soda		2 tbsp
9 g	10 ml	Salt	⅓ oz	2 tsp
1.36 kg	1.42 l	Persimmons, ground	3 lb	1½ qt
605 g	632 ml	Milk	1 lb, 5⅓ oz	2⅔ cups

Procedure

1. Cream the sugar, butter or margarine, and vanilla.
2. Sift together flour, baking powder, soda, and salt. Add alternately with persimmons and milk to creamed mixture.
3. Yield: 9¾ lb/4.42 kg of batter.
4. Scale 4 lb, 14 oz/2.21 kg into each of 2 serving pans (10 × 12 × 2 in). Cover tightly and steam for 2 hours.
5. Serve with a lemon sauce.

Note: If desired, 1 qt/947 ml of dates plus 2 cups/474 ml of water may be substituted for the 1½ qts of ground persimmons.

CHAPTER 15 _Pastry_

Pastry, Filling, and Icing

Tender, flaky, sweet-flavored pastry is a first essential for good pie. Pastry flour and lard or hydrogenated fat are the chief ingredients for plain pastry. When lard is used, chill all of the ingredients before mixing. Work quickly and lightly.

For rich pastry, cut half of the fat into the dry ingredients until it is the size of rice. Add the remainder of the fat and cut it into the mixture, until it is the size of peas. Beware of pressing fat into the flour. A mealy crust, rather than a flaky one, will result if fat is melted and absorbed by the flour, or if the size of the fat particles is too small. Add liquid, immediately and in small amounts, to different areas of the mix. Toss the mix lightly in each area as the liquid is added. Use barely enough liquid to moisten the dough so that it will hold together. Chill for a few minutes before rolling. Avoid excess pressure on dough in handling or rolling.

Graham Cracker Pie Crust
8 Pies (9 in)
Bake, 375°F/190°C, 6–8 min

Metric		Ingredients	U.S.	
Weight	Volume		Weight	Volume
1.02 kg	2.37 l	Graham Crackers	2 lb, 4 oz	115 crackers
227 g	237 ml	Sugar	8 oz	1 cup
14 g	30 ml	Cinnamon	½ oz	2 tbsp
114 g	237 ml	Flour, all-purpose	4 oz	1 cup
681 g	789 ml	Butter or Margarine, melted	1 lb, 8 oz	3 ⅓ cups

Procedure

1. Crush graham crackers.
2. Mix dry ingredients; then blend thoroughly with graham crackers.
3. Add melted butter or margarine and mix.
4. Yield: 4½ lb/2.04 kg. Press 8 oz/227 g of mixture firmly over the bottom and up sides of 8–9″ pie tins. Reserve 8 oz/227 g of mixture to sprinkle on tops of pies (1 oz/28 g per pie).
5. Bake 6 or 8 minutes at 375°F/190°C or chill for 45 minutes.

Pie Crust, No. 1

8 Pies (9 in)

Bake, 425°F/218°C, 10 min

Metric		Ingredients	U.S.	
Weight	Volume		Weight	Volume
907 g	947 ml	Lard or Shortening	2 lb	1 qt
1.82 kg	3.79 l	Flour, pastry	4 lb	4 qt
	35 ml	Salt	1⅙ oz	2⅓ tbsp
605 g	632 ml	Water	1 lb, 5⅓ oz	2⅔ cups

Procedure

1. Blend lard lightly into flour and salt.
2. Add cold water a little at a time, distributing the water evenly through the mixture. Add only enough water to make the dough hold together.
3. Yield: 8 lower crusts of 8 oz/227 g each and 8 upper crusts of 6 oz/170 g each.
4. Roll lower crusts; place in pie pans, allowing ¾ -in extra width of pastry around edge to build up edges or to overlap top crusts of double-crust pie.
5. For single-crust pies, flute the edges, prick uni- formly over the bottom of the shells, and bake at 425°F/218°C for 10 minutes.
6. For double-crust pies, brush the edge of the bottom crust with milk or water, fill, and cover with top crust that has been slashed several times to make an attractive design. Fold extra ¾-inch width of lower crust over top crust and flute edge. Brush top crust with thin cream and sprinkle with granulated sugar before baking.

Pie Crust, No. 2

8 Pies (9 in)

Bake, 425°F/218°C, 8–10 min

Metric		Ingredients	U.S.	
Weight	Volume		Weight	Volume
28 g	30 ml	Salt	1 oz	2 tbsp
64 g	118 ml	Powdered Sugar	2¼ oz	½ cup
1.70 kg	3.56 l	Flour, cake	3 lb, 12 oz	3¾ qt
907 g	947 ml	Lard	2 lb	1 qt
340 g	355 ml	Water, cold	12 oz	1½ cups

Procedure

1. Sift together salt, powdered sugar, and cake flour.
2. Blend in lard lightly.
3. Cool mixture in refrigerator.
4. Add cold water slowly, mixing lightly until dough holds together.
5. Yield: 8 lower crusts (8 oz/227 g) and 8 upper crusts (6 oz/170 g).

Basic Chou Paste

(for cream puffs or éclairs)
48 Puffs
Bake, 400°F/205°C, 35–45 min

| Metric | | | U.S. | |
Weight	Volume	Ingredients	Weight	Volume
454 g	947 ml	Flour, A.P.	1 lb	1 qt
907 g	947 ml	Water	2 lb	1 qt
	5 ml	Salt		1 tsp
21 g	22 ml	Sugar	¾ oz	1 ½ tbsp
454 g	474 ml	Butter or Margarine	1 lb	2 cups
907 g	947 ml	Eggs (16 lge)	2 lb	1 qt

Procedure

1. Measure flour.
2. Heat water, salt, sugar, and butter or margarine to melt fat. Then bring to a rapid boil over high heat.
3. Dump in all of flour, remove pan from heat and stir until smooth, thick paste is formed and leaves side of pan.
4. Stir in eggs, one or two at a time until mixture is shiny and smooth. Let cool 15 or 20 minutes. (The paste may be refrigerated for later baking if desired. Remove from refrigerator and let stand at room temperature 30 or 40 minutes before shaping.)
5. Puffs may be shaped with pastry tube or a No. 16 scoop (1/4 cup/59 ml). Place 3 inches apart on greased baking sheet.
6. Bake at 400°F/205°C for 35 to 45 minutes.
7. Cut shells while hot.

Chocolate Éclair Icing

50 Éclairs

| Metric | | | U.S. | |
Weight	Volume	Ingredients	Weight	Volume
43 g	90 ml	Cocoa, unsweetened	1 ½ oz	6 tbsp
454 g	829 ml	Powdered Sugar	1 lb	3 ½ cups
	1 ¼ ml	Salt		¼ tsp
	5 ml	Vanilla		1 tsp
114 g	118 ml	Cream	4 oz	½ cup
66 g	78 ml	Butter or Margarine, melted	2 ⅓ oz	⅓ cup

Procedure

1. Thoroughly blend cocoa, sugar, and salt.
2. Add vanilla, top milk, and melted butter and stir until smooth.

Custard Filling for Cream Puffs (or Éclairs)
5 qt/4.74 l

Metric		Ingredients	U.S.	
Weight	Volume		Weight	Volume
1.36 kg	1.42 l	Sugar	3 lb	1 ½ qt
283 g	474 ml	Cornstarch	10 oz	2 cups
	10 ml	Salt		2 tsp
3.63 kg	3.79 l	Milk	8 lb	1 gal
510 g	474 ml	Egg Yolks (24 med)	1 lb, 2 oz	2 cups
227 g	237 ml	Butter or Margarine	8 oz	1 cup
28 g	30 ml	Vanilla	1 oz	2 tbsp

Procedure

1. Combine sugar, cornstarch, and salt. Stir in milk gradually. Heat to boiling and cook for 2 minutes, stirring continually.
2. Remove from heat. Beat egg yolks. Add a small amount of hot mixture to yolks, then stir yolks into hot mixture and cook for 2 minutes longer, stirring constantly. Remove from heat and stir in butter or margarine and vanilla.
3. Let cool. Fill cream puffs with pastry tube or a No. 12 scoop.

Puff Paste
50 Puffs
Bake, 425°F/218°C

Metric		Ingredients	U.S.	
Weight	Volume		Weight	Volume
57 g	59 ml	Butter or Margarine	2 oz	¼ cup
756 g	1.60 l	Flour, all-purpose	1 lb, 10⅔ oz	6 ¾ cups
	3 ⅓ ml	Salt		⅔ tsp
28 g	1 med	Egg White	1 oz	1 med
	2 ½ ml	Cream of Tartar		½ tsp
454 g	474 ml	Water, cold	1 lb	2 cups, approx.
709 g	789 ml	Shortening or Butter	1 lb, 9 oz	3 ⅓ cups

Procedure

1. With pastry knives or blender, work butter and flour together thoroughly.
2. Make well in center of flour and add salt, egg white, and cream of tartar. Mix only until blended. Add cold water, gradually working by hand until sufficient water has been added to make a firm, pliant dough. Cover with cloth. Let stand for 12 minutes. Weight: 3 lbs/1.36 kg.
3. Roll out into rectangular shape, 1 inch thick. Place one half of butter or margarine on one third of dough. Fold and roll out. Add remainder of shortening. Fold, being sure that all of shortening is enclosed. Refrigerate for 15 minutes.
4. Roll ¾-inch thick and fold from opposite ends as before. Let stand for 10 minutes. Roll to 1-inch thickness and fold again. Place in refrigerator overnight.
5. Roll to thickness of pie crust. Bake over back of muffin pans at 425°F/218°C until light brown.

Almond Cracker Crust

8 Pies (9 in)

Bake, 375°F/190°C, 6–8 min

| Metric | | Ingredients | U.S. | |
Weight	Volume		Weight	Volume
595 g	789 ml	Butter or Margarine, melted	1 lb, 5 oz	3 ⅓ cups
114 g	178 ml	Powdered Sugar	4 oz	¾ cup
1.36 kg	2.84 l	Graham Crackers	3 lb	150 crackers
114 g	178 ml	Almonds, ground (may be omitted)	4 oz	¾ cup

Procedure

1. Grind graham crackers.
2. Blanch almonds by heating in water just below the boiling point, until skins are easily removable. Remove skins and grind almonds.
3. Combine graham crackers, almonds, and powered sugar thoroughly. Mix in melted butter.
4. Yield: 5 lb/2.27 kg. Press 8 oz/227 g in each of 8 pie tins, reserving 1 lb/454 g (or 12 oz/340 g if almonds are omitted) for sprinkling on pie tops.
5. Bake 6 or 8 minutes at 375°F/190°C.

Chocolate Crumb Crust

8 Pies (9 in)

Bake, 350°F/177°C, 10 min

| Metric | | Ingredients | U.S. | |
Weight	Volume		Weight	Volume
1.02 kg	2.13 l	Chocolate Wafer Crumbs	2 lb, 4 oz	2 ¼ qt
454 g	474 ml	Margarine, melted	1 lb	2 cups

Procedure

1. Crush or grind chocolate wafers into fine crumbs.
2. Mix well with melted margarine.
3. Scale 6 ½ oz/184 g into each of 8 9-inch pie pans, and press into shape.
4. Bake at 350°F/177°C for 10 minutes. Cool well before filling.

Fruit Pies

Fresh Apple Pie
8 Pies (9 in)
Bake, 400°F/205°C, 15 min
350°F/177°C, 30 min

Metric		Ingredients	U.S.	
Weight	Volume		Weight	Volume
6.35 kg	13.26 l	Apples, tart (peeled and sliced, E.P.)	14 lb	3 ½ gal
1.59 kg	1.66 l	Sugar	3 lb, 8 oz	1 ¾ qt
28 g	60 ml	Cinnamon	1 oz	4 tbsp
170 g	355 ml	Flour	6 oz	1 ½ cups
9 g	10 ml	Salt	⅓ oz	2 tsp
227 g	237 ml	Butter or Margarine	8 oz	1 cup

Procedure

1. Peel and core apples and slice thin.
2. Place 1 ¾ lb/793 g of apples in each of 8 unbaked pie shells.
3. Combine sugar, cinnamon, flour, and salt. Sprinkle 8 oz/227 g of mixture over each pie. Dot each pie with 1 oz/28 g butter or margarine.
4. Cover with top crust. Brush with milk, sprinkle with a little granulated sugar, and bake at 400°F/205°C for 15 minutes, then at 350°F/177°C, for 30 minutes or until apples are tender.
5. Serve plain or with warm spiced cream.

Note: If apples are not tart, add ½ cup/59 ml of lemon juice to recipe.

French Apple Pie
8 Pies (9 in)
Bake, 400°F/205°C, 15 min
350°F/177°C, 45 min

Metric		Ingredients	U.S.	
Weight	Volume		Weight	Volume
5.44 kg	11.36 l	Apples (fresh E.P., sliced)	12 lb	12 qt
	2 No. 10 cans	(canned)	12–14 lb	2 No. 10 cans
907 g	947 ml	Granulated Sugar	2 lb	1 qt
114 g	118 ml	Lemon Juice	4 oz	½ cup
227 g	474 ml	Flour, all-purpose	8 oz	2 cups
9 g	10 ml	Salt	⅓ oz	2 tsp
	20 ml	Cinnamon		4 tsp
	10 ml	Nutmeg		2 tsp
454 g	474 ml	Shortening	1 lb	2 cups
1.36 kg	1.89 l	Brown Sugar	3 lb	2 qt

Procedure

1. Mix apples, granulated sugar, and lemon juice and put in unbaked pie shells.
2. Mix together remaining ingredients and spread over apples.
3. Bake at 400°F/205°C, for 15 minutes and at 350°F/177°C for 45 minutes, or until apples are tender.

Apple Pie (Canned or Frozen Apples)
8 Pies (9 in)
Bake, 400°F/205°C, 15 min
350°F/177°C, 30 min

| Metric | | Ingredients | U.S. | |
Weight	Volume		Weight	Volume
5.90 kg	6.63 l	Apples, pie pack	13 lb	2 No. 10 cans
1.82 kg	1.89 l	Sugar	4 lb	2 qt
9 g	10 ml	Salt	⅓ oz	2 tsp
	30 ml	Cinnamon		2 tbsp
	15 ml	Nutmeg		1 tbsp
170 g	355 ml	Flour, all-purpose	6 oz	1 ½ cups
227 g	237 ml	Margarine	8 oz	1 cup
227 g	237 ml	Lemon Juice	8 oz	1 cup

Procedure

1. Chop apples slightly.
2. Combine sugar, salt, spices, and flour and blend into apples. Heat apples and stir in margarine until melted. Mix in lemon juice.
3. Use approximately 3 ½ cups to fill each pie. Cover with top crust.
4. Bake at 400°F/205°C for 15 minutes and then at 350°F/177°C for 30 minutes.

Ginger Apple Pie
8 Pies (9 in)
Refrigerate

| Metric | | Ingredients | U.S. | |
Weight	Volume		Weight	Volume
		Crust		
1.14 kg	2.37 l	Gingersnap Crumbs, fine	2 lb, 8 oz	2 ½ qt
454 g	553 ml	Butter or Margarine, melted	1 lb	2 ⅓ cups
454 g	474 ml	Sugar	1 lb	2 cups
		Filling		
737 g	770 ml	Lemon-flavored Gelatin	1 lb, 10 oz	3 ¼ cups
1.82 kg	1.89 l	Water, boiling	4 lb	2 qt
9 g	10 ml	Salt	⅓ oz	2 tsp
3.63 kg	3.79 l	Applesauce, strained	8 lb	1 gal

Procedure
Crust

1. Mix ingredients together.
2. Yield: 4 ½ lb/2.04 kg. Press 8 oz/227 g in each pie pan. Save remaining 8 ounces for sprinkling on top, 1 ounce per pie.

Filling

1. Dissolve gelatin in boiling water.
2. Add salt and applesauce and chill until thick.
3. Place in crumb shells and cover each pie with 1 ounce of crumb mixture or with a layer of whipped cream, sprinkled with 1 ounce of crumb mixture. Use 1 ½ qt/1.42 l of whipping cream for 8 pies.
4. Refrigerate until ready to serve.

Apple Scotch Pie

8 Pies (9 in)

Bake, 400°F/205°C, 30 min

Metric		Ingredients	U.S.	
Weight	Volume		Weight	Volume
1.36 kg	1.89 l	Brown Sugar	3 lb	2 qt
907 g	947 ml	Water	2 lb	1 qt
170 g	178 ml	Vinegar	6 oz	¾ cup
5.44 kg	11.36 l	Apples, frozen or fresh, E.P.	12 lb	12 qt
170 g	355 ml	Flour, all-purpose	6 oz	1 ½ cups
9 g	10 ml	Salt	⅓ oz	2 tsp
76 g	79 ml	Lemon Juice	2 ⅔ oz	⅓ cup

Procedure

1. Cook 1 ½ lb/681 g of the brown sugar with the water and the vinegar until mixture boils.
2. Add the apples and simmer until tender. Remove the apples from the syrup.
3. Mix the remaining 1 ½ lb/681 g of brown sugar with the flour and the salt. Add slowly to syrup and cook until mixture thickens.
4. Remove from stove and add ⅓ cup/79 ml lemon juice and cooked apples.
5. Yield: 7 qt/6.63 l. Place 3 ½ cups/829 ml in each of 8 unbaked pie shells. Cover with a top crust and bake at 400°F/205°C for 30 minutes.

Peach Pie

8 Pies (9 in)

Bake, 400°F/205°C, 15 min

350°F/177°C, 45 min

Metric		Ingredients	U.S.	
Weight	Volume		Weight	Volume
5.44 kg	6.63 l	Peaches, pie pack	12 lb	2 No. 10 cans
1.36 kg	1.42 l	Juice and Water	3 lb	1 ½ qt
170 g	284 ml	Cornstarch	6 oz	1 ⅕ cups
1.36 kg	1.42 l	Sugar	3 lb	1 ½ qt
14 g	15 ml	Salt	½ oz	1 tbsp
	5 ml	Nutmeg		1 tsp

Procedure

1. Drain peaches. Add enough water to juice to yield 1 ½ qt/1.42 l of liquid. Heat juice to boiling point. Combine cornstarch, sugar, and salt. Add to hot juice, stirring constantly until smooth and thickened. Remove from heat.
2. Add nutmeg and peaches and blend.
3. Yield: 7 ¼ qt/6.86 l. Pour 3 ½ cups/829 ml of mixture into each of 8 unbaked pie shells. Cover with top crust, brush with thin cream, sprinkle with granulated sugar, and bake at 400°F/205°C for 15 minutes, and then reduce to 350°F/177°C for 45 minutes.

Dried Apricot Pie

8 Pies (9 in)
Bake, 400°F/205°C, 15 min
350°F/177°C, 45 min

Metric		Ingredients	U.S.	
Weight	Volume		Weight	Volume
2.72 kg	5.68 l	Apricots, dried	6 lb	6 qt
1.36 kg	1.42 l	Apricot Juice	3 lb	1 ½ qt
1.82 kg	1.89 l	Sugar	4 lb	2 qt
114 g	190 ml	Cornstarch	4 oz	⅘ cup
9 g	10 ml	Salt	⅓ oz	2 tsp
227 g	237 ml	Lemon Juice	8 oz	1 cup

Procedure

1. Cook dried apricots in water to cover, until tender. Drain off juice.
2. Add water, if necessary, to make 1 ½ qt/1.42 l of juice. Heat juice in double boiler.
3. Blend sugar, cornstarch, and salt. Add to hot juice. Cook until thick, stirring constantly. Remove from heat and add lemon juice.
4. Pour thickened juice over fruit.
5. Yield: 7 qt/6.63 l. Pour 3 ½ cups/829 ml in each unbaked pie shell. Cover with upper crust.
6. Bake at 400°F/205°C for 15 minutes and at 350°F/177°C for 45 minutes.

Apricot and Pineapple Pie

8 Pies (9 in)
Bake, 400°F/205°C, 15 min
350°F/177°C, 45 min

Metric		Ingredients	U.S.	
Weight	Volume		Weight	Volume
2.50 kg	2.37 l	Apricots, canned, halves	5 lb, 8 oz	2 ½ qt
2.27 kg	2.37 l	Pineapple, canned, diced	5 lb	2 ½ qt
1.02 kg	947 ml	Apricot Juice	2 lb 4 oz	1 qt
907 g	947 ml	Pineapple Juice	2 lb	1 qt
170 g	284 ml	Cornstarch	6 oz	1 ⅕ cups
1.36 kg	1.48 l	Sugar	3 lb	6 ¼ cups
	5 ml	Salt		1 tsp

Procedure

1. Combine apricot juice with pineapple juice and heat in double boiler.
2. Blend sugar, cornstarch, and salt and add to hot juice. Cook until thick, stirring constantly. Remove from heat and pour over drained combined fruit.
3. Yield: 7 qt/6.63 kg. Pour 3 ½ cups/829 ml of filling in each unbaked pie shell. Cover with upper crust.
4. Bake at 400°F/205°C for 15 minutes and at 350°F/177°C for 45 minutes.

Apricot Pie

8 Pies (9 in)
Bake, 400°F/205°C, 15 min
350°F/177°C, 45 min

Metric		Ingredients	U.S.	
Weight	Volume		Weight	Volume
5.44 kg	6.63 l	Apricots, pie pack	12 lb	2 No. 10 cans
1.59 kg	1.66 l	Sugar	3 lb, 8 oz	1 ¾ qt
170 g	296 ml	Cornstarch	6 oz	1 ¼ cups
1.36 kg	1.42 l	Juice	3 lb	1 ½ qt
	5 ml	Salt		1 tsp
57 g	59 ml	Butter or Margarine	2 oz	¼ cup
57 g	59 ml	Lemon Juice	2 oz	¼ cup

Procedure

1. Drain juice from apricots and add water to make 1½ qt/1.42 l. Heat to boiling.
2. Combine sugar and cornstarch and add gradually to hot juice, stirring constantly until smooth and thickened.
3. Remove from heat. Stir in butter or margarine until melted. Add lemon juice and apricots.
4. Fill unbaked pie shells with 3½ cups/829 ml (approx.) per pie. Cover with top crust.
5. Bake at 400°F/205°C for 15 minutes and then 350°F/177°C for 45 minutes.

Dried Prune and Apricot Pie

8 Pies (9 in)
Bake, 400°F/205°C, 15 min
350°F/177°C, 45 min

Metric		Ingredients	U.S.	
Weight	Volume		Weight	Volume
1.82 kg	3.08 l	Prunes, dried	4 lb	3 ¼ qt
1.36 kg	2.84 l	Apricots, dried	3 lb	3 qt
681 g	711 ml	Prune Juice	l lb, 8 oz	3 cups
681 g	711 ml	Apricot Juice	1 lb, 8 oz	3 cups
1.36 kg	1.50 l	Sugar	3 lb	6 ⅓ cups
114 g	189 ml	Cornstarch	4 oz	⅘ cup
9 g	10 ml	Salt	⅓ oz	2 tsp
	2 ½ ml	Nutmeg		½ tsp
	5 ml	Cinnamon		1 tsp

Procedure

1. Cook apricots and prunes. Pit prunes. Drain off juice from each fruit. Add water, if necessary, to get 3 cups/711 ml of each juice.
2. Heat combined juices in a double boiler.
3. Blend sugar, cornstarch, salt, nutmeg, and cinnamon and add to hot juice. Cook until thick, stirring constantly.
4. Pour thickened juice over combined fruit.
5. Yield: 7 qt/6.63 l. Pour 3½ cups/829 ml of filling into each unbaked pie shell. Cover with upper crust.
6. Bake at 400°F/205°C for 15 minutes and at 350°F/177°C for 45 minutes.

Purple Plum Pie

8 Pies (9 in)
Bake, 400°F/205°C, 15 min
350°F/177°C, 45 min

Metric		Ingredients	U.S.		
Weight	Volume		Weight		Volume
5.44 kg	6.63 l	Plums, purple	12–13 lb		2 No. 10 cans
1.59 kg	1.66 l	Juice and Water	3 lb, 8 oz		1 ¾ qt
283 g	474 ml	Cornstarch	10 oz		2 cups
57 g	90 ml	Orange Rind, grated	2 oz		6 tbsp
681 g	770 ml	Sugar	1 lb, 8 oz		3 ¼ cups
227 g	237 ml	Orange Juice	8 oz		1 cup
	10 ml	Cinnamon			2 tsp
	5 ml	Salt			1 tsp

Procedure

1. Drain plums and pit. Add enough water to juice to yield 1 ¾ qt/1.66 l. Make a smooth paste of 2 cups/474 ml of cold juice and cornstarch. Heat remainder of juice and orange rind to boiling point. Add cornstarch mixture and stir until thick and smooth. Remove from heat.
2. Add sugar, orange juice, cinnamon, and salt. Blend. Add plums.
3. Yield: 7 qt/6.63 l. Pour 3 ½ cups/829 ml of filling into each of 8 unbaked pie shells. Top with crusts and brush with thin cream. Sprinkle with granulated sugar and bake at 400°F/205°C for 15 minutes, and then reduce to 350°F/177°C for 45 minutes.

Rhubarb Pie

8 Pies (9 in)
Bake, 400°F/205°C, 30 min

Metric		Ingredients	U.S.		
Weight	Volume		Weight		Volume
4.08 kg	8.51 l	Rhubarb, fresh, diced, E.P.	9 lb		9 qt
2.04 kg	2.13 l	Sugar	4 lb, 8 oz		2 ¼ qt
	5 ml	Salt			1 tsp
37 g	60 ml	Lemon Rind, grated	1 ⅓ oz		4 tbsp
227 g	378 ml	Cornstarch	8 oz		1 ⅗ cups

Procedure

1. Clean rhubarb and cut into 1-inch pieces.
2. Combine sugar, salt, lemon rind, and cornstarch, mixing evenly. Blend with rhubarb. Place 1 ¾ lb/793 g in each of 8 unbaked pie shells. Cover with top crust, brush with thin cream, sprinkle with granulated sugar, and bake at 400°F/205°C for 30 minutes.

Cherry Pie

8 Pies (9 in)
Bake, 400°F/205°C, 15 min
350°F/177°C, 45 min

| Metric | | Ingredients | U.S. | |
Weight	Volume		Weight	Volume
4.54 kg	5.68 l	Cherries, pie pack, well-drained	10 lb	6 qt
1.82 kg	1.89 l	Juice and Water	4 lb	2 qt
283 g	474 ml	Cornstarch	10 oz	2 cups
2.72 kg	3.08 l	Sugar	6 lb	3¼ qt
9 g	10 ml	Salt	⅓ oz	2 tsp
57 g	59 ml	Lemon Juice	2 oz	¼ cup
	1¼ ml	Almond Extract		¼ tsp
	10 ml	Red Coloring, liquid		2 tsp

Procedure

1. Drain cherries. Add enough water to juice to yield 2 qt/1.89 l. Heat juice to boiling point. Combine cornstarch, sugar, and salt. Add to hot juice, stirring constantly until smooth and thickened. Remove from heat.
2. Add lemon juice and almond extract. Blend. Add cherries.
3. Yield: 8 qt/7.57 l. Place 1 qt/947 ml of mixture in each of 8 unbaked pie shells. Cover with top crust, brush with thin cream, sprinkle with granulated sugar, and bake at 400°F/205°C, for 15 minutes, and then at 350°F/177°C for 45 minutes.

Raisin Pie

8 Pies (9 in)
Bake, 400°F/205°C, 15 min
350°F/177°C, 45 min

| Metric | | Ingredients | U.S. | |
Weight	Volume		Weight	Volume
2.72 kg	4.26 l	Raisins	6 lb	4½ qt
2.72 kg	2.84 l	Water	6 lb	3 qt
227 g	415 ml	Cornstarch	8 oz	1¾ cups
681 g	711 ml	Sugar	1 lb, 8 oz	3 cups
	5 ml	Salt		1 tsp
170 g	178 ml	Lemon Juice	6 oz	¾ cup
37 g	60 ml	Lemon Rind	1⅓ oz	4 tbsp
227 g	237 ml	Orange Juice	8 oz	1 cup
37 g	60 ml	Orange Rind	1⅓ oz	4 tbsp

Procedure

1. Heat raisins and water to boiling point.
2. Combine cornstarch, sugar, and salt. Add to raisin and water mixture, stirring until thickened and smooth.
3. Remove from heat and add remaining ingredients. Blend.
4. Yield: 8 qt/7.57 l. Place 1 qt/947 ml of mixture in each of 8 unbaked pie shells. Cover with a top crust, brush with cream, sprinkle with granulated sugar, and bake at 400°F/205°C for 15 minutes and at 350°F/177°C for 45 minutes.

Berry Pie
8 Pies (9 in)

| Metric | | Ingredients | U.S. | |
Weight	Volume		Weight	Volume
5.44 kg	6.63 l	Berries (canned)	12 lb	2 No. 10 cans
		Berries (frozen)	12 lb	7 qt
227 g	378 ml	Cornstarch	8 oz	1 ³/₅ cups
1.82 kg	1.89 l	Sugar	4 lb	2 qt
57 g	59 ml	Lemon Juice	2 oz	¼ cup
	5 ml	Salt		1 tsp

Procedure

1. Drain berries. Heat juice to boiling point. Combine cornstarch, sugar, and salt. Add to hot juice, stirring constantly until smooth and thickened. Remove from heat.
2. Add lemon juice and berries. Blend.
3. Yield: 7 qt/6.63 l. Pour 3½ cups/829 ml of mixture into each of 8 unbaked pie shells. Top with crust, brush with thin cream, sprinkle with granulated sugar, and bake at 400°F/205°C for 15 minutes, and then reduce to 350°F/177°C for 30 minutes.

Strawberry Pie
8 Pies (9 in)

| Metric | | Ingredients | U.S. | |
Weight	Volume		Weight	Volume
3.63 kg	7.57 l	Strawberries, washed and capped	8 lb	8 qt
85 g	178 ml	Cornstarch	3 oz	¾ cup
9 g	10 ml	Salt	⅓ oz	2 tsp
907 g	1.01 l	Sugar	2 lb	4 ¼ cups
1.36 kg	1.42 l	Whipping Cream	3 lb	1 ½ qt

Procedure

1. Select large berries and arrange in a close layer in each of 8 baked pie shells.
2. Crush the remainder of the berries and heat. Mix cornstarch, salt, and sugar and add to hot strawberries and juice. Cook until clear.
3. Pour the hot mixture over the berries in the crusts.
4. Chill and cover with whipped cream.

Note: Fresh raspberries may be substituted.

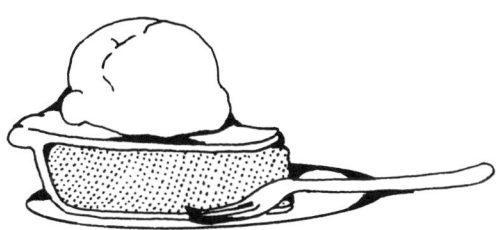

Custard Pies

Rhubarb Custard Pie

8 Pies (9 in)

Bake, 375°F/190°C, 50–60 min

Metric		Ingredients	U.S.	
Weight	Volume		Weight	Volume
2.72 kg	3.08 l	Sugar	6 lb	3 ¼ qt
170 g	284 ml	Cornstarch	6 oz	1 ⅕ cups
4.54 kg	9.46 l	Rhubarb, diced, fresh	10 lb	10 qt
340 g	316 ml	Egg Yolks (16 med)	12 oz	1 ⅓ cups
454 g	474 ml	Orange Juice	1 lb	2 cups
76 g	120 ml	Orange Rind	2 ⅔ oz	8 tbsp
9 g	10 ml	Salt	⅓ oz	2 tsp
		Meringue		
454 g	474 ml	Egg Whites (16 med)	1 lb	2 cups

Procedure

1. Mix all ingredients together, except for egg whites. Put in unbaked pie shells. Bake at 375°F/190°C for 50 to 60 minutes.

2. Let cool slightly. Cover with meringue and brown.

Variations

1. Use whole eggs in pie and cover with lattice pastry.
2. Use no meringue. Cool and serve with whipped cream.

Persian Pecan Pie

8 Pies (9 in)

Bake, 450°F/232°C, 5 min

300°F/149°C, 35 min

Metric		Ingredients	U.S.	
Weight	Volume		Weight	Volume
1.82 kg	1.89 l	Sugar	4 lb	2 qt
2.27 kg	1.89 l	Corn Syrup, dark	5 lb	2 qt
1.82 kg	1.89 l	Eggs (32 lge)	4 lb	2 qt
198 g	237 ml	Butter or Margarine, melted	7 oz	1 cup
35 g	37 ml	Vanilla	1 ¼ oz	2 ½ tbsp
907 g	1.89 l	Pecans	2 lb	2 qt

Procedure

1. Cook sugar and syrup to 228°F/109°C.
2. Beat eggs and add hot syrup slowly. Add butter or margarine, vanilla, and pecans.
3. Pour 1 qt/947 ml into each of 8 unbaked pastry shells. Bake at 450°F/232°C for 5 minutes. Reduce heat to 300°F/149°C and continue baking for 35 minutes.

Custard Pie

8 Pies (9 in)
Bake, 450°F/232°C, 10 min
350°F/177°C, 40 min

| Metric | | Ingredients | U.S. | |
Weight	Volume		Weight	Volume
1.36 kg	1.42 l	Eggs, beaten (24 lge)	3 lb	1 ½ qt
907 g	1.01 l	Sugar	2 lb	4 ¼ cups
14 g	15 ml	Salt	½ oz	1 tbsp
4.99 kg	5.21 l	Milk	11 lb	5 ½ qt
43 g	45 ml	Vanilla	1 ½ oz	3 tbsp
	10 ml	Nutmeg, grated		2 tsp

Procedure

1. Beat sugar into the eggs. Add salt, milk, and vanilla.
2. Yield: 8 qt/7.57 l. Brush bottoms of unbaked pie shells with slightly beaten egg white, to help prevent soaking of crust while baking. Pour 1 qt/947 ml of mixture into each crust. Sprinkle each top with ¼ tsp/1 ¼ ml of grated nutmeg.
3. Bake for 10 minutes at 450°F/232°C and at 350°F/177°C for 40 minutes or until inserted silver knife comes out clean.

Caramel Pecan Pie

8 Pies (9 in)
Bake, 350°F/177°C, 15 min
300°F/149°C, 45 min

| Metric | | Ingredients | U.S. | | |
Weight	Volume		Weight		Volume
2.37 kg	3.31 l	Brown Sugar	5 lb,	4 oz	3 ½ qt
3.30 kg	2.37 l	Corn Syrup, light	7 lb,	4 oz	2 ½ qt
1.36 kg	1.42 l	Eggs, well-beaten (24 lge)	3 lb		1 ½ qt
28 g	30 ml	Vanilla		1 oz	2 tbsp
100 g	118 ml	Butter or Margarine, melted		3 ½ oz	½ cup
907 g	1.89 l	Pecans, unsalted, roasted	2 lb		2 qt

Procedure

1. Combine all ingredients except for pecans and beat until well-mixed.
2. Yield: 8 qt/7.57 l. Pour 1 qt/947 ml in each of 8 unbaked pie shells. Sprinkle the top of each pie with 4 oz/114 g of pecans.
3. Bake at 350°F/177°C for 15 minutes and at 300°F/149°C for 45 minutes.
4. Serve with or without whipped cream.

New England Squash Pie (with Candied-Ginger Meringue)

8 Pies (9 in)
Bake, 400°F/205°C, 15 min
350°F/177°C, 45 min

Metric		Ingredients	U.S.	
Weight	**Volume**		**Weight**	**Volume**
4.08 kg	4.26 l	Squash, cooked, mashed	9 lb	4 ½ qt
454 g	474 ml	Granulated Sugar	1 lb	2 cups
454 g	632 ml	Brown Sugar	1 lb	2 ⅔ cups
14 g	15 ml	Salt	½ oz	1 tbsp
	25 ml	Nutmeg		1 ⅔ tbsp
	10 ml	Ginger		2 tsp
	22 ½ ml	Cinnamon		1 ½ tbsp
1.19 kg	1.24 l	Eggs, slightly beaten (21 lge)	2 lb, 10 oz	5 ¼ cups
1.82 kg	1.89 l	Milk	4 lb	2 qt
907 g	947 ml	Half and Half	2 lb	1 qt
		Candied-Ginger Meringue		
454 g	474 ml	Egg Whites (14 lge)	1 lb	2 cups
	5 ml	Salt		1 tsp
340 g	355 ml	Sugar	12 oz	1 ½ cups
114 g	118 ml	Candied Ginger, chopped	4 oz	½ cup

Procedure
Filling

1. Drain off excess water before weighing squash.
2. Weigh and sift dry ingredients. Add to squash and stir until mixed.
3. Add slightly beaten eggs, milk, and top milk. Mix.
4. Yield: 9 qt/8.51 l. Pour 4 ½ cups/1.07 l into each of 8 unbaked pie shells that have been brushed with slightly beaten egg whites to help prevent soaking. Bake in hot oven at 400°F/205°C for 15 minutes; then reduce to 350°F/177°C for 45 minutes, or until an inserted silver knife blade comes out clean.

Candied-Ginger Meringue

1. Have egg whites at room temperature.
2. Add salt and beat until a slight peak can be made.
3. Gradually add sugar and beat until stiff but moist.
4. Fold in ginger.
5. Spread on squash pie, about 15 minutes before it is done, and bake at 350°F/177°C for 12 to 15 minutes or until meringue is a light, golden brown.

Coconut Custard Pie

8 Pies (9 in)
Bake, 450°F/232°C, 15 min
350°F/177°C, 20–25 min

Metric		Ingredients	U.S.	
Weight	**Volume**		**Weight**	**Volume**
227 g	711 ml	Coconut	8 oz	3 cups
681 g	711 ml	Sugar	1 lb, 8 oz	3 cups
1.36 kg	1.42 l	Eggs, beaten (24 lge)	3 lb	1 ½ qt
14 g	15 ml	Salt	½ oz	1 tbsp
4.08 kg	4.26 l	Milk	9 lb	4 ½ qt
43 g	45 ml	Vanilla	1 ½ oz	3 tbsp

1. Sprinkle 1 oz/28 g of coconut in each of 8 unbaked pie shells.
2. Beat sugar into the eggs. Add salt, milk, and vanilla.
3. Yield: 6 ½ qt/6.16 l. Pour 3 ¼ cups/770 ml of filling in each shell.
4. Bake for 15 minutes at 450°F/232°C and at 350°F/177°C for 20 to 25 minutes, or until inserted silver knife comes out clean.

Pumpkin Pie
8 Pies (9 in)
Bake, 425°F/218°C, 15 min
350°F/177°C, 45 min

| Metric | | Ingredients | U.S. | |
Weight	Volume		Weight	Volume
793 g	829 ml	Eggs, slightly beaten (14 lge)	1 lb, 12 oz	3 ½ cups
2.15 kg	2.84 l	Pumpkin, solid pack	4 lb, 12 oz	3 qt
1.36 kg	1.42 l	Sugar	3 lb	1 ½ qt
19 g	20 ml	Salt		4 tsp
14 g	40 ml	Cinnamon	½ oz	8 tsp
7 g	20 ml	Ginger	¼ oz	4 tsp
	10 ml	Cloves		2 tsp
2.95 kg	3.08 l	Evaporated Milk	6 lb, 8 oz	3 ¼ qt

Procedure

1. Blend pumpkin into eggs. Add sugar, salt, and spices.
2. Stir in milk. Pour 1 qt/947 ml into each of 8 unbaked shells.
3. Bake at 425°F/218°C for 15 minutes. Reduce heat and bake at 350°F/177°C for 45 minutes or until custard tests done (inserted knife blade comes out clean).

Sweet Potato Pie
8 Pies (9 in)
Bake, 425°F/218°C, 10 min
350°F/177°C, 40 min

| Metric | | Ingredients | U.S. | |
Weight	Volume		Weight	Volume
3.18 kg	3.31 l	Sweet Potatoes, mashed	7 lb	3 ½ qt
1.42 kg	1.54 l	Sugar	3 lb, 2 oz	6 ½ cups
1.14 kg	1.18 l	Eggs, beaten (20 lge)	2 lb, 8 oz	5 cups
	10 ml	Cinnamon		2 tsp
	10 ml	Mace		2 tsp
	5 ml	Nutmeg		1 tsp
	20 ml	Salt	⅔ oz	4 tsp
2.95 kg	3.08 l	Milk	6 lb, 8 oz	3 ¼ qt

Procedure

1. Mix together mashed sweet potatoes, sugar, beaten eggs, cinnamon, mace, nutmeg, and salt.
2. Add milk. Blend.
3. Yield: 8 qt/7.57 l. Pour 1 qt/947 ml of mixture into each of 8 unbaked pie shells that have been brushed with slightly beaten egg white. Bake at 425°F/218°C for 10 minutes; then reduce to 350°F/177°C for 40 minutes, or until a silver knife comes out clean.

Cream Pies

Basic Vanilla Cream Pie
8 Pies (9 in)

Metric		Ingredients	U.S.	
Weight	Volume		Weight	Volume
3.63 kg	3.79 l	Scalded Milk	8 lb	1 gal
283 g	474 ml	Cornstarch	10 oz	2 cups
1.36 kg	1.42 l	Sugar	3 lb	1 ½ qt
	10 ml	Salt	⅓ oz	2 tsp
510 g	474 ml	Egg Yolks, beaten (24 med)	1 lb, 2 oz	2 cups
227 g	237 ml	Butter or Margarine	8 oz	1 cup
28 g	30 ml	Vanilla	1 oz	2 tbsp

Procedure

1. Mix cornstarch, sugar, and salt and gradually stir into scalded milk, stirring constantly until thickened and smooth.
2. Add a little of the hot mixture to beaten egg yolks, stirring; then add egg mixture to hot mixture slowly, stirring. Cook 2 minutes. Remove from heat.
3. Add butter and vanilla. Cool. Pour into cooled baked pastry shell.
4. Yield: 2 ½ cups/592 ml per baked pie shell. Top with meringue.

Note: See Meringue for Pie recipe for use of egg whites.

Variations for Basic Cream Pie

1. Almond Cream—Add ½ tsp/2 ½ ml almond extract to recipe and 1 ½ qt/l.42 l of shaved almonds sprinkled on top of meringue.
2. Blueberry Cream—Fold 2 lb/907 g blueberries, fresh or frozen, into filling.
3. Graham Cracker—Use either of the two graham cracker pie crust recipes.
4. Banana Cream—Slice layer of bananas in baked shell (approx. 1 banana per shell). Cover with cold filling. Top with meringue or whipped cream.
5. Coconut Cream Pie—Add 8 oz/227 g of coconut to the cold filling. Sprinkle another 8 oz/227 g of toasted coconut on meringue before browning.
6. Date Cream Pie—Add 1 ¼ lb/567 g of chopped dates to cold filling.
7. Fruit Topping—Omit meringue and top cream filling with bright colored fruit that has been thickened with cornstarch and sweetened (similar to commercial pie filling).
8. Jam Cream Pie—Spread approximately ½ cup/118 ml jam in each baked pie shell. Cover with cold filling.
9. Pineapple Cream Pie—Add 1 qt/947 ml drained, crushed pineapple to cold filling.

Meringue for Pies

8 Pies (9 in)

Bake, 350°F/177°C, 12–15 min

Metric			U.S.	
Weight	Volume	Ingredients	Weight	Volume
454 g	474 ml	Egg Whites (16 med)	1 lb	2 cups
	7 ½ ml	Cream of Tartar		1 ½ tsp
	5 ml	Salt		1 tsp
454 g	503 ml	Sugar	1 lb	2 ⅛ cups

Procedure

1. Have egg whites at room temperature. This gives maximum volume.
2. Add cream of tartar and salt to egg whites and beat until frothy.
3. Add sugar gradually, beating constantly. Whip egg whites until they are stiff, but not dry, until they stand in peaks that lean over slightly.
4. Spread on pies sealing edges to crust. Bake at 350°F/177°C for 12 to 15 minutes or until golden.

Lemon Meringue Pie

8 pies (9 in)

Bake 350°F/177°C, 12–15 min

Metric			U.S.	
Weight	Volume	Ingredients	Weight	Volume
1.82 kg	2.01 l	Sugar	4 lb	8 ½ cups
340 g	569 ml	Cornstarch	12 oz	2 ⅖ cups
9 g	10 ml	Salt	⅓ oz	2 tsp
2.72 kg	2.84 l	Water, boiling	6 lb	3 qt
57 g	118 ml	Lemon Rind	2 oz	½ cup
340 g	316 ml	Egg Yolks, beaten (16 med)	12 oz	1 ⅓ cups
567 g	592 ml	Lemon Juice	1 lb, 4 oz	2 ½ cups
114 g	118 ml	Butter or Margarine	4 oz	½ cup
		Meringue		
454 g	474 ml	Egg Whites (16 med)	1 lb	2 cups

Procedure

1. Combine sugar, cornstarch, and salt. Add slowly to boiling water and lemon rind, in double boiler. Cook until thick and the cornstarch loses its raw taste, stirring constantly.
2. Add beaten egg yolks gradually, first adding a small amount of the cooked mixture to egg yolks. Cook for about 5 minutes.
3. Remove from heat and add lemon juice and butter or margarine. Let mixture cool slightly before adding lemon juice to lessen chance of hydrolizing cornstarch. Cool the custard.
4. Pour into baked pie shells. Cover with meringue and brown in oven.

Butterscotch Meringue Pie

8 Pies (9 in)

Bake, 350°F/177°C, brown

Metric		Ingredients	U.S.	
Weight	Volume		Weight	Volume
3.63 kg	3.79 l	Milk	8 lb	1 gal
312 g	521 ml	Cornstarch	11 oz	2 1/5 cups
	7 1/2 ml	Soda		1 1/2 tsp
19 g	22 ml	Salt	2/3 oz	1 1/3 tbsp
1.59 kg	2.13 l	Brown Sugar	3 lb, 8 oz	2 1/4 qt
283 g	296 ml	Butter or Margarine	10 oz	1 1/4 cups
756 g	789 ml	Eggs, separated (15 med)	1 lb, 10 2/3 oz	3 1/3 cups
14 g	15 ml	Vanilla	1/2 oz	1 tbsp

Procedure

1. Make a paste of 2 cups/474 ml cold milk and cornstarch. Scald remainder of milk, soda, and salt.
2. Add cornstarch mixture to scalded milk, stirring until thick and smooth and the cornstarch has lost its raw taste.
3. Heat brown sugar and butter in a skillet slowly for 20 minutes or until thick. Then add to above mixture, stirring until smooth.
4. Add a little of hot mixture to beaten egg yolks, stirring. Add egg mixture to hot mixture, stirring until eggs are cooked (for about 5 min). Remove from heat. Add vanilla.
5. Yield: 5 qt/4.74 l. Pour 2 1/2 cups/592 ml of filling into each of 8 baked pie shells. Top with meringue and brown in 350°F/177°C oven.

Persian Butterscotch Pie

8 Pies (9 in)

Metric		Ingredients	U.S.	
Weight	Volume		Weight	Volume
227 g	237 ml	Butter or Margarine	8 oz	1 cup
1.02 kg	1.42 l	Brown Sugar	2 lb, 4 oz	1 1/2 qt
454 g	474 ml	Granulated Sugar	1 lb	2 cups
1.21 kg	1.26 l	Water, hot	2 lb, 10 2/3 oz	5 1/3 cups
1.81 kg	1.89 l	Milk	4 lb	2 qt
189 g	316 ml	Cornstarch	6 2/3 oz	1 1/3 cups
85 g	158 ml	Flour, all-purpose	3 oz	2/3 cup
567 g	592 ml	Eggs, beaten (10 lge)	1 lb, 4 oz	2 1/2 cups
28 g	30 ml	Vanilla	1 oz	2 tbsp

Procedure

1. Combine butter or margarine and brown sugar and cook until well-melted.
2. Brown white sugar until lightly carmelized. Combine with butter or margarine and brown sugar mixture.
3. Stir in water until sugars are dissolved (the carmelized sugar will tend to harden upon adding water—continue stirring until it has dissolved). Add 1 1/2 qt/1.42 l of milk.
4. Blend cornstarch and flour with remaining 2 cups/474 ml of milk and add to sugar mixture. Cook until thick (about 20 minutes).
5. Add a little of the hot mixture to beaten eggs, stirring; then add egg mixture to hot mixture, slowly, stirring. Cook for about 3 minutes.
6. Remove from heat and add vanilla. Cool.
7. Pour filling into 8 baked pie shells. Garnish with whipped cream if desired.

Raisin Meringue Pie

8 Pies (9 in)

Bake, 350°F/177°C, 12–15 min

Metric		Ingredients	U.S.	
Weight	Volume		Weight	Volume
283 g	474 ml	Cornstarch	10 oz	2 cups
681 g	741 ml	Granulated Sugar	1 lb, 8 oz	3 1/8 cups
681 g	947 ml	Brown Sugar	1 lb, 8 oz	1 qt
9 g	10 ml	Salt	1/3 oz	2 tsp
681 g	1.07 l	Raisins	1 lb, 8 oz	4 1/2 cups
	5 ml	Nutmeg		1 tsp
	7 1/2 ml	Cinnamon		1 1/2 tsp
	2 1/2 ml	Cloves		1/2 tsp
340 g	316 ml	Egg Yolks, beaten (16 med)	12 oz	1 1/3 cups
3.63 kg	3.79 l	Buttermilk	8 lb	4 qt
227 g	237 ml	Shortening	8 oz	1 cup
454 g	474 ml	Egg Whites (16 med)	1 lb	2 cups

Procedure

1. Mix cornstarch, sugars, salt, raisins, and spices.
2. Combine beaten egg yolks and buttermilk and add to dry ingredients. Mix well.
3. Cook in double boiler until thick and cornstarch has lost its raw taste, stirring constantly. Remove from heat and add shortening (butter or margarine).
4. Let cool. Yield: 6 qt/5.68 l. Place 3 cups/711 ml of filling in each baked pie shell.
5. Cover with meringue and brown in oven.

Chocolate Cream Pie

8 Pies (9 in)

Bake, 350°F/177°C, Brown

Metric		Ingredients	U.S.	
Weight	Volume		Weight	Volume
3.63 kg	3.79 l	Milk	8 lb	1 gal
1.36 kg	1.50 l	Sugar	3 lb	6 1/3 cups
9 g	10 ml	Salt	1/3 oz	2 tsp
312 g	521 ml	Cornstarch	11 oz	2 1/5 cups
340 g	316 ml	Egg Yolks, beaten (16 med)	12 oz	1 1/3 cups
454 g	474 ml	Chocolate, unsweetened, melted	1 lb	2 cups
28 g	30 ml	Vanilla	1 oz	2 tbsp
454 g	474 ml	Egg Whites (16 med)	1 lb	2 cups

Procedure

1. Scald milk in double boiler.
2. Combine sugar, salt, and cornstarch and add to hot milk. Cook until thick and the cornstarch loses its raw taste, stirring constantly.
3. Add beaten egg yolks to hot mixture gradually, first adding some of hot mixture to egg yolks. Cook 5 minutes.
4. Add melted chocolate and stir well.
5. Remove from heat. Add vanilla. Cool.
6. Yield: 5 1/2 qt/5.22 l. Put 2 3/4 cups/652 ml filling into each baked pie shell.
7. Cover with meringue. Brown in oven.

Chocolate Sundae Pie
8 Pies (9 in)

Metric		Ingredients	U.S.	
Weight	Volume		Weight	Volume
3.63 kg	3.79 l	Milk, scalded	8 lb	1 gal
907 g	1.01 l	Sugar	2 lb	4 ¼ cups
227 g	379 ml	Cornstarch	8 oz	1 ⅗ cups
9 g	10 ml	Salt	⅓ oz	2 tsp
28 g	60 ml	Gelatin	1 oz	4 tbsp
227 g	237 ml	Milk, cold	8 oz	1 cup
340 g	316 ml	Egg Yolks, beaten (16 med)	12 oz	1 ⅓ cups
28 g	30 ml	Vanilla	1 oz	2 tbsp
454 g	474 ml	Egg Whites, beaten (16 med)	1 lb	2 cups
1.36 kg	1.42 l	Whipping Cream	3 lb	1 ½ qt
114 g	237 ml	Chocolate, semi-sweet, shaved	4 oz	1 cup

Procedure

1. Scald milk in double boiler.
2. Combine l lb/454 g of the sugar with cornstarch and salt. Add to scalded milk. Cook until cornstarch loses its raw taste, stirring constantly.
3. Soak gelatin in cold milk.
4. Add beaten egg yolks to hot mixture gradually, first adding a small amount of the hot mixture to egg yolks. Cook for 5 minutes.
5. Remove from heat. Add softened gelatin and vanilla. Cool slightly.
6. Beat egg whites with remaining 1 lb/454 b sugar and fold into slightly cooled mixture.
7. Yield: 7 ½ qt/7.10 l. Pile 3 ¾ cups/889 ml into each baked pie shell. Cover with a layer of whipped cream and sprinkle ½ oz/14 g shaved chocolate on each pie.

Lemon Sponge Pie
8 Pies (9 in)
Bake, 350°F/177°C, 40 min

Metric		Ingredients	U.S.	
Weight	Volume		Weight	Volume
227 g	237 ml	Butter or Margarine	8 oz	1 cup
2.72 kg	3.02 l	Sugar	6 lb	12 ¾ cups
227 g	474 ml	Flour, sifted	8 oz	2 cups
28 g	30 ml	Salt	1 oz	2 tbsp
511 g	474 ml	Egg Yolks, beaten (24 med)	1 lb, 2 oz	2 cups
454 g	474 ml	Lemon Juice	1 lb	2 cups
76 g	118 ml	Lemon Rind	2 ⅔ oz	½ cup
3.18 kg	3.31 l	Milk	7 lb	3 ½ qt
681 g	711 ml	Egg Whites, beaten (24 med)	1 lb, 8 oz	3 cups

Procedure

1. Cream butter or margarine and sugar.
2. Add flour, salt, beaten egg yolks, lemon juice, lemon rind, and milk. Mix well.
3. Fold in beaten egg whites.
4. Yield: 2 ½ gal/9.46 l. Place 5 cups/1.18 l of filling in each unbaked pie shell.
5. Bake at 350°F/177°C for 40 minutes or until silver knife comes out clean.
6. Serve with or without whipped cream.

Lemon Cream Pie
8 Pies (9 in)

Metric		Ingredients	U.S.	
Weight	**Volume**		**Weight**	**Volume**
2.84 kg	2.96 l	Milk	6 lb, 4 oz	3 qt + ½ cup
106 g	178 ml	Lemon Rind, grated	3¾ oz	¾ cup
227 g	379 ml	Cornstarch	8 oz	1⅗ cups
1.14 kg	1.24 l	Sugar	2 lb, 8 oz	5¼ cups
19 g	20 ml	Salt	⅔ oz	1⅓ tbsp
425 g	395 ml	Egg Yolks, beaten (20 med)	15 oz	1⅔ cups
567 g	592 ml	Lemon Juice	1 lb, 4 oz	2½ cups
114 g	118 ml	Butter or Margarine	4 oz	½ cup
567 g	592 ml	Egg Whites (20 med)	1 lb, 4 oz	2½ cups

Procedure

1. Scald milk and lemon rind in double boiler.
2. Blend cornstarch, half of sugar (1¼ lb/567 g), and salt and add to hot mixture, stirring constantly. Cook until cornstarch loses its raw taste.
3. Add beaten egg yolks, first blending with a small amount of hot mixture. Cook for 5 minutes.
4. Remove from heat. Add lemon juice and butter or margarine. Cool in refrigerator.
5. Beat egg whites with remaining 1¼ lb/567 g of sugar and fold into cold mixture. Pour into 8 baked pie shells.
6. Serve plain or with whipped cream, or top with a meringue, and brown in oven.

Maple-Pecan Cream Pie
8 Pies (9 in)

Metric		Ingredients	U.S.	
Weight	**Volume**		**Weight**	**Volume**
3.63 kg	3.79 l	Milk, scalded	8 lb	1 gal
227 g	379 ml	Cornstarch	8 oz	1⅗ cups
907 g	1.01 l	Sugar	2 lb	4¼ cups
14 g	15 ml	Salt	½ oz	1 tbsp
454 g	474 ml	Milk, cold	1 lb	2 cups
28 g	60 ml	Gelatin	1 oz	4 tbsp
368 g	355 ml	Egg Yolks, beaten (18 med)	13 oz	1½ cups
	10 ml	Maple Extract		2 tsp
510 g	533 ml	Egg Whites, beaten (18 med)	1 lb, 2 oz	2¼ cups
227 g	415 ml	Pecans, chopped	8 oz	1¾ cups

Procedure

1. Scald milk in double boiler.
2. Combine cornstarch, 1 lb/454 g of sugar, and salt. Add to scalded milk, stirring constantly until thickened and smooth, and the cornstarch has lost its raw taste.
3. Soak gelatin in cold milk.
4. Add a little of the hot mixture to beaten egg yolks, stirring; then add egg mixture to hot mixture slowly, stirring. Cook for 5 minutes. Remove from heat and add softened gelatin and maple extract. Cool slightly.
5. Beat egg whites with remaining 1 lb/454 g of sugar. Fold into slightly cooled mixture. Cool thoroughly and pour into baked pie shells.
6. Sprinkle each pie with 1 oz/28 g chopped pecans, or cover with whipped cream, and then sprinkle with chopped pecans. Use 1½ qt/1.42 l of whipping cream for 8 pies.

Strawberry Cream Pie
8 Pies (9 in)

Metric		Ingredients	U.S.	
Weight	**Volume**		**Weight**	**Volume**
907 g	1.01 l	Sugar	2 lb	4 ¼ cups
9 g	10 ml	Salt	⅓ oz	2 tsp
227 g	379 ml	Cornstarch	8 oz	1 ⅗ cups
3.63 kg	3.79 l	Milk, scalded	8 lb	1 gal
340 g	316 ml	Egg Yolks, beaten (16 med)	12 oz	1 ⅓ cups
28 g	60 ml	Gelatin	1 oz	4 tbsp
227 g	237 ml	Milk, cold	8 oz	1 cup
28 g	30 ml	Vanilla	1 oz	2 tbsp
1.82 kg	2.84 l	Strawberries, fresh, whole	4 lb	3 qt
		Meringue		
454 g	474 ml	Egg Whites (16 med)	1 lb	2 cups
227 g	711 ml	Coconut, toasted	8 oz	3 cups

Procedure

1. Mix sugar, salt, and cornstarch. Add slowly to scalded milk in double boiler. Cook until cornstarch loses its raw taste, stirring constantly.
2. Add a little of the hot mixture to beaten egg yolks, stirring; then add egg mixture to hot mixture slowly, stirring. Cook for 5 minutes.
3. Soften gelatin in cold milk.
4. Remove hot mixture from heat and add gelatin and vanilla. Cool.
5. Fold in strawberries. Pour in baked pie shells.
6. Cover with meringue and toasted coconut. The meringue may or may not be browned.

Strawberry Ice Cream Pie
8 Pies (9 in)
Bake, 350°F/177°C, Brown

Metric		Ingredients	U.S.	
Weight	**Volume**		**Weight**	**Volume**
3.03 kg	4.74 l	Strawberries	6 lb, 10⅔ oz	5 qt
567 g	889 ml	Powdered Sugar	1 lb, 4 oz	3 ¾ cups
3.41 kg	4.74 l	Ice Cream, vanilla	7 lb, 8 oz	5 qt
907 g	947 ml	Egg Whites (32 med)	2 lb	1 qt
907 g	1.01 l	Sugar	2 lb	4 ¼ cups

Procedure

1. Wash and stem strawberries and cut in half.
2. Spread evenly on the bottom of 8 baked pie shells.
3. Sprinkle 2 ½ oz/71 g of powdered sugar over berries in each shell.
4. Spread with layer of vanilla ice cream.
5. Make meringue of egg whites and granulated sugar.
6. Cover ice cream with meringue and brown quickly in a 350°F/177°C oven. Serve immediately.

Berry Cream Pie
8 Pies (9 in)

| Metric | | Ingredients | U.S. | |
Weight	Volume		Weight	Volume
		Cream Filling		
2.95 kg	3.08 l	Milk	6 lb, 8 oz	3 ¼ qt
793 g	829 ml	Sugar	1 lb, 12 oz	3 ½ cups
227 g	379 ml	Cornstarch	8 oz	1 ⅗ cups
9 g	10 ml	Salt	⅓ oz	2 tsp
57 g	59 ml	Butter or Margarine	2 oz	¼ cup
19 g	20 ml	Vanilla	⅔ oz	1 ⅓ tbsp
		Berry Sauce		
3.18 kg	3.79 l	Fresh Berries (Blueberries, Loganberries, Boysenberries, or Huckleberries)	7 lb	4 qt
907 g	947 ml	Water	2 lb	1 qt
907 g	947 ml	Berry Juice	2 lb	1 qt
114 g	190 ml	Cornstarch	4 oz	⅘ cup
907 g	1.01 l	Sugar	2 lb	4 ¼ cups
9 g	10 ml	Salt	⅓ oz	2 tsp
1.14 kg	1.18 l	Whipping Cream	2 lb, 8 oz	5 cups

Procedure
Cream Filling

1. Scald milk in top of double boiler. Combine sugar, cornstarch, and salt. Add mixed dry ingredients to milk, stirring constantly. Cook until mixture is thick and smooth and there is no starchy flavor. Remove from heat and add butter or margarine and vanilla. Cool thoroughly.
2. Yield: 3 ½ qt/3.31 l. Pour 1 ¾ cups/415 ml into each of 8 baked pie shells.

Berry Sauce

1. Cook berries with 1 qt/947 ml of water until tender. Drain berries. Add enough water to juice to yield 1 qt/947 ml.
2. Combine cornstarch, sugar, and salt. Add dry ingredients to fruit juice, stirring constantly. Cook until mixture is thick and smooth. Remove from heat and cool thoroughly. Add fruit.
3. Yield: 4 qt/3.79 l. Pour 2 cups/474 ml of the berry sauce over cream filling in each pie shell.
4. Whip cream and spread on top.

Note: Frozen or canned berries may be used.

Toasted Coconut Cream Pie

8 Pies (9 in)

Bake, 350°F/177°C, 12–15 min

Metric		Ingredients	U.S.	
Weight	Volume		Weight	Volume
28 g	60 ml	Gelatin	1 oz	4 tbsp
227 g	237 ml	Milk, cold	8 oz	1 cup
3.63 kg	3.79 l	Milk, scalded	8 lb	1 gal
9 g	10 ml	Salt	⅓ oz	2 tsp
567 g	632 ml	Sugar	1 lb, 4 oz	2 ⅔ cups
227 g	379 ml	Cornstarch	8 oz	1 ⅗ cups
425 g	395 ml	Egg Yolks, beaten (20 med)	15 oz	1 ⅔ cups
454 g	1.42 l	Coconut, toasted	1 lb	1 ½ qt
567 g	592 ml	Egg whites (20 med)	1 lb, 4 oz	2 ½ cups

Procedure

1. Soften gelatin in 1 cup/237 ml of cold milk.
2. Combine salt, sugar, and cornstarch. Add to scalded milk, stirring constantly until thickened and smooth and the cornstarch has lost its raw taste.
3. Add a little of the hot mixture to beaten egg yolks, stirring; then add egg mixture to hot mixture slowly, stirring. Cook for 5 minutes. Remove from heat and add softened gelatin. Stir until dissolved. Add 8 oz/ 227 g of the toasted coconut. To toast coconut, place in a moderate oven 350°F/177°C. Watch carefully and toss with fork to brown evenly.
4. Yield: 5 qt/4.74 l. Place 2 ½ cups/592 ml of filling in each baked pie shell. Cover with meringue and sprinkle remainder of toasted coconut on meringue. Meringue may or may not be browned.

Sour Cream Raisin Pie

8 Pies (9 in)

Bake, 350°F/177°C, Brown

Metric		Ingredients	U.S.	
Weight	Volume		Weight	Volume
2.72 kg	2.84 l	Sour Cream	6 lb	3 qt
1.02 kg	1.07 l	Sour Milk or Buttermilk	2 lb, 4 oz	4 ½ cups
907 g	1.42 l	Raisins	2 lb	1 ½ qt
340 g	316 ml	Egg Yolks, beaten (16 med)	12 oz	1 ⅓ cups
227 g	379 ml	Cornstarch	8 oz	1 ⅗ cups
	5 ml	Nutmeg		1 tsp
	10 ml	Cinnamon		2 tsp
	2 ½ ml	Cloves		½ tsp
114 g	118 ml	Lemon Juice	4 oz	½ cup
9 g	10 ml	Salt	⅓ oz	2 tsp
2.27 kg	2.49 l	Sugar	5 lb	10 ½ cups
454 g	474 ml	Egg Whites (16 med)	1 lb	2 cups

Procedure

1. Mix all ingredients except for egg whites and cook to custard-like consistency in double boiler, stirring constantly.
2. Yield: 6 qt/5.68 l. Cool and place 3 cups/711 ml of filling in each of 8 baked pie shells.
3. Cover with meringue and brown in oven.

Chiffon Pies

Lemon Chiffon Pie
8 Pies (9 in)

| Metric | | Ingredients | U.S. | |
Weight	Volume		Weight	Volume
43 g	60 ml	Gelatin	1 ½ oz	6 tbsp
227 g	237 ml	Water, cold	8 oz	1 cup
28 g	30 ml	Sugar	1 oz	2 tbsp
28 g	45 ml	Lemon Rind, grated	1 oz	3 tbsp
114 g	118 ml	Water	4 oz	½ cup
596 g	553 ml	Egg Yolks (28 med)	1 lb, 5 oz	2 ⅓ cups
340 g	355 ml	Lemon Juice	12 oz	1 ½ cups
681 g	1.21 l	Sugar	1 lb, 8 oz	5 ⅛ cups
793 g	829 ml	Egg Whites (28 med)	1 lb, 12 oz	3 ½ cups
454 g	474 ml	Sugar	1 lb	2 cups
1.36 kg	1.42 l	Whipping Cream	3 lb	1 ½ qt
114 g	178 ml	Powdered Sugar	4 oz	¾ cup
	5 ml	Vanilla		1 tsp

Procedure

1. Soften gelatin in 1 cup of cold water.
2. Boil the 2 tbsp/28 g of sugar, grated lemon rind, and water, to make a syrup.
3. Beat egg yolks in double boiler and gradually add lemon juice, syrup, and 1 ½ lb/681 g of sugar, beating until mixture starts to thicken. Remove from heat and add softened gelatin. Stir until dissolved. Put in refrigerator to cool.
4. Beat egg whites until they begin to peak. Slowly add 1 lb/454 g of sugar, beating until stiff but moist.
5. When gelatin mixture is slightly thickened, fold in the egg white mixture.
6. Whip cream, adding powdered sugar and vanilla. Fold into lemon chiffon filling.
7. Pile into 8 baked shells. Place in refrigerator to set.
8. Whipped cream may be piled on top instead of folded in, if desired.

Maple Nut Pie
8 Pies (9 in)

| Metric | | Ingredients | U.S. | |
Weight	Volume		Weight	Volume
425 g	711 ml	Cornstarch	15 oz	3 cups
	3 ¾ ml	Salt		¾ tsp
1.28 kg	1.78 l	Brown Sugar	2 lb, 13 oz	7 ½ cups
2.72 kg	2.84 l	Water, boiling	6 lb	3 qt
397 g	415 ml	Egg Whites, stiffly beaten (14 med)	14 oz	1 ¾ cups
	3 ¾ ml	Maple Flavoring		¾ tsp
340 g	711 ml	Walnuts, chopped	12 oz	3 cups

Procedure

1. Combine cornstarch, salt, and brown sugar. Add slowly to boiling water, stirring constantly until mixture is thick and clear.
2. Fold into stiffly beaten egg whites. Add maple flavoring and nuts.
3. Pour into 8 baked crusts and chill.

Ambrosia Chiffon Pie
8 Pies (9 in)

| Metric | | Ingredients | U.S. | |
Weight	Volume		Weight	Volume
737 g	770 ml	Orange-flavored Gelatin	1 lb, 10 oz	3 ¼ cups
907 g	947 ml	Water, boiling	2 lb	1 qt
9 g	10 ml	Salt	⅓ oz	2 tsp
	5 ml	Orange Rind, grated		1 tsp
510 g	474 ml	Egg Yolks (24 med)	1 lb, 2 oz	2 cups
1.14 kg	1.24 l	Sugar	2 lb, 8 oz	5 ¼ cups
1.36 kg	1.42 l	Orange Juice	3 lb	1 ½ qt
227 g	237 ml	Lemon Juice	8 oz	1 cup
681 g	711 ml	Egg Whites (24 med)	1 lb, 8 oz	3 cups
340 g	1.07 l	Shredded Coconut	12 oz	4 ½ cups

Procedure

1. Dissolve gelatin in boiling water and add salt and orange rind.
2. Beat the egg yolks with 1 ¼ lb/567 g of sugar. Add gelatin mixture. Place in double boiler. Cook until eggs thicken mixture, stirring constantly. Remove from heat.
3. Add orange and lemon juice. Cool in refrigerator until partly thickened.
4. Beat egg whites gradually. Add remaining 1 ¼ lb/ 567 g of sugar and fold into thickened mixture.
5. The coconut may either be folded into the cold mixture at the same time that the egg whites are folded in, or it may be sprinkled on top.
6. Pile the mixture into 8 baked pie shells (9 in). Allow to set. Serve with or without whipped cream.

Pumpkin Chiffon Pie
8 Pies (9 in)

| Metric | | Ingredients | U.S. | |
Weight	Volume		Weight	Volume
1.25 kg	1.66 l	Brown Sugar	2 lb, 12 oz	1 ¾ qt
511 g	474 ml	Egg Yolks, beaten (24 med)	1 lb, 2 oz	2 cups
2.04 kg	2.60 l	Pumpkin, cooked	4 lb, 8 oz	2 ¾ qt
28 g	60 ml	Cinnamon	1 oz	4 tbsp
	10 ml	Ginger		2 tsp
	5 ml	Mace		1 tsp
9 g	10 ml	Salt	⅓ oz	2 tsp
57 g	120 ml	Gelatin	2 oz	8 tbsp
454 g	474 ml	Water	1 lb	2 cups
14 g	15 ml	Vanilla	½ oz	1 tbsp
681 g	711 ml	Egg Whites (24 med)	1 lb, 8 oz	3 cups
340 g	355 ml	Granulated Sugar	12 oz	1 ½ cups

Procedure

1. Combine brown sugar, egg yolks, pumpkin, spices, and salt. Cook in double boiler until thick.
2. Remove from heat and add gelatin that has been softened in water. Add vanilla. Cool in refrigerator until slightly thick.
3. Beat egg whites, gradually adding granulated sugar. Fold into the chilled pumpkin mixture.
4. Pour into 8 baked pie shells, and serve with or without whipped cream.

Banana Chiffon Pie

8 Pies (9 in)

Metric		Ingredients	U.S.	
Weight	Volume		Weight	Volume
57 g	120 ml	Gelatin	2 oz	8 tbsp
907 g	947 ml	Water	2 lb	1 qt
1.82 kg	1.89 l	Bananas, mashed	4 lb	2 qt
114 g	118 ml	Lemon Juice	4 oz	½ cup
38 g	60 ml	Lemon Rind	1 ⅓ oz	4 tbsp
9 g	10 ml	Salt	⅓ oz	2 tsp
907 g	1.01 l	Sugar	2 lb	4 ¼ cups
510 g	474 ml	Egg Yolks, beaten (24 med)	1 lb, 2 oz	2 cups
681 g	711 ml	Egg Whites (24 med)	1 lb, 8 oz	3 cups

Procedure

1. Soak gelatin in 2 cups/474 ml of water.
2. Cook remaining 2 cups/474 ml of water, bananas, lemon juice, lemon rind, salt, sugar, and beaten egg yolks until a soft custard is formed, stirring constantly.
3. Remove from heat. Add softened gelatin and cool until thick, but not set.
4. Beat egg whites until stiff but moist, and fold into banana mixture. Pile mixture into baked pie shells and chill.
5. Serve with or without whipped cream.

Chocolate Chiffon Pie

8 Pies (9 in)

Metric		Ingredients	U.S.	
Weight	Volume		Weight	Volume
57 g	118 ml	Gelatin, granulated	2 oz	½ cup
907 g	1.01 l	Sugar	2 lb	4 ¼ cups
5 g	1 tsp	Salt		1 tsp
170 g	355 ml	Milk, nonfat dry	6 oz	1 ½ cups
170 g	158 ml	Egg Yolks, slightly beaten (8 med)	6 oz	⅔ cup
1.36 kg	1.42 l	Water, cool	3 lb	1 ½ qt
907 g	1.26 l	Chocolate, semi-sweet pieces	2 lb	5 ⅓ cups
114 g	118 ml	Margarine	4 oz	½ cup
28 g	30 ml	Vanilla	1 oz	2 tbsp
1.81 kg	2.84 l	Whipped Topping, non-dairy	4 lb	3 qt

Procedure

1. Combine gelatin, sugar, salt, and milk and mix thoroughly in a sauce pan.
2. Combine egg yolks and water and stir into dry ingredients. Blend thoroughly.
3. Heat slowly over low heat. Add chocolate pieces. Stir, until melted.
4. Remove from heat and add margarine and vanilla. Beat in mixer or with rotary beater until smooth. Cool until moderately thickened.
5. Fold mixture into non-dairy topping, whipped until stiff. (Beat at low speed.)
6. Scale approximately 1 lb, 8 oz/681 g into each pie shell.

Note: Use chocolate wafer crumb crust and top with whipped cream topping and nuts or shaved chocolate.

Strawberry Chiffon Pie
8 Pies (9 in)

Metric		Ingredients	U.S.	
Weight	Volume		Weight	Volume
2.42 kg	3.79 l	Strawberries, fresh	5 lb, 5 ⅓ oz	4 qt
1.14 kg	1.24 l	Sugar	2 lb, 8 oz	5 ¼ cups
737 g	770 ml	Strawberry Gelatin	1 lb, 10 oz	3 ¼ cups
1.36 kg	1.42 l	Water, hot	3 lb	1 ½ qt
114 g	118 ml	Lemon Juice	4 oz	½ cup
9 g	10 ml	Salt	⅓ oz	2 tsp
454 g	474 ml	Egg Whites (16 med)	1 lb	2 cups
454 g	474 ml	Whipping Cream	1 lb	2 cups

Procedure

1. Crush strawberries with 2 lb/907 g of sugar.
2. Dissolve gelatin in boiling water. Cool slightly and add to strawberries. Add lemon juice and salt. Cool in refrigerator until partly thick.
3. Beat egg whites. Add 8 oz/227 g of sugar gradually. Fold into slightly thickened mixture.
4. Whip cream and fold into mixture.
5. Pour into 8 baked pie shells, and serve with or without whipped cream.

Pineapple Chiffon Pie
8 Pies (9 in)

Metric		Ingredients	U.S.	
Weight	Volume		Weight	Volume
43 g	60 ml	Gelatin	1 ½ oz	6 tbsp
227 g	237 ml	Water, cold	8 oz	1 cup
511 g	474 ml	Egg Yolks (24 med)	1 lb, 2 oz	2 cups
681 g	711 ml	Pineapple Juice	1 lb, 8 oz	3 cups
681 g	741 ml	Sugar	1 lb, 8 oz	3 ⅛ cups
14 g	15 ml	Salt	½ oz	1 tbsp
907 g	947 ml	Pineapple, diced	2 lb	1 qt
681 g	711 ml	Egg Whites (24 med)	1 lb, 8 oz	3 cups

Procedure

1. Soften gelatin in cold water.
2. Beat egg yolks in double boiler, gradually adding pineapple juice, ½ lb/227 g of the sugar, and the salt. Beat until the mixture begins to thicken. Remove from heat. Add softened gelatin and stir until dissolved. Stir in diced pineapple and cool in refrigerator until slightly thick.
3. Beat egg whites until they begin to peak, then slowly add 1 lb/454 g of sugar, beating until stiff but moist. When pineapple mixture is slightly thick, fold in egg-white mixture.
4. Pile into eight baked pie shells. Let cool until set.
5. Serve with or without whipped cream.

Frozen Pies

Sponge Cake Lining for Frozen Pies
8 Pies (9 in)
Bake, 500°F/260°C, 8–10 min

Metric		Ingredients	U.S.	
Weight	Volume		Weight	Volume
510 g	533 ml	Eggs, separated (9 lge)	1 lb, 2 oz	2 ¼ cups
283 g	296 ml	Sugar	10 oz	1 ¼ cups
283 g	592 ml	Flour, cake	10 oz	2 ½ cups
	5 ml	Salt		1 tsp

Procedure

1. Beat egg yolks in mixer slowly. Add 5 oz/142 g of sugar. Beat for 10 minutes, or until thick and lemon colored. Remove from mixer.
2. Fold in sifted cake flour gradually and lightly.
3. Add salt to egg whites and beat until they first begin to peak; then slowly add remaining 5 oz/142 g of sugar. Beat until stiff but moist. Fold in egg yolk mixture.
4. Pencil off 8 circles, 9 inches in diameter, on brown paper. Placed paper on large baking sheets.
5. Spread circles with sponge mixture, smoothly and evenly.
6. Bake quickly at 500°F/260°C for 8 to 10 minutes.
7. Remove from oven and immediately peel off paper and shape in 9-inch pie pans. If crust cools too much before placing in pie pans, reheat briefly in oven.

Frozen Pie Base
8 Pies (9 in)

Metric		Ingredients	U.S.	
Weight	Volume		Weight	Volume
756 g	789 ml	Eggs (15 med)	1 lb, 10 ⅔ oz	3 ⅓ cups
681 g	741 ml	Sugar	1 lb, 8 oz	3 ⅛ cups
21 g	45 ml	Gelatin	¾ oz	3 tbsp
114 g	118 ml	Water, cold	4 oz	½ cup
2.50 kg	2.60 l	Whipping cream, whipped	5 lb, 8 oz	2 ¾ qt
454 g	829 ml	Powdered Sugar	1 lb	3 ½ cups

Procedure

1. Whip eggs with granulated sugar in a double boiler over boiling water, 15 to 20 minutes, or until eggs are partly cooked and mixture is light.
2. Beat mixture on machine at medium speed until cold (about 20 to 30 min).
3. Soak gelatin in ½ cup/118 ml cold water; then dissolve over hot water. Add to mixture.
4. Add flavoring desired, as suggested under the following variations.
5. Combine with whipped cream, sweetened with powdered sugar.
6. Fill sponge cake pie crusts and place in freezing chamber overnight or until frozen.

Flavoring Variations

Vanilla: Increase whipping cream to 3 qt/2.84 l and add 2 tbsp/30 ml vanilla.
Chocolate Chip: Fold in 12 oz/340 g chocolate chips.

Chocolate: Add 1 pint/474 ml chocolate syrup. After filling pie pans, sprinkle with 8 oz/227 g chocolate shavings; then place in freezing chamber.

Metric		Ingredients	U.S.	
Weight	Volume		Weight	Volume

Eggnog

Metric Weight	Metric Volume	Ingredients	U.S. Weight	U.S. Volume
114 g	118 ml	Lemon Juice	4 oz	½ cup
114 g	118 ml	Brandy	4 oz	½ cup
14 g	15 ml	Rum Flavoring	½ oz	1 tbsp
	12 ½ ml	Nutmeg, grated		2 ½ tsp

Note: Add lemon juice when whipping eggs and sugar. While stirring in gelatin, add the brandy and the rum flavoring. After filling pie pans, sprinkle with nutmeg before placing in freezing chamber.

Lemon

Metric Weight	Metric Volume	Ingredients	U.S. Weight	U.S. Volume
38 g	60 ml	Lemon Rind, grated	1 ⅓ oz	4 tbsp
28 g	30 ml	Sugar	1 oz	2 tbsp
114 g	118 ml	Water	4 oz	½ cup
454 g	474 ml	Lemon Juice	1 lb	2 cups

Note: Boil down lemon rind with sugar and water to make a syrup. Add lemon syrup when whipping eggs and sugar.

Maple Nut

Metric Weight	Metric Volume	Ingredients	U.S. Weight	U.S. Volume
	10 ml	Maple Extract		2 tsp
	5 ml	Vanilla		1 tsp
340 g	711 ml	Nuts, chopped	12 oz	3 cups

Note: Add the flavorings when whipping eggs and sugar. Stir in gelatin, combined with 8 oz/227 g of the chopped nuts. After filling pie pans, sprinkle with remaining chopped nuts before placing in freezing chamber.

Mocha

Metric Weight	Metric Volume	Ingredients	U.S. Weight	U.S. Volume
114 g	118 ml	Fresh Coffee	4 oz	½ cup
7 g	8 ml	Vanilla	¼ oz	1 ½ tsp
340 g	355 ml	Water	12 oz	1 ½ cups

Note: Boil down coffee, vanilla, and water. Strain. (This should give about 1 cup/237 ml of extract.) Add the coffee extract when whipping eggs and sugar.

Orange

Metric Weight	Metric Volume	Ingredients	U.S. Weight	U.S. Volume
38 g	60 ml	Orange Rind, grated	1 ⅓ oz	4 tbsp
28 g	30 ml	Sugar	1 oz	2 tbsp
114 g	118 ml	Water	4 oz	½ cup
454 g	474 ml	Orange Juice	1 lb	2 cups
114 g	118 ml	Lemon Juice	4 oz	½ cup

Note: Boil down the orange rind with sugar and water to make a syrup. Add orange juice, lemon juice, and orange syrup when whipping eggs and sugar.

Peach

Metric Weight	Metric Volume	Ingredients	U.S. Weight	U.S. Volume
907 g	947 ml	Peach Pulp	2 lb	1 qt
28 g	30 ml	Sugar	1 oz	2 tbsp
	1 ¼ ml	Almond Extract		¼ tsp

Note: Pass peaches through coarse sieve or chop fine. Add sugar. Add peach pulp, almond extract, and dissolved gelatin to the cold egg and sugar mixture.

Strawberry

Metric Weight	Metric Volume	Ingredients	U.S. Weight	U.S. Volume
907 g	947 ml	Fresh Strawberry Pulp	2 lb	1 qt (2 ½ qt fresh berries)
28 g	30 ml	Sugar	1 oz	2 tbsp
57 g	59 ml	Lemon Juice	2 oz	¼ cup

Note: Use fresh or frozen strawberries. Crush. Add strawberry pulp, lemon juice, and dissolved gelatin to the cold egg and sugar mixture.

Metric		Ingredients	U.S.	
Weight	**Volume**		**Weight**	**Volume**
		Tutti-Fruiti		
114 g	118 ml	Candied Cherries, chopped	4 oz	½ cup
57 g	59 ml	Candied Pineapple, chopped	2 oz	¼ cup
57 g	79 ml	Almond, toasted, chopped	2 oz	⅓ cup
28 g	30 ml	Pistachio Nuts, chopped	1 oz	2 tbsp
	1 ½ tsp	Rum Extract		1 ½ tsp
		Sprinkle Mixture		
142 g	158 ml	Candied Cherries, chopped	5 oz	⅔ cup
85 g	118 ml	Almonds, toasted, chopped	3 oz	½ cup
85 g	118 ml	Pistachio Nuts, chopped	3 oz	½ cup

Note: While stirring in gelatin, add fruits and nuts that have been marinated in rum extract. After filling pie pans, sprinkle top with sprinkle mixture before placing in freezing chamber.

Cheese Cakes and Pies

Three-Step Cheese Cake
6 Cakes (9 in)
Bake, 300°F/149°C, 20–25 min

Metric		Ingredients	U.S.		
Weight	**Volume**		**Weight**		**Volume**
1.08 kg	96 crackers	Graham crackers	2 lb,	6 oz	96 crackers
298 g	355 ml	Butter or Margarine, melted		10 ½ oz	1 ½ cups
511 g	533 ml	Cream Cheese	1 lb,	2 oz	2 ¼ cups
681 g	711 ml	Eggs, slightly beaten (12 lge)	1 lb,	8 oz	3 cups
681 g	711 ml	Sugar	1 lb,	8 oz	3 cups
28 g	30 ml	Vanilla		1 oz	2 tbsp
	1 ¼ ml	Salt			¼ tsp
1.36 kg	1.42 l	Sour Cream, thick	3 lb		1 ½ qt
170 g	178 ml	Sugar		6 oz	¾ cup
14 g	15 ml	Vanilla		½ oz	1 tbsp

Procedure

1. Grind graham crackers and mix with butter or margarine. Pat 4⅔ oz/132 g into bottom and sides of 6 pie pans (9 in). Bake shells at 350°F/177°C for 5 minutes. Cool.
2. Mash cream cheese to soften. Blend with eggs (low then medium speed) until smooth. Add sugar, vanilla, and salt.
3. Pour into shells. Bake at 300°F/149°C for 15 minutes. Cool for 4 minutes.
4. Blend sour cream, sugar, and vanilla until smooth. Divide evenly and spread over tops of cheese cakes.
5. Bake for 5 minutes at 300°F/149°C. Cool. Chill in refrigerator for 24 hours or overnight.

Cheese Cake with Berry Glaze

6 Cakes (9 in)
Bake, 350°F/177°C, 20 min
400°F/205°C, 8 min

Metric		Ingredients	U.S.	
Weight	Volume		Weight	Volume
1.02 kg	115 crackers	Graham Crackers, crushed	2 lb, 4 oz	115 crackers
170 g	178 ml	Sugar	6 oz	¾ cup
340 g	355 ml	Butter or Margarine, melted	12 oz	1 ½ cups
2.04 kg	2.13 l	Cream Cheese	4 lb, 8 oz	2 ¼ qt
681 g	711 ml	Sugar	1 lb, 8 oz	3 cups
14 g	15 ml	Vanilla	½ oz	1 tbsp
14 g	15 ml	Lemon Juice	½ oz	1 tbsp
681 g	711 ml	Eggs, well-beaten (12 lge)	1 lb, 8 oz	3 cups
2.04 kg	2.13 l	Sour Cream, thick cultured	4 lb, 8 oz	2 ¼ qt
170 g	178 ml	Sugar	6 oz	¾ cup
14 g	15 ml	Vanilla	½ oz	1 tbsp
340 g	355 ml	Egg Whites (12 lge)	12 oz	1 ½ cups

Procedure

1. Blend graham cracker crumbs, sugar, and melted butter or margarine.
2. Pat mixture into sides and bottom of six 9-inch pie pans.
3. Blend well cream cheese (at room temperature) with the 3 cups/711 ml sugar, 1 tbsp/15 ml vanilla, and lemon juice.
4. Pour eggs into cream cheese mixture, and stir until well-blended and smooth. Divide the mixture into crumb-lined pans. Bake in moderate oven (350°F/177°C) for 20 minutes.

5. While cheese cake is baking, mix sour cream with ¾ cup/178 ml sugar, and 1 tbsp/15 ml of vanilla. Just before removing pan from oven, beat egg whites until stiff and fold into sour cream mixture.
6. Spread over top of hot cheese cake. Return to hot oven (400°F/205°C) and continue baking 8 minutes or until topping is set. Cool. Cover with strawberry or raspberry glaze.

Berry Glaze

2.72 kg	4.26 l	Strawberries or Raspberries, fresh	6 lb	4 ½ qt
1.36 kg	1.42 l	Sugar	3 lb	1 ½ qt
212 g	355 ml	Cornstarch	7 ½ oz	1 ½ cups
14 g	15 ml	Lemon Juice	½ oz	1 tbsp

Procedure

1. Clean berries and crush until slightly juicy.
2. Blend sugar and cornstarch and add to crushed berries. Heat, stirring constantly and cook until thickened. Remove from heat and stir in lemon juice.

3. Cool and spoon berry mixture over top of cheese cakes. Chill until set.

Zwieback Crust for Cheese Cake
50 Servings

| Metric | | Ingredients | U.S. | |
Weight	Volume		Weight	Volume
454 g	632 ml	Brown Sugar	1 lb	2 ⅔ cups
	10 ml	Cinnamon		2 tsp
454 g	1.42 l	Zwieback, ground	1 lb	1 ½ qt
198 g	237 ml	Butter or Margarine, melted	7 oz	1 cup

Procedure

1. Combine brown sugar and cinnamon. Add to zwieback crumbs and mix.
2. Add melted shortening and blend thoroughly.
3. Yield: 2 ½ lb/1.14 kg. Line 2 pans (12 × 20 × 2 in and 10 × 12 × 2 in). Fill with cheese cake mixture or cover bottom of each of 8 deep cake pans with 5 oz/142 g of the mixture.

Cottage Cheese Pie, No. 1
8 Pies (9 in)

| Metric | | Ingredients | U.S. | |
Weight	Volume		Weight	Volume
397 g	415 ml	Eggs, separated (7 lge)	14 oz	1 ¾ cups
454 g	474 ml	Sugar	1 lb	2 cups
9 g	10 ml	Salt	⅓ oz	2 tsp
454 g	474 ml	Milk	1 lb	2 cups
57 g	118 ml	Gelatin	2 oz	½ cup
454 g	474 ml	Water, cold	1 lb	2 cups
1.82 kg	1.89 l	Cottage Cheese	4 lb	2 qt
156 g	158 ml	Lemon Juice	5 ½ oz	⅔ cup
14 g	20 ml	Lemon Rind	½ oz	4 tsp
907 g	947 ml	Whipping Cream	2 lb	1 qt
595 g	947 ml	Powdered Sugar	1 lb, 5 oz	1 qt
19 g	20 ml	Vanilla	⅔ oz	4 tsp
907 g	1.89 l	Graham Crackers, crushed	2 lb	2 qt
454 g	532 ml	Butter or Margarine, melted	1 lb	2 ¼ cups
227 g	237 ml	Sugar	8 oz	1 cup
9 g	20 ml	Cinnamon	⅓ oz	4 tsp

Procedure

1. Beat egg yolks slightly.
2. Combine sugar, salt, and milk and heat in double boiler. Add egg yolks by first adding a small portion of hot mixture to yolks, stirring. Cook until of custard consistency (so that mixture coats a spoon).
3. Soak gelatin in cold water and add to hot custard, stirring until dissolved. Add cottage cheese, lemon juice, and rind. Cool.
4. Whip cream and fold into above mixture when it begins to thicken. Beat egg whites until they peak; then add powdered sugar and vanilla. Beat until stiff but not dry. Fold in.
5. Yield: 6 qt/5.68 l.
6. Combine cracker crumbs, butter or margarine, sugar, and cinnamon. Mix well.
7. Yield: 3 qt/2.84 l. Line 9-inch pie tins with 6 oz/170 g of crumb mixture, pressing down firmly. Pour 3 cups/711 ml of filling into each crust. Sprinkle tops with remaining crumbs.
8. Chill thoroughly, preferably overnight.

Note: If non-dairy, whipped topping is used that is sweetened, reduce amount of powdered sugar about one-third.

Cottage Cheese Pie, No. 2

8 Pies (9 in)

Bake, 325°F/163°C, 1 hr

Metric		Ingredients	U.S.	
Weight	Volume		Weight	Volume
1.82 kg	2.01 l	Sugar	4 lb	8 ½ cups
99 g	207 ml	Flour, all-purpose	3 ½ oz	⅞ cup
3.63 kg	3.79 l	Cottage Cheese, cream style, ground and whipped	8 lb	4 qt
605 g	632 ml	Cream	1 lb, 5 ⅓ oz	2 ⅔ cups
1.36 kg	1.42 l	Eggs, slightly beaten (24 lge)	3 lb	1 ½ qt
37 g	40 ml	Vanilla	1 ⅓ oz	2 ⅔ tbsp
14 g	15 ml	Salt	½ oz	1 tbsp
302 g	316 ml	Lemon Juice	10 ⅔ oz	1 ⅓ cup

Procedure

1. Sift sugar and flour together and add to whipped cottage cheese.
2. Add cream, eggs, vanilla, salt, and lemon juice.
3. Yield: 7 ½ qt/7.10 l. Pour 3 ¾ cups/889 ml of mixture into each of 8 zwieback pie crusts.
4. Bake at 325°F/163°C for 1 hour or until silver knife comes out clean.

Cottage Cheese Cake

50 Servings (2 ½ oz/71 g)

Bake, 350°F/177°C, 1–1 ¼ hrs

Metric		Ingredients	U.S.	
Weight	Volume		Weight	Volume
2.04 kg	2.13 l	Cottage Cheese, cream style, ground	4 lb, 8 oz	2 ¼ qt
198 g	415 ml	Flour, all-purpose	7 oz	1 ¾ cups
793 g	869 ml	Sugar	1 lb, 12 oz	3 ⅔ cups
9 g	10 ml	Salt	⅓ oz	2 tsp
397 g	355 ml	Egg Yolks, beaten (18 med)	14 oz	1 ½ cups
1.02 kg	1.07 l	Milk	2 lb, 4 oz	4 ½ cups
28 g	30 ml	Vanilla	1 oz	2 tbsp
511 g	533 ml	Egg Whites (18 med)	1 lb, 2 oz	2 ¼ cups
227 g	237 ml	Sugar	8 oz	1 cup

Procedure

1. Mix cottage cheese and flour. Add 1 ¾ lb/793 g of sugar and blend. Add salt and beaten egg yolks. Mix well.
2. Add milk and vanilla and blend well.
3. Beat egg whites with ½ lb/227 g of sugar and fold in.
4. Yield: 11 lb, 2 oz/5.05 kg.
5. Place in pans (12 × 20 × 2 in and 10 × 12 × 2 in) that have a zwieback or pastry lining, or in 8 deep cake pans.
6. Bake at 350°F/177°C for 1 to 1 ¼ hours.

Tarts

Blueberry Tarts
48 Tarts (½ cup/118 ml)

| Metric | | Ingredients | U.S. | |
Weight	Volume		Weight	Volume
106 g	178 ml	Cornstarch	3¾ oz	¾ cup
907 g	947 ml	Sugar	2 lb	1 qt
907 g	947 ml	Water, boiling	2 lb	1 qt
3.06 kg	5.68 l	Blueberries, fresh or frozen	6 lb, 12 oz	6 qt
114 g	118 ml	Butter or Margarine	4 oz	½ cup
681 g	711 ml	Cream Cheese	1 lb, 8 oz	3 cups
907 g	711 ml	Almond Paste	2 lb	3 cups
	48 shells	Pastry Tart Shells, baked, ½ cup/118 ml capacity		48 shells

Procedure

1. Combine cornstarch and sugar. Stir into boiling water. Cook and stir until thickened. Add blueberries and butter. Continue cooking until thoroughly heated and butter has melted. Remove from heat.

2. Blend cream cheese and almond paste and spread a heaping tbsp/15 ml of the mixture in the bottom of each tart shell. Top with the blueberries. Chill. Garnish with whipped cream or whipped topping.

Date Tarts
50 Tarts

| Metric | | Ingredients | U.S. | |
Weight	Volume		Weight	Volume
1.02 kg	1.42 l	Brown Sugar	2 lb, 4 oz	6 cups
340 g	355 ml	Margarine or Butter	12 oz	1½ cups
340 g	711 ml	Nuts (Walnuts)	12 oz	3 cups
907 g	1.42 l	Dates	2 lb	1½ qt
114 g	118 ml	Lemon Juice	4 oz	½ cup
340 g	355 ml	Eggs, beaten (6 lge)	12 oz	1½ cups
	50 shells	Pastry Tart Shells, baked		50 shells

Procedure

1. Cook brown sugar and butter or margarine for a few minutes, using low heat.
2. Add nuts and dates. Reheat.
3. Add a little of hot mixture to beaten eggs, stirring, then add egg mixture to hot mixture. Cook slowly until thickened (about 5 min). Cool. Add lemon juice.

4. Yield: 2½ qt/2.37 l. Fill 50 baked tart shells, using a No. 20 scoop.

Note: These are rich.

APPENDIX

Table A–1
Approximate Equivalents in Metric and U.S.
Measures of Weight

grams	ounces	pounds	kilograms	ounces	pounds
1	.035		.756	26.67	1 ⅔
5	.175		.793	28	1 ¾
15	.525		.832	29.33	1 ⅚
28.35	1	¹⁄₁₆	.850	30	
43	1.5		.907	32	2
57	2	⅛	.964	34	2 ⅛
71	2.5		1.000	35.28	2.2
76	2.67	⅙	1.020	36	2 ¼
85	3		1.135	40	2 ½
114	4	¼	1.25	44	2 ¾
128	4.5		1.36	48	3
142	5		1.59	56	3 ½
151	5.33	⅓	1.81	64	4
170	6		2.04	72	4 ½
198	7		2.27	80	5
227	8	½	2.50	88	5 ½
255	9		2.72	96	6
283	10		2.95	104	6 ½
302	10.67	⅔	3.18	112	7
312	11		3.63	128	8
340	12	¾	4.08	144	9
368	13		4.54	160	10
378	13.33	⅚	5.44	192	12
397	14		5.90	208	13
425	15		6.35	224	14
454	16	1	7.26	256	16
510	18	1 ⅛	8.17	288	18
529	18.67	1 ⅙	9.07	320	20
567	20	1 ¼	10.89	384	24
605	21.33	1 ⅓	12.70	448	28
623	22		13.60	480	30
681	24	1 ½	14.51	512	32
737	26		18.14	640	40

Table A–2
Approximate Equivalents in Metric and U.S.
Measures of Volume

milliliters			cups	quarts	liters	cups	quarts	gallons
5	= 1 tsp	= 1/48			.947	4	1	1/4
15	= 1 tbsp	= 1/16			1.07	4 1/2	1 1/8	
30	= 2 tbsp	= 1/8			1.18	5	1 1/4	
59.2			1/4	1/16	1.42	6	1 1/2	
78.9			1/3		1.66	7	1 3/4	
118.3			1/2	1/8	1.89	8	2	1/2
158			2/3		2.13	9	2 1/4	
178			3/4		2.37	10	2 1/2	
237			1	1/4	2.84	12	3	3/4
266			1 1/8		3.31	14	3 1/2	
296			1 1/4		3.56	15	3 3/4	
316			1 1/3	1/3	3.79	16	4	1
355			1 1/2		4.26	18	4 1/2	1 1/8
395			1 2/3		4.74	20	5	1 1/4
415			1 3/4		5.68	24	6	1 1/2
474	= pint =		2	1/2	6.63	28	7	
533			2 1/4		7.57	32	8	2
553			2 1/3		8.51	36	9	2 1/4
592			2 1/2		9.46	40	10	2 1/2
632			2 2/3		11.36	48	12	3
652			2 3/4		13.25	56	14	3 1/2
711			3	3/4	14.19	60	15	3 3/4
770			3 1/4		15.14	64	16	4
789			3 1/3		18.92	80	20	5
829			3 1/2		22.71	96	24	6
869			3 2/3		30.28	128	32	8
889			3 3/4		37.85	160	40	10

WEIGHT AND VOLUME MEASURES

The recipe ingredient measurements in this book are given in metric weight and volume in the left hand columns and U.S. weight and volume on the right of ingredients. Perfect agreement between metric and U.S. measures is not essential for practical purposes. Measurements of grams and milliliters may be taken at the nearest multiple of 5, except for minute quantities of leavening, spices, and extracts. For this, a teaspoon measure is used.

Table A–3
Approximate Weight and Volume Equivalents of Foods

Metric		Ingredients	U.S.	
Weight	Volume		Weight	Volume
1.7 g	5 ml	Allspice		1 tsp
28 g	75 ml	Allspice, ground	1 oz	5 tbsp
151 g	237 ml	Almonds, slivered	5 1/3 oz	1 cup
454 g	711 ml	Almonds, whole	1 lb	3 cups
227 g	237 ml	Anchovies	8 oz	1 cup
7 g	15 ml	Anise Seed	1/4 oz	1 tbsp
454 g	474 ml	Apples, canned pie pack	1 lb	2 cups
454 g	829 ml	Apples, peeled, diced	1 lb	3 1/2 cups
454 g	947 ml	Apples, peeled, sliced	1 lb	1 qt
454 g	474 ml	Applesauce	1 lb	2 cups
255 g	237 ml	Apricot juice	9 oz	1 cup
454 g	947 ml	Apricots, dried, not packed	1 lb	1 qt

Metric		Ingredients	U.S.	
Weight	Volume		Weight	Volume
454 g	474 ml	Apricots, pie pack	1 lb	2 cups
454 g	533 ml	Apricots, stewed halves	1 lb	2 ¼ cups
454 g	592 ml	Avocado, diced	1 lb	2 ½ cups
454 g	18–22 slices	Bacon, raw, hotel-sliced	1 lb	18–22 slices
114 g	237 ml	Bacon Bits	4 oz	1 cup
170 g	237 ml	Bacon Fat	6 oz	1 cup
28 g	40 ml	Baking Powder	1 oz	2 ⅔ tbsp
170 g	237 ml	Baking Powder	6 oz	1 cup
454 g	711 ml	Bananas, diced	1 lb	3 cups
454 g	474 ml	Bananas, mashed	1 lb	2 cups
454 g	4 small	Bananas, whole	1 lb	4 small
454 g	474 ml	Barley	1 lb	2 cups
2 g	15 ml	Basil Leaves		1 tbsp
2 g	15 ml	Bay Leaves, crushed		1 tbsp
454 g	829 ml	Beans, string	1 lb	3 ½ cups
454 g	592 ml	Beans, white, kidney, lima	1 lb	2 ½ cups
454 g	711 ml	Beef, cooked, diced	1 lb	3 cups
454 g	474 ml	Beef, raw, ground	1 lb	2 cups
312 g	237 ml	Beef Base	11 oz	1 cup
454 g	553 ml	Beets, cooked, diced	1 lb	2 ⅓ cups
454 g	533 ml	Blueberries, canned	1 lb	2 ¼ cups
454 g	829 ml	Blueberries, fresh	1 lb	3 ½ cups
57 g	237 ml	Bran (All-Bran)	2 oz	1 cup
396 g	947 ml	Bread Crumbs	14 oz	1 qt
227 g	237 ml	Butter	8 oz	1 cup
340 g	947 ml	Cabbage, E.P.	12 oz	1 qt
396 g	947 ml	Cake Crumbs	14 oz	1 qt
7 g	15 ml	Caraway Seeds	¼ oz	1 tbsp
5 g	15 ml	Cardamom, ground		1 tbsp
454 g	711 ml	Carrots, cooked, diced	1 lb	3 cups
454 g	711 ml	Carrots, raw, sliced	1 lb	3 cups
454 g	474 ml	Catsup	1 lb	2 cups
454 g	947 ml	Celery, diced	1 lb	1 qt
28 g	30 ml	Celery Salt	1 oz	2 tbsp
28 g	60 ml	Celery Seed	1 oz	4 tbsp
7 g	15 ml	Celery Seed	¼ oz	1 tbsp
454 g	947 ml	Cheese, cheddar, grated	1 lb	1 qt
454 g	474 ml	Cheese, cream	1 lb	2 cups
114 g	237 ml	Cheese, Parmesan, grated	4 oz	1 cup
454 g	474 ml	Cherries, maraschino, chopped	1 lb	2 cups
454 g	553 ml	Cherries, maraschino, whole (100)	1 lb	2 cups
454 g	533 ml	Cherries, Royal Anne, canned	1 lb	2 ¼ cups
454 g	711 ml	Chicken, cooked, diced	1 lb	3 cups
28 g	90 ml	Chili Powder	1 oz	6 tbsp
71 g	237 ml	Chives, snipped	2 ½ oz	1 cup
114 g	237 ml	Chocolate, grated	4 oz	1 cup
255 g	237 ml	Chocolate, melted	9 oz	1 cup
170 g	237 ml	Chocolate bits or chips	6 oz	1 cup
28 g	79 ml	Cinnamon, broken stick	1 oz	⅓ cup
28 g	60 ml	Cinnamon, ground	1 oz	4 tbsp
7 g	15 ml	Cinnamon, ground		1 tbsp
28 g	40 ml	Citric Acid	1 oz	2 ⅔ tbsp
184 g	237 ml	Citron, chopped	6 ½ oz	1 cup
454 g	474 ml	Clams, chopped meat	1 lb	2 cups
28 g	75 ml	Cloves, ground	1 oz	5 tbsp
2 g	5 ml	Cloves, ground		1 tsp
85 g	237 ml	Cloves, whole	3 oz	1 cup
114 g	237 ml	Cocoa	4 oz	1 cup
76 g	237 ml	Coconut, flaked or shredded	2 ⅔ oz	1 cup
454 g	1.42 l	Coconut, medium shredded	1 lb	6 cups
57 g	237 ml	Coffee, instant	2 oz	1 cup

| Metric | | Ingredients | U.S. | |
Weight	Volume		Weight	Volume
454 g	1.18 l	Coffee, regular grind	1 lb	5 cups
1.5 g	5 ml	Coriander Seed		1 tsp
454 g	474 ml	Corn, whole kernel	1 lb	2 cups
454 g	592 ml	Corned Beef, canned	1 lb	2 ½ cups
454 g	3.79 l	Cornflakes	1 lb	4 qt
114 g	237 ml	Cornflake Crumbs, commercial	4 oz	1 cup
170 g	237 ml	Corn Grits	6 oz	1 cup
156 g	237 ml	Corn Meal	5 ½ oz	1 cup
142 g	237 ml	Cornstarch	5 oz	1 cup
312 g	237 ml	Corn Syrup	11 oz	1 cup
454 g	474 ml	Cottage Cheese	1 lb	2 cups
454 g	711 ml	Crabmeat, canned, flaked	1 lb	3 cups
454 g	1.42 l	Cracker Crumbs	1 lb	6 cups
454 g	40 units	Crackers, graham	1 lb	40 units
454 g	108 units	Crackers, square soda	1 lb	108 units
454 g	947 ml	Cranberries, fresh	1 lb	1 qt
454 g	474 ml	Cranberry Pulp	1 lb	2 cups
454 g	474 ml	Cream	1 lb	2 cups
28 g	45 ml	Cream of Tartar	1 oz	3 tbsp
454 g	829 ml	Cucumbers, diced	1 lb	3 ½ cups
454 g	50–60 slices	Cucumbers, ⅛-in slices	1 lb	50–60 slices
1.6 g	5 ml	Cumin, ground		1 tsp
454 g	711 ml	Currants	1 lb	3 cups
28 g	60 ml	Curry Powder	1 oz	4 tbsp
2 g	5 ml	Curry Powder		1 tsp
454 g	711 ml	Dates, chopped	1 lb	3 cups
454 g	592 ml	Dates, pitted	1 lb	2 ½ cups
2 g	5 ml	Dill Seed		1 tsp
454 g	711 ml	Eggs, hard-cooked, chopped	1 lb	3 cups
57 g	1 lge	Egg, raw, whole	2 oz	¼ cup
454 g	947 ml	Eggplant, diced, raw	1 lb	1 qt
454 g	474 ml	Eggs, raw, whole, fresh (8)	1 lb	2 cups
454 g	474 ml	Eggs, whole, frozen	1 lb	2 cups
170 g	355 ml	Egg Solids, whole (plus 1 ⅞ cups water = 1 doz eggs)	6 oz	1 ½ cups
28 g	1 white	Egg White, raw, medium size	1 oz	1 white
454 g	474 ml	Egg Whites, raw (16)	1 lb	2 cups
21 g	1 yolk	Egg Yolk, raw, medium size	¾ oz	1 yolk
510 g	474 ml	Egg Yolks, raw (24)	1 lb, 2 oz	2 cups
170 g	237 ml	Farina, raw	6 oz	1 cup
454 g	632 ml	Figs, dried, chopped	1 lb	2 ⅔ cups
454 g	711 ml	Fish, cooked, flaked	1 lb	3 cups
454 g	.947–1.07 l	Flour, bread, sifted once	1 lb	4–4 ½ cups
142 g	237 ml	Flour, buckwheat, sifted once	5 oz	1 cup
454 g	.947–1.18 l	Flour, cake, sifted once	1 lb	4–5 cups
454 g	.711–.947 l	Flour, graham	1 lb	3–4 cups
454 g	.947–1.18 l	Flour, pastry, sifted once	1 lb	4–5 cups
454 g	947 ml	Flour, potato, sifted once	1 lb	4 cups
454 g	1.18 l	Flour, rye, sifted once	1 lb	5 cups
454 g	.711–.947 l	Flour, whole wheat, stirred	1 lb	3–4 cups
28 g	8 cloves	Garlic	1 oz	8 cloves
4.5 g	15 ml	Garlic Powder		1 tbsp
454 g	553 ml	Gelatin, flavored	1 lb	2 ⅓ cups
198 g	237 ml	Gelatin, flavored	7 oz	1 cup
151 g	237 ml	Gelatin, granulated	5 ⅓ oz	1 cup
28 g	45 ml	Gelatin, granulated	1 oz	3 tbsp
85 g	118 ml	Ginger, candied, chopped	3 oz	½ cup
28 g	60 ml	Ginger, ground	1 oz	4 tbsp
1.6 g	5 ml	Ginger, ground		1 tsp
454 g	474 ml	Ginger Ale	1 lb	2 cups
454 g	947 ml	Grapenuts	1 lb	1 qt

| Metric | | Ingredients | U.S. | |
Weight	Volume		Weight	Volume
454 g	533 ml	Grapes, purple	1 lb	2 ¼ cups
454 g	711 ml	Grapes, white, seedless	1 lb	3 cups
454 g	6 med	Green Peppers	1 lb	6 med
454 g	711 ml	Ham, cooked, diced	1 lb	3 cups
454 g	474 ml	Ham, ground	1 lb	2 cups
340 g	237 ml	Honey	12 oz	1 cup
114 g	237 ml	Horseradish, grated	4 oz	1 cup
227 g	237 ml	Horseradish, prepared	8 oz	1 cup
2.72 kg	3.79 l	Ice Cream	6 lb	1 gal
227 g	237 ml	Lard	8 oz	1 cup
142 g	237 ml	Lemon, thinly sliced	5 oz	1 cup
227 g	237 ml	Lemon Juice	8 oz	1 cup
28 g	45 ml	Lemon Rind, grated	1 oz	3 tbsp
454 g	4 lemons	Lemons, whole, size 300	1 lb	4 lemons
184 g	237 ml	Lentils	6 ½ oz	1 cup
454 g	2 heads	Lettuce, medium-size heads	1 lb	2 heads
227 g	947 ml	Lettuce, shredded	8 oz	1 qt
454 g	592 ml	Macaroni, cooked	1 lb	2 ½ cups
511 g	947 ml	Macaroni, cut, A.P.	18 oz	1 qt
128 g	237 ml	Macaroni, cut, A.P.	4 ½ oz	1 cup
1.6 g	5 ml	Mace, ground		1 tsp
312 g	237 ml	Maple Syrup	11 oz	1 cup
2 g	15 ml	Marjoram Leaves		1 tbsp
454 g	474 ml	Marmalade	1 lb	2 cups
454 g	1.89 l	Marshmallows	1 lb	2 qt
454 g	474 ml	Mayonnaise	1 lb	2 cups
454 g	592 ml	Meat, cooked, diced	1 lb	2 ½ cups
454 g	415 ml	Milk, evaporated	1 lb	1 ¾ cups
227 g	237 ml	Milk, fresh	8 oz	1 cup
312 g	237 ml	Milk, sweetened condensed	11 oz	1 cup
454 g	1.30 l	Milk Solids, instant, nonfat	1 lb	5 ½ cups
454 g	947 ml	Milk Solids, regular, nonfat (3 ½ qt/3 ¼ l water = 1 gal/1.9 l)	1 lb	1 qt
28 g	15 ml	Molasses	1 oz	1 tbsp
312 g	237 ml	Molasses	11 oz	1 cup
454 g	474 ml	Mushrooms, canned	1 lb	2 cups
454 g	1.42 l	Mushrooms, fresh, chopped	1 lb	6 cups
454 g	1.66 l	Mushrooms, fresh, sliced	1 lb	7 cups
28 g	60 ml	Mustard, dry	1 oz	4 tbsp
1.5 g	5 ml	Mustard, dry		1 tsp
28 g	30 ml	Mustard, prepared	1 oz	2 tbsp
283 g	237 ml	Mustard, prepared	10 oz	1 cup
28 g	45 ml	Mustard Seed	1 oz	3 tbsp
3.2 g	5 ml	Mustard Seed		1 tsp
2.72 kg	3.79 l	Noodles, cooked	6 lb	1 gal
454 g	652 ml	Noodles, cooked	1 lb	2 ¾ cup
340 g	947 ml	Noodles, raw, dry	12 oz	1 qt
28 g	60 ml	Nutmeg, ground	1 oz	4 tbsp
2 g	5 ml	Nutmeg, ground		1 tsp
114 g	237 ml	Nuts, chopped	4 oz	1 cup
114 g	237 ml	Oatmeal, raw	4 oz	1 cup
454 g	504 ml	Oil	1 lb	2 ⅛ cups
170 g	237 ml	Olives, chopped	6 oz	1 cup
2 g	5 ml	Onion Powder		1 tsp
454 g	711 ml	Onions, chopped	1 lb	3 cups
28 g	20 ml	Onions, grated	1 oz	1 ⅓ tbsp
454 g	947 ml	Onions, sliced	1 lb	1 qt
227 g	237 ml	Orange Juice	8 oz	1 cup
85 g	237 ml	Orange Rind, grated	3 oz	1 cup
454 g	947 ml	Orange Rind, ground	1 lb	1 qt
454 g	592 ml	Oranges, diced	1 lb	2 ½ cups

| Metric | | Ingredients | U.S. | |
Weight	Volume		Weight	Volume
454 g	2 oranges	Oranges, 150 size	1 lb	2 oranges
2 g	15 ml	Oregano leaves		1 tbsp
21 g	1 lge	Oyster	¾ oz	1 lge
454 g	533 ml	Oysters	1 lb	2 ¼ cups
114 g	237 ml	Paprika	4 oz	1 cup
6 g	15 ml	Paprika		1 tbsp
28 g	178 ml	Parsley, chopped	1 oz	¾ cup
454 g	6 ½ halves	Peaches, canned, 40 count	1 lb	6 ½ halves
227 g	237 ml	Peaches, canned, sliced	8 oz	1 cup
454 g	711 ml	Peaches, fresh, sliced	1 lb	3 cups
255 g	237 ml	Peanut Butter	9 oz	1 cup
198 g	237 ml	Pears, cooked, diced	7 oz	1 cup
454 g	711 ml	Pears, fresh, diced	1 lb	3 cups
227 g	237 ml	Peas, canned, drained	8 oz	1 cup
454 g	711 ml	Peas, frozen	1 lb	3 cups
454 g	553 ml	Peas, split	1 lb	2 ⅓ cups
142 g	237 ml	Pecans, chopped	5 oz	1 cup
114 g	237 ml	Pecans, whole	4 oz	1 cup
28 g	60 ml	Pepper, ground	1 oz	4 tbsp
7 g	15 ml	Pepper, ground	¼ oz	1 tbsp
227 g	237 ml	Pickle Relish	8 oz	1 cup
454 g	711 ml	Pickles, chopped	1 lb	3 cups
170 g	237 ml	Pimiento	6 oz	1 cup
454 g	8–12 slices	Pineapple, canned, sliced	1 lb	8–12 slices
255 g	237 ml	Pineapple, crushed	9 oz	1 cup
227 g	237 ml	Pineapple Juice	8 oz	1 cup
227 g	237 ml	Pineapple Tidbits	8 oz	1 cup
142 g	237 ml	Poppy Seed	5 oz	1 cup
8 g	15 ml	Poppy Seed	⅓ oz	1 tbsp
85 g	947 ml	Potato	3 oz	1 qt
283 g	947 ml	Potato Chips, crushed	10 oz	1 qt
227 g	237 ml	Potatoes, sweet, cooked	8 oz	1 cup
454 g	533 ml	Potatoes, white, cooked, diced	1 lb	2 ¼ cups
454 g	4 med	Potatoes, white, cooked, whole	1 lb	4 med
198 g	237 ml	Potatoes, white, mashed	7 oz	1 cup
227 g	237 ml	Prune Juice	8 oz	1 cup
454 g	553 ml	Prunes, cooked	1 lb	2 ⅓ cups
454 g	474 ml	Prunes, cooked, pitted, chopped	1 lb	2 cups
142 g	237 ml	Prunes, 30/40, raw	5 oz	1 cup
567 g	947 ml	Prunes, 30/40 size	20 oz	1 qt
454 g	592 ml	Pumpkin, cooked	1 lb	2 ½ cups
454 g	592 ml	Raisins, seeded	1 lb	2 ½ cups
454 g	711 ml	Raisins, seedless	1 lb	3 cups
454 g	770 ml	Raspberries, fresh	1 lb	3 ¼ cups
454 g	947 ml	Rhubarb, raw, cut	1 lb	1 qt
454 g	592 ml	Rice, cooked	1 lb	2 ½ cups
198 g	237 ml	Rice, uncooked	7 oz	1 cup
114 g	947 ml	Rice Krispies	4 oz	1 qt
1.2 g	5 ml	Rosemary Leaves		1 tsp
454 g	789 ml	Rutabagas, E.P., raw, cubed	1 lb	3 ⅓ cups
2 g	5 ml	Saffron, ground		1 tsp
454 g	474 ml	Salmon, canned	1 lb	2 cups
454 g	711 ml	Salmon, fresh, cooked, flaked	1 lb	3 cups
28 g	118 ml	Sage, powdered	1 oz	½ cup
1.5 g	5 ml	Sage, powdered		1 tsp
28 g	30 ml	Salt	1 oz	2 tbsp
454 g	474 ml	Salt Pork	1 lb	2 cups
2 g	5 ml	Savory, ground		1 tsp
5 g	15 ml	Sesame Seed		1 tbsp
170 g	237 ml	Sherbet	6 oz	1 cup
227 g	237 ml	Sherry	8 oz	1 cup

Metric Weight	Metric Volume	Ingredients	U.S. Weight	U.S. Volume
198 g	237 ml	Shortening, melted	7 oz	1 cup
227 g	237 ml	Shortening, solid	8 oz	1 cup
454 g	770 ml	Shrimp	1 lb	3 ¼ cups
28 g	35 ml	Soda	1 oz	2 ⅓ tbsp
28 g	30 ml	Soup Base	1 oz	2 tbsp
213 g	237 ml	Soybeans, dried	7 ½ oz	1 cup
454 g	947 ml	Spaghetti, uncooked, broken	1 lb	1 qt
454 g	474 ml	Spinach, canned	1 lb	2 cups
454 g	592 ml	Spinach, freshly cooked	1 lb	2 ½ cups
454 g	474 ml	Spinach, frozen	1 lb	2 cups
454 g	4.74 l	Spinach, raw	1 lb	5 qt
454 g	711 ml	Strawberries, fresh, whole	1 lb	3 cups
454 g	533 ml	Strawberries, frozen, sliced	1 lb	2 ¼ cups
170 g	237 ml	Sugar, brown	6 oz	1 cup
227 g	237 ml	Sugar, white granulated	8 oz	1 cup
454 g	829 ml	Sugar, white powdered	1 lb	3 ½ cups
454 g	592 ml	Tapioca, minute	1 lb	2 ½ cups
28 g	45 ml	Tapioca, minute	1 oz	3 tbsp
454 g	1.42 l	Tea	1 lb	6 cups
3 g	15 ml	Thyme Leaves		1 tbsp
454 g	474 ml	Tomatoes, canned	1 lb	2 cups
142 g	237 ml	Tomatoes, fresh, peeled, quartered	5 oz	1 cup
227 g	237 ml	Tomato Puree	8 oz	1 cup
454 g	533 ml	Tuna, canned	1 lb	2 ¼ cups
28 g	50 ml	Turmeric, ground	1 oz	3 ⅓ tbsp
2 g	5 ml	Turmeric, ground		1 tsp
454 g	829 ml	Turnips, diced	1 lb	3 ½ cups
28 g	30 ml	Vanilla	1 oz	2 tbsp
227 g	237 ml	Vinegar	8 oz	1 cup
85 g	237 ml	Walnut Halves (33 halves)	3 oz	1 cup
425 g	947 ml	Walnuts, English, chopped	15 oz	1 qt
227 g	237 ml	Water	8 oz	1 cup
28 g	237 ml	Watercress	1 oz	1 cup
156 g	237 ml	Wheat, bulgar	5 ½ oz	1 cup
255 g	237 ml	White Sauce	9 oz	1 cup
66 g	50 ml	Worcestershire Sauce	2 ⅓ oz	3 ⅓ tbsp
28 g	4 pkgs	Yeast, active dry	1 oz	4 tbsp or 4 pkgs
14 g	1 cake	Yeast, compressed	½ oz	1 cake
454 g	32 cakes	Yeast, compressed	1 lb	32 cakes

Table A–4
Abbreviations

ml	milliliter	gal	gallon
dm	demiliter	pkg	package
l	liter	wt	weight
oz	ounce	vol	volume
lb	pound	lge	large
		med	medium
tsp	teaspoon	sm	small
tbsp	tablespoon	in	inch
c	cup	min	minute
qt	quart	g	gram
°F	degree Fahrenheit		
°C	degree Celsius		
psi	pressure per square inch		
cm	centimeter		
in	inch		
A.P.	as purchased		
E.P.	edible portion (less preparation waste)		

Item	Amount	Approximate Equivalent
Baking Powder	1 tsp/5 ml	¼ tsp/1 ¼ ml soda + ⅝ tsp/3 ¼ ml cream of tartar
		¼ tsp/1 ¼ ml soda + ½ cup/118 ml sour milk or buttermilk
		¼ tsp/1 ¼ ml soda + ¼ to ½ cup/59 to 118 ml molasses
Butter	227 g/8 oz	equal quantity of margarine or 198 g/7 oz oil, clarified chicken fat, or
	1 cup	hydrogenated fat + ½ tsp/2 ½ ml salt
Chocolate	28 g/1 oz	3 tbsp/45 ml cocoa and 1 tbsp/15 ml fat
Cornstarch	1 tbsp/15 ml	2 tbsp/30 ml flour or 2 tsp/10 ml arrowroot
Egg, whole, large	1	14 g/½ oz or 2 tbsp/30 ml whole egg solids + 2 ½ tbsp/37 ½ ml water
yolk	1	10 g dried yolk + 2 tsp/10 ml water
white	1	4 g dried white + 2 tbsp/30 ml water or 28 g/1 oz frozen white
Flour, all-purpose	237 ml/1 cup	237 ml/1 cup less 2 tbsp/30 ml cornmeal
		237 ml/1 cup graham or rye flour
		355 ml/1 ½ cup bread crumbs
		237 ml/1 cup oatmeal
Flour, all-purpose (thickening)	1 tbsp/15 ml	½ to ¾ tbsp/7 ½ ml to 11 ¼ ml arrowroot, waxy maize, or cornstarch
		2 tbsp/30 ml cornmeal, granular wheat, or tapioca
		1 whole egg, 2 egg yolks or 2 whites
Garlic Powder	¼ tsp/1 ¼ ml	2 medium size cloves
Chips	¼ tsp/1 ¼ ml	2 medium size cloves
Ginger, ground	¼ tsp/1 ¼ ml	1 tsp/5 ml minced fresh ginger root
		2 tsp/10 ml chopped crystallized ginger
Green Pepper	1 ½ lb/681 g	4 oz/114 g dried
Horseradish	2 tbsp/30 ml prepared	1 tbsp/15 ml dry mixed with 1 tbsp/15 ml water and 1 tbsp/15 ml vinegar
Lemon Peel, dry	1 tsp/5 ml	1 tsp/5 ml fresh grated or ½ tsp/2 ½ ml extract
Milk, whole	237 ml/1 cup	118 ml/½ cup evaporated + 118 ml/½ cup water
		60 ml/¼ cup nonfat milk solids + 1 tbsp/15 ml butter and 158 ml/⅔ cup water
Sour or buttermilk	237 ml/1 cup	1 tbsp/15 ml lemon juice or vinegar + fresh milk to make 237 ml/1 cup
Whipped Cream	474 ml/2 cups	237 ml/1 cup instant dry milk + 237 ml/1 cup ice water (beat to soft peaks), add 60 ml/¼ cup lemon juice (beat until stiff and fold in) 118 ml/½ cup sugar
Mushrooms, dried	3 tbsp/45 ml	114 g/4 oz fresh or 57 g/2 oz canned
Mustard, dry	1 tsp/5 ml	1 tbsp/15 ml prepared
Onions, dried	1 tbsp/15 ml	2 tbsp/30 ml chopped fresh or 1 small
Onion Powder	1 tbsp/15 ml	4 tbsp/60 ml chopped fresh
Orange Peel, dry	1 tbsp/15 ml	1 tbsp/15 ml fresh grated or ½ tbsp/7 ½ ml extract
Parsley, dry	1 tbsp/15 ml	3 tbsp/45 ml fresh chopped
Soup Stock	3.79 l/1 gal	4 oz/114 g concentrated soup base + 3.79 l/1 gal water
		12 bouillon cubes + 3.79 l/1 gal water
		2 qt/1.89 l canned bouillon or consommé concentrated + 2 qt/1.89 l water
Sugar, granulated	227 g/8 oz	316 ml/1 ⅓ cup brown sugar
		355 ml/1 ½ cup powdered sugar
		296–355 ml/1 ¼–1 ½ cup corn syrup less 60–118 ml/¼–½ cup liquid in recipe
		237 ml/1 cup honey less 59–78 ml/¼–⅓ cup liquid in recipe
		316 ml/1 ⅓ cup molasses less 79 ml/⅓ cup liquid in recipe
Yeast, active dry	1 pkg	1 cake compressed
	15 g/½ oz	28 g/1 oz compressed
	43 g/1 ½ oz	114 g/4 oz compressed yeast
	183 g/6 ½ oz	454 g/1 lb compressed yeast

Item	Size	Use	Yield				
			grams	ounces	tsp	tbsp	cup
Scoop	No. 100	Dainty Cookies	10	.35	2	⅔	1/48
	No. 70	Small Drop Cookies	11	⅜	2	⅔	1/48
	No. 60	Small Drop Cookies	15	½	3	1	1/16
	No. 40	Medium Drop Cookies	23	⅖	5	1 ⅗	
	No. 30	Large Drop Cookies	28.35	1	6	2	⅛
	No. 24	Sandwich or Cream Puff Filling	38	1 ⅓	8	2 ⅔	
	No. 20	Sandwich Fillings, Salads, Muffins, Desserts	42	1 ½	10	3 ⅓	
	No. 16	Entrées, Muffins, Desserts	57	2	12	4	¼
	No. 12	Entrées, Salads, Croquettes, Vegetables	76	2 ⅔	14	4 ⅔	⅓
	No. 10	Meat Patties, Cereals, Croquettes, Vegetables	92	3 ¼	19 ½	6 ½	⅜
	No. 8	Meat Patties and Casserole Dishes	114	4	24	8	½
	No. 6	Main Dish Salads	170	6	36	12	¾
Ladles	1 oz	Sauces, Relishes	28.35	1	6	2	⅛
	2 oz	Gravy, Sauces	57	2	12	4	¼
	4 oz	Creamed Dishes and Vegetables	114	4	24	8	½
	6 oz	Stews, Baked Dishes, Chili, Creamed Dishes, Vegetables	170	6	36	12	¾
	8 oz	Soups, Chili, Stews	227	8	48	16	1
	12 oz	Large Soup, Goulash	340	12	72	24	1 ½
	24 oz	Kitchen Dipper	681	24	144	48	3
	32 oz	Quart Dipper	907	32	192	64	4
Demiliter Measure			496	17 ½	105	35	2 3/16
Liter Measure			1000 (1 kg)	35.28	210	70	4 ⅜
2-quart Measure			1990 (1.8 kg)	64	384	128	8

Pans, Cake, Oblong 7 × 11 × 1 ½ in/18 × 28 × 4 cm. Cut 3 × 4 = 12 cuts 2 ⅓ × 2 ¾ in/59 × 69 mm
Cut 4 × 4 = 16 cuts 1 ¾ × 2 ¾ in/44 × 69 mm
Square, 9 ½ × 9 ½ in/24 × 24 cm   Cut 3 × 4 = 12 cuts 3 ⅙ × 2 ⅖ in/80 × 67 mm
2 layers   Cut 3 × 7 = 21 cuts 1 ⅓ × 3 ⅗ in/34 × 91 mm
Round, 8 in/20 cm in diameter, 2 layers = 12 cuts
12 in/30 cm in diameter, 2 layers = 30 cuts
Tube pan, 10 in/25 cm in diameter = 12 to 16 cuts
Loaf pans for bread, cake, and meat loaf
9 × 5 × 3 in/22 ½ × 12 ½ × 7 ½ cm =   12 slices ¾ in/19 mm thick
14 slices ⅝ in/15 mm thick
16 slices ½ in/12 ½ mm thick
3 × 6 ½ × 2 ⅜ in/7 ½ × 16 ½ × 6 cm =   10 slices ⅝ in/15 mm thick
12 slices ½ in/12 ½ mm thick
Baking sheet for meat patties, bar cookies, and cakes
Approx. 18 × 26 × 1 in/46 × 66 × 2 ½ cm
Cut 6 × 8 = 48 units 3 × 3 in/76 × 76 mm
Cut 5 × 12 = 60 units 3 ⅗ × 2 ⅛ in/91 × 55 mm
Pie, 8-in/20 cm (1 ½ to 3 cups/355 to 711 ml filling) = 6 cuts
9-in/23 cm (1 ¾ to 2 lb/793 to 907 g filling) = 6 to 8 cuts
10-in/25 cm (2 to 2 ½ lb/.907 to 1.14 kg filling) = 8 cuts
Serving pan, 12 × 20 × 2 in/30 × 50 × 5 cm. Cut 6 × 8 = 48 2 × 2 ½ in/50 × 63 mm
Cut 5 × 6 = 30 2 ⅖ × 3 ⅓ in/67 × 84 mm
Cut 4 × 6 = 24 3 × 3 ⅓ in/76 × 84 mm
10 × 12 × 2 in/25 × 30 × 5 cm. Cut 3 × 5 = 15 2 ⅔ × 3 ⅓ in/67 × 84 mm
Cut 4 × 4 = 16 2 ½ × 3 in/63 × 76 mm
Pudding pan, 15 ½ × 10 ½ × 2 ¼ in/39 × 26 × 6 cm

A pastry bag with tip desired may be used for portioning meringue for shells, filling cream puffs, stuffing eggs, and adding dressing to salads.

Table A–7
Cooking Temperatures*

Term	Fahrenheit	Celsius (Centigrade)	Suggested Use
Low	212	100	Boiling Water at Sea Level
Very Slow	250	121	Meringue Shells
	275	135	Less tender meats
Slow	300	149	Roast beef, lamb,
	325	163	Poultry, veal
Moderate	350	177	Cakes, casseroles
	370	188	Deep-fat frying
Hot	400	205	Baking vegetables
	425	218	Muffins, cookies
	450	232	Biscuits, pastry
Very Hot	475–525	246–274	Baked Alaska
Extremely Hot	550–575	288–301	Broiling meats

*Note: To convert Fahrenheit to Celsius temperature, subtract 32 from the Fahrenheit temperature, multiply by 5, and divide by 9.

Table A–8
Approximate Percentage of Edible Portion in Fresh Fruits and Vegetables.*

Percentage calculated on the basis of one pound as purchased			
	%		%
Apples	76	Lettuce, leaf	67
Asparagus	56	Mushrooms	97
Avocado	72	Okra	78
Banana	67	Onions, mature	89
Beans, green or wax	88	Orange sections	56
Beans, lima	38	Parsnips	85
Beets	76	Peaches	76
Blueberries	86	Pears	78
Broccoli	61	Peas, green	38
Brussels Sprouts	74	Peppers, green	82
Cabbage, green	79	Pineapple	52
Canteloupe, served without rind	50	Plums	94
Carrots	82	Potatoes	81
Cauliflower	55	Potatoes, sweet	80
Celery	75	Radishes	63
Chard	77	Rhubarb, partly trimmed	86
Cherries, pitted	89	Rutabagas	85
Cranberries	97	Spinach, untrimmed	74
Cucumber, unpared	95	partly trimmed	92
pared	73	Squash, acorn	88
Eggplant	81	Squash, Hubbard	66
Endive, chicory, escarole	74	Squash, zucchini	98
Grapefruit, sections	47	Strawberries	89
Grapes, seedless	95	Tomatoes	91
Honeydew melon, without rind	57	Turnips	81
Kale	74	Watermelon	47
Lettuce, head	75		

*In order to find the quantity to purchase, divide the recipe amount by the percentage yield. (Example: Apples for salad calls for 4 lb and, divided by 76, indicates that approximately 5 ⅓ lb should be purchased.) Adapted from FOOD BUYING FOR TYPE A SCHOOL LUNCHES, U.S. Dept. of Agriculture PA-270, Revised 1972.

INDEX

Italian
    delight (noodles), 102
    macaroni, 98
    spaghetti, 105
    stew (veal), 169

J

Jambalaya, 113
Jellied
    beet salad, 287
    carrot and pineapple salad, 279
    grapefruit and apple salad, 275
    ham loaf, 182
    rhubarb pudding, 432
    veal loaf, 169
Jelly roll, 362
Jewel salad, 275
John Marzetti, 162

K

Kolache, 36

L

Lamb, 171–175
    baked steaks, 174
    barbecued shanks, 171
    curry, 172
    French stew, 173
    mixed grill, 175
    pinwheels, 175
    roast, 171
    shashlik, 174
    stew, 172
    time required for broiling (table), 147
    time required for cooking with moist heat (table), 148
Lasagna, 101
Leg of veal, roast, 166
Lemon
    baked fish, 129
    bars, luscious, 382
    chiffon pie, 467
    cream pie, 463
    cream rice pudding, 406
    frozen pie, 472
    honey salad dressing, 317
    lime punch, 47
    meringue pie, 459
    meringue pudding, 422
    nut frosting, 370
    orange frosting, 369
    orange punch, 46
    pineapple cocktail sauce, 231
    pudding, 409
    sauce (sweet), 256
    slices (cookies), 396

sponge pie, 462
sponge pudding, 408
Lentil
    patties, 122
    soup, 70
Light Christmas cake, 354
Lima beans
    baked, 117
    with green pepper and pimiento, 117
Lime
    jelly salad, 273
    pear mold, 273
Lining, sponge cake, for frozen pies, 471
Little red hens, 195
Loaf
    caramel ham, 184
    carrot, 122
    celery pecan, 119
    cheese meat, 159
    chicken, 196
    glazed ham, 180
    ham and rice, 183
    jellied ham, 182
    jellied veal, 169
    meat, 158
    meat with vegetable protein, 160
    meat, cold (beef), 161
    meat, Italian glacé, 160
    salmon, 140
    turkey, 199
Loaf breads, quick, 20–26
    applesauce raisin, 20
    apricot orange, 21
    banana, 20
    Boston brown, 21
    carrot, 23
    cranberry nut, 22
    date-nut, 24
    nut, 25
    peanut butter, 22
    poppy seed-lemon, 26
    praline coffee cake, 25
    prune, 24
    raisin orange, 23
Loaf breads, yeast, 26–33
    cheese, 27
    cranberry anadama, 28
    dark rye, 30, 31
    four grain, 32, 33
    fruit, 29
    herb, 32
    orange, 28
    orange rye, 30
    potato raisin, 31
    slices in commercial, 320
    white, 27
    whole wheat, 33
Lobster (or crab) Newburg, 133
Loganberry punch, 49
Lorenzo, crab, 133
Louisiana spice cake, 359

Luscious lemon bars, 382
Lyonnaise carrots, 211

M

Macaroni
    broccoli and cheese, 99
    and cheese, 98
    cooking of (table), 90
    Italian, 98
    John Marzetti, 162
    Milanese, 97
    and mushroom casserole, 99
    pineapple salad, 299
    and vegetables, 100
Macaroon cream pudding, 402
Mandarin apricot sauce, 249
Mandarin carrots, 213
Maple milk drink, 52
Maple nut pie, 467
Maple pecan cream pie, 463
Marinades, 229, 242–243
    simple, 242
    teriyaki, 243
    wine, 242
Marmalade
    pinwheels, 2
    rolls, 36
Marshmallow and fruit cream pudding, 435
Marshmallow sauce, 250
Mashed potatoes, 223
Mayonnaise, 309. See also Dressings, salad
    cocktail sauce, 230
    cooked base, 310
Measures
    equivalent volume, 480–485
    weights, 479–485
Meat
    cooking of (tables), 145–148
    and egg salad sandwich, 326
    purchasing, 145
    storage, 145
    use of vegetable protein, 146
Meatballs
    Norwegian, 155
    Oriental, 164
    Swedish, 156
Meat hors d'oeuvres, 60
Meat loaf, 158
    cheese, 159
    cold, 161
    Italian glacé, 160
    with vegetable protein, 160
Meat salad sandwich, 326
Meat sandwich suggestions, hot, 337
Meat salads. See Salads
Meat sauce, 246
Medley, vegetable salad, 280
Medley of vegetables, 212
Melba sauce, 249